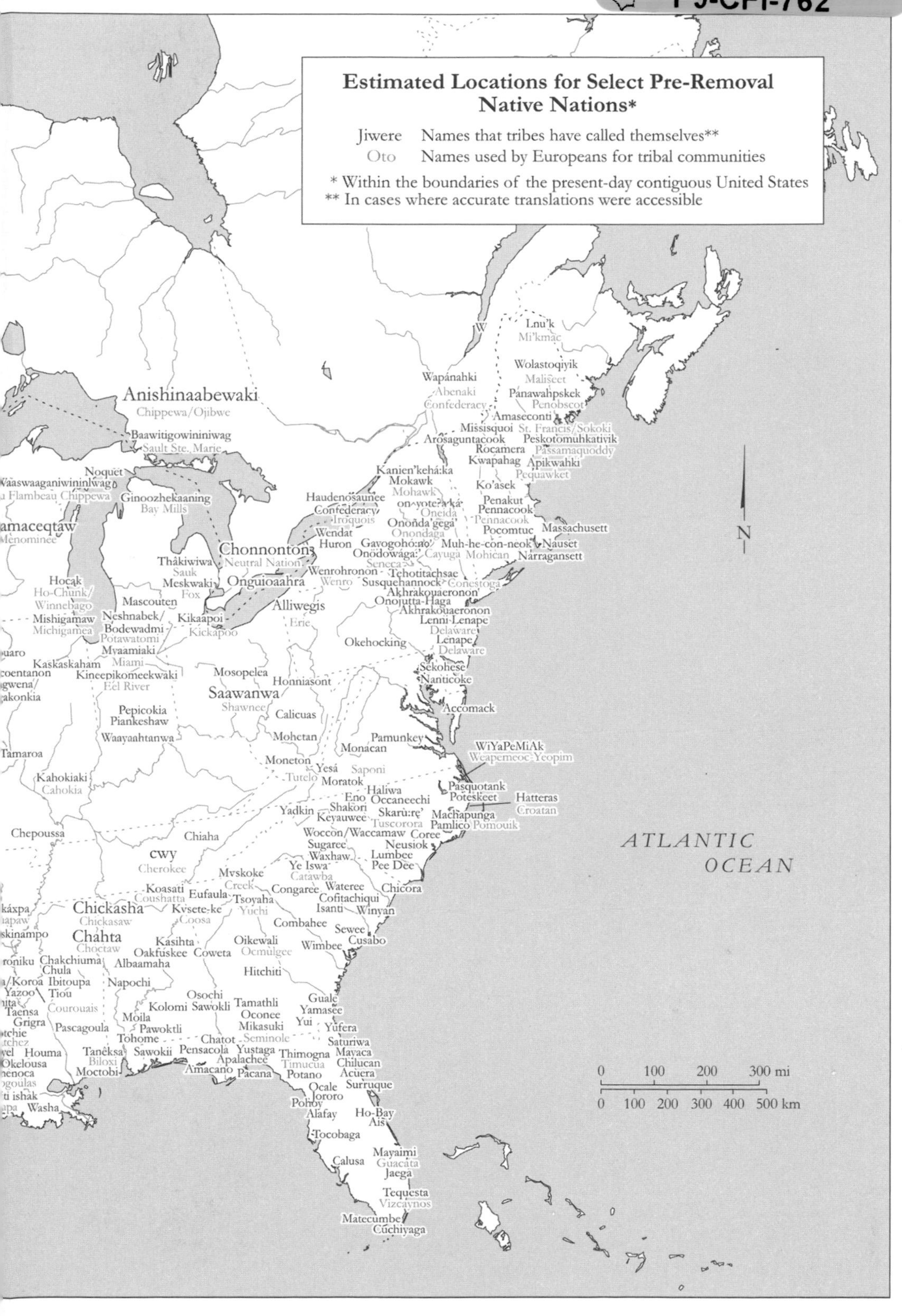
Estimated Locations for Select Pre-Removal Native Nations*
Jiwere Names that tribes have called themselves**
Oto Names used by Europeans for tribal communities
* Within the boundaries of the present-day contiguous United States
** In cases where accurate translations were accessible
Anishinaabewaki
Chippewa/Ojibwe
Baawitigowininiwag
Sault Ste. Marie
Noquet
Ginoozhekaaning
Bay Mills
Menominee
Thâkiwiwa
Sauk
Meskwaki
Fox
Hocąk
Ho-Chunk/
Winnebago
Mascouten
Mishigamaw
Michigamea
Neshnabek/
Bodewadmi
Potawatomi
Kikaapoi
Kickapoo
Myaamiaki
Miami
Kaskaskaham
Kineepikomeekwaki
Eel River
Pepicokia
Piankeshaw
Waayaahtanwa
Tamaroa
Kahokiaki
Cahokia
Chepoussa
Chonnontons
Neutral Nation
Onguioaahra
Alliwegis
Erie
Wendat
Huron
Wenrohronon
Wenro
Haudenosaunee
Confederacy
Iroquois
Kanien'kehá:ka
Mokawk
Mohawk
Onoñda'gegá'
Onondaga
Gayogohó:nǫ'
Cayuga
Onödowága:
Seneca
Tehotitachsae
Susquehannock
Conestoga
Akhrakouaeronon
Onojutta-Haga
Okehocking
Mosopelea
Saawanwa
Shawnee
Honniasont
Calicuas
Mohetan
Moneton
Tutelo
Yesá
Saponi
Moratok
Monacan
Pamunkey
Lenni-Lenape
Delaware
Lenape
Sekohese
Nanticoke
Accomack
WiYaPeMiAk
Weapemeoc Yeopim
Pasquotank
Poteskeet
Hatteras
Croatan
Haliwa
Eno
Occaneechi
Shakori
Keyauwee
Yadkin
Skarù:rę'
Tuscorora
Machapunga
Pamlico
Pomouik
Woccon/Waccamaw
Coree
Sugaree
Neusiok
Waxhaw
Lumbee
Ye Iswa
Catawba
Pee Dee
Chiaha
CWY
Cherokee
Mvskoke
Creek
Koasati
Coushatta
Eufaula
Tsoyaha
Yuchi
Kvsete-ke
Coosa
Congaree
Wateree
Chicora
Cofitachiqui
Isanti
Winyan
Chickasha
Chickasaw
Chahta
Choctaw
Combahee
Sewee
Wimbee
Cusabo
Kasihta
Oakfuskee
Coweta
Oikewali
Ocmulgee
Albaamaha
Chakchiuma
Chula
Ibitoupa
Napochi
Tiou
Courouais
Yazoo
Taensa
Grigra
Hitchiti
Osochi
Kolomi
Sawokli
Tamathli
Oconee
Mikasuki
Seminole
Moila
Pawoktli
Pascagoula
Tohome
Chatot
Houma
Tanêksa
Biloxi
Sawokli
Pensacola
Yustaga
Apalachee
Amacano
Pacana
Moctobi
Okelousa
Washa
Guale
Yamasee
Yui
Yufera
Saturiwa
Thimogna
Timucua
Mayaca
Chilucan
Potano
Acuera
Surruque
Ocale
Jororo
Pohoy
Alafay
Ho-Bay
Ais
Tocobaga
Calusa
Mayaimi
Guacata
Jaega
Tequesta
Vizcaynos
Matecumbe
Cuchiyaga
Wapánahki
Abenaki
Confederacy
Lnu'k
Mi'kmac
Wolastoqiyik
Maliseet
Panawahpskek
Penobscot
Amaseconti
Missisquoi
St. Francis/Sokoki
Arosaguntacook
Peskotomuhkativik
Passamaquoddy
Rocamera
Kwapahag
Apikwahki
Pequawket
Ko'asek
Penakut
Pennacook
on^yote?a·ká
Oneida
Pocomtuc
Massachusett
Muh-he-con-neok
Mohican
Nauset
Narragansett
ATLANTIC
OCEAN
N
0 100 200 300 mi
0 100 200 300 400 500 km

The Rediscovery of America

THE HENRY ROE CLOUD SERIES ON AMERICAN INDIANS AND MODERNITY

Series Editors

Ned Blackhawk, Yale University
Joshua L. Reid, University of Washington
Renya K. Ramirez, University of California, Santa Cruz

Domestic Subjects: Gender, Citizenship, and Law in Native American Literature (2013), by Beth H. Piatote

Hollow Justice: A History of Indigenous Claims in the United States (2013), by David E. Wilkins

For a Love of His People:The Photography of Horace Poolaw (2014), edited by Nancy Marie Mithlo

The Sea Is My Country: The Maritime World of the Makahs (2015), by Joshua L. Reid

Indigenous London: Native Travelers at the Heart of Empire (2016), by Coll Thrush

Memory Lands: King Philip's War and the Place of Violence in the Northeast (2018), by Christine M. DeLucia

Our Beloved Kin: A New History of King Philip's War (2018), by Lisa Brooks

Indigenous Visions: Rediscovering the World of Franz Boas (2018), edited by Ned Blackhawk and Isaiah Lorado Wilner

A Journey to Freedom: Richard Oakes, Alcatraz, and the Red Power Movement (2018), by Kent Blansett

Assembled for Use: Indigenous Compilation and the Archives of Early Native American Literatures (2021), by Kelly Wisecup

"Vaudeville Indians" on Global Circuits, 1880s–1930s (2022), by Christine Bold

The Makings and Unmakings of Americans: Indians and Immigrants in American Literature and Culture, 1879–1924 (2022), by Cristina Stanciu

The Rediscovery of America: Native Peoples and the Unmaking of U.S. History (2023), by Ned Blackhawk

The Rediscovery of America

✦

Native Peoples and the Unmaking of U.S. History

Ned Blackhawk

Yale UNIVERSITY PRESS   NEW HAVEN AND LONDON

Published with assistance from the income of the
Frederick John Kingsbury Memorial Fund.
Published with assistance from the foundation
established in memory of Philip Hamilton McMillan
of the Class of 1894, Yale College.

Yale University Press books may be purchased in quantity
for educational, business, or promotional use. For
information, please e-mail sales.press@yale.edu
(U.S. office) or sales@yaleup.co.uk (U.K. office).

Set in 10/14 Scala Pro type by Motto Publishing Services.
Printed in the United States of America.

Library of Congress Control Number: 2022944823
ISBN 978-0-300-24405-2 (hardcover : alk. paper)

A catalogue record for this book is
available from the British Library.

This paper meets the requirements of
ANSI/NISO Z39.48-1992 (Permanence of Paper).

10 9 8 7 6 5

To Maggie,
with love

and

to the Native American Cultural Center community,
with gratitude

Contents

Maps

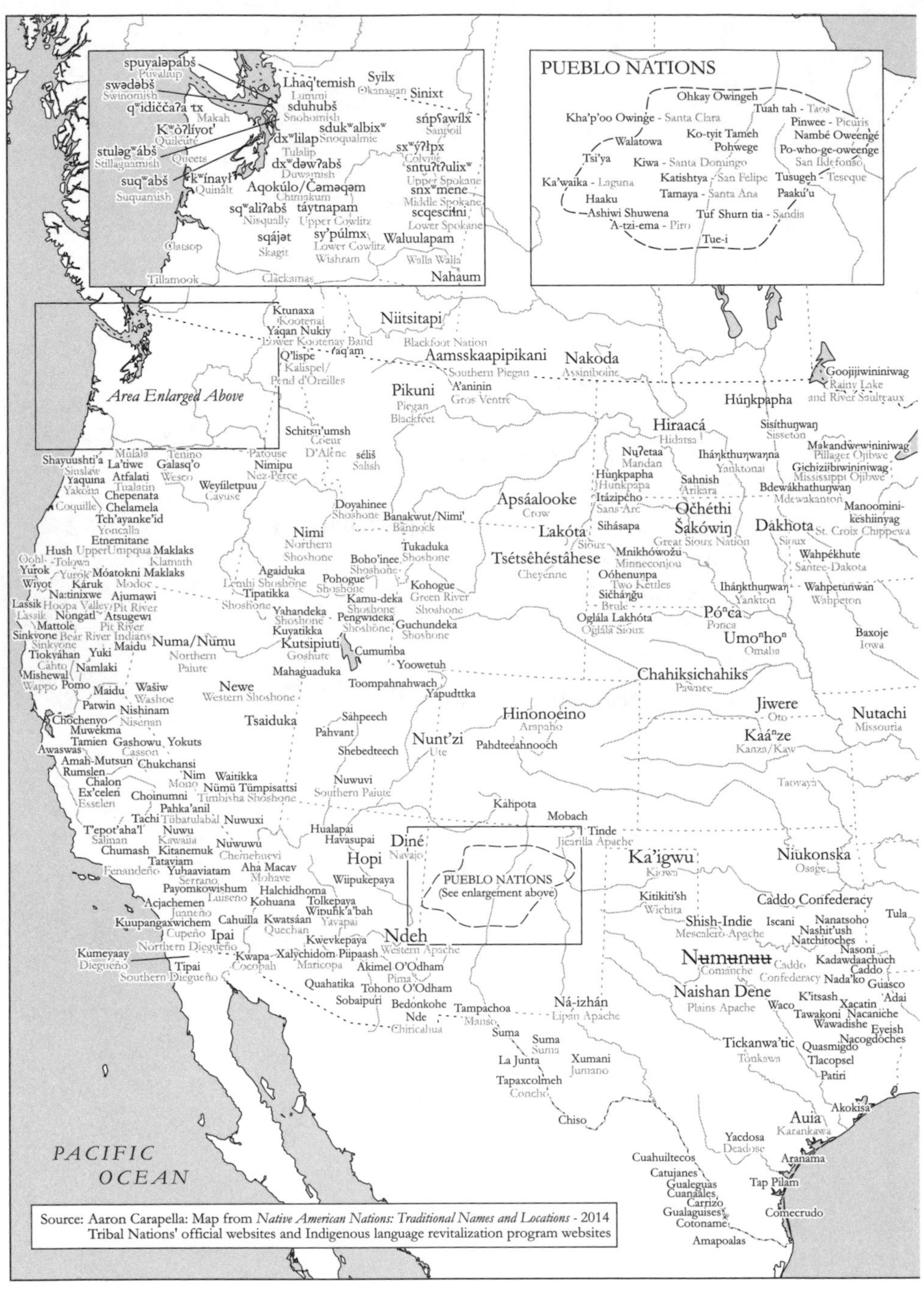

Source: Aaron Carapella: Map from *Native American Nations: Traditional Names and Locations* - 2014
Tribal Nations' official websites and Indigenous language revitalization program websites

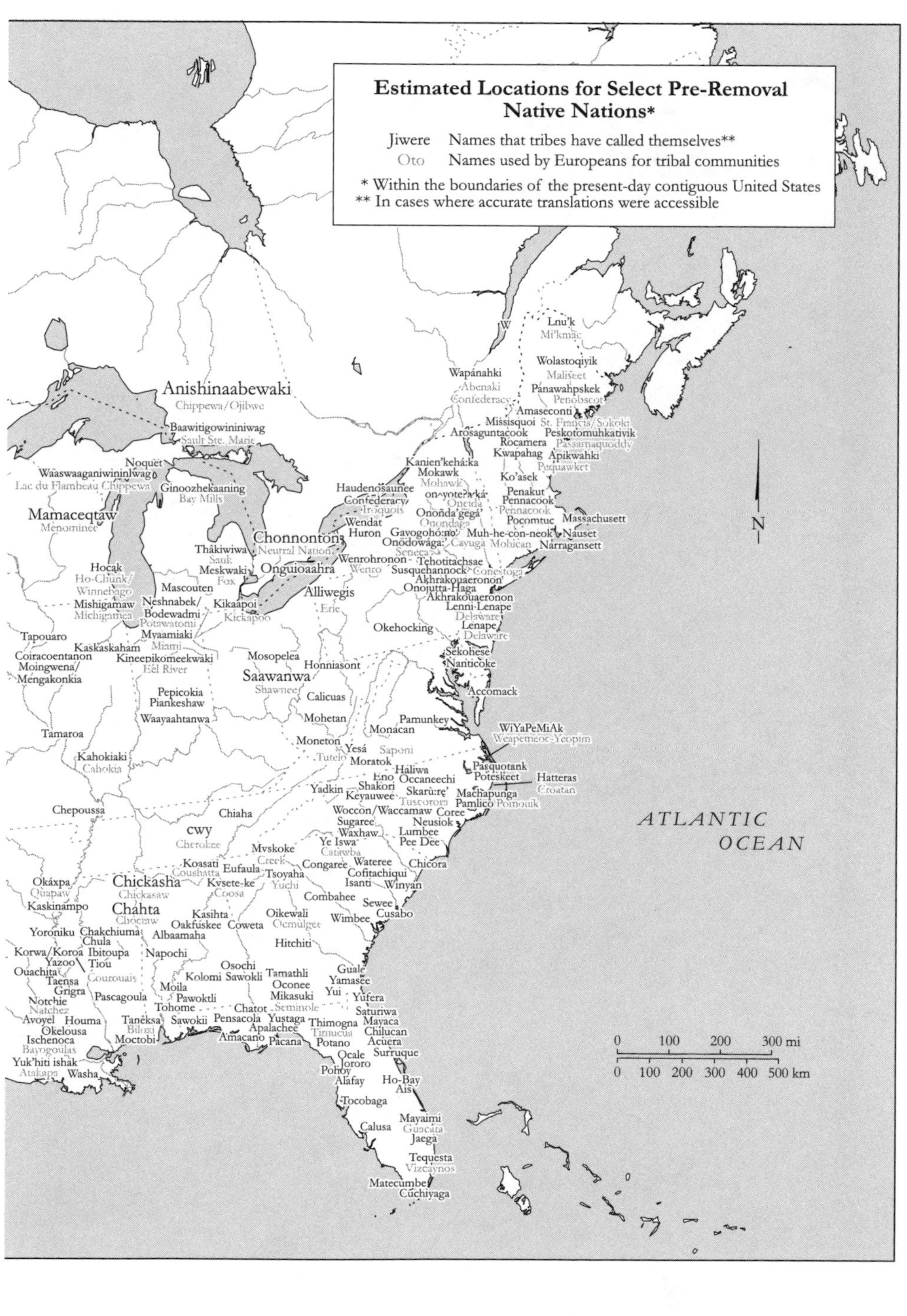

Estimated Locations for Select Pre-Removal Native Nations*
Jiwere Names that tribes have called themselves**
Oto Names used by Europeans for tribal communities
* Within the boundaries of the present-day contiguous United States
** In cases where accurate translations were accessible
Lnu'k
Mi'kmac
Wolastoqiyik
Maliseet
Wapánahki
Abenaki
Confederacy
Panawahpskek
Penobscot
Amaseconti
Missisquoi
St. Francis/Sokoki
Arosaguntacook
Peskotomuhkativik
Passamaquoddy
Rocamera
Kwapahag
Apikwahki
Pequawket
Ko'asek
Penakut
Pennacook
Pennacook
Pocomtuc
Massachusett
Muh-he-con-neok
Mohican
Nauset
Narragansett
Anishinaabewaki
Chippewa/Ojibwe
Baawitigowininiwag
Sault Ste. Marie
Noquet
Waaswaaganiwininiwag
Lac du Flambeau Chippewa
Ginoozhekaaning
Bay Mills
Mamaceqtaw
Menominee
Kanien'kehá:ka
Mokawk
Mohawk
Haudenosaunee
Confederacy
Iroquois
on^yote?a·ká
Oneida
Onoñda'gega'
Onondaga
Wendat
Huron
Gavogoho:no'
Onödowága:
Seneca
Cayuga
Chonnonton
Neutral Nation
Thâkiwiwa
Sauk
Meskwaki
Fox
Onguioaahra
Wenrohronon
Wenro
Tehotitachsae
Susquehannock
Conestoga
Akhrakouaeronon
Onojutta-Haga
Akhrakouaeronon
Lenni-Lenape
Delaware
Lenape
Delaware
Hocąk
Ho-Chunk/
Winnebago
Mascouten
Mishigamaw
Michigamea
Neshnabek/
Bodewadmi
Potawatomi
Kikaapoi
Kickapoo
Alliwegis
Erie
Okehocking
Tapouaro
Kaskaskaham
Coiracoentanon
Moingwena/
Mengakonkia
Myaamiaki
Miami
Kineepikomeekwaki
Eel River
Mosopelea
Honniasont
Sekohese
Nanticoke
Saawanwa
Shawnee
Accomack
Pepicokia
Piankeshaw
Calicuas
Waayaahtanwa
Mohetan
Pamunkey
Monacan
WiYaPeMiAk
Weapemeoc-Yeopim
Tamaroa
Moneton
Tutelo
Yesá
Saponi
Moratok
Kahokiaki
Cahokia
Haliwa
Pasquotank
Poteskeet
Hatteras
Croatan
Eno
Occaneechi
Shakori
Yadkin
Keyauwee
Skarù:rę'
Tuscarora
Machapunga
Pamlico
Pomouik
Chepoussa
Chiaha
Woccon/Waccamaw
Coree
Sugaree
Neusiok
Waxhaw
Lumbee
ᏣᎳᎩ
Cherokee
Ye Iswa
Catawba
Pee Dee
ATLANTIC
OCEAN
Mvskoke
Creek
Kosati
Coushatta
Eufaula
Congaree
Wateree
Chicora
Cofitachiqui
Okáxpa
Quapaw
Chickasha
Chickasaw
Tsoyaha
Yuchi
Isanti
Winyah
Kvsete-ke
Coosa
Combahee
Kaskinampo
Chahta
Choctaw
Sewee
Kasihta
Oikewali
Ocmulgee
Wimbee
Cusabo
Oakfuskee
Coweta
Yoroniku
Chakchiuma
Chula
Albaamaha
Hitchiti
Korwa/Koroa
Ibitoupa
Napochi
Yazoo
Tiou
Ouachita
Osochi
Guale
Taensa
Courouais
Kolomi
Sawokli
Tamathli
Yamasee
Grigra
Moila
Oconee
Notchie
Natchez
Pascagoula
Pawoktli
Mikasuki
Yui
Yufera
Tohome
Chatot
Seminole
Saturiwa
Avoyel
Houma
Tanēksa
Biloxi
Sawokii
Pensacola
Yustaga
Thimogna
Timucua
Mayaca
Okelousa
Apalachee
Chilucan
Ischenoca
Bayogoulas
Moctobi
Amacano
Pacana
Potano
Acuera
Yuk'hiti ishak
Atakapa
Washa
Ocale
Surruque
Jororo
Pohoy
Alafay
Ho-Bay
Ais
Tocobaga
Mayaimi
Guacata
Calusa
Jaega
Tequesta
Vizcaynos
Matecumbe
Cuchiyaga
0 100 200 300 mi
0 100 200 300 400 500 km
N

The Rediscovery of America

Introduction

Toward a New American History

How can a nation founded on the homelands of dispossessed Indigenous peoples be the world's most exemplary democracy? This question haunts America, as it does other settler nations.[1] Among historians, silence, rather than engagement, has been the most common response, together with a continued unwillingness to see America's diversity from the vantage point of those most impacted by the expansion of the United States.[2]

This is not that surprising. Like most countries, the United States has celebrated its past. Its revolutionary leaders understood America to be both a nation-state and an idea. As George Washington wrote in June 1783:

> The citizens of America, placed in the most enviable condition, as the sole Lords and Proprietors of a vast Tract of Continent, comprehending all the various soils and climates of the World, and abounding with all the necessaries and conveniences of life, are now by the late satisfactory pacification, acknowledged to be possessed of absolute freedom and Independency; They are, from this period, to be considered as the Actors on *the most conspicuous theater, which seems to be peculiarly designated by Providence for the display of human greatness and felicity.*[3]

Historians have largely followed suit in focusing on Europeans and their descendants: Puritans governing a commonwealth in a wilderness; pioneers settling western frontiers; and European immigrants huddled upon Atlantic shores.[4] Scholars have long conflated U.S. history with Europeans, maintaining that the United States evolved from its British settlements.[5]

In more complex narratives, a multicultural America struggles to extend its national promise to every one of its citizens and live according to its founding proclamation that all are created equal. Despite assertions to the contrary, American democracy arose from the dispossession of American Indians. If history provides the common soil for a nation's growth and a window into its future, it is time to reimagine U.S. history outside the tropes of discovery that have bred exclusion and misunderstanding. Finding answers to the challenges of our time—racial strife, climate crisis, and domestic and global inequities, among others—will require new concepts, approaches, and commitments. It is time to put down the interpretive tools of the previous century and take up new ones.[6]

✦

Even the word *America* refers to Europeans and discovery. In 1507 cartographers Matthias Ringmann and Martin Waldseemüller renamed the recently encountered "fourth part" of the world after Americus Vesputius (Vespucci), its supposed discoverer.[7] Unlike Columbus in the 1490s, in 1503 Vespucci claimed to have found not passage to Asia, but something more—he claimed to have discovered "a new world."[8]

For centuries America and the New World have been ideas that convey a sense of wonder and possibility made manifest by discovery, a historical act in which explorers are the protagonists. They are the drama's actors and subjects. They think and name, conquer and settle, govern and own. They are at the center of Washington's "most conspicuous theater," just as Native Americans remain absent or appear as hostile or passive objects awaiting discovery and domination.[9]

Indigenous absence has been a long tradition of American historical analysis. Building upon a generation of recent scholarship in Indigenous history, this book joins the many scholars who are creating a different view of the past, a reorientation of U.S. history.[10] A full telling of American history must account for the dynamics of struggle, survival, and resurgence that frame America's Indigenous past. Focus upon Native American history must be an essential practice of American historical inquiry. Existing paradigms of U.S. history remain incomplete when they fail to engage the field. We need to build a more inclusive narrative, and this cannot be accomplished simply by adding new cast members to the dramas of the past. Our history must reckon with the fact that Indigenous peoples, African Americans, and millions of other non-white citizens have not enjoyed the self-evident truths of equality, life, liberty, and the pursuit of happiness proclaimed at the nation's founding as inalienable rights belonging to all. Many people have remained historically excluded from the nation and exploited by its citizens. Native peoples were not granted U.S. citizenship until 1924, by which time the federal government had seized hundreds of millions of acres of land from Native nations in more than three hundred treaties.[11] Tens of thousands of Native peoples were killed by settler militias and U.S. armed forces during the Civil War era, and government-sponsored campaigns of child removal from reservation communities resulted in 40 percent of Indian children being forcibly separated from their families and taken to boarding schools by 1928.[12]

Pervasive violence and dispossession are more than sidebars or parentheses in the story of American history. They call into question its central thesis. The exclusion of Native Americans was codified in the Constitution, maintained throughout the antebellum era, and legislated into the twentieth century: far from being incidental, it enabled the development of the United States. U.S. history as we currently know it does not account for the centrality of Native Americans.

Scholars have recently come to view African American slavery as central to the making of America, but few have seen Native Americans in a similar light. Binary, rather than multiracial, conceptions dominate studies of the past in which slavery represents the antithesis of the American idea. Leading scholarship considers it both America's original sin and its foundational institution.[13] "In the American book of genesis," we are told in a recent best-selling history of the United States, "liberty and slavery became the American Abel and Cain."[14] But can we imagine an American Eden that is not cultivated by its original caretakers? Exiled from the American origin story, Indigenous peoples await the telling of a history that includes them. It was their garden homelands, after all, that birthed America.

Building a new theory of American history is no small undertaking. It will take years and will require the labor of generations of contributors. It will need new themes, new geographies, new chronologies, and new ideas that better explain the course of American history. It is a simultaneous challenge and opportunity, one that falls particularly hard on tribal members who continue to bear the burdens of explaining Indigenous experiences, history, and policies to non-Native peoples.

Encounter—rather than discovery—must structure America's origins story. For over five hundred years peoples have come from outside of North America to the homelands of Native peoples, whose subsequent transformations and survival provide one potential guide through the story of America. Native peoples collectively spoke hundreds of languages and lived in societies ranging from small family bands to large-scale empires with emperors and vassal subjects. Their encounters with newcomers began in well-documented form with Spanish explorers in the 1490s.

Understanding the formation of the earliest American colonies requires seeing Indigenous societies in motion, not stasis. Like the oceans upon which newcomers traveled, North America's earliest colonies experienced waves of turbulence within preexisting Indigenous geographies. From the foods they ate to the economies that sustained them, colonists depended on Indigenous peoples. To conceive of their composition, survival, and growth otherwise is fallacy. Indigenous-imperial relations explain the distinctions among Europe's American colonies, several of which, including colonial New Mexico, had been a part of European empires longer than they have been a part of the United States.

As the following chapters show, European contact sent shockwaves across Indigenous homelands, reverberating in many forms, some of them undocumented. Scholars have spent over fifty years attempting to measure the impacts of these intrusions. They suggest that the worlds of Native peoples became irrevocably disrupted by the most traumatic development in American history: the loss of Indigenous life due to European diseases. Epidemics tore apart numerous communities and set in motion large-scale migrations and transformations. North America's total population nearly halved from 1492 to 1776: from approximately 7 or 8 million to 4 million.[15]

The almost unimaginable scale of death and depopulation calls into question celebratory portraits of the nation's founding, and also helps to explain the motivations for American Indian trade, diplomacy, and warfare, all of which shaped the evolution of European settlements. From the rise of New France in 1609 to the colonization of California in 1769, the economic, diplomatic, and military influence of American Indians were key factors in imperial decision making. The treaties with Indigenous nations ratified by the U.S. Senate constitute the largest number of diplomatic commitments made by the federal government throughout its first century. These truths show that it is impossible to understand the United States without understanding its Indigenous history.

✦

Revising interpretations of the past is an inherent part of the study of history, and as each generation reinterprets, it does so in response to new circumstances, ideas, and conditions. In the early twenty-first century, a new paradigm, "settler colonialism," became popularized by Commonwealth scholars dissatisfied with historical frameworks that naturalize the process of Anglophone global expansion.[16] Committed to assessing colonialism as an ongoing process, these scholars launched new methods, concepts, and historical approaches that centered upon Indigenous peoples. They called into question the founding narratives of nation-states, exposing how mythologies like the Puritan "errand into the wilderness" or the democratic nature of "frontier" settlements do more than erase Indigenous peoples—they turn history itself into nature and excise the violence of colonialism.[17] Moreover, as Commonwealth nations such as Australia and Canada offer national apologies and establish truth and reconciliation commissions to assess their respective histories of Indigenous forced acculturation, many have asked the historical community to examine the broader question of Indigenous genocide.[18] Using the definitions established by the UN Convention on the Prevention and Punishment of the Crime of Genocide (1948), historians have located genocide across Native American history.[19]

Identifying American history as a site of genocide complicates a fundamental premise of the American story. Indeed, histories of Native America provide the starkest contrast to the American ideal. Native American studies scholars often view the conquest of the Americas as an ongoing process marked by mass violence that connects diverse Native nations.[20]

This book seeks to move toward reconciling these contested meanings of America. Drawing upon a wealth of recent scholarship, it aims to distill new insights into a single volume and synthesis, offering heuristics for building a new American history.

While the field of settler colonial studies has revealed the ongoing legacies of global colonialism and practices of Indigenous resistance, it nonetheless has limitations.[21] It often foregrounds Indigenous "elimination" as the defining aspect of Native American history and minimizes the extent of Indigenous power and agency.[22] It also struggles to assess changing power dynamics over time and leaves less space for recognizing Indigenous sovereignty across vast swaths of territories and over long periods.[23] To build a new theory of American history will require recognizing that Native peoples simultaneously determined colonial economies, settlements, and politics and were shaped by them.

Native American and Indigenous studies scholars have responded to the erasure of Native peoples from academic disciplines by emphasizing survival rather than elimination.[24] The founding of the Native American and Indigenous Studies Association (NAISA) in 2008 expanded professional opportunities for Indigenous scholars across the world.[25] Native scholars who once fought for visibility within established scholarly disciplines now interrogate those disciplines, collaborate with tribal communities, and build on the concept of "survivance" first articulated in 1993 by Ojibwe literary critic Gerald Vizenor.[26]

This book, indebted to these scholarly developments, seeks to recognize the extraordinary diversity of Native Americans as well as their equally extraordinary agency, which is essential to rediscovering American history. If the existing paradigms of U.S. history have been maintained by excluding Indigenous people, historicizing the agency of Indigenous peoples offers vital ways to remake these paradigms. Like all peoples, Native Americans have emerged as diverse peoples through centuries-old contests, continuities, and traditions. To understand such diversity and agency requires historicization.[27]

The Rediscovery of America: Native Peoples and the Unmaking of U.S. History traces a particular form of Indigenous agency—the dialectic of Indian-newcomer relations that developed over centuries of interactions, bringing new communities together in inextricable and enduring ways. The following twelve chapters examine specific paradigms of U.S. history—from the Spanish borderlands to the Cold War era—to expose the centrality of Indigenous peoples within them. Dialectics of transformation inform each chapter, none of which begins in a time before encounter. All the chapters focus on the interrelatedness of Native-newcomer relations, collectively asking whether there is potential for building an alternate American story that is not trapped in the framework of European discovery and European "greatness."

In a nation that has always been more diverse than its historical paradigms indicate, confronting such centuries-long dialectics is an essential, if daunting, challenge. The fact that American history flattens the actual diversity of the country's past deepens the need to rethink the field's foundations, especially as many recent syntheses downplay the "colonial era," suggesting that what matters most is the drafting of the U.S. Constitution.[28]

The mythology of America's founding offers limited spaces for Native Americans. The Declaration of Independence called Native peoples "merciless Indian savages" even as they remained an ever-present influence on interior colonial settlements.[29] More experienced leaders than Thomas Jefferson, such as George Washington, advocated diplomacy over violence and drew upon existing Indian treaties to expand federal authority. As the first six chapters of this book suggest, looking at the full complexity of Native American history in the revolutionary period creates a deeper understanding of social—and eventually national—power.

✦

When and where does the story of America start, and who constitutes its central cast? What are the main subjects, or acts, of this national drama? Are the English colonies the site of the origins of America? Did those who proclaimed themselves "We, the People" ever intend to relinquish their exclusive control? What were the legacies of the expansion of the United States across Indigenous homelands in the nineteenth century? How have Native nations responded to the overwhelming presence of federal power within their everyday lives?

Scholars have worked for generations to answer these questions, and starting in the late twentieth century, scholarly as well as tribal projects began to expose a rich historical universe that had been previously neglected. From the Makah Cultural and Research Center in Neah Bay, Washington, to the Mashantucket Pequot Museum and Research Center in Mashantucket, Connecticut, for example, nearly two hundred tribal museums and cultural centers now articulate the histories of these respective Native communities.[30] New source materials—oral traditions, ethnographies, Indigenous languages, and the archival records from multiple empires—have also helped create new historical and literary studies.[31]

Native Americans have now emerged from the shadows of historical neglect in their full complexity, living in varied societies, speaking centuries-old Indigenous languages, and governing often vast territories. Many continue to live in the homes of their ancestors and tend gardens that predate European arrival, such as the twenty-one Pueblo Indian nations of Arizona and New Mexico, who maintain North America's oldest continuously inhabited communities.

This rediscovery of American history continues to swell. Each year new courses, publications, and partnerships between tribal communities and non-tribal institutions continue to shape the practices of researchers, teachers, tribal members, and students of all ages who yearn for more accurate, multiracial histories. Tribal governments have grown in their size and capacities, providing the clearest examples in American politics of the inherent sovereignty of tribal communities. Some, like the Navajo Nation, govern hundreds of thousands of citizens across millions of acres. Others employ thousands of Native and non-Native workers in their industries and economies.[32] These nations reside within the borders of the United States, where they maintain autonomy, sovereignty, and power in concert with the federal government.[33]

If our schools and university classrooms are to remain vital civic institutions, we must create richer and more truthful accounts of the American Republic's origins, expansion, and current form. Studying and teaching America's Indigenous truths reveal anew the varied meanings of America.

✦

This book seeks to reorient U.S. history by redressing the absence of American Indians within it. Covering five hundred years of history, it builds on the work of many other scholars while recognizing that not all peoples, themes, and places can be held within a single study. American history developed out of the epic encounter between Indians and European empires and out of the struggles for sovereignty between Native peoples and the United States. American Indians were central to every century of U.S. historical development.

The Rediscovery of America: Native Peoples and the Unmaking of U.S. History seeks to combine multiple streams of U.S. and Native American history. Rather than seeing U.S. and Native American history as separate or disaggregated, this project envisions them as interrelated. It underscores the mutually constitutive nature of each; the two are and remain interwoven.

There have been few overviews or single-volume interpretations of Native American history. Even as the temporal, spatial, and ethnographical diversity of the subject has made a single interpretation difficult, scholars, teachers, and educators have developed new interpretive paradigms, fashioned new regional histories, and contributed to a vast rediscovery of new periods, places, and themes. Previously ignored, Native American history has become a flourishing field. As the following pages reveal, its insights unsettle operative assumptions about U.S. history.

Notwithstanding its growth, Native American history remains encumbered by many challenges. The habits of previous generations remain calcified. College campuses, textbooks, and public memorials continue to exclude Native peoples. As Pawnee scholar Walter Echo-Hawk maintains, "The widespread lack of reliable information about Native issues is the most pressing problem confronting Native Americans in the United States today."[34]

More studies are needed to historicize Native Americans and assess how Native agency and power have shaped tribal and non-tribal communities. The twelve chapters here seek to denaturalize familiar subjects and expose undetermined, contingent moments of social formation. They offer alternative temporalities of U.S. history; locate Native Americans within larger global contexts; and establish the enduring sovereignty of Native communities as a defining thread of U.S. politics.

Part I—"Indians and Empires"—underscores the centrality of violence to the making of early America. Its first chapters examine sixteenth- and seventeenth-century Spanish, English, Dutch, and French foundations of empire in North America, while subsequent chapters examine the collision of French and English empires and the place of American Indians in the origins of the American Revolution and specifically during one determinative moment: the clash between Pennsylvanian settlers and British imperial authority in the aftermath of the Seven Years' War. This clash—involving settler militias known as the Black Boys—erupted in the aftermath of Pontiac's War and British officials' failed attempts in 1764 and 1765 to establish authority across Great Lakes Indian homelands. As the endnotes to these chapters indicate, studies of Indian-settler conflicts in the Ohio River Valley remain among the most studied areas in American Indian history, with prominent works published annually. How scholars in the fields of U.S. constitutional history and the history of the early Republic have missed this profusion of scholarly work remains an implicit question throughout these chapters.

Part I closes with "Colonialism's Constitution," which provides a suggestive bridge to part II, "Struggles for Sovereignty," arguing that it is impossible to understand the making of the U.S. Constitution outside the context of Native history. The chapter analyzes the emerging structures of national governance in the Articles of Confederation and later in the U.S. Constitution, highlighting how the federalist system arose out of efforts to incorporate interior lands, the use of the inherited "treaty-making" powers of the Articles to negotiate land cessions, and the establishment of the supremacy of federal authority over Indian affairs. In the minds of many founders, the constitutional position of Native peoples was akin to that of foreign nationals, as the commerce clause of the Constitution suggests: "The Congress shall have Power . . . to Regulate Commerce with foreign nations, and among the several states, and with the Indian Tribes." This founding perspective reflected the philosophies of Native people, who have advocated now for centuries for recognition of their autonomous but shared jurisdiction with the federal government. The history of the Republic and of tribal nations has remained indelibly shaped by this constitutional distinction.[35]

The following chapters in part II focus on the struggles of sovereignty between the United States and Native nations. They assess U.S. democracy, racial formation, and Indian removal through a comparative and relational lens and highlight how Indian affairs remained at the center of early U.S. statecraft. Two of the United States' earliest foreign policy determinations—Jay's Treaty and the Louisiana Purchase—evolved from treaty-making practices that started with Indians. These findings suggest the need to reorientate nineteenth-century U.S. history away from its usual focus on eastern North America and to highlight continental transformations attending U.S. expansion. Several chapters locate U.S. expansion within preexisting Spanish, Mexican, Russian, English, and French imperialism, and the histories of California and Colorado highlight transformations engulfing Indian communities during these periods of rapid settlement and gold rush developments.

The later chapters in part II highlight Native American responses to the growth of U.S. power after the Civil War. During Reconstruction, new institutions of federal authority—the army, treaty makers, and other agents of Indian affairs—created vast structures across western North America. Forts, reservation agencies, and boarding schools inaugurated the Reservation Era (1870s–1920s), when federal leaders such as U.S. Army captain Richard Henry Pratt, the founder of the Carlisle Indian Industrial School and architect of its military-style pedagogy, sought to transform Native people by removing children from their families and destabilizing tribal governments.

As these chapters highlight, for half a century displacing children and alienating reservation lands defined U.S. policy. Over seventy-five thousand children were removed to federally funded boarding schools and nearly a hundred million acres of reservation lands became further dispossessed. By 1912 Congress had placed Indian communities under its "absolute jurisdiction and control," as Public Law 219 established.[36]

This doctrine of congressional authority over Indian affairs, known as "plenary power," lies at the heart of these chapters. In the late nineteenth and early twentieth centuries, a new generation of Native American activists responded to these intrusions, and the book's last chapters examine how such activism shaped the contours of federal policy, particularly during the Indian New Deal and Cold War era. The analysis draws on studies of reservation activism, the Society of American Indians (SAI), and the publications by its leaders, including Laura Cornelius Kellogg (Oneida), Zitkála-Šá (Dakota), Henry Roe Cloud (Ho-Chunk), and Elizabeth Bender Cloud (Ojibwe), among others.

As a generation of activists confronted governmental intrusions and false promises, their efforts challenged mythologies of American innocence and sought new interpretations of history. Kellogg's advocacy was steeped in efforts to restore historic practices of Indigenous governance, particularly the gendered forms of authority within Iroquois (Haudenosaunee) communities. Roe Cloud, Bender Cloud, and other SAI members developed inter-tribal, coalition-building institutions that proved essential throughout the Cold War. Bender Cloud became the only co-founder of the two primary national Indian rights organizations of the modern era: the SAI in 1911 and the National Congress of American Indians (NCAI) in 1944.

The book concludes with assessments of the surprising paradoxes of Native resurgence in the twentieth century. In addition to foregrounding the agency of Native peoples, this examination invites scholars to see Native actors as agents in complex and contradictory structures. Federal-Indian relations have enmeshed Native nations in challenging doctrines of law and policy, particularly during two recent eras: termination (1953–70s) and self-determination (1975–present).

This history highlights the challenges inherent in the exercise of tribal sovereignty, and it begins by showing how New Deal–era reforms were initially used against Native nations by Senate and federal leaders such as Bureau of Indian Affairs (BIA) commissioner Dillon Myer. These officials tied the prospects for land settlements to acceptance of policies designed to "terminate" tribal sovereignty. As termination undermined Native nations, it fueled a generation of Indian activists, including reservation leaders such as Ada Deer (Menominee) and urban and non-reservation members, including those in the American Indian Movement (AIM). At the close of the 1960s, Native activists seized not only Alcatraz Island in San Francisco Bay but also the United States' attention, landing Indigenous militancy and activism on the front pages. Such activism proved essential in transforming national policies, aided by the legislative advocacy of Native leaders such as Deer.

The last decades of the twentieth century revealed the radical potential of reform movements. To navigate the structures of U.S. dominion required engaging with its institutions of law making, specifically Congress and the federal courts. Native peoples have long sought redress through both formal and informal processes—advocacy and activism have often been two sides of the same coin within Native politics. By the end of the twentieth century, after five hundred years of contact with Europeans, a new generation of Native leaders had endured the turbulent challenges of the Cold War era and entered the dawn of the new century, positioned to ensure that their communities never again faced elemental threats to their existence.

Part I
Indians and Empires

✦

A 1613 engraving of the July 1609 battle between Samuel de Champlain, his men, their Native allies, and Mohawk soldiers. (Beinecke Rare Book and Manuscript Library, Yale University.)

E
B
C
C
C
C
C

1 • American Genesis

Indians and the Spanish Borderlands

It would be an endless story to attempt to describe in detail
each one of the many things that are found there.
—*Juan de Oñate (1599)*

Over two months had passed since the twelve horsemen left the colony. It was autumn 1776, and the party had traversed hundreds of miles across some of the most treacherous terrain in North America. The nights were cold, followed by long, occasionally waterless days. Suddenly: snow. At first it dotted the peaks along the western horizon, and then it enveloped them, sometimes falling "all day . . . without ceasing."[1] Lacking firewood, they "suffered greatly from the cold" accompanied by a relentless north wind.[2]

Led by two Spanish friars, Francisco Atanasio Domínguez and Silvestre Vélez de Escalante, the party had not seen another European since July, when they had left New Mexico. For months they had journeyed through Ute and Paiute homelands in Colorado and Utah in the late summer months, occasionally befriending and following Native guides. Only a few of the Indians they encountered spoke any Spanish. Though most had never seen Europeans, they knew from the reports of others that equestrian travelers brought violence and suffering, and many avoided the party.[3]

This was the first attempt by the Spanish crown to link Spain's oldest North American colony, New Mexico, founded in 1598, with its newest in California, colonized in 1769. The party expected to find navigable rivers, trails, and people to assist them in their journey to the garrison at Monterey, but they did not make it anywhere near the Pacific. Cold and hungry, in western Utah the friars abandoned their attempt and instead started a month-long return route to New Mexico, where the familiar smells of roasted chilies and piñon fires awaited.

Had they continued, the party would have struggled to pass through Western Shoshone homelands across Nevada and would have confronted the virtual impossibility of crossing the Sierra Nevada Mountains in winter. Returning south to New Mexico and its centuries-old missions and settlements made the most sense. The decision saved their lives and along with them their maps and journals, which became a part of the imperial archive. Subsequent explorers—including Americans Meriwether Lewis and William Clark—would benefit from these documents, while others would later study the party's crossing—the first recorded—of the Colorado River in what later became known as the Grand Canyon.[4]

On November 14, the party arrived in familiar territory, the outskirts of the Hopi village of Mishongnovi in Arizona. This, the region's principal village on Second Mesa, had long-standing relations with the crown. The community was characterized by verdant fruit and vegetable gardens, which produced bountiful harvests of corn, squash, melons, and beans.[5]

Though relieved to be back in the colonial world with its recognizable bounties, the party still had a lengthy journey ahead. Santa Fe and other settlements along the Rio Grande were still a week away, and they remained burdened by the harsh winter conditions and dwindling food supplies. After two further days of riding, they halted for the evening.[6] Desperately hungry, the friars ordered another one of their horses to be killed, but they were careful to instruct their party "that no one was to approach" the Hopi cattle around them, even if they appeared to be "runaways or public property."[7]

The men were disgruntled. Horses were their personal property, and they had already been asked to butcher many during their journey. Ten days earlier, as they considered their descent down to the north side of the river, even their horsemeat had run out. "We had not eaten a single thing today," the friars recorded—breakfast consisted of "toasted pads of low prickly pear cactus."[8] Surely now that they were back in the empire, they could seize a calf from this distant Pueblo community, one infamous for its resistance to Spanish authority.[9] Who would care?

This scene might appear minor in the annals of Spanish colonialism, which brought death, disease, and devastation, and later dispossession to tens of millions of Indigenous peoples. But colonialism is also a lived reality. Since 1492 its everyday manifestations and interactions have shaped the modern world. As with the events that precipitated the American Revolution, these 1776 encounters highlight aspects of daily life within a sprawling empire that predated English settlement and vastly exceeded it in size.

Spain's American empire stretched across the hemisphere from Argentina to New Mexico, where nearly one hundred Pueblo communities confronted the Spanish in the 1500s.[10] From Taos Pueblo in the east to the Hopi Pueblos in the west, New Mexico formed New Spain's northernmost border. When Domínguez and Escalante ventured into the continent, they did so as agents of an empire that used everyday negotiations to develop the world's largest colonial dominion. Nearly a dozen generations had expanded Spain's archipelago of American possessions, which remained surrounded by vast territories of Indigenous lands.[11]

Within this empire, Spanish-Indian relations were governed by countless agreements and rules of behavior, both formal and informal, reinforced by the overlapping institutions of church and state.[12] Inhabited by approximately 75 million Native peoples in 1492, the Americas were not so much discovered by Spanish colonialists as created by the generations of Spanish-Indian relations that followed.[13] Even as Spain introduced violence, disease, and carnage across the hemisphere, throughout the centuries it had come to depend on the negotiated relations of power that wedded Natives and newcomers together.

The Indigenous peoples of Spanish America inhabited a colonial order that had been forced upon them, and they lived the imposition in an everyday struggle for survival.[14] The initially deadly, confusing, and complex encounters between Native peoples and Spanish colonists eventually transformed as Indigenous peoples and Spanish settlers came to coexist in the same social order.[15] While subordinate to Spanish officials, settlers, priests, and soldiers, Native peoples within the empire were subject to the law and had rights and responsibilities that came with the vassal status they occupied in the colonizers' legal culture.[16] Across a sprawling empire, Indians had legal rights, and they exerted them. They had not only agency but power.

Across the northernmost reaches of the Spanish empire—the Spanish borderlands—the power of Indigenous nations often rivaled that of Europeans. The Ute of Colorado and the Comanche of the southern Plains dominated Spanish New Mexico and Texas throughout the 1700s and 1800s.[17] Comanches were "so superior . . . in firearms as well as in numbers," a Texas presidio commander reported, "that our destruction seems probable."[18] Within each colony, dozens of Pueblo towns, Apache bands, and Coahuilteco-speaking villagers maintained cultural, religious, and economic autonomy throughout the colonial era and into the nineteenth century.[19] These Native nations had endured the initial disruptions brought by Europeans and carved out autonomous spaces within colonial societies and across their expanding hinterlands.

Far from the urban centers of empire where colonial authority was concentrated, Indigenous power flowed across the borderlands. Spain's imperial control was not evenly exerted across its extensive domain, and its claims could be exercised only on limited corridors of lands.[20] Throughout the Spanish borderlands, Native nations were constituents within a multi-polar world of overlapping and at times contested sovereignties. Despite Spain's long-standing presence, beyond the Rio Grande no one held easy or exclusive dominion. Many peoples—both Spanish and Indigenous—vied for supremacy. Starting in the 1500s and for the next two hundred years, Indigenous peoples and Spanish settlers traded, raided, warred, and made peace together. They bartered in villages and at seasonal markets, fought as allies against common enemies (both imperial and Indigenous), and coexisted across generations and centuries, eventually blurring the boundaries between Native and newcomer and forming a constellation of diverse ethnicities and communities.

The Spanish borderlands extended across three thousand miles: from California's missions across Arizona and Mexico through central Texas to the Mississippi Gulf coast and to the Florida coast. There, on the Atlantic at St. Augustine, El Castillo de San Marcos, the oldest fort in North America, guarded Spain's first North American settlement. Founded in 1565, St. Augustine served as an outpost to protect Spanish ships heading north from Cuba. Its turrets faced the sea and sought to keep other imperial forces from moving into the Caribbean—the initial nucleus of Spain's American empire.

New Mexico was in the heart of the borderlands. Throughout the seventeenth century, it was home to more Native peoples than other American colonies—nearly eighty thousand Pueblo community members at the time of contact.[21] The Pueblo speak several distinct languages across dozens of village communities and practice a centuries-old religion, maintained even after they adopted a nominal Catholicism.[22]

As many as seventy-five to one hundred Pueblo villages greeted Spanish conquistador Francisco de Coronado in 1540.[23] Many Pueblo villages, including Acoma, Taos, and Pecos, held two thousand to three thousand people and traced their origins back to the early second millennium. Others were smaller, with only several hundred inhabitants. All had their own religious and political leaders and grew corn, beans, and squash—the staples of North America's Indigenous economies.[24]

Domínguez and Escalante knew this world well. They had both traveled from Mexico to missionize the Pueblos earlier.[25] By refusing to allow their men to poach in November 1776, they were respecting the negotiated forms of Indigenous power that lay at the heart of their society. They understood the value of Hopi property and the need to protect it, and they respected Hopi law as part of an empire that depended on the maintenance of laws, traditions, and customs. Even though the authority of the crown diminished with distance and violent coercion continued, to take the Hopi cattle would be to defy the political and religious logics that guided them. It would be a crime.[26]

The laws that govern societies often appear natural. They seem to flow from a seemingly universal understanding and become normalized through repetition and practice.[27] But the friars and their men did not have a shared understanding of justice. On more than one occasion, the men broke ranks and traded illicit goods with interior Utes in defiance of the friars and the Spanish governors, whose prohibitions, or *bandos*, had attempted to limit such trade.[28] These religious leaders understood everyone to be members of a single social order, and their moral and political responsibility was to follow norms. Representatives of cross and crown, the friars were resolute in normalizing the rule of law.[29]

Native peoples across the Spanish empire lived in an increasingly varied, hierarchical, and expansive colonial society. They encountered soldiers, priests, and generations of settlers in the markets, on military campaigns, and in church services. Spain's American empire revolved around Native peoples, and the Spanish relationship to the Indigenous population was fundamentally different than that of Europe's other empires.

Unlike those in England's and France's North American colonies, Native peoples formed Spain's largest laboring classes. They became converted by the millions and learned the Spanish language as early as the 1500s. Indios became, moreover, a racially classified people in European law, subject to Spain's New Laws of 1542 that held, among other provisions, that Native peoples from Spanish domains could not be enslaved.[30] In 1549 Catalina de Velasco, an "India" servant of twenty, visited the missionary Bartolomé de Las Casas at the monastery of San Pablo in Castile. She successfully petitioned him to intercede with his Spanish superiors for justice, claiming that she had been "stolen and brought as a child to these kingdoms" and was being unjustly held.[31] Indigenous peoples across the Spanish empire, like Catalina de Velasco, used the law to navigate the rapacious forms of colonial violence unleashed after 1492.

To know America and its history requires knowledge of these centuries of Spanish injustice and Indigenous negotiation, the recent studies of which have recast the temporal and spatial boundaries of early American history. Recurring themes in this scholarship are the adaptations of Native peoples to Spanish empire and the incorporation of European imports into Native worlds. Spanish-introduced technologies, religious practices, clothing, and currencies changed everyday life across the Americas while Native labor, foods, knowledges, and minerals shaped Spain's political economy. The horse and cattle herds that prompted disagreements such as that between the friars and their men were not indigenous to the Americas, and neither were Hopi peach orchards or the Spanish lingua franca that first echoed across the region in the 1520s.

Spain's Earliest American Conquests

Before the conquest of Mexico in 1519, Spanish settlements were limited to islands in the Caribbean. Puerto Rico, Jamaica, Cuba, and Hispaniola were taken following Columbus's final voyages, and they provided launching points for further expeditions like Juan Ponce de León's 1513 exploration of Florida.[32] The lands claimed for the Spanish crown formally became extensions of the Spanish kingdom rather than colonies.[33]

Cruelties and violence against Native peoples characterized the first half century of Spanish imperialism. On his second voyage, Columbus enslaved "five hundred and fifty souls . . . around two hundred of [whom] died" before reaching Spain, and he cast those who died "into the sea."[34] Slavery, overwork, famine, and European pathogens killed Native peoples across the Caribbean, creating the most horrific of all chapters in Native American history.[35] Native communities throughout the region sought to drive the invaders out, but in vain—Taino, Arawak, Carib, and numerous other peoples were decimated.[36]

The New Laws of 1542 had emerged partly in response to the brutalities of conquest. Bartolomé de Las Casas first came to Hispaniola in 1502 as a landowner who participated in raids against the native Taino population. Living among the generation of men—*hidalgos*—who had come to the Americas in search of wealth and power, he saw firsthand what he described as the "horror and dread" of conquest.[37] The Spanish passed along their aspirations to fame and fortune—and the accompanying violence—to their sons.[38]

Ordained as a priest on Hispaniola in 1510, Las Casas left the Americas in the 1530s, having witnessed countless scenes of suffering and death. In the solitude of Spanish monasteries, he worked to change how the Spanish empire treated Native people. He understood what was happening in the Americas. He had seen children like Catalina de Velasco trafficked, held against their will, beaten, branded, chained, and raped by soldiers, ship captains, crew members, and property owners in Spain. Though Las Casas had once believed in the practice of fortune seeking, he changed his mind in the face of colonialism's brutality. "Who of those born in future generations will believe this?" he asked after witnessing the depopulation that the Spanish caused.[39]

Juan Ponce de León, by contrast, unashamedly sought fortune. An impoverished noble in Spain, he accompanied Columbus to the Caribbean in 1493 and participated in many conquests thereafter. He fought across Hispaniola throughout the 1490s and helped defeat the Taino in what was their first organized military confrontation with the Spanish in 1495.[40] In 1509 he led the subjugation of nearby Puerto Rico where, as the island's first governor, he founded its first Spanish settlement, divided its Indian slaves among his men, and led a succession of attacks upon the remaining Taino villages.

De León governed through terror. He used attack dogs so mercilessly that "the Indians were more afraid of ten Spaniards with the dog, than one hundred without him."[41] He so perfected this terror by hunting Indians with greyhounds in Hispaniola that a new word was coined to express casting a victim to the dogs: *aperrear.*[42]

The rapaciousness of Spanish colonialism originated in the centuries-long consolidation of monarchial power in Iberia during the Reconquista.[43] A distinctive masculine culture of violence had taught generations of Iberian men like de León to be experts in the technologics of violence. After 1492 these men increasingly sought their fortunes abroad.

Those who sought wealth and glory overseas came mostly from impoverished families.[44] The Spanish crown's professional soldiers and naval officers remained in Europe, where they were needed to lead the endless European wars. The men who initially came to the Americas were not formally trained or disciplined soldiers; they were neither paid for military service nor forced into it.[45] They were fortune seekers who did not hesitate to use violence in order to obtain it.

Failing to find abundant mineral wealth in the Caribbean, the conquistadors continued exploring the western waters and larger basin around them. Many obtained land grants across the growing archipelago of colonies, receiving property title from the crown in exchange for their participation.[46] Many conquistadors, including Columbus, were fervently religious, so they believed their task included spreading Christianity as well. Thus, for those willing to risk life and limb against Native peoples, the opportunities were spiritual as well as material.

But the Spanish conquistadors perpetrated horrors on a previously unimaginable scale. They brought with them deaths due to military campaigns, indiscriminate violence, animal attacks, slavery and forced labor, and above all European pathogens. Of the 3 million inhabitants of Hispaniola at the time of Columbus's arrival in 1493, only five hundred remained fifty years later.[47] The Spanish conquest was simultaneously a holocaust.

The Meeting: Spanish and Nahua Empires in Mexico

After the Caribbean, Spain expanded into Mexico, which quickly became the center of its American empire. Home to tens of millions of Native peoples, Mexico was governed by an empire of its own, the Aztec, or Nahua, empire.[48] Led by the emperor Montezuma, the Nahuas had consolidated power during the previous centuries, incorporating millions of surrounding peoples under their sovereignty through trade, warfare, and tribute.[49] As much as any factor, the Nahua language united the empire.[50] Politically, the empire dominated from its capital of Tenochtitlan, a city ten times larger than Seville, where Spanish ships started their voyages across the Atlantic.[51]

The Nahua governed millions from one of the earth's greatest cities, their influence extending throughout central, southern, and even northern Mexico. Though only limited trade connected the Rio Grande Pueblos with this imperial colossus over one thousand miles to the south, knowledge of the northern cities soon came to entice Spanish conquistadors.

As along the Rio Grande, horticultural villages thrived throughout the Nahua world. Semi-autonomous Native villages formed a vast, interconnected network of politically identifiable ethnic states, known in Nahuatl as *altepetls*.[52] Nominally under the distant authority of Tenochtitlan, these self-governing communities were ruled by a dynastic ruler known as a *tlatoani*. Their political structures often emerged from amalgamations of earlier communities or recent migrants to central Mexico, including northern Chichimecas, who had migrated into central Mexico generations beforehand.[53] Much like European villages claimed by distant urban monarchs, the *altepetls* had their own religious structures and markets.[54] Unlike the Taino, Arawak, and other Caribbean societies, these sedentary horticulturalists inhabited an institutionally varied and ethnically heterogeneous world, a world that had developed longstanding patterns of engagement with distant Nahua authorities.

The heterogeneity of the Nahua empire enabled the Spanish to conquer it. When Montezuma met Hernán Cortés on November 8, 1519, two vast empires, each commanding millions, came face-to-face for the first time.[55] Now European and American empires confronted one another, linking their civilizations, continents, and indeed two hemispheres. The forging of a truly interconnected, global society had now begun.

The world of Nahua-speaking *altepetls* had many tensions. Some, like the Tlaxcalans, maintained their autonomy but chafed under Montezuma's rule. They allied with Cortés during the Spanish-Aztec War (1519–21) and joined Spanish campaigns thereafter.[56] Tlaxcalan leaders were so proud of their service with Cortés that they traveled to Spain to present gifts to the crown and to argue that Indians who had befriended the Spanish were deserving of recognition.[57] Indigenous allies became essential auxiliaries in the Spanish-Mesoamerican War (1517–50), of which the Spanish-Aztec War was the central theater.[58]

Indigenous-Spanish alliances grew common in sixteenth-century New Spain, as the Spanish viceroyalty of Mexico was known. Spanish racial and legal categories—eventually known as *castas*, or castes—did not yet exist and would take generations after conquest to fully evolve.[59] Spanish leaders and their growing number of Native allies availed themselves of opportunities to cooperate or exploit existing rivalries. In 1524 a Spanish army led by Pedro de Alvarado exploited long-standing antagonism between Quiché and Cakchiquel Maya in the south of Mexico. De Alvarado came with Spanish recruits and hundreds of Xochimilco Nahua auxiliaries conscripted from Mexico City as well as with recently imported Africans, who in the 1490s had been enslaved in the Caribbean, laboring alongside Taino and other Natives.[60]

De Alvarado deftly pitted these rival Mayan groups against one another; just as Tlaxcalan soldiers had joined Cortés on final assaults against Tenochtitlan, de Alvarado used Nahua troops throughout this invasion. In two months, he extended Spanish influence south into the Mayan highlands and claimed Guatemala for the crown.[61] Protracted battles followed, however, as did years of recurring conflicts.

From the perspective of North America, the Meeting and the subsequent wars of conquest enmeshed the most densely populated portions of the Americas within the deadly currents of European empire. Giant tentacles of influences now stretched across the Atlantic, each season securing firmer, more grounded moorings. As in the Caribbean and soon the Andean world, Europeans consumed Indigenous resources, lives, and labor. Father Toribio de Benavente wrote of the conquest that Native captives "were brought into Mexico City in great flocks, like sheep, so they could be branded easily."[62] These disruptions radiated north, arriving with conquistadors in the 1530s and 1540s, creating the Spanish borderlands and laying the foundations for the emergence of other American colonies.

De Soto and Coronado across the Spanish Borderlands: 1539–42

In 1539 and 1540 two unrelated Spanish *entradas* (invasions) crisscrossed North America.[63] Both came to plunder Indigenous communities and to find additional worlds to conquer. One arrived via the Caribbean and moved into Florida and the Southeast; the other moved from Mexico north along the Rio Grande and then onto the Plains. They were led, respectively, by Hernando de Soto and Francisco Vázquez de Coronado.

Each expedition failed to secure wealth for their leaders but succeeded in laying claims to Florida and the Rio Grande, respectively, which became the first European possessions in North America and eventual hubs of Spanish colonialism in the Southwest and Southeast. Each also laid waste to countless Indian villages, mapped the continent's lands, and then departed without conquering anyone. De Soto died of disease along the Mississippi in 1542, while Coronado died in Mexico City twelve years after returning. His chief lieutenant, García López de Cárdenas, died in a Spanish prison, convicted for defying crown orders not to attack Indian villages without provocation.[64]

These first North American campaigns shared much in common. Their leaders disregarded evidence that there were few prosperous Indigenous kingdoms awaiting them in the north: no mineral wealth was to be found among the many Pueblo villages that Coronado visited, and de Soto's most valued theft was a trunk of coastal pearls. Both ignored their men's exhortations to return to Spanish ships or settlements in order to avoid prolonged confrontations with resident Indians.

After landing on the Floridian coast in 1539 and wintering nearby, de Soto inched through Georgia and the Carolinas with a party of nearly seven hundred. Months passed and then seasons. His search of Carolina's coastal and Piedmont communities having come up empty, he ordered his men to march west across the Appalachians—mountains that English traders would not traverse for well over a century.[65] Knowing that Native kingdoms had formed in the Andean and central Mexican highlands, he was convinced that he would find others in the Appalachians.

Upon eventually reaching the Mississippi, he refused to follow it toward the Caribbean and back to the empire, though he knew that the river offered the possibility of return. Spanish explorers had known of this nautical entryway to the northern lands since the days of Ponce de León.[66] But de Soto carried on, and his party traversed the river's slow currents for unknown points to the west.

Through 1541 de Soto was on a random, destination-less journey marked by recurring frustrations, recrimination, and battles with local communities. On more than one occasion, he asked local Native leaders whether they knew of nearby gold deposits or how to get to the Pacific Ocean, which he knew was off to the west somewhere. Native peoples suggested that elusive minerals were only days of travel away, incensing de Soto, who became aggressive and used terror as his preferred method of diplomacy. In March 1542, in retaliation against a town that had sent his men farther into the Arkansas backcountry, he commanded his men to slaughter the town, known as Nilco.[67] The Spanish arrived on foot and horseback, surprising the unsuspecting village:

> The cries of the women and children were so loud that they deafened the ears of those who pursued them. A hundred or so Indians were killed there and many were badly wounded with the lances, [but] were let go in order that they might strike terror into those who did not happen to be there. There were men so cruel and such butchers that they killed old men and young men and all they came upon without any one offering them little or much resistance. . . . Some they lanced and let them go in that condition; but on seeing a child or woman, they would capture and deliver such a person [into slavery]. . . . Of the Indians at Nilco, eighty women and children were seized.[68]

News of the massacre spread as its wounded survivors ran off and regrouped. The dead, the survivors' wounds, and the enslavement of Nilco's captured women and children communicated the lessons of encounter.

In May 1542, sick and dispirited, de Soto, the would-be conqueror, died, along with half of his party. Most of the men's horses were so debilitated that they could no longer carry their owners, having not been fitted with horseshoes in months. The expedition's return in September 1543 was the end to a forgettable moment of failed exploration, one of at least six expeditions to Florida that failed between 1513 and the 1560s.[69]

North American history originates amid such chaos and failure. Across the continent, Spanish (and later French, Dutch, and English) exploration was often marked by failures. Historians have tended to see these events from the perspective of European national history, narrating the explorers' arrival, departure, and fate as the main features of analysis.[70] Histories of failure are by definition unnationalistic, and for many, de Soto and Coronado are best known as namesakes for American car manufacturers, not for massacring Indian peoples. Borderlands history invites a deeper look at past failures because failures tell stories that unmake national histories.

They also tell stories of encounter and survival.[71] The most devastating consequences of these earliest Spanish expeditions came not from Spanish metals, men, or missionaries. De Soto's crossbows, lances, and swords took several hundred lives, but his horses and domesticated pigs brought with them invisible microbes that destroyed those who never met his expedition.[72] Thousands of Native peoples across the southeastern chiefdoms that de Soto visited died following his arrival. Acute infectious diseases like smallpox, measles, yellow fever, typhus, whooping cough, influenza, and plague struck the region.[73] By the next European intrusions into the region, few of the concentrated kingdoms de Soto encountered still existed. In 1567, when Juan Pardo retraced de Soto's expedition across the Carolina Piedmont, the region was in transition, and the concentrated power of chiefdoms de Soto encountered was weakening.[74]

As a result, Native communities throughout the seventeenth century recast themselves. After de Soto's travels, Indigenous communities experienced generations of largely unrecorded migrations and demographic collapse while at the same time resisting the growing external pressures of the traffic in Indian captives.[75] Old societies rapidly regrouped into new ones in a process scholars now refer to as *ethnogenesis*—the creation of new ethnic communities and social identities out of the remains of former societies.[76] Histories relating these events help us understand Native North America after 1492 and offer alternatives to European-centered narratives. They provide a more accurate story of American genesis.

Along the Rio Grande, Coronado and later Spanish conquistadors encountered nearly one hundred Pueblo villages that constituted a world of Native communities across the Southwest. Within this world, as Domínguez and Escalante learned, old communities such as the Hopi and emergent Native powers such as the Comanche had survived the calamity of colonialism, even making colonialism their own. Born of colonialism, their power undermined the Spanish empire—and outlasted it.

The Colonization of the Silver Frontier: The Mixtón War of 1540–41 and After

Following Cortés's negotiations with Nahua leaders and continuing the sixteenth-century *entradas* across north-central Mexico, colonial violence or-

After conquering Tenochtitlan, Hernán Cortés summoned Indigenous nobles to Coyoacán, demanding they submit to Spanish dominion and pay tribute to Emperor Charles V. In response to the refusal of several lords, Cortés set mastiffs on them, continuing a form of Spanish terror unleashed in the Caribbean in the 1490s. According to the Nahuatl gloss on this codex, seven Indigenous nobles died in the attack. This work was created by an unidentified Nahua artist in 1560. (Bibliothèque nationale de France.)

ganized the emergent world of New Spain. As in the Caribbean, Spanish governance required violence and monopolized its use.[77]

After the conquest, Cortés established his headquarters in Coyoacán, a village on the outskirts of Tenochtitlan. Central Tenochtitlan remained in ruins following the battles of 1521, so Cortés received delegations of Native leaders at Coyoacán. They needed to understand that the Nahua empire had fallen and that the Spanish were now the rulers—those who failed to understand the new power dynamics and refused to submit faced Cortés's wrath.[78] In response to one recalcitrant delegation, Cortés unleashed a pack of mastiffs on the visiting nobles, allowing the ravenous creatures to kill some of them.[79] A Nahuatl codex gloss reproduces the scene of carnage and shows the demoralized survivors chastised by one of Cortés's lieutenants.[80]

The Spanish used terror not only to control Indians physically but also to sow fear. Murders and massacres communicated destruction, but they also communicated power, informing the war's survivors of the region's new realities. Even when idle, Spanish weapons, horses, dogs, metals, and guns served to remind Native communities that the conquest never ended.[81]

The vast distances between the Rio Grande and Tenochtitlan witnessed cycles of Spanish aggression and Native resistance throughout the sixteenth century. One episode, the Mixtón War, became one of northern Mexico's most decisive military campaigns and the most threatening revolt in colonial Mexico before the independence rebellions of 1810.[82] It erupted in 1540 after numerous settler soldiers joined Coronado's expedition to the north, leaving behind less defended settlements.

A part of the Chichimeca War, as the subjugation of Mexico's northern communities was known, the Mixtón War required the mobilization of tens of thousands of Spanish soldiers, Native allies, and horses. They targeted Caxcanes peoples who were members of a confederacy known as the Gran Chichimeca, which attempted to stop a decade of Spanish advances from Compostela and Guadalajara.[83] Initially, a force of fifteen thousand Chichimecas easily defeated the four hundred Spaniards and their Native allies who had unwisely engaged in battle before their reinforcements arrived. Encouraged by their victory, the Chichimecas attacked at Guadalajara, besieging dozens of Spanish mounted soldiers behind fortified walls.[84]

Unbeknownst to the Caxcanes, two decades of rule in Mexico had brought to the Spanish not only countless riches but also millions of subject peoples. Conquistadors learned in the Caribbean that to exploit American wealth required the subjugation of its peoples. Their service, labor, and loyalties were harnessed to imperial purposes, and those that fought with the Spanish became known as *indios amigos*—auxiliaries who marched north against the Caxcanes.[85]

The army of Mexico's first viceroy, Antonio de Mendoza, included thirty thousand Tlaxcalan and Nahua soldiers.[86] They proved decisive in the defeat of the Caxcanes during the Mixtón War, which raged for two years. Their service reinforced Spanish authority across New Spain, demonstrating to the crown that its authority rested in part on the loyalty of Native peoples.[87]

Capitalizing on Indigenous rivalries, the Mixtón War included soldiers on both sides whose villages shared deep animosities. Numerous Indigenous communities from central Mexico—the Nahua, the Otomís, and the Tarascans—had tried to subjugate these northern peoples, whose homelands between northern Mexico's two principal mountain chains—the Sierra Madre

Oriental and the Sierra Madre Occidental—had been the highway to northern trade and travel.[88]

With the Chichimecas defeated, the Spanish could turn to extracting profits from a stable New Galicia. These efforts were led by Cristóbal de Oñate, who became the most successful settler in New Galicia. A captain under the infamous conquistador Nuño Beltrán de Guzmán, de Oñate had led the establishment of Guadalajara in 1531.[89] He held a lieutenant governorship until 1545 and then helped to finance the growth of the region's mining industry at Zacatecas until his death in 1567. These mines soon became among the most profitable spots on earth.[90]

Mexico's silver industry, together with the mines at Potosí in the Andes, helped to revolutionize the monetary systems of Europe. For centuries after 1492, silver poured into Spain, forty-eight thousand tons from Mexico alone.[91] By 1585 imported bullion amounted to 25 percent of the crown's total revenue, rescuing the Spanish from their imbalances of trade with Asia.[92]

Although the Spanish conquistadors had been obsessed with finding gold, silver had a far greater impact. Indigenous laborers extracted nearly a hundred times more silver than gold in the Americas. As in Peru, nearly all the excavation work in Mexico was done by hand.[93] Hauling ore through cavernous tunnels, workers carried it in baskets and ascended the steep mine shafts with ladders.[94] As soon as it was removed from the ground, the silver was separated from the ore using mercury, on which the Spanish crown maintained a monopoly.[95] By 1700 the largest silver mine in the Americas, Potosí in Peru, elevation thirteen thousand feet, was among the largest cities in the world with more than one hundred thousand inhabitants, Indigenous and Spanish.[96]

Once transported across the Caribbean and onto galleons heading to Seville, American silver was again remade into Spanish pesos, French pences, and English pennies.[97] American silver provided a common universal currency in Europe, helping to move economies away from barter to trade and launching the mercantile and later commercial revolutions. Indigenous-mined silver expanded European commerce globally.[98]

Silver mines became the centers of power in northern New Spain. Subsequent outposts for travel, trade, and communication followed, as did continued Indigenous conflicts throughout the century. Increasingly, the crown worked to both missionize and pacify the region's Native communities. Spanish leaders encouraged the resettling of their Native allies from central Mexico—Tarascan, Otomí, and Tlaxcalan—to northern districts. For these Indigenous settlers, the opportunity for agricultural autonomy and pastoralism was appealing and constituted a form of Indigenous settler colonialism in which Spain's Native allies aided in the dispossession of other Native nations and benefited from such service by receiving titles to their lands.[99] The notion of Indigenous settler colonialism might challenge how we understand global history, but the currents of colonization flowed across sixteenth-century New Spain in uncommon and varied directions. And it was these currents that laid the foundations for the acquisition of more northern lands across the Spanish frontier in North America.

Juan de Oñate and the Conquest of New Mexico

Like other Spanish *hidalgos*, Cristóbal de Oñate passed on to his children both fortune and ambition. His son Juan continued his father's legacies, writing that as soon as he was "old enough to bear arms" he began fighting northern Mexican Indians, including the "Chichimecos and Gua[chi]chiles."[100] Like his father, Juan hoped to secure new riches in the north and to broaden Spanish dominion. Born amid the violence that characterized Mexico's sixteenth-century silver frontier, he expanded Spain's empire into the Rio Grande Valley and became the first governor of its northernmost settlement, New Mexico.[101]

In New Mexico, Pueblo Indians became Juan de Oñate's primary targets. He planned to bring these northern communities into submission to both cross and crown. Following Coronado's *entrada* in 1540, Spanish colonial policies had begun to change. After passage of the New Laws of 1542, reforms were initiated by the Spanish crown, which attempted to incorporate Native peoples as vassals and subjects of Spanish political and religious authority. Mandatory labor requirements (*servicio personal*) gradually ceased throughout the 1540s, making material payments the primary form of compulsory tribute required in New Spain.[102] Additionally, some empowered and emboldened Catholic priests, like Mexico's first bishop, Juan de Zumárraga, attempted to limit outright abuses against Native peoples. Zumárraga oversaw educational, cultural, and spiritual reforms that sought to build Christian and enlightened institutions within the colonial enterprise.[103]

Missionaries sometimes walked barefoot and traveled unarmed, in stark contrast to colonial officials. Starting in the 1570s, Jesuit missionaries unaccompanied by soldiers expanded their efforts across New Spain, while Franciscan missionaries worked closely within colonized settlements at the many silver mines established in the wake of the Mixtón War.[104] The Spanish colonial world became increasingly characterized by a growing administrative duality between church and state. The divide became particularly apparent along the Rio Grande.[105]

Unlike participants in previous Spanish expeditions, Oñate was heading north to stay. It had taken him three years to convince three hundred settlers to join him. He was accompanied by a thousand head of cattle and eighty wagons, one hundred equestrian soldiers, a small number of Indian auxiliaries, and two African laborers, Luis and Manuel, whose attempts to escape Spanish bondage eventually cost them their lives.[106] His goal was to settle the region, to subjugate the region's Native communities, and to prospect for new mining areas. Father Alonso Martínez accompanied him as head of a small number of Franciscans.[107]

Initially, Oñate's efforts went smoothly. He claimed possession of the region at El Paso on April 30, 1598, proceeded slowly north along the Rio Grande, and encountered Pueblo communities that provided no organized military resistance. But the Spanish found many Pueblos deserted and sent scouts around to neighboring villages to encourage compliance.

Eventually, at a large gathering at Santo Domingo Pueblo, north of present-day Albuquerque, in July, Pueblo leaders—Pamo, Poquia, Pestaca, Atequita, Paquia, and Poloco—welcomed Oñate, the friars, and their accompanying soldiers. They agreed that their communities would submit to Spanish authority of their own accord. Oñate's secretary recorded, "They accepted our king, Don Philip, as their king and freely rendered him obedience and vassalage, without being compelled to do so by anyone."[108] Whether their submission was truly voluntary, the Pueblo leaders knelt and kissed Oñate and Martinez's hands.[109] Oñate estimated that 60,000 Native peoples lived across the region, a far more conservative estimate than that of Antonio de Espejo, who in 1583 claimed it to be home to 183,000.[110]

The gathering, held in the central plaza, surrounded by Santo Domingo's multi-storied adobe homes, cemented Spanish claims to New Mexico. The four previous Spanish expeditions had brought violence and chaos to Pueblo communities, and memories of these encounters lasted for decades. The Native leaders who now welcomed the Spanish clearly understood that Spanish authority had descended upon them. One hundred soldiers astride European horses communicated the seriousness of the Europeans' purpose. With hundreds of settlers moving north along the Rio Grande, Oñate had arrived to govern, and he now moved farther north, settling comfortably into the pueblo of Yunque (Yugewinge) in late summer. Like Cortés at Coyoacán, he and his men expropriated the Pueblo's homes and made them their own. They renamed the village San Gabriel, the first Spanish capital of New Mexico. By summer's end, the main party of the expedition had arrived, and on September 8, the first sermon was preached in its newly constructed church.[111] This journey had ended with a new Spanish homeland secured.

Pueblo communities harbored grievances about the colonization of their homelands. They had navigated Spanish intrusions before, but they had never formally submitted to Spain's political and religious leaders. The Spanish leaders asked for obedience to both "God and the king," and they had arrived divided into two distinctive classes of men: priests and soldiers.[112] Accustomed to their own political, ceremonial, and spiritual authorities, the Spanish drew sharp divisions between secular and religious power, unlike their Pueblo hosts, whose joint religious and political institutions structured everyday life.[113] This distinction and this contrast would shape the daily negotiations of Pueblo communities with Spanish rule. The missionaries expected Pueblo labor for the construction of churches and the homes of religious leaders. They suppressed Pueblo ceremonies and religious life and condemned Pueblo ceremonial structures, known as *kivas*, as well as their prayer sticks, dances, and offerings of cornmeal.[114]

Not all the Pueblos readily accepted Spanish dominion. But, as the Spanish had done in central Mexico, Oñate used threats of violence to achieve domination in his July meeting with Pueblo leaders at Santo Domingo: "The governor explained to them that they should realize that by rendering obedience and vassalage to the king our lord they would be subject to his will, orders, and laws, and that, if they did not observe them, they would be severely punished."[115]

The conflict that shaped Spanish-Pueblo relations started in December 1598. As the Spanish traveled on Pueblo trails, they came to Acoma Pueblo, fifty miles west of the Rio Grande. There, Oñate's sub-commander, Juan de Zaldívar, and a party of thirty soldiers stopped. The pueblo, one soldier recalled, was located on a towering rock with only a few paths to the top, and its defenses were strong.[116]

Zaldívar left half of his party with their horses and scaled the mesa with the remainder. When they reached the village, they demanded flour, water, and foods. A cry shot up across the village, signaling an attack from armed and concealed Acoma soldiers who, together with the elderly men and women of the village, attacked the soldiers, killing most, including Zaldívar. A hail of "arrows, stones, and other missiles" fell upon the Spanish force. A few soldiers survived only by jumping from the cliff onto the rocks below.[117]

Within a few weeks, Zaldívar's brother Vicente arrived at Acoma and after days of struggle set fire to the pueblo and laid it to waste.[118] Eighty Acoma men and five hundred women and children were captured; hundreds perished or fled. Juan Blázquez de Cabanillas of Castile believed that the pueblo should be forever erased. Acoma must "not be inhabited again," he informed Oñate.[119]

Far from a vengeful exercise of power, Zaldívar's attack was part of a careful response emanating from Oñate that aimed to communicate the strength of Spanish authority. The governor ordered Spanish participants to testify, requested reports from Franciscans, and had his secretary compile an extended record of the events. Violence was used but not haphazardly—Oñate understood that the indiscriminate use of violence would not yield stable governance or equally shared justice. New forms of punishment were needed.

The battle also galvanized the settlers' emergent identity and strengthened their faith in the sanctity of their mission, providing them with essential experiences and narratives of survival. Grieving, funerals, and masses memorialized the Spanish losses and served to celebrate heroism. But Spanish soldiers also participated in the punishment that followed and benefited from it.

The lives of the hundreds of Acoma captives would never be the same again. Spanish conquest had destroyed their village and killed their family members. Testimonials from six Pueblo witnesses indicated that the pueblo had been divided about attacking the Spanish. Several Pueblo suggested that there were those within the community who did not join or did not support the attacks, while others described a united community: the old people and other leading Indians did not want peace, and Acoma women "took part in the demonstrations and the fighting . . . [because] they were together with the men."[120]

On February 12, 1599, after weeks of collecting testimonies, Oñate made his judgment "in a public meeting." He and his sub-commanders gathered again at Santo Domingo, bringing with them their captives. He began, "I must and do sentence all of the Indian men and women from the said pueblo under arrest." He then meted out the following sentence:

> The males who are over twenty-five years of age I sentence to have one foot cut off and to twenty years of personal servitude [slavery].

> The males between the ages of twelve and twenty-five I sentence likewise to twenty years of personal servitude.
>
> The women over twelve years of age I sentence likewise to twenty years of personal servitude.
>
> Two Indians from the province of Moqui [Hopi] who were present at the pueblo of Acoma and who fought and were apprehended, I sentence to have the right hand cut off and to be set free in order that they may convey to their land the news of this punishment.
>
> All of the children under twelve years of age I declare free and innocent. . . . I place the girls under the care of our father commissary, Fray Alonso Martínez, in order that he . . . may distribute them in this kingdom and elsewhere. . . .
>
> The boys under twelve years of age I entrust to Vicente de Zaldívar. . . .
>
> The old men and women, disabled in the war, I order freed and entrusted to the Indians of the province of the Querechos that they may support them and may not allow them to leave their pueblos.
>
> I order that all of the Indian men and women who have been sentenced to personal servitude shall be distributed among my captains and soldiers in the manner which I will prescribe and who may hold and keep them as their slaves for the said term of twenty years and no more.[121]

Oñate's sentence was carried out in several locations. The first punishment was carried out that day at Santo Domingo. The next came at nearby villages where Pueblo captives had their hands and feet cut off.[122] The punishments—painful, humiliating, and terrifying—were witnessed by entire communities. They ended on February 15 at the pueblo of San Juan Bautista. There, "where his majesty's army is stationed . . . other Indians both men and women who had been condemned to become slaves" were distributed among Oñate's men.[123] The five hundred became the personal possessions of the soldiers. The Spanish had not found mineral wealth in their first year of conquest, but hundreds of enslaved Pueblo people offered the forms of potential profit and pleasure that had characterized over a century of Spanish colonialism.[124]

Pueblo Struggle and Survival: The 1600s

Throughout New Mexico's earliest years, Pueblo slaves, labor, and resources built the colonial economy. As in central Mexico and across the silver frontier, Native peoples worked throughout the province, developing its institutions of trade, commerce, religion, and governance. Pueblo communities built churches. They turned over portions of their harvests to Spanish *encomenderos*. They learned to herd sheep, horses, and cattle and, often by the dozens, they cooked and cleaned within Spanish households both ecclesiastical and secular.[125]

Each Pueblo household was required to provide annual tributes of one *fanega* of corn (approximately two and a half bushels) and tithed a large piece of woven cloth, a buffalo hide, or a deerskin.[126] The massacre at Acoma had started over the usurpation of Pueblo foods, and in its wake the Pueblos endured generations of labor and resource impositions that taxed their communities and assaulted their lands.

Pueblo communities maintained subsistence economies that followed seasonal cycles. Developed across generations, cycles are tied to ceremonies: daylong retreats, prayer sessions, and dances, among other religious practices, without which harvests cannot be conducted.[127]

As the Spanish came to understand, violent intrusion into village life and seizure of Pueblo resources threatened Pueblo subsistence and upset ritual and ceremonial life. The Pueblos came to fear such intrusion and confiscations as much as they feared natural disasters.

At the time of Oñate's *entrada*, Pueblo communities were stable, prosperous, and diverse. Indigenous peoples lived in the most densely settled portions north of central Mexico and spoke four to five languages that included dozens of dialects. They traded, intermarried, and shared customs that celebrated the return of spring and the arrival of harvest rains.

They endured after the conquest, but starting in the mid-1600s their numbers declined precipitously. Partly due to the violence and the accompanying terror brought by Spanish rule, hundreds fled the region, migrating west to more distant villages at Hopi and Zuni. Others began long-term patterns of dispersal and reconsolidation that diminished their total number of villages, which numbered eighty-one in 1598.[128] Pueblo communities suffered the death, disease, and displacement that had taken so many Indigenous lives across New Spain. Entire villages south of the new capital of Santa Fe, established in 1610, were vacated; eleven of the fourteen Piro-Tompioro communities were empty by the end of the 1630s, while in the middle Rio Grande region, only five of the eighteen Tiwa Pueblos remained.[129] By 1643 Governor Alonso Pacheco de Herédia reported that only thirty-eight pueblos remained under his jurisdiction.

Pueblo dispersal occurred for multiple reasons. Spanish labor, resource, and religious demands taxed smaller villages disproportionately. As more Spanish settlers, soldiers, and priests arrived, these demands required greater concentrated labor from individual communities. Moreover, proximity to Spanish settlements, roads, and trails generated recurring challenges. Spanish seizures of Pueblo women called for increased communal defenses or migration away from offending settlements. In times of drought, Spanish herds consumed the water needed for crops. Additionally, colonial leaders had forced Pueblo farmers to plant alfalfa and grains, and these were often consumed by livestock.

But dispersal also occurred because European pathogens ruptured the fabric of social life. As in the Caribbean, the Southeast, and central Mexico, diseases aided the expansion of colonialism. Reports from the 1630s and 1640s attest to a "very active prevalence . . . of small pox and the sickness which the Mexicans called *cocolitzli*."[130] These new diseases arrived from Mexico, brought by human and animal hosts. In 1640 alone, as much as 10 percent of the region's entire Pueblo population died due to these epidemiological invasions.[131]

The disruptions of colonial violence also affected other Indians, whom the Spanish termed *indios bárbaros* (savage Indians). They were migratory peoples outside of the colony who targeted Pueblos across portions of the province away from the protection of Spanish soldiers.

These Indian nations also shaped the evolution of colonial New Mexico and were shaped by it. They obtained new technologies from Spanish settlements and Pueblo communities—metal tools, European cloths, livestock, new foods, and horses. At first drawn to summer trade fairs, these Indian nations began to arrive throughout the year, bringing their allies with them and helping to build expansive trading and raiding economies. Such trade, travel, and raids characterized much of the centuries that followed. The Pueblo, now in a new landscape dominated by surrounding Native powers and Spanish colonists, consolidated against their many new enemies, foreign and domestic.

The Pueblo Revolt of 1680

The seventeenth-century world of the Southwest came to revolve around three heterogeneous, distinctive sets of social communities: Spanish settlers, soldiers, and friars; Pueblo villagers; and the exterior Native nations who came to be known as Apaches, Navajos, and Utes. Four generations after the conquest, in 1680, a monumental reordering of this world occurred following a series of events as revolutionary as the conquest itself. In an impressive display of unity, organization, and military strategy, the northern Pueblos revolted against New Spain. They did so in response to generations of Spanish dominion and innumerable acts of aggression, intimidation, and violence. And they succeeded.

Starting in August 1680, Pueblo villagers burned most of the churches their ancestors had constructed, killed the priests who ran them, and drove Spanish settlers into Santa Fe. There, on August 13, Governor Antonio de Otermín ordered all remaining priests, settlers from the north, and available soldiers to the capital. All the nations were to join together to destroy the capital, his lordship determined, and the Spanish huddled together in their primary government offices, *casas reales*, preparing themselves to be "ready for the enemy's assault."[132]

The Pueblo Revolt was arguably the first American Revolution and recast Spanish-Pueblo relations with far-reaching consequences across the continent. The revolt followed decades of growing repression of Pueblo leaders and those who continued to maintain Pueblo ceremonial and spiritual practices. In spite of endless punishments (hanging, beatings, enslavement, imprisonment) the Spanish failed to break the cultural practices of the Pueblo.[133] The punishments fueled resentment and despair, heightened by particularly onerous labor demands.[134] Hopi leader Edmund Nequatewa told of the labor drafts used to construct Spanish churches in which his ancestors were forced to retrieve pine and spruce from the nearby San Francisco Peaks to make into beams: "These beams were cut and put into shape roughly and were then left till the next year when they had dried out. Beams of that size were hard to carry and the first times they tried to carry these beams on their backs . . . if any gave out on the way he was simply left to die. There was great suffering. Some died for lack of food and water, while others developed scabs and sores on their bodies."[135] Now, despite several generations of coexistence, Pueblo and Spanish communities confronted one another in a week-long battle in Santa Fe.

Initially surprised, defeated, and discouraged, the Spanish nonetheless possessed military and tactical advantages. Outnumbered by an estimated force of five hundred Pueblos gathered on the outskirts of town, the one hundred Spanish soldiers had two small cannons, their guns and swords, and perimeter defenses to protect them. They awaited the arrival of additional settlers, who continued to stream into the city, but they also feared, correctly, that Pueblo soldiers from more distant villages were on their way. After a series of street battles and a surprise Spanish offensive that claimed approximately three hundred Pueblo soldiers, the governor decided to abandon the town altogether, retreating south a week into the fighting. Smoke from Santa Fe's burned-out buildings filled the sky, as did plumes from nearby Pecos Pueblo, whose monumental forty-foot church had once been the tallest structure in northern New Spain.[136]

The days, weeks, and years ahead brought surprising and lasting outcomes. Under the leadership of Popé—a religious leader from Ohkay Owingeh Pueblo who was approximately fifty at the time of the revolt—Pueblo soldiers had united against the Spanish, pledging near-complete disassociation from them. They burned churches and Catholic icons—crosses, *santos*, and altars. They targeted governmental houses and the records held within them, and they moved to cleanse themselves of Spanish influences. Unwanted marriages consecrated by Catholic sacraments were undone. Spanish technologies like horse saddles were burned.

By rejecting Spanish practices, beliefs, and institutions, Pueblo leaders reaffirmed and revitalized their own, performing their traditional dances to celebrate the victorious and memorialize the dead.[137] They had finally obtained their long-desired religious, cultural, and political autonomy. But governing was not easy when most communities resisted centralized leadership.[138] The unity of the revolt weakened. As the threat of Spanish rule faded, local leadership returned to Pueblo villages, limiting the revolutionary leadership structures that Popé had established.[139]

Not every Pueblo community had joined the revolt, and within those that had, not all were equally militant. The mission church at Acoma endured. It had been constructed after the village's painful experience with Oñate, completed by those who had lost family members during the massacre—too much destruction had already been visited upon this community. Hundreds of Pueblo citizens joined Otermín's party as it moved south. Many settled with them into Paseo del Paso along the southern Rio Grande. There, these refugees built new villages for themselves, consolidating initially into smaller missions, then reconsolidating again in 1684 due to Apache attacks.[140]

By extinguishing Spanish sovereignty in the region, the Pueblo Revolt

In 2005 Cliff Fragua (Jemez Pueblo) carved this marble statue of Popé to represent New Mexico in the U.S. Capitol Building. Popé holds a knotted cord like those sent to each pueblo in the days leading up to the 1680 Pueblo Revolt. Each knot represented one day, allowing Pueblo leaders to count down to the coordinated campaign against the Spanish. Popé bears scars on his back from the whipping he endured from the Spanish for participating in cultural ceremonies. (Courtesy of Cliff Fragua and Pamela Agoyo. Architect of the Capitol.)

ablished Indigenous villages' independence, freeing them to govern selves without oversight, taxes, or labor drafts. But even though Spanish governance had been intrusive, deadly, and violent, it had also been protective, and without Spanish soldiers, horses, and technologies, the Pueblo became more vulnerable to exterior attacks, which became more frequent. Throughout the many years of Spanish absence, Indian raiders targeted Pueblo fields and especially their corrals, where seized Spanish horses were stabled.

When Otermín attempted a reconquest in 1681, he was shocked to see former churches now used as stables. Most had burned-out roofs that had fallen in, leaving behind large open interiors with surrounding walls of thick adobe. Moreover, although he and subsequent Spanish leaders heard Pueblo complaints about attacks from neighboring nations, none understood the extent of the transformations now unleashed upon the continent. Surrounding Native nations that had once been entirely pedestrian now incorporated runaway, stolen, and traded horses into their societies. Before 1680 this transformation had been slow and gradual, but afterward an equestrian revolution engulfed the region.[141] None could have anticipated the far-reaching impacts that these Native raids would eventually bring, as worlds of Indigenous power increasingly stretched across the continent.

New Mexico's Growing Heterogeneity and Diversity: The 1700s

The world that Domínguez and Escalante described was created in the aftermath of the Pueblo Revolt. New Mexico was now shaped by the Indigenous powers surrounding the province. Bands of Ute Indians had become key allies of New Spain; they welcomed and guided the friars through their homelands and had even invited Spanish governors to send parties of exploration. Utes now grazed horse herds across great mountain valleys and migrated seasonally onto the Plains and to New Mexico for trade, diplomacy, and recreation. Dozens of similar equestrian powers had grown in size and stature across the eighteenth century.[142]

As Domínguez and Escalante knew, the Pueblo world of 1776 was one of autonomy, not submission. Pueblo authority was recognized and upheld by Spanish leaders and settlers. Hopi communities that had incorporated Spanish cattle into their economies held clearly recognizable property rights, though they had long withstood efforts to reestablish missions among them. They had maintained their traditions and resisted the Spanish state throughout the eighteenth century.[143]

Within missionized Pueblo communities, villagers outwardly worshipped Catholic deities, including saints, but they did so in conjunction with their own ceremonial and spiritual beliefs. The feast days of saints became celebrated across the Pueblos, held in tandem with Pueblo religious cycles and dances. Religious coexistence and pluralism persisted even after the Reconquista of New Mexico. When Spanish forces again marched north in 1692, they reextended Spanish sovereignty over the northern Rio Grande, but this time they did so in far different ways than Oñate. Following a decade of equestrian raids, many Pueblos were willing to accept Spanish protections, but only in exchange for greater cultural autonomy and religious freedom.

Such adaptation made eighteenth-century New Mexico far different than New Mexico in the seventeenth century. Now Pueblo soldiers accompanied Spanish governors onto the Plains in search of Native and French rivals. They suffered joint victories as well as defeats, including the devastating loss on the Plains in 1720 known as the Villasur Massacre, in which a joint French-Pawnee force from New France routed New Mexico's leading military unit under the command of New Mexico's lieutenant governor, Pedro de Villasur.[144]

The new loyalties paralleled other new social formations. Starting in 1754 groups of *genízaros*, or detribalized Indians, began successfully petitioning Spanish governors for land. Largely servants or domestics within the colonial economy, they were neither formally recognized members of Pueblo communities nor part of the surrounding equestrian communities that came into the region each summer by the thousands. Born of colonialism, they were a unique caste, or *casta*, from the borderlands.[145]

In 1776 there were 149 families of over 650 *genízaros* in four village settlements, and their numbers grew thereafter.[146] Their autonomy underscored the growing hybridity of the region. They were, in essence, diasporic Indigenous peoples. Their shared backgrounds, common experiences, and social connections helped create a communal identity in a world increasingly characterized by ethnic diversity and the diversity of experience.

After two centuries, New Mexico had become the largest, most heavily settled, and oldest continuously governed part of the Spanish borderlands. Spanish settlements along the Rio Grande came to coexist with older institutions of Pueblo governance, religion, and culture in a pattern that characterized the region throughout the Spanish era and into the modern world. The continuity to the present day of Pueblo linguistic, cultural, economic, and political autonomy distinguishes the region from all others in North America.

Although inherently violent and subordinating, colonialism across the Southwest was never complete or totalizing. At times it was as generative as it was destructive. After the Pueblo Revolt and for the century that followed, no single group was supreme in the Southwest. Power required constant negotiation between and among communities.

Settler communities negotiated power according to Spanish codes of masculinity, femininity, and class, excluding racialized groups like the *genízaros* and remaining committed to (often mythic) claims of racial purity.[147] Informal and formal forms of Spanish authority framed the world of possibilities within the colony, while outside it, the equestrian powers dominated a re-created North American landscape.

The Spanish missions in Texas, Louisiana, and Florida, located in places controlled by large Native powers, were never as developed as New Mexico. Coastal settlements like St. Augustine were principally strategic outposts for ships heading from the Caribbean to Spain. These less densely settled and missionized regions became increasingly coveted by other powers, particularly England, France, and later the United States, which eventually acquired them through treaty, conquest, or purchase.

For Native peoples in these regions, the limitations of imperial authority brought both autonomy and challenges. Across the American Southeast, as pathogens unmade countless Native worlds, emergent confederations of Native communities coalesced in the face of diseases but experienced new pressures from their many neighbors, both Native and imperial. The Southeast became a world shattered by the first century of Spanish colonialism, and its Native peoples coped with waves of largely undocumented disruptions.[148]

The Spanish empire remained committed to its northern frontier, largely because Mexico had become such a prosperous mining economy. Domínguez and Escalante had traveled north to Santa Fe as part of a broader imperial effort to connect New Mexico and California, whose settlement had just begun. Bordered to the far west by a Pacific empire whose center was the Philippines, New Spain formed a vast global order that by the mid-1700s had begun to fall into administrative and financial decline. Numerous attempts to reform this sprawling empire sought to stabilize existing institutions of governance and prevent further encroachments from England, France, and even Russia. As we shall see, throughout the last decades of the 1700s, new missionaries, naval expeditions, and explorers filtered throughout northern New Spain, further disrupting Native worlds across Arizona, into California, and farther north into the Pacific Northwest.[149]

Select Fortifications Established by European Powers Before 1787
French
Spanish
British
American
Dutch
Cities
San Francisco
Monterey
Santa Barbara
San Diego
PACIFIC OCEAN
Santa Fe
Albuquerque
Tucson
Tubac
Terrenate
Altar
Fronteras
Janos
El Paso
Carrizal
Horcasita
Principe
Buenavista
Conchos
San Saba
San Antonio de Béjar
San Juan Bautista
Santa Rosa
Monclova
Natchitoches
San Francisco de los Dolores
Fort St. Louis
Nuestra Señora de la Bahía de Espíritu Santo

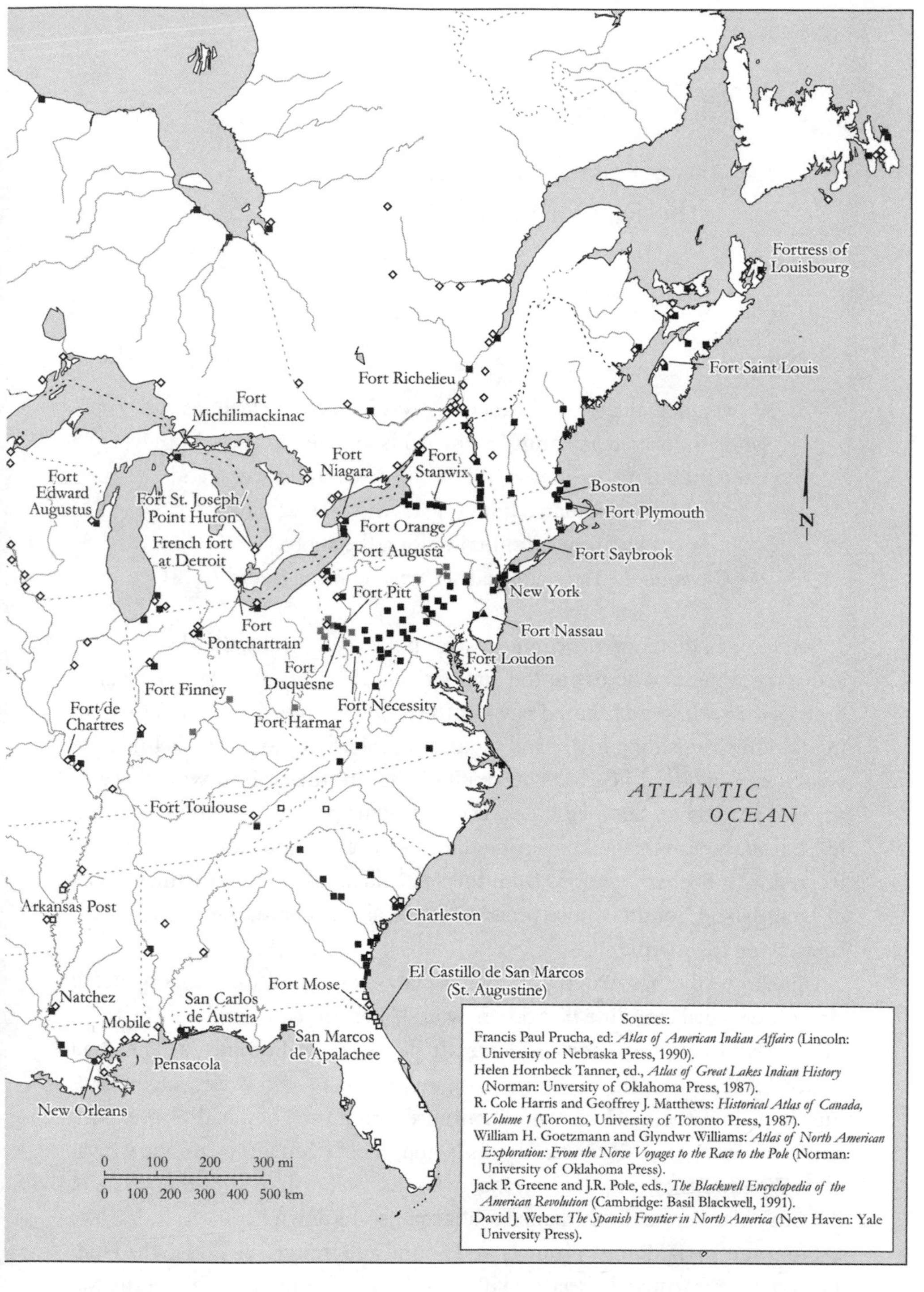
Fortress of Louisbourg
Fort Saint Louis
Fort Richelieu
Fort Michilimackinac
Fort Niagara
Fort Stanwix
Fort Edward Augustus
Fort St. Joseph/ Point Huron
Boston
Fort Plymouth
Fort Orange
French fort at Detroit
Fort Augusta
Fort Saybrook
Fort Pitt
New York
Fort Pontchartrain
Fort Nassau
Fort Duquesne
Fort Loudon
Fort Finney
Fort Necessity
Fort de Chartres
Fort Harmar
ATLANTIC OCEAN
Fort Toulouse
Arkansas Post
Charleston
Natchez
Fort Mose
El Castillo de San Marcos (St. Augustine)
San Carlos de Austria
Mobile
San Marcos de Apalachee
Pensacola
New Orleans
N
0 100 200 300 mi
0 100 200 300 400 500 km
Sources:
Francis Paul Prucha, ed: Atlas of American Indian Affairs (Lincoln: University of Nebraska Press, 1990).
Helen Hornbeck Tanner, ed., Atlas of Great Lakes Indian History (Norman: Unversity of Oklahoma Press, 1987).
R. Cole Harris and Geoffrey J. Matthews: Historical Atlas of Canada, Volume 1 (Toronto, University of Toronto Press, 1987).
William H. Goetzmann and Glyndwr Williams: Atlas of North American Exploration: From the Norse Voyages to the Race to the Pole (Norman: University of Oklahoma Press).
Jack P. Greene and J.R. Pole, eds., The Blackwell Encyclopedia of the American Revolution (Cambridge: Basil Blackwell, 1991).
David J. Weber: The Spanish Frontier in North America (New Haven: Yale University Press).

2 • The Native Northeast and the Rise of British North America

We weighed anchor, and sailed eastward . . . eighty leagues . . . [and] discovered a triangular-shaped island, ten leagues from the mainland. . . . It was full of hills, covered in trees, and highly populated [judging] by the fires we saw burning continually along the shore.

—*Giovanni da Verrazzano, description of Block Island (1524)*

Seen from a distance, the campfires lit up the evening sky. Sparks flickered above the water and across to the approaching ship. Families laid their children down to sleep and shared news of the day while preparing for the morning to come. Nets hung to dry and mounds of colorful quahog shells lined the shores and middens nearby. The smell of the fire intermixed with those of smoked seafood and tanned hides. Eventually the people, hundreds of them, fell asleep, secure in the knowledge that they lived comfortably on an island blessed with timber, bounties from the sea, and access to the warm currents of Long Island Sound, whose broad expanse also sheltered neighboring villages along the mainland.

Unable to find a suitable port, Verrazzano continued on, moving north along the jagged coastline that others would later call New England. By then, Block Island's Narragansett residents already knew of Europeans. They had traded for their wondrous, if often dangerous, metals and wares, incorporating them into their fishing and farming economies. They had also experienced the ravages of European diseases and, most enduringly, military invasion. Whether they knew of Verrazzano's 1524 visit or had seen the masts of the *Dauphine* across the darkened sea remains unknown.[1]

From southern Maine to Long Island Sound and from Cape Cod to the Hudson River, approximately 150,000 villagers lived in the shared world of the Native Northeast. Native presence—rather than a wilderness or absence—distinguished the region.[2]

Across the Native Northeast, dozens of Native nations maintained shared economies, religious traditions, architecture, and the Algonquian language.[3] Verrazzano noted the less populated Maine coastline dominated by the Wabanaki Confederacy where "the people were quite different."[4] Many of these northern communities did not combine fishing and hunting with the horticulture so common across the Native Northeast. He also considered those of the south to be "as beautiful of stature and build as I can possibly describe. . . . They are taller than we are. . . . Their manner is sweet and gentle; very like the manner of the ancients."[5] Had they possessed "the skilled workmen that we have," he contemplated, they may have rivaled the ancients in other areas: "they would erect great buildings, for the whole maritime coast is full of various blue rocks, crystals, and alabaster, and for such a purpose it has an abundance of ports and shelter for ships."[6]

Verrazzano described a wondrous, nearly mythical Algonquian world. A century after his encounters and his imaginative ruminations, settlers arrived, Puritans whose orthodoxies precluded such assessments and whose diseases and violent practices upended this world.[7]

In Puritan accounts, this region's Indigenous history possesses nothing remarkable, certainly nothing comparable to classical Europe. Many histories of the United States have taken this same tack, as the Native Northeast seems to provide a familiar past that is easily understood because of its simplicity. Since Puritan settlement in the 1620s, the superiority of Europeans to this world has been proclaimed, fueling construction of ancient edifices of a different kind. Molded not of the region's alabaster but from ideas of immutable difference, an ideological mortar undergirds study of the Northeast. It was an idea so pervasive that the insights of the first European to venture ashore, who uttered "various cries of wonderment" at what he encountered, are completely overshadowed.[8]

Despite recent scholarly and tribal efforts to the contrary, in the American historical imagination the history of New England still remains synonymous with colonial America. The histories of British North America and its thirteen Atlantic colonies are still understood as the canvas of early America, an era initially dominated by Massachusetts's economic and demographic growth.[9] To know early America is still to know British America, and to know British America is to know New England.

The Violent Origins of British North America

While the prospects of exploring lands across the Atlantic enticed mariners like Verrazzano, others sought financial and religious opportunities. Among the English, financiers organized land companies such as the Virginia Company, which was expected to return profits by any means. Over time, others in England imagined new lives for themselves, especially in the aftermath of the Protestant Reformation. Such reformers aspired to live according to a particular theological form. They imagined new societies for themselves and expected Native peoples to either disappear or assimilate to become God's children.[10]

Unlike in other American colonies, religious motivations attracted settlers of a different kind to the Northeast. Drawn from more affluent sections of English society, New England settlers created a different colonial society. It became the only region in the Americas with comparatively even European gender ratios. It was also home to North America's earliest academic colleges, its first printing presses, first self-governing legislatures, and most diversified economy. The Northeast attracted English colonists who wished to remain in a colder but ultimately healthier environment than the Chesapeake region or the Caribbean.[11]

As in other colonies, the newcomers' adaptation to the land required violence against Native peoples. This conquest became both spiritual and military. In the 1620s the first group of Massachusetts Bay colonists brought Bibles, candles—and "90 bandeleers, for the muskets, ech with a bullet bag; 10 horne fllaskes, for the long . . . peeces"; their ships also carried a hundred sharpened "swoordes."[12] These swords were not to become ploughshares, as the first generation of Puritan settlers seized Algonquian lands, particularly during campaigns against Pequot villages during the battle for Long Island Sound, known as the Pequot War (1636–37).[13]

This campaign began in Block Island. Historians have often lost sight of how this war fueled the rise of England's American empire.[14] In under two decades, Puritans expanded along Long Island Sound, forming "united" colonies—Rhode Island and Connecticut—along the way. This brought stability for their trade with the Chesapeake and Caribbean and vanquished the Pequot, who had dominated this sheltered coast. Their defeat and near displacement accelerated the growth of Puritan society.[15] Moreover, the battle for Long Island Sound expanded opportunities for other English colonies. It influenced the rise of other settlements, including those organized around African American slavery, which expanded throughout the late 1600s. England's transatlantic slavery had followed the trafficking of Native people by earlier English mariners and Spanish slavers. Although written out of history, thousands of Native people became captives across the Atlantic world. Indeed, an "Algonquian diaspora" erupted across the seventeenth-century world. From the Great Lakes to London and from Quebec to North Africa, Native captives circulated across a global nexus of enslavement.[16]

Of the 150,000 Native villagers living in the Northeast in 1600, less than 10 percent remained a century later: 90 percent perished due to European diseases, settlement pressures, warfare, and enslavement. Those who survived experienced dispossession and soon comprised a caste of unfree laborers within colonial society. As in the Spanish empire, Indians became the first racialized labor force in North America.[17]

The conquest of the Native Northeast also transformed England's oldest American colony. Founded in 1607, Virginia's first two decades stood in marked contrast to Massachusetts's. Whereas New England's villages mushroomed, the first generation in the Chesapeake languished. Of the six thousand colonists who went to Virginia, only twelve hundred survivors remained by 1620. Diseases initiated a form of "seasoning" for indentured English laborers, who died in waves attempting to adjust to plantation labor. Unlike Massachusetts, which Governor John Winthrop compared to "a paradise," Virginia was described by its settlers in letters sent home as a death-filled world.[18]

Two different economic changes characterized Virginia and Massachusetts in the 1600s: the transition away from indentured servitude in the Chesapeake and the transformation of Algonquian lands into Puritan pastures. Soon, plantations and family farms dominated the economy of British North America.[19] Each region also supported the other in symbiotic and circular ways. Puritans produced silverware, domestic linens, and food that ran plantations—both in the Chesapeake and the Caribbean—while building the ships that carried plantation exports to market. Such inter-regional trade also increased migration and traffic across the Atlantic.

Despite their differences, each colony's formation required similar practices of Indigenous land theft, which culminated in the 1670s. In Virginia the colony's "ordeal" centered upon developing alternative labor systems to stem the political instability posed by English laborers. Their uprising during Bacon's Rebellion (1676–77) momentarily overthrew the region's planter class and changed its racial calculus.[20] Similarly, the "Second Puritan Conquest," known as King Philip's War (1675–76), reconfigured the Indigenous demography of the Northeast and made Puritan settlers, finally, the region's dominant social community. Comprising roughly 30 percent of the region's population in 1670, Native peoples were soon outnumbered ten to one, a demographic catastrophe that continued. At Block Island, Native people totaled fifteen hundred in 1660. A century later, only fifty-one remained.[21]

For Native peoples in both regions, these cataclysms heralded an ascendancy of English hegemony. The Puritan-Algonquian collision that began in 1620 wrought demographic, economic, and racial legacies that defined much of seventeenth-century American history. European-introduced diseases, enslavement, military campaigns, and ideological justifications aided colonization. As with the Spanish conquest of New Mexico, these conquests were neither inevitable nor predestined—they hinged on individual decisions and happenstance, the consequences of which were never fully foreseen or anticipated.

Moreover, this dispossession foreshadowed subsequent forms of colonialism. With the establishment of slave-labor regimes and racially exclusive political systems, over time within British North America only certain types of people did certain types of work. The collective labor of African Americans, in particular, helped the colonists eventually secure their independence.[22] Within this devil's bargain, dispossessed Indian lands served as tender. Historians have failed to recognize this essential truth: Indigenous dispossession fueled the rise not only of British North America but also of its foundational institution of chattel slavery. The English conquest of Native American lands laid the foundations for American slavery, an institution preceded by traffic in Indian captives. Begun years before English colonies emerged, Indian slavery facilitated the earliest years of Puritan settlement, particularly through the use of captives and translators such as Tisquantum (also known as Squanto).

Nearly a million Native Americans were enslaved across the Americas during the sixteenth and seventeenth centuries.[23] Housed within colonial homes, trafficked out of Boston and later Charleston, and sent across the Atlantic, a maritime Indigenous diaspora radiated from England's earliest colonies. Such enslavement paralleled the continent-wide displacement of Algonquian peoples.[24] By the end of the seventeenth century, the Indian slave trade—especially in the Southeast—exceeded the African trade: before 1715 more Indians were exported from Charleston than Africans imported from West Africa.[25]

These slaves experienced various forms of captivity. Like Columbus before them, English mariners ferried captives across the Atlantic, both as signs of more marvelous possessions to come and to aid in colonization.[26] As captives became the first trafficked peoples of early America, they learned to navigate global networks of slavery and in the process learned how to aid English explorers and colonists. Through their language skills, understanding of climate and geography, and other forms of cultural knowledge, captives in England, aboard ships, and even back in North America influenced colonization. Few understood at the time that the initial practices of Indigenous dispossession would eventually fuel the rise of a slave-holding republic in the century that followed.

Ideologies of Difference: Puritanism

Puritans believed that scripture foretold reforms to come, and scholars have long emphasized the centrality of religion in motivating English colonization. To understand the "new English" requires examination of their views on Christian texts.[27] Just as the Apostle Paul had done in the Macedonian city of Philippi, Puritans sought to build new societies among unconverted peoples. Like Paul, they hoped to build religiously organized colonies in which church and state would be intertwined.[28]

According to the New Testament, Philippi was "the chief city of that part of Macedonia" that became "a colony" of believers who abided "certain days."[29] Puritan settlements viewed themselves similarly. They believed that they were sanctioned by Providence rather than by monarchs and that individuals' concentration of political authority created a violent English culture. Religion, more than politics or economics, compelled seventeenth-century reformers to fight English authority or to migrate away.[30]

Facing recurring conflict, groups of Puritans aspired to establish new societies devoted to Christian purity. They hoped to live "as a city upon a hill," as Governor Winthrop likely preached aboard the *Arbella*, one of eleven Puritan ships destined for the Northeast in 1630.[31]

Winthrop had heard sermons about such a place. "Of such a Colony we reade in *Acts* 16.12," John Cotton preached in *God's Promise to His Plantation.* This tract opens with examples explaining why certain people come to live in certain places, based on "Gods soveraignty over all the earth and the inhabitants thereof."[32] Cotton highlighted the emergence of Philippi as the first place in Europe where the gospel was preached.[33] Cotton is now credited with issuing this iconic metaphoric simile—"a city upon a hill"—a description not for a single settlement but applicable to an expanding transatlantic congregation engaged in colonization.[34]

As Puritans debated the justifications that "may warrant . . . removeall" from Europe, such debates generated new interpretations.[35] Native peoples attracted attention within this expanding faith, and for good reason. As in Philippi, Indians were to become converts within a new order. Their salvation both awaited and enticed.

In 1629, as the company's charter was granted, the Great Seal of the Massachusetts Bay Company was created. It featured an image of a Massachusetts Indian with the reference: "COME OVER AND HELP US"—referencing Acts 16.9, which describes Paul being beckoned by the "man of Macedonia" to "come over . . . and help us."[36] Such imagery and references resonated with Cotton's audiences. "When God gives other men hearts to call us," he intoned, "God makes room for us . . . [because] The earth is the Lords."[37] Massachusetts and eventually New England became landscapes of intended reform and conversion, twin logics that guided the earliest years of the colony. Nothing mattered more within this anticipated city upon a hill.[38]

This metaphor for understanding early America drew upon long-standing presumptions about the sanctity of spiritual colonization. It was an inherently colonial ideology. None could escape its emphases on predetermination. Indeed, for Puritans, America was now becoming a central stage in a larger religious drama that they believed was entering its final stages. Just as the Romans had brought Christianity to Britain, Puritans attempted to convert the inhabitants of the Americas in the next stage of Western civilization.[39]

Furiously upheld and violently imposed, the Puritan worldview conflicted with the Native Northeast. The Algonquian world resisted its conversion and fought to ward off religious as well as other colonial intrusions. Although the region's Native peoples survived this century of radical disruption and eventually learned to use Christian principles against Puritan colonizers, they had more than English settlers to confront.[40] The livestock, microbes, and material products that accompanied the settlers also refashioned their world.[41] Moreover, these were not the only disruptions reshaping the region. By the time the *Mayflower* landed at Plymouth in 1620, the region was already undergoing colonization.

The Native Northeast on the Eve of Colonization

In the first decade of the seventeenth century, European empires disrupted the Native Northeast. Microbes swept across its shores, bringing diseases from trade networks. Such networks had developed before 1524, when Verrazzano documented various protocols utilized by Native communities when first encountering European ships, including the use of small vessels to meet Europeans at sea rather than on land and other strategies designed to limit European exploration. Such trade became more institutionalized throughout the sixteenth century as vessels returned annually to fish, trade, and explore.[42] As we shall see in the next chapter, French trapping incorporated the Northeast into the continent's emergent fur trade. Samuel de Champlain visited Massachusetts Bay in 1605 and 1606 in search of furs, but he found greater success with Abenaki traders who trapped in Maine's many watersheds for furs. Within a decade, twenty-five thousand furs flowed annually onto French ships. As in New France, the trade revolved around the gendered economies of Native villages in which Native women processed, tanned, and bound animal products.[43]

The fur trade brought not just trade goods but also germs. As early as 1610, Native leaders informed European leaders of the diseases. Membertou of the Mi'kmaq Nation told French officials that his people had once been "as thickly planted there as the hairs upon his head," but their numbers had dwindled following contact. Seventeenth-century diseases became essential to European expansion. Diseases generated demographic and ecological changes that have taken scholars centuries to understand.[44]

The fur trade's new demands upon Abenaki women fostered a greater reliance on southern New England's horticulture. Across eastern North America, corn, beans, squash, and pumpkins provided many of the nutrients that sustained Native economies. Their harvests also remained under the jurisdiction of Native women, who decided when, where, and how to plant and gather these bounties. Women, according to Roger Williams, "set or plant, weede, and hill, and gather and barne all the corne, and Fruites of the field."[45] As the fur trade taxed Abenaki labor production, New England's Native gardens attracted more Indian traders from the north.[46]

The sheltered coast of Long Island Sound and calmer waters of Cape Cod Bay provided a nearly limitless bounty from the sea. The combination of its horticultural villages, seasonal hunting, and maritime harvests made New England the economic epicenter of the northern Atlantic. The diversity of the region's food ways and its integrated economies made the area among the most productive in the world.[47]

After contact, however, these regional trade routes carried European diseases. Just a few years before Puritan settlement, the Great Pandemic of 1616–19 fractured the region. This catastrophe originated from French contact zones to the north and Dutch settlements to the south. Over two-thirds of the coastal population of Massachusetts perished during this outbreak. Their deaths enabled English colonization. When the *Mayflower* anchored at Plymouth in 1620, fewer than two thousand of Cape Cod's twenty thousand inhabitants remained.[48] Puritan immigrants remarked the unburied dead, whose "bones and skulls," according to a contemporary, were comparable to "a new found Golgatha."[49]

Durable English settlements became possible only in the aftermath of such trauma. English villages at Plymouth (1620), Salem (1626), and Boston (1630) took form upon the once developed landscapes of the Native Northeast. Surviving Native people understood this ecological dispossession. After the founding of Providence, Miantonomo, a Narragansett sachem from Rhode Island, explained: "These English having gotten our land, they with scythes cut down the grass, and with axes fell the trees; their cows and horses eat the grass, and their hogs spoil our clam banks. . . . Our father [once] had plenty of deer and skins, our plains were full of deer, as also our woods."[50]

Diseases combined with settlement pressures to create, in the famous words of historian Francis Jennings, "a widowed land," the ashes of which provided the sediment for empire. "Incapable of conquering true wilderness," he writes, "Europeans were highly competent in the skill of conquering other people. . . . They did not settle a virgin land. They invaded and displaced a resident population."[51]

English Enslavement of Native Peoples: Tisquantum's Travels

Diseases became the primary but not exclusive agent of destabilization. The taking of captives also transformed the Native Northeast. It fueled apprehension and conflict with European newcomers. Seventeenth-century European mariners routinely captured Native people. When invited to board their ships, Native leaders declined or hurried away. As early as 1602, a Wampanoag party off Martha's Vineyard, when seeing gestures to board a European ship, promptly "refused and . . . departed."[52]

Begun in the earliest years of Anglophone exploration, the Indian slave trade shaped settlement thereafter, particularly because captives helped English financiers, cartographers, and officials come to know North America.[53] Largely the domain of captains attempting to learn more about the region or interested in increasing their fortunes, this initially haphazard traffic mushroomed throughout the century. For example, the enslaved labor and knowledge of Indian captives aided captains Edward Harlow and John Hunt. Each returned to Europe with cargos of Indian slaves, in 1611 and 1614, respectively.[54] Hunt, according to John Smith, had "abused . . . and betrayed twenty seauen [seven] of these poore innocent soules" from the Pawtuxet and Nauset Nations and "sould" them in Spain.[55] Memories of his betrayal stayed with tribal members for generations, while at Málaga, his captives garnered eight *reales* each.[56] They included Tisquantum (Pawtuxet), eventually known as Squanto, from Massachusetts Bay.

Captured in 1614, Tisquantum became New England's best known captive. His life highlights the forms of enslavement that preceded settlement in the region, the devastating impacts of European diseases, and the incredible determination of Native survivors to reunite with their devastated communities.

While hundreds of captives were either seized or killed in the Northeast before the arrival of the *Mayflower*, only a few are named in English records. Of these, Tisquantum and only a handful of others ever returned. Groups of Indians were captured routinely enough to form identifiable communities not only in London but also across the British empire.[57] The steady shipment of Indians to Bermuda, for example, initiated the formation of diasporic Indigenous communities, whose legacies continue to the present.[58] The early seventeenth-century traffic brought seven Abenaki slaves to London.[59] Those named are Tahanedo, Amoret, Mandeddo, Sassacomoit, and Skicowares, who had all been taken by James Rosier and presented to Ferdinando Gorges, commander at Fort Plymouth. A leading financier, Gorges supported numerous settlement efforts, and these Abenaki five aided Gorges's intiatives to map the Northeast while also helping to build a small Algonquian-speaking community in London.[60]

As in other slaving frontiers, ship captains struggled to get captives aboard. According to Rosier, five or six crew members were needed to subdue each victim. As he recounted, "Our best hold was their long haire."[61] Once in England, Gorges commissioned other slaving campaigns and enlisted captives in various exploratory efforts.[62] In 1606 he ordered Mandeddo and Sassacomoit to assist Captain Henry Challons in charting the region's coastline, recognizing the utility provided by those who knew the region best. Challons's dreams were, however, short-lived. Attacked by Spanish ships, he, his men, and their Indian guides were killed or captured.

Wounded by Spanish rivals, Sassacomoit again became enslaved. Like Tisquantum, he was taken to Spain. His captivity, journey to England, and return to North America with Nicholas Hobson in 1614 remain chapters of an untold epic, one of countless Indigenous biographies either erased or simply lost within the currents of early American history.[63] That so many Native peoples' lives were cut short by European exploration, slavery, imperial rivalry, and transatlantic migration has escaped the attention of historians.[64] Sassacomoit's odyssey anticipated that of Tisquantum.[65] Along with thousands of others, they were trafficked across a triangular trade that linked London, the Northeast, and Iberia.[66] The trade in slaves became critical to New England's formation as captives and other Native peoples fueled the geographic and imaginative worlds of English officials.[67]

Unlike Sassacomoit, whose life after 1614 remains undocumented, Tisquantum is better known. "Also called Squantum," he was, as Governor William Bradford described him on March 22, 1621, "the only [surviving] native of Patuxet, where we now inhabit." Bradford knew of his time in England and viewed it matter-of-factly. He "was one of the twenty captives that by Hunt were carried away, and had been in England."[68]

What made Tisquantum remarkable was his relationship with the Plymouth colony. "A spetiall [special] instrument sent of God," as Bradford later described him, he aided the Puritans during their first winter in 1621. Their relationship became so close that they consulted one another, dined together, and may have even shared living space. Most notably, "Squanto," according to Bradford, "directed them how to set corne, wher to take fish, and to procure other comodities."[69] His "useful services to the infant settlement," Bradford summarized, "entitle him to grateful remembrance."[70] For the Puritans, it was his service that became the basis for such remembrance, not that he had once lived in England.

Tisquantum, likely in his mid-twenties at the time of his enslavement, learned English during his captivity. While he was gone his community endured the Great Pandemic and dispersed, and his family died. Bradford described him as not only abandoned but also forsaken: he lacked both a family and a people. But these tragedies did not define his life, and he remained close to the English to the end of his life. According to Bradford, he "desired . . . that he might go to the Englishman's God in heaven, bequeathing divers of his things to . . . his English friends, as remembrances of his love."[71] He died in the village where he had been raised, surrounded by newcomers.

Contrary to his portrayal as a diasporic wanderer, Tisquantum's return highlights key struggles occurring across the Northeast, struggles during which Natives and European newcomers at times turned to one another.[72]

After living among financiers in London, he returned to the Northeast in early 1619. He had been gone for over five years. He came close to returning in 1618, having made it as far as Newfoundland with a group of other English explorers. There, he met Thomas Dermer, who had traveled with Captain John Smith and now worked for Gorges. According to Bradford, Dermer "took Tisquantum with him to England" to coordinate with Gorges, who was organizing additional explorations.[73]

While American history is often told as a story of the one-way migrations of Europeans, Tisquantum now made his third and fourth transatlantic journeys.[74] During his half decade in Europe, he learned the social world of his captors, adopted at least one of their languages, and navigated European trade networks from Spain to England. He did so after arriving into what must have seemed a babel of Mediterranean, African, and other Indigenous tongues within Iberian slave markets. He would also have encountered new forms of clothes, foods, smells, and facial brands.[75]

For Dermer, Tisquantum was not simply a "heathen" but a path to fortune. Although we have no records of their conversations, he grew enthralled with Tisquantum's reminiscences and organized a return expedition around them. He found only devastation. A decade of disease and raiding for captives had left his village abandoned. Overgrown and infested fields mirrored the untrodden pathways in and out of his former home.

In a state of shock, Tisquantum stayed with Dermer's party throughout the summer of 1619, continuing to aid its exploration and diplomatic efforts. He even interceded on Dermer's behalf after his capture by neighboring villagers. Tisquantum, however, remained devastated by the loss of his family, wondering how to search for his dispersed relatives. In this era of change, his odyssey continued.[76]

Tisquantum spent a year with Dermer. In the summer of 1620 they traveled to Martha's Vineyard, where they encountered other Native peoples who had also been held in England, including the Wampanoag sachem Epenow. Gorges had "acquired" him from Harlow in 1611, keeping him at Fort Plymouth with other captives, including Sassacomoit.[77]

Unlike Tisquantum, however, Epenow returned to an intact community whose safety was his responsibility. As he looked across the bow of yet another English ship, his suspicions grew. In England, he had been publicly exhibited and humiliated. Observing English customs, Epenow knew that there was an insatiable interest in tales about his homelands. English leaders made inquiries particularly about gold, a mineral similar to the Great Lakes copper so coveted across the Northeast. Epenow likely manipulated such interests and, like Tisquantum, used stories to facilitate his return.

As Harlow's vessel approached land, Epenow literally jumped ship. He escaped under a flurry of arrows coming from his community. It is unclear how the Wampanoags knew he was returning. Presumably they persisted in hoping, as had he, for his return, scanning the horizon for the masts of English ships that might be carrying him.

Tisquantum did not share Epenow's anti-English sentiments. His time in England was spent dining among financiers, not being paraded before onlookers. In the complex world of the Northeast, individuals who had survived the Great Pandemic turned to one another as well as to powerful newcomers for survival. As he had done earlier, Tisquantum assisted Dermer and his crew. He was, however, unsuccessful, as their party was attacked. Dermer received fourteen wounds and died in Virginia, where he had fled in search of English doctors. Tisquantum became a captive once more. At least now he knew the language of his captors.[78]

Puritan Settlement upon a Widowed Land

It is unclear how Tisquantum arrived at Plymouth in March 1621. He may have been exchanged between villages within the Wampanoag Confederacy or directed as an emissary to the English settlers by confederacy leaders.[79] Wampanoag leaders understood his utility in negotiating with the newly arrived Puritans.

Once among the English, he famously helped with the settlement's survival. Praise for his assistance abounds.[80] In the Native Northeast, a mastery of languages was now as important as mastery of the sea, and the captive trade had yielded a bilingual man. He may have tried to gather together the remaining survivors of his Patuxet community and reestablish their home. But amidst the devastation, he used translation, conversion, and even friendships as strategies for survival.[81]

Tisquantum's ability to move freely within the growing settlement helped it succeed. He gained the trust of Bradford and other Puritan leaders and advised them on agriculture, fishing, and diplomacy. He brokered the earliest agreement between Plymouth and the neighboring Wampanoag Confederacy, led by the Pokanoket leader Massasoit, an agreement we know as Thanksgiving.

The first year of settlement had been difficult. Nearly half the settlers died of disease or exposure. Under such pressures, mediation and trade, not just their unwavering faith in Providence, were key to the Puritans' survival.[82] The ability of English settlers to make partnerships grew from the region's disruptions, particularly its cycles of disease and captive taking. Death stalked Plymouth as it did Native families. It compelled unanticipated compromises, such as Thanksgiving. A curiously imagined event that mythologizes the Puritans' first year, the holiday forgets the decades of European exploration, the recent deaths, and perhaps above all the long-standing maritime economies that nourished life. It imagines poultry as the region's staple. If named at all, the Wampanoag appear as the region's only Indians and the Puritans the only Europeans. As always, "Squanto" remains a go-between, perpetually stuck in-between nations even at an event that he organized.[83]

As those gathered knew all too well, Plymouth was just one of several European outposts forming across the Atlantic world. Twelve months earlier, the *Mayflower* had missed its anticipated arrival in Virginia, ending up closer to the Dutch on the Hudson and the French farther north.[84] Other English colonies were also forming. In the West Indies, colonists settled in the Caribbean between 1624 and 1632: St. Christopher, Barbados, Nevis, Montserrat, and Antigua.[85] Barbados and later Jamaica became the most profitable colonies in the English empire, key links to New England's economy.

Native powers in the lands between Massachusetts Bay, Cape Cod, and Narragansett Bay were under the jurisdiction of the Wampanoag Confederacy. They called these ancestral grounds Wôpanâank which, like all Native landscapes, were marked by place-names, familiar paths, commemorative locations, and religious sites.[86] It was a region full of bounty—but one now racked by the aftermath of disease.

To their south in Rhode Island and Connecticut, the Puritans confronted Narragansett and Pequot communities, rival confederacies that threatened both Puritan and Wampanoag authority.[87] These confederacies had survived the Great Pandemic in greater numbers than the Wampanoag of Massachusetts. As Dutch trader Johannes de Laet reported in 1625, "There are few inhabitants near the mouth of the [Connecticut] River," but farther up "they become numerous."[88]

Death and disease destabilized Wôpanâak to such an extent that the political and social networks that structured the region were eroding. Displaced villagers often allied together into new alliances or joined other confederations, spreading contagion and generating instability and conflict. Native communities now concentrated into more remote, fortified villages, in post-contact settlement patterns that diverged from centuries of pre-contact residential practices in which villages developed almost entirely around coastlines or watersheds.[89]

With their numbers so diminished, the Wampanoag remained vulnerable, and they became ready allies with Puritan newcomers.[90] In this era of growing conflict, Wampanoag leaders worked to keep their authority intact. Trade, diplomacy, and even alliance with Europeans offered paths of survival.[91]

Violence and warfare were, of course, well known across the Native Northeast. Ritualized forms of combat provided conflict resolution, honorific gain, and material benefit. Violence within communities was largely allowed by elite authorities, both male and female "sachems," who were entitled to leadership roles by descent.[92] These structures endured after the arrival of Europeans, but colonization displaced other forms of Indigenous autonomy. As among the Iroquois Confederacy, discussed in chapter 3, colonization bred new motivations for warfare and introduced new technologies of violence. Seventeenth-century warfare was more violent than that of previous generations, and deepened conflicts among the region's communities.[93]

Arriving with firm ideas of cultural, religious, and racial difference, Puritan leaders looked askance at their Indian neighbors. They believed that they had to rectify the providential misfortune of the Natives' religion, so opposed to Puritanism.[94] Governor John Winthrop, who led the Great Migration of 1630–42, chose Massachusetts Bay in part because he believed that "god had consumed" the Indians "in a miraculous plague."[95] As he wrote to his wife in England, Providence both protected and provisioned his settlement: "My dear wife, we are here in a paradise. Though we have not beef and mutton . . . yet (God be praised) we want them not; our Indian corn answers for all."[96]

A decade after settlement, Puritans still remained a small percentage of the region's population. Fourteen thousand came during this migration while one hundred thousand Englishmen migrated to the Chesapeake and the Caribbean throughout the century. By 1650, more colonists lived in the West Indies (forty-four thousand) than in Virginia (twelve thousand) and New England (twenty-three thousand) combined.[97]

Demographically, the Puritan colonies resembled other seventeenth-century confederations, such as the Wendat in Ontario, the Iroquois of Iroquoia, and the Powhatan of Virginia. Each of these powers consisted of tens of thousands and controlled expansive territories. Collectively, they all shaped the emerging economy and diplomacy of eastern North America.[98] While powerful, Puritan New England by 1634 was contained along the coastline.

Events of the mid-1630s transformed Puritan colonization into an eventual engine of Indigenous dispossession. Following a dozen years of settlement, internal divisions bred a religious crisis that spilled out of the colony's boundary. Led by Roger Williams, groups of separatists broke from Massachusetts and established in 1636 other "united colonies" to the south.[99] Simultaneously, rivalries between English and Dutch traders brewed along Long Island Sound. These divisions and conflicts soon initiated more permanent forms of colonization while breeding regional wars that targeted Indigenous communities.

As opposed to resource-based or extractive colonial systems—from the French fur trade to the Spanish silver empire—Puritan colonization sought to transform American landscapes. Land enclosures, imported domesticated livestock, and invasive crops remade the Northeast's ecology.[100] Moreover, unlike other colonies, Puritan settlements revolved around the labor of families—not servants, company employees, or slaves who had to be contracted, imported, or enslaved. While village economies were tied to the empire, family-run farms nourished Puritan bodies and spirits.[101]

Considering themselves a chosen people, Puritans interpreted their "good works" as signs of a predetermined salvation. Successful harvests, new congregations, and growing settlements all became further evidence of the righteousness of their values and their providential fortune. Puritan separatists like Williams may have argued about the forms of the spiritual practices necessary to achieve salvation, but none questioned the forms of labor needed to build their kingdom. Religious ideology fueled economic growth and justified the expropriation of Indigenous lands.

The sheltered coast of Long Island Sound became the primary site in the struggle for the region's future. As with Williams's settlement in Rhode Island, Puritans looked south to expand. They eyed the Sound, its nearby islands, and interior waterways, particularly the Connecticut River, which drains much of the Native Northeast. Moving south, Puritans expanded along the coast and then into the interior. As in other colonies, expansion occurred for economic reasons and generated violence.

Wampum and Anglo-Dutch Rivalry on Long Island Sound

In the 1630s Long Island Sound remained a center of Indigenous economic, political, and cultural power. It sheltered Pequot villages from the North Atlantic and attracted European traders, including early seventeenth-century Dutch explorers such as Adrian Block. Block had come to New Holland to trade but saw his fur-laden ship catch fire in New York in 1613. He decided to build a smaller vessel, the *Unrest*, to traverse the Sound before returning to Holland. He landed on Block Island in 1614. Like John Hunt, who captured Epenow the same year, Block also enslaved Indians, taking them back to Holland to aid colonization.[102]

Despite such intrusions, the Sound remained comparatively removed from colonial disruptions, particularly diseases. Both the Pequot and the Narragansett escaped the worst of the Great Pandemic. Pequot villages were drawn into the orbit of Dutch traders who came seasonally to trade furs. For over a dozen years, the Dutch also monopolized one of early America's most profitable resources, *wampumpeag*, or wampum, which brought an economic revolution to the Northeast. The economic power of the Dutch and Pequot over this trade soon initiated Puritan reprisals.[103]

Known for their beauty and sociopolitical power, wampum "strands" or "belts" consist of woven strings of small, symmetrical purple and white beads made from the quahog and whelk shells that flourish along the Sound.[104] The use of wampum is recorded in the epics and diplomatic accords of the Iroquois Confederacy. Its cultivation across the Native Northeast remains less recognized.[105]

The process of producing wampum was complicated, requiring an incredible amount of artisanal labor featuring strict divisions along lines of gender and age. Throughout the 1600s, Native women and children collected shells from ocean beds, clam banks, and deep waters, and men drilled and assembled them. The painstaking craftsmanship that wampum required meant that before contact it was never made in large quantities. The market of the fur trade, however, accelerated its production. The arrival of European metal tools also brought adaptations that led to more and more intricate forms of beadwork.[106]

Once woven, wampum strands became signs of social and political power. Leaders amassed and displayed them, distributing belts as symbols of their authority. Belts also conveyed spiritual power and were used for ceremonial purposes in tribes across eastern North America. Some, such as the Iroquois Confederacy, were particularly invested in their use: Iroquoian epics require annual and ceremonial recitation, and wampum belts assisted such presentation and documentation.[107]

Throughout the 1620s, the trade in wampum exploded. As one Dutch official wrote, Indian traders arrived at their many posts "for no other reason than to get *sewan* [wampum]."[108] Dutch traders increased wampum's production and circulation, linking it with the fur trade, which the Dutch and their Iroquois allies dominated. The Dutch quickly used wampum to attract more furs.[109]

Initially, the trade benefited Pequot producers and their Dutch partners alike. Dutch traders traveled north to Pequot communities, bringing with them the most desired goods in the Americas: metals, cloth, wares, and quality guns. Never large in numbers, Dutch traders undertook the arduous interregional journeys between Fort Orange (Albany), New York, and the Sound and returned with stacks of furs bound for Europe.

The wampum trade facilitated the Dutch monopoly and allowed for more complex exchanges.[110] Initially, Dutch traders ferried manufactured goods to Pequot and Mohawk villagers, who incorporated metals, wares, and cloth into their village economies. Pequot villages could offer mainly wampum for Dutch goods, while the Mohawk offered furs. As European traders discovered the shells' desirability with their many Indigenous partners, transportation costs plummeted. Instead of ferrying manufactured goods to the Mohawk, the Dutch added wampum to their manifests. Soon, along with guns, wampum became the most desired Dutch trade good. It weighed far less than other goods. It did not require transatlantic shipment. The Dutch, essentially, provided a more advantageous route for this once overland trade, expanding its production and distribution. Famous as middlemen in Europe, the Dutch became similarly positioned in the Northeast, ferrying Indigenous resources—wampum and furs—between the Pequot and Iroquois.[111]

Like minerals drawn from the earth, shells only possess the values attributed to them. Their economic and symbolic powers are culturally and socially determined.[112] Such strands held centuries of sociocultural value and stretched dozens and even, on occasion, hundreds of feet in length. Collectively, the belts consisted of millions of quahog and whelk shells. Their circulation was so common that in 1637 Puritan leaders collected tribute from Native villagers on Block Island of "100 fathoms of beads annually."[113] Decades of similar payments followed, and by 1657 one tribute payment included a million shells, valued at £700.[114] Wampum provided one of the earliest universal equivalencies of value—or currencies—across colonial America. It came to be used in all forms of transactions from tribute to trade and from debt relief to war bounties.[115]

Increasing values, however, created conflicts between colonists and their Native allies. In 1626 one of the earliest Dutch reports about Plymouth stated that the English newcomers "come near our places to get wampum."[116] Unlike the Dutch, Puritan settlers initially sought limited trading relations with regional Native powers and mainly traded corn. Corn, however, was hard to transport, and its value fluctuated relative to the size of annual harvests.[117] The English needed different trade goods to compete with Dutch traders.

Wampum provided the alternative. Its desirability prompted English leaders to encourage its circulation, because wampum also helped to foster debt or dependency on English trade. The more Puritans required wampum payments, the more many smaller tribes became indebted, and indebtedness facilitated land cessions. From its limited pre-contact circulation, wampum flowed across the Northeast. Puritan leaders understood this exchange system and began to exploit it.[118]

During the first years of the Great Migration in the 1630s, Puritan settlements remained relatively isolated. A dozen church communities from Salem to Plymouth threatened neither New Holland nor the Pequot Confederacy. From 1633 to 1636, however, demographic changes altered the balance of power: a smallpox outbreak hit, facilitating Puritan expansion into Narragansett lands in Rhode Island. As with the Great Pandemic earlier, diseases preceded English expansion and once again aided the rise of British North America.[119]

As Native villages suffered, English ambitions grew. The Dutch were a formidable trading power, but they were hardly a threat to Puritan colonists and their Native allies—including eventually Narragansetts, Mohegans, and other allies in Massachusetts. Many of these Native communities vied for access to the Pequot-dominated shell beds of Long Island Sound and also looked to exploit the fur trade along the Connecticut River where Dutch posts were established. Furs and wampum remained the region's primary trade goods,

This wampum belt, composed of buckskin and primarily dark purple quahog shells, was crafted by a Haudenosaunee artist circa 1775–1800 and belonged to the Miami chief Shepoconah (also known as Deaf Man). For centuries before and after European contact, quahog shells circulated widely across eastern North America, conferring social and political authority and cementing multilateral commitments between eastern North America's many nations, both Indigenous and non-Indigenous. (Cranbrook Institute of Science, Photographer: Michael Narlock.)

and interior Puritan settlements held the potential to not only displace Pequot hegemony but also extend English influence into the fur trade.

Unlike the Great Pandemic, the Epidemic of 1634 hit Native villages already in conflict with settlers. Diseases from this outbreak killed an estimated three thousand to four thousand soldiers across the Sound. This loss combined with the arrival of several thousand new settlers continued to destabilize Pequot spheres of influence. Indigenous political authority across the region was eroding, particularly as the stream of English settlers increased during the Great Migration.[120]

Nonetheless, for nearly a generation after 1620, conflicts between Puritans and Native peoples were more often civil than violent. Debates over land title, destruction of crops by livestock, theft of goods, and terms of exchange comprised the quotidian nature of these conflicts. Even though the threat of violence simmered beneath such disputes, mechanisms for adjudication—particularly compensation—had emerged.[121] With extreme infractions such as murder, however, when mechanisms of restitution no longer worked, the potential for violence escalated.

Dutch, Puritan, and Native leaders understood that enslavement—like murder—created conflicts. Mediation, compensation, and redress became forms of resolution. However, as the wampum trade deepened existing Indigenous rivalries and imperial competitions, a series of English murders at sea increased conflicts on land.

In 1634 John Stone, a Virginia-based trader, arrived at the Sound after being exiled from Massachusetts following his assaults upon a married woman. This crime had led to his conviction, a £150 fine, and the lifetime prohibition "upon pain of death to come here no more."[122] Like other Virginians, he was more interested in profits than Providence and had heard of the wealth to be made in furs and wampum. Arriving in Connecticut, he captured two Pequot men to show him the way up the Connecticut River.[123] As his ship docked that evening, Pequots and their Niantic allies boarded. In the ensuing melee, Stone was killed and his ship destroyed.

Despite his banishment, Massachusetts officials responded to Stone's killing. They made growing demands for compensation. The Pequots, as was their custom, attempted to make restitution for Stone's murder with payments of wampum.[124] But the English saw his death as an opportunity to make larger demands on a Native power weakened by smallpox. Governor Winthrop declined compensation, envisioning more punitive forms of redress.

When another English trader, John Oldham, was killed sailing toward Block Island in July 1636, Winthrop mobilized a hundred-man militia to exact punishment, even though Oldham's death had already prompted a retaliatory attack that had killed ten Native soldiers and rescued Oldham's remaining crew. The militia sailed from Boston under John Endicott, to whom Winthrop gave a "commission":

> To putt to deathe the men of Blocke Iland but to spare the woemen & Children & to bringe them away, & to take possession of the Iland. & from thence to goe to the Pequodes to demande the murders of Capt. Stone & other English & 1000: fath[om] of wampum for damages . . . & some of their Children as hostages: which if they should refuse they were to obtaine it by force.[125]

Few directives in American history have been so forthright. Winthrop ordered Endicott to kill the men at Block Island, enslave the island's women and children, and then seize Pequot wealth. As he remarked, "No man was impressed for this service, but all went voluntaryes."[126] The histories of wampum, enslavement, and English ambition now converged. The battle for Long Island Sound had begun.

The Battle for Long Island Sound: The Pequot War (1636–37)

Endicott failed to enslave Block Island's Narragansett women and children or to kill its men. He spent two days in August "searching the Iland, & could not finde the Indians."[127] He had orders to follow wherever they had gone and hurried to reassemble his militia for the coming encounter. Before leaving, he reported on the island's geography, noting that it had become "all ouer growne with brushe."[128] Diseases, growing conflicts, and Puritan invasive species had already reconfigured the island's ecology, and Endicott punished resident islanders even further, setting ablaze sixty of "their wigwams & all their mattes, & some corne & staved 7: Canoes."[129] As his officer John Underhill reported, "Wee burnt and spoyled both houses and corne in great abundance."[130]

Within weeks of the invasion, Narragansett leaders from across the Sound traveled to Boston to negotiate. Miantonomo, "the sachem of the Narragansett," met with Winthrop in October and pledged his full support for Puritan operations.[131] In addition to confirming that the Narragansetts "would deliver our enemies to us, or kill them," the two leaders drafted a nine-article treaty.[132] The first three articles made preparations for war. They established "a firm peace between us . . . and their confederates"; ensured "neither party to make peace with the Pequods without the other's consent"; and required both "not to harbor the Pequods."[133] The third article was ominous, as earlier forms of diplomacy and compensation were now changing. A war of annihilation had begun. Not only would this war remake the Native political world, it also laid the foundations for the future expansion of English authority.[134]

As they arrived at Pequot villages on the Connecticut River, Endicott and Underhill were welcomed. The murder of Oldham, let alone Stone, had occurred seasons beforehand and among distant people. As Winthrop later suggested, the convicted Stone, "for whom this war was begun . . . [was] none of ours."[135] Surely, trade and diplomacy would continue; however, Stone's death became justification for conflict. When Pequot leaders attempted mediation, the English issued ultimatums, the severity of which caught the Pequot off guard. According to Underhill, "They [were] not thinking we intended warre."[136] Then Endicott issued the only remedy the Puritans would accept for their grievances: the decapitated heads of those who had killed Stone.

Bodily dismemberment remained a symbol of power in both England and New England. The punishment was used to extend authority over poor, Indigenous, colonized, and enslaved peoples and provided a public warning against challenging imperial power.[137] For the Puritans, skulls also conjured the authority of an omnipotent god whose capacity for vengeance was deeply imprinted upon their theology.[138] When asked, "What doe you come for?" by Pequot leaders, the English replied that they required human skulls; otherwise, Underhill warned, "Wee will fight."[139]

Fight they did, but they did not receive Pequot heads. When the Pequots did not submit, the English attacked. They pillaged their town, destroyed its fields, and ransacked homes before setting them ablaze.[140] "The Narragansett men told us after that thirteen of the Pequods were killed, and forty wounded."[141] This August 1636 attack and the Pequots' counterattacks at Fort Saybrook became the opening theaters of the Pequot War.

Within a year, the Pequot Confederacy had been destroyed. Most men were either killed or enslaved, and many women and children were also captured. Hundreds retreated farther into the interior, finding shelter among communities less reliant on the Sound.[142] On May 25, 1637, "the general defeat of the Pequods at Mistick," according to Winthrop, became the single deadliest conflict in the region's history.[143] Surrounding the second-largest Pequot fortification along the Mystic River, Underhill, a hundred Puritan militia members, and several hundred Narragansett allies annihilated the village of four hundred. Returning east, they then "fell upon a People called the Nayanticks, belonging to the Pequot, who fled to a Swamp for refuge."[144] Many died. The Mystic Massacre, according to Winthrop, became another sign of providential glory. It "happened the day after our general fast," he wrote, and initiated "a day of thanksgiving kept in all the churches for the victory obtain[ed] against the Pequods."[145] The massacre became the most commemorated moment in the Puritan settlement of North America.

When the war ended, the central forts of the confederacy lay in ruins. The Pequots fled south along the Sound and north into the interior. The killing continued because no one would harbor them. The English continued their demand for skulls, and threatened any tribe providing refuge with a similar fate. Days after the Mystic Massacre, Wyandanch, a Montauk sachem from Long Island, canoed to Fort Saybrook to ask Puritans if they were at war with all Indians. The fort's commander replied that they were not, but warned, "If you have Pequits with you . . . we might kill all you . . . but if you will kill all the Pequits that come to you, and send me their heads, then . . . you shall have trade."[146] Puritan retribution was now feared across the Sound. Pequot "heads and hands" had become simultaneous trophies of war and signs of allegiance.[147] As one English official exalted, "The Pequots now become a Prey to all Indians."[148]

In August Winthrop recounted the last vestiges of Pequot resistance and detailed the efforts of those who still pursued them:

> Eighty of their stoutest men, and two hundred others, women and children, were at a place within twenty or thirty miles of the Dutch, whither our men marched, and, being guided by Divine Providence, came upon them, where they had twenty wigwams . . . by a most hideous swamp, so thick . . . men could hardly crowd into it. Into this swamp they were all gotten. . . . Then our men surrounded the swamp . . . and shot at the Indians, and they at them, from three of the clock in the afternoon till they desired parley and offered to yield. . . . So they began to come forth, now some and then some, til about two hundred women and children were come out . . . then the men told us they would fight it out; and so they did all night. . . . Not one of ours was wounded. . . . Them as were left . . . escaped.[149]

From the captured Pequot women, the English learned that they had slain half of the remaining Pequot sachems. Among the survivors, fifteen of the boys and two women were enslaved and taken to Bermuda. Many were divided among Puritan homes as slaves. Since the war began, Winthrop concluded, "we had now slain and taken, in all, about seven hundred" as well as seized most of the Pequot's remaining "kettles, trays, [and] wampum."[150]

Shortly after the war, Puritan forces arrived at Block Island and continued their assaults, killing whomever they could find and burning their property. Once dialogues of peace began, Native leaders recognized the new realities of power in the region. Much had changed since the Oldham conflict two summers prior. Now they submitted "themselves to become tributaries [and to pay] one hundred fathom wampompeague."[151] A few weeks later in Boston, Miantonomo met with the settlement's governor, deputy, and treasurer. He too understood the realities that the war had established, acknowledging "that all the Pequod country and Block Island were ours [the Puritans'], and promised that he would not meddle with them but by our leave."[152] Puritans now controlled access to Block Island, the northern Long Island Sound, and its central watershed, the Connecticut River.

The battle of Long Island Sound continued after 1637. Pequot sovereignty diminished not only because of Puritan campaigns from the north but also due to southern Dutch advances. An imperial vise squeezed the Sound's Indigenous peoples, strengthening each zone of European settlement.

✦

The expansion in Puritan hegemony generated increased opportunities for English settlement, trade, and missionization. Many interpreted English triumph as divine intervention, especially as the Puritan population grew. Of the fourteen thousand who journeyed to New England by 1640, less than 5 percent had died from disease, and only one English ship out of nearly two hundred was lost at sea.[153] While in England Oliver Cromwell disparaged the Northeast as "poor, cold, and useless," the New English, as they called themselves, were consolidating power over an expanding commonwealth.[154] By 1700 Boston boasted fifteen shipyards that produced more ships than all other English colonies combined; in a nautical world, the city was second only to London.[155] Moreover, the Puritans' diversified farming, fishing, and trading dominated England's inter-regional trade across America's coastline, stabilizing British North America throughout the 1600s.

3 • The Unpredictability of Violence

Iroquoia and New France to 1701

> They . . . asked me as a token of great friendship and rejoicing to have muskets and arquebuses fired off. . . . I did so and they uttered loud shouts of astonishment, especially those who had never heard or seen the like.
>
> —*Samuel de Champlain (June 18, 1609)*

A generation had passed since Samuel de Champlain had regaled a gathering of Algonquin leaders near Quebec with his nearly magical military prowess, but now, in the 1630s, those Native leaders who survived the carnage that followed hardly remembered the warm summer days before they first heard the sound of gunfire. From the Hudson River to the shores of Lake Michigan and from the Chesapeake to the gulf of the St. Lawrence River, Native peoples fought each other using metals and newly acquired guns. The violence shattered Indian communities and shocked Europeans, as it combined with the scourge of European diseases to cause devastation. The lethal combination of disease and warfare remade the human geography of North America and defined an entire century of American history. By 1776 there would be fewer living souls on the continent than in 1492.[1]

As in British North America, the first generation of French colonization witnessed both setbacks and successes. By the time of Champlain's death on Christmas Day, 1635, the French had expanded New France, as a string of settlements lined the St. Lawrence. At Quebec and Trois-Rivières, churches, fields, and stone walls dotted the shorelines. Montreal was founded in 1642, becoming the colony's economic hub. Like their Dutch counterparts in New Holland, these settlements drew furs from the continent's interior and channeled them to the Atlantic.[2]

Across the interior, Native peoples navigated many challenges. In the St. Lawrence Seaway and Great Lakes, a new world emerged, one that differed from the previous one and was forged by violence, disease, and disruption.[3]

Many Native nations did not survive the lethal combination of disease and warfare that reverberated across their homelands. Diseases in particular destabilized the long-standing rhythms of village life and strained the religious systems that provided solace amid the violence. The additional threats of war and enslavement only further devastated Indian communities, as traumas radiated out from zones of European settlement.

Indigenous histories invite new interpretations of American history. The demographic losses of English laborers in the Chesapeake are dwarfed by American Indian and African mortality rates from the Middle Passage. The struggles of French or Puritan communities to endure oceanic travel and survive cold winters appear small compared to the trials of America's most beleaguered families, particularly the struggles of Indian nations in the 1600s.

Despite currents of death and diseases, many thousands did survive, particularly within the expanding spheres of the Iroquois Confederacy. This is essential for understanding not only how these communities developed thereafter but also for how early America evolved. As was the case for Native nations across the Americas, Iroquois peoples responded to the cycles of colonialism and shaped the continent's historical development. They came to control many aspects of the economic, social, and political affairs in eastern America during the seventeenth and much of the eighteenth century.[4]

Unlike many of their rivals, like the Wendat (Huron) Confederacy, the Iroquois survived the wave of warfare and disease that came to their homelands, albeit transformed. Their conflicts with New France in the seventeenth century reflect larger patterns of Indigenous struggles across North America. They often became more powerful than the Dutch, French, and later English colonists around them. Moreover, they played a significant role in the revolutionary struggle of the eighteenth century.

Initial Encounters: Champlain and the Iroquois Confederacy

Among the most feared combatants of early America, the Iroquois of central New York and eastern Canada are known for their consummate oratory and political organization. Archaeology, documentary records, and oral histories reveal the formation of a Great League of Peace in the pre-contact era when five different nations—the Mohawk, Oneida, Onondaga, Cayuga, and Seneca—united around a set of teachings, rituals, and practices.[5] At the time, such unity quelled strife between discordant villages and positioned the Iroquois to better harness, compared to other Indian nations, the violent advantages of contact. They shared a system of clans and chieftainships, representative councils, and governing practices including the annual recitation of beaded wampum belts that recorded Iroquoian epics and philosophies. Using shared values and ceremonies for peace, by 1600 the Iroquois had developed a confederation capable of withstanding the turbulence of contact.[6]

The French charted the Atlantic and St. Lawrence River, the great nautical highway into the Great Lakes from 1534 to 1609.[7] They soon claimed possession of the region and its peoples, but French relations with Algonquian-speaking peoples formed the basis of New France. Indian affairs, above all other concerns, fueled the expansion, texture, and fate of France's New World empire.[8]

As the French ascended the St. Lawrence, they came into conflict with the Iroquois, especially the Mohawk Nation, which represented the symbolic Eastern Door of the Iroquois Confederacy. Between the first expeditions of Jacques Cartier (1534) and Samuel de Champlain (1608), Mohawk communities struggled to keep their Algonquian-speaking rivals from gaining access to French goods, alliance, and weaponry.

As in so much of early America, absences cloud our understanding of these early encounters. Cartier encountered unidentified Native peoples along the Atlantic who had already traded with Europeans. They held up furs and indicated a desire to trade. After these coastal encounters, his ships headed up the St. Lawrence, encountering Montagnais villagers, who succeeded in courting French favor and enlisting the newcomers into alliance against their Mohawk enemies. They attempted to deny Mohawks access to French metals and weaponry.[9]

Inter-tribal rivalries predated French arrival and shaped the subsequent century of French imperialism. Early French voyages also engendered epidemiological and ecological chaos. In 1534 Cartier wrote of crops and orchards lining the St. Lawrence, but by the time of Champlain's arrival, villages were abandoned and gardens overgrown.[10]

As would be the case across the continent, the 1500s were merely the prologue to European diseases, trade goods, and violence. The specifics within this prologue remain largely unknown. Indian families migrated to ward off encroaching pathogens, limiting or abandoning altogether their horticultural and hunting grounds. Others, including the Iroquois, increased their raiding and captive taking to supplement economies and replace lost family members.[11]

Moreover, violence flowed from settlements. Champlain's 1608 founding of Quebec and his administration's Indian policies inaugurated many of the dynamics of seventeenth-century American history. From expanding the fur trade to charting the Great Lakes, Champlain established the foundations of empire and governed a rapidly expanding territory. Over the next thirty years, missionaries, traders, and officials coursed across the continent.

While no clergy boarded Champlain's ships, Jesuit priests followed. They became among the most informed, active, and visible agents of empire. Across the Great Lakes, they founded nearly three dozen missions by century's end.[12] By 1700 France laid claims to two-thirds of North America, from eastern Canada to the Mississippi and New Orleans.[13]

As New France became the largest colony in early America, its traders, explorers, and missionaries navigated many of the continent's major rivers—including the Missouri, Mississippi, and Ohio. They did so generations before their English rivals, laying claim in 1673 to the headwaters of the Mississippi and in 1682 to Louisiana.[14] Although this was often unrecorded, their travels depended upon the assistance of Native guides, translators, and laborers as well as hundreds of Indian villagers who housed French newcomers. These villagers, as we shall see in chapter 4, formed the center of France's empire.[15]

French governance, however, was nominal across the region optimistically known as "New France." French officials didn't really understand this territory and its peoples: few had ever traversed the colony's entire realm, whose northern and western perimeters were never formally determined.

For many French newcomers, including Champlain, New France was a stepping-stone for greater imperial glories. In 1624, after "sixteen years" of "laborious zeal . . . in the discoveries of New France," Champlain remained convinced that the Great Lakes offered a "means of reaching easily the Kingdom of China," a geographic chimera that enticed French explorers for generations.[16] Such a discovery would be a marvelous achievement for himself and the crown, adding immeasurable duties paid into royal coffers. Champlain had spent a decade circumnavigating the Great Lakes and believed that such a journey could be accomplished "without much difficulty."[17]

Illusions of discovery have obscured history's more important insights. The thoughts of Europeans have often dominated narratives of history. Such narratives erase not only Indigenous peoples but also the transformations emanating from colonial settlements, which radiated deadly change. In July of 1609, during Champlain's first full year as governor, he, his men, and several hundred of their Montagnais and Algonquin allies gathered to fight Mohawk forces (see the illustration at the opening of part I). The Mohawks were clad in reed-woven armor and gathered along the shores of the lake that now carries Champlain's name. As much as any moment in early America, this attack reveals the extent to which warfare would change across the century. This battle altered the nature of war. Its consequences spilled across the continent.[18]

Encountering a Mohawk encampment with more than twice as many men as their own forces, Champlain reported:

> They said that as soon as the sun should rise, they would attack us, and to this our Indian [allies] agreed. . . . Having sung, danced, and flung words at one another for some time, when daylight came, my companions and I were still hidden, lest the enemy should see us, getting our fire-arms ready as best we could. . . . After we were armed with light weapons, we took, each of us, an arquebus and went ashore.[19]

The resulting battle and the imagery it inspired mark the incident's significance in colonial history: a 1613 engraving of the conflict is the only surviving portrait of Champlain despite three decades of exploration, many trips across the Atlantic, and frequent visits to royal courts.[20]

For the Mohawks and members of the Iroquois Confederacy, this battle communicated the violent lessons of European colonialism. "Our [allied] Indians," Champlain wrote,

> told me that those who had the three big plumes were the chiefs . . . and I was to do what I could to kill them. . . . I marched on until I was within some thirty yards of the enemy, who as soon as they caught sight of me halted and gazed at me and I at them. . . . I took aim with my arquebus and shot straight at one of the three chiefs, and with this shot two fell to the ground. . . . I had put four bullets [*balles*] into my arquebus. . . . The Iroquois were much astonished that two men should have been killed so

> quickly, although they were provided with shields made of cotton thread woven together.

After his men opened fire and their Mohawk adversaries retreated, Champlain and his men "pursued them and laid low still more of them."[21]

These events hint at larger questions. How did Iroquois soldiers become feared combatants? How did communities so seemingly ill prepared for European-informed warfare become such dreaded antagonists? In their first recorded battle with Europeans, the Mohawks were defeated: their chiefs were targeted and their retreating soldiers pursued and killed. From Champlain's perspective, victory was easy.

In fact, by century's end Iroquois soldiers would leave their villages more often to talk than to fight. They soon initiated a global form of Indigenous shuttle diplomacy that made them courted guests in colonial and European capitals. The first portrait paintings ever rendered of any American Indian would be made a century later. In London portraits of four "Mohawk Kings"—Iroquois leaders who traveled to England after a "Great Peace" held at Montreal in 1701—were commissioned. Iroquois affairs concerned European leaders so much that Iroquois leaders, not New France's founder, would be invited to sit for portraiture.[22]

Throughout the century, everyday life within Iroquois villages shifted with the currents of diplomacy, trade, and warfare. Villages disbanded and regrouped. New peoples became incorporated, and new polities emerged. As communities moved or expanded, additional fields were cleared to make way for the essential foods of Iroquoia—the "three sisters" of corn, beans, and squash. And, everywhere animals became hunted, especially those with valuable furs to trade. The spatiality of Iroquoia shifted.[23] The Confederacy's influence soon extended across new regions and included new dependent peoples. To be an Iroquois man was soon to live a life in seasonal motion: not only fighting, raiding, and trading across the expanding colonial world but also speaking, deliberating, and visiting with Dutch, French, and other Euro-American settlements.

Similarly, life for Iroquois women changed. For centuries, Iroquois women have held power within their villages and across the Confederacy. Iroquois clans are matrilineal, and children are expected to remain members of their mother's clan. Farming rights, the rights to appoint and remove political leaders, the right to demand retribution for lost lives, and other communal powers have remained under the jurisdiction of women throughout Iroquois history.

As stipulated during the founding of the Great League, senior women,

John Verelst, *Tejonihokarawa (Baptized Hendrick). Named Tee Yee Neen Ho Ga Row, Emperor of the Six Nations*, 1710. Portrait of Tee Yee Neen Ho Ga Row, or Hendrick Tejonihokarawa, one of the four reported Mohawk leaders who traveled to London in 1710 on a diplomatic mission. Tejonihokarawa holds a wampum belt in his hand as a symbol of diplomacy and a wolf crouches behind his cape, illustrating his clan affiliation. (Source: Library and Archives Canada/John Petre collection/ e011179910_s1.)

known as clan mothers, held the highest forms of communal authority. They selected the chiefs who inherited the Confederacy's primary (or federal) chieftainships. Women named the individuals who succeed deceased leaders. Mohawk women initiated this process following Champlain's attack.[24] As Iroquoia endured the lethal combination of warfare and disease, women dominated the daily life of village politics and economies even more. "No one was there," reported Dutch trader Harmen Meyndertsz van den Bogaert during his 1634 winter tour of Mohawk villages, "but women."[25] The identification of village sites, the organization of community farms, the raising and education of children were all within their jurisdiction. Such authority increased the more Iroquois men traveled following the arrival of Europeans.

New forms of warfare, new strategies of survival, and new structures in village life characterized Iroquoia in the 1600s. Champlain's first cracks of fire initiated infernos of transformation. Unbeknownst to any at the time, other Europeans were making inroads south of Lake Champlain, adding additional combustibles to early America's cauldron of violence.

The Centrality of Violence in the Atlantic World

Members of the Iroquois Confederacy deliberated on how to respond to French aggression. French soldiers possessed terrifying weapons, and they had allied with their Montagnais rivals, who instructed the Europeans on how best to kill them. The newcomers had come by sea, claiming that there were many more like them.

The first year of Champlain's reign was followed by another year of French attacks upon the Mohawk. In June 1610 Champlain joined five hundred Montagnais and other allies and descended the Richelieu River, often referred to as the Iroquois River. There, Mohawk defenders had built a temporary palisade from which they launched stone-tipped arrows and insults. One archer struck Champlain near his earlobe. The governor and his arquebusiers responded with attacks that wore down Mohawk defenses. Nearly a hundred were killed and a dozen captured. These losses represented a high percentage of the Mohawks' military, as their population ranged between five thousand and eight thousand.[26]

For the Mohawks, it was clear that neither open-field nor defensive engagements worked against European newcomers, who combined superior armaments and numerous allies. So challenging were French advantages that throughout Champlain's nearly thirty-year governorship, the Mohawks limited their raids upon French settlements, including along the St. Lawrence and Ottawa Rivers, thereby enabling a growing exchange between interior peoples and French traders. French military advantages curbed Iroquois power in the colony's first decades, enabling the expansion of New France into the continent.

Like other colonial leaders, Champlain used violence not only to subjugate Native peoples but also to stabilize his authority. Across the Atlantic world, everyone understood that violence and the use of military technologies—ships, guns, horses, metals, and cannons—enabled colonization. Violence was as necessary for French expansion as rain was for its vineyards.

Even before they had landed, Champlain's ships had confronted armed Basque whalers whose obstructions were surmountable "only by force." He responded not with immediate violence—which would have endangered his plans for settlement—but threats of it, informing these sailors that his mission was supported by French king Henry IV. The authority of France was behind his effort, he told them. Similar to the Spanish Requerimento and its performative claims of title to lands the Spanish had never known, Champlain projected the authority of a monarch over France's recently claimed possessions. He compelled subservience to a recognized sovereign within an expanding if undetermined jurisdiction.[27]

Such projections by themselves never reached that far. Monarchical authority needed to be asserted and reinforced. Champlain understood that violence was crucial and showcased his technologies of violence, using them not just to kill but to display French power. Whether welcoming allied Indian leaders with gunfire or beginning holidays with cannon fire, the sound of arms became a growing feature of seventeenth-century life. New audible features also characterized Indian communication. Native trade fairs, diplomatic gatherings, and arrivals to the shoreline now also commenced with gunfire. Gunfire became a new habitus of *habitation.*[28] In fact, as Champlain lay dying, the sound of Quebec's cannons on Christmas morning 1635 were among the last sounds he heard.[29]

While violence was an essential institution of colonialism, it was never enough to achieve permanent goals of empire. As political theorists have long maintained, violence fails to create stability. It destroys relationships—between individuals, communities, and nations—and does so unpredictably.[30] Once it is initiated, none can predict its ultimate course. While threats upon a population do over time result in compliance, more enduring stability requires shared understandings of power and of the legitimate use of violence. The Basque whalers understood as much when they recognized that their interests were best served by heeding a distant monarch and the ships under his command.[31]

Nor could violence ever be completely monopolized. As in New Spain, Native peoples across North America quickly adopted the advantages that Europeans brought. Raiders took weapons as spoils of war and plundered Indians who were allied with Europeans or had traded with them. They stole their metals, cloths and, if possible, guns. Increasingly, they took captives to trade in colonial slave markets.

Colonial leaders understood the inherent disruption that violence brought and attempted to regulate the gun trade. Across colonial America, however, farmers, artisans, and even servants participated in it.[32] Paradoxically, the profitability of gun trading undermined the stability of the colonial settlements that engaged in it. Over time, alliances of protection, beneficial trading relations, and even conversion and intermarriage offered protections to both Indians and Europeans. Constant violence between Indians and settlers was too unpredictable to maintain.

The French, however, initially believed that the Iroquois could be driven to submission. The Mohawks had been defeated in each of the colony's first two summers, and the Iroquois were the hereditary enemies of Champlain's allies: the Montagnais, Wendat (Huron), and Algonquin Nations. Since the days of Cartier, the Iroquois were at odds with these nations, and this dissension facilitated settlement, expansion, and soon missionization. Native allies enlisted the French to dislodge the Iroquois Confederacy's power.[33]

Champlain wanted to help his allies. In early autumn 1615 he launched his third campaign against the Iroquois, attacking Onondaga in what was an invasion of Iroquoia itself.

Home to the central council of the Confederacy, the longhouses of Onondaga form the heart of Iroquoia. They receive delegates from across the Five Nations and have done so for hundreds of years. Its leaders are the "fire keepers" of the Confederacy who hold responsibility for convening gatherings, keeping records, and issuing deliberations. Onondaga's status as the central body within the Confederacy was so recognized that representatives to the Articles of Confederation in the 1770s referred to their newly formed body as holding its "council fires." Just as he had targeted Mohawk leaders in 1609, Champlain now attacked the Confederacy's legislative leaders.[34]

Unable to draw soldiers into an open confrontation, Champlain laid siege to the village of Kaneenda. Upon his arrival at "the enemy's fortress," he reported, the Onondagans retreated in the presence of Europeans: "As soon as they saw us and heard the arquebus-shots . . . they quickly withdrew into their fort." A large village consisting of over twenty longhouses, Kaneenda withstood Champlain's initial assaults. From inside its thick walls, archers rained waves of arrows and pushed back French soldiers and their allies. For days Onondagas repulsed Champlain's assault.[35]

Although they were familiar with fighting alongside Frenchmen, Champlain's Native allies did not follow his command structure. They chose to deliberate rather than simply accept his imperatives.[36] Hoping for the arrival of five hundred additional allies, Champlain had little choice but to accept his allies' deliberations, but after their assaults were thwarted he grew incensed at their harsh words. His allies saw little hope for victory, as Onondaga's reinforced and imposing walls held strong. Few French allies wanted to continue fighting through the many days that a siege of this magnitude required. It had become the longest and most difficult battle in the short history of New France—and the French were losing.[37] Unlike in the Mohawk campaigns, this battle also included women, children, and the elderly.[38]

To avoid defeat, Champlain proposed something unusual. He ordered his men to build an elevated "war machine," a wooden cavalier, a platform common in medieval Europe. Upon completion, this platform reached "within a pike's length" of the village walls and allowed soldiers to "ascend the cavalier from which they fired incessantly upon the enemy." "We should . . . place four or five of our arquebusiers to fire many volleys over the top of their palisades," he further instructed.[39]

While deadly, the platform did not break the village defenses. Provisioned with thousands of arrows, throwing stones, and water to douse enemy fires, Kaneenda held out. Like their Mohawk brethren, Onondagan archers again targeted Champlain, wounding him in the leg. "Never was [such] great consternation seen," wrote seventeenth-century historian Christian Le Clercq.[40] In vain opposed to his allies' decision to withdraw, Champlain was forced to bear their anger, insults, and disappointment with their European partners.

This failed assault haunted him throughout his governorship. His campaign, the third and largest in six years, was the first European attempt to subjugate the Iroquois, an ambition that would not be realized until the American Revolution. The siege in the heart of the Iroquois Confederacy lasted nearly a week. It came during harvest season—at the end of the Green Corn moon cycle—and targeted noncombatants.[41] For the first time in North American history, it utilized military constructions designed to benefit those who had guns.

The Iroquois did not confront the French in battle again during Champlain's lifetime. They learned to avoid such combat, understanding that the

French and their allies were too difficult to engage. A détente emerged among the Iroquois, the French, and the "Northern Alliance" of Native allies who became drawn into the colony's seasonal rhythms of economic, political, and religious life. These first decades of New France's existence (1608–38) stand in contrast to the remainder of the century, when Iroquois war soon brought the colony to its knees, destroyed much of the Northern Alliance, and drove Native peoples across the Great Lakes region into diaspora.[42] Champlain died believing that he had thwarted the threat of the Confederacy, but Iroquois actions and recalibrations soon proved otherwise.

The Rise of the Dutch-Iroquois Alliance

For decades, the Iroquois remained at a disadvantage. They were attacked by French leaders, excluded from trade along the St. Lawrence, and in conflict with France's allies. In addition, English settlers in the Chesapeake and Dutch traders along the Hudson River had formed colonies that engulfed those regions in similarly disruptive dynamics. From 1607 to 1609, three European empires had expanded almost simultaneously across the northern, eastern, and southern borders of Iroquoia, sending shockwaves into the Confederacy.[43]

As the first members of the Confederacy to combat Europeans, the Mohawk developed solutions to redress the Confederacy's disadvantages. They found strategies that soon characterized the Confederacy's broader foreign policy and, like the Europeans around them, they used violence.

The establishment of New France pressured Mohawk villages and weakened their military capacity. The spread of diseases compounded the disadvantages.[44] The Mohawk were faced with an expanding empire out of Quebec and at a remove from Dutch networks along the Hudson. Their northern Native enemies used European metals and French soldiers, while they confronted Native rivals to the south—Mahican, Delaware (Lenape), and Munsee—who, like them, traded with the Dutch. Mohawk leaders realized that these Dutch trading relations brought dangerous but also transformative possibilities. Controlling them became imperative.[45]

Inspired by the wealth the Spanish had amassed by colonization, the Dutch oversaw an empire that ranged from Guyana to Indonesia. Throughout the 1600s, Dutch businessmen looked for new trading opportunities, positioned themselves atop the Atlantic's mercantile networks, and worked to avoid labor-intensive, agricultural-based colonies. Europe's leading merchants, Dutch traders soon dominated key arteries of the Atlantic trade.[46]

Compared to France and Spain, Holland was a small nation, its popul numbering roughly 1.5 million—less than one-tenth the size of France. I a small pool of emigrants because there were few incentives to emigrate. The Dutch became different imperialists than their many rivals. Their aim was to trade.[47]

In North America Dutch activity revolved around trading manufactured goods for American resources. Native peoples were essential to Dutch fortunes. In 1609 Dutch traders began offering metals, cloth, and wares for trade. In exchange, Native people harvested furs, provided food and hospitality, and even joined military actions. The relationship lasted for a whole generation before permanent settlers and Dutch families arrived to build New Amsterdam in the mid 1620s.[48]

Laden with furs, Mohawks traveled to Dutch trade fairs. Notwithstanding their defeats, the Mohawk still wielded significant influence, particularly to their south. Other than New France and its Northern Alliance, only the Iroquois posed real threats. As Champlain had learned in 1615, they continued to exert military and political authority, and during this first generation of Dutch trading, the Mohawks began expanding.[49]

Iroquois expansion started with the Mohawks and continued for the next half a century, fueled by their political union, united by language and religion, and by the enduring pressures of colonialism. It was the Iroquois—not the French, the Dutch, or the English—who expanded into the headwaters of the Ohio River, which flows to the Mississippi and offers strategic advantages across the Trans-Appalachian West.[50]

In their earliest years, Dutch traders attempted to mediate tensions between Mahican and Mohawk rivals. They sought peace between them so as to protect exchange. In April 1613 Dutch leaders even attempted a trilateral agreement—the first North American treaty between Native peoples and Europeans—in which Mahicans exacted tribute on Mohawks coming to trade.[51] Conflict ensued, however, leading to the abandonment of some trading sites, including Fort Nassau in 1617. Nonethless, Mahican-Dutch trading continued unabated, and following the 1621 establishment of the West India Company, Dutch settlement and trade increased. It included the founding of Fort Orange, near present-day Albany, in 1624. American furs had helped to grow a new artery of the Atlantic economy.[52]

The Mohawks worked to subvert and then destroy Mahican advantages. In 1624, as Mahican leaders exacted tribute from visiting Iroquois traders, they also invited to New Holland Northern Alliance traders from Quebec to the Hudson, welcoming those most likely to raid Iroquois villages. Furs taken during Canadian winters were thicker and more profitable than those of the Northeast, and these northerners hoped to extract better returns from the Dutch.[53]

In response, Mohawks attacked Mahicans and the few Dutch leaders who fought alongside them. Near Fort Orange, they destroyed a Mahican party that included Daniel van Kriekenbeeck, a Dutch commander. The Mohawks regretted his death and "wished" to excuse their actions.[54] It was not their desire to kill the Dutch, they reported; they intended not to attack Europeans but only their Native rivals.

Reflecting the West India Company's overarching philosophy, Fort Orange's leaders worked to quell inter-tribal conflict. They followed up with Mohawk leaders after conflicts and worked to stabilize tense environments. They even criticized Kriekenbeeck's decision—a "reckless adventure"—to ally himself with the Mahicans. Dutch leaders expressed hopes that they could "prevent discontent" among all the nations devoted to trading with them.[55] They hoped to be neutral regarding their many partners and worked to avoid becoming embedded in historic antagonisms between Indigenous rivals.

The Mohawk-Mahican War ended in 1628. Mohawk soldiers had driven Mahicans east of the Hudson River and away from Fort Orange, and now they fought to keep them out. They monopolized the Dutch trade for themselves, driving non-Iroquois traders away from Fort Orange. In a short period, they gained access first to Dutch goods and then to Dutch guns. By 1634 Mohawk villages had acquired various types of metals—"chains, bolts . . . iron hoops, spikes"—that they had stolen from their rivals or gained in trade.[56] They also welcomed Dutch leaders into their villages, deepening the mutualism between them. The Mahican, in contrast, became displaced and needed to reconstitute themselves. The effects of warfare and disease had reduced their initially promising ties with the Dutch.[57] They became the first Algonquian-speaking nation dispersed in what became a broader Iroquois-influenced diaspora.

The Iroquois and Wendat Confederacies in the Age of Disease

These developments suited the Mohawks well. The Dutch traded cloth, metals, and wares. Unlike the Spanish, English, or French, they openly and consistently traded guns. Starting in the 1630s, they brought guns and ammunition to Fort Orange. Dutch gunsmiths welcomed Indian traders, sharing their knowledge on how to load, aim, fire, and fix them. Ammunition, of course, needed constant resupply and also dry storage, which led to a range of storage devices designed by Native people.

Ultimately, the Dutch-Mohawk gun trade changed the calculus of seventeenth-century politics because these were not just guns but guns of superior quality. Other European nations' efforts paled in comparison to the Dutch production of arms.[58] Mohawk and Iroquois soldiers now possessed the technologies of violence that had eluded them in their struggles with Champlain. What might be termed the southern strategy of the Iroquois now paid off.

Champlain and his men had used the French wheel lock, often referred to as an arquebus. Despite its advantages, it was not durable and was prone to clogging, making it costly to fix.[59] As in New Spain, these were weapons for governors, not Indigenous allies. Although these guns had ensured early military successes against the Iroquois, throughout the 1600s the French were increasingly using a sixteenth-century technology in a seventeenth-century world. In contrast to the Spanish, New France's monopoly on violence became short-lived.

The Dutch traded the flintlock, or snaphance. It was lighter than the arquebus, compact, and better suited for use in forests. Starting in the 1630s, Iroquois hunters, keen to acquire furs to trade for flintlocks, adapted their economies accordingly, in the process depleting the fur-rich animal populations across their own homelands. In the winter of 1634–35, when Harmen Meyndertsz van den Bogaert became the first European to record peaceful travels though Iroquoia, he "repeatedly" witnessed excitement for Dutchmen and their guns.[60] Everywhere, people wanted him to shoot his guns and, essentially, to confirm the new truths circulating across Iroquoia. The presence of the Dutch, he wrote, "caused [so] much curiosity in the young and old" that they "could hardly pass."[61]

Moreover, if he needed any additional evidence of the fur trade's ubiquity, his stomach reminded him. At one village he "ate beaver meat here every day." Finally, on New Year's Eve, among the Oneida, the Dutchmen consented to fire their guns, informing a village leader at Onneyuttehage that there would indeed be an evening celebration: "I told him I would fire 3 shots this evening, and they said that it was good and they were very pleased. . . . This evening we fired 3 shots in honor of the year of our Lord and Redeemer Jesu Cristo."[62]

In contrast to Champlain's first shots fired in Iroquoia, van den Bogaert's represented an alliance. By 1642 Mohawks had obtained enough firearms—

approximately three hundred—to have gained fluency in this recently distributed trade item.[63] They soon acquired more, trading thousands of pelts for hundreds of guns.[64]

Although armed with the best guns available, Iroquois leaders confronted many other challenges besieging Iroquoia. The outbreak of diseases became recurring traumas across the region. As Europeans ventured into Indian homelands, diseases followed them. A smallpox outbreak was reported across Iroquoia in 1634. It was the first of three in under six years. These outbreaks also devastated New France's Indian allies.[65] As much as any other force, epidemics shaped Indian survival strategies and determined the texture of diplomacy.

Unlike guns, immunities could not be bought, stolen, or procured, let alone monopolized. Diseases targeted all. Without immunities to many Old World communicable diseases, Native communities struggled against measles, smallpox, and influenza. While numerous diseases already existed across the Americas, including tuberculosis, pneumonia, and typhoid, many European diseases did not.[66]

At the crossroads of African and Asian trade networks, Europeans had suffered disease-ridden centuries, especially in northern and eastern Europe. Such exposure and the use of domestic livestock combined to foster greater immunities throughout Europe's populations. Even though the specter of disease haunted their memories and folklore, Europeans emerged from the dark ages primed for global encounters. History, not biology, provided clear—if unseen—advantages.

The inverse characterized Native America. Waves of contagion rolled across eastern America, crashing with unrecorded fury. The outbreaks became more frequent as colonies grew. Invasive species, colonial agricultural practices, and the depletion of fisheries and game compounded the shock, producing social conditions that increased the severity of pandemics.[67] Among the Mohawk, van den Bogaert noted the effects of that year's smallpox outbreaks.[68]

The clearest evidence of these pandemics was left by missionaries. The Iroquois refused missionization throughout the first half of the seventeenth century; therefore, we have fewer accounts of their daily lives, since these were often written by missionaries. In New France, by contrast, Indian villages began accepting missionaries as representatives of their French allies. As early as 1637, Jesuits established *réductions* (reserves) for Native converts outside Quebec at Sillery.[69] While acceptance was not synonymous with conversion, Jesuits observed, wrote about, and tried to remedy the challenges confronting their Indian allies. They did so particularly across the western reaches of New France in the Great Lakes region. The most detailed Jesuit accounts originated from western villages across New France's Northern Alliance, including the Wendat Confederacy. This confederacy lived around Georgian Bay, east of Lake Huron in Huronia, or Wendake.[70]

Also referred to as the Huron, the Wendat maintained political, economic, and clan structures similar to those of the Iroquois. They were comprised of four principal nations with eight clans and spoke an Iroquoian dialect, Nadowekian. Their confederacy consisted of roughly twenty to thirty palisaded villages with an estimated thirty thousand people.[71] The Iroquois and Wendat Confederacies paralleled each other, and their fortunes became forever intertwined in the generation to follow. In the early 1630s, disease and suffering linked them most.

Many Wendat died during the smallpox epidemics, their deaths recorded by the Jesuit fathers. Arakhie, a Wendat boy "eleven or twelve years old," held great promise, according to Father Paul LeJeune. His name translated as "closing day," and he was "like a little sun which arose before the eyes." Strong, intelligent, and responsive to the Jesuits, Arakhie was "obliging, and of agreeable conversation." When the boy died of smallpox, the Jesuit father could not bear to record his death and waited until he "was ready to write about it," until he could describe the loss without tears.[72]

Like Arakhie, many Wendat leaders died during these smallpox epidemics, including two chiefs, Taretande and Aenon, who represented various anti- and pro-French factions, respectively. They both died in 1637, and Aenon was buried in a French cemetery at Trois-Rivières following a summer of shuttle diplomacy—in response to their diminishing numbers, he had hoped to assemble Wendat villages into a great central location, a "Centre Lieu," that could be fortified through French alliance and trade. He had also tempered many of Taretande's anti-Jesuit rebukes, some of which had been delivered during Jesuit ceremonies. He did so with pragmatism. The "Wendat need for firearms," he informed his people, complemented "the French need for able-bodied men," and he envisioned Wendat leaders like himself working toward maintaining such an alliance.[73] His hopes, like those of so many others, perished during these diseased years: "The epidemic prevailed . . . he summoned the interpreters, offered a present to Monsieur the Governor, and begged him to favor the Hurons."[74]

An estimated five hundred Wendat died during the 1636 epidemic, including 20 percent of the village of Ossossane. The deaths began there with ten in eight days. The Wendat "country," expressed one leader, "is going to ruin. . . . Every day it is worse than before; this cruel malady has now overrun all the cabins of our village."[75] Wendake was descending into chaos.

The ravages of disease were evident throughout the 1630s. Peeling skin, fevers, interminable diarrhea, and blindness were commonly identified by observers.[76] Disease stalked village life and compounded colonialism's burdens. People worried about the causes of the devastation. Many "tribes believe that we poison and bewitch them," Le Jeune wrote. "They say that we have infected the waters."[77]

An elder Wendat, Anne, lost two daughters and a niece to the epidemics, and she was left to raise her orphaned grandchildren. Approximately seventy, she had survived the outbreaks but was now blind and weak. Like many, she had also adopted the new Christian faith. She believed, as many did, that baptism could stave off epidemics, even though the acceptance of this sacrament had not saved her daughters. Few came to Anne's assistance, and the Jesuits believed that she was shunned because of her faith. (So strong was this feeling of Christian separateness that Christian and non-Christians soldiers often refused to fight together.)[78] Anne was unable to gather without sight; starvation soon took two of the children under her care. They had survived the disease's outbreak but not its aftermath.[79]

The seventeenth-century shockwaves that reverberated throughout Iroquoia and the Great Lakes region require thought and contextualization. We tend to focus on the fact that germs caused these deaths, but we sidestep the many social stresses that accompanied disease. The dynamics of colonialism made diseases only one deadly vector in a world that faced the broader challenges of European expansion.

This point is important because in the face of this devastation, the Wendat Confederacy initiated political and military responses that drew them further into cycles of destruction. Like the use of violent technologies, diseases compelled communal decisions that accelerated the use of force in ways not anticipated. Both Wendat and Iroquois villages endured waves of pathogens in the 1630s. In their aftermath, they attempted to render anew their disordered worlds.

Origins of Iroquois Expansion

Aenon had traveled to Trois-Rivières in August 1637. Departing from Georgian Bay, his party traveled down the Ottawa River to the St. Lawrence. They made good time, their canoes powered by soldiers. Having fallen "sick upon the way," Aenon was buried on August 6, alongside Frenchmen who had helped to build the settlement.[80]

The day following his burial another disaster occurred. After a delegation of canoes had departed for Wendake, one returned and reported, "They have encountered the Iroquois." The others "had been captured."[81]

Initially French leaders "gave no credit" to their allies' concerns. "These barbarians are often alarmed without cause," reported Le Jeune. But with the appearance the next day of an Iroquois canoe "in the middle of the great river . . . we knew by this that there were many of them." A small French vessel ventured out, returning to report that "there were about five hundred men well armed." The boat fired its "brass cannon," killing "some crawling into the reeds" "skillfully."[82]

Much to the Jesuits' relief, Governor Charles-Jacques Hualt de Montmagny was already at the settlement. He "put everything in so good order" and calmed his countrymen and their allies. Like Champlain before him, he had hundreds under his command and dispatched a canoe to get reinforcements. The settlement remained secure. No one, however, controlled the river's waters, where the Iroquois continued their attacks. Despite the presence of an armed French ship, they destroyed a flotilla of ten Wendat canoes. Montmagny took this additional attack "greatly to heart." He despaired that "he could not drive these rovers away from us as we had so few men."[83]

As much as any other, the day of August 6, 1637, highlighted the lethal threat that diseases and warfare now constituted. Within hours, disease had taken a respected Wendat leader and warfare had killed soldiers under his command. Wendat allies had made the journey safely up the St. Lawrence. They did not, however, survive to return. In the days that followed, more Wendat lost their lives or were captured, and for the first time, the French heard the sounds of Mohawk guns.[84]

After the arrival of "two shallops, well equipped for war," Montmagny counterattacked: "We set sail as promptly as possible; the night favored us with a good wind . . . and we ascended to the river, where we expected to find these barbarians. . . . It was already broad daylight when we approached. We perceived a quantity of smoke. . . . But, when we reached the place whence this smoke came, we found . . . [they] had flown thence. One day sooner, and we would have had a battle." Unsuccessful in their pursuit, the French were dismayed to find not only the desecration of the "crossbar" from "a cross . . . erected the year before" but also an Iroquois message upon it. The governor and the Jesuits "studied it carefully." "Upon this plank," the Iroquois "had painted the heads of thirty Hurons, whom they had captured. . . . The different lines indicated the quality and age of the prisoners . . . [including] two heads much larger than the others, to represent two Captains whom they had in their clutches."[85]

Captives soon reshaped Iroquoia and Wendake. Nearly three thousand Wendats, or approximately 15 percent of all Wendats, became Iroquois captives.[86] In a historical process that has generated much debate, new practices of violence interconnected Iroquoia and its many neighbors. In this often apocalyptic world, captivity had become another radius of transformation, one that possessed both deadly and regenerative possibilities.

Starting in the 1620s, Iroquois raids against the Mahicans expanded. To their north, the Iroquois attacked French settlements, their allies, and the Native peoples who had come to live among them.[87] They pushed south and east, raiding not only across the Hudson but also into the Connecticut River Valley. There, in a reversal of fortunes, Mahicans now paid tribute to Mohawk leaders. Iroquois raids ranged even into Maine, where in 1647, after a months-long campaign, raiders returned with twenty Abenaki captives, their communities having become allied with Mahicans.[88] The attacks eventually subsided when these eastern communities obtained their own firearms, often from English traders specializing in traffic in arms.

The Iroquois incursions into Wendake were the most deadly. Starting in the late 1630s and for fifteen years after, the Wendat and Iroquois Confederacies collided. From roughly 1637 to 1652, this collision ended in the dispersal of the Wendat. It also brought similar effects to societies around them, particularly communities around Lake Erie.[89] By 1650 southern Ontario had been overrun by Iroquois soldiers who used the region to procure furs for themselves and to establish grounds to attack farther west into the Great Lakes. Wendake, according to *The Historical Atlas of Canada*, now became only "seasonally occupied."[90]

To many observers around the Atlantic region, this collision seemed to defy logic. The violence, pain, and brutality involved made little sense to European chroniclers, who were accustomed to more institutionalized forms of torture and warfare. French leaders tried to remain outside of what they regarded as the "madness" of inter-tribal conflict.[91] Infamous for their practices of captivity, the Iroquois became feared not only as skilled adversaries but as terrifying ones. In 1722, after a century of war, Bacqueville de la Potherie published his multivolume *Histoire de l'Amérique septentrionale.* "When one speaks in France of the Iroquois," he began volume 3, one often hears that there is "nothing in the world as cruel as an Iroquois war."[92]

Like all historians, Bacqueville de la Potherie was writing after the fact. Unlike most, he attempted to convey how the preceding century had made Iroquois warfare so brutal.[93] After two decades of French colonization, the Mohawks had driven the Mahicans away to gain access to Dutch trading centers. Epidemics had arrived in the 1630s. Now, and for half a century to follow, Mohawks and other Confederacy nations raided widely. They did so armed with guns superior to those acquired by their Native rivals.

Economically, Iroquois hunters now trapped far less than they had beforehand. It had become easier to steal furs than to trap them. By 1656 Iroquois traders brought nearly fifty thousand skins a year to Fort Orange, a ninefold increase from the 1630s. Harvested from across the Great Lakes region, the skins had been hunted, processed, and transported by tribes whose stolen labor now fueled Iroquois and Dutch fortunes.[94]

An escalation in captives exploded in similar proportion. Like piracy, captive raids accelerated in the aftermath of disease. Van den Bogaert noted the presence of disease among the Mohawk in 1634, but his records did not convey the extent of it. Of the eight villages he described, the Mohawk abandoned nearly half of them. Approximated at eight thousand during the 1620s, their population had fallen to fewer than three thousand by 1634. While estimates are hard to determine for the other Five Nations, epidemics fractured Iroquoia as they did Wendake.[95]

Among the Iroquois, diseases transformed captivity into an essential institution. The thirty Wendats captured in 1637 were taken for potential adoption, which occurred to replace lost family members whose responsibilities were too essential to abandon. Affective ties between family members and duties within clans structured village life across Iroquoia, and captive taking enabled these ties to continue. After severe population losses, the Five Nations embarked on efforts to "requicken" the league and to adopt Wendats.[96] The painting, for example, that the Iroquois had left for Governor Montmagny to discover had not only images but also colors upon it: "All these heads were scrawled in red, except one, which was painted black."[97] Red colorings identified those intended for adoption, or requickening. Mohawks similarly painted the face of Pierre-Esprit Radisson after he was captured as a teen outside of Trois-Rivières in 1651. While he may not have understood it at the time, "the red colour," one biographer has written, "meant that he had already been chosen as a candidate for adoption."[98]

In contrast to other seventeenth-century North American slaves, captives taken by Indians were taken for incorporation, not exchange. Indigenous slavery did not evolve in the same way as Atlantic slavery; this traffic did not center exclusively on economics. Indigenous slavery in New France was driven less by a demand for slaves than by the demographic and cultural imperatives of enslavement.[99]

In response to population losses, Iroquois raiders attempted to capture their enemies in order to bring them into their own village structures. Captives became kinsmen. They did so, however, only through suffering. Iroquois captors used violence to bind, transport, and incorporate captives. They tormented captives ritually in order to break down their identities.[100] To become a naturalized member of the Confederacy one had to disavow one's previous nation and accept, through violence, a new identity.

This violence was predictable. In the process of detribalization, family and clan leaders decided who would assume positions in Iroquois society. Captives were told the names, clans, and family positions of those who had perished. They were expected to assume these positions and names themselves. After suffering multiple abuses, Radisson recalled that "among the tumult I perceived my father and mother, with their two daughters. The mother pushes in . . . directly to me . . . calling me often by my name." As in a matrilineal culture, Radisson's new Mohawk mother identified him by the name of her lost child. She then removed him, "drawing me out of my rank," and placed "me into the hands of her husband, who then bid me have courage."[101] His new mother had sanctioned her new son's position within her family.

Captives knew that pain was a mechanism to achieve their anticipated transformation. Those unable to endure the pain or whose resistance became uncompromising did not survive. Tortured in ways that included days-long bindings, gauntlets, fire brandings, and fingernail removals, captives experienced harms intended to destroy their previous selves. To a surprising degree, such "ceremonial requickening" worked. Potentially as many as ten thousand were naturalized into Iroquois families in the half century following the epidemics of the 1630s.[102]

Even as captives became initiated into Iroquois society, they also brought with them elements of their previous societies. Hunting routes, village locations, and strategic information facilitated Iroquoian expansion. Captured

Europeans and Natives from distant regions added new cultural and linguistic fluencies into the Confederacy. The process of captive adoptions also created new soldiers. As Nicolas Perrot observed, the Iroquois "spared the lives of the children, who became, when grown, so many soldiers in their service."[103] The economics of the fur trade, the demography of diseases, and the cultural imperatives of captivity fueled Iroquois motivations for warfare.

The Effects of Iroquois Assaults on Wendake: 1648–53

Often called the "beaver wars," "Iroquois wars," or "mourning wars," Iroquois warfare reshaped the Great Lakes region and prompted reprisals from across the Atlantic. Scholars have long debated the causes and effects of these wars of the forest that cascaded out of Iroquoia in annual waves and raged so intensively or with such ferocity.[104]

This brutal history has overshadowed the origins of this warfare. Much is to be gained by viewing these conflicts in time and space. When Champlain invaded Iroquoia in 1615, he confronted archers using stone-tipped arrows. By contrast, on Sunday morning, July 3, 1648, a thousand Iroquois soldiers annihilated the palisaded Wendat village of Teanaostaiaé. They carried the most advanced weaponry in North America and attacked villagers who had missionaries among them and were attending a church service.[105] Nothing about these two battles resembled the other. Additionally, as evidence of the escalating violence of this era, over seven hundred were captured or killed, including a Jesuit priest who began the day celebrating mass and died attempting to baptize the wounded. Following the destruction, over one thousand Wendats fled.[106]

Such annihilation was just the beginning. Iroquois raiders aimed not only to limit these French allies but to displace them entirely, seizing them and their lands.[107] Ten percent of Wendake's population of nearly twenty-thousand were killed, captured, or exiled this one morning—and this attack was but one of seventy-three Iroquois raids of the era.[108] Hundreds of grieving, starving families fueled a diaspora that spread across the Great Lakes region.[109]

As the dispersed fled, their crisis enveloped others. They carried the disruptions from their own worlds into those around them. Initially, Indian communities around Lake Erie—peoples known as Neutral (Attawandaron) and Erie—accepted Wendat refugees. Where the refugees fled, however, Iroquois soldiers followed. As one priest wrote in 1651:

> The number of captives was exceedingly large. . . . This loss was very great, and entailed the complete ruin and desolation of the Neutral nation; the inhabitants of their other villages, which were more distant from the enemy, took fright; abandoned their houses, their property, and their country; and condemned themselves to voluntary exile. . . . Famine pursues these poor fugitives everywhere and compels them to scatter through the woods and over the more remote lakes and rivers.[110]

Within these new communities, the Wendat situation became dire. Food was hard to find. Some ate moss, bark, and fungus, but these were inadequate to support large numbers of families.[111] To an extent comparable only to the epidemics of the previous decade, famine shadowed Wendat life. Winters became a time of particular despair, especially for communities who had dispersed before their fall harvests.[112]

By 1650 an Indigenous remapping of the continent was underway—and gaining momentum. As the Iroquois displaced Wendat, Petun, Nipissing, Neutral, Erie, and neighboring Algonquian-speaking peoples, their attacks radiated into adjacent regions.[113] The raids drove refugees farther west, where they encountered other resident powers such as Siouan-speaking Ho-Chunk, Dakota, and Lakota peoples. To avoid conflict with these nations, the dispersed retreated onto peninsulas, along lakeshores, and into defensive locations. They feared Iroquois raids from their east and confronted new rivals to their west.[114]

In the years that followed, migration reconfigured French imperialism. As displaced Wendat and other allies of New France confronted Great Lakes–area nations, such as the Ho-Chunk and Menominee in Wisconsin, they turned to the French for support. In a seeming inversion of colonialism, these reestablished communities worked with French officials to rebuild security, understanding the necessity of mutual aid and protection. The French mediated conflicts across a vast region, providing gifts and governance that held a shattered world together. Throughout the Great Lakes region, an assemblage of Algonquian-speaking peoples, particularly Anishinaabe villagers across the north, worked with each other to find stability. The fate of New France—and soon the continent—hinged on the relationships, forged at Indigenous coun-

cil fires and in growing ties to French leaders, that developed across this interior world.[115]

The French called this interior world the *pays d'en haut*, high country, because the area holds the headwaters of so many watersheds.[116] The geography of this dispersal stretched from Lake Superior on the Chequamegon Peninsula through the Illinois country. Green Bay lay near its center. Jesuit missionaries quickly arrived there, following their converts and attracting more.[117] Throughout this reconstituted region, Indians from across the Ohio River Valley and southern Ontario rebuilt their lives among resident Native peoples, including Anishinaabe, Potawatomi, and Wyandot villages around Lake Michigan. The eastern homelands of the Wendat had become emptied due to Iroquois raids, and by drawing the French farther into the interior, these new settlements increased the expanse of European influences. That is, Indigenous military affairs and village realignment drew the French empire deeper and deeper into the heart of the continent over a century before English was spoken along the upper Mississippi.

These histories highlight the far reach of colonial violence and reveal its effects on populations removed from the sites of colonization. They undo long-standing assumptions about Indian peoples remaining removed from European influence, and show the centrality of Indian peoples to the continent's historical evolution and the growth of European colonies.

Iroquois warfare also initiated an imperial reordering beyond the Great Lakes.[118] In under five years, Iroquois soldiers had attacked communities from Maine to Michigan. From 1647 to 1651, their attacks decimated France's closest allies and curbed the colony's western trade altogether. Such attacks spiraled across a thousand miles. Not since the introduction of maize in the second millennium had such changes radiated so broadly across the region.[119]

Flush with their successes in the west, Confederacy members nonetheless struggled for stability in the aftermath of the Wendat dispersal. Seneca leaders prioritized the Confederacy's ongoing western advances and envisioned further advantages across the Ohio River Valley. They also held the longest-standing animosities with many western nations, several of which had launched similar attacks upon them.[120] Mohawks, in contrast, prioritized their Hudson-based trading relationships, which at times included heeding Dutch calls to arm. As Mohawks understood, Dutch fortunes were threatened by challenges from New England and, after 1638, New Sweden, whose growth south of New Holland prompted Dutch-Swedish conflicts.[121]

As the Iroquois attempted to harness the power of Wendake for themselves, they displaced their historic enemies and adopted many of their resources. The Wendat maintained bountiful fields across Ontario's rich southern soils, while the colder, fur-bearing watersheds across Georgian Bay also surpassed those of Iroquoia. Their excess production of corn had once complemented the economies of their northern neighbors, many of whom lived in regions ill suited for cultivation.[122] These neighbors became preeminent trappers and eventually fueled the growth of England's most northern American settlement at Hudson's Bay. (The Hudson's Bay Company was chartered in 1670 in the years following the Wendat dispersal.)

Trading relations across the continent were now upended by Iroquois warfare. Not only did the Iroquois use these conquered lands for their own, they severed them from New France. Starting in 1647, Wendats no longer traveled to French trade centers. The 1650s became a time of destitution among refugee communities and a time of scarcity across New France.[123]

With their trade cut off and their allies fleeing, French officials struggled to regain stability as the colony endured Iroquois raids on outlying settlements, trading convoys, and missions. Various peace initiatives were attempted with Iroquois leaders, including a short-lived treaty from 1653 to 1657 in which French leaders abandoned any protections for their Wendat allies.[124] For the first time since Champlain, French governors attempted neutrality in the region's violence. They tried to step outside of the internecine violence they had initiated. In the process, they isolated their long-standing Indian allies, and by May 1656, French cannons, guns, and officers remained silent as Mohawks raided the easternmost Wendat settlement at Île d'Orléans outside Quebec.

Only hundreds of feet from the city's walls, this island sits at the mouth of the river's estuary. Killing or capturing seventy Wendats, Mohawk leaders returned downriver past French settlements whose leaders failed to intercede. Outraged religious leaders vented their frustrations to no avail. The Ursuline leader Marie de l'Incarnation wrote bitterly to her son about the actions of this "infidel nation that does not know Jesus Christ."[125]

For the Iroquois, the benefits of war outweighed those of peace. Confederacy members held long-standing patterns of conflict resolution, but disagreements about war and peace quickly became too pronounced to resolve, fostering pro- as well as anti-Francophone factions.[126] In 1656 Jesuit missionaries

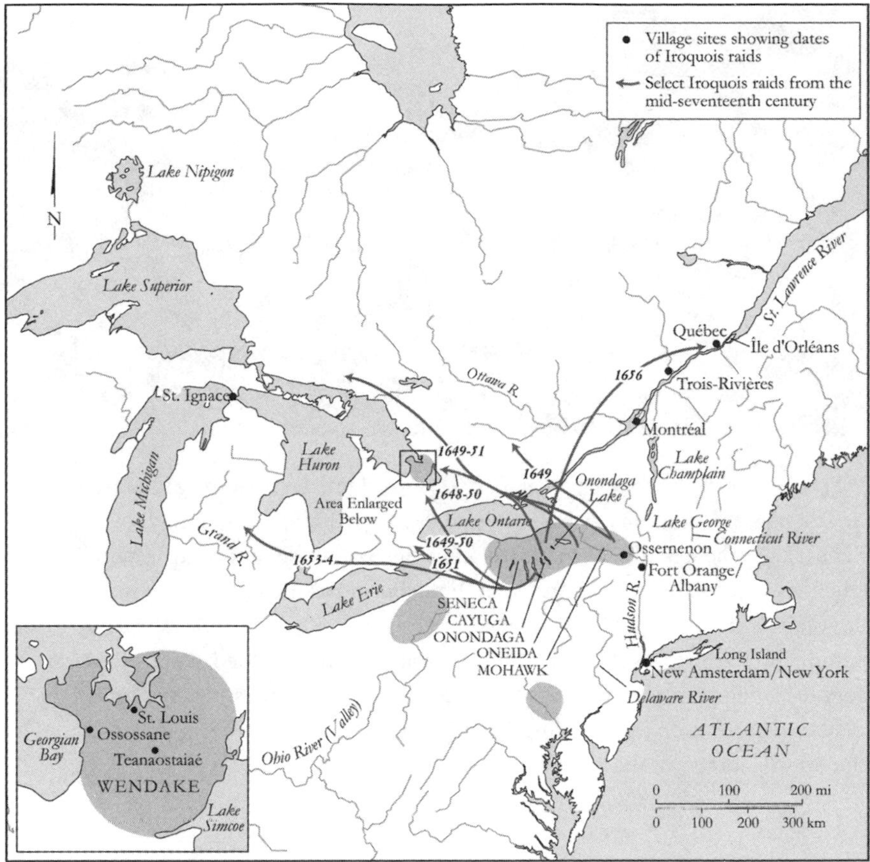

finally succeeded in establishing a mission among the Onondaga. They not only evangelized among the recalcitrant Iroquois but also served their former Wendat followers, who were now naturalized into the Confederacy.[127]

While factionalism divided Confederacy members, the Iroquois had withstood the first half century of European colonization and navigated Dutch, French, Swedish, and English influences throughout the 1600s. Their power destabilized French settlements to such an extent that the Iroquois could maraud western trading convoys for furs to trade with the Dutch. The weakened French colony had now become a magnet that drew vulnerable traders into Iroquois raiding paths.

Eventually, to stabilize its American empire, the French monarchy intervened. Louis XIV ordered increased troops to Canada, including over a thou-

G. Peter Jemison, *Iroquois Creation Story II*, 2015. Jemison's painting is based on the Iroquois creation story as it was told in 1899 by Chief John Arthur Gibson (Seneca). On the left, Sky Woman falls from the Sky World onto a turtle's back, which becomes the Earth. On the right, Jemison shows the world, including the plants and animals, that Sky Woman's descendants create on Turtle Island. By including the expression "Water Is Life," the artist connects the Iroquois creation story to contemporary movements to protect Indigenous land and sovereignty, including protests on the Standing Rock Reservation to stop the Dakota Access Pipeline. (Courtesy of the artist.)

sand of France's elite soldiers—the Carignan-Salières Regiment. At a time when the civilian population in New France was roughly three thousand, the military soon totaled one-third of the colony's European population.[128] If one saw a European man, he was likely wearing a uniform. The Sun King appointed his second-ranking officer, the marquis de Tracy, to command these troops. His mission: "to destroy [the Iroquois] completely."[129]

The Iroquois and the Remaking of New France

French leaders on both sides of the Atlantic understood the disruptions caused by Indigenous warfare. Leaders from New France regularly crossed the Atlantic to request reinforcements, as Pierre Boucher from Trois-Rivières attempted in 1661.[130] Royal officials, however, left the colony in the private hands of associates who managed the Compagnie des cent-associés.[131] As in the Chesapeake, a conglomerate acting on behalf of "one hundred associates" contracted laborers to run the colony's economy. But Iroquois warfare now brought down the company.

Louis XIV and his advisors began new reforms. They needed greater authority to build a prosperous colony integrated into France's mercantile networks, and war was antithetical to prosperity. Officials devised strategies to limit conflict.[132]

New garrisons were established and provisioned, and campaigns and invasions of Iroquoia were launched with hundreds of soldiers who, unlike most of the company's contracted workers, often stayed on as settlers after their tour of duty.[133] A lasting peace between New France, its Indian allies, and the Iroquois was established in 1701 and defined French-Iroquoian relations during the reign of Louis XIV.[134] The reorganization of New France, no less than the building of Versailles, the various European campaigns, and the growth of hegemonic absolutism characterized the king's reign.[135]

In 1663 Louis XIV revoked the charter of the Compagnie des cent-associés and appointed the marquis de Tracy lieutenant general of France's overseas colonies. He arrived at Quebec in August 1665, in command of eight companies of soldiers aboard two ships of nearly four hundred tons. He immediately set about restructuring the colony's defenses, beginning the construction of a fort at the entrance of the Richelieu River.[136] After their campaigns against the Mohawks, a hundred Iroquois arrived at Quebec "to conclude the 'traitté de paix'" (treaty of peace).[137]

The regiment's arrival answered a generation of settler appeals.[138] As Marie de l'Incarnation wrote,

> I should never have dared hoped to see such magnificence in . . . Canada, where when I first came I saw nothing. . . . According to the calculations of the army's march, battle should have been joined in the first [Mohawk] village. . . . These barbarians have good forts, they have cannon, and they are valiant, and doubtless it will not be easy to vanquish them. But our French soldiers are so fervent they fear nothing. . . . They undertook to carry cannon on their backs over very difficult rapids and portages. They have even carried shallops [ships], which is an unheard-of thing.[139]

The French eagerly observed the Iroquois wars and the efforts of France's military leaders to resolve them.

Lasting peace took a generation to materialize. Despite the redoubled French commitment to New France, the Iroquois Confederacy continued its western and southern expansion and often allied with English officials, who had acquired New Holland in 1664. As France was England's principal antagonist, a series of wars engulfed their American colonies, and a generation of reforms in both New France and British North America flowed from the 1660s.

Most notably, while Iroquois raids in the Great Lakes region continued to yield captives and furs, they prompted greater reprisals. The Iroquois were on the defensive by 1665, as French leaders worked to supply their western allies.[140] The growing influence of English traders also prompted the French to fuel resources into the interior. While Iroquois raiders had dominated seventeenth-century warfare, their dominance was ending.

Violence had come to constitute a vast geography of its own, an expansive region stretching from the Great Lakes, across the upper Ohio River Valley, and to Quebec, with Iroquoia near its center. Twelve hundred French soldiers succeeded in limiting Iroquois power in the east, but they could not subdue the Confederacy, and they remained unable to thwart Iroquois offensives in the Great Lakes.[141] Seneca and Cayuga raids reached as far as St. Louis in 1684. But they now generated commensurate reprisals. Governors invaded Iroquoia in 1687 and 1693, targeting and burning Iroquois villages. Like earlier invasions, these campaigns had been authorized by the French monarchy and drew allied Indian villagers from across the Great Lakes region.[142]

The final French invasion of Iroquoia came in the summer of 1696. With a force of over two thousand soldiers and Native allies, it demonstrated the growing capacity of New France to deliver violence into the heart of Iroquoia. Like previous campaigns, it failed to generate lasting victories, particularly as Onondaga villagers retreated, burning their longhouses before the French advance. In a further sign of weakness, the campaign was shadowed by Mohawk raiders who broke off to attack French settlements after the French departure. Regardless of directives from Versailles, Iroquoia remained unconquerable.[143]

Although the French and their allies had unwoven Iroquois hegemony, neither side could claim supremacy. The Confederacy still exerted its influence across great distances and over many peoples, but at great cost. French soldiers now staffed interior forts and for the first time, armed their Native allies. Better-equipped allies now shaped the fortunes of French imperialism and reversed Iroquoian assaults.[144] Since Champlain, French governors had never intentionally armed Native peoples with guns, but after 1665 this became colonial policy.[145]

A century of horrific violence was followed by an enduring peace. After a generation of failed initiatives, two thousand Indian delegates from across North America prepared to arrive in Montreal in July 1701. Within Confederacy longhouses, across Great Lakes villages and council fires, and onto the Mississippi's prairie plains, Native chiefs, clan matriarchs, and community members discussed past losses, implored their leaders for justice, and hoped for a future without bloodshed.

The Great Peace of 1701

In early July 1701, after a year of provisional agreements, large convoys of Great Lakes Indians left for Montreal. Representing Anishinaabe and other Algonquian-speaking villages, these convoys also included Iroquoian-speaking Wendats (exiled from Wendake); Siouan-speaking Dakota, Ho-Chunk, and Lakota peoples as well as others from across the interior. They were joined by Abenakis and New France's eastern Indian allies and by leaders from each of the Five Nations.[146]

Ultimately, representatives from over forty Native nations came together.[147] Days of rejoicing followed. Peace was to be restored across the region, prisoners returned, and spheres of autonomy respected. The French governor, the chevalier de Callières, agreed that he and other officials would now arbitrate grievances and work to resolve disputes between various nations. Speaking in the metaphorical language typical of such diplomacy, Callières expressed much "satisfaction in seeing all my children united" and distributed wampum belts to each delegation.[148] By signing or leaving their marks on the treaty, Native signatories committed themselves and their respective village kinship relations to the processes of peace.[149]

The French narrative describing these fateful days, paternalistic in tone, overstates the extent of European authority and ignores the cultural diversity and interdependence of those assembled. In fact, all were children of this new world, born from the encounters initiated by European and Indigenous warfare. Unlike in the days of Champlain or during the Iroquois attacks upon Wendake, none could unilaterally hold power. Mutual coexistence, recognition, and diplomacy were intrinsic to their collective survival. As the Great Peace suggested, the differences between Europeans and Natives had become less determinative than their commonalities. Matters of war and peace—of life and death—required the presence and participation of peoples from across the continent.

After 1701 new forms of trade, diplomacy, and alliance both built this world and held it together. The unfamiliar, frozen lands that Champlain optimistically called "New France" had become home to ten thousand settlers. It included missions, forts, and outposts that stretched up the Mississippi, across each of the Great Lakes, into the Atlantic. "Indian" families welcomed traders, priests, and leaders into their villages, blurring the boundaries of these categories while establishing new ones, such as Métis, or "mixed-blood."

Iroquois influences and Great Lakes Indian responses shaped the evolution of the French empire. Triangulated relations of war, trade, and now peace enveloped all, and this varied history was recorded across a range of Indigenous traditions, from Iroquois wampum belts to pictographic Anishinaabe "doodem" marks, which provided "a visual metaphor for Anishinaabe readers" of larger sets of political, cultural, and allegorical associations.[150]

At the dawn of the eighteenth century, Louis XIV claimed much of North America. The uncharted territory of Louisiana and the settlement at St. Louis even carried his name. The Grand Settlement of 1701 made such claims more than imagined fictions. Agreeing to limit their Great Lakes raids in exchange for jurisdiction over Native villages across the Ohio River, the Iroquois emerged from a century of war intact and sovereign. They had lost tens of thousands to diseases and warfare but had incorporated many others to survive. They soon welcomed a sixth nation, the Tuscarora from the Southeast, facilitating their evolving strategy of dealing with New France and British North America: playing each against the other.

Similarly, across New France and into the *pays d'en haut*, new relations flowed from 1701. The shared European-Algonquian world of the seventeenth century continued, but it changed.[151] New settlements, such as Detroit, were founded after the Great Peace, drawing settlers, military leaders, and traders farther into the continent. These included aspiring men like Antoine Laumet de Lamothe, sieur de Cadillac, who made great promises to the region's Indian peoples.[152]

Much like imperial officials from the era, historians have tried to find distinctions across this landscape, giving the impression that Europeans knew the lands they claimed and controlled the peoples upon them. Understanding the constellation of French, English, Dutch, Iroquoian, Algonquian, and Siouan-speaking communities that shaped the composition of New France requires seeing past outdated ethnographic and spatial categories that frame many approaches to the past. As we shall see, the greatest imperial struggle of the century to follow both began and ended in this interior world, making a full accounting of early America impossible without attention to its history.

4 • The Native Inland Sea

The Struggle for the Heart of the Continent, 1701–55

The true point of view in the history of this nation is not the Atlantic coast; it is the Mississippi Valley.
—*Frederick Jackson Turner (1892)*

Like other cities, Mandan towns were noticeable before being seen. Sounds traveled across the calm waters of the Missouri River, whose winding path gathers momentum each spring when mountain snows begin to melt. Beginning in Montana, flowing through the Dakotas, between Nebraska and Iowa, and across Missouri, this watershed drains much of the continent. The longest river in North America, it is fed by dozens of eastern-flowing rivers and carries their waters to the Mississippi and ultimately to the Gulf of Mexico. For millennia, its waters have nourished life across the heart of America.

Smoke from roasted corn, drying meats, and morning meals signaled the concentrated nature of this community. Guests would recognize the busy routines of spring and summer days, particularly the work of farming that occurred outside the town's palisaded walls. In their nearby gardens, Mandan women cultivated at least nine varieties of maize. As in much of eastern America, a gendered political economy sustained this world. Theirs was a maize-based diet, infused with the seasonal harvests of bison, fish, and game obtained through trade or from the labor of the men.[1]

Mandan towns were, however, situated in less than temperate environments. Their residents' work was done within a short growing season, concluding before the much longer winters. Some estimate the Mandan growing season was little more than 120 days. Busily pounding and turning the earth, Mandan women sowed into July, hoping to steal away one last green-corn harvest before early frosts. By that time, the principal work of the year was done—the sowing, planting, and harvest complete.[2]

After the winter thaws, traders, often in the thousands, ventured to these towns. In spring 1739 Pierre Gaultier de Varennes de La Vérendrye reported that "two hundred lodges of them came; sometimes even more come."[3] As with the trade fairs of New Mexico, these guests traveled to Mandan "forts," exchanging hides, meats, and the many wares processed during the long winter "for grain and beans, of which they have an ample supply."[4]

Often staying for months, the guests formed temporary ethnic enclaves surrounding the village. According to La Vérendrye, they "are not all of the same tribe" and hailed from across the West. Some had even traded in New Mexico and had spent time among those who "were white like them, . . . had beards, and . . . prayed to the great Master of Life in books."[5] Situated at the geographical heart of the continent, these Indigenous towns drew travelers such as La Vérendrye from distant corners.

Scholars estimate that these visiting lodges held extended families of eight to twelve. Two hundred to three hundred lodges brought, then, several thousand to the fifteen thousand to twenty thousand within the Mandan's river community. Seasonal trade made the six central Mandan villages among the most densely inhabited sites in North America.[6] Boston, New York, and Philadelphia had a combined population of thirteen thousand in 1690.[7] With a population size similar to that of Mississippian-era urban centers such as Cahokia, the Mandan sustained North America's largest urban network until the age of the American Revolution, when New York finally overtook these earlier Indigenous cities.[8]

Later Euro-American travelers such as Meriwether Lewis and William Clark also visited. In 1804 the American explorers had entered the Louisiana territory recently purchased by their president, Thomas Jefferson. Like La Vérendrye, they hoped to trace the Missouri to its headwaters, where they hoped to find a route to the Pacific. By the time of their arrival, however, Mandan villages had endured smallpox outbreaks and other colonial disruptions. They were now confronted with the equestrian powers around them, particularly the Lakota (Sioux). Mandan leaders, Clark recorded, informed "us that the Sioux [now] settled on the Missourie above, threaten to attacked them this winter, and have treated . . . [Mandan emissaries] Verry roughly."[9]

Scholars have studied the inter-tribal conflicts that led to the decline of the sedentary Mandan world, and often frame histories of the American West in terms of the tensions between the Mandan and their Lakota neighbors.[10] But this riverine world was defined by connections as much as by conflict.[11]

Nearly a century before Lewis and Clark, La Vérendrye came from the far eastern corner of an interconnected world, the interior world of the Native Inland Sea.

Born in 1685 at Trois-Rivières, he was the son of the town's governor, an office second in importance only to the governor of Montreal.[12] He grew up during the Indigenous struggles that forged New France, living through the final Iroquois campaigns and the Grand Settlement of 1701.[13] He received military instruction in Europe, where he was captured in battle, and he returned to North America to lead campaigns in the Northeast, across the *pays d'en haut,* and onto the Plains, which he charted. His life intersected with the economic dynamism of the Mandan, whose leaders he courted and whose history he recorded. He lived in a world defined by Native and non-Native peoples.[14]

Throughout the eighteenth and nineteenth centuries, inhabitants of the Inland Sea routinely traveled the nearly two thousand miles that separated Trois-Rivières and Double Ditch, the largest Mandan village. The social relations, diplomatic accords, and economic nodes that they defined at the heart of the continent determined the continent's future.

With its western reaches along the Missouri and its eastern arteries stretching across the St. Lawrence, this interior world was dominated by the rivers and passages of the Great Lakes. It included countless trails and roads, forest and open hunting grounds, prairie gardens, lakes and dunes, and Native villages that formed communication and transportation networks that circulated the goods, peoples, and information that fueled North America's greatest transformations. From the rise of the continental fur trade to the eventual struggle between France and Britain known as the Seven Years' War, this interior world was the beating heart of the continent. The war spread from here across the continent, into Europe, and across the high seas; in 1763, at the former French fort at Detroit, the war's last battles occurred, setting in motion frontier conflicts that eventually toppled British North America.[15]

At the heart of this interior world were Native nations, particularly the Anishinaabeg (Ojibwe). For centuries, Anishinaabeg and other Algonquian-speaking peoples have lived here, maintaining seasonal, semi-migratory economies centered on freshwater resources: fish, wild rice, and furs. Over one hundred contemporary Ojibwe communities in the United States and Canada reside between the Lake of the Woods in the west to Lake Ontario in the east, two dozen of which are currently federally or state-recognized tribes in Michigan, Wisconsin, and Minnesota.[16] They speak related dialects of Anishinaabemowin, the Ojibwe lingua franca.

Ojibwe communities settled the northern Great Lakes region in the sixteenth century, separating from other Algonquian speakers, the Potawatomi and the Ottawa. Their homelands are known as Anishinaabewaki, or "Ojibwe territory," which eventually spanned both sides of the international border in the aftermath of the American Revolution.[17] Throughout the colonial era, the Ojibwe comprised the largest of the Native Inland Sea's social communities, and they began to confront the deluge of settler colonialism in the early decades of the nineteenth century.

Like other Algonquian-speaking communities, the Ojibwe combine fishing, hunting, and gathering. Their economies revolved around numerous foods and medicines. As with the Mandan, their economies followed seasonal and gendered labor routines. Families migrated seasonally between villages and the campsites along the streams that connected the interior's lakes, ponds, and waterways. Wild rice beds, berry harvests, and spring maple sugars fueled a domestic economy run by women, while hunting, fishing, and trapping drew men away from village work. The growth of the fur trade further accelerated gendered divisions, eventually bringing new divisions of labor and property.[18]

In the eighteenth century, bonds of commerce, diplomacy, and warfare linked the interior's Algonquian-speaking communities with the French empire. Familial, religious, and social ties also wedded village societies with French imperial authority. From the Great Bend of the Missouri to the estuary of the St. Lawrence and from the mouth of the Mississippi to the northern Great Lakes, Native peoples controlled essential arteries, and thus access, into the continent. Powerful allies, trading partners, and antagonists, Native villagers shaped the contours of the century's crucible of war.[19] Few would go untouched by these global conflagrations.

After 1701: The Reconfiguration of Iroquois Power in the Eighteenth Century

La Vérendrye lost his father—the governor of Trois-Rivières—at age four and began his military career in Europe at twelve. He returned to Quebec as a young man.[20] Had his father lived, La Vérendrye's adolescence might have been spent along the St. Lawrence, whose spring thaws heralded the beginning of New France's annual commerce. He might have attended the Grand Settlement in 1701. Father and son would have joined Governor Louis Hector de Callières during the evenings and celebrated the "Great Peace" established between France and forty Native nations to celebrate that the Iroquois wars were over, ending decades of warfare.

In these days of hope and optimism, his father would have stood by the governor's side when he welcomed the Odawa leader Outoutagan, the first Native leader received.[21] They would have heard the rejoicing on the island's shoreline where encampments had formed. Only three days earlier, seven hundred western leaders had brought their canoes ashore near the juncture of the Ottawa and St. Lawrence Rivers.[22] They were soon joined by hundreds of Iroquois delegates as well Abenaki, Mi'kmaq, Mohegan, and other leaders from the Northeast.[23]

For many, the 1701 gathering was the largest of their lives. In July Montreal's population nearly doubled with the arrival of two thousand Native guests.[24] These included Dakota and Ojibwe leaders from the communities that La Vérendrye later visited during his 1739 travels. By then he was a father and had enlisted his sons in an attempt to discover an overland passage to the Pacific.[25]

The Grand Settlement at Montreal occurred at the same time as an English-Iroquois conference held at Albany. After the conquest of New Holland, Albany became the most northern capital of England's thirteen colonies, and in 1701 Iroquois leaders convinced English officials to recognize Iroquois autonomy between New France and British North America and suzerainty over a string of dependent villages across the Ohio River.[26] This shaped English, French, and Iroquois diplomacy for the next half century as maintaining stability between France and England became essential components of Iroquois politics. As New York's Indian Affairs secretary Peter Wraxall recalled: "To preserve the Balance between us and the French . . . is the[ir] great ruling Principle."[27]

Until the 1740s, relations between the Confederacy and interior communities remained largely outside European control. The agreements of 1701 recognized Iroquois autonomy over much of the trans-Appalachian world, especially the Ohio River Valley, where the Confederacy maintained power and autonomy. The Iroquois not only influenced, as Wraxall suggested, the balance of power between France and England but also possessed the power to incorporate others into their union, even those at war with the English. In 1715, following the colonization of South Carolina and warfare between the Tuscarora and Carolinian settlers, Iroquois leaders welcomed Tuscarora members into the Confederacy. These southern enemies of the English now became the Confederacy's Sixth Nation, learning the Confederacy's teachings and covenants while expanding its size through a process of naturalization.[28]

In addition to remaining neutral in conflicts between France and England, the Iroquois recognized French alliances with Native nations across the interior. They curbed their western advances and sanctioned French expansion across the continent. The founding of Detroit in late 1701 highlighted the far-reaching effects of the Great Peace and with it the changing diplomacy of the Confederacy, whose western reaches now ended there. Soon, Fort Pontchartrain on the Detroit River signaled entryway into a Franco-Algonquian world, one that soon attracted diverse Francophone, Algonquian, and even dissatisfied Iroquoian residents.[29]

Iroquois power determined much of the Ohio River's subsequent development. Both French and English leaders feared the other might enlist the Confederacy in the cascading conflicts between France and Britain during the eighteenth century. Maintaining Iroquois neutrality became essential to the stability of each European empire, while staying removed from European conflicts sheltered Iroquois and their dependent villages from war.[30] In this trilateral world, the Iroquois Confederacy and its allies were one essential pillar.

Neutrality and warfare, however, were not the only diplomatic practices connecting these diverse communities. Trade tied all together. It provided lifelines of support, and at Albany, Iroquois leaders received assurances there would be continued markets for their goods. Securing partners for their furs—and receiving trade goods and ammunition in return—resolved long-standing tensions for the Confederacy that followed the English conquest of New Holland in the 1660s. After 1701, the Iroquois more easily traded with English settlers and used colonial ports and forts to supply themselves. Trade with England assured that they would never again find themselves shut out of European markets, as they had throughout much of the 1600s.

The Iroquois wanted to maintain a three-tiered balance of power between the French and their many Algonquian-speaking allies; the Iroquois and their dependent villages; and the diverse but connected thirteen English colonies. This political triad endured throughout the first half of the eighteenth century, making the agreements of 1701 among the most diplomatically influential moments until the Treaty of Paris in 1763 formally ended the Seven Years' War. As we shall see, that war erased the triadic diplomacy and ultimately the French North American empire altogether.[31] The fate of North America increasingly revolved around this interior world, and within this world, French-Indian relations proved decisive.

Trade, Mediation, Justice, and Religion: French Ties across the Interior

As a cadet, La Vérendrye trained alongside those who had fought in the final campaigns against the Iroquois. He heard men complain of their inability to dislodge the villages of the Confederacy. He listened as they took issue with then governor Louis de Buade de Frontenac's shifting strategies. He was, however, too young to follow one of the era's other great developments: the arrival of western Native allies. As in the days of Champlain, Native delegations arrived every year, coming now from more distant lands. In 1695 an unnamed Dakota ambassador arrived representing twenty-two villages from the Mississippi. Concerned about the growing French alliance with Ojibwe communities, he requested a meeting with Frontenac in which he asked for the same forms of "iron and ammunition" provided to the governor's Ojibwe allies.[32] The Dakota leader relayed that his communities were hesitant to ally with the French, but that access to French weaponry might change their minds.

When French officials faced west, they confronted a complex Indigenous universe.[33] Governors at Montreal, settlers from Trois-Rivières, and monarchs at Versailles all understood the importance of the interior, but they understood it differently than those who shaped it. They read or heard fictional accounts of "noble savages" that circulated in philosophical circles and formed a mythology of empire that was at odds with how the empire actually worked. French leaders knew that the interior had absorbed the brunt of Iroquoian campaigns in the 1600s, and now, following the Grand Settlement, it posed new opportunities as well as challenges, but they did not necessarily recognize that the fate of New France revolved around the Native Inland Sea.[34]

Countless forms of everyday relations tied French and Native peoples together, molding the landscapes of the eighteenth-century interior. They included trade and commerce; political mediation and dispute resolution; religious conversion and syncretism; intermarriage and kinship incorporation;

Painted circa 1780 by a German immigrant in Quebec, these studies of French and Indian inhabitants of the interior show the melding of European and Indigenous cultures, particularly through commonly shared forms of clothing, accessories, and cooking implements. (With permission of the Royal Ontario Museum © ROM.)

and military affairs and alliance. All were interrelated. All entangled Native and non-Native peoples in webs of dependency, obligation, and allegiance. From New Orleans to the St. Lawrence, such economic, political, social, religious, and military relations formed the infrastructure of New France. As Native peoples and French traders, priests, settlers, and officials confronted one another, they constructed the ties that held the empire and interior villages together.

As Frontenac heard, trade goods provided essential technologies for interior peoples. European guns, cloths, and "iron" were particularly coveted. Each became incorporated into Native military, domestic, and industrial relations. European-made metal scrapers, for example, facilitated the processing of furs and animal hides; kettles the boiling of water; and guns, hatchets, and knives subsistence hunting and community defense.

As with the diffusion of horses from New Spain, French goods radiated across the continent. They arrived, however, in streams, not waves. Only seventy French canoe loads, for example, reached Great Lakes villages in the late 1680s. While such deliveries included over five hundred guns and two thousand iron hatchets, they entered an Indigenous world inhabited by at least one hundred thousand people.[35]

Many interior communities were, in fact, comparable in size to the great Mandan villages on the Missouri. In 1670 approximately twenty thousand Ojibwe resided in settlements around Green Bay. Farther south, another twenty thousand confederated Illinois, Miami, and Shawnee lived within a cluster of villages across Illinois. At Fort Michilimackinac in Michigan's Upper Peninsula, seven thousand resided in 1695. At the time of the Grand Settlement, the interior included more people than any neighboring region, equaling Iroquoia, Quebec, and New England combined. French goods never arrived in numbers sufficient to replace Indigenous technologies, and as with so many other facets of everyday life, European material goods existed alongside Native ones.[36]

While precise population figures are impossible to determine, interior Native peoples vastly outnumbered French colonists, missionaries, and soldiers. Moreover, as threats of Iroquoian violence continued, Native migrations, resettlements, and mission abandonments were routine, further confounding French officials. Following the 1696 death of Father Charles Albanel, the mission settlement at Sault Ste. Marie collapsed. The next year posts at Michilimackinac and St. Ignace also closed.[37] As they had for centuries, Native villagers maintained seasonal settlements, and their mobility complicated imperial efforts to classify the interior.[38]

One thing was certain—trade goods cemented relations between peoples. The French bestowed trade goods as "gifts" to allied communities. They did so for many reasons, including protection, as in 1680 when the Illinois chief Oumahouha "adopted" a Jesuit priest "as his son . . . and Monsieur de la Salle

had made him presents in order that he might take good care of me."[39] Such gifts met Native community needs and linked them with French imperial goals. Trade, in essence, became more than simple economics. It rooted communities, cultures, and traders together in social, political, and military entanglements. As in the Iroquois wars of the previous century, trade became an essential component of everyday life. To trade was to live.[40]

Commerce, however, also generated conflicts. Equitable terms of exchange and competition for guns, hatchets, and knives generated endless tensions.[41] Additionally, alcohol accompanied the fur trade. Like metal and gun technologies, the introduction of this trade good bred violent interactions. During the Great Peace negotiations, Outoutagan shared more than his own community's concerns when he implored Callières to "prevent the sale of alcohol to *anyone* among his allies."[42] Conflicts within villages, between neighboring nations, and among Indians and Frenchmen beleaguered Native and French leaders. Violence, as always, challenged social order.

These conflicts demanded mechanisms for resolution. As Indigenous and imperial sovereignties collided, new juridical practices emerged. Across New France, mediation became a second key realm of Indigenous-imperial politics. Leaders traveled, often for days on end, to seek mediation. Unlike in other parts of North America or along other "gun frontiers," Native and imperial leaders sought to alleviate tensions.[43] Native leaders demanded audiences with French governors, and they were received by them. Governors, meanwhile, expected Native loyalties in return for commercial, military, and other protections. Over time, appeals, mediation, and deliberations became essential to everyday politics.

When Frontenac and other governors received Indian guests and listened to their concerns, they offered remedies that ranged from the payment of goods to the release of prisoners. In addition, governors stationed officials at forts, settlements, and missions. The presence of officials, according to Bacqueville de la Potherie, reassured Native villagers, many of whom "believed [themselves] protected from the insults of [their] neighbors" if they "possess Frenchmen." Such officials, he continued, became "mediators in all disputes."[44]

Resolution, however, did not always happen, particularly in criminal matters such as theft and murder. Cross-cultural murders challenged Franco-Indigenous relations. In the lower Mississippi, French leaders initially required capital punishment for those who killed Frenchmen, as in 1716 when three Natchez soldiers killed four *voyageurs*. When the Natchez presented only two of the culprits along with another community member in his stead, the governor took the lives of their leaders, provoking an escalation of violence. Warfare raged for years, and in 1731 Natchez soldiers destroyed a settlement of two hundred colonists, capturing over a hundred women, children, and African slaves.[45]

New practices of mediation replaced normative forms of European justice. On April 25, 1723, for example, a French trader at Fort de Chartres, near the confluence of the Missouri and Mississippi rivers, killed a soldier from the fort during an argument. The soldier's comrades, who looked to the newly established Provincial Court for redress, expected the death penalty for the trader. But the trader had close ties with nearby Kaskaskia villages of the Illinois Confederation and was essential to their economy. Within four days of the killing, three Kaskaskia chiefs arrived to intercede on his behalf and ask for his release.[46] They had come to save his life.

Court officials did not initially welcome their appeal. "It is a serious matter to grant you the life of a man," they insisted: "He has killed, and understand, today . . . that the Grand Chief of the French, the King, your Father and ours, desires that every murderer be punished with death. With us such crime cannot go unpunished."[47]

The chiefs replied that they understood the gravity of their request. They listened patiently to French imperatives. As one chief stated, "Behold, it is the first time that I appeal to thee. . . . It is in the name of all my nation that I ask thee to spare the life of one of thy own children." They reminded the French that they too had lost lives in defense of the French community. Only recently, several priests had been murdered by their rivals. "We at one time wept over a White Collar," one leader testified. When asked by the French to retaliate, he "went to war . . . [and] saw the blood of several of my warriors spilt."[48] They worried that their Chickasaw and Fox enemies would interpret the killing of one of their own as a sign of weakness, and that an execution would invite further violence.

In publicly requesting mercy for their ally, the chiefs made themselves vulnerable and linked their authority with that of the French. Invoking shared authority did not always work, but they believed that this shared authority transcended that of "the King," whose sovereignty was recognized but not always followed. Their appeals were more than symbolic. In the interior, alliances required maintenance, and authority was expected to be deliberative, consensual, and nonhierarchical. While French and Native allies maintained different understandings of power, they worked to ensure stability between them. The fate of their world rested on negotiation. Kaskaskia leaders made formal requests and linked them to their own losses. They expected recognition and remedies. "Do not embarrass me," one chief said. "I beg you."[49]

To be received and yet not have one's needs recognized violated the evolving politics that held this world together. Unilateral authority was dangerous. As among the Natchez, it threatened stability. By the end of May, French leaders finished deliberating. They informed the Kaskaskia that "no other nation but you would have obtained what has been granted."[50] The trader was set free and his life restored due to Native appeals on his behalf. Thus ended the first formal criminal trial by the French in Illinois.

No group of French leaders understood the power of the interior's Native peoples better than Jesuit "white collars." Committing themselves to those with "whom we are to spend the rest of our lives," Jesuit priests began missionizing in the seventeenth century.[51] Known also as "black robes," they maintained different understandings of power than governors and traders. They appealed to a higher authority and, like commerce, mediation, and justice, religion became a fourth realm that connected Native and imperial worlds.

In English accounts of New France, Jesuit missions play a large part. Missions were among the first nodes of European influence, and churches often the most permanent European-designed structures across the region. The missions often preceded the establishment of forts, settlements, and towns.[52]

These histories were not always complimentary toward the missionaries. The nineteenth-century historian Francis Parkman argued that the efficacy of Catholicism was limited because the Jesuits professed "mediaeval type[s] of Christianity" full of backwards "superstitions."[53] Such teachings, he maintained, were anathema to the spirit of individualism destined for the continent.

Descended from the Puritans, Parkman spent decades compiling a seven-volume series dedicated to the history of France and England in North America, including *The Jesuits in North America in the Seventeenth Century* (1867).[54] His antipathy toward Indians ran even deeper than his anti-Catholicism: "The Indian [was] hopelessly unchanging . . . [and as] mutable as the wind."[55] Describing them as both unchanging and changeable, Parkman uses Native people to critique absolutism.

Jesuit conversions were much less successful than Parkman and others have emphasized. While their copious reports highlight their perseverance, Jesuits made few inroads in converting the Anishinaabe. Ojibwe cultural practices, kinship organization, and cosmologies outlasted Jesuit teachings. At Fort Michilimackinac, for example, Jesuit fathers spent decades trying to win over the settlement's several thousand villagers but attracted few full-time adherents.[56]

Jesuit missions became enclaves within an Indigenous world. The spring and summer brought renewals of many kinds, and when Ojibwe parents and children looked at the early summer sky, they saw not an unchanging, celestial heaven described by priests but a seasonal vision of hope and opportunity. It was *Ode'imini-giizi*, or the time of the "Strawberry Moon."[57] Wild rice, maple syrup, and medicine harvests, ceremonies, and celebrations occurred not according to Christian calendars but according to changes in the earth and sky. Lakota villages also remained committed to their theology, so much so that Jesuits asked the King for telescopes from his personal collection to try to convince the skeptical Lakota that the skies above them followed Western temporalities and rhythms. Their request: "a case of mathematical instruments, a dial plate of universal astronomy . . . and a telescope six or seven feet long."[58]

The tools and books of the priests did little to alter Indigenous cultures. Indigenous knowledge explained the composition of the universe and offered lessons on how to survive within it. This was knowledge that gave meaning to everyday life and linked spiritual and earthly realms in song, kinship, and stories.[59]

When we focus on the successes or failures of missionaries, we tend to miss the many quotidian acts of translation, counseling, and communication that priests did provide. From baptisms to burials, Jesuits became the most visible representatives of empire at a time when few other Europeans were consistently present in the interior. At the trial at Fort de Chartres in 1723, the Kaskaskia chiefs asked the court to allow a priest to inform the imprisoned trader of their appeal: "Would there be any harm if the White Collar, who is our interpreter, informed the prisoner what you have promised us?" They were also the empire's most prolific scribes.[60]

Intermarriage, Kinship, and Sexuality

As priests, soldiers, and officials traveled across the interior, they wrote letters that circulated across the Atlantic. From the earliest Jesuit priests in the 1630s, chronicles of the North American interior fascinated French society. In 1725, for example, when the commander of the outpost to Missouri tribes, Étienne de Véniard de Bourgmont, arrived in Paris with a delegation of Illinois, Missouri, and Osage leaders from Louisiana, they were received by civil and royal leaders, including King Louis XV and his family members.[61]

Most French traders, however, appear in documents only fleetingly, like the incarcerated trader at Fort de Chartres. As a result their work in securing the empire, through their ability to travel, trap, learn Native languages, and become accepted by Native communities, is not always visible in documentary sources.

But many traders helped to secure the empire by becoming kinsmen to Indian families, gaining social standing within village societies. As husbands to Indian women and fathers to Métis children, French voyageurs and coureurs des bois became part of elaborate Native kinship systems.[62] Their social and intimate ties shaped economic and political relations, creating alliances and cementing trading partnerships.[63]

Like La Vérendrye, men left their homes along the St. Lawrence and migrated into the interior. Many stayed, married, and raised families with Native partners.[64] These social, kinship, and familial relations shaped the Native Inland Sea, becoming among the most visible legacies of French colonialism in North America.[65]

As French and Indigenous sovereignties collided, so too did their gender systems. Before the Grand Settlement, few French women ever ventured into the interior. Not until the 1730s did the sight of French women become commonplace in the interior. Such sightings were so unusual earlier that Madame Le Sueur's arrival at Fort Saint Louis in the 1690s created a sensation. She had to consent to her public display so that resident Native peoples could view her.[66]

Not all French men sought relations with Native women, or with women at all. Most notably, priests professed a lifetime of celibacy, a vow that few Native peoples in the eighteenth century ever took up or followed. Among Indian communities two-spirit "berdaches" (individuals with the social attributes of men and women) and an acceptance of homosexuality and same-sex relationships drew French attention and scorn.[67]

In 1680 the Illinois's largest village numbered "seven or eight thousand," and within it, relayed Father Zenobius Membré, "hermaphrodites are numerous." This community, he continued, included men and women "tall of stat-

This painting of an unidentified Indigenous woman in the Native Inland Sea illustrates how French trade goods and styles influenced Great Lakes Indian fashion in the eighteenth century. (Mackinac State Historic Parks Collection.)

ure, strong and robust" and many "boys dressed as women." "These boys," he continued, "are employed only in women's work, without taking part in the chase or war."[68] Since the French recognized hunting and warfare to be male economic and military realms, young men who did not participate in these gendered relations provided different labor. They did "women's work."

The Ojibwe term *hemaneh* refers to individuals who are "half man, half woman." Among interior communities, such two-spirit individuals held recognized social authority. They assisted in village economies and maintained religious and cultural practices. The study of such individuals has often been used by contemporary scholars as "a quest for examples of primordial homosexuality" rather than recognition of Indigenous peoples' "alternative gender practice[s]."[69] Such gender practices structured Illinois society, and many European commentators believed that they had favorable effects on their landscapes, which, according to Membré, became filled with a "richness and fertility," providing "them fields everywhere."[70]

Throughout the colonial era, the interior world included hundreds of distinct communities, many of which maintained rich economies full of healthy and able children. Many Algonquian-speaking communities, including the Ojibwe, became allied with French traders, officials, priests, and even family members. Such alliances originated in the harrowing challenges of the seventeenth century and endured throughout the 1700s. These bonds drew European resources, leaders, and settlers farther into the heart of the continent. Ultimately, the French empire became rooted in this interior world.

Native peoples had been initially reluctant to receive many French influences, but over time they incorporated new goods, peoples, and ideas into their societies. By 1750 such ties were so well established that they could only be displaced by warfare. The revolutionary conflicts that followed turned the interior into a key realm within the struggles of the Atlantic world. With their French allies beside them, Native peoples defended their homelands against growing waves of intruders. The fate of the continent was determined by the struggles at its center.

Indigenous Warfare and Captivity along the Violent Edges of Empire

Warfare was common across the Native Inland Sea. Seventeenth-century wars established the form of the French empire and eighteenth-century conflicts helped to expand it. From New Orleans to the eastern Great Lakes, Indian and French allies enlisted one another in a seemingly never-ending cycle of conflicts. Some were fought against large confederations, such as the Fox Indians of Wisconsin, who refused to be incorporated into French alliances.[71] Other campaigns targeted imperial Spanish and English forces encroaching into French spheres. In 1720 a joint Pawnee-French expeditionary force ambushed the New Mexican forces of Lieutenant General Pedro de Villasur along the Loop River in Nebraska, killing him and one-third of New Mexico's garrison.[72] Other conflicts were resource-driven efforts by tribes to secure more "gifts" from French officials, including Choctaw soldiers in Mississippi who expected compensation for their services to the crown and retaliated when French coffers ran dry.[73]

Violence seeped into everyday life, becoming habitual over time, in spite of the ceaseless efforts of Native and imperial leaders to mitigate it.

As in New Spain, new forms of captive raiding accompanied the growth in militarism. Slave trafficking brought streams of slaves into settlements, onto French plantation colonies, and eventually to France itself.[74] The captives were procured through warfare. As in New Spain, the captives were overwhelmingly women and children.[75] In 1742, when Dakota leaders returned to Montreal to continue their decades-long effort to curb the French arms trade, they were stunned to find "two of our children" within nearby households, both of whom "started to weep as soon as they saw us."[76] These children had been taken near the Mississippi headwaters and trafficked over a thousand miles to labor in Montreal, where nearly 15 percent of all households had Indian slaves.[77] Outraged, the Dakota leaders returned west, breaking off negotiations and carrying word of the traffic of their young.

Home to the Dakota, Lakota, Anishinaabe, and Ho-Chunk, the western Great Lakes region provided the most Indian slaves. The Dakota children had been taken in 1741 along with two hundred others by their Cree and Assiniboine enemies. The raids grew from existing rivalries, which accelerated following European contact. They were also the extensions of previous conflicts: in this case, the regional conflagration that had culminated in the Fox Wars.

After the Grand Settlement, which Fox leaders had signed, a confederation of Fox, Ho-Chunk, and Menominee Indians formed across Wisconsin. Situated along the major arteries of the Fox and Wisconsin rivers, they controlled vital access and trade routes. But they never fully allied with the French. The confederation included communities that held long-standing animosities against the Ojibwe and other French allies that threatened to explode into uncontrollable violence.

In 1733, in an effort to ward off further aggression, Kiala, a Fox war chief, offered himself as ransom to French authorities in exchange for peace. In April he and three other leaders made themselves hostages to safeguard their community. Conflicts had raged for years, culminating in massacres of Fox villages the previous year. When reports of a potential alliance between the Fox and nearby Sauk reached France, councilors to Louis XV agreed that "the joining of the Sacs with what remains of the Foxes" abrogated Kiala's efforts.[78] The Fox, according to French leaders, could not be trusted.

From Kiala's prison in Quebec, the governor ordered him to board the *St. François,* destination Martinique, where he was to be sold into plantation slavery. Raised in the western reaches of New France, this leader's life was now decided at its eastern terminus. His life ended in enslavement and diaspora in the Caribbean.[79]

Wars now brought allies closer together and conditioned them for future conflict, unlike the chaotic violence of the previous century. French and Algonquian leaders determined the targets of their violence in conflicts that were now better coordinated, used advanced weaponry, and included diverse combatants. Before battle, one might encounter soldiers from numerous tribes, *voyageurs* and their Métis sons, and French officials gathered together while priests offered Latin prayers of blessing. During combat, French commands intermixed with those of Algonquian chiefs while new pidgin expletives flew. Most also now used modern guns, powder, and metal weaponry.

This partnership presented a paradox for the French. Village leaders, endowed with bronze or cast-iron medals from the French, represented both their own communities and the crown. These "medal chiefs" collaborated with French officials on policies and especially on military affairs.[80]

French leaders wanted to reverse this balance of power and to turn their Indian allies into subjects, but they lacked the power to do so. Away from forts, imperial authority diminished. At times it disappeared altogether. Despite expeditions such as La Vérendrye's, the western reaches of New France remained uncharted.[81] Even within settlements at Detroit, Michilimackinac, or Vincennes, Indian peoples comprised the majority. French officials often joined inter-tribal wars because Native peoples had convinced them to do so. The interests of their village allies had become the interests of their empire.

Alliances and Tensions: The Origins of the Seven Years' War

Shared antagonisms shaped the French-Algonquian alliance. French animosities toward British colonists, however, posed challenges when interior Indian allies did not share them. While French and British conflicts dominated European politics throughout the first half of the eighteenth century,

France's Indian allies expressed little interest in French fortunes outside North America.

French leaders attempted to transform disinterest to allegiance. When Bourgmont took a delegation of Illinois, Missouri, and Osage leaders to Paris in 1725, they visited influential leaders as well as landmarks.[82] Bourgmont's intention: to court Natives as allies, cement their loyalties, and establish further diplomatic efforts.

Back in Louisiana, however, few believed the wonders described by the returning delegates. They wondered how Frenchmen who struggled to feed themselves and smelled due to infrequent bathing could come from a land of palaces and tree-lined boulevards. "They have bribed you . . . to make us believe all these beautiful fictions," one listener stated.[83]

Interior communities were indifferent to European conflicts. Rather than compelling loyalties, they created emptiness—both in words and resources. When French-English hostilities spilled across the Atlantic during the War of the Austrian Succession, or King George's War (1740–48), British blockades curbed shipments and closed ports, thereby limiting the importation of manufactured goods and the export of furs. Notably, in 1745 British forces seized the massive Fortress of Louisbourg at the mouth of the St. Lawrence, halting the arrival of all French ships to Quebec, Montreal, and interior settlements.[84]

Louisbourg controlled entries into the St. Lawrence. It also protected fishing vessels across the Grand Banks, one of the world's deepest fisheries. All European leaders understood its importance to New France, and it was returned at the Treaty of Aix-la-Chapelle, which ended the war. By then, however, the conflict had already begun to sever French control over the interior.

During the conflict, backcountry British traders moved to fill interior demand. In one of the most important economic developments of the era, they traveled across the Ohio River Valley and began trading in a region that had been only partially resettled following the Iroquoian wars of the late 1600s. What Native peoples learned about these English traders threatened French ambitions because "backcountry traders," as they became known, brought manufactured goods in far greater quantity than the French. They also traded them at lower rates. Arriving overland from Philadelphia and Virginia, English traders began establishing interior trading posts in the 1740s, doing so to meet Native demand and occupy a comparative advantage opened by British blockades.[85]

Offering colonial-produced metals, alcohol, and cloth, these posts attracted Miami, Shawnee, and Algonquian traders from across the Ohio River Valley, although they remained nominally attached to French commanders. No European empire, however, exerted control over the Ohio River's headwaters, which were prime hunting lands for the Seneca and other members of the Iroquois Confederacy and its dependent allies. In fact, the region around the headwaters came to include communities of breakaway "Ohio Iroquois," often referred to as "Mingos."[86]

Tanaghrisson, a Seneca "half chief," presided over several of these settlements. During King George's War, he attracted English traders—and benefitted from their business. While he was careful to let traders and resident Natives know that any land cessions would be subject to the Confederacy's Grand Council at Onondaga, in reality these settlements were liminal spaces outside the reach of centralized authority. They revealed the weaknesses of the Iroquois, who could not always control their dependent allies or prevent them from attracting English traders.[87] Before long these settlements also attracted migrating Indians from the East whose familiarity with English traders encouraged English trade. One such trader was George Croghan, who had fled British authority and soon became one of the region's most successful entrepreneurs.[88]

The Grand Settlement of 1701 recognized Iroquois suzerainty over the Ohio River and its headwaters. That authority, however, had grown weaker, especially when French-allied Indians arrived to trade with Croghan and other traders and when new village leaders such as Tanaghrisson attempted to secure their own fortunes.[89]

The stream of goods and Indian allies leaving New France now threatened the empire. While settlements in New France had grown in population throughout the 1700s, they were dwarfed by the English colonies. Virginia's population had more than doubled since 1701 and included an African slave population that had grown from 300 in 1650 to 150,000 a century later.[90]

For New France to survive, it was a necessity to keep interior Indian allies connected to French traders, forts, and officials. Gifts and trade facilitated the many forms of alliance that held the interior together. Without goods to exchange, French *voyageurs* essentially worked without pay and had little to offer their Indian partners other than empty promises. Such conditions became acute during King George's War, when French storage rooms sat empty and stacks of furs awaited export. In 1745, as Louisbourg fell, the governor-general attempted to ameliorate such concerns, granting license-free usage of interior posts "in order to maintain the savages of the post until times change."[91] For much of the eighteenth century, furs had once been a predominately French trade. In the 1740s, English traders encroached upon this French monopoly.[92]

As English traders continued to provide actual goods, they did so across a string of overland posts. For the French, a simple solution emerged: English traders needed to be both expelled and prevented from returning. As departing governor-general Roland-Michel Barrin, marquis de la Galissonnière, told his successor, it was vital to prohibit "every attempt of the English to settle" west of the Alleghenies.[93]

French expeditionary initiatives began in the spring of 1749. King George's War was now over, and Louisbourg reoccupied. Leaders in Quebec believed it was time to organize a series of expeditions aimed at reclaiming possession of the Ohio River. They planned a series of new forts to prevent English trespass to retain Indian traders at their existing forts and to keep the Great Lakes fur trade moving through Montreal.

Unlike the explorations of La Vérendrye, these were large military campaigns, not the travels of small groups. With more than two hundred soldiers and three dozen Indian allies, Detroit's commander Pierre-Joseph Céloron de Blainville departed Montreal in June for a three-thousand-mile journey. His travels became a show of force. While offering select gifts to Indian allies, he also carried metals of a different kind: lead plaques to be planted throughout the region. The inscription of the first, laid on July 29, read:

> In the year 1749 during the reign of Louis XV . . . we . . . have buried this plaque at the confluence of the Ohio and Tchadakoin [Conewengo] . . . as a monument of the renewal of possessions which we have taken of the said river Ohio and of all those that fall therein and of all the lands on both sides, unto the sources of these said rivers.[94]

It stayed in the ground only briefly, as English traders dug it up to send to New York.

Céloron returned in November with disappointing news. Since leaving Montreal in June he had witnessed dozens of pack trains of pelts heading toward English colonies. He had chastised the drivers about their illegal actions and made them take notes back to the English complaining that their trade was "contrary to the preliminaries of peace signed at Aix-la-Chapelle."[95] Céloron's travels convinced him that only permanent forts—and not displays of metal plaques—could prevent English traders from doing business with interior Indians.[96] He was not authorized to attack English subjects in these disputed lands, but his travels revealed that a larger expedition was needed, one able to stay in the region and fortify it.

More than double the size of Céloron's, the new expedition began construction on a string of outposts. The largest was named Fort Duquesne in honor of the governor-general, the marquis de Duquesne. It sat at the confluence of three rivers—the Ohio, Allegheny, and Monongahela—and it was as large as any interior fort except Detroit and Niagara.

The Beginnings of the First World War

After so many years of austerity, Native communities were unresponsive and even hostile to Céloron's visit. Some fled his arrival, some chastised him, and all offered ambivalent responses to his imperatives to stop trading with the English. While Native leaders joined Céloron in enacting the rituals of diplomacy—with Céloron "forgiving" their transgression of allowing Englishmen in and sharing "pipes of peace" with Shawnee leaders—their mutual faith was dissipating.[97]

Céloron's had been the largest European campaign in the interior, surpassed only by the French-Algonquian invasions of Iroquoia the previous century. Two hundred and fifty soldiers represented a serious deterrent, especially when few European soldiers remained stationed in North America. Most were in seaports, hundreds of miles from the Ohio River. Few English soldiers had ever seen the interior.[98] It had been the English navy that had defeated French forces during King George's War. English colonists' appeals for maps of the interior usually fell on deaf ears.[99] What English military officials knew of New France and its interior allies came from diplomatic gatherings, French publications, and hearsay.

The first shots of the Seven Years' War, also known as the French and Indian War, came in these contested lands at sunrise on May 28, 1754. In a clearing nearly six miles from Great Meadows on the Maryland-Pennsylvania border, a twenty-one-year-old colonel from Virginia, George Washington, had constructed a makeshift fort appropriately named Fort Necessity. Virginia's governor Robert Dinwiddie had ordered him to assemble an expeditionary force to head to the Ohio River's disputed headwaters, where hundreds of French soldiers were continuing Céloron's fort building.

Washington's regiment totaled nearly 160. They had little idea where they were going or how many they might confront. They lacked training, supplies, and intel.[100] Their morale was also limited; men and officers openly complained about their wages. All had either been promised interior lands in exchange for their service or stood to benefit from interior land acquisition. Everyone knew that while backcountry traders profited, they represented but one head of a larger economy of expansion. English colonists aspired to take as much Indian land as possible to establish farms in the interior.[101] Washington's interests in preventing French fortification arose from both duty and greed. He anticipated profiting from interior land speculation.[102]

The Great Meadows appeared a good spot to rest, reconnoiter, and await reinforcements. The area was clear, watered by a stream, and full of grass for their few horses. Washington had divided his forces the day before, a small error in what became a series of them. As the prospects of battle grew, his miscalculations turned deadly, and his leadership over the ensuing six weeks cost many Virginians their lives and ended up driving the English from the Ohio. By summer's end and for the first time, French authority became established over these contested lands. And war had begun.

Washington's miscalculations stemmed from a misreading of local Native politics. Most notably, on May 28 he discovered that he had mismanaged Tanaghrisson's advice and misgauged his motivations. Both were fortunate to survive.

A longtime ally of English traders, Tanaghrisson had learned of an encroaching party of thirty-five French soldiers under the leadership of Ensign Joseph Coulon de Villiers, sieur de Jumonville. Their mission was diplomatic: to determine whether English soldiers had indeed reached French-claimed territories, and if they had, to send word back to Fort Duquesne and initiate council with English leaders. De Jumonville was instructed to tell the Virginians to withdraw. This reconnaissance party had no intention of combating the Virginians, who outnumbered them fivefold. England and France were not at war, as the peace from 1745 still held.

With his forces divided, Washington grew nervous. Unsure of what to make of French encroachment, he blindly followed Tanaghrisson and a dozen soldiers through the night. Together, they encircled de Jumonville's party before it broke morning camp.[103]

Four different accounts—including reports by Washington and testimonies relayed by a French soldier—survive of this encounter, which began as an ambush and turned into a massacre. In each account, after an initial volley from their elevated perimeter, Tanaghrisson and his soldiers descended upon the French forces and killed de Jumonville with a hatchet. He was pursuing strategies best aimed at improving his community's interests, not Washington's.

Unbeknownst to Washington, French fortifications threatened the village autonomy of Tanaghrisson and other "Ohio Iroquois." These communities had a decade-long partnership with English traders, and they coolly received Céloron and his news of expanded imperial authority. We "live in a Country between," he had told French leaders in 1752, and this breakaway Iroquois leader knew that his profitable trading would shrivel under expanded French authority.[104] The loyalties of Native people across the Ohio were becoming contested, and Tanaghrisson also feared that his people might face retaliations from Iroquois Confederacy leaders, who had also expressed dissatisfaction with his autonomy. His decision to escalate violence foreclosed the possibility of diplomacy, particularly as he dismembered the highest-ranking French officer in a public form.[105]

A young officer without battlefield experience, Washington became overwhelmed by the morning's violence. Like many officers across the colonial world, he had dreamed of battlefield glory but now stood shaken by his first encounter with battle.[106] His report masked the insubordination of his allies and the subsequent killing of wounded soldiers, whose weapons, uniforms, and supplies ended up with Tanaghrisson. Sanctioning such actions, he reported: "We killed Mr. *de Jumonville*, the commander of that Party, as also nine others."[107] Responsibility, he reluctantly concluded, lay with him.

The morning began a series of subsequent miscalculations, all combining to create a cascade of disasters. In particular, continued misunderstandings of Indian affairs became more and more deadly for the Virginians. Upon receiving reinforcements that more than doubled his numbers, Washington continued toward Duquesne. He did so, however, without realizing the difficulty of the terrain ahead or the total number of French soldiers stationed therein. Most parties traveled the interior via rivers. He had chosen to go overland.

Washington also underestimated the allegiances of resident Native peoples. While Native communities had benefited from their trade with the English, they had done so in the *absence* of French trade during the war. Céloron's expedition was the first in a series of renewed efforts to secure interior allegiances and resolidify the region's long-standing alliance system.[108] French leaders understood the importance of reasserting their ties with resident Indians and sent over a thousand soldiers with accompanying supplies and ammunition to trade. All had familiarity with interior affairs. All also learned of the death and dishonor recently suffered by de Jumonville. Many, in fact, had arrived at Duquesne under the leadership of his brother, Captain Louis Coulon de Villiers. He now sought retribution.[109]

Washington headed west, unaware of these developments. He knew little of the patterns of French-Indian diplomacy or the composition of the forces awaiting them. He assumed that Tanaghrisson would enlist resident Native peoples to rise up against the new French fortress. He was mistaken.

Upon arrival in late June at the interior post known as Gist's settlement, Washington and Tanaghrisson were joined by George Croghan and local Mingo, Shawnee, and Delaware leaders. For three days, each implored these Native leaders to join in an assault against Duquesne. They, however, offered no support.[110] Despite their partnerships with English traders, these Native communities knew the composition of the French force awaiting them. They had seen the size of the growing fortifications and heard the determination of French commanders. To make an assault was pointless.

While unsuccessful, these meetings likely saved Washington and his men's lives. They were not only outnumbered but also exhausted from days of travel, and a frontal assault on Duquesne would have proven futile. Such delay, however, threatened Tanaghrisson because, as the English now retreated back to Great Meadows, they were not only abandoning their planned assault on Duquesne but also isolating Tanaghrisson and his allies. While Washington believed Fort Necessity could withstand "the attack of 500 men," Tanaghrisson thought different.[111]

Tanaghrisson understood that the hardening resolve of his Ohio River compatriots signaled more than an unwillingness to join the British. These communities were becoming realigned with the French, who were turning Washington's anticipated allies into potential combatants. For the French, the Ohio River Valley was the key to securing their interior empire, and its security was their highest priority.[112] Trade goods flowed from Duquesne.

Additionally, resident Natives were unimpressed with Washington and his inexperienced forces.[113] Although Tanaghrisson made the trip back to Fort

Necessity, he quickly departed for one of Croghan's remaining posts.[114] His morning gamble to escalate the violence against the French had failed. He could neither enlist the Virginians to assault the French fort nor compel resident Ohio Indians to stay away from the French. The space of liminal authority from the 1740s that had benefited him so well had disappeared. Moreover, he knew French retaliation was coming.[115] In early October, he died of disease at a time when French influence seemed all but certain to expand.

With his men driven hard in the heat, Washington's forces returned to Fort Necessity on July 1. Their retreat was becoming a fiasco. So many animals had died that the soldiers dragged their own wagons of supplies and artillery.[116] Meanwhile, Coulon de Villiers had left Duquesne with six hundred men and one hundred Native allies. They were right behind the Virginians.

They attacked on the morning of July 3. Rain had fallen throughout the night, and unlike Duquesne and other forts, Fort Necessity had neither palisaded walls nor rooms for shelter. Washington, having anticipated taking Duquesne, had left Fort Necessity without establishing barracks for his troops. During the night, they had not slept well in the rain and were exhausted from their campaigning.

Throughout the morning attack, French assaults pinned the Virginians behind the fort's makeshift walls and in its few trenches, now full of mud. By nightfall, their discipline was gone. "It was no sooner dark," wrote one of Washington's commanders, "than one-half of our Men got drunk," breaking into casks of rum brought by recent supply trains.[117] Moreover, the rains had made their powder ineffective, and they were outnumbered. Seven hundred armed men, including a hundred allied Indian soldiers, surrounded them. The shouting of Algonquian and French orders intermixed with the sounds of gunfire.

Historians debate why the French-led forces ceased their assault. Coulon de Villiers reportedly gained the retribution he had sought and sent emissaries offering peace for the next morning, July 4. As Washington's forces staggered out of the fort, French leaders offered lenient terms of surrender. In what would become a recurring feature of the war, the French and their Indian allies had lost only three fighters compared to one hundred English casualties. Other relationships also died at Great Meadows. "What is most severe upon us," wrote one English survivor, were that the soldiers fighting in alliance with the French "were all our own Indians, Shawnees, Delawares, and Mingos."[118]

The same communities Washington had lobbied days before had now fought against him. His failure to understand their motivation was now seen as betrayal. Animosities resonated among the colonists, whose disgust for the French was only matched by their feelings about Indians. It was a hatred that hardened in the generation that followed.[119]

For the French, the summer was a time of triumph. Within days, French and Indian forces burned Fort Necessity and nearby trading posts. After five years, they had achieved the authority that Céloron promised, repelling colonial traders and restoring ties with resident communities. They had also defeated and demoralized the first British expedition into the region. They had dispatched it with unexpected ease, and their terms of surrender were made in exchange for Washington's pledges to persuade his superiors to not return.

But Washington did return in the following summer of 1755—with a force ten times larger than before. While the summer of 1754 had favored French fortunes, the following six years reversed them, doing so in ways that were as unbelievable as they were inexplicable. The French soon lost not only their forts on the Ohio but also on the St. Lawrence and the Mississippi. By the end of 1760, Louisbourg, Quebec, and Montreal had all fallen to British invasion, with eighteen thousand soldiers witnessing their final surrender.[120] Thousands of Acadian settlers were also expelled, and at the Treaty of Paris in 1763, King Louis XV ceded France's entire claims to North America. More territory in North America changed hands in 1763 than in any other time in U.S. history.[121]

After 1763 New France was no more. Duquesne had initially held out but fell to English forces, which replaced it with a fort eight times larger. The English had suffered defeats in the early years of the war but had reorganized their naval, diplomatic, and military strategies. They had initiated total war in North America and across the globe, where the English navy blockaded French forces in North America, Europe, the Caribbean, India, West Africa, and the Philippines.

Prime Minister William Pitt led such expansion, and English officials named their new fort at Duquesne after him. The town around it also became known in his honor: Pittsburgh. Striking the French empire at its weakest points in North America, Pitt achieved supremacy in ways previously unimagined. French mariners had navigated the St. Lawrence for over two centuries. Now the English had removed the French altogether from North America.[122]

An Interior Still at War

By war's end, English fortunes had never seemed stronger. Starting in 1760, British officers arrived at interior forts and claimed them as their own, appointing themselves the new rulers. Although the future was uncertain across the Great Lakes region, Britain had won the greatest war in world history. It essentially redrew the Grand Settlement of 1701, which had maintained multilateral relations for half a century and preserved local autonomy along the Ohio River. By expelling the French and claiming their territories, Britain had assumed the balance of power in eastern America. It now attempted to connect former French forts with its Atlantic colonies.

Numerous signs highlighted Britain's ascendancy. During the war, settlers established countless farms often alongside forts for protection. As new forts were built or captured, these nodes of power attracted additional settlers, who further cleared the land and displaced its game. Along the Susquehanna River, British soldiers at Fort Augusta protected nearby settlements and farms. "Every thing grows finely here," reported one lieutenant at war's end.[123] He may have noticed the changing harvests of the previous years. In 1757 farmers grew turnips and watermelons. In 1758 cabbage, potatoes, marigolds, and fruit trees appeared. By 1760 oats and hay were harvested to feed the fort's growing supply of livestock. Forty-one cows had arrived with troops in 1756, domesticated livestock that soon included sheep, chickens, and hogs.

Outraged Iroquois leaders appealed to colonial officials, reminding them of their long-standing promises of neutrality and of British recognition of Iroquois lands. "You told me . . . you would build a Fort against the French, and you told me you wanted none of our lands," a Seneca leader told colonial officials in 1762.[124] Farms threatened the region's long-standing Indian trading networks, depleted game, contributed to the deforestation of hunting lands, and soiled fresh waters. Trade, and not settlement, according to Oneida leader Sagugusuniunt, remained "the [only] way for us to live peaceably together."[125]

Across eastern North America, the war and its aftermath upset economic relationships. Forts protected farms, migrants, and livestock. Settlements transformed interior relations because settlers grew weary of approaching Indian traders, viewing them as enemies. "At present your People cannot distinguish Foes from Friends; they think every Indian is against them,"

Interior North America, the Progress of the Seven Years' War, and Associated Conflicts, 1754–1765

KEY

1 Virginia-Pennsylvania-Ohio Backcountry

2 Nova Scotia (Acadia)

3 Hudson River-Lake Champlain-Richelieu River Corridor

4 Mohawk Valley-Lake Ontario-Upper St. Lawrence Valley

5 Battle and Siege of Minorca, 1756

6 Central European Operations, 1756–1762

7 Operations in Bengal and Battle of Plassey, 1757

8 Siege of Louisbourg, 1758

9 West African expeditions, 1758

10 Québec and the Upper St. Lawrence Valley

11 The Eastern Caribbean

12 British Naval Operations from Gibraltar

13 British Operations on the Coast of France

14 Upper Great Lakes

15 The Cherokee War, 1759–61

16 Operations on the Coromandel Coast, 1758–60

17 Newfoundland expeditions, 1762

18 Siege of Havana, 1762

19 Conquest of Manila, 1762

20 Pontiac's Rebellion, 1763–65

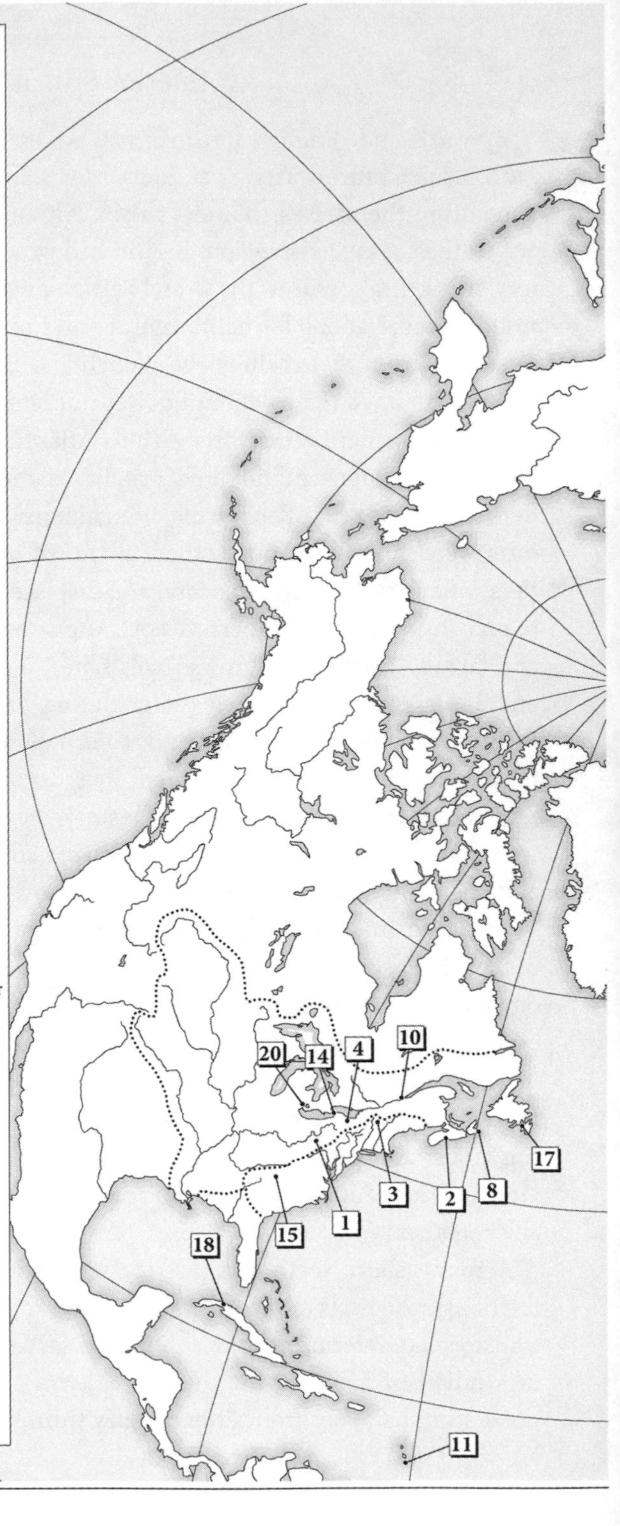

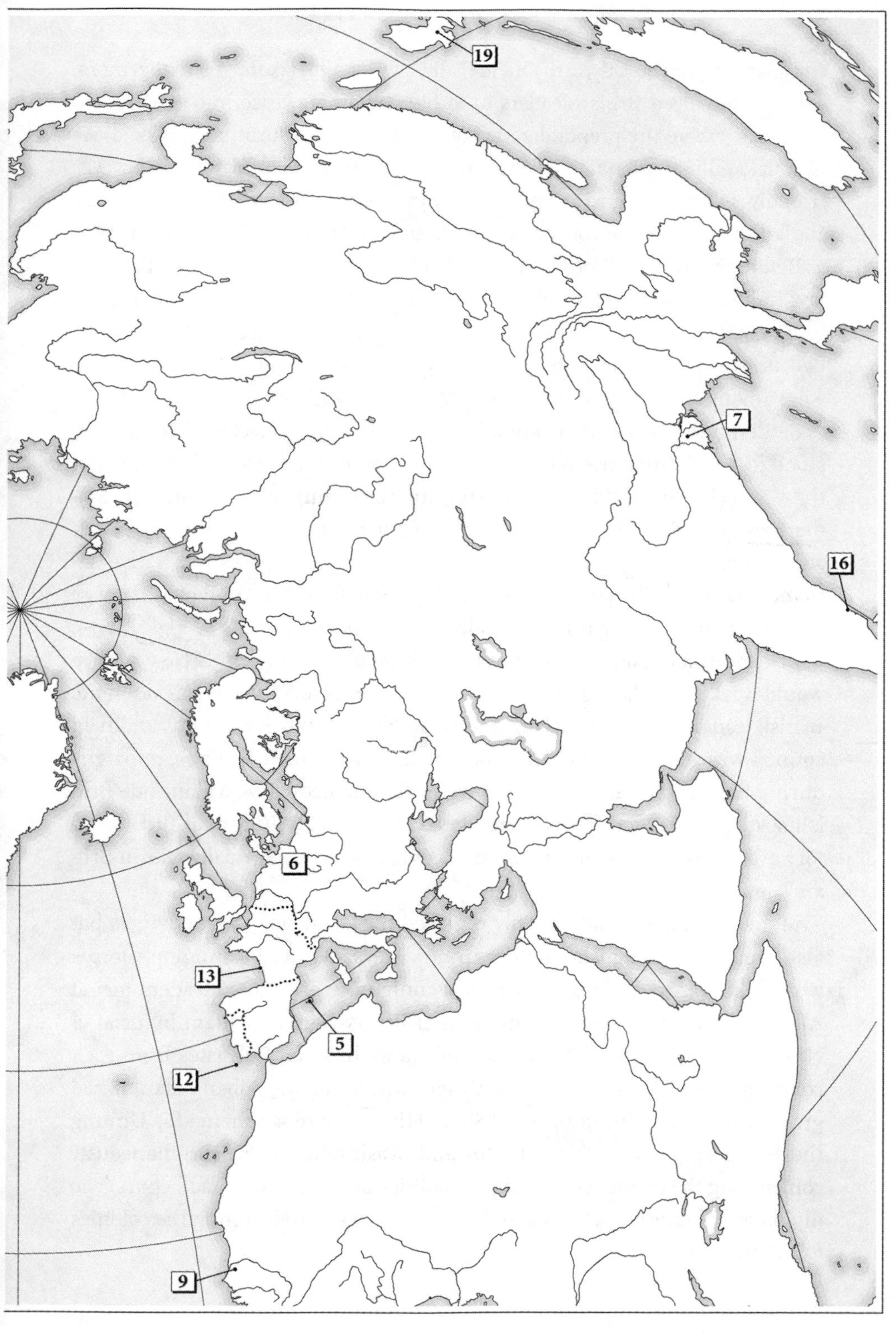
19
7
16
6
13
5
12
9

complained Scarouyady, an Oneida ally of Tanaghrisson.[126] Furthermore, settlers convinced British leaders to forbid Indian entrance into settlements and forts, where the preponderance of power and ammunition was held. As Colonel William Clapham of Fort Augusta instructed, no Indian "however friendly, should . . . be admitted."[127] Only in rare instances of diplomacy could Indians be allowed, he continued, and then with "the guard turned out."[128]

Before the war, such prohibitions would have been inconceivable. Britain's few Indian allies traded, dwelled with, and counseled Euro-Americans. They fought, camped, and resided alongside British encampments. Washington had implored Tanaghrisson and his soldiers to stay at Fort Necessity. They were among his only interior allies.

Settlers and many soldiers knew little of such shared histories. They understood fear and difference more clearly. "For you to keep soldiers there, is not the way to live peaceable," Sagugusuniunt noted, imploring, "Call your Soldiers away . . . these Soldiers must go."[129] British leaders had once taken such adjurations seriously, but the time for entertaining Iroquois and Native demands was past. The politics of neutrality had defined the Iroquoian strategy of playing both ends against the middle, which now no longer worked.

British leaders had once worried that Iroquois alliance with New France would weaken England's interior possessions, but New France was no more. British leaders had previously traded favorably with the Six Nations and held council with their leaders. The Iroquois had also joined British campaigns during the war. Seven hundred, for example, watched in 1760 alongside British soldiers as French forces surrendered at Montreal. With total British victory over France, however, Indian threats grew weaker, especially within Britain's growing colonies.

Moreover, the war had not only removed the colonists' oldest enemies but also brought the English together in new ways. While Washington's forces were falling apart at Great Meadows, a conference of colonial leaders met at Albany. It included Benjamin Franklin of Pennsylvania, William Johnson of New York, and Thomas Hutchinson of Massachusetts. Delegates from each colony gathered to draft a Plan of Union. Known as the Albany Plan, it had grown from Franklin's proposed "Short Hints toward a Scheme for Uniting the Northern Colonies."[130] Franklin and Washington were simultaneously confronting the challenges of interior politics before the war had begun. The diplomacy of interior politics and the crisis of war were bringing the colonies together.

Colonial legislatures, however, denied this plan for inter-colonial cooperation. The challenge of shared expenses was particularly divisive. Nonetheless, the Albany Congress established two superintendents of Indian Affairs, divided into northern and southern regions.[131] Johnson now held the northern appointment, a position he used to navigate Iroquoian diplomacy for the coming generation. He had also married into the Mohawk Nation. His wife, Molly Brant, was the Mohawk leader Joseph Brant's sister.

As would become clear in the decades ahead, Indian affairs required centralized, or federal, authority. The colonies could not manage Indian affairs individually, only collectively. Ineffective when managed on a colony-to-colony basis, Indian affairs required inter-colonial coordination and consensus between colonial leaders. Indian conflicts brought colonists such as Washington and Franklin together in new political forums and eventually in new political forms. Such forms became codified during the Revolution and constituted afterward during the drafting of the U.S. Constitution. Similarly, contests over Indian lands drew colonists together, positioning them against not only the Indians who held those lands but also the monarchy that claimed them.

In 1760 the struggle for the interior was growing, not ending. British leaders soon learned the hard lessons that had beleaguered French governors. Force, authority, and even violence extended only so far in the Native Inland Sea. Trade, diplomacy, gifts, and mediation not only smoothed social conflicts but also continued to be requisite forms of politics. These were hard lessons for the British to learn, and they were learned only through the difficult experiences of continued warfare and then revolution that followed.

✦

While the Mandan and Native Nations of the western Great Lakes area remained removed from the conflicts of the 1750s, throughout the years ahead, warfare again returned to the region. In fact, generations of conflict followed as the struggle for the heart of the continent escalated in scope and form. For more than half a century, Indigenous peoples confronted imperial and eventually U.S. national leaders, both on the battlefield and in various diplomatic forums.

Bamewawagezhikaquay lived through the fateful decades after this half a century of war. Born in 1800 in Sault Ste. Marie, she grew up there in a bilingual Ojibwe- and English-speaking household, surrounded by many French former fur-trading families. All of the city's families had lived through the transitions from French to British and finally to U.S. rule.

Her Ojibwe name translates as "Woman of the Sound the Stars Make Rushing through the Sky," but she is better known as Jane Johnston Schoolcraft, the name she took after her marriage to Henry Rowe Schoolcraft.[132] He arrived in 1822 as federal Indian agent. They married the next year.

Widely regarded as the first American Indian poet, Bamewawagezhikaquay coined the term "Native Inland Sea" in an unpublished poem, "Lines Written at Castle Island, Lake Superior," in 1838.[133] It was originally written in Ojibwe before being translated. Like her other works, her poem celebrates the "sweet delight" of Anishinaabewaki, particularly the nautical world of its lakes, rivers, and islands. "Here," she writes, "only nature reigns." Her poetry offers a critique of the forces of colonialism that have undercut Anishinaabe autonomy. "Far from the haunts of men," she continues, "here, there are no sordid fears, no crimes, no misery, no tears, no pride of wealth; the heart to fill, no laws to treat my people ill."[134]

Two years later another writer, from the eastern fringes of the region, popularized a different vision of an Inland Sea. The second-to-last novel in what became the most celebrated and serialized series in nineteenth-century America, James Fenimore Cooper's *The Pathfinder* (1840) is subtitled "The Inland Sea." Unlike Bamewawagezhikaquay's poem, it opens from an exterior, nearly aerial perspective: "The sublimity connected with vastness, is familiar to every eye. . . . Towards the west . . . ranged an ocean of leaves, glorious and rich in the varied and lively verdure of a generous vegetation."[135] Vast, beautiful, and seemingly beyond definition, the interior provides the frame and content for Cooper's novel and for the rest of the "Leather-stocking" tales, including *The Last of the Mohicans* (1826). Cooper's is an imaginative world set during the eighteenth century away from the Atlantic. His "Inland Sea" sits apart from the cities, leaders, and processes that birthed the U.S. Republic. It is home to a proximate but distant world whose peoples and landscapes possess great beauty but are full of danger. Each requires a process of submission in order for the region's destiny to be achieved.

These contrasting visions of the American interior emerged after the revolutionary conflicts of the late eighteenth and early nineteenth centuries. Both Bamewawagezhikaquay and Cooper came from worlds imprinted by the processes of U.S. expansion. Their varied understandings of the region's history and its people still remain unreconciled.

5 • Settler Uprising

The Indigenous Origins of the American Revolution

This land where ye dwell I have made for you and not
for others. Whence comes it that ye permit the Whites
upon your lands? Can ye not live without them?
—*Teaching attributed to Neolin, the "Delaware Prophet" (1763)*

"But now behold!" declared Nathaniel Ames of Dedham, Massachusetts, in his 1763 farmer's almanac. "The Farmer may have land for nothing."[1] The greatest military victory in English history had expelled the French from the continent altogether and given the British empire global reach. One could now traverse British North America from Florida to Hudson's Bay. As Horace Walpole, the future Earl of Orford, rhetorically asked: "Is this not magnificent? A senate regulating the Eastern and Western worlds at once? The Romans were triflers to us." The British were now, he concluded, "confessedly the masters of Europe."[2] For individuals ranging from English barons to Massachusetts farmers, the outcome of the war held the potential for seismic transformations. Most important for Ames was the availability of land. The farmer, he continued, could now obtain "enough [land] for himself and all his sons, be they ever so many."[3]

Optimism pervaded English colonies after 1760. Each had struggled through the previous decade of war and now gazed upon an interior free of European rivals. Lands for the taking seemed to beckon to a triumphant empire. The coronation of King George III in 1760 had coincided with the fall of Montreal, generating even greater enthusiasm across colonial capitals. Everywhere colonists rejoiced. In Boston, one professed, "I have been here about sixteen years and I don't know of one single man but would risque his life and property to serve [the] King."[4] Another Bostonian echoed at a town meeting: "The true interests of Great Britain and her [colonies] are mutual, and what God in his providence has united, let no man dare attempt to pull asunder." His euphoria continued: "We love, esteem and reverence our mother country and adore our king."[5]

The war had generated shared experiences across the colonies. The King's Protestant subjects on both sides of the Atlantic shared identities based partly on their antagonisms against French Catholics, whose expulsion now signaled continued glory.[6] Throughout the British Atlantic, all seemingly understood that the war had changed the world.[7]

The war in the interior, however, had not ended. Independent Indian villages remained unconquered after the French withdrawal. Many had formed coalitions and confederations.[8] In the interior South, across Iroquoia, and throughout the Ohio River Valley, Indians still remained powerful adversaries. Their power "is generally known and understood," wrote one Carolinian during the war. When "they are our friends they are the Cheapest and Strongest Barrier for the Protection of our Settlements; when Enemies, they are capable of . . . [rendering] those Possessions almost useless."[9] Indians in the interior remained sovereign. They were allies to be courted and antagonists to be feared.

Most Indians had not lost any lands during the Seven Years' War. Even those allied with the French had been defeated but not conquered. As one Anishinaabeg leader matter-of-factly expressed to British leaders: "Although you have conquered the French, you have not . . . conquered us."[10] French Colonel Bougainville—who had witnessed the fall of Montreal in 1760 and would later, as a colonial ally, see the British surrender at Yorktown—understood the nature of Indian power, remarking not only that raids against interior settlements proved impossible to defend against but that Indian dominance had forced the French into perpetual dependence: "One is a slave to Indians in this country. They are a necessary evil."[11] The French had lost the war, not their Indian allies. New France had been subdued by the financial resources poured into the conflict by a determined British Parliament. The supremacy of the British navy enabled an economic explosion across British North America's major seaports.[12] Additionally, a robust colonial militia ensured its naval and demographic supremacy, as more than forty thousand served in the war's American theater.[13]

Native people had fought battles against Europeans before. As in earlier eras, the war's aftermath became as critical as its conduct. When the French flag at Detroit was lowered for the final time in December 1760, a thousand Indian people gathered.[14] They did not weep for the French departure but greeted the newly arrived British officials, reminding them, "This land is ours, and not yours."[15] The future was uncertain but they hoped to maintain autonomy for themselves and garner trade, ammunition, and supplies as they had from the French. The war's aftermath would be conducted, they hoped, on their terms.

Violence erupted following the French expulsion. When British officials tried to impose rule upon undefeated Native villagers, conflicts over trade, ammunition, and diplomacy returned the region to a state of war. During a two-year "rebellion" named after the Odawa leader Obwandiyag, or Pontiac, British officials learned that peace in the interior could be as costly as war. They had not considered that after the French withdrawal, political and economic realities would change for Native people. As Pontiac and his followers destroyed interior forts and captured settlers, they fought British forces with a growing fury.

Often seen as a tragic ending to Indian power in the Great Lakes, Pontiac's uprising in fact bred a restoration of a different kind across what historians have called the "Middle Ground."[16] This restoration gave rise to a world of British imperial regulations that sheltered Indian villages in ways that would have seemed incomprehensible in 1760. Such compromises—including enforcements of the Proclamation Line of 1763—soon became revolutionary as they unraveled the shared sensibilities that pervaded the colonies following Britain's global triumph. As was true in earlier eras, the interior added unanticipated political, economic, and military fuel to imperial affairs, breeding greater conflict and soon revolution. The interior, in short, helped to sever the colonists from their crown, and many of their anti-monarchical beliefs originated from their experiences settling the interior and fighting Native peoples for it.[17]

The Treaty of Paris redrew boundary lines and added new territories to the growing list of British colonies. Expectant British conquerors, however, became unanticipated mediators across former New France, and the growing allegiances between Indian and British leaders became valuable fodder in colonists' critiques of their monarch. Through rapidly expanding communication networks, colonists leveled charges against the crown that hinged on colonial fears of Native peoples.[18] As Thomas Jefferson wrote in the Declaration of Independence, the British crown had encouraged "merciless Indian savages" to attack "the inhabitants of our frontiers."[19] Such peoples, he suggested, knew only one law—the rule of warfare—and they had "resolved on the total extermination of all the settlers of our north and south-western frontiers," according to an early nineteenth-century history of the conflict.[20]

Labeled as surrogates, or proxies, operating on behalf of a distant tyrant, Native peoples were vilified in a larger ideological transformation that distanced colonists from their British kinsmen.[21] British policies that continued interior trading, diplomatic, and political relations with Indian peoples galvanized the revolutionary struggle as colonial resentments against Indians fueled ambitions for independence.

Across multiple military theaters and within countless political discourses, Native peoples shaped the origins of the Revolution. Across the Pennsylvanian backcountry, their vilification united colonists around latent fears and, ultimately, a common cause.[22] Indeed, the first shots fired by colonists against British officers occurred on March 5, 1765, when interior rebels under the leadership of James Smith and the "Black Boys" called for insurrection. Throughout that fateful spring, they attacked supply trains, lay siege to British forts, and evaded prosecution. They circulated notices and posted them along roads. Their concern: the renewal of trade and diplomacy with interior Native nations.

Smith's uprising occurred at the end of Pontiac's War. He, his men, and every official in Pennsylvania were already familiar with another settler rebellion that began during the war's first winter in December 1763.[23] That uprising, led by the "Paxton Boys," targeted missionized Conestoga Indian villagers who "had lived in peace for [nearly] a century in the neighborhood of Lancaster County."[24] A diverse community of Native nations, they had lived there since 1701, allied with Pennsylvania's leaders. Because of Pontiac's War, however, colonists feared that this community had been trading with Pontiac's forces. Vigilantes killed dozens of unarmed Native men, women, and children. They also marched on Philadelphia "with a view to assault the barracks and murder the Indians."[25]

Pennsylvania's settler rebellions of 1763, 1764, and finally 1765 targeted Native peoples and the institutions of British authority surrounding them. British leaders simultaneously struggled to enforce policies in the interior and prosecute those who violated them. Throughout the 1760s, Governor John Penn lost the authority to do both. In 1768 he received a note of sympathy from his Virginian counterpart, who shared similar concerns about western settlers: "I have found by experience it impossible to bring anybody to Justice for the Murder of an Indian, who takes shelter among our back [country] Inhabitants. It is among those People, looked on as a meritorious action."[26]

Indian Groups, Regions, and Topography of the North American Interior
Proclamation Line, 1763
Proclamation Boundaries, 1763
Hudson Bay
PAYS D'EN HAUT (NOTIONAL LIMITS)
OJIBWAS (CHIPPEWAS)
Lake Superior
ANISHINAABEWAKI (Ojibwe Territory)
Sault Ste-Marie
Straits of Mackinac
MICHILIMACKINAC
FT. LA BAYE (FT. EDWARD AUGUSTUS)
WINNEBAGOS
SAUKS
KICKAPOOS
FOXES
POTAWATOMIS
Lake Michigan
OTTAWAS
Lake Huron
MASCOUTENS
WYANDOTS
FT. ST. JOSEPH
MIAMIS
(WEAS)
Ouiatenon
Detroit
Lake Erie
FT. SANDUSKY
FT. MIAMI
Maumee R.
Lake Ontario
Niagara
SENECAS
CAYUGAS
ONANDAGAS
ONEIDAS
TUSCARORAS
MOHAWKS
(MINGOS)
Allegheny R.
WESTERN DELAWARES
EASTERN DELAWARES
Muskingum R.
SHAWNEES
Pickawillany
Great Miami R.
Scioto R.
Ohio R.
Wabash R.
Missouri R.
St. Louis
FT. CHARTRES (Kaskaskia)
St-Genevieve
Vincennes
Kentucky R.
Kanawha R.
Monongahela R.
See Detail Map Below
MONTAGNAIS
St. Lawrence R.
MALECITES
Québec
QUÉBEC (1763)
Montreal
WESTERN ABENAKIS
EASTERN ABENAKIS
MAINE (Mass.)
N.H.
Portsmouth
Connecticut R.
Hudson R.
N.Y.
MASS.
Boston
R.I.
Hartford
CONN.
Newport
New Haven
N.J.
New York
Perth Amboy
PENNA.
Philadelphia
Burlington
Newcastle
Baltimore
MD.
DEL.
Chesapeake Bay
Williamsburg
VIRGINIA
ATLANTIC OCEAN
APPALACHIAN MOUNTAINS
Holston R.
NORTH CAROLINA
New Bern
CHICKASAWS
CHEROKEES
CATAWBAS
Tennessee R.
Coosa R.
SOUTH CAROLINA
GEORGIA
Charleston
Savannah
Mississippi R.
UPPER CREEKS
FT. TOULOUSE
Alabama R.
LOWER CREEKS
WEST FLORIDA (1763)
Mobile
APPALACHEES
Pensacola
New Orleans
Apalachicola R.
Gulf of Mexico
0 MILES 200
0 KILOMETERS 200
FT. DUQUESNE (PITTSBURGH)
FT. LIGONIER
Youghiogheny R.
FORBES ROAD
Carlisle
Susquehanna R.
Ohio R.
FT. NECESSITY
FT. BEDFORD
FT. LOUDOUN
FT. CUMBERLAND
FT. FREDERICK
Monongahela R.
BRADDOCK'S ROAD
Baltimore
Winchester
Shenandoah R.
Alexandria

Seasons before the passage of the Stamp Act of 1765, violence between interior settlers and Native communities destabilized the power of imperial authority and galvanized solidarities among interior settlers.

Historians have long focused on other moments of revolutionary formation. In the process, they have erased the centrality of Native peoples to the Revolution and, ultimately, the course of American history. To understand the Revolution—its origins, course, and legacies—without American Indians is like a one-handed clap, an empty if excited gesture that perpetuates longstanding traditions of assessing only the rivalries and eventual dominance among Euro-Americans. Focus upon the colonies' "ordinary people" misses the power of Native peoples and their influence in fostering new political identities.[27] As many have suggested, the Revolution became both a war for a new political order—for independence—and a struggle for the future of eastern North America.[28]

The ramifications spilled into the decades that followed. By the 1780s, the settler "sons" that Nathaniel Ames anticipated were children in a new national community. In this Republic, land remained the cornerstone of a new political system, one still rooted around "life and property" but now applicable only to men of European ancestry. Race, gender, and property converged to determine—to constitute—the new union's political subjects, upending previously established norms, including diplomatic practices between Indians and Europeans. The Republic did continue long-standing customary practice of treaty negotiations with Native leaders but did so in ways that sought land cessions from, and eventual authority over, Native peoples.[29]

The Unexpected Costs of the Seven Years' War

By the end of 1760, Quebec, Montreal, and then Detroit had surrendered. Despite the general euphoria across the colonial world, the costs of securing new territories, dispatching French prisoners, returning soldiers to Europe, caring for the sick, administering seventy-nine new forts, and adjudicating interior conflicts beleaguered policy makers.[30] While the French withdrawal had ballooned its empire, Britain emerged from the war mired in debt. So too did its colonies: in Boston one in seven received poor relief and sixteen of the city's wealthiest traders threatened to move their business due to increased taxes levied by the Massachusetts legislature.[31]

Amid economic and political transitions, Britain's secretary at war Welbore

Ellis asked General Jeffrey Amherst to submit a plan for the "future Defense of North America." Amherst gave the response desired, that the plan would be "as little expensive" as possible.[32] Throughout 1760 he worked to redeploy and demobilize England's costly army; for example, on October 25 he ordered that "all the Rangers away [in Canada]" should be paid off to "get rid of the expence as soon as possible."[33] As he toured the former strongholds of New France, the conquering general shifted from military affairs to austerities; however, no one grasped the extent of the financial challenges.

Britain had employed 167,000 sailors and soldiers around the globe, more than double the entire French settler population of New France. Many were not actually British but came from India, Germany, Switzerland, and southern Europe.[34] These combatants had neither volunteered nor been conscripted. They fought on behalf of the empire, but required compensation for doing so.[35]

The total military salaries exceeded £18 million annually, an astronomical commitment for this single conflict. In North America, colonial militiamen also required payment. Massachusetts had fielded over ten thousand, nearly 25 percent of its eligible male population, and the colony's debts soon exceeded £350,000, with interest accruing.[36] As Benjamin Franklin wondered in 1758, "Can England possibly bear the continuance of a war at so enormous an expence?"[37] Massachusetts was home to 250,000 colonists, and Britain's largest American colony teetered on insolvency. Victory had not come easily nor without cost, and Britain's national debts grew to over £130 million.[38]

While the British navy and army continued the war in the Caribbean and elsewhere, demobilization brought some cost reduction. By the end of 1760, however, ten thousand soldiers remained in North America under Amherst's command, and each still required annual payment of £36. In addition to securing French Canada, Britain obtained other colonies across the Americas, including East Florida and West Florida (from Spain); the French so-called ceded islands of Dominica, Grenada, St. Vincent, and Tobago; and even the Falkland Islands. Around the globe, the British empire grew in both size and cost.[39]

New acquisitions required settlers. They also needed troops, administrators, and the suppression of hostilities with Indigenous peoples and former African slaves. All required funding. For example, conflicts with free "Black Caribs" on St. Vincent continued until 1773, when the British made a peace that reserved a quarter of the island for their exclusive use. In Florida, organizers of settlements seemed to have forgotten the previous hardships associated with prior plantation experiments in the Chesapeake and coastal Georgia, relying on indentured servants and violence. The humidity, dense growth, and mosquitoes made the settlement of East Florida deadly. Moreover, colonial governors, such as Francis Ogilvie, governed with an iron fist. After three runaway servants were captured, he ordered them executed; however, he offered one a pardon should he be willing to perform the killing of the others.[40]

Slave revolts remained constant preoccupations of colonists and policy makers. All understood that the fortunes produced by slavery were only possible through violent suppression. Unanticipated wartime shortages had made life even harsher across plantation economies, spurring not only threats but outright revolts. In Jamaica, many had recently survived the Middle Passage and retained African leadership structures and military tactics.[41] In April 1760, five thousand slaves organized the island's largest revolt, destroying plantations, settlements, and mills before retreating into the hillsides to establish maroon communities. British retaliations were swift and included soldiers from Canada outfitted aboard naval ships that had blockaded French coastlines. Brutal conflicts ensued, in which British leaders showed less leniency than they had at either Quebec or Montreal. They tortured and executed without restraint. A hundred impaled heads lined Jamaican crossroads thereafter as planters pleaded for more soldiers to garrison their colony, run on terror.[42]

In many ways, the war's aftermath precipitated greater crises than the war itself. Resource shortages, spiraling costs, rebellions, and far-flung acquisitions plagued British leaders. The war—which had erupted in the American interior—had now bred an imperial behemoth, the size of which the world had never seen. Maintaining it required a larger naval and military administration than ever before.[43] Victory threatened to sink the empire.

Cultural Hybridity and Indigenous Power After 1760

At the center of this evolving crisis remained the North American interior, abandoned by the French but controlled by Native peoples. The Native Inland Sea had shaped the outbreak of war in 1753, and it now generated continued transformations. Starting in 1760, resident Odawa, Potawatomi, and Wendat Indians around Detroit organized revolts against British policies.[44] They had not lost any lands during the war and now sought to maintain their sovereignty.[45]

Like other Algonquian speakers, they had been close allies of New France, living, trading, and fighting together with French residents. Since the fort's founding in 1701, they had enjoyed the autonomy provided by French alliance.[46] Determined to retain it, they resisted English policies that threatened the region's economic and diplomatic practices.

Not all Native peoples of the interior, however, had been allies of the French. As we have seen, many Ohio River Indians sought refuge away from French, English, and Iroquoian dominion. They also wanted autonomy, including the ability to continue their trade with whomever they liked. Soon after the French surrender, they joined a rising confederation in the Great Lakes area comprised of former French allies and recent Native migrants from eastern America, principally Pennsylvania.

Innumerable French-introduced customs continued after 1760. From everyday fashion to foods and beverages to games played by children born to French and Indian parents, New France remained imprinted upon Native communities. To take just one pedestrian example, French and Native peoples had developed forms of moccasins, including the single and two-piece center-seam style known as *soulier à pièces*. Often adorned with ribbons, metals, beads, porcupine quills, and animal hairs, such durable footwear was common throughout the interior.

After 1760 these moccasins were exported east to backcountry British settlers who found Euro-American shoes impracticable and uncomfortable. Deerskin footwear far better suited the everyday challenges of interior hunting, canoeing, trading, and socializing.[47] Whether they knew it or not, British settlers walked upon well-trodden cultural ecologies.

Language, particularly the language of diplomacy, remained the most audible legacy of French settlement. A colloquial and Algonquian-influenced dialect pervaded the *pays d'en haut*. Vernaculars for trade, inter-cultural exchange, and politics lasted for generations.[48] A linguistic revolution paralleled the region's political evolution, particularly in communities that became named after or associated with French place-names, for example, Fond du Lac and Lac du Flambeau.[49] Over time, French names took on political meanings within this Algonquian-speaking world, forming a lingua franca that framed subsequent deliberations, treaty councils, and relations with the federal government.[50]

British commanders either spoke French or had translators who could. Thousands of French settlers, or *habitants*, remained throughout the interior world, and they were expected to take oaths to their new monarch and become his subjects. At Detroit, "all the inhabitants," Amherst relayed in January 1761, "gave up their arms & took the oath of Allegiance."[51] Trepidation, however, remained.

The war had wrought disasters for French families. English forces expelled thousands of Acadians from eastern Canada while blockades of the St. Lawrence brought famine and curbed exports. "There were about 1000 souls in Detroit," Amherst noted. "They had about 3000 packs of skins . . . [but] there had been no opportunity of selling them since [Fort] Niagara was taken."[52] Nervous French farmers planted their crops in the spring of 1760 unsure whether their harvests might feed English soldiers rather than their children.[53]

Interior communities were often comprised of dozens of extended French families. At Detroit, nearly a hundred houses surrounded the settlement's main building, Fort Pontchartrain, which dominated the city's riverfront. Three of its four bastions faced the river, the anticipated site of attack. While the fort did not see military conflict during the war, it remained a center for trade, communication, and diplomacy.[54] Supplies and ammunition, however, dwindled so much that French commanders instructed Indian allies to venture to British forts to trade—ironically, given that the war had been started to prohibit such trade. Even at Fort Pitt, however, the war limited provisions, as meat, dry goods, and even gunpowder arrived either spoiled or wet from Philadelphia.[55] Without being told directly, France's Indian allies knew the war was lost.

Detroit in 1760 was a microcosm of the interior's diversity and challenges.[56] As British solider Dietrich Brehm reported, the city's fields were "extremly good, producing, winter wheet, Indian corn, good Grass, and all sort of Garden Stuff and Fruit lik Aples, Pears and Pikhes." The city's diverse residents additionally "have tryed Wines from France, which grow extremely well."[57] Native villagers had formed communities along both sides of the river. These included Algonquian-speaking Ojibwe, Odawa, and Potawatomi as well as Iroquoian-speaking Wendat. The differences between these communities were less pronounced than their commonalities. Intermarriage linked these villages, as did webs of trade, diplomacy, and kinship.[58] Such communities, however, remained distinct. They remained "allies to each other," remarked interior trader cum Indian agent George Croghan.[59]

In December 1760 Irish, German, English, and American-born soldiers arrived to occupy the city. Many came from Fort Pitt and had witnessed the raids that had plagued backcountry settlements during the war. The fate of nearly two thousand captives remained an ongoing diplomatic crisis: to release British captives required sizable crown resources for ransom. Captive taking also weakened the crown, exposing its inability to protect its subjects. Across the trans-Appalachian frontier, fear of Indians combined with a distrust of governance. Increasingly, settlers doubted the capacity of any authority to protect them.[60]

The experiences of war would not be forgotten across the backcountry. Desires for retribution pervaded Indian and non-Indian communities. Native peoples viewed colonists' arrival with suspicion and worried whether British leaders would continue existing policies. By contrast, settlers grew concerned when their officials continued the trade and diplomatic practices that Native peoples desired. After 1763 these desires grew incompatible. In the interior, colonists' attitudes about Indians and government were changing. While Pennsylvania had historically been defined by its commitments to peace, it now faced the irrepressible challenges of frontier conflict.[61]

Religious Diversity across the Interior

While the polyglot composition of the British forces at Detroit paralleled the diversity of the Indians around them, imperial officers deepened rather than eased tensions. British leaders, reported a Shawnee leader, "tell us that they regard us as dogs, that they are masters of all the Land, and they have overthrown our French father."[62] Unlike in the French era, British leaders dismissed calls for mutualism—the basis for alliance. They also denigrated Indian leaders, considering them haughty, entitled, or both.[63] French mediation, diplomacy, and rituals of governance had characterized the region's political culture. Now British commanders had arrived with little appreciation for such customs and their long-standing history.[64]

Derisive words soon led to hostile behaviors. The customary language of mediation that had characterized Indian-imperial relations was eroding. "Indians," Amherst determined in 1760, "always . . . do mischief."[65] His impressions had solidified by 1763, when he underscored the need for constant guard against "an *Enemy* [who] in *some Degree* must always be Lookt upon [as such], altho' it is unnecessary to Let them know it."[66] In more than one way, the language of diplomacy had changed.

Unlike language, religion remained a less apparent register of French influences. Despite the early presence of missionaries in the 1630s, Great Lakes Indian communities continued generations-old spiritual practices that were viewed as at odds with the ecclesiasticism of Jesuit fathers, although Jesuits did find similarities in many Anishinaabe practices.[67] Native and French leaders emphasized thrift, not greed, called for open declarations of faith to the supernatural, and valued general truthfulness. Jesuits, however, condemned many customs, such as divorce or premarital sex, viewpoints that made little sense to Native peoples. Over a century after missionization, the differences between Native and French religions were as apparent as their congruences.[68]

Adaptation, however, continued. Many Native peoples yearned for a French return to America. Even though French soldiers and friars had departed, the syncretism that they had imparted endured. Many Indians had accepted select Christian teachings—such as learning to study the Bible. Others had adopted new clothing, or settled into religiously organized villages. In Lancaster County, Pennsylvania, the Conestoga Indians had formed pacific, religiously minded, and semi-agricultural communities working in close social and religious partnership with Quakers, Moravians, and Mennonites.

Throughout the 1750s, cultural revivals emerged across North America.[69] In eastern and western Pennsylvania, the teachings and prophesies of Lenape (Delaware) leaders gained growing adherents. Near Wyoming and farther east along the Susquehanna, male and female prophets preached prophecies that combined teachings from Native and European religions.[70] Such individuals had lived through the pressures of British settlements around them. They had attempted to find stability within the colonial world. They and their communities, however, had usually found rejection, dispossession, and betrayal.[71]

Christian missionaries had been the first to ally with Indian peoples over land, rights, and protection. Missionaries, one Indian leader suggested, treated Native peoples better than colonists and other imperial officials. They "did not come to buy or sell, or get Gain, but came in Love and Respect . . . and desired their Well-doing both here and hereafter."[72] Native communities had also welcomed religiously minded settlers among them, including German-speaking pacifists, who reportedly were "truthful and . . . venerated by the Indians of those regions."[73]

In Pennsylvania, Quakers, Moravians, and other Protestant faith keepers emerged as allies of resident Lenape peoples. In the 1740s, Moravians served as key mediators in diplomatic accords forged before the outbreak of the Seven Years' War.[74] They established religious houses and villages for Indian converts along the Susquehanna at Shamokin and across the Alleghenies at Gnadenhütten.[75] They served as translators between colonial officials and Lenape people.

Such religious ties, however, could not keep settlement pressures from infringing upon Native homelands. Many Lenape took flight west and were among the thousands of Algonquian-speaking peoples from the mid-Atlantic and Northeast who formed part of "the Algonquian diaspora"—a continent-wide migration of Algonquian peoples away from British North America. To survive, the Lenape migrated.

Many migratory communities found the autonomy available in the Ohio River region preferable to living within or near British colonies. Indeed, as we have seen, the upper Ohio River had been a land of opportunity for Native migrants.[76] It retained hunting grounds, bountiful fields, and easy access to waterways. Most important, it was outside the jurisdictions of New France, British North America, and Iroquoia, the latter two recognized as the region's principal colonizing powers.[77] The Alleghenies separated the region's interior valleys and created a semi-autonomous borderlands between Iroquoia and New France.[78] Throughout the first half of the eighteenth century, the region saw comparatively less warfare and provided choice hunting and trading routes away from the colonial centers east of the mountains. It soon attracted migratory Native peoples and backcountry traders.[79]

The Lenape brought with them memories and stories. Like other migrants, these refugees knew of a fundamental duplicity of the British: the hypocrisy between colonists' professed Christian principles and the practice of taking Indian lands.[80] Few other peoples had experienced such simultaneous spiritual and settler colonialisms, and while they reveled in their autonomy, they remembered the losses associated with their homelands. They told stories of family who had passed on or had been killed by colonists; of burial grounds that became largely untended, disturbed by colonial expansion; and of the many ways newcomers had desecrated their homelands. They also noted how colonial leaders regularly sided with the Iroquois over them, as in 1737, when Iroquois leaders skillfully enlisted Pennsylvania into recognizing Iroquois authority over Lenape lands in what became known as the Walking Purchase.[81] Bitterness informed their knowledge of colonial society.

Unsurprisingly, spiritual power guided Native peoples through their migrations and resettlements. While the term *diaspora* implies a separation from one's ancestral homelands, it also connotes continuing connections of culture, language, history, and religion. Spiritual ties with interior tribes increased as the Lenape and other interior peoples interacted and, together, expanded upon shared religious traditions. Common enmity against the British underlay their increasingly shared interior world.

After their migration to the interior, Lenape leaders began to impart visions of a shared destiny for the continent's Indian peoples. The Seven Years' War was eroding the autonomous spheres of the Ohio River while also signaling an end to Indian autonomy within French settlements. To many, these outcomes were related. Did not the war's aftermath and the triumph of the British threaten all Native people? As Indian leaders communicated to French leaders in Illinois during the war: "All that the Delawares and Shawannays [Shawnees] told us is now come to pass. . . . The English sought to become Masters of all, & would put us to death."[82] The message also included the suggestion: "They told us also, Our Brethren, let us die together."[83]

Long recognized among the Anishinaabe as distant relatives from the sacred eastern direction, or *Waban*, the Lenape held standing among interior Indians. Pontiac and other regional leaders took such calls for cultural purification seriously and matched them with their own political and military ambitions to unite against the British.[84] Most notably, Neolin, often called "the Delaware Prophet," articulated visions of strength and rebirth through unification. A millennialist vision of a bountiful future emerged from his teachings. In this future, Native peoples from all tribes would revitalize longstanding practices, curb their dependency on European technologies, and forge new relations with one another outside the disruptive realms of Europeans. These teachings attracted a broad following, and soon they informed military reactions against newly arrived British rulers.

Neolin and the Troubled Aftermath of War

The exact causes of Pontiac's War remain debated. Pontiac's and Neolin's visions remain visible largely through the recollections of others. While many have written these Indian leaders out of history, their combined movements shaped the post-1763 world.

Pontiac was born along the Ottawa River around 1720, and he and his family migrated to Michilimackinac when he was a young man.[85] When exactly he moved south to Detroit is unclear. He was reported fighting with the French there in 1746. He is also believed to have fought in 1755 against Washington and General Braddock during their ill-fated attempt to seize Fort Duquesne. He thus traversed the Native Inland Sea multiple times and knew intimately its dozens of Indian tribes, who lived across hundreds of villages.[86]

He also knew that the Great Lakes were home to thousands of French traders and officials in the Illinois country. In contrast to the French, English-speaking officials, missionaries, and settlers spoke rudely and without deference to Indian leaders accustomed to the politics of consensus. They also spoke in contradictions. Their words were often at odds with their actions. General John Forbes, for example, told Lenape leaders in 1762 that "the English have no intention to make settlements in your hunting country beyond the Allegheny hills." Lenape sovereignty, he said, remained intact. Settlers, he continued, "shall be desired for your conveniency to erect some store houses in order to establish and carry on a trade."[87] Colonel Henry Bouquet had made similar assurances a few years earlier: "We are not . . . here to take Possession of yr hunting Country in a hostile manner."[88] Trade, peace, and order remained the professed goals of British leaders.

The experiences of Neolin and other Lenape members told otherwise. Neolin, who lived in the Ohio River country at Tuscarawas, closely followed British-Lenape negotiations during these fateful transitions. The prominent Lenape chief Tamaqua resided there. Starting in 1758 Tamaqua led delegations to Fort Pitt, Lancaster, and Philadelphia to discuss the region's future. He worked with Bouquet to ensure that British leaders abided by their pronouncements, especially regarding interior settlements. Tamaqua commanded such attention that his arrival at Fort Pitt in 1759 was met with a cannon salute. Throughout the final years of the war, he affirmed his peoples' commitments to peace both in words and followed up with deeds, returning a hundred British captives taken during the conflict.[89]

As commander of Fort Pitt, Bouquet tried to implement what he believed to be Britain's postwar policies. He attempted to keep Indians and settlers apart, sought the return of captives, and secured trading goods for Native communities, many of which had faced lean times during the war. He was successful in the second two endeavors but failed in the first. In the fall of 1761, he ordered squatters to return east of the Appalachians. Like other British commanders, he used violence to enforce his orders, and the following spring he sent soldiers to burn the cabins of those who remained.[90] As with Tamaqua, Bouquet's actions followed his words, and while nervous about growing settlements around them, Lenape leaders were pleased by Bouquet's enforcement of his professed commitments. Led by Tamaqua, they arrived in August 1762 at Lancaster in a "cavalcade" for negotiations.[91]

Elsewhere, however, British leaders and settlers behaved differently. They viewed bilateral deliberations with suspicion and grew angry about perceived favoritism toward Indians. The use of the king's soldiers to drive away settlers outraged both settlers and more distant land speculators, for whom the exercise of military authority brought moral and economic worry.

Washington was among them. He spent much of 1759 and 1760 trying to convince Virginia's colonial governor to compensate him with interior lands. In 1754 Virginia's Governor Dinwiddie had promised two hundred thousand acres of Ohio lands to those who enlisted in Washington's regiment, and he now worked to obtain his share. Like many plantation owners, he eyed interior lands for speculation. To diversify their holdings, Washington's generation understood the need to broaden their properties, especially those who relied on the unpredictability of seasonal tobacco production.[92] As they had before the war, Washington and others of the Ohio Company continued to vie for interior lands. They lobbied leaders in Virginia and London. King George III, they hoped, would heed their concerns and respond to their petitions.

It is unclear when Neolin and later Pontiac lost faith in British promises. The sheer number of interior Indian leaders like Tamaqua who tried to find mediated solutions suggested, potentially, diplomacy's futility. From declining game to growing restrictions on Indian trading supplies, Lenape and other Native peoples faced growing challenges. The British curb on gift giving was particularly hard. It deprived Native hunters of gunpowder and undercut their masculine authority to provision their families and villages.[93]

After 1760 Indian leaders shuttled endlessly between British forts and colonial capitals attempting to overcome what many viewed as impossible obstacles. After a decade of warfare, peace and diplomacy brought little resolution, and they increasingly seemed destined to fail. By 1762 those who favored mediation or had accommodated British authority after the fall of Duquesne began losing political influence.[94] For many Native people, a new destiny was needed.

For Neolin, the problems posed by Europeans were pervasive and systemic. All colonists, he believed, were to blame. Colonialism was the root problem and needed to be disrupted altogether to bring liberation and renewal to Indian homelands. Destructive influences—alcohol, economic dependency, declining game, disease, and above all dispossession—needed to be curbed. Radical reform appeared the only solution. For Neolin and his followers, there was only one path forward, and it started within.

In the last years of the war, Neolin began traveling to share a prophecy. He spoke about powerful teachings that had been revealed to him by the "Master of Life." He told how he had encountered in a dream a divine, almighty God who was as kind as he was powerful. "Clothed all in white," this deity spoke with an assuring resonance. In his vision, Neolin had jettisoned his possessions and ascended a mountain to meet him. After being seated, the "Lord said to him":

> I am the Master of Life, and since I know what thou desirest to know, and to whom thou wishest to speak, listen well to what I am going to say to these and to all the Indians: "I am he who had created the heavens and the earth, the trees, lakes, rivers, all men, and all that thou seest and hast seen upon the earth.
>
> "Because I love you, ye must do what I say and love. . . . I do not like that ye should drink . . . that ye should fight one another . . . or run after the wives of others; ye do not well. . . . When ye wish to go to war, ye conjure and resort to the medicine dance, believing that ye speak to me; ye are mistaken. . . .
>
> "This land where ye dwell I have made for you and not for others. Whence comes it that ye permit the Whites upon your lands? Can ye not live without them? Ye could live as ye did live before knowing them. . . . Ye had no need of gun or power, or anything else. . . .
>
> "Here is a prayer which I give thee in writing to learn by heart and to teach to the Indians and their children."[95]

Neolin's message of unity and reform rebuked Native peoples as much as colonists. It offered guidance. Temperance, cultural renewal, self-sufficiency, and faith were the keys to overcome their challenges. According to these teachings, Native peoples alone possessed the solutions to their worldly problems. They had power and were encouraged by a divine presence to harness it.

Neolin's teachings spread across the Native Inland Sea. From the Seneca at the "western door" of the Iroquois Confederacy to the Illinois country, Native peoples gathered to hear the prophet and his disciples. The above quotation was recorded in 1763 by a Detroit *habitant*, Robert Navarre. Like many French subjects, Navarre knew the region's Indians. He had seen them suffer from the cold and lack of provisions. He now recorded Neolin's prophecy, as relayed by Pontiac, before a council of Odawas, Potawatomis, and Wyandots. Pontiac had heard the prophecy and encouraged others to follow these new principles. He also wanted them implemented through force. Pontiac's and Neolin's visions converged in May 1763.[96] They made it a year unlike any other in American history.

Pontiac's Uprising and the Revolutionary Costs of Peace

The year began well for England. On January 21, the victorious "proclamation for declaring a Cessation of Arms" arrived aboard the *Pitt Packet*.[97] Amherst spent that evening drafting letters to governors informing them of the empire's collective triumph. Three days later, the proclamation made it into colonial newspapers, and the formal Treaty of Paris was signed in February. Although official word of the treaty did not reach the interior for some time, festivities erupted across the East. Euphoria pervaded seaports, family farms, and plantation households.

The year that began with so much promise, however, ended in disaster. Renewed warfare, colonial massacres, growing military regulations, and mob violence erupted as the chaos across the interior spilled toward the Atlantic. Pontiac and Neolin had harnessed one end of the Native Inland Sea's discontent with British rule. Fatefully, they directed it against British leaders as well as unwelcome settlers in western Pennsylvania. They captured soldiers and settlers, including the entire regiment at Fort Edward Augustus in Wisconsin, whose members they ferried to Montreal in June for ransom. Despite Bouquet's initial misreading that this conflict "will end in nothing," the interior was again at war.[98]

Exhausted by a decade of conflict, Pennsylvania's settlers added their own fuel to this cauldron of instability. England's global victory in the Seven Years' War unleashed an elemental struggle—the principal conflict in American history—between "Indians" and "whites" for control of the frontier.[99] For the next half century, protracted conflicts engulfed the Ohio River region as white settlers poured into the interior Indian lands that backcountry traders, missionaries, and French officials had navigated for over a century.

With decades of military experience, Pontiac understood that his Native alliance was outnumbered by British forces and that their officers could draw upon the burgeoning streams of settlers. Pontiac also knew that his forces would over time be overwhelmed by Britain's technologies and endless supply lines. Such had been the fate of the French empire, which Indians had watched disintegrate. Stacks of furs sat rotting without access to markets; guns became useless without ammunition; and French and Indian families starved.

To implement a rebellion required coordination, unification, and above all surprise. The prophet had helped. His vision provided motivation and networks of communication.[100] Time would be of the essence. Prompted by beaded "war belts" readable only by Native leaders circulating throughout the winter, spring became the time of action. In a series of assaults that ranged from northern Michigan to the Appalachian backcountry, allied Indian forces destroyed nine out of fourteen British forts. Indian soldiers closed roads, captured livestock, and sacked settlements. They aimed to expel British soldiers and colonists both.[101]

It was a bold and ambitious attempt to reverse the region's new imperial order, and for a while it succeeded. Fort Pitt, however, was too large to overtake, and Detroit, surprisingly, held out during a seven-month siege. Pontiac commanded forces around the city and attempted to enlist *habitants* to join them. Many, like Robert Navarre, lived alongside the Indian villages that surrounded Fort Pontchartrain and recorded key elements of this growing conflict.[102]

Alliance leaders also turned west to remaining French allies in Illinois. The commander of Fort de Chartres, Pierre-Joseph Neyon de Villiers, spent much of 1763 attempting to explain that France was no longer at war with England. He urged diplomacy, not insurrection. Native peoples, however, did not fully believe him and hoped that other remaining French allies still held on to visions of a Franco-Algonquian alliance returning. Surely, they also reasoned, the French king wanted retribution for the losses of the previous decade.

Pontiac even ventured to Fort de Chartres in early 1764. He spoke with Neyon of their long-standing relationship and about his new spiritual imperatives. "Thou goest against the Master of Life," he reportedly informed Neyon. "I pray thee to talk no more of peace with the English." He further suggested that in addition to his Ottawa and Michigan communities, he spoke for eastern Shawnee, Lenape, Iroquois, and Ojibwe allies: "in short all the nations of the Continent."[103] Unlike in previous generations, Pontiac was not requesting French authorization to fight but inviting them to join a continent-wide effort.

Pontiac was successful early on, but three of the four principal interior forts—Pitt, Detroit, and Niagara—successfully resisted. While much smaller than Detroit, Michilimackinac held similar strategic value because of its position between vital bodies of water. It finally fell to alliance forces on June 2. They used the subterfuge of playing lacrosse outside its walls before storming the fort under the guise of retrieving a lost ball. Ojibwe women had hidden weapons in their trade packs to arm the soldiers.[104] It was the largest victory for the alliance.

The three surviving forts had their own supply systems, which alliance members targeted but could not destroy. Native forces could hamper overland travel, but British ships traveled the waters of the Native Inland Sea unimpeded. They resupplied Detroit throughout the summer and into the fall. Vessels such as the *Huron* carried multiple four-pound cannons and swivel guns that bombarded shoreline villages across Lakes Erie and St. Clair.[105]

On occasion Pontiac outmaneuvered English troops attempting to encircle his forces. His numbers at Detroit had doubled to nearly a thousand by summer, and each side believed it possessed the power to overwhelm the other. In late July 60 out of 250 of the fort's soldiers were either killed or wounded in a failed morning assault.[106] Indian soldiers also captured soldiers and craft heading to resupply these beleaguered encampments. On June 16 Amherst recorded that a contingent of ten "batteaus" with ninety-six men and "139 barrels of provision" had been attacked en route to Detroit. Most of these men, boats, and supplies never made it to the straits. They returned to Niagara with only two boats and forty men.[107] In what would become a defining military feature across the region, neither side was able to subdue or expel the other.

While such conflicts paled in comparison to the monumental battles of the Seven Years' War, they stirred comparable alarm. With few soldiers still stationed in America, England's hold on the interior appeared weakened, if not entirely relinquished. By October, Bouquet (now a general) estimated that six hundred settlers had been killed and thousands driven away from their farms.[108]

Moreover, successful Indian conflicts generated alarm and reminded colonists of their previous experiences at war. Their experiences of 1763 rekindled the years of warfare that preceded them when all settlers had suffered or knew someone who had. Over 40 percent of the interior's settler population lived in a "war zone." In Pennsylvania fears became so pervasive that, notwithstanding their victory over France, the English could not govern. In fact, that colony's overall per capita death toll was equivalent to the number of Pennsylvanians killed in the Civil War.[109]

As Pontiac's alliance offered a unifying umbrella for discontented Natives, it was countered by an equally resolute force of settlers. These forces operated against the proclamations of British leaders, such as Bouquet, and colonial legislative leaders, including Benjamin Franklin.[110] A nearly primordial battle had unfolded, as powerful newly constituted Indigenous and settler communities vied for supremacy over the eastern gateways to the Native Inland Sea.

Despite their familiarity with imperial policy and colonial politics, nothing could have prepared Pontiac, Neolin, and other Native leaders for the growing divisions within colonial society. These divisions hardened after Pontiac's misnamed "rebellion." In fact, by year's end, a rebellion of a different kind had broken out as backcountry settlers marched on colonial capitals.

Western Pennsylvania and the Crisis of British Imperialism

The Seven Years' War had turned the world upside down, and Pontiac's War of 1763 wrought further instability. However, unlike in 1755, when backcountry settlers worried about being "alarm'd at the slightest notice in the night," Pennsylvanians would not be unprepared this time.[111] Like Pontiac, Neolin, and their followers, colonists also used violence to make their fortunes. In this they acted not just outside British rule but against it.

British imperial leaders faced vexing challenges. Every day Governor John Penn received petitions from settlers requesting assistance against Indians whom the crown attempted to mollify. As during the previous decade, Penn's government was divided on how best to fund western defenses. It became mired in a political morass that Penn called simply "the old dispute."[112]

The situation in 1763, however, was different. Following Pontiac's string of victories, colonists formed volunteer militias quickly and with ease, a testament to the martial culture that had grown during the war.[113] Unlike in 1754, when settlers flooded into forts, interior settlers organized, and they did so across ethnic divides. They bridged linguistic and religious divisions and in the process developed new solidarities and racial identities of whiteness.[114]

British officials initially looked favorably upon such volunteerism. Solidarities and loyalties were to be celebrated. As General Thomas Gage reflected on the region's previous conflicts, he noted the common ties among those who "will of their own accord associate themselves for their mutual defense."[115] Unlike during the Seven Years' War, the difficulty of mustering volunteer forces no longer beleaguered British officers.[116] It was, however, the collective actions of such organized militia that soon generated concern.

In many ways, Pontiac's War unleashed sets of Anglophone ambitions that intersected before diverging. When directed against Indians, violence cemented social ties between settlers, created experiences that transcended ethnic, class, and religious differences, and linked colonists with imperial policy goals. The Seven Years' War had bred such commonalities. Now, as Pontiac's War ignited common enmities, it also fueled calls for even greater forms of retribution. Bouquet and Amherst, for example, were shocked by the seeming betrayal of the Indian leaders whom they had courted. Each fatefully began policies that aimed to "extirpate that Vermine," in Bouquet's words, legitimating commonly shared anti-Indian hatreds across the colonies.[117]

Having led Britain through the bloody conquest of New France, Amherst had little hesitation heeding such calls. Most notoriously, and for the first time in recorded history, he issued orders to pass smallpox-infested blankets among interior tribes. "We must," he wrote, "Use Every Stratagem in our Power to Reduce them."[118] All prisoners "be put to death, their extirpation being the only security for our future safety."[119]

After a decade managing interior affairs, Amherst had grown tired of the time-consuming diplomacy, gift giving, and politics required to convince Indian leaders to follow British policies. In October he simply chose not to receive his deputy Sir William Johnson's Iroquois delegation: "I thought it best not to see them for they would have kept me two days, tho' they had nothing to say." Indians were too hard to comprehend. To Amherst, they were prone to time-consuming communal deliberations and also beholden to what he believed were unnatural forces, such as dreams. Violence, as he informed Johnson, was the correct path: "I told him I proposed to collect 3,000 men to proceed by Niagara for the punishment of the Indians who have committed hostilities. . . . He thought the Senecas, Delawares, and Shawn[ee] deserved the most severe punishment and he said should be tortured."[120] Although his orders were known only within his chain of command, no doubt they would have pleased backcountry settlers, many of whom shared a broadening hatred of Indians. They also, however, resented their own officials' inabilities to stabilize interior relations, and they quickly organized violent responses of their own.

Such violence was as much a sign of weakness as strength. The illusion of British forces marching to assured victory against interior Indians reflected Anglophone hubris. Much like Washington at Great Meadows, Bouquet and Amherst did not comprehend the spiraling conflicts around them. Given the extent of British victories, they believed that they held the power to determine interior policies. After their unprecedented military achievements, how could they fail to manage the war's aftermath? They had given their king a continental and global empire. Surely, they believed, defeated Indians with little ammunition posed a limited threat.[121]

In a year of such turbulence, Pennsylvania offered the clearest expression of the interior's broader reverberations and ultimate legacies. Governor John Penn was heir to a position held by his grandfather, William Penn, after whom the colony was named.[122] William Penn's policies of pacifism and tolerance had distinguished the colony. Penn had learned the Lenape language—so "that I might not want an Interpreter on any occasion"—and had negotiated countless agreements with many tribal leaders.[123] He oversaw the maintenance of the colony's expansion and navigated complex inter-tribal and multi-imperial landscapes. While often idealized, such practices bred patterns of Indian and white coexistence.

Unlike in the Chesapeake and New England, no state-driven practice of removal emerged before 1750. Pennsylvania had had few Indian wars. The colony's biggest challenge in Indian affairs involved negotiations *between* rival

Indians, particularly the Iroquois Confederacy, whose long-recognized influence west of the Alleghenies endured throughout the 1760s.[124] Only a few years prior, in October 1758 at the Treaty of Easton—which was held just before the English assault on Duquesne—Iroquois, Lenape, and colonial leaders had negotiated the continued recognition of Iroquoian suzerainty over lands west of the Allegheny Mountains.[125] Additionally, in the 1750s a group of "prominent Quakers," including Israel Pemberton, had formed the "Friendly Association for Regaining and Preserving Peace with the Indians by Pacific Measures" to negotiate inter-cultural affairs.[126] In matters of Indian policy, Pennsylvania was different.

Something happened, however, that changed the colony's relationship with Indians. Many have labeled such changes "revolutionary" and assessed their impacts on the clashes between crown and colonist in the decades that followed. The changes of the 1760s are essential for understanding the Revolutionary War that followed. These changes centered foremost on Indian affairs. During Pontiac's War they took violent expression. Nothing in the colony would ever be the same again.

The Conestoga Massacre of 1763 and the Expansion of Racial Violence

British leaders made new policies and attempted reforms. The Treaty of Paris had been signed in February, Pontiac's War launched in May, and the first effort to regulate interior lands—the Royal Proclamation of 1763—promulgated on October 7. The last was in some ways a response to the second, although in retrospect it failed to achieve what it intended.

Ironically, from London's perspective, Pontiac's War illuminated the need not for the expulsion of Britain from America but for land reforms. Regulating interior lands now became a "royal" priority. The proclamation attempted such redefinition. Many have written about its detailed provisions and how they ultimately collapsed.[127] According to British leaders, to stabilize North America new colonies were needed in the territories acquired from France, as was a boundary demarcating the western limits of Britain's existing colonies.

An unprecedented world war had started in the interior, and now another war with Native peoples had broken out farther west. Wars were costly and bred instability. Separating colonists from Indians and regulating commerce now became "royal" policies, as did the granting of land titles to those, such as George Washington, who "have served in North America during the late war."[128] "Everything else," from the Great Lakes to Florida and from the Mississippi River to the Appalachians, was now reserved for the use of the Indians.[129] Taxing commerce, managing land reforms, and preserving stability became Britain's postwar policies.

As taxes, land reforms, and the rule of law became the policies of the day, colonists grew impatient and dissatisfied. Bouquet's expulsion of settlers in 1762 had upset many, while colonial planter elites remained frustrated in their efforts to obtain promised lands. Moreover, colonists believed that their voices did not receive sufficient audience in London.

Scholars have long focused on colonial resentments over taxation—debates about which began pervading northern legislatures in 1764 following the American Duties Act. However, interior land concerns as well as the crown's conciliatory relations with Indians upset settlers just as much if not more than policies of taxation. Taxes were levied largely in seaports, which held only a small percentage of British North America's total population. While the cost of living had doubled during the war in both New York and Philadelphia, farmers welcomed the higher prices that their produce received.[130] After the Treaty of Paris, the stability of interior farms elicited the deepest passions, and in 1763 settler fears revolved around concerns from the west, not the east.[131]

Such fears erupted in late 1763, bringing Pennsylvania to the verge of civil war. Those who suffered most were Indians allied with the colony. As Edward Shippen of Lancaster wrote to his son in June, colonists feared that Pontiac's attacks to their west represented "a deep plan for the extermination of us all."[132]

Indians were not to be trusted, and nor were British leaders working toward diplomatic resolution. Settlers denounced authorities for using public funds to support so-called friendly Indians while doing little to protect whites.[133] Many believed that Amherst bore responsibility for the growing frontier conflicts, which by July had forced 1,384 settlers off their Pennsylvanian farms.[134] As Shippen wrote, Amherst "ought immediately . . . to have sent up Men." Shippen had further recommendations: "A good reward offered for Scalps would be the most effectual way of quelling the Indians." Militia efforts at Lancaster, he continued, were also underway: "The Rev. Mr. Elder writes me . . . to desire me to try to animate our folks this way to hire a number of men and send them up to guard the Frontier at Paxton. . . . [Where there] is a quantity of Indians on an Island below who behave in a very insolent manner."[135] Outraged by the violence of Pontiac's War and the perceived favoritism in Indian policies following the proclamation, groups of frontier settlers now organized themselves. They did so against the same Indian communities that British leaders wanted to secure as partners and allies. Colonists now used violence without the consent of British officials and threatened those who defied them.

On December 14 several dozen attacked the town of missionized Indians at Conestoga Creek, east of the Alleghenies along the Susquehanna.[136] Few of these "Christian Indians" had ties to Neolin, let alone Pontiac's soldiers to the west who had sacked English forts.[137] Six were killed. Others, as Shippen wrote to Governor Penn, such as "Bill Sawk and some other Indians [who] were gone towards Smith's Iron Works to sell brooms," fled. "Where they are now, we can't understand."[138]

Militiamen destroyed homes and killed unarmed defenders. Many of the Indians had lived for decades in the town, which had been established three generations before as a protectorate for Lenape, Iroquois, and regional Native families who, upon the appointment of each new colonial governor, "promise ourselves your favour and protection."[139]

The Conestoga worked as broom and basket makers, domestic servants, and farm hands, and they learned to write and read English and attend Sunday services. They believed that they were protected by the colonial legislature with which they had worked. They were mistaken. Vigilantes, calling themselves Paxton Boys after a nearby Scotch-Irish settlement, justified their attack as self-defense. They maintained that the Conestoga community had been aiding interior war parties, thereby jeopardizing their settlements and families.[140] Fears of inter-tribal trade now motivated colonists to massacre.

At the end of December, vigilantes again resorted to racial violence, invading the Lancaster jail and massacring fourteen Conestogas to whom the sheriff had offered protection. As word spread that they intended to kill every Indian in Pennsylvania, the Paxton Boys' popularity grew. They now believed they could take down the colonial capital.

In February five hundred Paxton Boys marched on Philadelphia, announcing that they would kill the remaining 140 Indians who sheltered there as well as Israel Pemberton, whom they regarded as the colony's leading Indian sympathizer. Benjamin Franklin and other colonial leaders intercepted the mob, heard their complaints, and offered them immunity if they went home. City leaders also began organizing their own citizen soldiers.[141] All were British subjects who lived in the same colony, but they came from different worlds: the backcountry and the seaport.[142]

Tensions between backcountry settlers and eastern leaders had percolated for many years. They boiled in the weeks after the December massacre when backcountry leaders issued a "Declaration of the injured Frontier Inhabitants" linking their frustrations with legislative leaders with recent Indian attacks.[143]

When the colony held its elections the next fall, such differences were exposed. Franklin lost reelection, defeated in part for his support of diplomacy with interior tribes and his denunciation of the Paxton Boys. Many German immigrants from interior communities resented Philadelphians' control of the colony's politics. "Never before in the history of Pennsylvania," according to Lutheran minister Heinrich Melchior Mühlenberg, "have so many people assembled for an election."[144] Starting in 1764, interior settlers demanded greater representation, accountability, and political influence. Increasingly, their political culture transformed colonial governance and brought a new language of politics to the colony.[145]

Interior rebels were exonerated for their transgressions of colonial authority. In fact, legislative leaders, including Governor Penn, continued to placate their demands throughout the year. Not only did Penn commit to mobilizing a regiment of one thousand to join interior conflicts, on July 7 he issued a declaration to "promise, that there shall be paid . . . to all and every Person . . . premiums and bounties for the prisoners and Scalps of the Enemy Indians."[146] The militarized political culture of the interior had now spread to the colony's legislature, transforming its racial politics away from diplomacy toward violence.

Among the possessions of the fourteen victims in Lancaster was a copy of "A Writing on Parchment, purporting An Article of Agreement between William Penn, Proprietary, & of Pennsylvania, and the King of the Indians inhabiting in or about the River Susquehanna, and other Indians."[147] It dated to April 1701, a time when agreements between colonial leaders and Native peoples had carried guaranteed assurances and protections. Those days had now passed as, very soon, would the governing authority of the crown itself.

Colonial Divisions and Endemic Indian Violence

Indian hating is an ideology that holds Native peoples are inferior to whites and therefore rightfully subject to indiscriminate violence. The events of December 1763 and 1764 form recognized chapters in the broad history of this ideology. Importantly, they also accelerated divides within colonial society. In under fourteen months, the outbreaks of violence initiated by the Paxton Boys

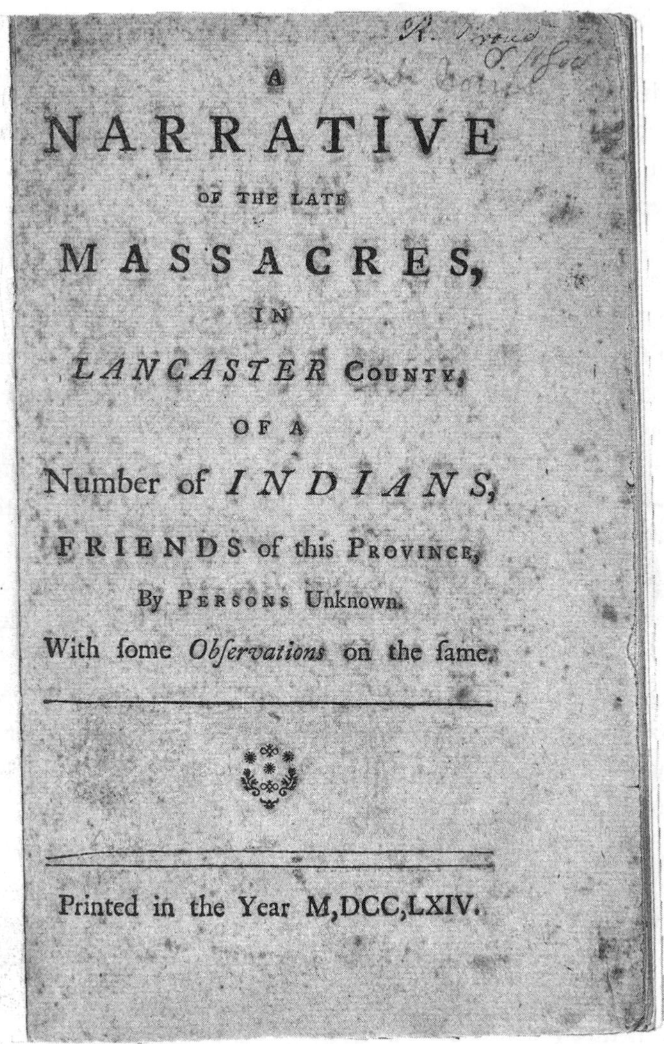

A
NARRATIVE
OF THE LATE
MASSACRES,
IN
LANCASTER COUNTY,
OF A
Number of *INDIANS*,
FRIENDS of this PROVINCE,
By PERSONS Unknown.
With ſome *Obſervations* on the ſame.

Printed in the Year M,DCC,LXIV.

In this thirty-page pamphlet published in 1764, Benjamin Franklin condemns the Paxton Boys' massacre of Conestoga Indian villagers in 1763, citing the incident as a violation of the diplomacy established between the Native nation and William Penn; a disgrace to Christian faith; and an insult to the British crown. Despite such public outcry, however, none of the perpetrators faced trials. In fact, in order to appease settler militia members who had marched into Philadelphia in pursuit of fleeing Native villagers, the Pennsylvania legislature incentivized further attacks on Indians, in July 1764 offering bounties for those who perpetrated such practices. This fueled subsequent attacks, including those by the Black Boys in 1765. (Reproduced with permission from the Historical Society of Pennsylvania.)

generated broader revolts, especially as Britain increased its diplomatic commitments to Native peoples after Pontiac's War.

The gulf between western settlers and colonial leaders was not new, but now it deepened.[148] Its potential for urban violence was, however, unprecedented. In fact, few colonial governments had been as threatened by their own settlers as was Philadelphia in the winter of 1764. Almost daily, Penn published proclamations, drafted letters to British officials, and made sets of inquiries about the nature of the spreading conflict.

His proclamation of January 2 offered £200 for the apprehension and prosecution of the massacre's leaders. It yielded few results. His government was so weak that Penn decided to send the remaining Conestoga refugees to New York for protection; however, Governor Cadwallader Colden stopped them at Albany, refusing them entry due to his own worries about encouraging militia violence.[149] By January 20, they had arrived at Trenton, where they were under the protection of English soldiers. They were cold, impoverished, and homeless—more in fact died from hunger and disease than were killed by the Paxton Boys. They soon came back to Philadelphia, where they resided in barracks, a temporary respite for those whose mere presence attracted vigilantes and repulsed the leaders of other colonies. As Colden saw it, "They consist of a number of rogues and thieves, runaways from the other Nations, and for that reason not to be trusted. . . . [They] are the most obnoxious to the People of this Province or any."[150]

When news of their return circulated, the Paxton Boys continued their threats, reporting that over a thousand more of their adherents would descend on Philadelphia to destroy the Moravian Indians. They threatened to mobilize even more if needed. Pacifist Quakers would be spared, unless they interfered, but the homes of those hiding Indians would be burned.[151] Civil strife and further violence loomed.

A popular newsman and elected leader, Franklin stood with the colony's leaders and the monarchy behind it. "Dr. Franklin" even carried loyalties in his title, having returned from England with an honorary degree, a sign to many of his aristocratic leanings and elite sensibilities.[152] As Penn published his proclamation against the vigilantes, Franklin wrote about "My love to England and my Friends there." He concludes one letter with expressions of faith in "the future Course of his Majesty's Reign, which I predict will be happy and truly glorious."[153] Like Governor Penn, he abhorred mob violence and believed in the rule of law. In his efforts to stop vigilantes, he turned to his trusted newspaper for defense.

As Conestoga Indians traveled across the winter landscape, Franklin wrote an impassioned pamphlet. He was not the only one; his was one of sixty-three publications concerning the massacres of the Conestoga Indians and the march of the Paxton Boys on Philadelphia.[154] Entitled *A Narrative of the Late Massacres, in Lancaster Country, of a Number of Indians, Friends of this Province, by Persons Unknown,* it is one of the few texts in colonial America to indict colonists of Indian hating.[155] While the moral iniquity of Franklin's fellow Pennsylvanians is its target, it also offers effusive praise for the "just and generous Actions [of] . . . the King's Forces." They had been called to protect the 140 remaining Conestoga, "now trembling for their lives." Their protection, Franklin concludes, "endear the Military to the Civil Power."[156]

"The only Crime" of the Conestoga, Franklin writes, "seems to have been, that they had a reddish brown Skin, and Black hair." Outraged, he asks for any evidence of their alleged participation in Pontiac's War: "I thus publicly call on the Makers and Venders of these Accusations to produce their Evidence. . . . What had little Boys and Girls done; what could Children of a year old, Babes at the Breast, what could they do, that they too must be shot and hatcheted?" Such action, he concludes, "is done by no civilized Nation . . . [especially] not against their Friends."[157] Printed in early 1764, the pamphlet circulated widely and is included in editions of Franklin's writings. It identified a common racial animus forming among the interior's "Christian White Savages," whose violent behaviors simultaneously bridged religious divides and became a dominant political force.[158]

Pontiac's War and the Political Culture of Interior Settlements

The Paxton Boys dispersed before reaching Philadelphia. They disbanded following a meeting at Germantown with Franklin and other colonial leaders. They did not, however, disappear. An interior political culture was forming that disdained Indians and the eastern officials who supported them. Penn wrote to Gage for increased troops to quell the unrest. But Gage, who had replaced Amherst in November, had little interest in policing mob violence. He was now charged with overseeing all of British North America, and his primary focus in 1764 was preparing for campaigns against Pontiac, not civil affairs.

Gage had been in North America for ten years. He commanded forces through a decade of war, peace, and now renewed mobilization. Before being recalled, Amherst had exhorted him to make no peace with interior Indians until they had been "Sufficiently Punished" and their leaders captured or executed.[159] With most of the interior forts destroyed, Gage's campaign in 1764 would be costly and consuming. Pennsylvania would have to defuse its own settlers.

Gage's persistence in prioritizing interior diplomacy reflected the commitments of British leaders. Civil authority was to be handled by governors. Matters of empire necessitated interior stabilization. Ironically, the commander of British forces became plagued in the years ahead by such colonial divisions. As Indian affairs became more violent, they spurred increased conflicts across society. An interlinked imperial and Indigenous paradox soon emerged: Indian confederations and British commanders directed their power at one another rather than at the most threatening communities on the continent—British settlers.

Pontiac's War ignited the collective action of Pennsylvania's settlers and their growing self-identification. After 1760 frontiersmen saw themselves as different from settlers to the east because of their dissimilar experiences and conditions. They derided easterners as "our fellow subjects who being remove[d] from danger, sit as ease and know not what we feel."[160] They viewed concentrated authority differently and came to resent it. As George Croghan noted, "It can not be even supposed that any Authority . . . will be paid any Regard to by those Unruly Settlers."[161]

Beginning in 1764, Gage underestimated the power of vigilantes and ultimately of organized rebellion. Amherst was recalled because of his losses to Pontiac, and Gage would similarly be dismissed a decade later after the battles of Lexington and Bunker Hill. In a little more than a decade, interior politics and settler rebellions deposed two of Britain's leading generals.

The crisis of Pontiac's War toppled more than England's military commanders. The structures of interior diplomacy, the Proclamation Line of 1763, and interior tribes' once-recognized authority crumbled in its aftermath because whereas Gage, Sir William Johnson in New York, and interior traders–cum diplomats like Croghan prioritized trade and diplomacy, the Paxton Boys and other rebels offered new alternatives.[162] While Johnson, Gage, and Croghan organized diplomatic solutions, settlers organized for violence. They unseated unpopular legislative leaders, blocked the passage of imperial supplies, and began raising a militia.

The settler rebellions that started in December 1763 at Conestoga continued with marches on Philadelphia in 1764 and into 1765, when Gage believed that Britain had finally achieved peace in the Great Lakes region. The siege of Detroit had ended in late 1763, and Pontiac began negotiating a truce. In early

1765, Croghan was ordered to Fort Pitt to begin loading provisions for five anticipated conferences with Pontiac that would mark an end to the war.[163]

The prospects of peace, however, stoked fears among settlers. Peace with Indians was to be feared, not celebrated—any forms of diplomacy suggested the continued autonomy of Indian peoples. When Croghan arrived in February at Fort Pitt to begin preparations to convene the region's Native leaders, he was optimistic. He aspired to restore lost trading partnerships and consolidate Britain's profitable new monopoly over interior furs. A world of peace, trade, and assurances, he and other officials believed, would bring stability and continued revenue. They were wrong. A revolution of settlers was forming, and its primary concerns were Britain's renewed commitments to provisioning Native peoples.

No longer called the Paxton Boys, these new rebels became known as the Black Boys because they "painted [their] faces red and black, like Indian warriors," as leader James Smith later recalled; they did so to impart "Indian discipline, as I know of no other at that time, which would answer the purpose."[164] At the core of their beliefs was the tenet that Native peoples deserved no place in the region. It was a belief they were willing to kill for. Just as the Paxton Boys had murdered with unbridled fury, the Black Boys also challenged the crown's authority with violence.[165] They attacked Indians and the British officials who provisioned them. More than anything, these settlers feared becoming involved in another prolonged war because, as Smith summarized, "the frontiers received no assistance from the state."[166] This fear of renewed conflict prompted their organization, their defiance, and their use of violence. Like Neolin and Pontiac two years prior, they believed in radical, not consensual, reforms.

Like all revolutionaries, the Black Boys used violence to build new forms of politics. Their performance of such violence was, however, uncommon. Not only did they dress similarly to Indians, they used the tactics of guerrilla warfare, which many had experienced during the preceding decade of war. For them, the Seven Years' War had never ended. After Pontiac's War, they dreaded what they termed "a third Indian war."[167] Their fear of Indians had hardened into hatred, and it soon spread in revolutionary waves.

"To Serve the Enemies of Mankind": The Indigenous Origins of the Revolution

Across the backcountry, print culture helped to foment rebellion. Notices appeared along Forbes Road from Philadelphia to Fort Pitt. Billets called on settlers to band together "to prevent the carrying [of] ammunition and the like to the Indians."[168] The three-hundred-mile road passed growing settlements of Scots-Irish settlers and drew tens of thousands of migrants west.[169] Taverns welcomed travelers and forts dotted the path as the road wound its way to Fort Pitt where, in March 1765, George Croghan waited.

Croghan had lived in the interior for two decades. To survive, he worked across its ethnic, racial, linguistic, and political divisions. Like his first posts discussed in chapter 4, his new home outside Fort Pitt appeared on the colony's maps. His standing had grown since the war. He spent much of 1764 in England meeting with state officials, discussing speculative land prospects, and hearing perspectives on Pontiac's War. He heard much disappointment about the military's response. As he wrote, "General Amhirsts Conduct is Condemd by Everybody and has been pelted away in the papers."[170]

Amherst and Pontiac had come to represent opposite poles of understandings about the interior's imbalance. Croghan now became the single individual charged with restoring equilibrium. After returning from abroad, he moved to convene what he anticipated would be an end to Pontiac's War. He hoped to bring stability to an interior world racked with conflict. To do so, he assembled in Philadelphia a supply train of over eighty packhorses carrying trade goods. It was one of the largest diplomatic efforts in U.S. colonial history.[171]

Loaded with clothes, wampum, beads, knives, alcohol, and ammunition, this supply train carried the goods that were to guarantee the empire's assurances. As they had for over a century, trade goods remained a lifeline for interior peoples. Both the Seven Years' War and Pontiac's War had erupted partly due to trade disputes. With imperial consent, Croghan returned to the interior to deliver the goods that all knew were needed for peace. Without trade, words were empty. Without exchange, peace was an illusion.

Starting on March 6, groups of armed rebels intercepted the supply trains. They burned them, forced the return of traders, and even laid siege to English forts in the region. These were insurgents, not thieves or "robbers, as they called us," Smith wrote.[172] Pillage was not their intention. They aimed to curb Indian access to trade, especially ammunition, and with it "the great danger the frontier inhabitants would be exposed to, if the Indians should now get a supply."[173] Like the Paxton Boys, the Black Boys sought to destroy what one leader termed the "independent commonwealths among us." Indians, above all others, "were our most dangerous enemies."[174]

Throughout March, raids, skirmishes, and confusion erupted across western Pennsylvania. Few officials understood the grievances or took seriously the power behind them. For example, after six of their men were captured, several hundred Black Boys under Smith's leadership surrounded Fort Loudon on March 9.[175] Its commander, Lieutenant Charles Grant, knew American warfare well. He had laid siege to Quebec and Montreal. He knew what sieges entailed and casually admitted Smith to negotiate, asking him "what he meant by appearing with such a mob before the King's Fort." When informed that they came for the prisoners, Grant responded with surprise, asking what Smith might do if the prisoners "were sent to Carlisle and escorted by the King's troops." To which Smith replied that "if they would not give up the prisoners . . . they were determined to fight the troops and die to a man."[176]

Uncertain about his jurisdiction over criminal affairs, Grant released the six in custody. He also exchanged captured Black Boys for several of his own scouts whom Smith now held. This and subsequent exonerations emboldened the Black Boys, seemingly implying imperial acceptance of their open flouting of authority. Throughout March, Smith continued to waylay English soldiers as well as officers. After Grant "refused" to give up "a number of riffles . . . we took him prisoner, and detained him until he delivered up the arms; we also destroyed a larger quantity of gun-powder that the traders had stored up [inside the fort], lest it might be conveyed privately to the Indians. . . . The king's troops, and our party, had now got entirely out of the channel of the civil war, and many unjustifiable things were done by both parties."[177]

Governor Penn, attempting to restore his administration's rule of law, arrived in Carlisle in April to convene a grand jury to indict those who intercepted the trade. He failed. The jury found "not sufficient testimony to convict a single person" and even went so far as to remind the court of their own hostility toward Native peoples.[178] The governor received not the justice he had anticipated but instead confirmation of the interior's independence. In the months to come, the Black Boys militia inspected all westbound vehicles for ammunition and other "warlike stores." They even issued their own passports.[179]

The foundations of British authority in the interior were now crumbling. An emergent settler sovereignty had formed.[180] Settlers used their own diplomacy, legal reasoning, and collective violence to secure their goals and establish their legitimacy. Unleashed in the first year of Pontiac's War, such sovereignty hardened into a new political movement. It was both distinctive and growing, and it now targeted English soldiers. As one of Governor Penn's allies had blithely observed about his office's authority, "There is no standing army to inforce its laws and support the government."[181]

Stopping interior trade, limiting the power of seaport elites, and driving Native peoples from the region formed the foundations of an emerging political culture that one scholar has termed "popular constitutionalism."[182] It was a violent political culture in which negotiations were best conducted between armed parties.

The start of the fall of the British empire in North America began on the Pennsylvania frontier, and it occurred on March 5, 1765, with Smith's first raid.[183] William Penn's "Peaceable Kingdom" had ended. A divided and contested landscape emerged, and across the interior, settlers celebrated the Black Boys in both verse and song, as an anthem attributed to Irishman George Campbell reveals:

> Astonished at the wild design [of British trading policies], frontier inhabitants combined, with brave souls to stop their career . . .
>
> On March the fifth, in sixty-five [1765], their Indian presents did arrive, In long pomp and cavalcade . . .
>
> Some patriots did their train surprise, And quick as lightning tumbled their loads, and kindled them bonfires in the woods, and mostly burnt their whole brigade.
>
> At [Fort] Loudon, when they heard the news, They scarcely knew which way to choose . . .
>
> At length some soldiers they sent out . . . And seized some men . . . [and] laid them fast
>
> But men of resolution thought, too much to see their neighbors caught, For no crime but false surmise
>
> They join'd a warlike band, and march'd to Loudon out of hand, and kept the jailors prisoners there, until our friends enlarged were, Without fraud or any disguise.
>
> Let mankind censure or commend, This rash performance in the end, Then both sides will find their account. 'Tis true no law can justify, to burn our neighbors property, But when this property is designed to serve the enemies of mankind. It's high treason in the amount.[184]

After 1765

Like autumn leaves, the origins of the American Revolution are debated in seasonal and colorful ways. Boston remains prominent in such assessments. For generations, it has been seen as the site of the first organized ur-

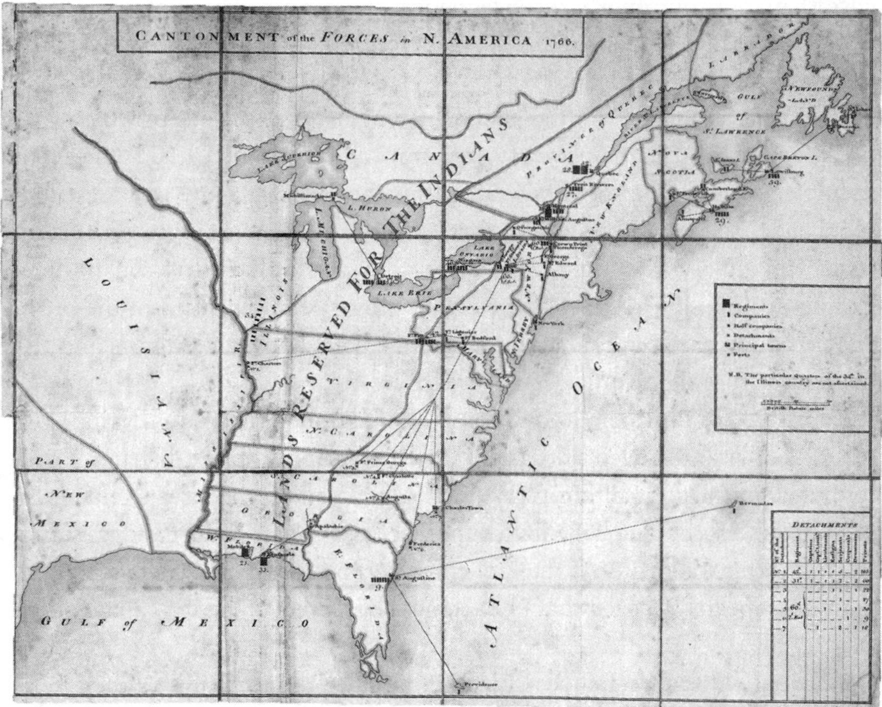

This map, issued by General Thomas Gage in 1767, shows the distribution of British forces in North America in 1766. The map designates lands west of the Appalachian Mountains as "Lands Reserved for the Indians," aligning with the political boundaries established by the Royal Proclamation of 1763. (William L. Clements Library, University of Michigan.)

ban "riots" in August 1765, when colonists organized to protest sugar and then stamp taxes.[185] A long-recognized crucible of the Revolution, the Boston Massacre of March 1770 remains a signature beginning, the sine qua non of the Revolution itself.[186]

While Indians and interior rebellions occasionally appear in such histories, neither has dislodged the proprietary hold of these more familiar assessments of the origins of the American Revolution. The Revolution, in nearly all narratives, originated in seaports, and the Enlightenment ideas of liberty, virtue, and self-representation continue to be seen as the principal forces motivating independence. Indeed, as Bernard Bailyn has suggested, "Ideas may be understood to have lain at the heart of the Revolutionary outbreak and to have shaped its outcome and consequences. . . . The outbreak of the Revolution was not the result of social discontent, or of economic disturbances in the colonies, or of rising misery."[187]

Numerous ironies surround such genealogies, the legacies of which continue to misconstrue the place of American Indians in the United States. For example, on July 15, 1776, eleven days after the issuing of the Declaration of Independence, Pennsylvanians continued the revolutionary processes that interior vigilantes had started. As a state, they wrote their first constitution. Benjamin Franklin was elected president after spending much of the previous decade working to bridge the social divisions between seaports and settlements across the colonies.

Completed in Philadelphia at the end of September, the Pennsylvania Constitution of 1776 reflected a decade of interior warfare and the distrust of concentrated and distant authority.[188] It was celebrated on the streets, eulogized in Sunday services, and contributed to the city's growing international standing as a refuge of virtue. As the French writer Joseph Cérutti later suggested, many Europeans believed that Philadelphia deserved "to be the capital of the world."[189]

Residents in the west choose Black Boy leader James Smith as their delegate to the constitutional convention. He was joined by his compatriot John Moore, who was assigned to a committee to write the state's "declaration of rights." Authority in the new government was "instituted for the common benefit, protection and security of the people, nation or community; and not for the particular emolument or advantage of any single man, family, or sett of men."[190]

Rooted in generations of concerns about concentrated familial, aristocratic, and monarchical authority, this constitution overturned the legitimacy of the former government. The crown was no longer sovereign. The state's people possessed authority under the principle of popular sovereignty. They—"the people"—would elect their representatives, justices of the peace, and state leaders.[191]

As Franklin had written in January 1764, "The mad armed Mob" shaped much of the region's politics, its principal target "the Assembly and their Friends."[192] Now, a decade later, the century-old assembly ceased to exist.[193] A new government had formed. It embodied a set of refined arguments and political tactics designed to appeal to all white men regardless of their ethnic, linguistic, and religious divides.[194] Despite their differences, they were now "the people." The structures of political authority in Pennsylvania had been inverted—indeed, revolutionized.[195]

Constituting the new states, keeping them united during war, and creating a "more perfect union" remained the challenge for Smith, Moore, Franklin, and others, such as Thomas Jefferson, who was also in Philadelphia in July 1776 to declare independence. Many returned eleven years later for a different Constitutional Convention, one where the place of Native Americans within the new union became debated and determined in enduring ways.

6 • Colonialism's Constitution

The Origins of Federal Indian Policy

> The white Americans . . . have the most rancorous antipathy
> to the whole race of Indians; and nothing is more common
> than to hear them talk of extirpating them totally from
> the face of the earth, men, women, and children.
> —*J. F. D. Smith (1784)*

In February 1783, another Treaty of Paris recognized the independence of the United States, and by year's end, the last American general completed his service. On December 23, 1783, after eight years of conflict, George Washington relinquished command of the Continental army and traveled to Congress to tender his resignation.[1] In early December, he had overseen the final British evacuations of New York, the demobilization of his troops, and their return to farms. It had been six years since he had visited Mount Vernon.[2]

Despite its many celebrations, 1783 had been a hard year for the general. It was even harder for his men. Shoes, gunpowder, and blankets were hard to come by.[3] Remembering his own struggles during the Seven Years' War to obtain interior lands as payment, Washington had grown weary trying to secure compensation for his soldiers. Many had not received payment in over two years. Every day the "crisis of 1783" deepened.[4] As he explained in May, it was better for the men to return to their homes unpaid rather than remain together "enraged, complaining of injustice."[5] Like other concentrations of power, angry veterans gathered together presented threats to republican liberties. With Christmas approaching, Washington finalized the army's demobilization, riding one last time as general.

So many bewildering changes had happened since his first days of combat at Great Meadows. In nearly thirty years, he had participated in countless battles in which thousands of Frenchmen, English soldiers, colonial militiamen, and Native soldiers had been killed. Over four thousand colonial forces had perished during the Revolution, all under his command.[6] In October 1781 seven thousand British soldiers surrendered at Yorktown. For the first time in his career, Washington received an enemy's formal surrender. Beforehand, he had lived in the shadow of defeat and had seen soldiers and noncombatants starve, freeze, and suffer. Following two cataclysmic wars and the fall of two empires, peace—at least for the colonists—had finally arrived.

While the battles with England had ended, conflicts of a different kind reoccurred. Congress, in particular, had become reviled. Even before the treaty, the new government was unpopular, and not only with its unpaid soldiers. Many elected to Congress were shocked by its inefficiency.[7] Meetings achieved little, debates wore on, and worries about finances seemingly drove all decisions. The former colonies were now independent, but they remained disunited.

Violence and protest also plagued the new Republic. By the time of Washington's retirement, Congress had moved to Annapolis due to growing protests in Philadelphia.[8] Only seven states bothered to send delegations—even Maryland's representatives were not present to receive their nation's conquering hero. As Thomas Jefferson wrote to James Madison on January 1, 1784, "Maryland is scarcely ever present, and we are now without a hope of it's [*sic*] attending till February."[9] Washington's decades of service, triumph at Yorktown, and celebrations of Evacuation Day were insufficient to draw a quorum to the Republic's legislature.

To many, the new union appeared more than ineffective: it seemed doomed. With fewer than nine states attending Congress, "we do nothing," Jefferson continued.[10] A hereditary leader or monarch seemed a potential outcome. As Boston merchant Benjamin Tappen wrote to future secretary of state Henry Knox, some form of absolutism was "absolutely necessary to save the states from sinking into the lowest abyss of misery."[11] Not only was Congress reviled but a common "disgust with the state leadership" further soured the nation's faith in government.[12]

Despite the uncertainties, Washington understood the necessary drama in front of him. Upon entry into Annapolis, he welcomed throngs of adoring citizens. They—and not their representatives—surrounded him in his last hours of service. As he later wrote, formally ending the "mighty Scene" of the Revolution was a necessity. The Revolution needed its requisite closing rituals, an end to what he termed "the Military Theatre" and the departure of its central protagonist.[13] Exact in his attire and ceremonial in his performance, he submitted his resignation and retired to Mount Vernon. Independence had been secured. Governing now awaited the deliberations of the people.

Thomas Paine in *Common Sense* had compared the spirit of 1776 to "the Birthday of a new world."[14] Many have lost sight of how nearly fatal a birth it was. After England had recognized American independence, it began the laborious tasks associated with its unexpected defeat. Fighting continued following the surrender at Yorktown. And now, throughout 1783, more people than ever were on the move: not only English soldiers still stationed across the Eastern Seaboard but also their thousands of Indian allies, including Iroquois soldiers stationed at British forts in eastern Canada. Where could those who fought with the English now seek refuge? Where could these and other "loyalists" turn for safety?

Those on the move also included nearly sixty thousand colonists as well as untold thousands of slaves who had sought freedom with English forces.[15] Former slaves included a "runaway" from the slave quarters at Mount Vernon, Harry Washington. Much to General Washington's dismay, Harry had left the United States for Nova Scotia in May. For eight years he lived in damp quarters outside Halifax and then joined a thousand African American refugees emigrating to Sierra Leone.[16] They included former slaves who had been children in Africa, including a one-hundred-year-old survivor of the Middle Passage who desired to "lay her bones" in the continent of her birth.[17] For so many the world had indeed been inverted by the war.

Virginia, Nova Scotia, and Sierra Leone became among the countless places interconnected by the Revolution. Throughout the 1780s, such interconnections grew. Space exploded for those in search of freedom and opportunities across the expansive former British empire. In particular, untold thousands headed into the American interior.

Even before the war ended, thousands of settlers had rushed into Kentucky. Across the trans-Appalachian West, they claimed Cherokee, Shawnee, and other Native hunting grounds as their own.[18] As it had in the previous half century, this interior world of the Native Inland Sea would determine much of the history of the new Republic. From Indian resistance to the enforcement of new national laws and policies, struggles over interior lands shaped the contours and eventual structures of the new American government.[19]

The colonization of the interior devastated the everyday lives of Native peoples and also contributed to the concentration of American political power. These interrelated processes of Indigenous dispossession and state formation originated in the aftermath of the Revolution. They continued for generations thereafter, laying the foundations of the early Republic.

Although unclear in 1783, the federal government's ultimate power, authority, and sovereignty over Native peoples (and of the American continent) became enshrined in the U.S. Constitution. Partly due to irresolvable struggles over interior lands and with Native Nations, America's Founding Fathers abandoned the first government of the United States—the Articles of Confederation—and adopted a new constitutional government in 1787. This originated from struggles to centralize power over the interior and expanded processes of colonialism thereafter.

While the Revolution changed the landscape for everyone, space shrank for some, including returning Virginian soldiers. After years of military service, many returned to the region's small-scale family farms and plantations. Like Washington, they settled into the familiar rhythms of agricultural production surrounded by their own slaves, or those of others, for whom the Revolution had brought only whispers of liberation.[20] Concentrated together across plantation counties and family farms, Virginians now constituted the largest state within the new Republic. Led by Washington, James Madison, Thomas Jefferson, James Monroe, and other gentry leaders, they were now sovereign across their far-reaching borders. The years ahead would determine what that sovereignty entailed.

American Indians and the Revolutionary Republic

For Native peoples, the Revolution itself was not a beginning. Nor was it an end, as its aftermath brought no semblance of peace. Across eastern America, the Revolution extended a generation of warfare and wrought destruction, death, disease, and displacement. For countless villagers, it deepened the challenges of procuring food, obtaining trade goods, and maintaining shelter, among other crises. Tens of thousands of Native forces had died during the conflict, the vast majority fighting as allies of the English. Colonial leaders had in fact targeted English-allied Native communities.[21]

Across Iroquoia and the interior South, American independence crystallized the defeats that revolutionary invasions had wrought. Thousands of Cherokee, Creek, and Iroquois soldiers died defending their homelands, while others fled into neighboring regions or abandoned hunting grounds altogether.[22] Unsuccessful in their alliances with England and now witnessing the rapid diminishment of their authority, Native communities relinquished claims to lands. Those who remained found themselves surrounded by settlers. During the decade of the Revolution, none suffered as heavily as interior Native communities.

The Continental army's invasions of Iroquoia in 1779–80 were determinative. Nearly eight generations after Samuel de Champlain had first attempted it, white soldiers occupied the Confederacy's central villages. While Champlain's last invasion of Iroquoia in 1615 had left him wounded and dispirited, in 1780 American general John Sullivan destroyed dozens of Iroquoian towns, hundreds of longhouses, and thousands of bushels of the "three sisters": corn, beans, and squash. American forces spent entire days burning the harvests of Iroquoian fields.[23]

Such scorched-earth tactics drove hundreds of Iroquois families to British forts for refuge. Poor shelter, limited supplies, and the cold took additional lives. One Onondaga chief reported that American forces had committed murder and rape: "They put to death all the Women and Children, excepting some of the Young Woman [*sic*], whom they carried away for the use of their Soldiers."[24]

The Cherokee had suffered similarly. Their leaders reported that revolutionary forces have "dyed their hands in the blood of many of our Women and Children, burnt 17 towns, destroyed all our provisions by which we & and our families were almost destroyed by famine."[25] Hunger now stalked the region, and in 1785 Cherokee leaders at the Treaty of Hopewell were forced to acknowledge themselves "to be under the protection of the United States of America, and of no other sovereign whosoever."[26]

Neighboring Creek Indians also suffered major losses. Their alliance with the British proved similarly ill fated. By war's end, Georgia's governor commented on recent Creek defeats: "[Their] bones now lay white upon the ground . . . Their women are now widows, and their children fatherless."[27] As among the Iroquois and Cherokee, independence underscored the growing power of the Republic over these lands and communities. Additional treaties soon secured settler authority even further.

Such defeats, however, did not mean dispossession. Treaties, after all, continued between Native communities and the federal government. In 1783, in one of its first acts, Congress adopted resolutions decreeing that "just and necessary . . . lines of property should be ascertained and established between the United States and them."[28] In 1787 such treaties became the "supreme law of the land" in the Constitution. Moreover, despite the bloodshed, Native peoples outside the original thirteen colonies maintained control over the majority of North America, which remained in 1783 predominately Indian Country.[29] From the Great Lakes to the Missouri River and through the Georgia backcountry, such "independent Indians" continued to control the continent.[30]

In 1776 few American settlers had crossed the Ohio River, let alone formed settlements across what would become known as "the Old Northwest." In fact, many believed that the Ohio River provided a natural and necessary boundary between the Great Lakes area and American settlers. Many also believed that the region remained poorly defined by the Treaty of Paris, particularly as English officers remained stationed across the Great Lakes.[31] As leaders of the confederated "United Indian Nations" declared to congressional agents at Detroit in 1786, "We again request of you . . . to order your surveyors and others, that mark out lands, to cease from crossing the Ohio."[32] Of all the regions during this revolutionary decade, the Ohio River remained engulfed in conflicts that showed no signs of abating. In March 1782 the Gnadenhutten Massacre of Christianized Indian converts by backcountry militiamen underscored the region's propensity for unmitigated violence.[33]

Throughout the ensuing decade, many insisted on the Ohio River as a physical and political boundary. In 1792 Indian women captured by the U.S. Army insisted that the Ohio River remain the boundary between their lands to the north and American lands to the south.[34] Relatedly, despite Sullivan's campaigns across Iroquoia, many northern territories remained vanquished but not incorporated into the Republic. A century and a half after its founding, Albany still remained the northernmost seat of colonial governance—home to officials with long-standing ties among the Iroquois. So while the specter of colonization haunted Indian communities, few conquests had secured the actual transfer of Indigenous lands to the United States. The Revolution had destabilized, devastated, and depopulated large swaths of interior homelands. It had not, however, conquered them.[35]

Moreover, little appeared certain in the wake of the Revolution. As with Congress's shifting locations, the form—and thus future—of the American government appeared undetermined. Its structure under the Articles of Confederation was ineffective. It did not have the revenue to maintain a standing army or the power to tax in order to do so. In Indian affairs, the Articles of Confederation gave the federal government powers over those Indians living outside the jurisdiction of any state but little clarity on anything else.[36] The Articles of Confederation constricted more than they confederated. As Alexander Hamilton wrote in 1782, only a stronger national government could override the "prejudices in the particular states"; however, Congress remained mired in debt, debates, and despondency.[37] It struggled to muster a quorum, and by 1786, after moving to New York, it achieved a quorum only 15 percent of the time.[38]

The French and English empires had collapsed in eastern North America due to their inabilities to govern interior lands. Each possessed navies, armies, colonies, cities, treasuries, and diversified economies.[39] They maintained superior systems of taxation, transportation, and communication.[40] The American Republic lacked such systems and could hardly envision them. Only in the 1770s had Philadelphia and New York grown larger than the pre-Columbian city-state of Cahokia, and no American seaport came close to rivaling either Paris or London in size or influence. In these empires, authorities regulated economies, governed agrarian populations, and managed bureaucracies that included centuries-old jails and judiciaries, police and constable units, and property and customs offices.[41]

On the seas, such disparities were even more apparent. It would take over a century before the American navy resembled those of the English and French, each of which controlled colonies, ports, and nautical offices across the globe. Moreover, after the Revolution, the standing army also shrank to 625 poorly paid and inadequately supplied soldiers.[42] How could a newly independent and agrarian country impose greater authority than these empires? Questions of national power perplexed the young Republic.

Interior Indian Lands and the Origins of American Federalism

Indian lands provided solutions to the Republic's economic dilemmas and helped the United States overcome its comparative disadvantages. In 1783 the interior offered the nearly limitless resources in one commodity that had drawn Europeans deep into the continent: furs. The fur trade flourished throughout the eighteenth and nineteenth centuries, as Francophone, Anglophone, and later American traders, such as John Jacob Astor, amassed spectacular fortunes. Astor became the wealthiest person in the Republic, later shifting his fortunes to real estate, as Indian-harvested furs helped to fuel the eventual rise of New York City's skyline.[43] As Thomas Jefferson suggested in 1784, Virginians should obtain not only access to interior lands but also "a monopoly of the Western & Indian trade."[44]

The interior, however, offered far more than furs and animal skins, such as deer and bison. Above all, it offered the prospect for property, especially as land ownership became synonymous with American democracy.[45] No other resource in American history has been so important, and interior lands became the nation's "treasure chest."[46]

After Yorktown, opportunities for surveying, purchase, and settlement fueled western expansion. With the war over, settlers rushed west into western Virginia and Kentucky, where fur traders cum surveyors such as Daniel Boone acquired title to tens of thousands of acres. Initially drawn to hunt and trade, settlers turned to land speculation, which became the region's dominant economy.

From 1782 to 1786, as deputy surveyor for Fayette County, Boone concluded 150 land surveys. Some totaled fifteen thousand acres. Working nearly every day, he traveled across, inspected, and drafted land surveys that claimed hundreds of thousands of acres, twenty thousand of which were done in his own name.[47] Every waking hour (except Sundays), he claimed an acre of interior land.

As land frenzy gripped the Republic, Boone was outpaced by more propertied interests such as Richard Henderson and John May, whose claims each reached into the hundreds of thousands. Like Washington, these Virginians fixated on the wealth of the interior. They understood the potential for capital accumulation and joined others in controlling the region's land holdings and its politics. Soon Virginians dominated the territorial governments of the interior.[48] And they were not alone. As Presbyterian minister David Rice wrote of his first trip to Kentucky, land speculation flowed "in such a torrent that it would bear down every weak obstacle that stood in its way."[49]

Land acquisition expanded the Republic's treasure chest, offering land in exchange for capital as well as opportunities for speculation. It also undercut the autonomy of Native peoples. Settler colonialism, by definition, advantages settlers over Indigenous peoples, and this deluge rapidly alienated millions of acres from tribes such as the Cherokee, whose recent military defeats confirmed their diminished powers. In a complex process of law, politics, and economics, tribes ceded large swaths of their territories to the Republic through treaties, thereby opening lands for survey, purchase, and eventual settlement.

During the late British period with conferences such as the 1768 Treaty of Fort Stanwix, treaties facilitated U.S. territorial acquisition. Initially ambiguous, this process became law under the Constitution in 1787 and was eventually clarified by the U.S. Supreme Court in *Johnson v. McIntosh* (1823), which upheld the supremacy of the federal government to oversee interior land acquisitions. These developments, however, had not yet occurred. In 1783 the Supreme Court, like the U.S. Constitution, did not exist.

Treaties are bilateral agreements between recognized sovereigns. In negotiations, Native leaders ceded not their primary homelands but unsettled hunting grounds and fought to retain the sites of their villages, graveyards, and sacred sites.[50] In Kentucky, vast hillside forests and bluegrass plains had provided hunting lands to generations of Cherokees to the south and to Algonquian-speaking Delawares, Shawnees, and Miami Indians to the north.[51] Throughout the 1780s, Kentucky's torrent of settlers had become a tidal wave. By 1818, as one guidebook boasted, "No where in America has the almost instantaneous change, from an uncultivated waste to the elegances of civilization, been so striking."[52]

The formation of Kentucky devastated the region's hunting economies and drove resident Native people north of the Ohio River and closer to British forces. Indian people throughout the Great Lakes region knew that British forces remained stationed across North America. Forts at Detroit, Michilimackinac, St. Joseph (Port Huron), Niagara, Montreal, and farther east at Louisbourg remained under English control. In 1794 the Jay Treaty clarified some of these ongoing border controversies.[53] Additionally, French and Spanish leaders claimed St. Louis and New Orleans and worked with regional Indian powers. Moreover, within English forts, British commanders said they were waiting for a resumption of conflicts, which they believed were certain to materialize. Indians would again be key allies during such conflicts and able to command resources, allegiances, and territorial control. Accordingly, from the perspective of interior Native communities, little about the Republic generated stability.

Yet one thing was certain: interior white settlements generated endless tensions with Native nations, particularly regarding land claims and the respective jurisdiction of tribal communities. As Seneca leader Red Jacket explained to New York leaders, "You tell us that our Country is within the lines of the States. . . . This surprises us, for we had thought our Lands were our own."[54] Red Jacket was not alone. Everywhere in 1783, confusion brewed. Was it the states, the larger national government, or individuals themselves who now controlled interior American lands?[55] Who held title to these newly acquired lands, particularly in states will ill-defined boundaries, including Virginia, New York, and Pennsylvania? Did states or the federal government have the power to tax interior acquisitions and their sales, and were smaller states destined to become dwarfed by the larger states in the Union?

After the Revolution these questions remained not only unsettled but seemingly unanswerable. They invited divergent opinions and bred growing conflicts. Clear answers often came only through force, as in Kentucky, where white settlers amassed in such numbers that they appeared to constitute their own nation. Like any treasure, the bounty of interior lands created both allure and division. All understood that possession brought not only wealth but power.

Managing claims to the interior and governing its transfer into the Union became leading practices of the new Republic.[56] Vexing questions of taxation were also linked to disputes over property. In 1783 returning soldiers looked to the national government to provide compensation for their service and relief from taxes. During the war, state legislatures passed measures designed to protect citizen-soldiers from debt collection, but a terrible recession beset the Republic, limiting such tax forgiveness.[57] During the Revolution, soldiers were authorized to use personal property, such as horses, to fulfill their debts. Increasingly, after the war they lost such rights and were expected to use silver or gold, which were always in limited supply.

As the national government struggled to pay back its wartime loans, state governments responded to their citizens' spiraling debts by printing new currencies. The problem, of course, was that such practices generated little national revenue, fueled inflation, and limited Congress's ability to pay the nation's debts.[58] Many, in fact, believed the printing of state currencies to be the single greatest threat to the national economy. At a time when citizens' loyalties remained overwhelming local—to their families, their towns, the states where they were born—farmers developed distrust of the national government. Congress had failed to pay its soldiers and now prohibited state legislatures from doing so. As they looked upon their new nation, many also gazed upon the firearms above their entryways with which they had gained fluency during the Revolution.

From Washington's resignation in 1783 to his election as president in 1789, the United States survived myriad problems. The central challenge of the era—nation formation—yielded a new government and a governing Constitution that remains among the most interpreted and influential texts in human history.

Indians and their lands informed the Constitution and influenced the deliberations of the "Founding Fathers." The anticipated prosperity of the interior provided the canvas upon which the strokes of the Constitution were painted. During this half decade, the enticement of Indian lands drew speculators such as James Madison, visitors such as the marquis de Lafayette, and settlers such as Daniel Boone deeper into the interior, where the power of Indian nations (and confederacies) weighed upon American policy makers. U.S. leaders adopted policies that stabilized the precariousness of the Union through interior land regulation, oversight, and eventual purchase, as Indian lands helped to fuel U.S. expansion.

As land speculation vexed the post-1783 interior world, white settlers and squatters confronted interior Native nations outside the institutions of the Republic. Managing interior white settlements and Indigenous nations became interrelated concerns for American leaders. To transform interior Indian homelands into stable farms, plantations, and eventual territories would not be easy. Nor would it be peaceful. For many, Indians were simply in the way. "Had it not been for the hostile appearances in the Indians," Massachusetts congressman Nathan Dane moaned to his state legislature, "7,000,000 acres of the land belonging to the United States would now have been surveyed, and ready for sale."[59] The wealth of the new nation resided in its interior. So, however, did its central antagonists. New battles were certain, and violence would be used on both sides. As U.S. treaty commissioners relayed to Indian delegates at interior treaty negotiations: "The arms of the United states are again exerted against you. . . . The United States wish to give you peace . . . but, if you foolishly prefer war, [our] warriors are ready to meet you in battle."[60]

The U.S. Constitution reflects such multi-polarity. In particular, it grants exclusive authority to the federal government to regulate trade and commerce with Native peoples. As article 1 establishes, the federal government holds the power to levy taxes, adjudicate disputes, and administer "commerce with foreign nations, and among the several states, and with the Indian tribes." These last five words identify Indian tribes as comparable to "states" and "foreign nations."[61] As it has been interpreted over time, the commerce clause recognizes the inherent sovereignty of Indian nations and the supremacy of the federal government in maintaining relationships with them. In this constitutional system, tribes possess authority over their lands, members, and those who pass through them. They exert such authorities through their own structures of governance and do so under the jurisdiction of the federal government, not the states.

Such recognition evolved out of the multilateral world of the founding of the United States. Framers understood Native nations to be powerful but struggled to identify such powers vis-à-vis those of the Republic. During the Constitutional Convention, drafters confronted the urgency of balancing individual and states' rights and to do so with limited national powers. All powers ceded by the states to the federal government followed this essential balancing act. Lodging Indian diplomacy as well as the power of treaty making along with other centralized powers with a "federalist" government, the Constitution established new doctrines of law and governance. Such doctrines, however, remained untested.

The Chaotic Interior and the Republic's Search for Order

Following the Revolution, settlers flooded interior Indian lands, doubling, tripling, and even quadrupling in number. In the summer of 1784, Spanish leaders in Louisiana heard of such invasions as Native leaders decried settlers who formed "like a plague of locusts in the territories of the Ohio River."[62] By century's end, western Pennsylvania held ninety-five thousand settlers, up from thirty-three thousand before the war. Kentucky's settlers had grown even faster, from twelve thousand in 1783 to seventy-three thousand in 1790.[63] Such settlements did indeed constitute an infestation. Settlers, as Washington complained, came to speculate, squat, and plunder, giving "great discontent to the Indians."[64]

Such an infestation eroded not only Indian autonomy but also attempts at national authority. Such expansion needed to occur through formal mechanisms of law and governance. Converting Indian homelands into American properties, Washington believed, would provide homes for citizens, fill the nation's depleted treasury, and ensure the country's stability and growth.[65]

Chaos, rather than order, accompanied expansion. Everywhere settlers were strapped for cash. So too were their leaders. In 1784 Jefferson had suffered the indignity and "mortification" of the arrival of debt collectors: "to have our horses turned out of the livery stable for want of money."[66] Interior settlers were even more challenged economically. They did not (yet) possess plantations, horse herds, or personal property and were less able to weather the economic crises that followed independence. They often used violence to secure resources. In Kentucky, male settlers often became territorial militiamen. Each year after independence, hundreds crossed the Ohio River to raid Indian villages, targeting Algonquian-speaking villages in southern Ohio and Indiana.

Raiders came for many things, including Indian trade silver, which had circulated across the region since the 1600s. The plunder of silver holdings accelerated colonization, providing the scarce hard currencies needed to obtain seeds, farming equipment, and related household goods. Raiding enabled settlers to overcome their lack of currencies while simultaneously destabilizing Indian sovereignty.

Since the earliest days of the French empire, Native allies had been gifted

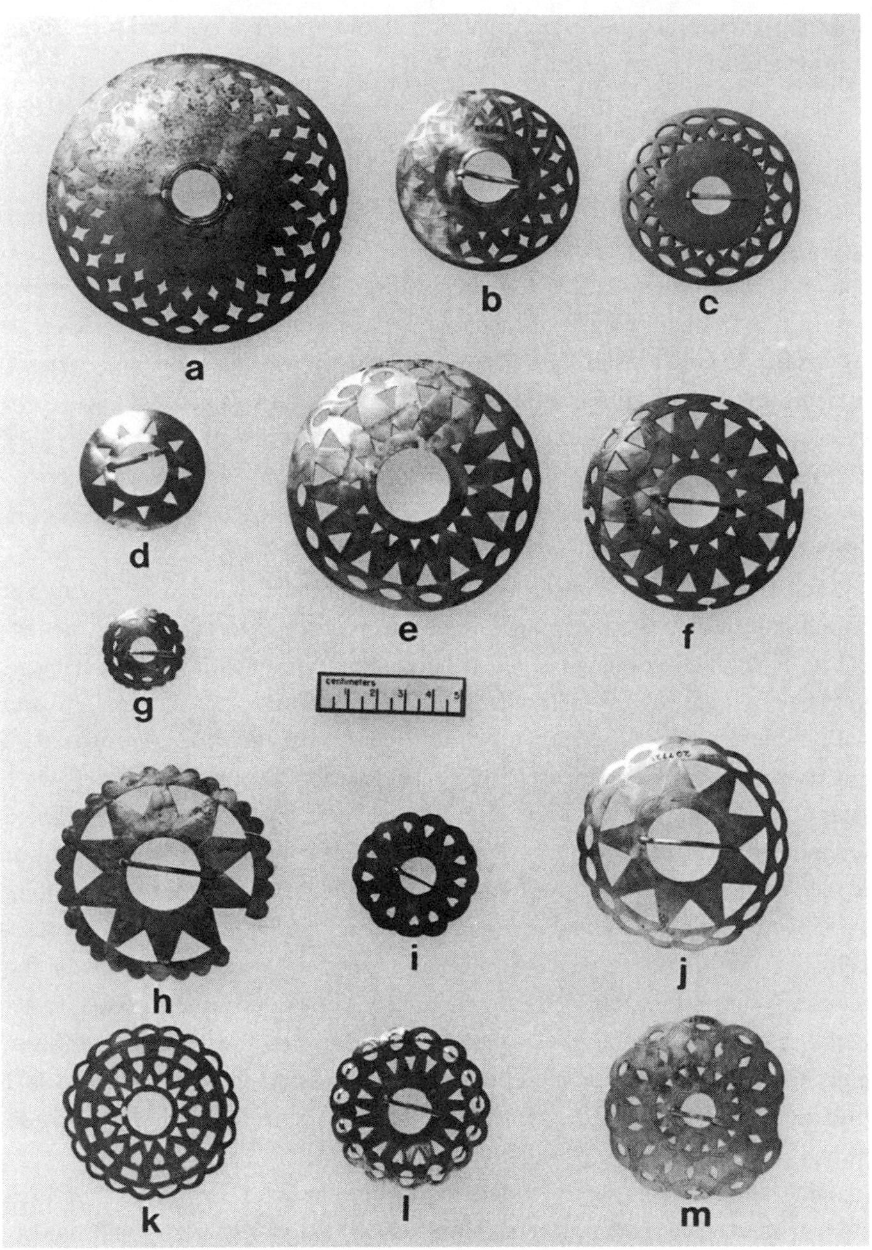

Generations of Great Lakes Indian families and individuals accumulated silver disk brooches across the Native Inland Sea. This image shows various brooches created in the late eighteenth to early nineteenth century. (© The Field Museum, Image No. A111317, Photographer Ron Testa.)

French silverware, jewelry, and ornaments. Silver was, in fact, ubiquitous. Beginning in the seventeenth century, silver coins, religious beads, and silverware were refashioned by Native craftspeople into other things. They molded, reshaped, and even recast them into forms of decoration. French traders came to understand the growing need for such items, and over time Francophone silversmiths made myriad trade items, including arm cuffs, small crosses, buttons, bells for women's dresses, and adornments for men's jackets. Some individual pieces of Native clothing came to hold dozens and at times hundreds of such "brooches," as they became known.[67] Trade silver so adorned nineteenth-century Native men and women that countless portraits of Native people showcased such silverware.[68]

For Native peoples, trade silver provided more than decoration. It became a means of securing wealth.[69] As silver adorned the body, in times of scarcity, Indian women used brooches as currency.[70] Easily detachable from jackets or dresses, these valued items circulated for generations, commonly traded both between Indian villages and within them.

Moreover, after independence, Indian silver increasingly provided Native villagers with unanticipated financial repositories. Throughout the eighteenth century, as silver became scarce in the colonial world, Great Lakes Indian villages retained an economic autonomy that supported their political independence. Some were as prosperous as their nearby Francophone and early settler neighbors. At a time of continental scarcity, Great Lakes Indians possessed bounties of silver.

Such prosperity can be measured in the region's silver trade. In 1767 George Morgan, a trader at Fort Pitt, received 201 silver brooches for his commerce with interior Native peoples. He also received hundreds of smaller "rings of stone," "small heart drops," and "silver Morris bells," among other items.[71] Unlike cloth, ammunition, or alcohol, silver was not consumable. It was reused and accumulated, and silversmiths from Detroit to Montreal expanded their silver production, particularly as the fur trade reached farther west. In 1801 one Montreal silversmith, Robert Cruikshank, produced over forty-nine thousand individual pieces.[72]

Aware of such silver trade networks, American settlers raided into "the Indian side of the Ohio," as the region became known. They returned with untold amounts of such plunder, which they quickly fashioned into coins and currency, as thousands of pieces of stolen silver ended up in Kentucky settlers' pockets. Flash-sale auctions popped up along the Kentucky frontier as returning raiders sold their loot and divided the profits.[73]

Such theft fueled Kentucky's growth. It also became a prelude to murder,

Alfred M. Hoffy's 1837 portrait of Tshusick, an Ojibwe woman who spoke French and English and lived in various village and fort communities across the Native Inland Sea. Upon her arrival in Washington, D.C., in 1826, she successfully navigated the city's social world, even receiving the valuable silver brooches that here adorn her chest. As in eighteenth-century portraits of Great Lakes Indians, her clothing reflects a fusion of European and Ojibwe styles. (Courtesy of the Library of Congress, Prints & Photographs Division, LC-DIG-pga-07591.)

as bounty systems in Indian scalps paralleled the expansion of the practice. Across the backcountry, state leaders offered rewards for Indian body parts. In Pennsylvania, Governor Joseph Reed offered $100 bounties for Indian scalps, as did leaders in South Carolina. In Kentucky, settlers eagerly extended such traffic to include body parts dug from resident Shawnee graves.[74] Violence, instability, and conflict resonated from Kentucky's proliferating settlements as settlers targeted nearby Indian villages across the Ohio River. Such raiding fueled the escalation of regional conflict and soon renewed global warfare during the War of 1812.

The first years of American independence along the Ohio presaged a violent future, and such violence—both ongoing and anticipated—fueled American debates about the nation's structures of government. From interior land policies to the determination of the size and purposes of a national army, the interior shaped the formation of the Republic.[75] The interior provided what many in Europe understood to be the Republic's future. As the Spanish Count d'Aranda anxiously wrote to the Spanish crown in 1783 after reiterating Spain's contestation of American claims to the lower Mississippi:

> A day will come when it [the United States] will be a giant, even a colossus. . . . The facility of establishing a new population on immense lands, as well as the advantage of a new government, will draw thither farmers and artisans from all nations. In a few years, we shall watch with grief the tyrannical existence of this same colossus.[76]

When States Illegally Seized Indian Lands: New York and Iroquoia in the 1780s

In New York, settlers similarly rushed into interior river valleys. They coveted in particular the lands of the Mohawk River Valley. Like Pennsylvania and Virginia, New York had undetermined western boundaries, and state competition over interior lands became a central problem under the Articles of Confederation. As early as October 1777, Congress debated proposals that aimed to grant the national government the exclusive authority to control, administer, and oversee the sale of western lands.[77] Congress, however, remained too divided to establish a national policy.[78] Many smaller states, such as Rhode Island and Delaware, hoped to limit the growth of larger states as growing problems of national governance emerged alongside the expansion of the Republic. Repeatedly, as American citizens eyed interior lands, their state governments also competed for them.

Who exactly held the authority to obtain western lands? Many in Congress believed that only a central governing body—the federal government—had the power to secure and administer interior land transfers. They called for increased federal powers. Other states and interior settlers believed that states held an independent right of discovery from their original crown charters. More worrisome, individual citizens often believed their personal claims trumped those of other claimants.[79] When in 1785 Congress sent General Josiah Hamar to compel settlers to leave contested lands, they argued that "Congress is not empowered to forbid" interior settlement and suggested they planned to create their own government.[80]

As had England earlier, the young Republic hoped to achieve land acquisition through treaty rather than costly wars. As Washington suggested, the Republic needed orderly mechanisms for regulating land acquisition and settlement. The Republic needed laws. As land fever gripped the nation, the right of individuals, states, and the national government to obtain clear title generated competing claims, particularly in Iroquoia.

Like Kentucky settlers, New York officials hoped to acquire as much land as possible. They aimed for the vast lands governed by the Iroquois Confederacy. For much of the eighteenth century, the Iroquois had thwarted competing imperial demands over an expanse of Ohio River territory between western Virginia and the Great Lakes. Much of this territory was inhabited by other tribes whose allegiances the Iroquois had cultivated. Confederacy leaders had blocked imperial efforts to claim the interior until 1768, when English officials finally acquired Iroquois cessations of Ohio River lands.[81]

Shortly after independence, national officials gathered in October 1784 at Fort Stanwix to accelerate the dispossession. They came this time not for the lands of other Indians, but for those of the Iroquois themselves. And they were not alone. Joining them from the start were New York State's leaders, whose simultaneous efforts made it unclear which authority—Congress's representatives or those of New York—held the authority to conduct such negotiations. As New York governor George Clinton declared: "I shall have no objection to . . . improving . . . the advantage of the United States, expecting however and positively stipulating that no long agreement to be entered into with Indians residing within the Jurisdiction of this State, *with whom only I mean to treat.*"[82] New York, Clinton claimed, held exclusive authority to negotiate with Native peoples within its borders.

Iroquois leaders, including Seneca leader Cornplanter and Mohawk leader Joseph Brant, attempted to safeguard Iroquois claims to Confederacy lands.

Surrounded by competing state and federal officials, they increasingly lost such efforts. "You are a subdued people," treaty commissioner Arthur Lee informed Iroquois leaders, echoing the words of U.S. general Philip Schuyler, who had proclaimed, "We are now masters of this Island, and can dispose of the Lands as we think proper or most convenient."[83]

Schuyler, Lee, and two other "Commissioners Plenipotentiary" represented the federal government.[84] They obtained at Fort Stanwix cessions of Iroquois lands "that the Six Nations shall and do yield to the United States."[85] However, as everyone understood, such treaties were meaningless as long as Indian soldiers remained motivated to fight for their continued independence, and numerous Iroquois leaders, including Brant, refused to sign the agreement. The prospects for continued warfare remained.

Additionally, New York officials continued to swarm Iroquois villages. In what would become a defining feature of early U.S. Indian policy, Clinton and other state officials competed with federal commissioners. They too negotiated a separate treaty with the Iroquois, undercutting national policy.[86] New York essentially pursued separate means to dispossess Indians, rewarding themselves and their allies with Iroquois homelands. Such efforts were not only unwelcomed by federal leaders but also illegal, because the Articles of Confederation granted only "the united states in congress . . . sole and exclusive right and power . . . [over] regulating the Indian trade."[87] A sign of the tensions between state and federal leaders, Lee posted armed guards during the October treaty negotiations to exclude the state's agents.[88] New York officials, however, employed gambits of their own in a series of land seizures, offering bribes, gifts, and hollow promises to secure lands from Iroquois leaders.[89]

As state governments seized Indian lands for themselves, national authority crumbled. Such tensions defined Indian policy throughout the post-independence period as states increasingly violated federal agreements, threatening Native villages as well as weakening the Union.

Virginians View Indian Lands: Washington's Proposal of 1784

Not only did New York and federal authorities vie with each other to obtain Iroquois lands, they were joined by leaders from other states. Many had come to gauge the value of Mohawk lands, whose dark soils appealed to coastal landowners. Such leaders included James Madison and James Monroe, who journeyed separately to Fort Stanwix from Virginia.[90] A slave state with a growing western population, Virginia had a political economy that differed from New York's, but it shared similar concerns on Indigenous diplomacy, land development, and the governance of interior settlers. The proceedings at Fort Stanwix attracted state leaders from nearby regions contending with similar problems.

Madison wrote of his travels to Thomas Jefferson, who had left for Paris that summer. Madison was excited to be in New York. He arrived with the Republic's second most famous military leader, France's marquis de Lafayette. "Wherever he passes," Madison informed Jefferson, "he receives the most flattering tokens of sincere affection." Lafayette had intended to stay at Mount Vernon, but "Genl. Washington was about setting out on a trip to the Ohio." Lafayette then developed a new plan: "to proceed immediately to New York . . . thence through Albany to Fort Stanwix where a treaty with the Indians is to be held."[91]

On September 30, the party from Virginia arrived in Iroquoia and "paid a visit to the Oneida Nation." Among these former wartime allies, "the Marquis was recd. by the Indians with equal proofs of attachment as have been shewn him elsewhere in America."[92] This nation of the Iroquois Confederacy, the only one to have allied with the colonists during the Revolution, the Oneida regaled the French leader.[93]

A congressional representative during the Revolution, Madison had returned to Virginia after the war without lands of his own. He was unmarried and lived in his father's home.[94] Land ownership and masculine authority were, of course, synonymous with revolutionary ideals of virtue, and unlike other Virginian leaders, Madison lacked these attributes. Older Virginian leaders recognized his energetic leadership and promoted his career. Washington encouraged him to head to New York and to assess the lands that Washington knew so well. He encouraged Madison's investment, as the Mohawk River offered "the very spot which his fancy had selected of all the U.S."[95]

Fourteen years beforehand, Washington began acquiring interior lands in return for his service to the crown after the Seven Years' War. He was among the first generation of Chesapeake leaders to expand their holdings into the interior and understood the need to complement his plantation-based economy with interior land development.[96] He differed in part from other Virginians, such as Jefferson, who spent his time in Europe declaring his disinterests in "the acquisition of Western lands." Unlike both Madison and Washington, Jefferson believed he had inherited sufficient wealth (despite the challenges that soon beset him): "I am one of eight children to whom my father left his share. . . . I never was nor am now interested in one foot of land on earth, off of the waters of James River."[97]

Washington's return to Mount Vernon had brought him face-to-face with the severity of postwar economy. His plantation was in disarray. Its economy had fallen into what he termed a "deranged situation."[98] Tobias Lear, his secretary, estimated that the war had cost the estate £10,000, a loss that would never be regained. Madison valued Washington's counsel, and understood that while Mount Vernon was vast in acreage (forty square miles), it was on exhausted soil.[99]

Agricultural study consumed much of Washington's first months back in Virginia. He applauded the opening of the Agriculture Society in Philadelphia, corresponded with English naturalist Arthur Young, and experimented with soil fertility by dredging from the bottom of the Potomac.[100] As he monitored the crop rotations across his estate's five main fields, his slaves dredged the river bottom, planted and harvested its fields, and applied fertilization.

Unlike along the Mohawk River or across the Ohio River, cash crops had been cultivated for decades across Potomac plantations. Slave owners understood that interior lands in proximity to rivers held the greatest wealth. Such lands, however, fueled great debates because interior rivers crossed state and political boundaries. Numerous leaders debated how best to harness the potential of interior lands and whether canals, roadways, or interior forts provided the best mechanisms for accessing the continent.

Washington understood these opportunities more clearly than others. Speculators across the nation realized the profits to be gained from the "opening" of Indian lands, but Washington's experience with interior land acquisition, management, and Indian affairs informed his views of the West at a time when Virginians came to dominate national politics.

Like Richard Henderson and John May in Kentucky, Washington had acquired tens of thousands of acres of interior lands. He was a leader in this regard and encouraged others, including Madison and Monroe, to do the same. Virginians understood that interior lands were essential not only for national growth but also for their own financial security. As he had learned during the Seven Years' War, Indian lands provided the perfect opportunity to complement the fluctuating cycles that plagued the tobacco economy.[101] Prosperity lay in the interior, particularly in soils that were neither weak nor exhausted.

Like other Americans, Washington ended the war with little gold or silver. He was wealthy but lacked money. He owned slaves, plantation lands, and the household itself at Mount Vernon. But the plantation's expenses outran its earnings.[102] He refused loans to many and grew concerned about the fate of his family's fortune. Indeed, as one biographer relays, Washington's "plans for a comfortable retirement rested on income" to be drawn from western lands.[103]

Washington's claims to interior lands were extensive, dating to his services under the crown. They included patents signed by former governor Dunmore that totaled thirty thousand acres, among these ten thousand acres that lay on the Ohio River in a region once dominated by the Iroquois Confederacy. Washington began attending to these lands and attempted to lease them throughout spring 1784. Leasing lands from afar, however, was challenging and dispiriting. As he informed Lafayette, he decided that he needed to visit them in person. He hoped that such a visit would clarify his claims, identify competent overseers, and recover rents.[104]

Leaving in September with a small party, Washington did not intend to survey new lands. He merely hoped "to secure what I have."[105] As the party moved along the Potomac, they passed into Pennsylvania, traveling along portions of the trail he took with Braddock in 1755, which subsequently became known as "the shades of death."[106] Little mention was made of the general's previous expeditions. Nor was there any recorded mention of his first combat at Great Meadows in 1754. As he recorded in his diary on September 12: "Stopped a while at the Great Meadows, and viewed a tenement I have there, which appears to have been but little improved."[107]

Few historical ironies, expressed satisfactions, or commemorations emerged upon his return to his first battlefield. The general's attention was elsewhere. He was focused not only upon the "present aspect" of his claim but also "the numbers of Persons & Pack horses going in" across the mountains.[108] They concerned him most. Migrants represented what he termed the "rage for speculating," a problem that he felt prevented existing lands from being "improved."[109]

Speculation had indeed become a national problem. And it was growing. "Men in these times," Washington wrote, "talk with as much facility of fifty, a hundred, or even 5,000 Acres as a Gentleman formerly would do of 1,000. . . . They roam over the Country . . . mark out Lands, Survey, and even Settle them," doing so without regard for current claimants, Indians, or existing laws.[110] Squatters, in particular, raised his ire. They broke the law but never the soil and claimed the land of others without improving it. As he wrote to

Henry Knox, he found "those in the vicinity of Fort Pitt [to be] people who set me at defiance, under the claim of pre-occupancy."[111]

Washington's visit to his Ohio River properties convinced him that stronger national authority was needed across the interior. Otherwise, he predicted, unregulated speculation would generate conflicts with tribes and challenge broader practices of state formation. Settlement "of the Western Country and making a Peace with the Indians are so analogous," he wrote, "that there can be no definition of the one without involving considerations of the other."[112]

Washington had a radical and far-reaching proposal for preventing such conflict and lawlessness. It recognized the sovereignty of tribes and understood that tribal authority was useful in curbing the lawlessness of settlers. As he wrote to Congressman Jacob Read:

> Declare all steps, heretofore taken to procure Lands on the No. Wt. [northwest] side of the Ohio, contrary to the prohibition of Congress, to be null and void. And that any person thereafter, who shall presume to mark, Survey, or settle Lands beyond the limits of the New States, and purchased Lands, shall not only be considered *as outlaws*, but *fit subjects for Indian vengeance*.[113]

Washington's proposal came in November, informed by his "western tour." He had been gone for a month and traveled seven hundred miles. The party passed his earliest battlefields as well as locations near Pittsburgh that had taken his name: Washington's Bottom, Washington's Lands, and the town of Washington itself. Pennsylvania had just named the surrounding county after him. Its namesake, however, found an unwelcoming reception upon arrival at his 2,813-acre tract. Indigent squatters were living there. Outraged by their refusal to leave, he contacted local authorities and took them to court for past-due rents. He also sought their eviction. He succeeded only in the latter, as they quickly migrated away for continued squatting. No rent was ever provided. The case lasted two years and, according to one biographer, pitted "the most powerful figure in the nation against a feisty delegation of impoverished farmers."[114]

On his other lands, Washington found a mill broken, fields overgrown and, worst of all, lands unleased.[115] Such lands needed to be "improved" and regulated. They lost value when they went untended. "The people of the Western Country hav[e] had no excitements to Industry," he wrote; they "labour very little."[116] Squatters sat on lands not to develop them but to profit by claiming ownership of them. As his experience suggested, when driven away, they continued farther west, thereby creating a cycle of underdevelopment that Washington found enraging and defeating. Squatting and lawlessness hindered both his own fortunes and those of the Republic.

Interior lands remained, then, not only underused but also devalued. As more western territories opened for settlement, existing possessions lost value. Surplus drove down values and inspired few citizens to lease the lands of others. Moreover, squatters, by definition, followed little authority. As Washington would learn as president, Kentucky settlers in particular followed few commands. They cared little for distinctions between peaceful and hostile Indians, holding, according to Henry Knox, an "equal aversion" to both.[117] Indian hating would become a pervasive ideology by the end of Washington's presidency. For now, he sought oversight for his possessions, contracting former soldiers to oversee his properties. He departed Pennsylvania generally satisfied with "the situation quality and advantages of the Land which I hold."[118] He returned to Virginia in October, just as deliberations at Fort Stanwix, which he had not followed, were developing. Of their outcome, he wrote to Read, "I pretend not to say."[119]

American Federalism, American Indians

Washington would never see the Ohio again, but his predictions about conflicts therein did come true. They soon dominated his first term as president when little preoccupied the Federalist administration more than struggling to deal with the interior's Native peoples.[120]

Unlike many of his contemporaries, Washington understood that centralized authority was needed to regulate interior lands and to establish diplomatic ties with Native nations. Such a "double" recognition eventually became shared by other national leaders, many of whom had modeled their own political and financial ideas after the general's.[121]

As Washington articulated, only a national government could establish diplomatic peace with Indians and regulate land acquisition. The two remained, as he had written, "analogous." Expansion required federal authority over interior lands and also recognition of the authority of tribes therein. In fact, U.S. jurisdiction ended where tribal sovereignty began. As Washington wrote, any white persons who "shall presume" to settle outside the boundaries of the Union became "outlaws." They were also "fit subjects" to the jurisdiction of Native nations. As they moved west, settlers left behind one political realm and entered the jurisdiction of others, as the interior remained a multilateral world where no single sovereign governed. The Virginia legislature held similar jurisdictional understandings and concerns about "the tranquility of our western inhabitants." It resolved in November 1784 that "speedy and exemplary punishment ought to be inflicted on every person doing injury to the subjects of Spain or the Indians in that quarter."[122] Settler expansion, in short, was so destabilizing that it required governmental oversight of some form.

Treaties established such jurisdictional divides. They concerned the fate of Native and non-Native peoples. For example, while the 1785 Cherokee Treaty at Hopewell dispossessed Cherokee of their hunting grounds across much of the South, it recognized their authority across their remaining homelands and outlined their jurisdiction. As article 5 states:

> If any citizen of the United States of America, or person not being an Indian, shall attempt to settle any of the lands . . . which are hereby allotted to the Indians . . . or having settled and will not remove from the same . . . *such person shall forfeit the protection of the United States,* and *the Indians may punish him or not as they please.*[123]

Although diminished territorially, Cherokee sovereignty remained. It was inherent. It was so ubiquitously recognized that it informed not only tribal communities but also American understandings of governance. Indian treaties concerned the "protection" of U.S. citizens, and accordingly helped to demarcate the nature and form of U.S. jurisdiction. As Washington indicated, Indian sovereignty helped to clarify when, where, how, and upon whom American laws operated. The sovereignties of Indian nations and of the United States were interrelated.[124]

Additionally, tribal sovereignty helped the Republic's economy. By establishing boundaries between Native nations and white settlements, diplomacy helped to bring, as Washington wrote, "consequently a higher price" for existing property. Lands, he wrote, "like other commodities, rise or fall in proportion to the quantity at market."[125] As he had seen in Pennsylvania, stability was impossible in "Settlements, where nothing is thought of but scrambling for Land."[126] Squatting and speculation would only bring additional "confusion and bloodshed," both of which diminished the value of existing properties.[127] Making peace with Indians brought order. Treaties established borders that were essential to peace and prosperity. For Washington, expansion was best conducted through shared processes of diplomacy and governance.

As the will of the people extended into the interior, so too did the required institutions of the state. Unlike French or British imperial claims, a civic ideology of state formation—"settler republicanism"—underwrote Washington's thoughts; individuals worked within established institutions of the state to incorporate interior lands.[128] Such expansion followed the forms of diplomacy and recognition that had emerged from generations of practices and understandings of sovereignty. Native sovereignty existed across the interior. Treaties brokered tribal relationships with the new Republic.

The Articles of Confederation, however, had failed to bring order. As early as 1780, the nation attempted a series of public land resolutions that aimed to regulate lands "for the common benefit of the United States."[129] Such laws reflected popular claims about the "common good," including those of Thomas Paine, whose 1780 text *Public Good* concerns "claims" to "vacant western territory." Such territories, he wrote, were "the common right" of all.[130] While rights to interior Indian lands were presumed by revolutionary leaders to be inherent to U.S. citizens, the new government was unable to regulate them effectively.

Unlike Paine, who had emigrated from England in 1776, Washington had decades of experience. His call for greater national authority drew upon years of travel, warfare, diplomacy, and now property management. As he wrote to Read, new national authority needed to be centralized under a stronger government. Only a federal government was positioned to regulate power across the interior.

Washington knew this world. John Adams and Thomas Jefferson, by contrast, had never fought interior battles, and they spent much of the post-1783 period in Europe. Thousands of Washington's men had died in conflicts with Native peoples and their allies, and he commanded the earliest battles in two global wars. He had given commands that Indian villages be burned, their lands occupied, and their women and children imprisoned. In fact, he had become so reviled among the Iroquois that he—and all those who subsequently have held the office of U.S. president—became known in Iroquois as "Conotocarious," which translates as "Town Destroyer" or "Devourer of Villages."[131] Adams, Jefferson, Madison, and Monroe—let alone Paine—had not experienced this interior world.

While Washington had encouraged the destruction of Indigenous communities, he also understood that the autonomy of tribes could never be extinguished. Only a federal government could effectively regulate relations with them. Moreover, he understood that the administration of Indian policy provided ways for curbing the lawlessness of U.S. citizens and improving the value of their lands. By demarcating the limits between Native and white settlements, treaties underscored the power that Indian sovereignty provided for national formation. Indian sovereignty offered mechanisms for enforcing U.S. laws. Settlers needed to recognize "the limits of the New States" and the consequences of transgressing them. Otherwise, they were to be considered as "outlaws" and "subjects for Indian reprisal." As with his expressed faith in deference and virtue, Washington understood that tribal sovereignty remained a determinative influence of republicanism. In his mind, Indians governed differently, and such differences mattered. As his November 1784 proposal outlined, such differences had the power to strengthen the capacity of the Republic.

The Failures of the Articles of Confederation

By the end of 1784, the Articles of Confederation were failing. "We have no politics," Henry Knox wrote to Washington in November. "Indeed, I do not know of any that are in operation," he continued, "excepting those creeping principles of self or local politics which are the reverse of what ought to actuate us."[132] Washington attempted to reassure his trusted aide. He told him of his current efforts to "connect the Western Territory" with eastern seaports. Since returning from the interior, Washington had also become engrossed in a series of infrastructure projects to "stimulate my Countrymen to the extension of the inland navigation of rivers Potomac and James."[133] Canals, expanded roads, and shared interstate financial commitments consumed his writings. Madison worked in a similar capacity to reform Virginia's ports.[134]

Washington's initiatives spoke to immediate challenges and highlighted vacuums of leadership at the national level. No individual or single office presided over the Republic. State legislatures held nearly unbridled autonomy and rarely cooperated on interstate commercial or infrastructure projects such as roads and canals.

It had been a year since Washington had resigned his command. He had seen how precarious politics had become. "No public money . . . is likely to be obtain[ed] from [Maryland]," he wrote to Madison, and he encouraged those in Virginia to apply "the wisdom of both assemblies" to fund his canal efforts.[135] Much more was needed, however, on a national level than the combined legislative funding from two of thirteen states.

Washington believed that the fate of the Union hung in the balance. Since no state or national government regulated western settlement, commerce, he hoped, could cement such limited policies. Without any commercial or political ties, moreover, he worried the West's interior settlements "will settler faster than any other ever did" and in doing so "they will become a distinct people from us." In the interior, new settlers will have "different interests, & instead of adding strength to the Union" may in fact become over time "a formidable and dangerous neighbour."[136] Interior nationalism was a growing threat. Washington believed that interior settlements might soon become foreign powers.

As with his November proposal to Read, herein lay interrelated problems. Neither interior Indian diplomacy nor western settlement followed established norms. Each occurred with a simultaneity characterized by neither stability nor certainty. White settlements of Indian lands brought conflicts that were often resolved through violence or through treaties, which settlers often rejected. Chaos rather than process reigned, particularly as settler leaders flouted the authority of treaty makers. They argued that negotiated settlements with Indian nations were an affront to their peace. As militia leader James McFarlane informed Indian agent Richard Butler, western Pennsylvanian settlers held an "absolute determination to be at war with the Indians."[137]

Indian treaties were only one realm of contestation between interior settlers and the federal government. As Pennsylvanian congressman William Findley expressed after the Whiskey Rebellion: when "a spirit of disorder is permitted to prevail, no character or interest in society will be secured from its effects."[138] In what was becoming a downward spiral, the absence of governmental institutions hindered attempts to build them. The limited presence of the federal government impeded attempts to establish authority of any kind, whether regarding Indian affairs or taxes of whiskey. In both examples, such absences generated settler violence, which threatened the broader legitimacy of the Union.

In addition to his contempt for interior squatters, Washington focused his ire on those state leaders who undercut national authority. Officials, he believed, should follow national laws before those of the states. They should not contribute to lawlessness. When informed of the tensions between state and national leaders at Fort Stanwix, for example, Washington replied:

> Much to the advantage it is said of the United States, but to the great disquiet of that of New York: fruitlessly, it is added by some, who assert that the Deputies on the part of the Indians were not properly authorized to treat—How true this may be, I will not pretend to decide; but certain it is in my opinion, that there is a kind of fatality attending all our public

> meetings—inconceivable delays—particularly states counteracting the plans of the United States when submitted to them. . . . In fact, our federal Government is a name without substance: No State is longer bound by its edicts, than it suits *present* purposes.

Ultimately, he believed, the state of American politics was bound to make them "victims of our own folly."[139] The federal government remained in conflict with those who placed their local interests over those of the nation.

The colonists had fought for a decade to secure their independence from England, but within twenty-four months of the Treaty of Paris, their Republic was teetering. State officials and western settlers operated with limited attachments to existing laws and used violence against peaceful as well as unallied Indians. Meanwhile, the most active governing bodies—state legislatures—remained uncooperative. They pursued efforts aimed at their individual state's improvement. Moreover, several states, such as Maryland and Rhode Island, rarely sent delegations to Congress, and the national government remained mired in debt. These were a few of the concerns confronting Washington as a citizen.[140] The problems inherent in the Articles of Confederation were apparent and growing, and many stemmed from the inability of the United States to impose jurisdiction over the interior. As Washington's experiences suggested, the nation's western treasure chest held the potential to expand or collapse the Union.[141]

Over a hundred thousand settlers moved into the interior between 1770 and 1790, and the Articles of Confederation finally began making laws aimed at their management. In 1787, before the Constitutional Convention, Congress passed the Northwest Ordinance, which established mechanisms for admitting new territories while prohibiting the expansion of slavery within them. Guided by an ambition to give the national government authority to regulate and tax interior lands, the Northwest Ordinance gave the federal government an exclusive authority to dispossess Native nations.[142]

Deep fissures, however, prevented the orderly transfer of lands. Northern and southern states remained embroiled in debates about the nation's new borders. The Northwest Ordinance provided a roadmap for incorporating these new lands into the Union; however, southern states desperately wished to keep these interior settlements allied with the South. Georgia and South Carolina still claimed much of what soon became known as the Deep South.[143] Increasingly, these agrarian economies contrasted with northern, merchant-based economies centered around Boston, New York, and Philadelphia. As merchant Benjamin Rush prophesized, "There is but one path that can lead the United States to destruction; and that is their extent of territory."[144] The interior simultaneously foretold American greatness and its demise.

In addition to sectional divides, violent conflicts between settlers and Native communities recurred across the interior. Hundreds of settlers died each year, while Native communities also mourned the loss of loved ones. Treaty negotiations continued, partly in an effort to keep Native communities from banding into larger confederations. However, the divided, bankrupt federal government lacked the capacity to compensate tribes for their lands. The Articles also lacked the ability to conquer them. As Knox bluntly informed Congress in 1787, the nation "was utterly unable to maintain an Indian war."[145] Despite shared optimism, a sobering reality had become clear: the interior was outside the limits of the nation's laws. While technically within its borders, settlers, Indian nations, and even Spanish and British rivals crisscrossed the interior. In its current configuration, the new nation could neither hold its newly acquired interior lands nor regulate its citizens within them. Equally evidently, it lacked the power to contend with the Indigenous peoples therein.

Indians and the U.S. Constitution

The drafting of the United States Constitution in 1787 remedied many of the failures of the Articles of Confederation. Emerging out of the Constitutional Convention, the Constitution offered a radical break. It created a powerful national government capable of better regulating interior lands, settlements, and peoples. It gave the national government centralized powers over land management, taxation, and Indian affairs, among other powers, and it authorized Congress to establish a standing army. It clarified the jurisdiction of states versus the federal government, established a judiciary and system of courts, and located political power in a three-tiered governing system.

A new government now ruled the Republic through a codified system of authorizations of power and through explicit grants and denials of such powers. Throughout the Convention and subsequent debates on ratification, these powers were debated and further enshrined in a series of amendments, the first ten of which became the Bill of Rights. Power—and limits upon it—informed the shape and meaning of authority in the new Constitution.

Such sovereign power, however, ultimately resided not with the government or its representatives. It lay with the nation's citizens.[146] For example, while states retained extensive sovereignty within their borders and upon the economies therein, federal laws such as the Northwest Ordinance governed the interactions between the states. No structures of authority, however, could make inviolate the form of representative government established by this system of governance. "The people" governed the Republic, and the Constitution, in its broadest conception of republicanism, ensured that individual liberties would not be threatened by concentrated forms of power.

For Native peoples, however, the view was different: the Constitution excluded them and aided in their dispossession. It offered little protection against the processes of colonization then underway. Moreover, it anticipated even greater land seizures to come. Forged by a nation born out of revolt, it emerged from three decades of interior warfare and positioned the new government to navigate its expansion through military and diplomatic tools. The Constitution now legitimated the process of American colonialism unleashed by the Revolution. It originated in a generation of Anglo-American struggles for political, economic, and social autonomy, and its framers worked to ensure Anglo-American supremacy over interior lands, Native peoples, and African American slaves. It became, in short, a constitution for colonialism.

Indians are formally mentioned twice in article 1 of the original Constitution.[147] Each reference—the prohibition against considering "Indians not taxed" in the allocation of congressional representation and the power of Congress to "regulate Commerce . . . with the Indian tribes"—centralizes federal authority over Indian affairs. Less explicitly, provisions regarding treaties, property, guarantees for common defense, and military affairs also applied to Indian relations.

Such delegated powers broadened the authority of the national government to project its power into the interior. In fact, the ability of Congress to tax in order to "provide for the common Defence" became exclusively used in Indian affairs throughout the decade ahead. Ultimately, the Constitution created a federalist system that was simultaneously weak and strong, one capable of projecting violence through an organized military rather than a series of state militia. This structure of government was also what the larger states and interior settlers wanted.[148] During the Convention, the lack of debate over Indian affairs revealed a rare consensus among the delegates.[149]

Emerging as it did after years of ineffective national policies, the new government was better positioned to navigate the challenges of the interior. Numerous representatives to the Convention understood that accelerated expansion awaited the nation. As Pennsylvanian delegate Gouverneur Morris explained, "All North America must at length be annexed to us."[150] South Carolina delegate Charles Pinckney similarly articulated the centrality of expansion to republicanism. There would now be, he stated, "more equality of rank and fortune in America than in any other country . . . as long as the unappropriated western lands remain unsettled."[151]

✦

As Jefferson would later suggest, an American "empire of liberty" had formed. Scholars have long labored to reconcile such apparent contradictions—empire versus liberty and freedom versus slavery. As the struggle of the interior suggests, such seemingly oppositional ideas remained in fact mutually constitutive. An empire is by definition imperial and unequal, and nations, like empires, create histories that seek to glorify their existence and expansion.

The Northwest Ordinance proclaimed that the United States would pursue a policy of expansion that was just to Native nations. Under the Constitution, a more powerful federal government increasingly sought to bring "civilization" to Indian nations. Masked under such vernacular veils, colonialism nonetheless continued to uncut the sovereignty of interior Indian nations, now through newly established forms and practices.

Part II
Struggles for Sovereignty

✦

This mural of Toypurina in Boyle Heights, Los Angeles, decorates the main wall of Ramona Gardens, a large public housing complex. It is one of three large murals dedicated to the Tongva leader in Los Angeles, a testament to her enduring legacy. (*Art Heals*, 2008, Mictlan Murals. Courtesy of the artists. Lead artist: Raul González. Assisted by: Joséph Montalvo, Ricardo Estrada. Photograph by Pete Galindo.)

7 • The Deluge of Settler Colonialism

Democracy and Dispossession in the Early Republic

In their places a new generation will arise.
—*Andrew Jackson (1814)*

Leopold Pokagon and his Potawatomi family were fortunate. They had survived the last campaigns of the "Removal Era," and remained in their southern Michigan homeland. They continued hunting, trading, trapping, fishing, and harvesting according to the seasonal cycles that had nourished their community since time immemorial. Things were quiet in the autumn of 1838 as seasonal colors surrounded their community, fading as the snows arrived.

But such stability was the exception. Earlier that year, U.S. soldiers had driven twelve hundred people from the region's other Potawatomi villages west, while in the South General Winfield Scott commanded seven thousand troops organized for Cherokee removal. The soldiers, he warned Cherokee leaders, stood ready "to hunt you down."[1] Nearly sixteen thousand Cherokee signed a petition presented to Congress to avoid their removal. It was to no avail.

In Michigan and Indiana, the army took the crying, cold, and confused Potawatomi through Illinois and across the Mississippi. In Kansas, they were forced into crowded settlements. A hundred children and elderly died along the way, adding to the thousands of Potawatomi lives already lost during this removal generation. In contrast, Pokagon's band continued to greet the morning sun upon their familiar rounds: river fishing holes, freshwater rice harvesting beds, and hunting grounds teeming with game.[2]

As primary *wkema*, or political leader, Pokagon had guided his community at Dowagiac since 1826.[3] Not since the seventeenth century had the region witnessed demographic and social upheavals on such a scale. The American newcomers held diplomatic gatherings with Potawatomi and other Native leaders. Each time, their confidence grew. So too did their threats. At the Chicago Treaty of 1833, white officials spoke with a particular urgency. "It is further agreed," the treaty commissioners stipulated, "that as fast as the said Indians shall be prepared to emigrate, they shall be removed." Ominously, the treaty established land cessions: the "said United Nation of Chippewa, Ottowa, and Potawatamie Indians, cede to the United States all their land . . . [of] about five millions of acres."[4]

Similar treaties flooded the U.S. Senate.[5] In September 1830, in the Treaty of Dancing Rabbit Creek, federal officials coerced Choctaw leaders into ceding over 10 million acres of their land. Two months later, officials planned the removal of "the balance of the nation, consisting of eighteen or nineteen thousand souls." Identifying the route of their removal, federal officials also reached out to local farmers. "You are requested to apprize the nearest settlers of the probable market they will soon have for their corn and cattle," Commissary General George Gibson instructed. "Hold out every proper inducement for them to raise both in quantities sufficient to meet the expected demand."[6]

For the Potawatomi, the Chicago Treaty was one of nine recent treaties ratified by the U.S. Senate, all since Pokagon had become band leader.[7] Like other *wkema*, he struggled to consent to such negotiations. He attempted to gauge the intentions of those gathered, particularly of those Native leaders who agreed to such cessions.[8] He had not signed the Chicago Treaty and now deliberated on how best to keep his community in their homelands, praying, as did the rest of his village, that the years of forced removal had finally ended.

Pokagon remembered an earlier time when the power of these newcomers remained far less determined. He was raised in the diverse, Algonquian-speaking villages that characterized Great Lakes Indian communities. Life within such villages was comfortable and comparatively prosperous.[9] White settlements were across the Ohio River, and settlers struggled to survive the winters of the Native Inland Sea.

His community had traded for generations with various newcomers—French, English, and Native traders who brought streams of products, including silverware, skins, and even silks.[10] Indian villages also knew how, when, and where to find the bounties of the earth. Such bounties sustained trade. Since the 1600s, Potawatomi villages had combined trading with the hunting and horticulture that formed the region's economy.

The War of 1812, however, had changed much across the region.[11] The defeat of the last military confederation led by the Shawnee leader Tecumseh had extinguished faith that a grand alliance with England might provide assistance against the newcomers. To many, it seemed that a wave of settlers had crashed upon the region, this tide engulfing all in its transformative wake.

Everywhere Native peoples struggled for air. Unlike the seventeenth-century challenges of colonialism, nineteenth-century "settler colonialism" threatened to extinguish the foundations of daily life.[12] Across the Native Inland Sea, Indians were now pressured to abandon their homes. They were encouraged to join others in a process of "removal." Those who remained faced growing threats, as newcomers provided few avenues for economic, political, and social survival.

Technically, treaties mandated that lands were to be provided to Native communities "in exchange" for their homelands. Such lands were to be protected by the government from the deluge. As Pokagon had seen, however, such stipulations did not yield guarantees. In 1830 the federal government passed the Indian Removal Act. It cast into doubt previous agreements and gave President Andrew Jackson an increased authority—soon to be declared unconstitutional—"to extinguish the Indian claim" within eastern states.[13] In that year's State of the Union address, Jackson applauded the passage of the legislation, noting that officials "now propose to acquire the countries occupied by the red men of the South and West . . . and . . . to send them to a land where their existence may be prolonged and perhaps made perpetual."[14]

In under three years, federal negotiators forced four treaties upon the Potawatomi. Each grew in intensity, culminating in the Chicago Treaty and the cession of 5 million acres. Other Indian nations endured comparable pressures as the "Removal Era" unleashed death, dispossession, and state-sanctioned violence throughout eastern North America. Despite their constitutional standing as the "supreme law of the land," treaties were broken with impunity. Existing treaties, as Pokagon witnessed, were now renegotiated—sometimes annually—and always under duress. Their guarantees, let alone supposed protections, carried little meaning.

Racial Formations and the Market Revolution

The 1820s had been a hard time for Pokagon to assume political leadership. His first year as leader in 1826 was the beginning not only of the "removal treaties" but also of the 363-mile Erie Canal.[15] The political economy of the Native Inland Sea would never again be the same, as now the region became connected to the Atlantic seaboard.

This meandering but revolutionary infrastructure stretched across New York State. Goods flowed from Lake Erie to the Hudson River, superseding both the St. Lawrence and the Mississippi as the primary arteries of the Native Inland Sea. In a development comparable to the discovery of the Northwest Passage, the canal positioned New York, not New Orleans or Montreal, as the terminus for the region's trade. Resources coming to and from the Great Lakes region now flowed across human-made trade routes.

The changes that followed were immediate and incalculable. White farms produced historic yields and settlers acquired acreage by the millions. They chased away game. They cut down forests and burned them to make way for agriculture. Their farms grew grains, pigs, and fruits by the boatload. Their leaders compelled Indians to leave.

Settlers renamed Indian villages and used a new name for the region altogether: the Northwest. New states were created, continuing the demographic transformations unleashed after the Revolution. Kentucky had four hundred thousand settlers when its most famous son, Abraham Lincoln, was a child. Less than 1 percent of its total population were "free persons of color."[16]

These decisive years established the economic and racial foundations of America. Treaties not only dispossessed Natives of their lands but also brought new meanings to them. As land acquired new names, it gained new value. It could now be exchanged and alienated. The Northwest Ordinance of 1787 made acquiring "private property" far easier in the Northwest than in New York, Pennsylvania, or Kentucky.[17] As George Washington had seen after the Revolution, squatters across the interior broke the law but not the soil, and throughout each year of the 1800s, thousands of new settlers moved across the Ohio River to acquire property. They included Lincoln's family, who helped to colonize Indiana. Soon the Lincolns moved to Illinois, where they joined thousands of others from Kentucky. In fact, six of Illinois's first seven governors hailed from Kentucky.[18]

As Michigan's Potawatomi communities looked south, they witnessed the deluge unfolding. They saw how the Erie Canal accelerated everything: trade, settlement, and commerce. Each fostered dispossession while new currencies, loans, and debts created additional losses for Native peoples struggling to maintain possession of their lands. Representatives of a new nation and economy had arrived—and they used every possible measure to undermine the power of Indian authority. As Pokagon had witnessed, the U.S. military resolved disputes in favor of settlers, using violence to pressure Native leaders to remove.

America's quickening economy, its burgeoning cities, and its expanding territories all contributed to the deluge of settler colonialism. Much like its English parent, the Republic entered a "crucible" after the Revolution.[19] Unlike in England, land rather than "steam power" combined with the cotton mill to fuel the "transformation of America" as the market revolution began.[20]

The deluge fueled three interrelated racial transformations in the early Republic: the state-sanctioned removal of Indigenous peoples; the expansion of white male constitutional democracy; and the expansion of African American slavery.[21] While often understood independently, each emerged in relationship to the other. As with its increased authority to acquire interior lands, the power of the federal government supported these new racial formations.

Treaties isolated Native peoples from their former imperial allies and divided them from each other. They not only extinguished Native people's ability to ally with European empires but also legitimated the authority within tribes of those who desired to trade with Americans.[22] Commerce enveloped Indian communities to such an extent that traditional hunters possessed comparatively "nothing now," as the Creek leader Hoboithle Mico complained.[23] Many communities encouraged intermarriage with white traders, even moving closer to settlements in order to trade. Such internal divisions became hallmarks of the era and hastened Indigenous dispossession.

Historians emphasize the political and constitutional challenges wrought by expansion but fail to highlight how Indigenous dispossession fueled the emergence of the settler colonial state. While the administration of federal lands created a bureaucratic problem of legibility across the continent, federal surveyors, army officials, and territorial leaders all traversed Indigenous lands.[24] The loss of such lands forever determined the political sovereignty that followed, as settlement and dispossession became two sides of the same coin.[25] In many ways, whether their lands became incorporated into the Republic as "slave" or "free" states mattered little to the Native peoples who had lost them.

However, these racial formations were interrelated. After the Revolution, Indigenous dispossession facilitated the growth of white male democracy and African American slavery. Each grew from the same trunk of expansion while also sowing the seeds of American disunion. Indeed, many of the nation's longest-standing racial inequalities remain rooted in this half century of racial formation, one in which American lawmakers struggled to establish legible distinctions between "red," "white," and "black" people. That struggle became ideological. It became social. It became political, and it eventually became legal.

Debates over the future roiled the nation. Moreover, a new social order governed the Republic as interior settlements and eventual states garnered increased authority. By 1830 the Republic's racial hierarchies seemed as natural as the seasons themselves; the market revolution so thoroughly structured society that many believed the nation's economy to be providential.[26] As one Indiana congressman suggested, manufacturing and commerce had become "the missionaries of freedom."[27] Indian lands provided the foundations for maintaining "the laws of commerce . . . and consequently the laws of God."[28]

A Deluge of Opportunities

Until the War of 1812, English ships plied the Native Inland Sea, and Native nations governed the interior. The Gulf states remained Chickasaw, Creek, and Choctaw homelands while Seminole bands dominated Florida. After the war, the power of the United States and its racial formations proliferated. All white men in the Union soon had the right to vote, and Indians across eastern North America lost over 100 million acres of lands. Starting in the 1820s, African American slavery reached Texas, where vast forests became cotton fields.[29]

As Indian homelands became farms and plantations, they broadened the market revolution that expanded the national economy. Across the "Old Northwest," farms produced vast exports while attracting endless imports. In its first decade alone, over $100 million in goods circulated via the Erie Canal.[30] By 1860 31 million barrels of grain flowed annually from Buffalo.[31] Exports were then sent on to New York City, whose populace surged after the canal's completion. Interior agriculture, in short, both transformed Indian hunting grounds and expanded the nation's economy.

The history of New York City highlights this growing intersection of settler colonialism and U.S. capitalism. After 1812 it became the financial hub of American commerce as well as the nation's primary entrepôt for European immigrants. In 1817 it opened its stock market—the first in the nation. In 1818 its harbors offered the first timed sailings to England. For the first time in the history of the Western Hemisphere, passengers could now obtain scheduled departures across the Atlantic. New York and the Erie Canal formed primary organs within the early Republic's economy.[32]

Like Cincinnati's, Pittsburgh's, and other cities', New York's population doubled after 1812 and then doubled again. By 1850 it exceeded half a million, a 1,300 percent increase since 1790.[33] Such growth made it among the most influential economic centers on earth. As global markets for cotton grew, for example, New York–based engineers often led the development of Latin Amer-

Painted just four years after the Erie Canal opened, J. W. Hill's 1829 watercolor illustrates the transformations unleashed by the canal across the "Old Northwest." The canal accelerated the emigration of settlers and the removal of Indigenous nations. Where forests once grew, fields and pastures now stretch behind the canal, and to the left, a team of horses pulls a packet boat carrying passengers and goods. (From The New York Public Library, https://digitalcollections.nypl.org/items/510d47d9-7ba7-a3d9-e040-e00a18064a99.)

ican, Asian, and Middle Eastern cotton industries. Louis Alexis Jumel and John Masterson Burke left the city to help build Egypt's and Mexico's cotton industries, respectively. Both had come to the city as young men and grown familiar with cotton production and its financing. They quickly followed the city's networks of capitalist development abroad, taking, in small measure, a part of New York with them.[34]

Of course, New York's economy predated the Republic. Home of the Dutch fur trade, the city had long been integrated into economies of the Native Northeast and across the continent. Indigenous-procured furs expanded its growth. The city's most famous entrepreneur, John Jacob Astor, made his fortune in furs. In 1808 he founded the American Fur Company, establishing its primary outpost at Astoria at the mouth of the Columbia River.[35]

Astor's efforts helped to cement American claims to the Pacific and broaden commerce with Asia; he built a fur-trading network that circled the globe.[36] Ships arrived annually at Astoria, its western terminus. They carried furs by the thousands and people drawn from all over the world. In 1813 twenty-four Native Hawaiians worked at Astoria, facilitating not only its economic productivity but also its social composition.[37]

An immigrant from the Swiss Alps, Astor had arrived in the city in 1784 at the age of twenty. His meteoric career embodied the city's development and the nation's changing political economy.

While the expansion of white male democracy may seem abstract, the transformations that linked men like Astor represented a social earthquake that remade white America. Across the early Republic, economic opportunities linked European immigrants and U.S. citizens, blurring the distinctions between them. New American race and gender relations were forming, revealing additional social changes fueled by Indigenous dispossession.

Whiteness, Gender, and Naturalization

Since the founding of Jamestown, distinctions between settlers had often been as important as their commonalities. Indentured servants in the Chesapeake, apprentices in New England, and tenants in the Carolinas all lived in worlds in which white men from higher classes governed. Those who governed held property, and property ownership formed the basis for the republican principle that those who could not support themselves lacked the independence to be active in politics.[38] To think otherwise was idealistic and wrong, as Judge James Kent explained: "Theories of government that suppose the mass of people virtuous and able, and willing to act virtuously are plainly utopian and will remain so."[39]

The Revolution changed such distinctions, but it did not do so universally.[40] Property owners continued to fear the landless around them, and tensions simmered throughout the early Republic. In the South, contempt for the poor approximated that shown toward blacks, as landowners treated servants contemptuously.[41]

While the Revolution and Constitution established new structures of governance, popular sovereignty remained restricted. A struggle between classes ensued. For two generations, state constitutions maintained "property qualifications" for political participation and office holding.[42] As late as 1829, Supreme Court justice John Marshall continued to endorse such restrictions; he "felt a deep respect for the rights of property."[43] Even though they shared the same skin color, white men with and without property held different legal and political rights.

Such restrictions also applied to white women, regardless of wealth. As in the colonial era, hierarchies of gender structured the early Republic even as new understandings of what that meant emerged.[44] The gendered character of the Republic generated distinctive forms of morality. Women's standing as mothers, wives, and caretakers offered guides of social restraints that served to safeguard the nation's virtue. After the Revolution, such virtuous designations legitimated a rise in domesticity, as a new gender system dominated public discourses and ultimately came to structure an emerging middle class.[45] In domestic spheres, female moral authority was supreme, providing the moral foundations upon which America's republican experiment increasingly stood.[46]

Territorial expansion and Indigenous dispossession complicated republicanism and its racial and gendered assumptions. Throughout the early 1800s, western migrants—single white men but particularly white families—recast the foundations of American democracy. In the interior, gender roles differed from those in the East. As white men more easily obtained property, authority came to rest on farms rather than in "middle-class" domestic spheres. Building settlements also required the labors of both men and women. Many of the energies of expansion centered around the daily tasks of farming, and settler families changed American politics. The word *husband*, for example, once meant "farmer" but came to mean a "married man."[47]

Settler colonialism and the political economy of settlement differentiated white families from their eastern contemporaries. It also strengthened legislated forms of marriage and heterosexuality across the Republic, cementing patriarchy as a familial cornerstone.[48] Across the interior, expanding forms of land ownership, agrarianism, and settlement challenged eastern property restrictions of republicanism. New participatory democratic practices followed.

As Thomas Jefferson suggested and the Northwest Ordinance legislated, interior lands were to be admitted "on an equal footing with the original states."[49] For men, such "equal" rights included mobility, ownership, and the franchise. Starting with Tennessee in 1796, interior states gained equal representation in the Union. Increasingly, American citizens shared a common white race, as whiteness came to bridge growing regional, sectional, and political divides.

Analyzing America's century of expansion, Frederick Jackson Turner identified an "antipathy to control" within frontier spaces as a distinctive characteristic of American identity. Such antipathies, Turner believed, "generated an intolerance of administrative government, and instead a more egalitarian, individualist, and self-governing ethos."[50] In many ways, frontier societies bred what would become American individualism, and they did so upon recently dispossessed Indian homelands.

Rights and liberties remained more elusive in eastern towns and seaports where land ownership and political power remained concentrated. The government issued a bevy of laws aimed at extending and protecting certain liberties. The Northwest Ordinance ensured that the colonization of interior territory would bring new territories into the Union on an "equal footing" with existing states, and in 1790 Congress passed the Naturalization Act.[51] Immigrants and new citizens were required to spend time in the country. They were expected to exhibit "proper and decent behavior" and refrain from criminal actions. Immigrants had to "abjure and renounce all allegiance and subjection to all and every foreign king, prince . . . and state, in all matters ecclesiastical as well as civil."[52]

When Congress used its constitutional authority to establish a path to citizenship, it added a key word to its legislation. Unlike the U.S. Constitution, the Naturalization Act used an explicit language of race to determine citizenship. Naturalization was reserved for "white" people. It was the first time the term appeared in national laws, and none in Congress objected to the restriction.[53] In the Militia Act of 1792, Congress similarly restricted military service to "whites," as the language of race became legislated and codified.[54]

Whiteness, like Indianness, is a social construction—an ideological habit that imagines similarities between different social communities. Such racial classifications took decades, even generations, to coalesce. Fueled by Indian dispossession, the Republic's new laws turned emergent social categories into hardened political identities. Throughout the early Republic, the United States became a country in which only white men held rights; the codification of "white" citizenship made explicit the exclusion of blacks, whether enslaved or free, rendering them outside the protection of the law.[55]

Such laws also distinguished others. Native peoples were not eligible for citizenship according to the Constitution or the Naturalization Act. "Free people of color" also found limited space within the Republic. Racism was pervasive. In settlements across the Northwest, settlers wanted the region to be entirely free of blacks.[56] Free blacks experienced as much discrimination as they had before the Revolution.[57] Most notably, slavery shaped understandings of personhood across the Republic: to be a citizen required classification as a member of the "white" race.[58]

After the War of 1812, such racialization intensified. Indeed, the generation after 1815 witnessed a growing commitment to excluding all non-whites from the American body politic.[59] Southern states had already started such restrictions, establishing in state constitutions the principle that only "freemen are created equal."[60] For African Americans, Indians, and other peoples of color, the claim that all men are created equal found immediate counter-assertions.[61]

Myth Making in the American Imagination

American historians have long assumed the nation's history to be that of Europeans and white Americans. Histories of early American religion, economy, and political ideology have, accordingly, fallen into separate fields of inquiry that often examine only the experiences of settlers. Not until the late twentieth century did historians begin approaching such questions in new ways. When, they asked, did the rise of "white" America actually begin, and why did a "consciousness of whiteness" emerge so quickly in the early Republic?[62] How did European immigrants like Astor so quickly come to share the same national identity as former colonists?

In *Democracy in America* (1832), Alexis de Tocqueville queried the meanings of the new nation. The "social state of Americans is eminently democratic," he begins. "From their beginning," American settlements "seemed destined to offer the development of freedom."[63] Much like J. Hector St. John de Crèvecoeur in *Letters from an American Farmer* (1782), de Tocqueville extols the American farmer, with his virtuous nature, as the embodiment of the new nation's political subject. The availability of land and its cultivation by small-scale farmers explained the rise of popular sovereignty and the participatory freedom of representative government. In many ways, according to de Tocqueville, the land itself possessed republican virtues. The "American soil," he writes, "absolutely repelled territorial aristocracy."[64]

De Tocqueville's optimism failed to recognize the vast differences within the nation and how whiteness cemented ties between them. Northeastern states faced cold Atlantic seasons while interior settlements wintered within forested lands. Carolinian slaveholders oversaw African American rice cultivation while backcountry traders carried alcohol and manufactured goods to Spanish and Indian villages. How could these diverse political communities come to form the "grand solidarity" that so many Europeans sensed within them?[65] Racial solidarity and myth making fueled the nation's growing self-conception.

While de Tocqueville wrote with confidence about America, the early nineteenth century offered limited actual histories about the nation. There were few libraries, and those that existed were not open to the public. Higher education remained limited to the sons of merchants, ministers, and property owners.[66] Only a handful of newspapers existed west of the Appalachians, and those that did continued to fan the flames of anti-Indian and anti-British sentiments. On the Fourth of July in 1808, a Kentucky newspaper reprinted the Declaration of Independence in full, putting its final grievance about "merciless savages" in italics.[67]

Moreover, nearly all of the nation's institutions of higher education were near the Atlantic. Attempts to build rural colleges failed to take off and only graduated few students. Dartmouth College's founder Eleazar Wheelock had once envisioned educating Indian students in New Hampshire's forests before he succumbed to others' interests. As Mohegan leader Samson Occom wrote: "The Poor Indians, they'll never have much benefit of it."[68]

Without books (or narratives from actual Native peoples), those describing America mythologized its history. They did so mostly in letters.[69] Letter writing remained the primary technology for communications, and thousands of correspondence chains crossed the Atlantic world.[70] Within such communications, writers appealed to a fictional past, one of simplicity and moral certainty.

These writers were in fact participating in something larger than political commentary. They were helping to build the imagination of the nation itself.[71] In these views, the violence and dispossession that structured American expansion became discounted and erased. The "happy" Puritan settlement at Nantucket, for Crèvecoeur, was not founded on violence: "Everything is modern, peaceful, and benign." As for Indigenous peoples, they were simply "hastening towards a total annihilation," in effect anticipating their own destruction.[72]

Such imaginings did more than excuse injustice. They resolved a classic philosophical paradox. Enlightenment thinkers such as Jean-Jacques Rousseau had long questioned the use of violence in the evolution of participatory democracy.[73] Viewing American history as a natural—and not violent—process, these writers erased the conflicts upon which political orders are founded.[74]

To many, the settlement of North America was bloodless. There were no struggles over land, and even the forest wars between empires were less consequential than those in Europe. Moreover, Indians did not constitute foreign states. Nor did they govern their territories. They were either not fully human or lived in primitive forms of development that required uplift—they were what Rousseau termed "noble savages." European settlers became the natural stewards of the land, entitled to its endless bounties. Much like Jefferson in *Notes on the State of Virginia* (1791), Crèvecoeur equated American farmers with Providence. According to Crèvecoeur, white Americans constituted a "race of cultivators."[75] As Jefferson had similarly noted about the yeoman farmer: "Those who labor in the earth are the chosen people of God."[76]

Expulsion or Incorporation: The Ambiguity of Indian Policy

Contradictory impulses characterized writers as well as those who governed the Republic. In the face of such contradictions, American leaders struggled to defend their commitments to republican virtue, particularly when revolutions in France and Haiti formed radically different governments with alternative notions of liberty.[77]

As revolution circulated across the Atlantic, each year brought added political transformation. American thinkers such as Thomas Jefferson advanced competing ideologies on how to govern the new Republic and how to conceive of their changing world. They were participating in a broader conversation about the origins of human nature.[78]

They also appealed to history. They imagined American history in mythic form and in particular believed the young Republic to be exceptional. Their government formed the culmination of centuries-old efforts to reform European politics and even Christendom. As a pastor proclaimed in Jefferson's home county, the "cause of liberty was the cause of God."[79]

Unlike their European counterparts, American leaders remained more attuned to racial differences. Their beliefs about race informed their answers to questions like citizenship, liberty, and intermarriage. It was a dark vision that they fashioned into laws to ensure racial purity. Indians lacked "reason" and failed "to change their pursuits with the change of circumstances" around them, Jefferson stated in his Second Inaugural Address.[80] Moreover, as he noted in *Notes on the State of Virginia*, when "an enemy is within our bowels, the first object is to expel him."[81]

Such expulsion proved impossible in 1776, when one in five people were slaves and Native nations dominated the interior South and Northwest. Throughout his life, Jefferson labored to justify what many viewed as the Republic's defining contradiction: American freedom had emerged alongside slavery and its most revolutionary texts were authored by slaveholders.[82]

More than any other writer, Jefferson became the leading authority on the differences between Indians and African Americans.[83] Appealing to science and reading broadly, he tried to resolve America's racial contradictions. He failed. In his seventies, he was concocting plans to remove African American children altogether from the South while supporting the calls for Indian removal.[84] He could not solve the nation's growing paradoxes.

Contradictory understandings fueled contradictory polices. As examined in chapter 6, the Constitution's opaque category of "Indians not taxed" excluded Native peoples from state representation and taxation. While ceding exclusive authority over Indian affairs to the federal government, the Constitution maintained the vagueness found in the Articles of Confederation, which held that Indians "were not members of any states."[85] Such ambiguity invited rancor, and James Madison in *Federalist 42* mocked this lack of clarity under the Articles. Such a designation, he suggested, "is not yet settled; and has been a question of frequent perplexity and contention."[86]

Contradictory and competing ideas soon hardened into contrasting policies. Ultimately, Jefferson's Indigenous "enemy . . . within our bowels" could be either assimilated or removed. While steeped in debates about the capacity of Indians to accept "civilization," both policies offered Native people little space for autonomy. Each in fact became prescriptions for violence. As the Republic obtained unexpected lands, arguments for removal and assimilation hardened into contrasting ideologies. Analogous to abolitionist debates about slavery, these ideologies bred national spokesmen, including Jefferson and Andrew Jackson.

An "Indian problem" quickly came to define the early Republic. By the time of Jackson's inauguration in 1829, the federal government maintained extensive practices of interior diplomacy and treaty making. These practices clashed with Jackson's belief that such treatment was too conciliatory. Others believed treaty making with Indians was unconstitutional. To many, the only forms of autonomy tolerable within the Union were for white citizens.

Early Federal-Indian Diplomacy

When Jefferson became secretary of state in 1790, he worked alongside leaders who had decades of experiences with Native nations. Washington had gained fame during the Seven Years' War and as president appointed Henry Knox secretary of war in 1789, a position Knox also held under the Articles. Like other military officers, these "federalist" leaders understood the nature of interior diplomacy. They held long-established relationships with Indian leaders.[87]

Diplomacy, trade, and the everyday chores of nation building characterized this first generation of policy makers. Given the diversity of practices, the varied personalities involved, and the contradictory motivations guiding them, no single federal Indian policy best describes the practices of the early Republic.[88] Contradiction more often than consensus guided Indian affairs as the first national government puzzled over questions of national authority.

Knox often courted Native leaders, plying them with trade goods and invitations to meet with Washington. Given the financial burdens confronting the Republic, Knox advocated for diplomatic and economic expediency. He knew that interior nations were powerful adversaries who maintained lands, soldiers, and even continued alliances with England. Knox occasionally encouraged assimilative changes among Native nations, recommending the spread of agrarianism. However, he wanted missionaries—not soldiers—to foster assimilation. As he encouraged: "They should be their friends and fathers."[89] Adopting a dualistic paternalism of Christian friendship and fatherhood, national leaders professed visions of interior coexistence with Native nations. The "Great Father" would guide their needed transformations, but the complete separation of the "races" was not national policy.[90]

An important but often forgotten infrastructure accompanied these efforts. With Washington's encouragement, interior trading houses replaced forts as the locus of federal power.[91] As he relayed in his Fifth Annual Message, Congress must create "ties of interest" with interior tribes:

> Next to a rigorous executive of justice on the violators of peace, the establishment of commerce with the Indian nations . . . is most likely to conciliate their attachment. But it ought to be conducted without fraud, without extortion, with constant and plentiful supplies, with a ready market for the commodities of the Indians and a stated price for what they give in payment and receive in exchange. . . . Should this recommendation accord with the opinion in Congress, they will recollect that it cannot be accomplished by any means *yet* in the hands of the Executive.[92]

Federal "peace medals" were conferred upon interior Native leaders. Such medals honored relationships between Native nations and the federal government. They recognized Native leaders who had kept relative accord within their communities. These medals were material forms of words spoken in council and written on treaties, and Indian leaders displayed them as affirmation of their community's recognized sovereignty. As Knox championed, missionaries also circulated across interior communities, spreading the Gospel and, importantly, modeling the virtuous practices of restraint and temperance that characterized republican ideology.[93]

Such practices evolved into the nation's "civilization" program.[94] Missionaries such as Isaac McCoy soon also advocated for educational opportunities for Indians, arguing that without formal Euro-American education and literacy, "they could not compete with our government."[95] Throughout the early Republic a small but influential number of Native students attended New England seminaries, including Moor's Charity School in New Hampshire and the Cornwall Mission School in Connecticut.[96] Native students enrolled in these institutions gained essential training, much of which they subsequently used to protect their communities against continued aggressions. Many of those who criticized removal policies in the decades to come did so after such education.

However, as was true during the colonial era, the behavior of the interior settlers did not match the ambitions of its leaders. Interior citizens disobeyed federal policies, often seizing Native lands or lives—or both. Kentuckians in particular routinely killed Native peoples. According to Knox, they targeted those "who prided themselves in their attachment to the United States." Limiting such aggression remained the nation's initial policy rather than the destruction or expulsion of interior nations. Besides, Knox concluded, "Blood and injustice . . . would stain the character of the nation, [and] would be beyond all pecuniary calculation."[97]

As Knox navigated the complexities of post-independence interior diplomacy, Jefferson was in Paris. He grew fond of the area surrounding the French-Italian border, writing in one letter: "If I should happen to die . . . I will beg you to send me here."[98] As ambassador to France, he worked to offset U.S. debts. He even participated in the drafting of France's own Declarations on the Rights of Man, his second declaration of independence in under fifteen years. He analyzed the French Revolution and its uncertain aftermath. In Paris he carried unpublished copies of his *Notes on the State of Virginia*, first published there in 1785 and then in London in 1787.[99] Jefferson had arrived in Paris after his wife Martha died in 1782. The city offered the middle-aged planter opportunities for travel, enrichment, and love affairs, including one with his fourteen-year-old slave Sally Hemmings.[100]

After years away from the challenges of interior diplomacy, land policies, and continued constitutional acrimony, his return in 1790 ushered him ba into an already formed government. Yes, he had drafted the Declaration c Independence and then worked with the nation's most important ally, but he had been abroad. In Washington's cabinet, Jefferson felt uncomfortable around the first political party, the Federalists. His deep faith in agrarianism and popular sovereignty contrasted with their views of national power. One cannot help but wonder whether his lack of familiarity with interior affairs informed his views. Unlike Washington and Knox, his expatriation during the 1780s contributed to the romanticized visions that pervade his writings. His continued focus on France, Haiti, and soon Louisiana dominated his presidency, with dire consequences for Native peoples.[101]

Slave Revolts and Interior Indian Campaigns, 1791–1800

For Jefferson, the specter that he feared most came to pass in September 1791. It came neither from North America nor Parisian guillotines. A "terrible Republic," he lamented, rose in Haiti, the former French colony of Saint-Domingue. It confirmed his never-ending fear of slave revolts expressed in *Notes on the State of Virginia*. "I tremble for my country," he wrote, referring to the potential of revolt in Virginia.[102] As the Haitian Revolution confirmed Jefferson's fears, it also shocked European leaders, for whom the notion that slaves could overthrow white rule and establish their own government was unthinkable.[103] "Never was so deep a tragedy presented," Jefferson wrote, "to the feelings of man."[104]

As much as any event before the War of 1812, the Haitian Revolution reshaped U.S. race relations. French efforts to retake the former colony floundered, threatening Napoleon Bonaparte's hopes of a renewed French empire in the Americas. As the 1790s wore on, the Haitian Revolution consumed U.S. foreign affairs and, unintendedly, helped to shift federal policies regarding Native peoples away from assimilation toward forced removal.[105]

American slavery also changed quickly after 1791. In 1793 the Fugitive Slave Act was passed. In 1794 Eli Whitney patented the cotton gin, and in 1800 Gabriel's Rebellion threatened slavery in Virginia. Jefferson was involved in each development, and each influenced Jefferson's visions of empire. As hundreds of Haitian refugees, including numerous interracial couples and families, landed in Philadelphia, they brought tales of revolt.[106] Their social practice of miscegenation contrasted with the Republic, where interracial marriages would have been illegal or at least condemned.[107] They also carried yellow fever, and in response Jefferson fled the city, sending back word of his worries about other insurrections.[108]

As secretary of state, Jefferson had also just received Whitney's application for a patent for his invention, which he understood to be a new technology of both science and commerce. Owner of 150 slaves, Jefferson had seen the growing demand for American cotton firsthand. He also knew of the difficulties inherent in manually removing seeds from cotton bolls. He told Whitney that his patent would be issued "immediately."[109] Finally, in 1800, after Gabriel's Rebellion as president-elect, he read the secret messages sent from Virginia governor James Monroe, who advocated expelling freed blacks from the state. Monroe believed such "persons" had become too "dangerous to the peace of society" and should therefore "be removed."[110] As Jefferson had similarly warned, "If something is not done . . . we shall be the murderers of our own children [for] the revolutionary storm, now sweeping the globe, will be upon us."[111]

Every day Jefferson confronted the challenges of slavery. In response to Monroe, he made inquiries about sending African Americans to Sierra Leone. The necessary expense and freed black resistance to such "colonization" scuttled these proposals. He inquired as well about ways to dispatch African Americans to Haiti.[112] From a broader perspective, it was becoming clear that slavery and slaveholders' fears of revolts threatened the Republic.[113]

Threats to the Republic came from both internal slaves and external Indian "enemies." After the Haitian Revolution, such threats grew interrelated. As interior Native nations continued to fight U.S. expansion in the Northwest, policy makers looked for new solutions other than the "civilization" program. Their searches grew more desperate after Native powers dealt crippling blows to the Republic and the threat of slave insurrections simultaneously grew.

Knox's support for the "civilization" program initially deepened after 1791 when campaigns along the Ohio River crippled the U.S. Army. Battles with confederated Algonquian-speaking peoples—what one scholar has called "the United Indian Nations"—cost over one thousand lives.[114] Costly expeditions led by Generals Hamar (1790), St. Clair (1791), and Wayne (1794) underscored the limitation of federal authority and the continued autonomy of Native nations. Deadly but not decisive interior wars characterized the first decade after independence.

St. Clair's 1791 defeat particularly highlighted such realities. His loss of nine hundred men underscored the sovereignty of Native nations across the Old Northwest.[115] The ability to protect a community and project violence against intruders had long been an essential component of Native power. Although outnumbered by settler populations, Native leaders defied U.S. policies on and off the battlefield, insisting to state leaders, "Money, to us, is no value" and that "no consideration whatever can induce us to sell our lands, on which we get sustenance for our women and children."[116] When they gathered on the banks of the Detroit River in 1793, United Indian Nations leaders offered assurances that they remained committed to peaceful coexistence. Such assurances, however, were possible only if the federal government "agree[s] that the Ohio [River] shall remain the boundary line between us."[117]

In December 1793, as Jefferson worried about slave insurrection, Native people lobbied to get the Ohio River recognized as the permanent boundary of the United States. They had rejected earlier boundary suggestions and attempts to dispossess their homelands.[118] American and foreign leaders recognized such continued Indigenous power in part because British soldiers remained allied with the region's Indians. Despite the provisions of the Treaty of Paris (1783), Native nations drew support at British forts at Detroit, Niagara, and Miami, among others. Such forts had not been abandoned.[119]

When Jefferson became president in 1800, he inherited these challenges. He tracked congressional debates and contemplated new solutions to interior Indian affairs. He looked in particular to legal precedents established in the Republic's first two international treaties—Jay's Treaty (1794) and the Treaty of San Lorenzo (1795). Each concerned interior land boundaries, and each arose in part from the practice of ratifying Indian treaties.

Ever fearful of slave uprisings, Jefferson learned from such debates arguments for a new constitutional authority. He soon sought to acquire territories from foreign powers in order to continue American expansion. His focus centered particularly on New Orleans and the mouth of the Mississippi River, where three-eighths of American agrarian exports were shipped to market. "There is on the globe one single spot," Jefferson wrote, "the possessor of which is our natural and habitual enemy. It is New Orleans." As president, he instructed his secretary of state, James Madison, to find any way, including force, of securing these territories. As Madison instructed American delegates in Paris, "Your discussions . . . may be held on the ground that war is inevitable."[120]

Indian Treaty Making and the Practices of Federal Power

When Jefferson became president in 1801, the government's executive and legislative branches had over a decade's experience in navigating interior relations with tribes and foreign empires. While new practices, particularly treaty making, expanded the authority of the federal government, many questions remained open. Under the Constitution, conquest through war and cessions by treaties were legitimate forms of land acquisition. But did the Constitution authorize the Republic to acquire lands in other ways? Could the federal government "purchase" lands, and if so, how were these lands to be added to the Union? And what was to be done with the Native and non-U.S. peoples upon them?

These questions exposed deep political factions. Madison's suggestion that "war is inevitable" was both a threat and justification. Under the Constitution, war became a legitimate means of territorial conquest. Diplomacy was, however, much easier, and treaties with Indians had added millions of acres of ceded lands to the Republic. It was in fact the practice of interior Indian treaty making that deepened the federal government's—specifically the Senate's—capacity to make treaties and to ratify binding agreements in the face of deepening partisan divides.

In many ways—from ratification to debates on their respective provisions, to the financing of annual budgets for interior forts, to annual tribal payments—treaties became the first instruments of American statecraft. At a time when the federal government struggled to field an army and to pay its debts, treaties became one of its most consistent forms of conflict resolution. Even more than the institutions of the "civilization" program—interior forts or "factory houses" or even missionaries—treaties became the primary institution of Indian policy. The fate of Native nations within the Republic became determined by treaties, nearly four hundred of which the Senate ratified from independence to the formal end of Indian treaty making in 1871.

Indian diplomacy shaped Federalist and Republican administrations. During Jefferson's administration, from 1801 to 1809, the Senate ratified thirty-three Indian treaties, including agreements with "Chickasaw, Choctaw, Creek, Seneca, Delawares, Cherokee, Saux and Foxes, Wyandot, Ottawa, Osage, and Chippewa," among others. Some included over a hundred signatories—such as the 1808 treaty with the Osage—while others involved a multiplicity of Native nations.[121] The 1807 treaty with the Ottawa included "the several nations of Indians, north west of the river Ohio on the one part, and the sachems, chiefs, and soldiers, of the Ottaway, Chippeway, Wyandots, and Pottawatamie nations of Indians, on the other part."[122]

As the U.S. Constitution maintains, treaties reflect "the supreme law of the land," and they provided the young Republic with mechanisms for establishing national peace, trade, and jurisdiction. Treaties ended wars, ceded lands, and over time clarified the constitutional authorities for diplomacy. It is hard to imagine the Republic's history without treaty law.[123]

The Constitution is clear on the exclusive power of the federal government to enter into treaties and manage Indian affairs. As we have seen, states ceded such authorities during the Constitutional Convention and recognized the need for federal authority to resolve interior land conflict.[124] In the first years of governing, treaties clarified such constitutional authority. For Native nations, they also provided resources, trade goods, and even precious currencies in exchange for land.[125]

The Constitution is less clear on how the federal government was to acquire additional lands, particularly those held by foreign powers. The Constitution's territories clause (article 4, section 3) establishes processes for adding new territories to the Union: "Congress shall have Power to dispose of and make all needful Rules and Regulations respecting the Territory or other Property belonging to the United States."

Such authority drew upon the language of the 1787 Northwest Ordinance, passed under the Articles of Confederation. However, upon what constitutional authority might the Republic add foreign territories and *their subjects* to the nation? These questions bedeviled the Republic and were not answered until after years of diplomacy with Indian nations.

The influence of tribes upon the federal government's development is overlooked. "We can never hope to succeed against the Indians," one congressman complained in 1792, "as long as Britain is suffered to retain" its alliances with them.[126] Confusion dominated political discourses.[127] Only after ratification did new forms of governance emerge, and they did so piecemeal. Federal officials responded to the challenges of Indian affairs by debating and testing sets of policies and practices. Inherited from the colonial era, treaties became an essential part of such deliberation. Indian affairs necessitated that the national government puzzle before it powered into its eventual form as an administrative state.

As the power of interior tribes weighed upon the branches of U.S. government, new forms of national power emerged.[128] Paradoxically for Native nations, such practices soon broadened to include the constitutional authority to secure lands not just from Indigenous but also from foreign nations. By broadening the powers of the federal government, Indian treaties established much of the "conceptual mastery" required for other forms of constitutional authority.[129] The power of the federal government to add Indian lands thus clarified other essential questions of national jurisdiction and assisted in its earliest foreign policy efforts, as Indian diplomacy preceded the nation's more famous episodes of foreign affairs.

For example, on May 25, 1789, in his first days in office, Vice President John Adams received a bulky package. As president of the Senate, he was responsible for administering senatorial procedures. The package had arrived from Knox, and it contained two treaties negotiated at Fort Hamar. Both had been drafted under the Articles and awaited ratification under the Constitution. These were the first treaties to come before the Senate.[130]

Many concerns confronted the Republic. Ratification had failed in Rhode Island and North Carolina, each rejecting the Constitution out of fear of the intrusion of centralized authority upon states' rights and individual liberties, respectively. Earlier that year, the nation's first election of congressional representatives drew sparse turnout; only eighteen men voted in one Pennsylvania county.[131] As Washington worried, the nation might soon be "shipwrecked in sight of the Port."[132] In August news arrived from France of its Revolution.

Few had anticipated dramatic changes in international relations. The Republic's first senators knew that their treaty-making authority would soon be required. There was much to clarify about the Constitution, which holds that the executive "shall have power, by and with the consent of the Senate, to make treaties, provided two-thirds of the Senators present concur."

In order to clarify the Constitution's treaty clause, Adams proposed that a committee assess the two treaties in consultation with the executive branch. They issued a recommendation in August on how to interpret the power of the Senate to fulfill such obligations. On September 8, the Senate resolved that Washington "be advised to execute and enjoin an observance" of the first treaty—the "Treaty with the Wyandot," signed January 9, 1789.[133] The Senate had now deliberated on the Republic's first treaty.

This recommendation supported Washington's general view of the treaty-making power. But it required greater clarifications. The Senate's response, he felt, failed to establish proper procedures for ratifying treaties. Without clear procedures, practice became unpredictable. As he wrote: "It strikes me that this point should be well considered and settled, so that our national proceedings, in this respect, may become uniform."[134] The Senate's recommendation and process of consideration were too ambiguous. He sent Knox to deliver the following meditations on the place of treaty making:

> It is said to be the general understanding and practice of Nations, as a check on the mistakes and indiscretions of Ministers or Commissioners,

> not to consider any treaty, negociated, and signed by such Officers, as final and conclusive until ratified by the sovereign or government from which they derive their powers: this practice has been adopted by the United States. . . . It would be adviseable to observe it in the conduct of our treaties with the Indians: for tho' such treaties, being on their part, made by their Chiefs or Rulers . . . [and] formed on our part by the agency of subordinate Officers, it seems both prudent and reasonable, that their acts should not be binding on the Nation until approved and ratified by the Government.

Washington included two questions for the Senate to consider with these treaties:

> The treaties with certain Indian Nations, which were laid before you with my message of the 25th of May last, suggested two questions. . . . 1st. Whether those Treaties were to be considered as perfected, and consequently as obligatory, without being ratified, if not, then 2ndly. whether both, or either, and which of them ought to be ratified?[135]

Washington asked for the treaties to be treated separately and for the Senate to vote upon them individually. He underscored the necessity of solidifying federal authority over such practices. No interior agreements could be conducted that did not have such "binding" power. Otherwise, he cautioned, the "mistakes and indiscretions of Ministers or Commissioners" might proliferate.

Washington understood that treaty making curbed the ability of individuals to act indiscriminately—particularly to acquire lands. He aspired to adopt "uniform" governing practices. Individual and concentrated interests, however, threatened the evolution and practice of legislative values, if not national priorities. The Senate needed to comprehend the enormity of this responsibility and treat it accordingly. Its recommendation that Washington "be advised to execute and enjoin an observance" was insufficient. It lacked clarity and foresight. Such a recommendation displayed little of the requisite conceptual mastery needed to tackle the challenges of interior and national governance.

By the end of September, the Senate had ratified the Wyandot Treaty and soon turned to additional treaties with the Six Nations, Creek, and Cherokee. The Republic's treaty-making powers had focused exclusively on Indian affairs. A total of eight treaties came before the Senate in its first six sessions.[136] To become "uniform" required the Senate to interpret its authorities and apply them to each treaty. Such procedural powers grew with each debate and formed the sediment upon which the Republic's international treaties were soon negotiated. These international negotiations often concerned Indian affairs also.

Jay's Treaty, the Treaty of Greenville, and Foreign and Domestic Affairs

Starting in 1794, the Senate began debating treaties that involved non-Indian signatories from Spain, England, and France. These debates grew contentious and raised unanswered questions about which branch of government should conduct foreign affairs. Such debates illuminated one of the dominant political questions of the time: toward which major European power should U.S. policy lean?[137] A ten-month period from November 1794 through August 1795 illuminates how "foreign" relations evolved from "domestic" Indian treaty making.

In August 1795, eighty-nine Native signatories from nine Nations affirmed their marks on the "Treaty With the Wyandot, etc., 1795" at Fort Greenville, Ohio. It had taken two months to negotiate and followed General Anthony Wayne's victory at Fallen Timbers the previous summer. In the treaty, the United Indian Nations ceded two-thirds of Ohio to the United States, which recognized their sovereignty over much of the Old Northwest. Article 3 is one of the longest ever written into an Indian treaty, a ninety-line provision establishing boundaries between "the lands of the United States and the lands of the said Indian tribes."[138] The treaty also allowed for U.S. forts to be stationed across the region.

Unlike constitutional rights for individual citizens, treaties provide "exchanges" between sovereigns. At Greenville United Indian Nations leaders exchanged most of Ohio in recognition of their sovereignty over their remaining homelands. The treaty also forbade unlicensed trading across the Old Northwest. Essentially, it attempted to build a mutually governed world where members of each sovereign power would prevent "private revenge or retaliation" against one another. "Instead," the treaty continues, "complaint shall be made by the party injured, to the other." The treaty also extended criminal jurisdiction over U.S. citizens, and it recognized the authority of tribal communities over "their towns," "hunting camps," and "boundaries of the land."[139] In addition, the treaty includes stipulations for continued diplomacy. Negotiated in painstaking detail over the entire summer, the treaty was meant to govern the region's future.

At Greenville the United States also asked to make earlier treaties "henceforth . . . void." In the process, it legitimated its own claims to the region and established the federal government's exclusive authority to acquire interior lands.[140] Article 5 in particular establishes the right of the federal government to acquire lands from Native nations:

> When those tribes, or any of them, shall be disposed to sell their lands, or any part of them, they are to be sold only to the United States; and until such sale, the United States will protect all said Indian tribes in the quiet enjoyment of their lands against all citizens of the United States, and against all other white persons who intrude upon the same.[141]

While in the short term the treaty limited the expansion of the United States, in the long term it preserved its authority to acquire such lands in the future. Three decades later, the Supreme Court affirmed the constitutionally recognized right of federal preemption in *Johnson v. M'Intosh* (1823).[142] The precedents for such deliberation began during these treaty negotiations.

The exclusive right of federal preemption arose from a long-standing history of interior diplomacy. It emerged in an imperial context because at Greenville Wayne held many advantages. Some he had achieved on the battlefield, reflecting the growing strength of his forces and their glistening arms. Equally important, Wayne carried powerful new words from England. There, a new agreement—Jay's Treaty—had just been signed in November 1794. Negotiated across the Atlantic, it placed additional pressure on Native nations to accede to U.S. demands. Jay's Treaty and the treaty of Greenville were simultaneous U.S. efforts to diminish Indian power.

Throughout 1794–95 the United Indian Nations confronted relentless pressures. As Britain agreed in the treaty to abandon its interior forts, Native leaders lost important allies, resources, and support. They lost even more, as they not only ceded vast lands but also abandoned long-standing efforts to get the Ohio River recognized as a formal U.S. boundary. They were losing more and more of the future, as they even allowed U.S. forts in the region. Such provisions reflected the growing power of the United States, which had successfully isolated many Native nations from their European allies.[143]

As in the Treaty of Paris of 1783, England in 1794 abandoned most of its commitments to Great Lakes Indians, though the United States did recognize select forms of Indigenous authority in Jay's Treaty. Of its many provisions, the treaty includes protections for "Indians dwelling on either side of the said boundary line" and recognizes Native rights "to pass and repass on land or inland navigation into the respective territories and countries of the two parties, on the continent . . . and to carry on trade and commerce with each other." The treaty underscores the sovereignty of Indigenous peoples, and these rights became guarantees of Native American rights in what would become international law. Such rights endure to this day, as Native peoples in both the United States and Canada draw upon such precedents to travel "freely" between the two states. Long before Canada became a confederation in 1867, Britain guaranteed the rights of Native peoples to travel through its lands. In no small measure, Indian affairs informed America's first "international" treaty.

Treaty Making and the Origins of the Louisiana Purchase

Jay's Treaty provoked rancorous debates across the Republic. Some scholars trace the evolution of the "first-party system" to the factions that emerged after its slim two-thirds passage of 20-10.[144] Washington even shut down House requests for additional information about budgetary finances in order to assure its passage.[145] As he had with the Wyandot Treaty of 1789, Washington placed treaty-making power with the Senate.

Like many southerners, Jefferson abhorred Washington and the federalists' decision. Jefferson and his followers believed that the process of treaty making required more deliberation.[146] Treaty making, they believed, was too important to leave to the executive and Senate. "The true theory of our constitution," Jefferson wrote, is "that when a treaty is made . . . the representatives are as free as the President & Senate to consider where the national interest requires or forbids their giving the forms & force of law."[147] Like many divides of the era, those provoked by Jay's Treaty revolved around visions of representative government and thus the meanings of democracy itself.[148]

There was, however, more to Jefferson's concerns. As the power of treaty making became concentrated away from the House, he worried that such power took governance away from the Republic's citizens. He was explicit about such concerns. The "powers of legislation" should be shaped by the House of Representatives:

> On the precedent now to be set will depend the future construction of our constitution, and whether the powers of legislation shall be transferred from the P. [president] Senate & H. of R. to P., Senate & *Piarningo* or any *Indian, Algerine* or any other *chief*.[149]

For Jefferson the powers of treaty making had become too concentrated in the hands of the executive and Senate. Such concentrated power deepened his greatest fears: the specter of multiracial diplomacy and its potential for black insurgency.

The rights of Native peoples had made their way into the Republic's first treaty with a European power. Jefferson found such developments repugnant. Treaty making should neither apply to Haiti nor elevate the rights of Indigenous peoples.[150] As president, he reversed such concentrations of authority—and did so by violating his own expressed concerns about the constitutional legitimacy of executive action.

In 1801 Jefferson worried that France might reassert its claims to Louisiana. He believed that he could develop the constitutional authority needed to acquire foreign lands. He also hoped to curb growing rivalries along the Mississippi and to secure U.S. sovereignty therein. In a world of such legal pluralism, U.S. claims to the Mississippi were but one of several. As U.S. diplomats in France worked to secure New Orleans or some other port along the Gulf Coast, they sought access to the mouth of the Mississippi and to limit restrictions over American exports.

No one anticipated that Napoleon's government would offer all of Louisiana. However, Napoleon was unable to reclaim Saint-Domingue. French forces disintegrated, overcome by disease and Haiti's revolutionary army.[151] Napoleon's war of reconquest cost soldiers, francs, and ships, and he offered all remaining French territories in North America to the United States.[152] Once hopes of a restored French empire had withered in the Caribbean, French imperialists no longer envisioned Louisiana as a breadbasket for Haitian plantations. Louisiana would not become a hinterland of cattle, timber, and gardens drawn from worlds in which Native peoples held long-standing authority.

Among their many advantages, Jefferson noted that additional western territories would provide new homelands for eastern Native nations. The Louisiana Purchase would provide lands to Indians on the east side of the Mississippi, and there was little doubt that treaties would facilitate such territorial exchanges. Jefferson, however, confronted a major problem: southern leaders had long expressed disdain at treaty making. As one Georgian representative complained about the Cherokee Treaty at Hopewell, it "violate[s] the retained sovereignty and legislative right of this State," and moreover, such "pretended" treaties were "repugnant to the principles and harmony of the Federal Union."[153] Jefferson understood that the Louisiana Purchase Treaty with France had to be different. He ensured that, unlike Jay's Treaty, it involved exclusively European signatories with scant attention to Native Nations. He also ensured that it was led by Virginians, not federalists like Jay. A vote on the treaty of cession was scheduled for October 17.

Serious challenges, however, remained. Most notably, Jefferson worried that the nation might acquire thousands of new subjects along with its new lands. Throughout the summer, he drafted letters to quell concerns and argued that the national government had authority to naturalize new subjects through treaties. Where such authority resided in the Constitution, however, remained unclear, and he even expected that Congress might need to alter it altogether. The treaty "will of course require an amendment of the Constitution," he wrote.[154] As he continued on August 9, the Constitution "has not given [the government] a power of holding foreign territory, and still less of incorporating it into the Union. An amendment . . . seems necessary for this."[155] As he noted to James Madison on the matter of naturalizing new subjects through treaty making:

> Louisiana as ceded by France . . . is made a part of the U.S. Its white inhabitants shall be citizens, and stand, as their rights and obligations, on the same footing with other citizens of the U.S. in analogous situations. . . . No new state shall be established, nor any grants of land made therein, other than to Indians, in exchange for equivalent portions of land occupied by them.[156]

New constitutional authority might provide precedent for subsequent incorporations, what Jefferson termed "analogous" situations, such as Spanish Florida. It too, he surmised, "shall become a part of the U.S. Its white inhabitants shall thereupon be citizens, on the same footing with other citizens of the U.S."[157]

In the space of a few years, Jefferson had changed his mind about the relative place of the House of Representatives in the treaty-making process. Now president, he understood that increased executive authority provided the constitutional powers needed to incorporate not only new lands but also subjects. Such naturalization differed from the Republic's previous laws, first established in 1790. Jefferson's new vision, however, was consistent with the nation's growing racial restrictions. While he hoped for involvement from the House of Representatives, Jefferson now embraced treaty making for naturalization and territorial expansion. Law making became even further concentrated in the executive and Senate, which now developed the constitutional powers to (1) obtain foreign lands via purchase and (2) selectively naturalize "white inhabitants." The protection of slaves as property was also written into the treaty.[158]

The logic of race informed Jefferson's visions of expansion. New white citizens existed in the Republic's adjacent territories—Louisiana, Florida, potentially Canada—lands that provided spaces not only for the mass deportation of Native peoples but also for the expansion of slavery. Jefferson felt comfortable adding white subjects to the Republic and protecting the property of slave owners. Race fueled his policies of expansion. He believed, as president, that he could broaden the Republic's democratic possibilities by naturalizing foreign "white" subjects, doing so in a process that he understood would also provide new strategies aimed at removing Native nations. A racial triad guided his philosophies: expansion fueled the naturalization of white subjects, the protection of slave owners, and Indian removal.

All three processes accelerated following the debates of 1803. Indeed, a new "kingdom" now became possible. Together with the development of the cotton gin, the Louisiana Purchase made possible the opening of new lands to slave cultivation while providing proximate territories for Indian removal. The lands along the Mississippi quickly became a kingdom for cotton, one populated with slaves trafficked from eastern southern states.[159] Removal targeted all Indian nations in between.

Indians and States' Rights in the South

The United States was founded upon the ideal of universal equality: "All men are created equal." The Constitutional Convention, Haitian Revolution, and Louisiana Purchase transformed and restricted that concept, creating forms of social and legal exclusion. The Republic's naturalization laws, structures of representative government, and gendered systems of property ownership excluded Native peoples, African Americans, and other men and women "of color." As the *Georgia Journal* wrote in 1825, "Indians" and "free negroes" were "of an inferior order," and in the minds of Jefferson and other founders, all people were not created equal.[160]

After the Purchase, new land seizures contributed to an explosion in slavery and its ideologies of racial superiority. By 1820 a domestic slave trade involving over a million slaves expanded across the "deep South."[161] Generating astronomical profits, cotton became king, and it did so upon former Indian homelands. Southern presidents from Jefferson through Jackson all championed the removal of Native nations. They understood that removal fueled slavery's expansion.

As in the Northwest, such dispossession was not natural. It resulted from the choices that politicians and their constituents made. Native peoples resisted such choices. They took to the battlefield. They published in English and new Native-language print culture—such as the *Cherokee Phoenix* newspaper.[162] Others took refuge in Appalachian forests or fled in advance of removal forces. Thousands died in deportation centers, where they were exposed to cold, hunger, and cholera.[163] Southern expansion followed different paths than in the Northwest. While the federal government oversaw military affairs, it developed a limited footprint in the interior South. By 1796, for example, the federal government had established twenty military posts in the Northwest, from Fort Mackinac in Michigan to Fort Finney in Kentucky to Fort Ontario in New York. In the South, by contrast, only four federal posts extended along fewer than fifty miles of the Tennessee River. One lone post, Fort Fidius, was established in Georgia.[164] Twenty years later, fewer than two hundred regular army troops were stationed in Georgia, Kentucky, and Tennessee combined.[165] For four decades after 1776, the federal government developed little infrastructure in the South.

Native nations, particularly Creek, Cherokee, and Choctaw communities, governed these lands. They determined the interior South's trade, travel, and politics. While the history of each nation is distinctive, they all incorporated Euro-American economies, education, religion, and governance, fusing them with their existing values to care for their citizens.

Such transformations became most visible when Native leaders adopted Western clothing, learned English, established Christian churches, and eventually sued in court. These nations had also welcomed white traders into their societies, and intermarriage created new class distinctions that correlated with federal emphases on agrarianism and private property. Gendered divisions of labor and American notions of patriarchy emerged, diminishing female authority.[166] Many leaders across each nation resembled the property owners of white settlements in both economic and social ways, including developing small to medium-sized plantations worked by slaves. Their political systems and skin color, however, differed—and that threatened southern white leaders.

Not all tribal members embraced such new practices. Dissension pervaded many nations, and compromises were forged. Among the Cherokee, new "hybrid system[s] of social welfare" blended key elements of Cherokee matriarchal systems with Euro-American institutions like schools, hospitals, and churches, in which women's authority dominated.[167] Such adaptation and hybridity characterized this period, as communities responded to threats to their homelands.

Unlike in the North, southern Native nations fought against territorial rather than federal forces. Leaders such as Andrew Jackson in Tennessee gained fame by leading local militiamen. During the Creek War of 1813–14, his forces killed over a thousand Creek soldiers, women, and children.[168]

Native nations found that the southern Americans they interacted with differed in mindset from northerners. Settlers like Jackson developed a southern culture in which forms of authority resided not only within their households but also in their states. In particular, Native nations faced a torrent of "states' rights" proponents who despised federal treaty making. Georgia's representatives routinely complained that treaties violated their sovereignty, and they were joined by a generation of southern leaders who espoused similar critiques of federal and Indigenous power.

The War of 1812 escalated such divisions. Outright denunciations of Native existence followed. A constitutional crisis emerged as many southern leaders did not believe that Native nations warranted inclusion within the United States. After the Creek War, Georgia's leaders passed legislation to extend jurisdiction over all lands "assigned to the Indians."[169] The state also extended its criminal laws over Native lands, in violation of established treaties. In 1819 it made further assertions: "The soil within her [Georgia's] boundaries should be subjected to her control, and . . . her police, organization and government should be fixed and permanent."[170] Across the South, states viewed Indian lands—recognized by the federal government and established by treaties—as their own. As was the case with their other grievances against the federal government, southern leaders abhorred what they believed to be federal intrusions into the sovereignty of their respective states.

Like Jefferson before he became president, Jackson felt equally disgusted with treaty making. It was "absurd," he declared, "for the sovereign to negotiate by treaty with the subject."[171] He believed that the federal government held exclusive power to shape the Republic's borders. In a defining constitutional crisis, competing visions of constitutional authority converged after Jackson became president in 1828 after an election in which he won over 96 percent of all votes cast in Georgia.[172] Such a crisis soon reached the highest court in the land, establishing fundamental doctrines in U.S. constitutional and federal Indian law.

Indian Removal and the Marshall Court

The actions of Georgia's leaders ran parallel to the Republic's limited capacity to manage the expansion of slavery. In fact, the two challenges intersected. Each year U.S. leaders attempted to manage slavery's expansion. They failed. States' rights proponents challenged federal treaties and remained defiant about their authority over Indian affairs. "The protection guaranteed by the United States to the Nations of Indians . . . is unconstitutional," declared the *Savannah Georgian* in 1826, "and a trespass on State sovereignty."[173] Disputes over Indian affairs exposed fractures within the Constitution.

Georgian leaders outlined a twofold critique of federal authority. First, they charged that treaties had unconstitutional standing vis-à-vis the state's jurisdiction. Second, they argued that it was the federal government's obligation to extend a state's sovereignty into such lands, thereby extinguishing Indian title altogether. As the federal government became more powerful, states' rights proponents came to believe that such powers should be vested in them rather than the nation. While treaties had helped the young Republic acquire much of the continent, states now looked to take over that function.

Georgia's leaders did more than advocate for the disavowal of treaties. They used violence to achieve it. In a series of repressive measures, Cherokee citizens were imprisoned, held without trial, and murdered. Georgia required state-issued passes for those traveling into Cherokee territories and oaths of allegiance to Georgia laws. Cherokee property was seized, and a militia unit, the Georgia Guard, enforced such harassment. As Secretary of War John Calhoun warned Cherokee leaders in 1824, their existence was "incompatible" with Georgia's. It was now impossible "for you to remain . . . as a distinct society or nation, within the limits of Georgia."[174]

The same secretary of war who threatened Indian leaders also oversaw the creation of the Office of Indian Affairs which, after the passage of the Indian Removal Act of 1830, coordinated removal. Many Cherokees felt betrayed. They had relinquished claims to millions of acres since the Revolution and had even allied with the United States in the War of 1812, doing so against their Creek neighbors in Alabama.

More so than the Creek, they built educational, governance, and social welfare programs that resembled Euro-Americans. Their newspaper the *Cherokee Phoenix* was published by editors, like Elias Boudinot, who attended boarding schools. Unlike southern newspapers, it used the Cherokee syllabary developed by Sequoyah.[175]

Conflicts with Georgia deepened throughout the 1820s. They exploded in 1830. After Jackson's election, Cherokee efforts to petition Congress, lobby federal officials, and generate national attention intensified but lost traction. Jackson had made removal the centerpiece of his presidency. As Vice President Martin Van Buren later recalled, "There was no measure, in the whole course of his administration of which he was more exclusively the author."[176] The passage of the Removal Act of 1830 divided Congress, passing by only five votes.

The act codified a generation of southern efforts to expel Native nations. But was it constitutional? Did Congress have the legislative authority to abrogate the commitments the federal government had made? Could Congress pass a law that defied ratified treaties, which reflect "the supreme law of the land," according to the Constitution? Cherokee legal activism now precipitated these questions.

For Native nations, the essential question raised by the U.S. Constitution was whether Native communities held authority over their own lands. Generations of practices and a body of international legal theory suggested that they did. Washington affirmed such sentiments and used treaty making to keep white settlers and Indians in separate jurisdictions.

Moreover, the Constitution is clear that Indian affairs fall under the jurisdiction of the federal government, whose powers transcend the authority of individual states. However, by categorizing "Indians not taxed" and equating tribes with "foreign nations," the founders left open questions of the standing of Native peoples within the Republic itself. If they could not vote or be naturalized, how exactly did they fit into the Republic?

Five decades of treaty making had established customary practices that recognized tribal authority. While their lands had become diminished, the Cherokee nonetheless held jurisdiction over these communities, their members, and even U.S. citizens who entered them. By targeting not only Cherokee members but also U.S. citizens, Georgia violated multiple national laws.

The Cherokee now argued that Georgia's efforts were unconstitutional. As the state attempted to legislate Indian communities out of existence, it now faced legal challenges about its jurisdiction to do so. Two cases before the Supreme Court would decide such questions as well as establish legacies to follow, and Chief Justice John Marshall oversaw each: *Cherokee Nation v. Georgia* (1831) and *Worcester v. Georgia* (1832).

Even though treaties created safeguards against settlers, protections from the federal government were weak. Once gold was discovered on Cherokee lands, Georgia accelerated its laws to abolish the Cherokee, calling for the redistribution of their 9 million acres to the state's counties. Other laws declared that after June 1830, all Cherokee land claims would be null and void. In fact, much of the impetus behind the Removal Act came from Georgia's congressional representatives—the act was passed on June 1, the same day Georgia passed its own state laws to that effect.

The Cherokee had used formal and informal networks to voice their concerns. In 1829 they formed a constitutional government similar to that of the Republic. They established their own presses, alphabet, schools, and diplomatic corps to lobby Congress. Famously, their leaders visited Washington under Chief John Ross in 1829. Staying throughout the months of Jackson's first term, they received support from many former members of the Adams administration.

They also enlisted the support of the former attorney general William Wirt, who joined their judicial intervention. Before their case was filed, however, Georgia demonstrated its contempt for their efforts. State police imprisoned and hanged Corn Tassel, a Cherokee leader, on trumped-up charges in a deliberate display of state power. Meanwhile, members of the Georgia legislature issued threats against Marshall and the national government, daring them to intercede.

In March 1831 the Cherokee filed a request for an injunction. The nation invoked its history of treaties with the United States and its standing as an independent government. They argued that the state's repeated encroachments into their lands breached their recognized sovereignty and equated themselves to a foreign government, given their long-standing history of treaty making. They further detailed how their economies were essential to their sovereignty and how their adoption of Christianity reflected their integration into U.S. society. Refinements of culture were also on display across their leadership classes, whose sensibilities mirrored those of Republic leaders.

The Cherokee, Choctaw, Creek, Chickasaw, and Seminole Nations had become known as the Five Civilized Tribes due to their incorporation of Euro-American institutions. Cherokee leaders were educated in American schools. Many, like Boudinot, had attended New England schools, and their new advocacy took them across the Republic courting allies.

Unfortunately for the Cherokee, the Supreme Court declined to hear their case. According to Marshall, the Cherokee did not constitute a "foreign government," as they maintained. While he recognized their uniqueness, he stated that the Court did not have the authority to take the case because Indian affairs were not comparable to U.S. relations with other nations. The Cherokee thus could not bring a case against Georgia directly. In a lengthy explanation, Marshall offered a pronouncement on the state of Indian affairs and outlined key features of the relationship between the national government and Indian tribes. Such clarifications were akin to the land and occupancy rights that the Court had held in his previous ruling, *Johnson v. M'Intosh*.

By not recognizing the Cherokee Nation as a separate sovereign, Marshall provided new definitions of Indian sovereignty. If not separate governments, then what were Indian tribes? "They may, more correctly perhaps, be denominated domestic dependent nations. . . . Their relationship to the United States resembles that of a ward to his guardian. They look to our government for protection; rely upon its kindness and its power; appeal to it for relief of their wants."[177] In his pronouncement, Marshall established definitions of what constitutes the standing of a tribe. He invented the term "domestic dependent nation," indicating that they were a government dependent upon a federal guardian.

The 1831 case was not the appropriate legal vehicle for challenging Georgia's laws. The next year such a case arose. Wirt again litigated, now on behalf of Samuel Worcester, a U.S. citizen working alongside Boudinot. Worcester was imprisoned by the state for traveling without a license. Georgia's laws, he argued, violated the treaty rights of the Cherokee and his constitutional rights. The case represented a clear conflict regarding federal authority over the rights of citizens.

Handed down on March 3, 1832, the ruling in *Worcester v. Georgia* articulated a new vision of Native political power. It confirmed the Cherokee government's authority to govern itself and those who entered its territories. Marshall further declared that the Cherokee Nation constituted

> a distinct community occupying its own territory, with boundaries accurately described, in which the laws of Georgia can have no force, and which the citizens of Georgia have no right to enter, but with assent of the Cherokee themselves, or in conformity with treaties, and with the acts of congress. The whole intercourse between the United States and

this nation, is, by our constitution and laws, vested in the government of the United States. The act of the state of Georgia . . . is consequently void.

Like their white neighbors around them, the Cherokee were under the jurisdiction of "the government of the United States." However, they retained sovereignty over their "own territory." The laws of Georgia thus did not apply. Its acts were "consequently void" and also, Marshall reasoned, "repugnant to the constitution, laws, and treaties of the United States."[178]

Marshall's decision eventually freed Worcester and caused euphoria across Cherokee communities. Boudinot, in Boston at the time, was delighted. "The question is for ever settled as to who is right," he declared, "and who is wrong."[179] The decision came nearly fifty years to the day that Parliament had surrendered after Yorktown, and after half a century of U.S. expansion. A clear doctrine of Indian law had now been established: tribes retained limited but nonetheless recognized forms of sovereign authority, enshrined through treaties under the "protection" of the federal government. Such authority extended over their members, their recognized territories, and U.S. citizens who entered upon them. It was an emergent doctrine, one recognized by the Supreme Court and rooted in decades of treaty making, customary practices, and war. Eventually, this doctrine elevated tribes to a separate plane of U.S. jurisprudence, one outside the jurisdiction of states, local governments and, at the time, the House of Representatives. Treaties were the ties that held this doctrine together. Just as they had structured the Republic, they now bound tribes to it.

✦

Augustine Clayton represented Georgia in Congress at the time. In 1830 he was a state judge who had ordered Corn Tassel's execution, earning support that he used to gain election to Congress. Clayton and Georgia's leaders had flouted Marshall's authority in 1830, and now they did so again. This time they were joined by President Jackson, who scorned Marshall and sat idly by as the nation veered toward a potential constitutional crisis. On the floor of the House, Clayton had warned that Georgia awaited "the application of a match to blow the Union into ten thousand fragments." Would Congress spark an inferno and blow "the Union to pieces?"[180]

The inferno that Clayton predicted arrived during the fiery trial of Abraham Lincoln's presidency. Its origins were forged in the inability of the federal government to resolve long-standing questions of constitutional authority. Worcester was freed by Georgia, which pardoned him after months of national pressure. He accepted the pardon and release, but his Cherokee compatriots now suffered. Just as the Union itself would be shattered in 1860, the Cherokee Nation was swept out of Georgia into fragments, destined, like so many Indian nations, for lands purchased from France a generation prior.

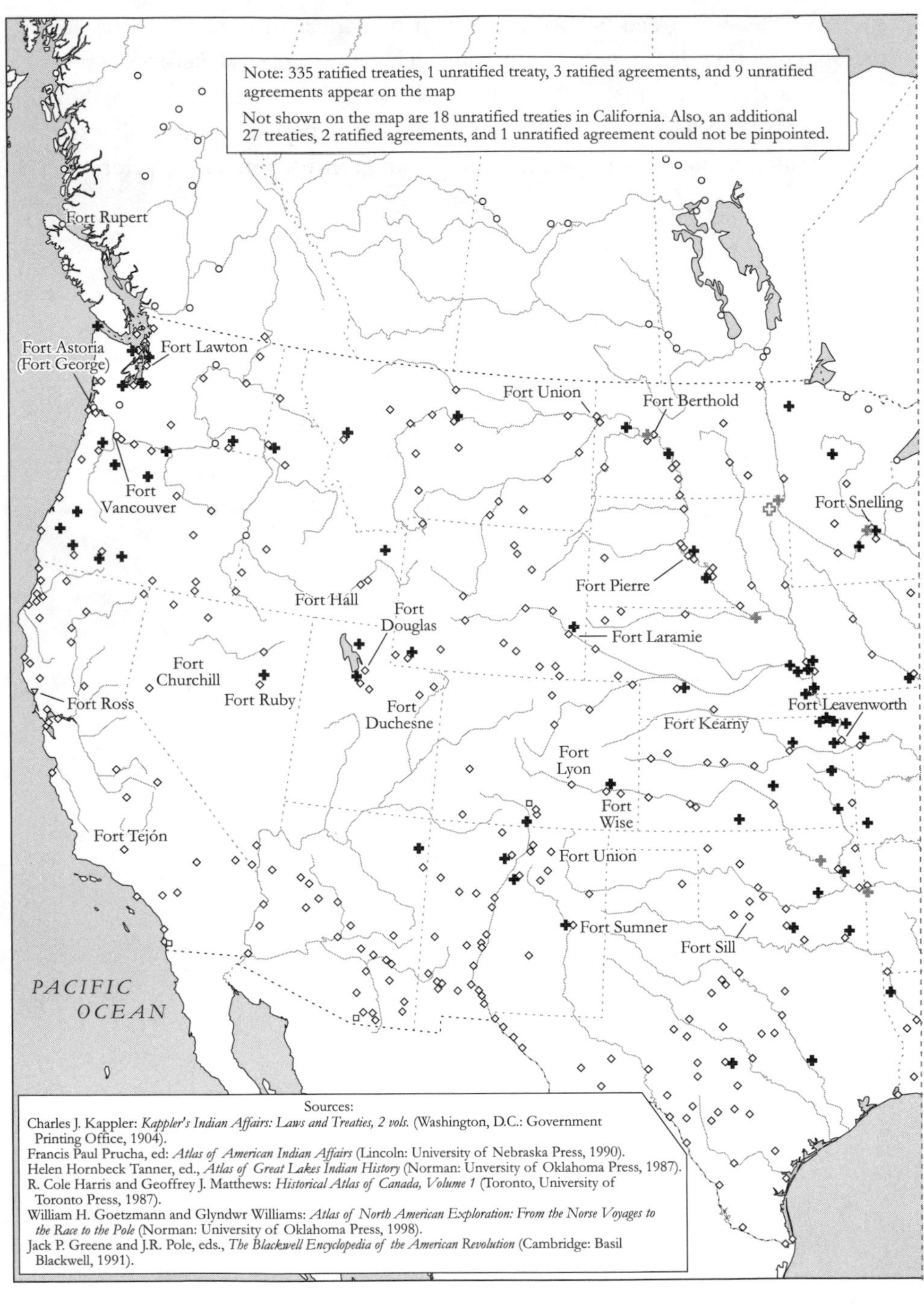

Note: 335 ratified treaties, 1 unratified treaty, 3 ratified agreements, and 9 unratified agreements appear on the map
Not shown on the map are 18 unratified treaties in California. Also, an additional 27 treaties, 2 ratified agreements, and 1 unratified agreement could not be pinpointed.
Fort Rupert
Fort Astoria (Fort George)
Fort Lawton
Fort Union
Fort Berthold
Fort Vancouver
Fort Snelling
Fort Pierre
Fort Hall
Fort Douglas
Fort Laramie
Fort Churchill
Fort Ruby
Fort Ross
Fort Duchesne
Fort Leavenworth
Fort Kearny
Fort Lyon
Fort Wise
Fort Tejón
Fort Union
Fort Sumner
Fort Sill
PACIFIC OCEAN
Sources:
Charles J. Kappler: *Kappler's Indian Affairs: Laws and Treaties, 2 vols.* (Washington, D.C.: Government Printing Office, 1904).
Francis Paul Prucha, ed: *Atlas of American Indian Affairs* (Lincoln: University of Nebraska Press, 1990).
Helen Hornbeck Tanner, ed., *Atlas of Great Lakes Indian History* (Norman: Unversity of Oklahoma Press, 1987).
R. Cole Harris and Geoffrey J. Matthews: *Historical Atlas of Canada, Volume 1* (Toronto, University of Toronto Press, 1987).
William H. Goetzmann and Glyndwr Williams: *Atlas of North American Exploration: From the Norse Voyages to the Race to the Pole* (Norman: University of Oklahoma Press, 1998).
Jack P. Greene and J.R. Pole, eds., *The Blackwell Encyclopedia of the American Revolution* (Cambridge: Basil Blackwell, 1991).

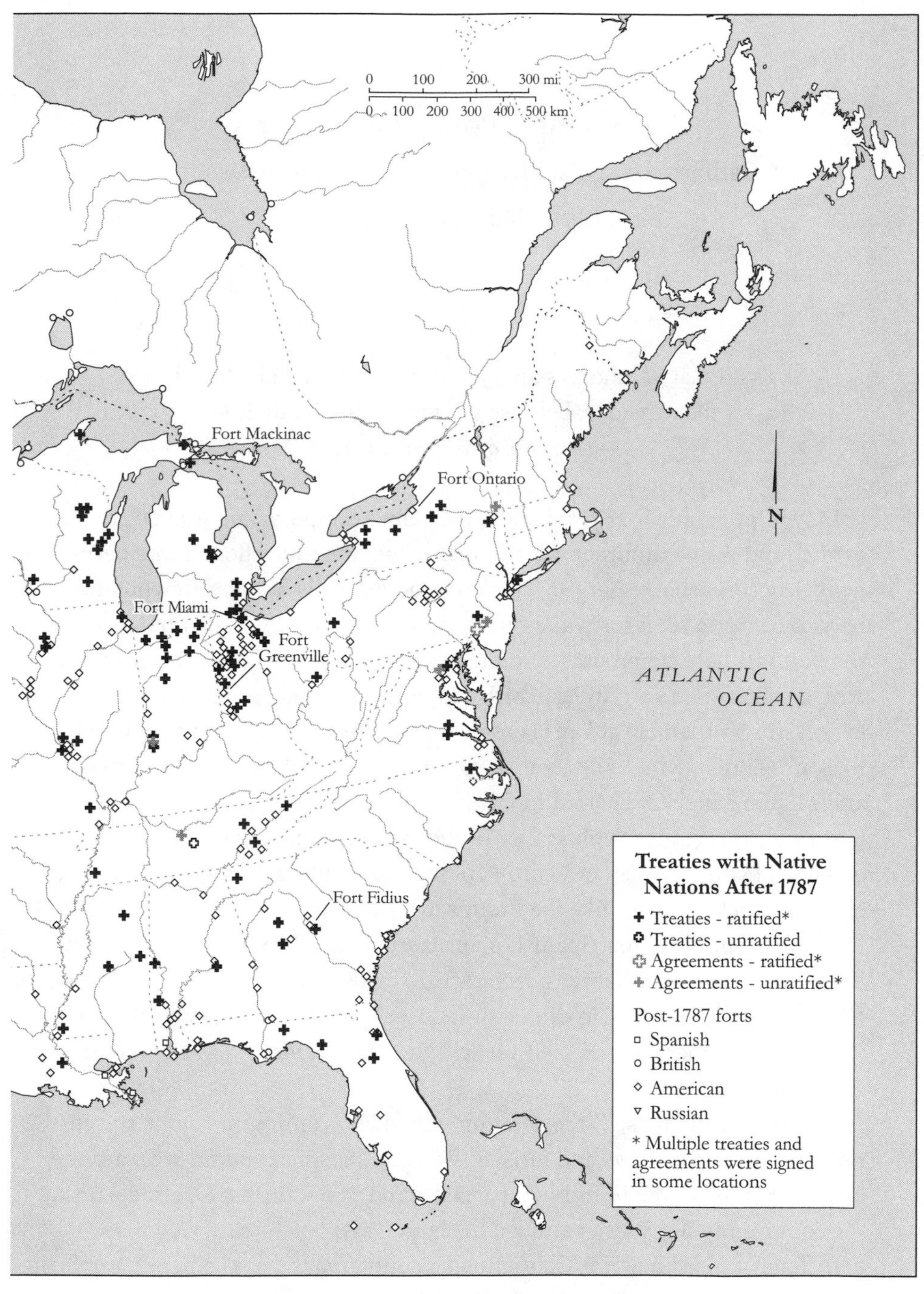

0 100 200 300 mi
0 100 200 300 400 500 km
N
Fort Mackinac
Fort Ontario
Fort Miami
Fort Greenville
Fort Fidius
ATLANTIC OCEAN
Treaties with Native Nations After 1787
Treaties - ratified*
Treaties - unratified
Agreements - ratified*
Agreements - unratified*
Post-1787 forts
Spanish
British
American
Russian
* Multiple treaties and agreements were signed in some locations

8 • Foreign Policy Formations

California, the Pacific, and the Borderlands Origins of the Monroe Doctrine

She said that . . . she was angry with the priests and all the others at the missions, because we were living on their land.
—*Response of Toypurina (1785)*

In 1775, after only four years, the settlement's temporary quarters were discarded, and the community moved north along the valley floor. More permanent structures soon emerged. Thick new adobe walls built by growing numbers of converts soon formed a quadrangle—the first European building in the basin. It held storerooms, a kitchen, three guestrooms and, most important, a church and sacristy.[1] Spanish religious and state leaders envisioned a long-lasting settlement at San Gabriel, the fourth and most interior of California's mission system. "The location is very good," Fathers Antonio Cruzado and Miguel Sánchez reported in 1783. "It has an oak grove quite close which is very advantageous for obtaining timber and firewood, and is within sight of a great plain."[2] As Father Pedro Font had noted in January 1776, "This is a country which . . . looks like the Promised Land."[3]

Throughout the 1780s, Spanish plans came to fruition. Franciscan leaders hoped to broaden San Gabriel's architecture and social community. Like their civil leaders, they worked to extend the authority of cross and crown along the Pacific. As in other parts of their vast empire, Alta California was designed to serve both majesties.

As the seasons passed, the mission expanded, coming to comprise separate dormitories for boys and girls, a two-room hospital and, in 1791, a stone church. Soldiers lived in mission barracks and maintained discipline within the community. They also patrolled the larger basin of Tovaangar, where resident Tongva, also known as Gabrielino, encountered the newcomers.[4] By 1780 the mission included 452 converts. By 1785 it had 843 full-time converts and had baptized over 1,200.[5] Its herds of livestock grew even faster, tripling in the same period from under one thousand to three thousand.[6]

The community's rising population was not attributable to a rising birth rate.[7] Fear compelled Tongva missionization and threats fueled the mission's growth. While friars proclaimed the spiritual glories to be found only under their direction, soldiers communicated more immediate lessons. Stationed in what many thought to be Spain's most "dreaded hinterland posting," they faced few constraints within the colony.[8] Their behavior ranged from uninterested to terrifying. "The soldiers, clever as they are at lassoing," Junípero Serra, father-president of California's missions, wrote of his compatriots at San Gabriel, "would catch Indian women with their lassos to become prey for their unbridled lust." Their husbands, fathers, and sons, he continued, "would try to defend their wives, only to be shot down with bullets."[9]

Violence in California came in many forms. Rape, murder, and torture became everyday acts of colonization. In the words of Viceroy Antonio María de Bucareli, such violence rendered those who resisted "so intimidated and frightened that they now wish nothing more than peace."[10] Mission priests required that Indians "live in the mission; and if they leave . . . they will go to seek them and will punish them."[11]

The violence was a part of a dual revolution sweeping the region. Spanish colonists targeted the social worlds of some sixty thousand coastal Californians, while their economies generated widespread ecological destruction.[12] While less visible than Spanish soldiers, environmental change wrought transformations that radiated across the region.[13] San Gabriel's sheep, cattle, pig, and horse herds consumed river waters, valley grasses, and seeds across both the basin and nearby foothills. Herds ate the seasonal foods that sustained Tongva communities. In turn, they also deposited tons of feces across riverbeds and waterholes, limiting access to freshwater.

Additionally, the mission's vineyards and fields paralleled the explosion of its livestock. From 1780 to 1785, its agricultural production grew from 1,892 *fanegas* (bushels) to 2,725, and new crops, such as hemp, were soon added.[14] These invasive species, whose seeds were often carried by birds and winds, contributed to Spain's biological imperialism.

Unsurprisingly, Tongva peoples attempted to impede encroachment on their land by new animals and unfamiliar peoples.[15] They killed sheep and cattle throughout the early years of colonization.[16] Pressured by so many forces, however, both visible and unseen, many reluctantly sought refuge within mission society, particularly since Spanish friars often distributed foods from their growing cornucopias. Tongva leaders, including Nicolás José and Toypurina, endured these early years of transformations until in 1785 they decided to destroy the mission altogether.[17]

As the mission system devastated California's Indigenous peoples, it also contributed to the expansion of the American Republic. When Spanish friars moved north, they extended a massive but weakening empire, adding strategic harbors, bountiful farms, and sprawling ranches. Native peoples remained at the heart of Spanish California, and its prosperity attracted traders, migrants, and soon other imperial agents across the eighteenth-century Pacific world.[18] Eventually comprised of twenty-one missions, colonial California linked Spain, Russia, Chile, and eastern North America, among other locales, in a complex "interdependence of places."[19]

California offered U.S. leaders opportunities comparable to the Louisiana Purchase. As navy officer John B. Prevost marveled about San Francisco in 1818: it was the "most convenient, extensive, and safe" port he had seen. "May we not infer," he wrote to his superiors, "views as to . . . [its] possession . . . and ultimately to the sovereignty of all California?"[20] After the Latin American independence movements of 1810–21 and then the 1846–48 war with Mexico, the United States did indeed acquire California and even more: northern Mexico. Upon delivery of the Treaty of Guadalupe Hidalgo of 1848 to Congress, President James Polk noted: "New Mexico and Upper California . . . constitute of themselves a country large enough for a great empire, and their acquisition is second only in importance to that of Louisiana in 1803."[21] Polk's presidency extended the dominion of the United States more than any other.[22]

As the Republic added Pacific regions to its domain, it acquired territories in which Native peoples retained varying forms of autonomy. Starting in 1769, California Indians along the coast became attached to missions, while interior equestrian societies formed confederacies that rivaled and outlasted Spanish as well as Mexican rule.[23] They also endured the violent traumas associated with colonial disruption and its attendant diseases and worked to incorporate thousands of former neophytes fleeing Spanish control.

California's interior and Sierra Nevada foothill communities suffered even greater losses in the transitions that followed, as violence facilitated incorporation into Polk's "great empire." Indeed, throughout the 1850s, California witnessed the most rapid economic and demographic transformation of any state in U.S. history. Beginning in 1846 and later in the gold rush era, the state endured a radical inversion of its human population that accelerated the dual revolutions of the colonial era.

In California more than in any other region, settlers used informal and state-sanctioned violence to shatter Native worlds and legitimate their own.

In February 1852, for example, the state legislature appropriated $500,000 to fund anti-Indian state militias as the violence that started in the gold rush era continued unabated. Such militia and military campaigns took thousands of Native Californians—estimated at between 9,492 and 16,094—and contributed to a demographic collapse that eventually reduced the state's Indigenous population from 150,000 in 1846 to 30,000 in 1873.[24] Such reduction followed the devastation that occurred in the Spanish era. Approximately 310,000 Native Californians lived in the region before missionization—a century later only 10 percent remained.[25]

Historians have rarely considered how such violence and colonization unmade Native societies while expanding the American Republic. As the United States encountered and then acquired Pacific territories, American leaders struggled to extend the nation's sovereignty over these distant lands and populations. While many leaders of the Republic aspired to a continental empire, building one was far more challenging. Naturalizing new subject populations and adding states to the Union's delicate balance between slave versus nonslave states troubled policy leaders throughout the era of Latin American independence. As argued in chapter 7, such fears had initially curbed Thomas Jefferson's interest in using treaties to acquire western lands.

As the Spanish colonization of California had revealed, a bountiful world lay on the Pacific coastline. As U.S. traders rushed to acquire its resources, particularly sea otter furs, their commerce fostered the incorporation of California and the Pacific Northwest into global networks.

The United States responded to such commerce and imperial competition by sending out federally chartered expeditions—including the Lewis and Clark Corps of Discovery in 1804, which explored the northern Louisiana territories acquired in 1803. After their journey across the continent, the United States also began seeking diplomatic measures to secure access to the Pacific. It did so at a time when ongoing conflicts with Britain intersected with the instabilities bred by Latin American revolutions. Such complexity along with continued Indian conflicts across Spanish Florida eventually compelled U.S. leaders to adopt a new policy forbidding European interference into affairs in the Western Hemisphere: the 1823 Monroe Doctrine.

As with the Louisiana Purchase Treaty of 1803, Indigenous peoples shaped this era of U.S. foreign policy formation. Their labors not only fueled the expansion of Spanish missions but also their autonomy and power across the Georgian backcountry generated southern counterattacks that ultimately led to Florida's incorporation into the Union. As was true throughout the colonial era, Indigenous labor, power, and resistance indelibly shaped the formation of colonial and national authority.

Across the Spanish borderlands such resistance formed an under-recognized dimension of U.S. political history, as many Native nations sought to secure "zones of refuge . . . outside the reach of the state" that only deepened the challenge of state incorporation.[26] As it added lands and finally clarified its southern boundaries in the 1819 Adams-Onís Treaty, the antebellum Republic struggled to incorporate Indigenous peoples. Such inability compounded other national challenges, most notably the constitutional failure of reconciling slavery within an expanding republic.

While targeting select Native nations, such as the Seminole of Florida, with military campaigns, the federal government lacked sufficient infrastructure and personnel to impose authority across its new lands. When the Republic broke apart in 1861, two competing nation-states claimed the West as their own. Each fought the Civil War, in part, to control the West's development, as numerous military theaters west of the Mississippi reveal. Reconstructing the Union afterward required resources, technologies, and armies as subjugating Native peoples to state authority became a defining hallmark of the era.

Mission Uprising: Persecution and Colonialism

Toypurina and Nicolás José had adjusted to life at Mission San Gabriel. Originally from the villages of Japchivit and Sibapet, respectively, by 1785 they had spent nearly a decade in the service of Spanish leaders. In 1778 José became the mission's first *alcalde* (magistrate).[27] As in other parts of the empire, municipal authority offered Indigenous leaders a modicum of autonomy. *Alcaldes,* for example, were among the few Natives who were permitted to ride horses.[28] Baptized at age twenty-six in 1774, José was also the first adult from his village to accept the new religious authorities surrounding him.

It is unclear how others from his village experienced mission life. As soldiers preyed on Native families, missions offered a degree of sanctuary. Friars professed to follow a different way of life through Catholic teachings. In one of the mission's earliest marriages, Nicolás José married Agustina María from an unspecified Tongva village. The two had been baptized together, and the mission's walls were still under construction when the couple received their most recent sacrament. Soon they welcomed their first child, Cosmé María, who was baptized on July 13, 1775.[29]

Spanish records highlight Nicolás José's growing standing within mission life. He served as witness in many marriages and became a *padrino* (godparent) to thirteen children, including one whose Indigenous parents came from outside California.[30] Such social bonds—known as *compadrazgo*—facilitated social advancement for both children and godparents, and dozens of Native children, most from Baja California, received mission baptisms in Alta California.[31]

Births, deaths, and marriages often provide documentation about the nature of mission life. Less is known of the mission community's experiential everyday lives, which changed as settlers moved into the region. As ranches and towns such as the pueblo of Los Angeles (1781) became established, Indigenous labor drafts fueled their growth, doing so in ways that undermined Catholic authorities.[32] Unlike in the missions, settlements offered "unbaptized Indians" more of a means to remain independent, and in Los Angeles, Tongva men and women became ranch workers, cooks, and domestic servants, among other vocations.[33] "The Indian plows, the Indian sows, the Indian reaps," complained Father José Señán to the viceroy in 1796. "In a word, he does almost everything."[34]

Records also convey the devastation brought by Spanish influences, particularly diseases. On October 28, 1775, less than three months after his baptism, Cosmé María was buried. Agustina María outlived her son, but she also died young, buried on June 5, 1783. Nicolás José remarried, but in 1784 his second wife also died. He lost three of his family due to pathogens, and he shared such tragedy with countless survivors. By 1784 half of all baptized Tongva children had died from disease, a decline commensurate with the rate across mission society more generally. Out of an estimated sixty thousand in 1770, California's coastal Native population had decreased to fifteen thousand in 1800.[35]

Much less is known of Toypurina. She was unbaptized in 1785 and remained away from the mission at Japchivit. Spanish authorities reported her to be a "wise" leader within her village, one with recognized power and authority.[36] She was twenty-five when she received messages from Nicolás José to organize an uncommon gathering. Its purpose: to determine whether to tolerate continued Spanish authority.

Franciscans had faced earlier uprisings. In November 1775 hundreds of Kumeyaay soldiers from sixty-five to seventy allied villages destroyed Mission San Diego, killing its priest and blacksmith and wounding soldiers.[37] Fires set by their forces also consumed its church, made of local tule reeds, similar to those initially used to build Mission San Gabriel.

The origins of such uprisings stemmed from abuses. One particular prohibition linked each: the violent persecution of religious practices away from the missions. Outside San Diego in October 1775, several baptized Indians were seized and whipped for attending dance ceremonies in a nearby village. Similarly, in October 1782 and October 1785, Spanish authorities prohibited the Tongva's annual Mourning Ceremony, reinforcing orders to "never allow baptized Indians to have dances in their villages."[38]

As Nicolás José testified in November 1785, within such ceremonies, all community members—baptized neophytes as well as unbaptized "gentiles"—danced together to ensure that "the souls of the deceased achieved release from the earth and entrance into the land of the dead."[39] As settler José Bandini recalled, "In order to perpetuate the memory of the dead, the rancherias are accustomed to unite annually."[40]

Outlawing ceremonies struck at the heart of California's Indian societies. "California Indians do not dance just for festivals," nineteenth-century Luiseño historian Pablo Tac wrote, but do so "in remembrance of the grandparents, uncles and aunts, and parents now dead."[41] Punishing those who attended deepened the sacrilege. In fact, Spanish chroniclers had written for centuries about the region's sacred dances, and Franciscans understood their importance. In 1542 explorer Juan Rodriquez Cabrillo noted:

> In their towns they have large plazas and circular enclosures around which imbedded in the ground are many stone posts. . . . In the middle of these enclosures there are many very thick timbers like masts sunk in the ground. These are covered with many paintings, and we thought they must worship them because when they danced they did so around the inside of the enclosure.[42]

Cabrillo was the first European to chart parts of California, entering San Diego Bay on September 28.[43] Subsequent explorers, including Sebastián Vizcaíno, who similarly charted the coastline, noted the importance of ceremonial dance grounds. Venturing onto Catalina Island on November 24, 1602, Vizcaíno noted "a great circle" within resident Native communities whose members "painted [figures within it] in various colors."[44]

Toypurina likely led her community's dances and ceremonies in 1785. She had learned of the restrictions and the intrusion of colonial authority into Japchivit. She knew the effects of Spanish abuses on those who had been terrorized. Ceremonies did not mend the wounds inflicted upon them but offered spaces for cleansing and renewal. After nearly a decade of colonization, many

Tongva reportedly sought "to undergo an extensive purification, which included a long course of sweating, the drinking of herbs, and other forms of purging."[45]

Colonial violence targeted women's bodies and also their authority. The imposition of monogamous marital practices, the gendered segregation of children, and the rigid enforcements of sexuality all highlighted patriarchal values at the center of Spanish colonialism.[46] Across California, patriarchy attempted to diminish Native women's authority and their communal institutions, such as the construction of child-rearing shelters and menstrual huts for coming-of-age ceremonies.[47] Spanish assimilationist practices attempted "to erase Native culture . . . [and] to erase from the cultural imagination Native feminisms."[48] Moreover, colonial leaders meted out punishments to "both sexes," which included "whipping, sometimes shackles, very seldom stocks, and also the lock-up."[49] Using torture and incarceration, missions drew upon centuries of Spanish colonial rule.

Repulsed by a decade of Spanish abuses, Toypurina joined Nicolás José and fellow Tongva leaders Temejasaquichí and Aliyivit to attack San Gabriel.[50] Enlisting seventeen tribesmen to join them, they planned to overrun the mission at dawn. Six of the seventeen had been baptized. They all knew the mission intimately.[51]

In contrast to the Mission San Diego uprising of 1775, death and torture did not follow the October 25, 1785, uprising. No one was killed, and certainly no regimes were overthrown. Notified in advance of the twenty-one approaching revolutionaries, the mission guard apprehended the insurgents. Four leaders were imprisoned, interrogated, and held until authorities in New Spain determined their fate. Soldiers administered immediate floggings to their seventeen compatriots, who received between fifteen to twenty-five lashes in front of the gathered mission community. As Governor Pedro Fages explained, the punishments were made "for their ingratitude, making ugly their perverseness, and showing them the deceit with which they allowed themselves to be dominated by the aforementioned woman and the powerlessness of their practices against we who are Catholic."[52]

After their verdicts, Nicolás José and Toypurina were both exiled north. He received six years of "hard labor in irons" in the presidio at San Francisco, while she was exiled to Mission San Carlos del Carmelo near Monterey.[53] It is likely that neither saw Tovaangar again. The last known document to mention Nicolás José dates to 1790, when he was still held in chains. Toypurina was baptized in March 1789 under the name Regina Josepha. She then married a

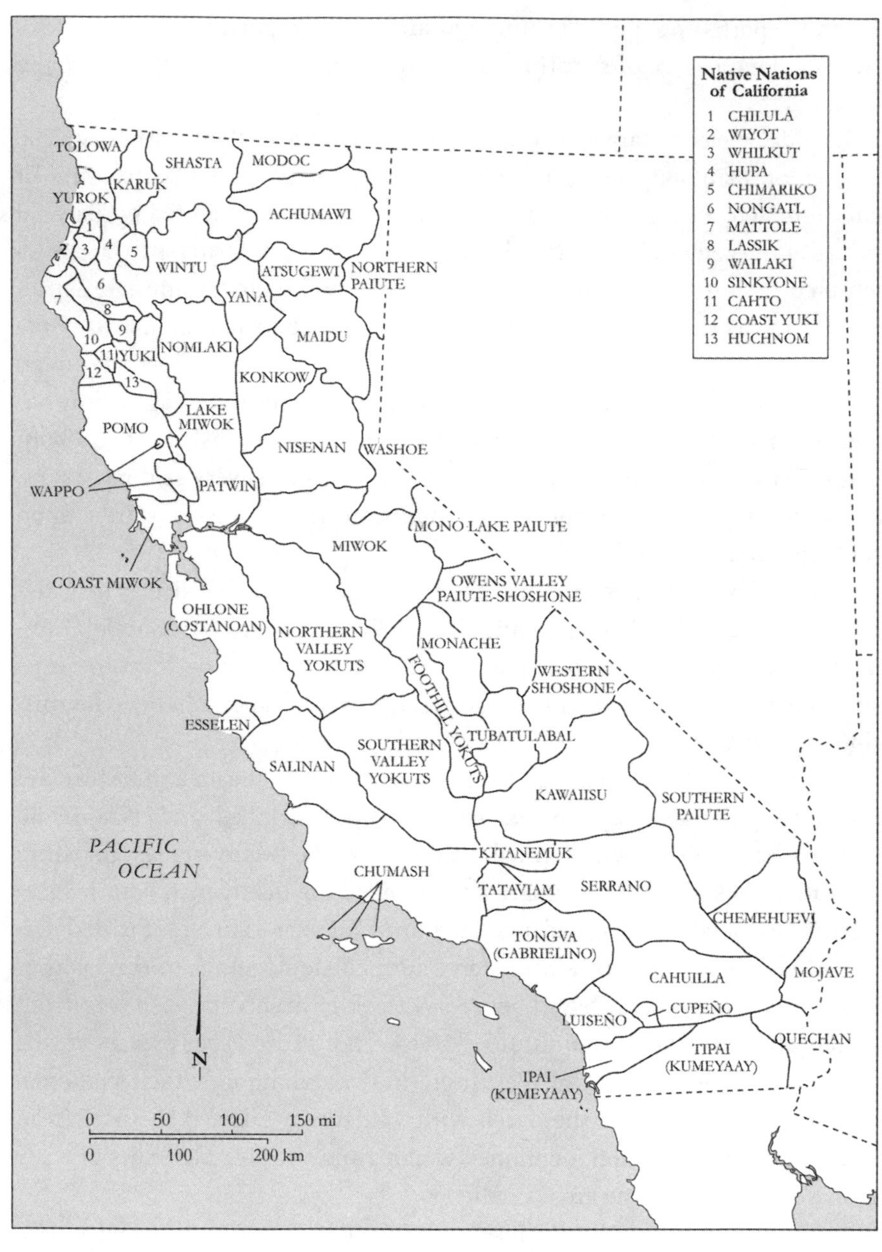
Native Nations of California
1 CHILULA
2 WIYOT
3 WHILKUT
4 HUPA
5 CHIMARIKO
6 NONGATL
7 MATTOLE
8 LASSIK
9 WAILAKI
10 SINKYONE
11 CAHTO
12 COAST YUKI
13 HUCHNOM
TOLOWA
YUROK
KARUK
SHASTA
MODOC
ACHUMAWI
WINTU
ATSUGEWI
NORTHERN PAIUTE
YANA
MAIDU
NOMLAKI
YUKI
KONKOW
POMO
LAKE MIWOK
NISENAN
WASHOE
WAPPO
PATWIN
MONO LAKE PAIUTE
MIWOK
COAST MIWOK
OWENS VALLEY PAIUTE-SHOSHONE
OHLONE (COSTANOAN)
NORTHERN VALLEY YOKUTS
MONACHE
FOOTHILL YOKUTS
WESTERN SHOSHONE
ESSELEN
TUBATULABAL
SOUTHERN VALLEY YOKUTS
SALINAN
KAWAIISU
SOUTHERN PAIUTE
PACIFIC OCEAN
KITANEMUK
CHUMASH
TATAVIAM
SERRANO
CHEMEHUEVI
TONGVA (GABRIELINO)
CAHUILLA
MOJAVE
CUPEÑO
LUISEÑO
QUECHAN
TIPAI (KUMEYAAY)
IPAI (KUMEYAAY)
N
0 50 100 150 mi
0 100 200 km

solider, Manuel Montero, from Puebla, Mexico, who was stationed at Monterey. By 1794, at age thirty-four, she had at least three children, the last being baptized that year. Five years later and of unknown causes, Toypurina died on May 22, 1799, at the Mission San Juan Bautista. She was buried the following day several hundred miles from Japchivit.[54] Both she and José had endured decades of colonial intrusions and witnessed the emergence of a vast new society. Each had developed strategies to endure the challenges wrought by invasion, and both died likely content that they had attempted to preserve their community's autonomy against the tides of colonialism.

Changes in California's Maritime Economy

By 1800 the mission system had wrought a generation of ecological and demographic change. In a destructive cycle, missions undercut the region's Indigenous populations and attracted settlers, immigrants, and other agents of change. As Nicolás José and Toypurina were escorted out of Tovaangar, for example, they headed toward the coastline—the most populous part of California. Here, they passed the mission of Chumash communities at Santa Barbara.

For generations, the coast's marine economies were visible from afar. Sturdy, oceangoing plank canoes known in Chumash as *tomols* crossed between nearby islands and coastal settlements.[55] "They maneuver the canoes as skillfully as they construct them. . . . The canoes can hold as many as ten men," Father Juan Crespí reported in 1769. "They use long oars with two blades and row with an indescribable ability and speed."[56] Beaches teemed with energy. Fishing, kelp and shellfish harvesting, and otter hunting fueled a maritime world as rich as any along the coastline.

Within missions, countless tasks structured the year's cycle of work. Santa Barbara's mission included horticulture, ranching, and maritime economies. Combining subsistence gathering, the production and maintenance of shells and beads for regional trade, and mission fieldwork, Chumash villagers maintained sedentary communities that were home to thousands.[57]

After colonization, however, work in mission gardens, across Spanish pastures, and within the mission itself required increased labor. For example, branding the mission's cattle and shearing sheep took weeks. After the herds grew, however, such tasks soon required months. In 1803 Chumash workers spent six summer weeks shearing the mission's eight thousand sheep.[58] They did this work in addition to maintaining their maritime and regional economies. They had also spent the spring sowing the mission's fields and tending its herds. Across the Americas, Indigenous labor fueled the rise and maintenance of colonial society—uncompensated labor that simultaneously expanded colonial economies and undercut Indigenous ecologies.

While vibrant and populous, much of the coastline was not conducive to oceangoing trade. *Tomols* traveled in groups of dozens but could not transport Spanish horses, sheep, and steer. Spanish ships often anchored in nearby island coves, sending supplies, soldiers, and sundries ashore aboard smaller craft. Like most coastal missions, Santa Barbara lacked deep-water ports, a challenge that had confronted Spanish mariners since Cabrillo.

Missionization eventually identified more sufficient harbors. After establishing a mission at Monterey in 1769, Spanish leaders further charted the region, and on October 31, de Portolá found "beyond all doubt" the long-rumored harbor of what became San Francisco. As he reported, "The country was plentiful in grass and all surrounded by very tall heights . . . [one] that opened only toward the bay."[59]

The port was situated between a short entryway known as the golden gate. It opened into a bay drained by the state's primary watersheds, the Sacramento and San Joaquin. These interior rivers were so vast that the Spanish would never traverse their headwaters. Nor would they cross the Sierra Nevada from which they drained. The Spanish did, however, transform the bay. They built a presidio and mission. Exiled prisoners such as Nicolás José were housed here, while the missions surrounding Monterey Bay housed the governor and other Spanish civil leaders. The centers of Spanish power developed in the north and along the coast.

If Native laborers built the foundations of colonial California, Pacific trade provided its structure. The problems of shipbuilding had plagued missions across northern Mexico. In Baja California, for example, the first ship, *El Triunfo de la Cruz*, was built and officially christened in 1719. Its cost, however, consumed "all the funds" in the missions' coffers.[60]

Alta California offered a new node in a world dominated by ships. San Francisco became the nucleus for its trade. Coveted by French, British, Russian, and U.S. leaders, it was, as one British diplomat reported, "the Key of the N.W. Coast of America."[61] French explorer Eugène Duflot de Mofras encouraged his leaders to seize it. He lamented their failure to obtain what he believed would have been "a magnificent establishment at so little expense."[62]

Frenchmen led the international traffic to California, introducing a range of flora and fauna. In 1786, after Jean-François de Galaup de La Pérouse traveled around Cape Horn, he stopped in the Chilean port of Talcahuano. Like most ships, La Pérouse's stopped in Chile to take on fruits, freshwater, and supplies, and to allow crew members recreation and rest. Charged by King Louis XVI to identify "all the lands which had escaped the vigilance" of English mariners, most notably Captain James Cook, La Pérouse traveled in two ships loaded with "a veritable arboretum" of "some fifty living trees and vines."[63] These included "Montmorency cherry trees, black heart cherry trees, white heart cherry trees, olive trees, quince trees, grape vines, fig trees, chestnut trees, lilac bushes," among other flowering plants such as roses.[64] His ships constituted nearly a "floating garden," and he arrived off Monterey in September.[65]

Bound by a shared faith and diplomatic accords between France and Spain, La Pérouse was feted in Chile before being received in Monterey. His arrival was noteworthy. He was the first foreign leader hosted by California authorities. Governor Pedro Fages organized much pageantry. His ships received, for example, a seven-cannon salute, which they returned in kind.[66]

Having spent most of his life at sea, La Pérouse delighted in coming ashore. He had suffered hardships to the north after his king directed him to take possession of the northernmost boundary of Spanish territory, which he named "Port des Français."[67] Such achievements, however, were clouded by the loss of two longboats and twenty-one men a few days after. Now, in Monterey, he exchanged his biotic bounties for those from California, including "forty head of beef, fifty-one sheep, 200 chickens, wheat, barely, peas, and . . . a barrel of milk a day."[68] His botanists "occupied every moment enlarging their collection of plants," identifying a dozen new species.[69] In return, La Pérouse reported: "We enriched the gardens of the Governor and the mission with differents [*sic*] seeds . . . which had kept perfectly and will provide them with added benefits."[70] Cherry trees, lilacs, and roses were carried ashore, as was his most lasting gift. "Our gardener gave the missionaries some potatoes from Chile, in perfect condition; I think this is not the least important of our gifts, and that this tuber will take perfectly in the light and rich soil of the Monterey district."[71] One of the crew also gifted the mission with a mill to replace the *matate* so commonly used to ground corn.[72]

La Pérouse had introduced new specimens, technologies, and products drawn from across the globe. He brought the primary food of highland South America to California and initiated the identification of the first plants from the Trans-Mississippi West.[73] And he was not alone. Generations of mariners followed, carrying Polynesian sandalwood, Alaskan-harvested furs, Australian trees, and U.S.- and English-manufactured wares, among other goods and species. Such trade further remade Indigenous societies, while also spurring increased imperial competition.

Imperialists from the North: The Russian-American Company

San Francisco provided markets to trade as well as warehouse storage for the new maritime economy. It became a site of diplomacy and commerce while maintaining its mission system. The northernmost port across the Spanish Pacific, it not only drew European traders coming from South America but also attracted traders from the north traveling from Asia. These included *promyshlenniki*, or fur trappers, from the Russian-American Company who brought furs drawn from Russia's coastal empire, which ranged from Alaska to northern California.[74]

Throughout the eighteenth century, Russian traders dominated the Pacific fur trade. They colonized Alaska, established its first settlements, and drew millions of rubles' worth from sea otters, which were initially traded at Chinese markets at Kyakhta along the Sino-Russo border. Modeled after the Hudson Bay Company and British East India Company, the Russian-American Company was established in 1799 by the tsarist government to administer and more effectively exploit Russian America.[75]

While controlled by Russians, the fur trade revolved around Aleut and Alutiiq hunters who were compelled to hunt and process furs. An extractive, violent form of colonization characterized the initial stages of the Russian presence in Alaska in which Native villagers became incorporated into forms of labor drafts that required annual payments in furs.[76] "Those who didn't pay" their tribute requirements, "they took their lives," reported Estéban José Martinez in 1786.[77]

While less valuable than northern Pacific furs, otters abounded throughout California's coastal waters. They teemed in maritime ecologies, as did seals, which were so bountiful in part because Native Californians were much less dependent upon them than were Native peoples in Alaska. These maritime resources increasingly drew Russian hunters farther south. Otters were in fact so abundant that many across the Russian empire referred to the Pacific as the "Otter Sea."[78]

As Monterey and San Francisco grew, they attracted Russian traders who used their provisions for supplies and ports for anchor. While tensions often pervaded relations between the two empires, traders built informal networks that linked rather than divided these overlapping powers. In 1807, for example, with its colony in Alaska suffering from malnutrition and recent warfare with Tlingits, commander in chief Nikolai Petrovich Rezanov traveled to San Francisco and opened diplomatic relations with the colony. Less warmly welcomed than La Pérouse, Rezanov nonetheless received provisions including several thousand pounds of "wheat, flour, barley, peas, beans, lard, salt, and a small quantity of dried meat" for the settlement at Novo Arkhangelsk (New Archangel).[79] He stayed over a month, using his time to plan future colonization efforts in the region, which eventually led in 1811 to the settlement at Bodega Bay, a Russian colony due north of San Francisco.[80] This second colony complemented the Russian post at Fort Ross, established farther north.[81]

As California attracted increased settlement and global traffic, U.S. traders also noticed the bounties of the Pacific. They too desired to join in its growing commerce. These included John Ledyard, who had attended Dartmouth College before joining Captain Cook's final Pacific journey (1776–79).[82] Ledyard grew up along the Connecticut coast, where ports such as New London and New Bedford served as eastern North America's principal hubs for whaling. Long familiar with oceanic traders and shipbuilders, he left his studies in New Hampshire and traveled the Pacific with Cook's expedition.

In the Pacific, Ledyard learned of the spectacular returns of the fur trade—fifteen hundred otter pelts, "which did not cost the purchaser sixpence sterling [a piece], sold in China for 100 dollars."[83] The Russian fur trade to China, however, followed a circuitous oceanic and then overland route to Kyakhta, whereas early British and U.S. traders moved fur directly to Canton and other ports. While the Spanish had initial trade advantages—Californian ports were founded in part to provision returning ships from Manila—the colony never approached the level of profitability drawn from the fur trade within Russian and Northwest coastal waters.[84]

British and other New England traders exploited resources that Spain never fully targeted, and Pacific-harvested furs provided healthy profits for ships to the Northwest coast. Fifteen U.S. ships traded across the "Otter Sea" in 1801, carrying their harvests to Chinese markets. Between 1805 and 1806, they sold $1 million worth and returned to U.S. ports with more than 10 million pounds of Chinese tea.[85] California provided safe harbors, provisions, and storage for these ships, as Native labor in missions paralleled the labor provided by Indigenous trappers. As with other borderlands societies, the foundations for trade depended upon Indians.

As the colonization of California attracted traders from across the globe, it also enabled the exploration of the Pacific Northwest. Many foreigners such as La Pérouse remained baffled about Spanish mariners' limited interest in harvesting the Northwest coast's resources. La Pérouse found it "perfectly unaccountable that the Spaniards, having so near and so frequent intercourse with China from Manilla, should have been hitherto ignorant of the value of this previous trade of furs."[86] Subsequent U.S. leaders had similar reactions, and they began acting on them, envisioning an American dominion across these bountiful lands and waters. U.S. claims to the Pacific became cemented in the Adams-Onís Treaty of 1819 in which Spain ceded Florida to the United States and established an international border between New Spain and the expanding American Republic. Such cession and recognition came as the Spanish empire had already begun to crumble.

The Pacific Coast in the Age of Revolution

While global trade networks expanded California's economy, the colony remained inexorably tied to Spain. Its main ports of trade crossed the empire—from San Blas in Baja California to Valaparíso and Talcahuano in Chile. The region's harbors provided anchorage for Spanish traders navigating the Pacific, particularly return trips for Mexican-bound Spanish ships traveling from Manila.[87]

While the area was dependent upon the sea for communication and trade, land expeditions also contributed to its formation. California's first heads of cattle and horses arrived not by sea but overland from ranching communities across northern Mexico. The same was true for many of its Spanish-speaking families.[88] As in New Mexico, the century-old *sistema de castas* (caste system) also arrived in the region, maintaining gendered and racial ideologies that corresponded with power and prestige.[89]

Within such hierarchies and global influences, intense and enduring localisms characterized the everyday worlds of Californian Indians. Coastal communities such as the Chumash and Ohlone (Costanoan) lived within missions that included by 1819 over twenty thousand neophytes.[90] Others were attached to nearby towns and ranches. Baptized by the thousands and congregated into colonial labor regimes, coastal Californians did not, however, share the same political and religious identities.

Local and inter-tribal differences persisted. Indeed, the twenty-one Spanish missions included Native peoples from hundreds of village communities and from dozens of language families. Before 1769, California was, in fact, among the most linguistically diverse areas on earth, and ethnographers have long assessed the complexity of the region's languages.[91]

Diversity came in many forms, and Spanish colonialism exacerbated Indigenous rivalries and divisions by importing Indigenous peoples from other parts of New Spain. As in colonial New Mexico, thousands of other Indians migrated into the region.[92] In 1785, when Toypurina was asked why she and Nicolás José had "come here armed to kill the priests and the soldiers," she replied that she "was angry with the priests and all the others at the mission, because we were living on their land."[93] Historians have often misread her indictments against the Spanish and "all the others" who constituted mission life.[94] These "others" included Indigenous peoples from neighboring villages as well as across New Spain, including Cochimí-speaking neophytes from Baja California, who arrived in "waves."[95]

When Juan Bautista de Anza arrived at San Gabriel in 1776, he led a procession of cattle, sheep, horses, women, friars, children, and other Indian laborers. "Our coming was a matter for great rejoicing by everyone," Font wrote.[96] However, "there was quite a commotion," Serra reported about such inter-Indigenous encounters, as many "did not know what to make of these [other Indigenous] families" who accompanied the conquest.[97] Indigenous newcomers also became mission Indians, underscoring the diversity of the region.

Toypurina and her compatriots understood the challenges of colonization. The myriad changes unleashed by new peoples and animals had motivated their anti-colonial revolt, and by 1800 a new demography structured the region: nearly twenty thousand mission Indians, an estimated two hundred thousand Native peoples across California's interior and northern regions, along with two thousand Spanish settlers, friars, and soldiers. California had become as diverse as any other place in North America.[98] It became only more so after 1810 when global revolutions broadened access to the Pacific.

Spain experienced major transformations during the Age of Revolutions, as new constitutional and political changes attempted to reform its global empire. Initially, in the 1760s, new "bourbon reforms" led to the expansion of its American empire and attempts to consolidate it.[99] From Texas to Monterey, Spain increased its military garrisons, established dozens of new missions, and organized exploratory campaigns.

California became the most successful of these reform efforts. It attracted traders, leaders, and mariners from across the empire. Cartographers and naturalists, for example, formed the Royal Scientific Expedition, which charted California and the Northwest. Leaving Acapulco in May 1791 under the leadership of Alejandro Malaspina, its botanists, artists, and explorers hailed from across the empire, providing many of the first "scientific" surveys of the Pacific coastline.[100] Its findings predated those of U.S. exploratory expeditions.

Like La Pérouse's, Malaspina's journey offered invaluable cartographic, ethnographic, and botanical findings.[101] It came during a period of imperial rivalries across the Northwest in which British and Spanish mariners contested their respective claims to sovereignty. Each also attempted to restrict Russia and France. As revolution consumed France in 1789, Spain interdicted several British trading ships across the Salish Sea, sparking what became known as the Nootka Sound Controversy in which Britain challenged Spanish claims on the grounds that Spain had not settled any parts of the region.[102] The threat was defused by 1792, but the region's future remained contested. Spain sent a seven-ship expedition to clarify its Pacific territories—the Expedicíon de Límites (Expedition of Limits or Boundary Survey).[103] Thereafter, Spain withdrew its claims to the Northwest and eased restrictions upon foreign traders in California, such as Rezanov. Foreign traders now operated freely north of San Francisco, particularly after 1808, when Spanish officials confronted the Napoleonic invasions of Iberia.[104]

Ships from Britain and the United States filled the vacuum created by Spanish liberalization. For nearly two decades after 1792, U.S. and British vessels were the only ones to visit the Northwest. Along the west coast of Vancouver Island, Friendly Cove and Nootka Sound provided trade, fresh water, and provisions. After 1778, when Cook had repaired and provisioned his ships there, American trading ships outnumbered their British counterparts by nearly eight to one (ninety-six to thirteen). However, British warships, the most powerful military technologies on earth, patrolled the Pacific.[105] As opposed to smaller commercial craft, they weighed hundreds of tons.

British and U.S. officials found themselves in conflict over these distant lands and waters. Each sent not only ships but also overland expeditions into the region. These intended to find rivers, particularly those that might provide outlets for interior furs. Scottish-born Alexander Mackenzie, for example, worked in Montreal with the North West Company. Starting in 1789, he continued the efforts of other company traders to locate a fabled river that flowed into the Pacific—what Cook had noted as "a fine spacious river" that traders believed to be interior lakes. Cook's river turned out, however, to be an inlet—known as Cook's Outlet—rather than a highway into the interior.[106]

By 1793 Mackenzie had reached both the Arctic and Pacific Oceans. His expeditions fueled British interests in solidifying monopolistic control over the continent's fur trade. Similarly, Meriwether Lewis and William Clark led the "Corps of Discovery." They too sought the headwaters of western rivers that many believed flowed to the Pacific. They became the first Euro-Americans to traverse the Missouri River to its headwaters.[107]

Departing St. Louis in 1804, they depended upon Mandan hosts during the winter and Shoshone guides throughout the summer. They ate salmon procured from Nez Percé traders, traveled with Métis guides, and traversed a continent inhabited by Native peoples. Rarely has a federally sanctioned expedition proven so reliant upon Indigenous knowledge, power, and hospitality.

After crossing the Continental Divide in August 1805, the party navigated the fast-rushing Columbia River to its mouth at Astoria, where they wintered, laying claim to the region. They also compiled critical information about the topography, ethnography, and climate of the West. What had once been the northern reaches of Spain's empire—first charted by Cabrillo in the 1540s—now became claimed by Britain and the United States. So distant from centers of empire, these agents and traders nonetheless charted the region's incorporation into the global economy.

As both nations claimed sovereignty across the region, each also threatened war. The inconclusive aftermath to the War of 1812 and its Treaty of Ghent (1814) provided little resolution other than a return to the prewar status quo.[108] For example, the only American settlement on the Pacific—John Jacob Astor's Astoria (1811)—returned after the war to U.S. sovereignty, despite its surrender to the British during the conflict.[109]

As disputes over the Northwest informed the struggle between these empires, tensions between Indigenous peoples and foreign traders shaped the course of this rivalry.[110] Soon, diplomatic resolution brought realignments that enhanced the national power of the early Republic. Indeed, less than a decade after the Treaty of Ghent, the United States in 1823 declared its most expansive foreign policy declaration, one that restricted foreign involvement in the Americas altogether while consolidating the nation's claims across North America. Maritime conflicts with Native peoples, in short, influenced the formation of a new "doctrine" named after the fifth U.S. president, James Monroe.

Attempted Incorporations of the Northwest

North of Astoria across Cape Flattery on the Olympic Peninsula, the Salish Sea begins. Extending to Fort Rupert on Vancouver Island, it includes the straits of Georgia and Juan de Fuca and the countless islands of Puget Sound and the Gulf of Georgia. The sea is home to the world's most diverse marine bioregion, its currents fueling nutrient-rich waters that absorb and emit the boundless energies that sustain life.[111] In particular, subsurface water-worlds of kelp beds and "dense marine forests" abound, rivaling the region's density of cedar, fir, and hemlock trees while supporting fish, marine mammals, and countless seabirds.[112] Scholars estimate that over two hundred thousand and potentially four hundred thousand Native peoples lived in the Northwest in the eighteenth century when, as in California, Indigenous peoples developed sustained relations with Europeans.[113]

These relations differed in shape and form from those in California. Few eighteenth-century forts or European settlements, for example, survived more than a few months in these wet and cold climates.[114] Despite its maritime and natural bounties, the region was too isolated for colonization and less hospitable for agriculture and livestock. It was also home to powerful Indigenous nations whose leaders commanded fleets of oceangoing canoes that could collectively hold hundreds of soldiers. In 1787, for example, when English trader John Mears arrived at Friendly Cove, two Mowachaht chiefs of the Nuu-chah-nulth, Maquinna and Callicum, approached in twelve canoes. Each canoe held eighteen men.[115] And these were only medium-sized vessels; the largest, according to John Jewitt, "will carry forty men, and are extremely light."[116]

Complex protocols evolved from these encounters, which occurred on coastlines rather than interior lands. Hesitant about these powerful newcomers, Native leaders worked to shape a borderlands world that focused on trade, diplomacy, and navigation rather than missionization or colonization. They were aided in part by imposing snow-capped mountains and rocky watersheds that limited navigation into the interior. Further, as in California, the absence of deep-water ports prevented colonial developments. Friendly Cove, the region's most visited port, was itself located on an island, thereby limiting the transmission of European herds, supplies, and settlers.[117] Additionally, perilous waters surround the region, including Cape Flattery at the tip of the Olympic Peninsula.

The coastal relations that developed contrasted with centuries-old, territorial-based forms of colonialism. For example, despite numerous formal ceremonies of imperial possession, the Northwest remained unincorporated into any empire during the maritime fur trade era (1778–1840s).[118] Not only were there few institutions of imperial authority, it was "exceedingly dangerous," as early traders complained, to allow Native peoples to gather together "without any controlling influence" upon them.[119] In many ways, "the state was absent" across the nineteenth century, and violence percolated beneath and across imperial-Indigenous relations.[120] Such statelessness, as we shall see also in Florida, informed the subsequent course of U.S. foreign policy formation. The region was contested by various traders, not statesmen. Individuals, such as John Jacob Astor, and companies, such as Canada's North West Company, vied for interior furs. Rather than colonization, extraction was their motive. Unlike Franciscans, these traders made few territorial claims or ideological demands. They were, however, far from friendly. Medieval forms of discipline helped to structure the region's few forts such as Astoria (1811) and Fort Vancouver (1818), comparable to European castles or walled villages. Authority centered not on "the rule of law . . . but the tactics of power."[121] Individual trading leaders attempted to wield absolute power and punished those who defied them.

Eventually, farms replaced forts. Starting in the 1840s, Native communities contended with growing numbers of settlers who claimed the region's sheltered river valleys and interior farmlands for themselves. Without a formal mechanism for diplomacy and communication, relations devolved into different forms of violence. In central and southern Oregon, settler colonialism and "genocidal warfare" emerged alongside the region's settler republicanism.[122]

Before the treaty period (1855–71), Native nations maintained sovereignty over the region in part by navigating the region's competing trade interests. They attracted resources from European and U.S. traders, particularly guns, metals, and cloths, and maintained social authority over their communities. They also held authority over the region's marine resources. These were substantial. As explorers were quick to notice, the bounties of the Salish Sea were resplendent, and they drove the Northwest's economies as well as cultures. Salmon and halibut, for example, provided annual runs that brought millions of protein-rich fish into the region.[123] Salmon returned fattened from their lives at sea to spawn across the region's rivers, the timing of their runs varying by species. Seasonal harvests attracted thousands of Native fishers to locales such as the Dalles on the Columbia River, accompanied by ceremonial practices designed to maintain their continuity. Comparable to the cod banks and lobster harvests that first attracted Europeans to the Northeast, these marine resources had sustained life since time immemorial. Indeed, more nonagricultural foods were harvested there than anywhere else on the continent.[124]

Europeans were amazed by these bountiful runs and Indigenous fishing skills. As Jewitt noted, "There are few people more expert in fishing."[125]

The fish both provided sustenance and enabled various technologies: making bones into threading needles, boiling skins into oils, and drying meats formed much of the subsistence economy. Such labor was largely done by women, who produced surplus materials for trade.

Indigenous hunters also harvested the region's largest bounty—migratory humpback, gray, and orca whales. Whaling in the Northwest diversified many coastal economies, sometimes to a remarkable extent. At the Makah village of Ozette on Cape Flattery, for example, remains uncovered during excavations indicate that whales accounted "for 75 percent [of] all meat and oil consumed."[126] Blubber and meat estimates at nearly a thousand metric tons were discovered at this single site.

Like salmon, whales also took on social importance, as the sea became the locus of the region's economy and its culture. Hereditary family rights, for example, determined the authority to hunt and gather at accustomed sites, forming customary laws within societies. "The whale is considered as the king's fish," Jewitt recalled of his stay among the Mowachaht, "and no other person is permitted to touch him until the royal harpoon has first drawn his blood."[127] Moreover, the redistribution of harvested meat sustained familial and clan prestige. The rights to hunt, fish, and gather across Makah and Nuu-chah-nulth communities, for example, hold deep cultural significance, and countless marine animals and mythic characters shape their folklore. Oral traditions of supernatural beings such as Thunderbird (T'iick'in) highlight his revered status in bringing whales to their communities.[128]

Such cultural values shaped Indigenous responses to European arrival. If sovereignty involves the power not only to command through force but also to govern through custom, then cultural practices establish imperatives that shape communal behaviors. In the Northwest, Indigenous sovereignty has long included the authority to redistribute wealth drawn from the sea. As traders flowed into the region, they offered manufactured goods—guns, knives, fishing hooks, and coppers—that became essential technologies in the region's economies and customs. "One can now buy the best English arms on this part of . . . America," one traveler remarked in 1802, and these could be obtained "more cheaply than in England."[129] The costs were comparatively lower because guns were purchased in large bundles (often of fifty) and were traded to foster dependency for associated trade items such as powder, shot, and flints.

Guns and trade goods conferred wealth. Those who possessed them held standing, and those who distributed them gained status within coastal communities. Traders understood the social values accompanying the trade, and many U.S. traders headed to England to obtain items needed for the Northwest. Jewitt, for example, had joined the *Boston* in Britain in 1802 after it had arrived from Massachusetts. Like many U.S. vessels, it traversed the Atlantic in order to go to the Pacific. It arrived in Britain "to take on board a cargo of such goods as were wanted for the trade, with the Indians of the North-west coast."[130]

Jewitt recorded one of the most extensive accounts from this early nineteenth-century world. He witnessed Maquinna's welcome of the *Boston* in 1803 and survived his unexpected attack thereafter. For a host of reasons—an imbalance of otter pelts for European markets, the disrespectful behavior of the ship's captain, John Salter, who had traded broken guns, and Maquinna's need to maintain his own standing as a leader—the Mowachaht leader surprised the American traders and executed the crew, save for Jewitt and the ship's sail maker, John Thompson. Their survival and subsequent writings revealed enduring features of Northwest culture.

As Maquinna's soldiers tore apart the ship and unloaded its cargo, the community's leaders prepared to celebrate. They sent word to surrounding villages to join this moment of victory. Inside Maquinna's longhouse, the chief surveyed his new bounty. With his family gathered, the village now welcomed "not less than twenty" neighboring canoes:

> Maquina invites them . . . and provisions are prepared for them, such as whale's blubber, raw herring spawn, and cold water, of which they appear to make a hearty feast. After the repast is over, they are ordered out of the house in order that preparation may be made for the dance which soon succeeded, and . . . our Chief exhibited his child with a masque on his face. . . . After the dance our Chief begins to give presents to the strangers. I saw him give one hundred muskets, four hundred yards of cloth, one hundred looking glasses, twenty barrels of powder.[131]

Maquinna's practices of redistribution enhanced his authority and brought prestige to his family and clan. In particular, he redistributed his new possessions in honor of his son, Sat-sat-sok-sis.[132]

Practices of redistribution pervade Northwest communities, which hold elaborate communal gatherings known as potlatches in order to preserve social authority, relay epic tales, and welcome newcomers into their societies. While giving "presents to strangers" may seem antithetical to private property, gift giving remains one of the highest honors within the region, and Maquinna and other Northwest coast leaders accrued standing by giving away their accumulated wealth.

Such wealth had historically been drawn largely from the sea, which now continued to bring riches to the region aboard foreign ships. Emblematized with carvings, crests, and "masques" of totemic imagery, these trading resources were sought by coastal leaders in part to redistribute them. On this one evening, one hundred guns, four hundred yards of cloth, one hundred looking glasses, and twenty barrels of powder distinguished the potlatch. This cornucopia of global wares all communicated Maquinna's growing standing.[133]

The Economic and Epidemiological Roots of Dependency

While the Northwest's Indigenous-imperial relations contrasted with more territorial forms of settler colonialism, they resembled other contests occurring across America's borderlands. From Alaska through the Columbia River Plateau and onto the Plains, Indigenous nations navigated recurring and deadly challenges, ranging from the violence of the gun trade to growing dependencies on textiles and metals, and labored to obtain resources needed to trade.

Violence always followed European trade. Foreign traders used hosts of enticements to attract Native peoples into their economies, and when these failed, violence often followed. Most notably, decades of violence, forced intermarriage, and compulsory tributes characterized Russian-Indigenous relations after unlicensed Russian traders, *promyshlenniki*, initiated the region's seal and otter trade starting in the mid-1700s. On Kodiak Island, *promyshlenniki* often held Aleut women captive in order to force their husbands, fathers, and sons to harvest abundant furs. They also raped them, spreading venereal diseases, abuse, and psychological harm. When the first Russian Orthodox missionaries arrived in 1794, they "were shocked" by such commonplace violence and disorder.[134] The island's Native population was also plummeting, from nearly six thousand in 1792 to under four thousand in 1806.[135]

South of Kodiak, Tlingit soldiers defied Russian attempts to conscript them. As British guns became more ubiquitous, the Tlingit exacted retributions that crippled Russian control. Most notably, in October 1804 outside the massive fort in Sitka, they killed and wounded 150 Russian-Aleut forces that commanded six cannon-laden ships, hundreds of Aleut kayaks, and nearly one thousand men with guns.[136] A decade of skirmishes followed as Tlingit soldiers continued ambushing traders, killing twenty-three and wounding eighteen in 1818. They simply "have more firearms than we," complained one Russian leader.[137]

Native nations endured colonial violence and also perpetuated it. Colonialism wrought such destruction that it compelled dependent communities to seize goods for market. As in eastern America, the overlapping trade in furs and guns incentivized hunters to deplete natural resources, to invade neighboring regions for their resources, and to monopolize trade networks. Indeed, the history of the western fur trade reads like an unfolding tragedy as Native, imperial, and unlicensed traders all competed for diminishing resources. Tlingit communities, for example, had fought Russians and their Native allies for decades, but only after the expansion of the gun trade did they obtain sufficient guns, powder, and metals to launch successful campaigns. Years of sorrow had preceded their victories, as incorporation into the global economy provided only select opportunities for preserving Indigenous autonomy. Moreover, incorporation fostered growing dependency upon market forces.[138]

While Native nations struggled to navigate such disruptions, they confronted other traumas. Colonialism always brought disease. As much as any two variables in the remaking of the Indigenous West, the combination of violence and diseases undercut the sovereign authority of tribal communities. Starting with the missionization of California in 1769 and extending until the great smallpox outbreak of 1837, every region of the West endured catastrophe. Diseases made these generations particularly deadly, and violence deepened the suffering.

Scholars often study Native American disease transmission in specific times and places. In cold and often impersonal frameworks, numbers of Native deaths are sketched, and if possible tallied. Like shadows down a descending staircase, clarity often grows faint, creating only a general, imprecise sense of the devastation.

California and the Northwest offer clearer registers. Their histories of population decline have been increasingly studied—if not firmly linked together. The history of disease in California is documented in "greater detail" than nearly anywhere in North America, partly due to Franciscan documents.[139] These histories underscore the catastrophic nature of colonialism.

In California as in Russian colonies, sexual violence pervaded mission life, and its results included declining fertility rates. Rather than becoming sites of community, missions became zones of contagion and infertility fueled by gonorrhea and syphilis.[140] As Father Ramón Olbés noted at Mission Santa Barbara, syphilis had become ubiquitous and lethal. "All are infected with it," he reported. "As a result births are few and deaths so many that the number of deaths exceed births by three to one."[141] Similar death rates were found in other missions. Throughout its history Mission San Carlos recorded twice as many deaths as births, including Toypurina's in 1799. Infant and child mortality rates also rose during these pandemics, collectively totaling 366 deaths per 1,000.[142]

Additional accounts fill Spanish chronicles. At Mission San Miguel, Franciscan leaders noted that among the mission's many diseases "the dominant malady . . . is venereal disease . . . [for which] there is no effective remedy."[143]

Governors and civil leaders detailed the costs of these social diseases, as did foreign visitors. As Georg Heinrich von Langsdorff, a German botanist working with Russian explorers, described:

> In New California not enough is being done in the area of health. Only the military has a doctor and a surgeon. . . . The Indians at the mission . . . frequently die. . . .
>
> The most terrible of all diseases . . . [syphilis] is found here in all of its variations. It is common among the Spanish and the Indians and causes even greater devastation, because absolutely no medical measures are taken to prevent it. The usual results are spots on the skin, horrible rashes, persistently running sores, painful aches in the bones, throat infections, loss of the nose, deformities and death. Among other complaints, I saw ophthalmia, rheumatism, virulent abscesses at the corners of the mouth and chronic diseases of various types, probably also thanks to Venus.[144]

Venereal diseases produced additional symptoms, including visible sores, bloody coughs, and uncontrollable discharges of the bowels. Such diseases were caused by sexual violence, not the invisible transmissions of smallpox and the like. These were social conditions, not strictly biological forms of colonialism, and they exacted deadly tolls.

Smallpox and the Reordering of Western Indian Societies

In the Northwest, diseases devastated Indigenous societies differently. Virgin soil outbreaks shook the foundations of society, often doing so outside the purview of Europeans. Few documents of Indigenous death rates exist for the first half century after contact, but numerous studies, oral histories, and sets of archaeological and historical analyses convey the destruction.[145] Transmissions arrived from the sea. They came overland, as overlapping disease vectors initiated traumas that soon facilitated the region's incorporation into other sovereignties.

Diseases also facilitated imperial expansion. Most notably, across the northern Plains in the 1780s, smallpox raged. Originating in central Mexico, it was part of a pandemic that engulfed much of the Spanish empire. Reaching into Central America and across North America, this outbreak became the most widespread recorded epidemic in the Americas.[146]

In 1782 the disease arrived as far north as Manitoba, where it devastated Cree and Chipewyans. Hudson Bay Company traders plying the West's lakes, rivers, and portages detailed this pandemic's rapid sweep. In his conversations with company workers, David Thompson estimated that potentially 60 percent of the region's population had perished. He recounted how traders relayed evidence of Native lodges full of rotting corpses that attracted wolves. He told of "survivors in such a state of despair and despondence that they could hardly converse."[147]

Four smallpox contagions were reported among the Mandan villages along the Missouri River. They started in 1781, and returned in 1801, 1831, and 1837.[148] As relayed in chapter 4, Mandan villages were home to the largest concentration of urban dwellers in eighteenth-century North America. When Lewis and Clark wintered there in 1804–5, they noted desolate villages and large earthen homes with decomposing roofs as the effects of disease destabilized the verdant gardens and urban cosmopolitanism that had characterized the community in earlier generations.

Having swept north from Mexico, the contagion moved west toward the Rockies. Among the Blackfoot Confederacy, leaders such as Young Man remembered the "tears, shrieks, and howlings of despair for those who would never return to us," and an annual communal history known as a "winter count" subsequently described the winter of 1781–82 as simply the time when "very few escaped death."[149] Traders reported that the total number of Blackfoot lodges declined by over 50 percent afterward.

After crossing the Rockies, the 1782 outbreak eventually swept down the Columbia River. It devastated Shoshone, Bannock, and Nez Percé communities throughout the Snake River watershed before moving north toward the Salish Sea where it crossed into Vancouver Island and the Fraser River Valley, reaching as far north as the interior Salish communities of Koia'um and Kalulaa'. Of the approximately twenty-five identified Salish communities along the Chilliwack River in 1782, all were abandoned by 1830, and many nearby Fraser River settlements had migrated farther up the river to avoid related colonial disruptions.[150] As in California, diseases brought not only dramatic depopulation but also migrations. Native peoples everywhere struggled to preserve autonomy and health in their transformed homelands.

These histories of death and disease often fall outside the register of U.S. history. They are, however, essential to its development; the history of the American Republic is as incomplete as it is inadequate without such considerations. The devastation not only contributed to the reshaping of the Indigenous nations but also enabled outsiders to exploit their territories.

Diseases challenged the ability of Native leaders to exercise authority and to respond to the threats of outsiders. Native nations in Oregon along the Columbia River, for example, entered into decades-long economic and social relations with British and U.S. traders. As a result, they contracted diseases. As the War of 1812 raged in the east, one Native leader at Fort George (Astoria), Caolp—a Clatsop headman and "medal chief" since the time of Lewis and Clark—spent early January 1814 burying the dead, which included a "poor girl [who] had died in a horrible condition, in the last stage of venereal disease, discolored and swollen."[151]

Disease undercut tribal capacities in countless ways and made those who survived more vulnerable. Nearby Klamath communities across the Klamath Basin, for example, endured so many raids from their equestrian rivals that they developed chants of lamentation. One, "Ko-I ak a nä'pka gatpam'nóka," has been translated as "Disastrous times we had when the Northern Indians arrived."[152]

Death caused by violence and disease also eroded the loose sovereignty of the West's existing empires. Spain, Britain, Russia, and the United States all competed with one another and also confronted internal threats to their claims. Eventually, and not by coincidence, U.S. settlers targeted Native lands already ravaged by violence and disease, viewing them as "empty" or as "deserts" of undeveloped potential.[153] Depopulated lands and destabilized communities became far more prone to colonization.

Missouri and the Crisis of Mexican Independence

Despite the fanfare upon Lewis and Clark's return to St. Louis, the United States did not initiate claims to the Pacific. While they had charted the Missouri's headwaters, crossed the Continental Divide, and navigated the Columbia to the Pacific, their overland route proved too perilous for subsequent travel. Moreover, the Republic was in no position to consolidate any claims. While the expedition's reports were published in a popular set of journals with an accompanying map, for nearly four decades, no other federally sanctioned overland expeditions touched the Pacific until John C. Frémont's travels in 1843.[154]

U.S. leaders confronted more immediate territorial worries, especially boundary concerns across the Spanish borderlands. California, New Mexico, and Texas were the three largest borderlands provinces, and each witnessed new governments during Mexico's independence movement (1810–21), when Spain lost its American empire.[155] From Florida to California, Spanish colonies teetered and soon collapsed, and in the decade that followed, the fate of Indigenous peoples was likewise recast.

Concurrently, the federal government set in motion its first plan for incorporating lands west of the Mississippi River into the Republic. "The people of the Missouri Territory have petitioned to be admitted into the Union," Indiana senator Waller Taylor wrote in January 1819. "No doubt but their wishes will be granted."[156] Taylor was correct. Missouri gained admission, but only after months of debates as northern representatives excoriated proposals for expanding slavery. As representative James Tallmadge declared:

> If a dissolution of the Union must take place, let it be so! If civil war . . . must come, I can only say, let it come! . . . I have the fortune and the honor to stand here as the representative of freemen, who possess intelligence to know their rights. . . . As their representative, I will proclaim their hatred to slavery in every shape.[157]

Missouri's statehood raised the specter of slavery's expansion and cast the Republic into a crisis. By establishing a geographic demarcation between free and slave states, the Missouri Compromise expanded slavery into former Spanish territories and forced southern leaders to defend an institution that Britain, France, and soon Mexico (in 1824) had abolished. Missouri also developed a constitution that limited free blacks, repudiated federal leaders, including Territorial Governor William Clark, and established a particularly virulent form of white supremacy that punished intermarriage and peoples of color. As W.E.B. Du Bois later noted, "The attitude of the West toward Negroes became sterner than that of the East."[158]

Slavery was often assumed to be a necessary part of the Republic's economy, culture, and politics. Agreeing, however, to its expansion confounded numerous administrations. "On such a question, one would think there could be no difference of opinion," one representative wrote in the *New Hampshire Patriot*. "It was something new to hear slavery justified and defended."[159] In 1821 a boundary line emerged that determined the admission of western territories into the Union.

If the Louisiana Purchase provided the frame and canvas for U.S. expansion, the Missouri Compromise offered the brushes and oils needed to render it. As much as any other era, the period after Mexican independence highlights how expansion destabilized the capacity of the federal government to solidify its western claims. Missouri's statehood, Texas's independence in 1836, and even the U.S. war with Mexico (1846–48) did not resolve the challenge of slavery's expansion, as competing political economies collided with preexisting Indigenous powers throughout the antebellum era.

The debate surrounding Missouri's admission was eventually forgotten. The boundary line became seen as a natural evolution of sectional politics. Deep divisions, however, accompanied the Union's process of expansion. The Republic's survival required constant negotiations, challenges that became more apparent as events across the Spanish borderlands raised new national claims. Soon, concerns about the boundaries between New Spain and the United States fueled the evolution of the Monroe Doctrine and thereafter the consolidation of U.S. territorial claims across much of North America.[160]

Borderlands Standoff: Florida and Spain's Crumbling Empire

East Texas and West Florida became the first parts of the Spanish empire to fall to U.S. expansionary pressures. In both regions, Spanish-Indian relations had shaped the evolution of distinctive societies, and in Florida, Indigenous powers such as the Creek and Seminole Nations had grown into formidable allies, traders, and antagonists. Long accustomed to fighting to preserve their autonomy, these Native nations shaped the Republic's evolving demarcation lines and, in turn, were devastated by them.[161]

The acquisition of Louisiana in 1803 forever changed the South. First Spanish and then a French possession, the lower Mississippi region now experienced exponential growth. Its land gained increased value and its settler population surged. As Postmaster General Gideon Granger explained when advocating for new postal roads through the region, "New Orleans will unquestionably be the place of deposit for the products of the Western World. . . .

[It will be] the greatest entrepot for merchandize in the world."[162] Goods, people, and livestock flowed across the region, bisecting Creek and other southern Indian homelands. From only 9,000 in 1810, Alabama's population mushroomed to 144,000 by 1820.[163]

In East Florida, Spain had developed centuries-old institutions and forts—such as the Castillo de San Marcos in St. Augustine—in addition to alliances with Native nations. As the Spanish envoy to the United States Minister Luis de Onís repeated in letters and eventual publications, Spain held a three-century claim to the region, dating to the early 1500s.[164]

Throughout the early 1800s and during the War of 1812, Native nations received support from Spanish settlements. In towns such as Pensacola, Spanish leaders encouraged Indian raids upon Georgian settlements. Creek leader Alexander McGillivray was in fact so familiar with Spanish settlers that he coauthored a letter of outrage to the Spanish king after the Treaty of Paris, complaining that Creek, Chickasaw, and Cherokee communities did not "forfeit our independence and natural rights" to Great Britain.[165]

Spain had long courted McGillivray and other Creek leaders, fighting alongside them in defense of their "mutual independence and prosperity."[166] The crisis of Latin American independence (1810–21), however, undercut Spanish, Creek, Chickasaw, and Seminole authority in Florida. As U.S. settlers proliferated, they rushed into Indian and Spanish lands and claimed them as their own.

Ironically, Spanish leaders had once envisioned naturalizing these U.S. citizens, hoping to turn those concerned about their weak national government into Spanish settlers. Those "who have lived under a precarious government," imagined Louisiana governor Bernardo de Gálvez in 1787, could be induced to follow Spanish sovereignty, one that "protects them, facilitates an outlet for their products, [and] decides their controversies with justice."[167] Others believed that settlers would eventually gravitate away from the Union in order "to maintain their independence" to avoid "the contrary and irreconcilable interests" caused by divisions such as the slavery question.[168] Onís even proposed that Spain and Britain ally with dissatisfied New Englanders to divide the Union into "two or three republics" in order to limit the rapaciousness of southern expansionists.[169]

According to article 3 of the Louisiana Purchase Treaty, Louisiana's residents were to be incorporated into the "Union of the United States and admitted as soon as possible."[170] However, the exact boundaries of these newly incorporated lands remained unclear. Also unclear to American leaders were the racial and religious compositions of their subjects. Generations of hybridity and interdependence were evident across the borderlands, and at settlement after settlement, U.S. travelers noted a variety of identities. Near Natchitoches in Texas, a "mixture of French, Spanish, Indian, and Negro blood" characterized the settlement in 1806, according to U.S. explorers Thomas Freeman and Peter Curtis.[171] Anti-Catholicism endured across the early Republic, as John Adams revealed in 1815. "The people of South America, he argued, "are the most ignorant, the most bigoted, the most superstitious of all the Roman Catholics of Christendom."[172] Most concerning, in West and East Florida, runaway slaves, African American freedmen, and Native peoples lived together, challenging both U.S. sovereignty and the nation's racial hierarchies.[173]

Spain had enlisted freed blacks into its militia and allowed the establishment of freed communities, such as Fort Mose outside St. Augustine. Fort Mose also supported Indian raiders who targeted U.S. plantations.[174] During the crisis of Latin American independence, U.S. leaders recommended the seizure of Spanish Florida, and Andrew Jackson led the First Seminole War in 1817 in order to achieve it.

Independence leaders from across Latin America had encouraged such seizures, hoping that U.S. alliances would further weaken Spanish forces. Many of Latin America's revolutionary leaders encouraged U.S. efforts to invade Florida and Texas. Various revolutionaries, Onís held, had helped to organize marauding parties that ranged from Galveston to Amelia Island, north of St. Augustine.[175] For the first time, the disruptions of Spanish colonial politics washed ashore on U.S. politics.

These forces attacked Spanish vessels and other travelers, including U.S. ships. Unsurprisingly, Monroe took issue with such insurgent diplomacy. He ordered the occupation of Amelia Island in December 1817. He also sought broader diplomatic resolution, commanding Secretary of State John Adams to resolve "the Florida Question."[176]

Scholars have struggled to connect Monroe's foreign policies with the nation's Indian affairs. Only recently have historians attempted to see Spanish-Indian affairs in Florida as an additional theater of the War of 1812, which is usually understood as ending with the battle of New Orleans in 1815.[177] Moreover, the Seminole War pitted the United States against not only Spain and Britain but also Native nations and African American freedmen. It also exposed how far U.S. leaders would go to restrict the ability of foreign nationals who aided black and Indian insurgencies. As Spain's foreign minister José

García de León y Pizarro summarized, Jackson's invasion and execution of prisoners of war were not only "repugnant to the laws of nations, and the principles which regulate the conduct of civilized Powers" but were initiated in order to bring "a forcible occupation" rather than "a peaceful acquisition."[178] Essentially, Jackson believed that American sovereignty included the right to employ armed forces extraterritorially to achieve national goals.[179]

While efforts to facilitate Indian dispossession and preserve African American slavery shaped U.S. diplomacy, there was little certainty in U.S. foreign affairs.[180] Unpredictability reigned. In Florida, African American freedmen had become integrated into Seminole society to such an extent that they lived within their societies and also joined Seminole raids on Georgian plantations. Such hybridity confounded U.S. leaders and justified their aggressions. As Congressman Henry Baldwin remarked, it was counterfactual to call "a gregarious collection of . . . outlawed Indians and runaway negroes a nation."[181]

Southern leaders were joined by northern representatives when they advocated new policies to entrench racial hierarchies, remove Indians, and consolidate U.S. sovereignty. These leaders included not only Presidents Monroe, Adams, and Jackson but also Senator Martin Van Buren and Secretary of War John C. Calhoun, who ordered the occupation of Amelia Island. Representatives of Virginia, Massachusetts, Tennessee, New York, and South Carolina, respectively, they all confronted overlapping geopolitical contests involving Native nations, European empires, and independent nations such as Venezuela.

Latin American revolutionary leaders often failed to register the extent of U.S. fears of miscegenation and slave revolts. When Simón Bolívar invited U.S. representatives in 1824 to join a Pan-American Congress, his invitation deepened, rather than alleviated, sectional tensions, as there was little common cause shared by these new republics.

Revolutionary visions of unity across the Americas collapsed in the face of an "American system" that supported U.S. racial politics and slavery.[182] "These [new] governments have proclaimed the principles of liberty and equality," proclaimed South Carolina's Senator Robert Hayne, and "have marched to victory under the banner of universal emancipation. You find men of color at the head of their armies, in their legislative halls, and in their executive offices." There should be only one foreign policy goal for the United States in the region, he continued: "to protest against the independence of Hayti."[183]

As Hayne's condemnation suggested, racial fears informed U.S. reactions to Latin American independence. Fears of Haitian influence, as argued in chapter 7, fueled Jeffersonian policies, and U.S. leaders continued to believe that Haitians were fostering independence movements across the hemisphere. For example, Haiti had offered asylum to Bolívar, who in 1817 used the Haitian port of Cayes to outfit vessels "against the Enemies of Venezuela."[184]

Moreover, Haitian newspapers such as *Le telegraph* circulated across the Caribbean, as did news about colonization efforts aimed at resettling freedmen in Haiti.[185] As Hayne and Calhoun knew well, slaves in South Carolina took particular inspiration from Haitian sovereignty. Denmark Vesey, who organized a slave revolt in South Carolina in 1822 and had spent his youth aboard ships traveling from Charleston to Saint-Domingue, drew upon Haitian revolutionary rhetoric. As with Gabriel's Rebellion of 1800 in Virginia, Vesey anticipated Haitian support for American slave uprisings, and he aimed to inspire other liberation movements. At his trial, one compatriot relayed that Vesey "had the habit of reading to me all the passages in the newspapers that related" to Haiti.[186]

As the Haitian Revolution had informed the Louisiana Purchase, so too did Haitian support for Latin America frame President James Monroe's diplomacy. The advocacy of "universal emancipation" became a threatening concept and practice, and it occurred amid ongoing conflicts between southern militia and Seminole soldiers.

The Seminole War and the Adams-Onís Treaty of 1819

By 1817 American racial animus toward Native peoples had hardened, and it now fueled the invasion of Florida. As the *Nashville Whig and Tennessee Advertiser* explained, Indians "know nothing of either law or reason. . . . Savages, in war, are to be brought to submission only through fear."[187] "Indians give no quarter," stated the *Albany Register*, and "of course they are entitled to none."[188]

Race also shaped national policies toward Latin America's new nations, in which people of color were now free and equal. U.S. policy leaders believed that freedom and equality did not apply to multiracial people and that therefore the Enlightenment principle of popular sovereignty did not extend to them. "The President is not prepared to say that Haiti ought to be recognized as an independent sovereign power," Secretary of State Henry Clay had written in 1826.[189] Those dark races who governed "armies . . . legislative halls, and . . . executive offices" remained outside the conventions of U.S. statecraft. They in fact resembled America's Indian nations and its borderlands communities.

The South's surging population growth had also fueled the growth of southern militias, and Jackson easily mustered an army to curb attacks upon Georgia's backcountry. With over three thousand men under his command, he also held a sweeping order from Calhoun: "to adopt the necessary measures to terminate a conflict which it has ever been the desire of the President . . . to avoid."[190]

Jackson ordered U.S. forces occupying Spanish settlements across West Florida to seize St. Augustine, beginning an occupation of both regions. A bevy of problems arose from such actions. Did Jackson have the authority to command an occupation of foreign territory? What to do with Spanish settlers who were white and may have once been U.S. citizens? And what of the region's other foreign nationals, especially British officials, who were stationed to aid Seminole and allied Indians? This last question had the potential to bring the United States back to war with Britain, especially after Jackson ordered the court-martial and execution of two British subjects, including a military officer.[191]

The laws of war did not allow for the execution of military prisoners. But was this international war, or was it war against Indians? During his campaigns against the Creek Confederacy during the Creek War of 1813–14, Jackson had insisted that the laws of war "did not apply to conflicts with savages."[192] He flatly refused to consider his campaigns against the Creek as a part of international diplomacy or subject to its protocols.[193] He conducted the Seminole War in similar fashion. In his mind, he was fighting Indians and runaway slaves, not foreign nations.

While Jackson believed that the laws of war did not apply to U.S. forces confronting Native nations, the Florida invasion was different. It involved both Spanish territorial leaders and British officials. Jackson, however, believed that Spain had licensed Indian raids upon the United States and thereby should be punished militarily while also forfeiting its territories. "The Spanish government is bound . . . to keep her Indians at peace with us," he explained. "They have acknowledged their incompetency to do this, and are consequently bound by the law of nations, to yield us all facilities to reduce them."[194] As with Calhoun's order to "adopt all necessary measures," Jackson considered all "facilities" permissible against the Seminole.

With U.S. forces occupying St. Augustine and the Gulf Coast to New Orleans, Spain had little power to counteract U.S. aggression. Moreover, Bolívar and independence leaders were making gains against Spanish forces. Spanish diplomats understood that U.S. ambitions also included Texas, particularly Galveston, whose port offered export possibilities for western cotton. Foreign Minister Pizarro understood that Spain no longer held power over Florida, and despite its historic relationship with Creek, Chickasaw, and Seminole nations, Spain now relinquished its centuries-old claims. "Negotiation based on the cession of the Floridas will be useless," he explained to the minister of war, "as we shall [soon] not have them to cede."[195]

Secretary of State John Quincy Adams agreed with Minister Luis de Onís, the Spanish envoy to the United States. Adams advocated quick negotiations. "Spain won't have the possession of Florida" for long, he wrote after Jackson's occupation.[196]

The resulting Adams-Onís Treaty of 1819 transferred Florida to the United States. It thereby clarified U.S. borders around the southeastern corner of North America. It also established the Republic's first internationally recognized border across the Trans-Mississippi West with Spain (and soon Mexico) and laid claims to the Pacific along the Forty-second Parallel. The agreement, often referred to as the Transcontinental Treaty, established for the first time boundaries between the Spanish empire and the American Republic.

Notably, the treaty also preceded the debates around Missouri statehood itself, and it informed the creation of the Missouri Compromise boundary line thereafter that demarcated slave versus free states.[197] The treaty of 1819, which originated from Spain's support for Indian allies, now not only shaped U.S. international boundaries and claims to the Pacific but also established the borderlines for the expansion of domestic slavery. Indian affairs thus influenced the nation's foreign policy deliberations and its domestic policies of expansion. What had begun as sporadic Seminole raids upon Georgia set in motion the expansion of two sets of U.S. borders.

With the treaty, the United States had now established its claims as a continental power. With the Missouri Compromise, the federal government also established the formal mechanism for incorporating lands from the Louisiana Purchase into the Union as either free or slave states. It had done so, however, at great cost: hundreds of casualties, millions of dollars, and the continued forced removal of tens of thousands of southern Indians, including now the Seminole. While it endured for decades, the Missouri Compromise in the aftermath of the U.S. war with Mexico (1846–48) eventually proved unable to maintain the Republic's balancing act of free versus slave states.

For now, U.S. claims to California were sown by the 1819 treaty. As the United States now claimed lands in Oregon, its traders continued to advocate for acquiring more Pacific lands, including California. Achieving this long-desired claim to the Pacific, the treaty, Adams said triumphantly, "forms a great epoch in our history."[198]

James Monroe, John Marshall, and the Doctrines of 1823

An engine of expansion had formed in eastern North America whose drive to add Indian lands had now broadened its capacity to add foreign appendages as well. Many believed Florida was just the beginning. Expansionists looked not only west to Texas and California but also south toward the Caribbean. They looked with worry as well as excitement because both Britain and France had an interest in Spain's former colonies. "It may be taken for granted that the dominion of Spain upon the American continents," Adams wrote in 1823, "is irrevocably gone. But the islands of Cuba and Porto Rico . . . she yet possesses the power of transferring her own dominion over them."[199] Many, especially Calhoun, called for Cuba's quick annexation while groups from New York and Philadelphia set out to establish the "Republic of Boriqua" in Puerto Rico.[200] The fall of the Spanish empire had created a seeming flash sale animating hopes for territorial acquisition.

Monroe shared Adams's concerns about Spain "transferring her own dominion." While fueling Jackson's popularity, events in Florida revealed the potential for borderlands crises to drag the Republic into conflict, especially with Britain. U.S. leaders expressed "serious inquietude" that Spain's possessions might fall under British control or that Spanish efforts to recolonize might bring other European powers into the hemisphere.[201] "The whole system of modern colonization is an abuse of government," Adams had written, "and it is time that it should come to an end."[202] Limiting foreign nations' ability to acquire Spanish possessions became national policy, as did limiting Spain's potential to colonize other borderlands regions.

In his address to Congress in 1823, Monroe issued a fifty-one-paragraph declaration outlining his administration's intention to prevent the transfer of European colonies. Along with principles of declared neutrality and prohibitions on future colonization efforts, his "Doctrine," as it became known, now constituted a declaration of foreign policy independence.[203]

Like the Declaration of Independence, the Monroe Doctrine also became a declaration of war against America's Indigenous nations, whose long-standing ability to ally with European powers became further inhibited. As Monroe proclaimed, "The American continents, by the free and independent condition which they have assumed and maintained, are henceforth no longer subjects for any new European colonial establishments."[204] The United States, he continued, would consider any attempt by European powers "to extend their system to any portion of this hemisphere as dangerous to our peace and safety."[205]

By 1823 the United States had navigated revolutions, wars, and independence movements. It had formed new governing structures and doctrines of power—such as the Constitution and Monroe Doctrine. New forms of law and jurisprudence accompanied these dramatic developments. Earlier that year, for example, the Supreme Court decided a case, *Johnson v. M'Intosh*, that offered a similar formulation of national power and judicial independence. It was one of John Marshall's defining cases, the first of "the Marshall Trilogy" involving Indian affairs.

Like the Adams-Onís Treaty of 1819, *Johnson v. M'Intosh* resolved a pressing concern. Unlike Marshall's later cases regarding the Cherokee, this dispute did not involve any individual Native plaintiffs or defendants. No one was imprisoned, like Samuel Worcester, or faced death, like Corn Tassel. The case involved a land dispute between two parties in Illinois, each of whom had purchased the same land—Johnson from a private company and M'Intosh from the federal government. Both claimed to have obtained ownership from Illinois and Piankeshaw tribal leaders. Their dispute raised the question of whether Indians could sell interior lands to individuals or strictly to the federal government.[206]

What seemed to be a simple concern raised questions about property, national power, and ultimately history. After independence, the United States received recognition of its sovereignty at the Treaty of Paris in 1783. It began formalizing interior acquisition and land cessions through Indian treaties, the Louisiana Purchase Treaty of 1803, and the Adams-Onís Treaty of 1819. Treaty, purchase, and conquest are the only forms of land acquisition authorized by the U.S. Constitution.

As every antebellum administration learned, adding new lands to the nation caused tensions. Expansion exposed political divisions and ultimately constitutional failures, such as regarding the issue of slavery. As Congressman John Tyler of Kentucky wrote during the Missouri Controversy, casual talk of disunion remained a constant: "Men talk of a dissolution of the Union with perfect nonchalance and indifference. . . . For myself, I cannot and will not yield one inch of the ground."[207]

Informed by the compromises of his time, Marshall attempted to stabilize the process of territorial acquisition and increase national powers over western lands. Siding with M'Intosh, he ruled that only the federal government had the power to acquire Indian lands because it held the exclusive authority, or supremacy, to acquire interior lands.

Whether Indians held title to their lands became the question in the case. In ruling that Native people could alienate their lands only to the federal government, Marshall established the precedent that Native nations held forms of recognizable land ownership but that such ownership was qualitatively different. He termed such ownership "Indian title," a form of property rights unique to U.S. law.[208] Native nations could cede lands to the federal government through treaties, as they had been doing for decades. In turn, they could also receive the federal government's recognition for their jurisdiction over such lands.

This case began Marshall's interpretation of the forms of Indian sovereignty established by the Constitution, upon which he later expanded in *Worcester v. Georgia* (1832). As the Monroe Doctrine decreed, the Marshall Court ruled that the United States held an authority above other powers: Indians, states, and foreign nations. The federal government held an exclusive right to both acquire and thus extinguish Indian title, and only the federal government had the constitutional power to receive the transfer of such lands. Such authority originated from what Marshall termed the "Doctrine of Discovery," which was a fictitious legal proclamation comparable, rhetorically, to Monroe's assertion of U.S. supremacy over the hemisphere. Discovery of a given territory, Marshall wrote, had "granted the discoverer the right, against other nations, to purchase Indian land."[209]

✦

Two national "doctrines" were articulated in 1823. One applied to foreign nations, the other to America's "domestic dependent nations." Both doctrines emerged out of the struggles for sovereignty during the era of Latin American independence. Each established preclusive federal powers to claim territory within its borders and to limit the claims of other nations. Both shaped the course of domestic and international law and established orthodoxies that deepened the federal government's administrative capacities.

Through their myriad actions, Native nations shaped these evolving structures of the U.S. nation-state. After 1823, however, they confronted that power without the protection of other foreign nations. While many continued to trade with British allies or encouraged Mexican leaders to reinstate the trading practices that had guided Spanish policy, the centuries-old system of playing rival Europeans against one another was nearly closed. The power of the United States grew ever more expansive throughout each decade that followed.

9 • Collapse and Total War

The Indigenous West and the U.S. Civil War

The very foundations of the Government are cracking. . . .
No mere policy or platform can outlast this storm.
—*Senator Timothy O. Howe (1861)*

The mountain passes, impenetrable in winter, displayed their deep and bright snowfall to the region's newcomers. Optimistic spirits filtered across the settlements where the Rockies and Plains collide. Each week of spring 1859, a new station, known as a road ranch, emerged. Hastily constructed, they enabled the passage of more prospectors, traders, and settlers. Like knots along an aging cord, a string of road ranches welcomed passengers and their tired animals along the six hundred miles to Colorado.

An air of inevitability also filtered across the Plains that spring. While immigrants in wagon trains or the occasional horse-drawn coach left colorful denunciations of the "suspicious eggs" and "rude and primitive shelter" provided by these makeshift operations, they celebrated them nonetheless.[1] The experience of the overland travel was not meant to be joyful. It was to be endured—the less time spent traveling the better. More efficient and shorter travel times became reason for jubilation, as distance itself was being conquered.[2] When two Concord coaches arrived in Denver on May 7 from Leavenworth, local newsmen rejoiced. "Bring out the Flags, and Let the Cannon Roar," they exclaimed, and a days-long festivity of parades, dinners, and toasts greeted the settlement's newest residents.[3]

With a gold rush in the nearby mountains, a palpable fever animated the region. Everywhere, newcomers filtered along the Front Range. They tracked the news circulating from the mines while awaiting word from their families to the east, more than halfway across the continent. Memories of places upon the Plains seemed like beacons upon the seas. Leavenworth, of all places, had become Denver's favorite sister city. It was "the greatest city in the East," as locals maintained. Its traders and massive freight trains kept the region supplied. They had all responded to the loud "Golden Echo" that rang down from the "Mineral Mountains" of the Colorado Territory.[4]

In the span of a few seasons, a new society had formed. It was growing, constantly reenvisioning its future. The string of overland stations, so initially welcomed, would have to go. The region's future would not be one of dirt roads plied by oxen, mules, and horses. It would consist of "iron arteries of inland commerce . . . over which the iron horse would yet snort on his road to the Pacific."[5] A glorious future awaited, filled with mythic machine-like creatures breathing not life, but commerce, across the continent.

Viewed as a cascading series of failed attempts to keep the Union together, the 1850s witnessed national crisis after national crisis: the end of the Missouri Compromise and the subsequent failure of the Compromise of 1850; the passage of the Fugitive Slave Law and the subsequent declaration of the *Dred Scott* decision; the rise of the Republican Party, committed to limiting slavery's expansion; and the eventual hardening of Confederate nationalism.

Sectional tensions exploded in the fall of 1860 with the election of Abraham Lincoln. As Denver prepared for the arrival of more immigrants, seven southern states formed the Confederate States of America. They were joined by four more, including Virginia, the largest state in the South. They elected their own president. Confederates seized Union forts, arsenals, and the U.S. Mint. The former United States of America was no more. The Union had collapsed.

The Civil War redefined the Republic. The deepening constitutional failures that had plagued the nation no longer found easy remedy in what Frederick Douglass termed "the old medicine of compromise."[6] "If the Union can only be maintained by new concessions to the slaveholders," he argued, "let the Union perish."[7] As Lincoln's law partner William Herndon recalled, before the war he "hated . . . the very name of Anti-slavery," but he had now grown into a champion of "universal freedom."[8] During the war, a broader potential of American freedom was unveiled. No longer constrained by the failures of the past, a new freedom was finally dawning. As Douglass declared, "It is difficult for us who have toiled so long and hard, to believe, that this event, so stupendous, so far reaching and glorious is even now at the door."[9]

The war brought the abolition of slavery and amendments to the Constitution. The Emancipation Proclamation of January 1, 1863, made the war into a conflict between societies, thereby ensuring that a Union victory would forever reconfigure the South's political economy and thus its social relations.[10] In this conflict—the largest ever fought in the Western Hemisphere—compromise became impossible.[11]

Every dimension of the state and the economy was mobilized in a "total war," but although the Union won the conflict the war did not result in a social revolution. The promise of Reconstruction remained unfulfilled—to this day, according to some. "The end is not yet," Douglass cautioned. "We are at best only at the beginning of the end."[12]

Within this epic, Lincoln forever stands tall. His letter of December 1, 1862, to Congress includes several of the most quoted words in U.S. history. "We cannot escape history," he wrote, concluding, "We shall nobly save, or meanly lose, the last best hope of earth."[13] Historians consider these words, like others he proclaimed during his presidency, "among the most eloquent ever composed by an American president."[14] They encapsulate the essence of the era, if not the nation itself.

There is, however, a limitation to this framework. The settler revolutions of the 1850s, including the California and Colorado gold rush, are often absent in studies of the Civil War. Far from being a transitory decade, the 1850s witnessed social revolutions that devastated Native communities and precipitated the national crisis at hand. Moreover, the Union victory served to consolidate these transformations as settlers recalibrated Indigenous worlds and increasingly drew upon the power of new national institutions to secure them. The West, in short, became absorbed into the nation's new political economy.[15] From the Willamette Valley in Oregon through the Sierra mining camps of California onto the central Plains and into the Mississippi headwaters, a demographic and economic deluge occurred, one of several booms in a "settler revolution" that swept the nineteenth-century world.[16]

Settler Booms and the Absence of the State

Settler booms not only destabilized Indigenous communities but also often led to their displacement. Rapid settlement also initiated acts of unmitigated violence that became genocidal, particularly in recently incorporated states and territories with limited forms of national authority.

Before 1850, for example, Minnesota had fewer than five thousand settlers. Euro-Americans knew it for its frozen lakes, endless forests, and exceptional cold—an American Siberia, as some referred to it. Dakota bands, estimated at twenty thousand earlier in the century, lived across its southern prairies, while Anishinaabeg (Ojibwe) and Métis bands controlled the northern woods and western lakes of Anishinaabewake (home of the Anishinaabeg).[17] These Native nations had long since adapted to the arrival of European traders, missionaries, and technologies. Surging immigration, however, brought farming to the region's rich prairie soils, engendering a settler boom.

Politics and diplomacy facilitated this boom. As in other parts of the Great Lakes region, treaty cessions confined Indians to reservations and opened remaining territory to settlement. The 1851 Treaty of Traverse des Sioux confined Dakota bands along the Minnesota River to a fraction of their former homelands, and in under a decade, the settler population grew thirty-fold to 150,000. Booster literatures now de-emphasized the cold, reclassifying the region as "a perfect Eden."[18]

Racial, economic, and political tensions brewed each season. As farms multiplied, game became scarcer. Indian families grew hungry while white farms overflowed with produce, grain, and livestock. Exports followed, as the region's farm surpluses mirrored its demographic swells. The number of pigs sent to slaughter in Chicago rose from twenty-two thousand in 1852 to five hundred thousand within a decade. Untold thousands arrived by railway from other farmlands, and by the time of the Civil War, the city held a million pigs in its pens. By 1877 they totaled 4 million.[19]

Such meteoric growth was not caused by the war but expanded by it. Beforehand, Denver, St. Paul, and other settler cities remained disconnected from the Union. The state was generally absent from the everyday lives of its citizens. Indeed, the nation's "conception of its duties" had changed little since the founding, as a limited national government governed an expanding populace across new territories.[20] In fact, the size of government and its limited involvement in the economy had fostered the growing conviction of many that the United States was a land of individualism and self-made men.[21]

In 1860 the federal government did not even tax its citizens. The army totaled sixteen thousand—less than 2 percent of its eventual total during the war—and most were stationed in forts ranging from San Francisco to St. Augustine.

Migrants did see U.S. soldiers along overland routes, such as Fort Lyons in Colorado, and they knew that territorial leaders, including Colorado governor John Evans, lived among them. By and large, however, most citizens lived their lives without interacting with government officials.[22] Throughout the antebellum era, a defining feature of American settler colonialism was the limited presence—and indeed absence—of the state.

By war's end, things had changed. A million soldiers served in the federal army—including 180,000 African Americans. Fifty thousand employees worked for the national government. For the first time, Congress imposed national taxes.[23] The size, power, and capability of the federal government had finally started to match its population and soon targeted its western lands for continued growth.

Wartime mobilization enabled the birth of the modern U.S. state and with it a concomitant rise in federal power over Indian affairs. Despite the scandal, graft, and failures of Reconstruction, a redefinition of the American body politic accompanied the war.[24] New national powers emerged: the draft, expansion of national tariffs and taxations, improved infrastructure, and new legislative powers, among many others. Signs of these new powers circulated across the continent. Citizens even carried them in their pockets, as Congress established the nation's first national currency, known as green backs due to their green ink.[25]

During the war, the government began exercising these powers. Sweeping legislation in 1862 included the Homestead Act, the Morrill Act, and the chartering of the Union Pacific Railroad. Each law extended federal authority over western lands, education, and infrastructure. For the time being, however, settler booms continued unabated and contributed more to the destruction of Indigenous worlds than any formal national policy. Indeed, the limited presence of the state engendered genocidal violence across the West.

The Dakota War and Indigenous Genocide

New national laws were meaningless without enforcement, and national power required an increase in the state's monopolization of violence. Starting in 1861, army officials attempted to mitigate conflicts with Native nations and to use diplomacy to extend U.S. sovereignty upon them. Violence, however, became ubiquitous after secession, when the Union diverted its few soldiers east. In fact, throughout the first years of the war, it seemed that the Union army was shrinking rather than growing.

In December 1862, as Lincoln prepared the Emancipation Proclamation, the six-month U.S.-Dakota War was ending. Throughout the month, roughly two thousand Dakota soldiers and their families remained incarcerated in Minnesota, most at Fort Snelling. Hundreds awaited execution. In November they had been marched across the territory. Prisoners and children had been attacked and killed by mobs in the streets of Minnesota cities such as New Ulm.

As they awaited execution, Lincoln signed an executive order on December 6 commuting the sentences of most soldiers, but thirty-eight remained scheduled for execution. On December 26, in the largest mass execution in U.S. history, they were hanged at Mankato for their participation in that summer's war. Combined, nearly a thousand settlers, Dakota community members, and U.S. soldiers lost their lives.[26]

The Dakota War and its aftermath reconfigured the human geography of the region. It brought the elimination of the Dakota reservation and a near diaspora of its people. In the 1851 treaty, the Sisseton and Wahpeton Dakota had ceded millions of acres in exchange for a reservation along the Minnesota River; the allocation of "one million six-hundred and sixty-five thousand dollars" to the tribe; and "money annuity, the sum of forty thousand dollars," among other stipulations.[27]

Like so many treaties, it was violated after ratification. Each spring, growing numbers of farmers squatted upon Dakota lands. They allowed their livestock to roam upon the river's beds and pressured the state to gain more lands. After 1860, not only did the annuity payments cease altogether, the few officials charged with provisioning Dakota families sold the agency's supplies to whites in what one decried as a "system of wholesale robberies . . . [in which] the Indians are greatly cheated by the traders."[28] Such illegal trade flourished across reservations during the war. When hungry Dakota families confronted agents at the reservation's supply centers, they were told to eat grass.

The executions at Mankato were followed by forced removal to the Dakota Territory, where Dakota bands joined their Siouan-speaking Lakota kinsmen. Such ethnic cleansing became the expressed aim of U.S. military leaders. Across the West, military officers often inherited command from local militias and came to share their anti-Indian ideologies. In Minnesota, as General John Pope ordered Colonel Henry Sibley in September 1862:

> It is my purpose utterly to exterminate the Sioux if I have the power to do so and even if it requires a campaign lasting the whole of next year. Destroy everything belonging to them and force them out to the plains. . . . They are to be treated as maniacs or wild beasts, and by no means as peo-

ple with whom treaties or compromises can be made. Urge the campaign vigorously; you shall be vigorously supported and supplied.[29]

One of over a hundred campaigns against Indigenous peoples fought during the Civil War and Reconstruction, the Dakota War became a campaign for Indigenous elimination.

Calls for the extermination of Native peoples were common throughout the era. U.S. soldiers and volunteers were ordered to carry out killings. As Lieutenant James Martin wrote from northern California in 1861, despite having "no means of finding out whether those that we may come upon are guilty or innocent . . . my instructions are to consider all who run . . . as hostile, and to fire upon them."[30] In January 1863, just weeks after the Mankato executions, Colonel Patrick Edward Connor surprised a northern Shoshone encampment along the Bear River near the Idaho-Utah border. Leading companies of California volunteers, his forces "destroyed over seventy lodges" in what historians generally recognize as the largest military massacre of Native Americans.[31]

The following year, in November 1864, as Colonel John Chivington led several hundred men of the First and Third Volunteer Cavalry out of Colorado's Fort Lyon to Black Kettle's Cheyenne and Arapaho village at Sand Creek, he reportedly shouted, "Damn any man who is in sympathy with an Indian!"[32] They too attacked at dawn, and like Connor, targeted women, children, and the elderly. They also came in winter because, as Governor Evans had reminded Cheyenne leaders beforehand, "The time when you make war best is in the summer. . . . My time is coming."[33] When Chivington's forces returned to Denver, revelers again lined the streets. The body parts of Cheyenne victims circulated as trophies.

To claim the Civil War was solely a conflict between the North and South is to miss this settler revolution and its transformative violence. Viewing the era as a conflict defined by "slavery" versus "freedom" also erases multiple campaigns of dispossession, removal, and even genocide. Such perspectives contribute to a story in which the abolition of slavery appears as the fulfillment of American freedom, obscuring a more complex and less celebratory past.[34]

California Militias at the Beginning of the Civil War

While army officials, newspaper writers, and national leaders understood violence against Indians to be central to the war's course, others protested its wanton application. As the commissioner of Indian Affairs William Dole reported in 1861 about the California campaigns, "This so-called 'Indian war' appears to be a war in which the whites alone are engaged. The Indians are hunted like wild and dangerous beasts of prey."[35] As the *San Francisco Herald* similarly noted, "The troops are not engaged in 'fighting' the Indians, but in slaughtering them."[36]

California experienced the most indiscriminate violence during the war, in which tens of thousands of Indians were killed. Such violence was initially perpetuated not by soldiers but by settler militia.

Before the war, differences between Union army "regulars" and "volunteers" were evident in easily recognized distinctions. Regulars wore uniforms, held salaried appointments, and were under the command of army leaders, many of whom were trained officers. None hailed from the far West—New Mexico, California, or Oregon—all of which only became U.S. states or territories after the Treaty of Guadalupe Hidalgo (1848). After secession, these differences started to blur. Many regulars returned east. Southern officers moved to join the Confederacy, and Union forces were similarly recalled. By the end of 1861, almost two-thirds of the Union army had been recalled.[37]

To strengthen its western posts, state and Union leaders called for volunteers. The first summons came on July 24, 1861, when California governor John Downey issued a call to form a regiment of infantry and a battalion of cavalry.[38] Such forces were to guard the Overland Trail that stretched across the Sierras to Fort Laramie, an arduous route of a thousand miles. By the end of August, more expansive plans were unfolding. Union leaders hoped to launch an invasion of Texas from California via northern Mexico to divert Confederate soldiers away from Missouri. They issued further calls for volunteers.[39]

Among white settlers, a surge of nationalism accompanied these calls to serve. Unlike in Oregon, where Confederate sympathies limited mobilization, Californians largely embraced the Union effort.[40] Across mining districts, interior ranches, and San Francisco, celebrations cheered the formation of volunteer units, several of which arrived from the mountains carrying staffs recently crowned with silver as gifts from Union supporters.[41]

For many, military service continued the violent service that they had provided as militiamen. Throughout the 1850s, twenty-three state-authorized militia units fought against Native peoples in Indian-hunting campaigns from the Mojave Desert to Humboldt Bay.[42] While these forces were comprised of local settlers, they received funding from state and eventually federal authorities.[43] On December 21, 1860, for example, the day after South Carolina seceded from the Union, California senator Milton Latham presented a bill to Congress for "expenses incurred in the suppression of Indian hostilities."[44] By the time of Lincoln's inauguration in March, Congress had appropriated up to $400,000 for nine militia campaigns over the previous six years.[45] The Union government funded campaigns against California's Native peoples before its battlefield encounters with the Confederacy. California Indians became in many ways the first casualties of the Civil War.

Across much of the West, campaigns against Native peoples, such as the Dakota War, elicited more passion than those against the Confederacy. In northern California, from Mount Shasta to Humboldt Bay, ranchers had long attempted to prevent Native communities from seizing their cattle. As the *Bulletin* of San Francisco reported on January 21, 1860:

> The Indians have again become very troublesome to the settlers of Mendocino country. . . . They have become so bad that the settlers have been compelled to organize themselves into a standing army, so to speak, by taking turns keep their stock . . . under constant guard. . . . The Indians had killed from ten to fifteen head of stock nightly. . . . On the 19th of December, the settlers turned out, and attacking the enemy succeeded in killing 32. . . . The aid of the state has . . . been asked, and will we trust be granted.[46]

The war now aided such efforts. With increased funding and assistance, it became easier to kill Indians and secure stock overnight. Starting in April 1861, Captain Charles Lowell launched a three-pronged invasion of the coastal forests east of Humboldt Bay. These campaigns reported killing more than two hundred Indians.[47]

More than in other western campaigns where U.S. soldiers often were stationed at military forts, settler militias in California operated outside the oversight of federal officials. They also fought Native nations that held limited prior alliances with Europeans. Coastal imperial powers, such as Spain, England, and Russia, had never expanded into the forested mountain terrain of redwood forests or the Sierra Nevada. Indeed, according to Lieutenant James Martin, Humboldt County was "in many places impassable" and remained "very favorable for the secretion of Indians."[48] Few northern California Native nations had incorporated guns or horses into their militaries.

Californian campaigns became known for their asymmetries of violence. These units developed the strategy of "killing the Indians in the mountains

. . . and kidnapping their children."[49] Destruction encouraged elimination. "The settlers are determined to exterminate them," reported the *Red Bluff Beacon* after an October 1861 massacre of Wailaki villagers at Horse Canyon in which two hundred died.[50] "The water in the creek became red," recalled Tome-ya-nem, a Konkow auxiliary member drawn from nearby Round Valley Reservation: "The old and the young alike . . . were strewn over the ground like dead leaves in the fall and for many days the sky was black with the ravens fattening on the dead."[51]

As Tome-ya-nem's testimony indicated, militia units on occasion relied upon Indian auxiliaries. Drawn from one of the state's few reservations, Tome-ya-nem lived at Round Valley, which became an inter-tribal community for those fleeing militia violence.[52]

The federal government had earlier attempted an alternate scenario to the genocide at hand. In 1851 and 1852, officials negotiated eighteen treaties across the state; however, bowing to California representatives, the Senate rejected these treaties, essentially authorizing the continued use of settler violence to aid colonization. Round Valley provided only limited shelter during these killing years. Vagrancy laws perpetuated the system of violence, and trafficking was established during the gold rush, as white settlers targeted Indian children within the reservation.[53] Nowhere was safe for Native families. Moreover, as California Indian Affairs superintendent George Hanson reported, whenever Indians left the reservation, they risked "being hunted down like wild beasts and killed."[54]

Such indiscriminate violence precipitated Indigenous guerrilla warfare and counter-reprisals by desperate Native survivors. Their responses, however, only deepened settler resolve and legitimated further reprisals. As San Francisco's *Daily Evening Bulletin* explained, "While we believe the manner in which the Indians are being exterminated is perfectly horrible, we are disposed to make every possible allowance for our own people."[55]

The *Daily Evening Bulletin*'s coverage followed the killing of a settler near Hydesville, which prompted the expansion of the Humboldt Home Guards militia to seventy-five men. Under the leadership of Captain G. W. Werk, it soon conducted fifteen engagements throughout 1861, killing seventy-five men and "a few women," with "nearly" as many wounded.[56] Werk reported no prisoners taken. He reported two men lost. His expedition, according to one of the few government reports on the subject, became "a mere series of Indian hunts, whose only object was to slaughter."[57] Werk's community had suffered one killing and the loss of two militia members during campaigns that claimed potentially two hundred Indians killed, wounded, or captured, as the asymmetrical violence of the 1850s continued on. As Civil War battles began in the east in July 1861, California's militia received additional federal funding. They still remained local units and were not yet institutionalized. By the end of 1861, however, many became absorbed into Union companies comprised of volunteers; a total of 15,725 enlisted.[58] Partly drawn from the state's militia units, these volunteers soon provided the bulk of western forces across the West, including in Utah, New Mexico, and Colorado, as "California Volunteers" facilitated the expansion of U.S. sovereignty across the West.

The Civil War and the Union's Ineffective Indian Office

Militias underscored a chilling reality: there was no consistent federal Indian policy nor clarity of national purpose.[59] The Union's attention was elsewhere. Other than Dole and a thin string of agents, few civilian officials were engaged in Indian affairs. A small handful of individuals were charged with overseeing policies across newly admitted states and vast territories. Their failures cost countless Native lives.

Few and far between, federal Indian officials remained understaffed and often came into conflict with settler populations. They consistently lacked resources to implement their policies, holding offices that in many cases were in name only. As Dole reported about Utah in 1862, "The Indian Service . . . cannot be otherwise than discreditable to the government, unless Congress shall, by liberal appropriations, enable our agents to conduct their operations upon a scale . . . corresponding with the absolute necessities of the Indians under their charge."[60] Such necessities were not being met, nor were the stipulations of treaties being followed. Everywhere, confusion reigned. Treaty obligations made by the federal government languished.[61]

Despite his stature, Lincoln had no answers to these challenges. As he informed a delegation of visiting Plains Indian leaders in 1863: "I can only say that I can see no way in which your race is to become as . . . prosperous as the white race except by living as they do, by the cultivation of the earth."[62]

Assimilation, land cessions, and eventual disappearance remained Lincoln's suggestions. Writing to Congress of the need to extinguish the "possessory rights of the Indians to large and valuable tracts of land," he offered abstract platitudes about the benefit that such actions would bring to "the welfare of the Indian."[63] In general, Lincoln devoted little attention to Indian policy during his presidency and deferred to army commanders in their campaigns in the West.[64]

Abolitionists and other social reformers also generally sidestepped the issue. The Civil War offered little national space for Indian affairs. As in California, select newspaper or editorial offices commented on ongoing atrocities but remained focused on other regional and national events. For many Union supporters, Native peoples provided useful, if simplified, contrasts to these other social challenges. "The Indian," as Douglass wrote, is "too stiff to bend . . . [and] retreats [from] your cities . . . your steamboats, and your canals and railways . . . he regards them with aversion."[65] The nation's Indian affairs seemed beyond repair.

Settler Colonialism and Infrastructure during the Civil War

The Civil War added fuel to the fiery trial consuming Native America. As in Colorado, Minnesota, and California, irreversible changes accompanied the settler booms of the era. Such booms were a part of a global explosion in people, livestock, and technologies that outpaced institutions of the nation-state. Like sudden storms, these settlements and herds eroded the economies of Native nations, and Native raiding became one of the few remedies to survive within ruptured worlds. Raids, counter-raids, and warfare followed.

Mobilization for total war consolidated these settler booms. During the Civil War, the army developed new forts, detention centers, and transportation systems, including the railway. Such consolidation comprises an essential chapter in the history of the Anglo world, whose total population grew from 12 million in 1780 to 200 million by 1930.[66] As in Australia, New Zealand, Canada, and much of South Africa, such growth occurred upon Indigenous homelands and came at their expense. The Civil War, in short, developed the administrative and military infrastructure that subsequently enabled the federal government to subjugate the West.

Denver's celebrated welcome of its first coaches and freight trains in 1859 underscored an essential truth about the era. While humans envisioned the region's future, animals—specifically oxen, horses, and mules—powered its movements. Stagecoaches and wagons were useless without them, and travel impossible. The first 5,434 white men and women who passed Council Grove, Kansas, in 1859 on their way to Colorado were outnumbered by oxen. Another thousand mules added additional support, while horse teams and cattle herds numbered nearly ten thousand.[67] Usually in teams of two to four, oxen drove in nearly one hundred thousand immigrants to Colorado, just as they had driven overland travelers to Oregon and California in the 1840s.

While many immigrants had seen railways in the East or even taken them to the edges of the Plains, they depended upon animals to carry their families and earthly possessions. Most adults walked rather than weigh down their carts. The fastest, if costliest, form of travel—stagecoaches—used horses and at times mules. They were notorious for their loud wheels and hard benches, but they required no walking.

Before the war, two- and four-legged locomotion was essential to continental travel. Steamboats plied the Mississippi, ferrying immigrants to launching points along the Missouri River, but feet and hooves carried them thereafter. In fact, so critical was the need for animal labor in the West that camels were imported to California—with limited success.[68]

Moreover, in regions where railways existed, their varied gauges and lack of standardization meant delays and the need to use multiple trains. When Lincoln left Chicago in February 1860 to address the Cooper Institute in New York, his travels took five trains, two ferries, and four days.[69] As many as twenty different gauges were used nationally. Railroads had yet to conquer the continent. In a divided nation, they were intended for regional travel.

As they had for generations, horses powered Colorado and continued to hold the keys to its future. Equestrian economies linked Indian trade and subsistence networks that centered around seasonal bison hunts. While dozens of different nations traveled across Colorado, the region was primarily home to Ute and Navajo (Diné) communities across its mountainous regions and Apache, Cheyenne, and Arapaho upon its southern, eastern, and northern plains. Kiowa, Lakota, Pawnee, and Comanche also concentrated upon its plains, while Pueblo horsemen and *Hispaño* traders known as *comancheros* also traveled across the region. White traders and "mountain men" traded in the mountains and out of depots, including Taos, and all traveled by horse.[70]

Stretching hundreds of miles, the central Plains had long provided a barrier to immigrant travel. The region had in fact witnessed a doubling of Native populations after 1820 as shifting pressures both pushed and attracted more Indian nations. Such Indigenous power only furthered Euro-American fears of overland travel; however, it was the endless, nearly sea-like distances of the Plains themselves that proved most jarring to newcomers. When, after days of uninterrupted riding in 1849, an army unit came within sight of trees along the Republican River, one private rejoiced, "Be Jesus we're in sight of land again!"[71]

To cover such distances required horses. To live within the region required herds of them. As many as eight to twelve horses per person characterized most equestrian powers, making a community of a few thousand home to tens of thousands of animals. When people gathered together for summer trade fairs or large diplomatic gatherings, horse herds sometimes extended miles on end, totaling over one hundred thousand in the central Plains. Across the southern Plains in Comanchería, horses circulated in similar numbers. As outsiders had long observed, the Comanche "knows more about a horse and horse-breeding than any other Indian," and "their wealth consisted" of them.[72]

Horses, like bison, require access to water and grasses. Seasonal rotations for equestrian pastoralism became an essential attribute of Plains Indian economies. Colorado's mountain parks and other alpine pastures provided coveted summer grasses for Ute, Cheyenne, and Arapaho as well as more distant Lakota and Comanche bands. Similarly, many New Mexican families who bristled under the Republic of Mexico sought refuge in the region's valleys, grazing horses and sheep along the San Luis Valley in partnership with Ute leaders.[73]

After the U.S. war with Mexico, conflicts intensified between Plains societies, as immigrant travel consumed pasturage and water sources. Twenty thousand travelers had journeyed across the Platte River Road before the California gold rush. After 1849, that number reached nearly two hundred thousand, with twice as many animals. Even as the number of immigrants declined, the number of livestock was large. In 1853 162,000 animals were counted at Fort Kearney, Nebraska, ten times the number of immigrants that year. As one commentator recalled, "It seemed as if Missouri would be totally drained of cattle."[74]

Native nations forged varied alliances to meet these challenges. As competition over the central mountain parks of the Rockies intensified, Ute bands developed ties with both New Mexican settlers in Colorado and U.S. leaders out of Santa Fe and Taos, where Indian agents such as Christopher Carson were stationed.[75] Utes confronted allied Cheyenne and Arapaho incursions throughout the 1850s, curbing their migration onto the Plains due to the presence of these rivals. Plains river valleys attracted large summer gatherings of Cheyenne, Arapaho, Kiowa, Comanche, and Plains Apache allies. In 1854 one encampment totaled over twelve hundred lodges of roughly eight thousand to ten thousand with an estimated forty thousand horses.[76]

These confederated allies ranged west into the Rockies. They also traveled east across Kansas and Missouri into Pawnee, Sac and Fox, Osage, Potawatomi, and other rivals' territories. Conflicts occurred, particularly as eastern Plains communities acquired greater access to firearms. For example, over a hundred from the 1854 summer gathering were killed or wounded along the Kansas River, including the Apache leader Bobtail Horse.[77]

Despite their use of guns, these eastern tribes often proved easier targets for raids. Given their close proximity to white immigrant trails, settlements, and eventual farms, Pawnee villagers suffered dual pressures, from both white intrusion and Indigenous adversaries. Like the Mandan, their horticultural villages had once teemed with trade and bounty. Estimated at a little more than four thousand in 1806, the Pawnee population had declined by 1859 to fewer than one thousand men, as warfare, disease, and starvation accompanied U.S. expansion.[78]

Inter-tribal conflicts intensified each summer before the Colorado gold rush. Grasses, timber, and water all become scarcer. Never had so many people and animals converged upon a single place within the central Plains.[79] Along the South Platte River in western Kansas, one traveler was amazed in 1857 to see a single herd of nine thousand sheep on its way to Oregon. Ecological and economic changes had uprooted the Plains just as such expansion had collapsed the Union.

The Hybridity of the Southwest

As the settler boom spread across the Plains, it became one of two transformative streams remaking the center of the continent. From the east came migrants, herds, and U.S. soldiers who staffed western forts, such as Leavenworth (1827), Kearny (1848), and Laramie (1849), that bookended road ranches across Kansas, Nebraska, and Wyoming.[80] While the explosion of immigration after the California gold rush ebbed in the early 1850s, migrants again poured into the region with the Colorado gold rush. By 1860 a total of more than three hundred thousand immigrants and at least five times as many animals had crossed the Plains.[81]

This eastern stream intersected with an older current that moved along a north-south axis. Originating within New Mexican settlements and extending through Texas and into northern Mexico, a continental trade in horses, furs, alcohol, and sheep radiated out of the Southwest. The Pacific fur trade at Astoria and across the Columbia River Basin formed a northern terminus for this trade, which starting in the 1820s sent hundreds of "mountain men," Hudson Bay Company brigades, and other traders into the Intermountain West.[82] Pressures from north and south converged, making these years among the hardest anywhere in Native America.

While often initially welcomed, trappers brought destructive influences. They in particular traded whiskey distilled at Taos, the principal source of alcohol in western North America.[83] They trapped in the spring and traded at summer gatherings known as rendezvous. Unlike immigrants, they resided in the region and often married into Native nations. Animals provided both the currency of this trade and its transport.

Like furs, horses and sheep formed arteries of trade, and they flowed from Mexico in the hundreds of thousands. Sometimes traded, they were often stolen by Indian nations. While the horse trade had expanded in the aftermath of the Pueblo Revolt, livestock herding was more recent. It grew in the late eighteenth century as more settlers gained land grants from Spain and Mexico. Soon over a million sheep were herded across New Mexico, providing endless targets for raiders. As New Mexico's superintendent of Indian Affairs James Calhoun decried in December 1850, "During the present month, a large number of sheep have been driven off by Indians. . . . It is estimated that near ten thousand were driven" from the region by Diné raiders.[84]

Equestrian nations maintained a complex political economy that combined pastoralism, migratory hunting and trade, and seasonal horticulture as well as raiding. While the U.S. war with Mexico had redrawn the West's political geography, it had neither dislodged its equestrian powers nor remade the political economy. Waves of immigrants and many new forts had not yielded a commensurate extension of U.S. sovereignty. Raids continued into the 1860s as equestrian spheres of influence undercut Union power. Tensions resonated. Few diplomatic resolutions appeared possible.

Looking north from New Mexico before the war, Calhoun wrote dispassionate reports about what was essentially a frenetic situation. Like superintendents in nearby Utah and soon Colorado, his office had few resources to manage Indian affairs among a constellation of nations: Diné and Jicarilla Apaches to the west; Mescalero Apaches and Comanches, Kiowas, and Wichitas to the east and south; Utes, Cheyenne, and Arapahos to the north; and dozens of resident Pueblo communities within the territory. Among the latter, he grew frustrated with attempts to determine the exact composition of their communities and governments.[85] As he reported, "The Pueblos of San Ildefonso, Pojoaque, Tesuque, and Nambé . . . have deceived those who have been charged with the taking of the Census." Moreover, he worried that "many are renouncing their Catholicism and joining the nomadic . . . tribes who encircle the territory."[86]

U.S. state power flickered across the antebellum West. While historians often presume that American territorial possessions were already predisposed to U.S. sovereignty, they were not. Before the Civil War, equestrians surrounded New Mexico's non-Indian populations. Moreover, Indigenous and other borderlands communities viewed U.S. officials with suspicion, sedition, or simply disinterest. As at the four Pueblos that Calhoun mentioned, they either deceived U.S. Census takers or practiced other forms of "refusal" to state officials and their accompanying property regimes based on gendered forms of patriarchal, familial authority.[87]

The heterogeneity of New Mexico particularly challenged U.S. officials. In addition to contending with the region's Native powers, Nuevomexicanos were discontented with the imposition of U.S. rule. The territory remained under military rule, and while the passage of the 1850 Organic Act had made "every free white male inhabitant" eligible for voting, racism clouded such eligibility.[88] Did former Mexican citizens qualify for U.S. citizenship, and if so, how about Pueblo Indians who farmed in sedentary villages? There were no clear answers. The most densely settled portion of Mexico seized by the United States, New Mexico did not become a state until 1912, even though some Union leaders supported its admission as a slave state in efforts to prevent secession.[89]

Everywhere the potential for violence remained. "There is a *great* and *deep* gulf between the Americans and Mexicans," Indian agent John Greiner reported. "There is hardly an American here [not] armed to the teeth."[90] U.S. leaders understood that the region's villagers were also allied with equestrian nations, which "encircle the territory." Utes, as Charles Beaubien reported from Taos in 1851, "are tampered with by Mexicans to effect our destruction. . . . Secret meetings have been held under various pretences for the purpose of organizing an insurrection [with] its object the extermination of the Americans and the Robbery of their Property."[91] While territorial leaders worked to incorporate Mexican leadership structures, such as the *ayuntamiento* system, into the county governments, outside the villages and across the Plains, U.S. sovereignty was limited, diffuse, and at times nonexistent.[92]

Treaty Making on the Northern Plains

On Wyoming's plains in 1851, U.S. officials attempted other forms of incorporation. Establishing peace and trade with Native nations had long guided federal Indian policy, and the treaty of 1851 at Fort Laramie became the West's most consequential initial attempt at incorporating Native nations into the folds of state power.

U.S. officials attempted to bring vast portions of the West under their jurisdiction. They hoped that diplomacy would aid efforts to establish overland roads, forts, and protections for immigrants while also establishing bounded territories for Native nations. Treaty negotiations provided diplomatic opportunities for Indian and white leaders, and nearly twelve thousand Native participants attended Fort Laramie. They brought approximately fifty thousand horses.[93]

Indian delegates came from as far away as Mandan-Hidatsa villages along the Missouri and from Shoshone camps north of Salt Lake. The majority were Lakota, Cheyenne, Gros Ventre, Arapaho, Crow, Arikara, and Assiniboine leaders.[94]

Evidence of that year's overland travel surrounded these leaders, but many had yet to witness the full effects of immigrant travel to California and Oregon. Chiefs Four Bears, Raven Chief, and Gray Prairie Eagle from Mandan-Hidatsa villages to the east were long accustomed to Plains trade and warfare. The transformations wrought by that year's immigrants, however, left them "with disbelieving eyes."[95] Carcasses of dead animals, broken wheels, abandoned kettles, and other debris littered immigrant roads. Moreover, the width of these trails were at times hundreds of yards. Surely, the chiefs queried officials, the lands from which so many people had come were now themselves abandoned and emptied?

Motivations to bring order to such chaos pervaded the gathering. Promises of government provisions and arms also drew Native communities from afar, but despite assuring words and grand promises, the treaty failed in nearly every regard. In contrast to New Mexico, with its fifty thousand villagers, the Plains presented a far different challenge for U.S. leaders. These lands were under competing Indigenous jurisdictions, all of which were contending with the ecological transformations attending U.S. expansion.

Despite the procession of overland travel immigrants came seasonally, and it was concerns between Native nations that dominated the conference. The arrival of Shoshone delegates under the leadership of Washakie, for example, almost drew the encampment into warfare. Lakota animosities, simmering since earlier conflicts with these eastern Shoshones, now threatened to explode.[96]

U.S. officials knew that warfare was antithetical to stability, and they attempted to establish clear boundaries between rival powers. They made generous pledges in terms of annuity payments that might foster greater dependencies. They also offered forms of redress for growing "depredations" committed against Plains communities by U.S. citizens.[97] As everyone knew, assaults against Indian peoples included not only violent attacks but also the destruction of grasses, elimination of timber, consumption of water beds, and overhunting of the region's bison herds.

The treaty of 1851 was a bold attempt to bring the northern Plains' most powerful tribes into a single agreement. In many ways, it represented a phase of U.S. policy making that disappeared in the years that followed. As in New Mexico, policies established after 1848 were often abandoned or achieved only minor results. Federally recognized boundaries between tribes became impossible to enforce. For many tribes, such failed diplomacy was abandoned but not forgotten. It would take a generation of treaties to establish a process to cede land and create reservations.

Early western treaties failed in part because western forts were few and far between. Problems arose around the distribution of the treaty's annuity payments. Perceived favoritism clouded many tribes' responses to Union promises, while subsistence demands compelled migration into adjacent territories contested by rivals. Bison herds recognized no jurisdictions, nor did hungry horse herds searching for scarce seasonal grasses. In addition, the treaty's provision to fund distributions of $50,000 worth of annuities was cut nearly 70 percent by the Senate. By 1855, for many nations in Montana, it was abandoned altogether.

For example, after the closure of fur posts along the Yellowstone (which had seen initial annuity distributions), Crow leaders were now encouraged to travel to Fort Union far to the east. To receive their promised annuities, they would have to travel hundreds of miles through Cheyenne, Arapaho, Lakota, and other hostile nations' land.[98] Moreover, with the near extermination of the West's mountain furs in the 1840s, U.S. annuities had become one of the few consistent sources of weapons, ammunition, and metal supplies, other than raiding. By 1851 the stream of mountain men carrying such trade goods had become a trickle. The 1850s, in short, had become an uncommonly dire period, and the federal government lacked both the authority and the institutions to remedy the hardships engendered by its citizens and their herds. By 1859 the federal government had dropped all pretenses of fulfilling the promises made in the 1851 treaty.[99]

Within Native nations, such unfulfilled treaties caused discord and bred factionalism. Tribal leaders who tried to abide by the agreements lost standing. Among the Crow, Chief Big Robber "is now despised by the other bands," trader Edwin Thompson Denig reported in 1856, due to his accommodation.[100]

Lakota leader Bear Ribs (Matȟó Thučhúhu) of the Húnkpapȟa band similarly attempted to follow the treaty, as had his father-in-law Chief Wanblíota of the Oóhenunpa band. Bear Ribs had grown close to Father Pierre-Jean de Smet, who had attended the treaty meeting and missionized out of Fort Pierre, established in 1855. Bear Ribs eventually resettled to the fort and took to farming. He and his followers also formed a new society within their community—the Society of Strong Hearts—which promoted practices of accommodation. As Lakota historian and author Josephine Waggoner has written, Bear Ribs and his "friendlies" now became nicknamed

> "The Fool Soldiers." . . . If the friendlies accepted anything from the government, they would be considered enemies of their nation and would be treated as such. The feeling ran so high against the friendlies taking annuities that boats coming up the [Missouri] river with goods were waylaid and fired into and sunk so the friendlies could not receive them.[101]

Such factionalism pervaded Native societies throughout the settler boom of the 1850s, deepening the growing ecological crises around them. As they confronted the destruction caused by immigrant travel and resource competition, many communities were fragmented. Peace and diplomacy grew strained by the ineffective policies and failed promises of the divided United States.

Oklahoma Indians and the Crisis of Secession

"If we surrender," Lincoln wrote in January 1861, "it is the end of us, and of the government." Each month of 1861 deepened the national crisis, especially after the war began in July. Lincoln's vision of "us and of the government" did not, of course, include Native nations, nor African Americans, nor Spanish-speaking villagers across the borderlands. The Union remained a white republic in which nearly 2 million voted for Lincoln as president.[102]

By the time of his inauguration, Congress had received hundreds of proposals that aimed to resolve the sectional crisis. A permanent western dividing line between the North and South was one of six constitutional amendments proposed by Kentucky senator John Crittenden. Slavery, in this compromise, would apply not only to all current territories, including New Mexico, but also to any "hereafter acquired." These were destined to include, Lincoln feared, Cuba and other Caribbean islands.[103]

The varied and frenzied proposals to keep the Union together paralleled the country's varied and frenzied Indian policies. Both efforts revealed irrepressible challenges that underscored the diffuse, contradictory, and decentralized nature of federal authority. The national government lacked sufficient powers to enforce its authority. To appease the South, some in Congress even proposed replacing the office of the president altogether with an executive council of representatives.[104] Seemingly, all possibilities to keep the Union together were considered. The eventual war did preserve the Union—and expanded its powers. Far from being abolished, the office of the presidency soon gained more authority than ever, including the power to proclaim slavery unconstitutional through executive order.[105]

Native nations had suffered before the war, and they now witnessed the Union's collapse. Indian traders at Fort Union in New Mexico observed the departure of military leaders to join the Confederacy. They also overheard heated deliberations. "Nothing is talked of here but secession," a soldier reported. "All the officers seemed for it."[106] The Union's skeletal army had been staffed by mainly southern officers, including New Mexico's Henry Hopkins Sibley, who boasted of his friendship with President Jefferson Davis.

After secession, Sibley rushed to Richmond to encourage Davis to invade New Mexico. Davis appointed him a brigadier general and "Commander of the Army of New Mexico." Eventually mustering an army of thirty-five hundred in 1862, Sibley soon marched north from Texas to capture Santa Fe and Colorado's gold mines, confronting Union forces at Glorieta Pass, New Mexico, as the region witnessed Confederate invasion.[107]As Lincoln awaited inauguration, Davis made it clear that war was inevitable. Northerners, he told an audience in Montgomery, would soon "smell southern gunpowder and feel southern steel."[108] For Davis, the West held potential gold for the Confederacy's coffers and potential overland railway routes for its cotton.

Appointed secretary of war in 1853, Davis knew the West as well as any Confederate leader. He had overseen the Pacific Railroad surveys conducted by the U.S. topographical engineers and pushed for the subsequent acquisition of Arizona's Gila Valley in the Gadsden Purchase of 1853.[109] He thought southern colonialism would facilitate not the expansion of "free labor" but the export of cotton. After secession, he worked to implement such a vision. Confederate gains, he envisioned, would secure territories upon which eventual railways would follow, thereby bypassing Union blockages. He knew also that pro-southern Democrats controlled the governments, congressional delegations, and many of the federal offices across Oregon and California, where Lincoln had received only limited support in 1860. Only seven of California's fifty-three newspapers endorsed Lincoln.[110] Home to nearly a quarter of a million southerners, the Pacific region, he hoped, would be a welcome addition to a Confederate empire.[111]

Confederate ambitions placed many tribes in a quandary. Such challenges were most pronounced for those in the South or bordering it, especially in "Indian Territory." The Union established the territory for tribes removed from eastern North America, principally members of the "Five Civilized Tribes" who had signed removal treaties exchanging Southeastern lands for those in Oklahoma. Congress set western boundaries of the Territory of Arkansas in 1819, and in 1824 it reserved the territory for the resettlement of southern tribes, many of which had long practiced African American slavery.[112] As the crisis deepened, many tribes became involved in secessionist politics. Their sovereignty, many believed, was best served by the Confederacy.[113]

With Texas to the west and Arkansas to the east, the Choctaws and Chickasaws were caught between states of the Confederacy. Each tribe had fought Jacksonian removal and adapted their governing structures in unsuccessful efforts to remain in the South. In Indian Territory, they subsequently developed stable economies, sending crops and cotton down the Red River to Louisiana while provisioning U.S. forts in the region. For over a generation, they lived off farming, ranching, and plantations. Slavery and cotton production became so commonplace that Chickasaws named their county with the largest number of plantations Panola, a variant of the Chickasaw word for "thread" and the Choctaw word for "cotton."[114]

After secession, tribal leaders understood that neutrality was not possible. Home to nearly one hundred thousand Native peoples from across North America, Indian Territory was now nestled within the Confederacy, and Confederate nationalism washed upon its shores. Indian people needed little motivation to resist the Union government that had removed them from their homelands.

On January 5, 1861, Chickasaw legislative leaders invited Choctaw, Creek, Cherokee, and Seminole leaders to join them "for the purpose of entering into some compact, not inconsistent with the Laws and Treaties of the United States, for the future security and protection of the rights and Citizens of said nations, in the event of a change in the United States."[115] By the end of February, efforts to maintain neutrality had dissipated. The Choctaw's General Council passed resolutions expressing their support for "the destiny of our neighbors and brethren of the Southern States," and they sent copies to Confederate governors informing them of their actions.[116]

Each tribe determined its own path for leaving the Union. Many were wracked by divisions between economically successful slave owners and smaller-scale farmers. Moreover, religious tensions became exposed because numerous communities had ties to missionary organizations from the North.[117]

The Confederacy moved to secure such allegiances and diminish such divisions. It established its own Bureau of Indian Affairs, formed its own Commission of Indian Affairs, and appointed a special agent, Albert Pike, for western tribes. Over a dozen treaties were signed by the end of 1861; all Five Civilized Tribes as well as Osages, Shawnees, Senecas, and Quapaws in Indian Territory agreed to remain under the authority of the Confederate States. They also, fatefully, agreed to "make themselves parties to the existing war."[118]

The Confederacy, however, needed more than loyalties. It also needed recruits, and Indian Territory became an independent military department. Like Sibley in New Mexico, Pike became a brigadier general, and thousands of Indian volunteers joined the Confederate army. These included a regiment of Cherokee Mounted Rifles as well as forces under the Cherokee secessionist Stand Watie. In 1864 he too became a brigadier general. At the end of the war he was the last Confederate general to surrender.[119]

As Pike had written to Davis, the war in Indian Territory would not be fought for Indians—far from it. It was fought for the preservation of slavery and the expansion of the Confederacy: "It is *we*, a thousand times more than they, who are interested to have this country, the finest in my opinion, on the continent, opened to settlement and formed into a state."[120] For Pike and Davis, the history of Indian Territory was preparation for the Confederacy's western growth. The countless years of toil that followed removal and brought the region into the South's economy were prologues to an expanded slave empire, one ruled by white men whose tolerance of Indian sovereignty remained as unclear as it was precarious.

Many tribal leaders understood the challenges of secession and appealed to Union forces for assistance. In January 1862, Lincoln ordered an invasion of Indian Territory, where the war was becoming a civil war within a civil war. As in many border states, discord pervaded the region. Thousands of tribal members disagreed with their respective nations' decision to secede. In late 1861, tensions among the Creek Nation broke into warfare, and Pike dispatched the First Regiment of Choctaw and Chickasaw Mounted Rifles to restore order.[121]

Despite the Confederacy's inroads, Union loyalties did not dissipate and continued to inform tribal politics. Despite the thousands lost along the Trail of Tears, Cherokee chief John Ross declared his commitment to maintaining his nation's treaties with the United States and to ensure its sovereignty. When Oklahoma tribes joined the Confederacy, however, such treaties no longer held, as secession now endangered a century of diplomacy and bilateralism with the United States.

For decades Ross worked to build and expand Cherokee sovereignty. A year after removal, he oversaw the redrafting of the Cherokees' constitution in 1839. Working from the nation's national capital at Tahlequah, Ross and a new National Council passed two hundred laws in its first twelve years and administered "the public school system, the national court system, including its supreme court, its male and female seminaries, and its national press."[122] Laws delegated powers within the community and proclaimed the nation's continued autonomy. A law enacted in December 1842, for example, established funds "to translate the Laws of the Cherokee Nation into the Cherokee Language" and to have "five hundred copies . . . distributed to the several Districts" across the nation.[123]

Rebuilding tribal governments had been hard before secession. It became even harder afterward as the war turned preexisting social divisions within tribal communities into hardened disagreements. Oklahoma's Civil War campaigns became unique in that they involved Indian combatants on all sides.

Like many nations, the Cherokee had incorporated slavery into their societies. Mixed-raced leaders, including Ross, built plantations in Indian Territory after losing farms and homelands during removal. Like their Chickasaw and Choctaw neighbors, they brought slaves to Indian Territory, and their new constitution established protections based on race. As article 3 held:

> No person shall be eligible to a seat in the National Council but a free Cherokee male citizen who shall have attained to the age of twenty-five years. The descendants of Cherokee men by all free women except the African race . . . shall be entitled to all the rights and privileges of this Nation, as well as the posterity of Cherokee women by all free men. No person who is of negro or mulatto parentage, either by the father or mother's side, shall be eligible to hold any office of profit, honor, or trust under this Government.[124]

Nestled in the corner of Indian Territory west of Arkansas and Missouri, the Cherokee Nation reinforced the institution of slavery. Like other members of the Five Civilized Tribes, they adopted slavery for their survival and prosperity. During the Civil War, many fought to maintain its future, particularly af-

This 1895 image illustrates the 1862 battle of Pea Ridge, in which Union forces defeated joint Confederate-Indian forces. Indian nations across Oklahoma and the West struggled for autonomy and survival during these decisive years. (The Florida Center for Instructional Technology.)

ter the early successes of the Confederacy. After the First battle of Bull Run in July 1861, many were convinced that the Union was doomed.

Surrounded by Confederate loyalists, Ross fled north to Kansas. By 1862 Cherokee refugees huddled in the snow at Union posts. So grave was their plight that Commissioner Dole left Washington to oversee the crisis. He found shocking destitution. As one surgeon detailed, "It is impossible for me to depict . . . their condition. Their only protection from the snow upon which they lie is prairie grass, and from the wind scraps and rags. . . . Why the officers of the Indian department are not doing something for them I cannot understand."[125] Dole estimated their numbers at six thousand and described their condition as "naked and starving."[126] He appealed to Congress for appropriations but understood that their plight had become dependent on Union victory.

Union campaigns took two years to regain control of Indian Territory. The most decisive victory occurred at Pea Ridge in March 1862, near the Arkansas-Missouri border. Union forces turned back a joint Confederate-Indian army force and curbed Confederate efforts to dislodge Missouri's Union loyalties. Pea Ridge became one of the few Union victories of 1862.[127] Subsequent campaigns brought carnage as well as changes in tribal leadership. With Ross in exile, Watie declared himself principal chief and passed a conscription law requiring all Cherokee boys and men over sixteen and under thirty-five to serve. He also led, as one Union officer described, "marauding parties" that "threatened" those who defied him and "murdered" with impunity.[128] Like Ross, he attempted to expand Cherokee sovereignty, doing so in partnership with the Confederacy.

In Kansas, Cherokee refugees joined Union forces before returning to their homelands to wage war. Not until May 1864, however, would federal funds arrive for the region's noncombatants, whose struggles for food and shelter continued.[129] Ross moved east to lobby for funding and to maintain commitments with the Union. He received assurances from Lincoln that the treaty with the Confederacy "would not be held against him personally or against the Cherokee Nation."[130] Like so many other promises, this commitment evaporated at war's end. A series of punitive Reconstruction treaties diminished the jurisdiction of the region's tribes and instituted a series of assimilative measures that eroded the power of tribal governments.[131] As we shall see in the next chapter, a new era of federal Indian policy emerged after the war when Congress extended its authority into Indian affairs in new, unconstitutional ways. As a result, Indian Territory experienced its own transformative boom of settlers, whose land seizures initiated a radical diminution of Indian authority.

Western Mining and Economic Booms

Many of the Civil War's largest changes came away from the battlefield, including a uniquely nineteenth-century form of settler colonialism—mining.[132] With reckless abandon, miners seized lands, resources, and Indigenous lives in a process of dispossession that shadowed the nation's war effort. Indeed, western mining initiated a torrent of ecological changes that refashioned Native America and subsidized the Union's mobilization for total war.

In 1860 Euro-American settlements had conquered neither the Plains nor the Inter-Mountain West. During the war, they metastasized. Unencumbered by antebellum compromises that mandated balanced territorial incorporation—"slave" versus "free" states—the Union added five western territories in under three years—Colorado and Nevada in 1861; Idaho and Arizona in 1863; and Montana in 1864. In 1864 Nevada achieved statehood. The federal government facilitated, encouraged, and profited from this incorporation.

These territories were overwhelmingly comprised of white male migrants.

Mines attracted tens of thousands of prospectors and prodigious infusions of capital. Contrary to popular conceptions, such investments surpassed the amounts of minerals extracted. More people, supplies, and mineral resources moved east to west than returned west to east.[133]

Freight companies supplied settlements with wagons, drafts animals, and supplies. Mule trains ferried goods up elevated trails, while hydraulic mining used waterpower to erode mountain deposits. By the time silver mines expanded into Colorado, towns like Aspen received one thousand tons of supplies a week. Mule trains carried everything, including luxuries such as pianos. In a constant cycle, men drove animals and materials up mountains where water and gravity powered their unnatural erosion.[134]

Life and work in mines differed from nearly all other nineteenth-century economies for white men. On farms or in cities, domestic and household labor maintained relatively even gender ratios. Mining communities were different. They consisted of migratory male "crews" and targeted lands, resources, and Indigenous peoples for exploitation.[135]

Such crews formed a central wave of the settler revolution remaking the West. In the mines and across supply chains, workers from similar backgrounds labored in temporary extractive economies. Virtually all workers who headed west to Colorado had Anglo or Germanic heritage.[136]

Drawn from the East, new laboring classes fueled territorial development. They also limited the mobility of other races. As detailed in the next chapter, these overwhelmingly male communities laid the foundations for a legal system that after the war developed gendered and racialized authorities to maintain white supremacy by protecting white property.[137]

Even in California, with its initial diversity of "crews," Euro-Americans comprised the largest number of workers and quickly remade the multiracial composition of the gold fields. Asian laborers, Mexican landowners and, as we have seen, Native peoples suffered, particularly as fluctuating mineral values destabilized the economy. Nearly five hundred San Francisco businesses went bankrupt in 1854–56. Twenty years later, during the Panic of 1873, three thousand companies folded. These depressions left many men unemployed, including fifteen thousand in San Francisco in 1873. Such instability deepened racial animosities and spurred racial violence and immigrant restrictions. After anti-Chinese riots in San Francisco, Congress passed the Chinese Exclusion Act of 1882, cementing racially restrictive immigration laws across the nation, as the demographic and economic transformations emanating from mines drove national politics.[138]

Ecologically, as mines sprouted across the West, they consumed water, timber, and other natural resources with a historic voraciousness. Mining in California extracted over $1.4 billion worth of ore, about one-third of which came before 1860.[139] Mines overwhelmed local Native ecologies. Writing of the tribes of Utah, Nevada, and Idaho in 1863, Dole explained, "The scarcity of game in these Territories, and the occupation of the most fertile portions thereof by our settlements, have reduced these Indians to a state of extreme destitution. . . . They have been almost literally compelled to resort to plunder to obtain the necessaries of life."[140]

Economically, mines contributed untold millions to the nation's economy. Starting in 1859, Nevada's Comstock Lode produced $292 million in two decades, with $30 million in 1864 alone.[141] Arizona's mines, according to General James Carleton, were "unsurpassed in richness, number, and extent by any in the world."[142] Most western territories, in fact, witnessed not one but multiple gold rushes. Colorado, Montana, and later Wyoming had forty among them.[143] Banks, newspapers, post offices, bars, hotels, casinos, and other services followed, as white men from across the continent flooded west.

This mining deluge shaped the fortune of a generation of young men, including America's most famous writer, who headed west during the war. Leaving Missouri for Nevada was the "turning-point of my life," remarked Samuel Clemens in 1910, one determined by "Circumstance" after "my brother [Orion] was appointed secretary of the new Territory of Nevada."[144]

The Clemens brothers moved west and avoided conscription. They left Missouri—a divided border state—in the summer of 1861 and crossed the continent via stagecoach. They arrived at the eastern slope of the Sierras, where Orion worked to facilitate Nevada's transition to statehood. The younger Samuel assisted as best he could. As territorial leaders debated the terms of potential statehood in meetings held in Carson City, Samuel hauled wood with local Paiute laborers. His future, however, was not in politics or mining. "I could not endure the heavy labor," he wrote in his *Autobiography*. "I could never learn to swing . . . a long-handled shovel."[145]

Samuel's future was in printing, which had been one of his earliest trades. Moving to Virginia City, home of the Comstock Lode, Clemens worked at the *Territorial Enterprise*. He used the pseudonym Mark Twain, an identity he had invented in the mining district. He spent the remainder of the war in Nevada and California mines and developed a jocular vernacular and literary style that launched a profitable career during Reconstruction.[146]

Although Twain saw "Circumstance" shaping his fortunes, politics more clearly determined his adulthood. As it had among the Cherokee, the crisis of secession had divided his homelands. The war turned his most recent livelihood—riverboat piloting—upside down. Suddenly, he wrote, "the boats stopped running." Moreover, he knew that his experiences as a river pilot might land him in the Union navy.[147] Or he might have been drafted into the army.

As he writes in *Huckleberry Finn* (1883), Twain "cleared for that country in the overland stage-coach," but, unlike Huck, he did so only after his brother's appointment as a territorial secretary.[148] Such patronage appointments became possible only because the mining explosion in Nevada hastened the incorporation of western territories. As with millions of others across the continent, the outbreak of the Civil War reoriented the Clemenses' lives. The war propelled them into mining communities, whose often driftless crews provided the basis for Twain's aesthetics of itinerancy.

Western mines also helped the Union win the Civil War. The cost of the war escalated to over $1 million a day. While taxes and tariffs provided the majority of national revenue, mining deposits supported national "banks notes" in a system of national banking that accompanied a national currency.[149] The costs of the war compelled Congress to expand the economy in production and scope. New markets in the West generated greater revenue, and Congress moved quickly in 1862 to pass laws to extend the economy west: the Homestead Act, Morrill Act, and Pacific Railway Act.

The West's agricultural productivity additionally aided the war effort. Western farms from Oregon to Nebraska not only fed Union forces but also provided exports to European nations suffering crop failures.[150] While unevenly distributed, wartime prosperity generated a social stratum of industrialists, financiers, and landowners who soon formed the nation's first class of millionaires. They helped to launch a new era in American life, one described by Twain in his 1873 satire, *The Gilded Age*.

California Volunteers outside of California: From Owens Valley to Bear River

Unlike units of "north-westerners" from midwestern states who comprised the majority of the Union army, western volunteers rarely saw the Confederate flag in battle. They rarely even saw the approach of uniformed soldiers.[151] They ended up stationed in western forts that lined emigration and postal routes. Their main targets were Indians, whose raids and movements Union forces attempted to prevent and police.

After deployment across the state in 1861, California units served Union efforts in other western theaters. Diverting thousands of its soldiers into other regions, the federal government also cut funding for the state's Indian affairs by 60 percent.[152] The demographic tidal wave of California settlement now reverberated back east across the Sierras, and thousands of Indigenous peoples were drawn into its turbulent wake.

In April 1862 California's Union forces expanded east of the Sierras. They invaded Paiute territories in what became known as the "first" Owens Valley War of 1861–62.[153] This year-long campaign targeted Paiute villages throughout the valley and nearby mountain strongholds, including an attack led by Lieutenant Colonel George Evans on April 9, 1862. This campaign targeted defensive fortifications that held between five hundred and seven hundred Paiute fighters, who had limited firearms.[154]

Nevada's Indian agent Warren Wasson attempted to broker a truce. As he reported to territorial governor James Nye, the Californian forces wanted "only to exterminate them."[155] The peace was temporary, and campaigns lasted into 1863. Over 330 Paiute deaths were recorded throughout the year.[156] Finally, on July 11, 1863, the remaining 850 survivors were marched south across the San Joaquin Valley to Fort Tejón, the lone interior southern California Indian reservation under federal jurisdiction.[157]

The violence of the Owens Valley War was as indiscriminate as it was sanctioned, and it mirrored that of other campaigns in the region. Captain Moses McLaughlin made the following demand of José (Chico) Pacheco, a Tubatulabal leader from the region west of the Sierra Nevada Mountains who served as McLaughlin's "guide and interpreter."[158] He required him to identify those who "had been engaged in the war," and once thirty-four had been identified, Pacheco reported, "they were all immediately taken outside the camp and shot and sabered by the soldiers."[159]

Indiscriminate violence followed Californians across the Sierras. Such "extreme punishments," McLaughlin reported, served to "crush the Indians . . . and save the Government some treasure."[160] No trial or intervention by military officials was offered, and there was no subsequent censure by civilian leaders. Far from it—the fiercest condemnation following the Paiute removal to Fort Tejón came from Edward Beale, the region's landowner who had used government funds to settle the region. He complained that his farm was now overrun by destitute Indians and that the fort's cattle were now being used to provision them rather than aid his farm.[161]

California volunteers sought military glory, and they grew frustrated by their inability to join eastern operations. They were deployed in the West, and they resented it. Colonel Edward Patrick Connor fomented such frustrations and learned to channel them against Indians. He directed campaigns in 1862–63 across Nevada, Utah, and Idaho that informed subsequent strategies against the Diné in Arizona and the Cheyenne and Arapaho in Colorado. Californian military practices increasingly shaped other Union efforts.

Leaving California in July 1862, Connor led seven companies of infantry over the Sierras. When they arrived at Fort Churchill near Carson City, Nevada, they were joined by one thousand additional California soldiers, many of whom had served in Owens Valley. Connor now took command of the Military District of Utah, which included Nevada Territory. He marched to Salt Lake City, home to roughly twelve thousand Mormon settlers. Utah's leaders, including Brigham Young, held long-standing tensions with the government and now professed neutrality during the war.[162]

Heading east, Connor stationed his forces at Fort Ruby, Nevada, a few days' ride from Salt Lake. In order to limit Mormon suspicions, he initially approached the city alone and in civilian dress. His disdain for Mormon "traitors" infused his reports, as did his responsiveness to demands from his soldiers to see more combat. Upon returning to Fort Ruby, he learned that his troops had requested that they be sent east to fight in Virginia. "Eating rations and freezing to death around sage brush fires," he reported, tested their patience.[163] Many had spent the year away from California. Isolated and limited service frustrated these volunteers.

In what would be a common situation throughout the war, cold, hungry, and impatient soldiers pressured their commanders to seek glory. Connor shared many experiences with the enlisted soldiers under his command. Before the war, he captained a state militia that guarded the Sierras. From his Stockton home he became a well-regarded officer across the region.[164]

Throughout 1861 Connor's forces increasingly sought out Indians. When news arrived of Western Shoshone raids along the Humboldt River, Connor dispatched cavalry units to "immediately hang them, and leave their bodies thus exposed as an example of what evil-doers may expect while I command this district."[165] He similarly ordered his men to "destroy every male Indian whom you may encounter in the vicinity."[166] Connor, in short, advocated indiscriminate slaughter and did so throughout 1862 before his most known attack in January 1863 along the Bear River in Idaho.

Federal forces in the West performed different political and military purposes than those in the South. They used violence to keep the Union together and did so by subjugating Native peoples. In Owens Valley and along the Humboldt, these were the first attempts by federal forces to project authority upon Paiute and Shoshone communities, and such campaigns became possible only after the founding of federal forts such as Fort Ruby. During the Civil War, soldiers extended U.S. sovereignty across the West, bringing new forms of military practices into areas that had never witnessed such concentrations of violence.

When Connor finally marched into Salt Lake City in October 1862, he led a sizable army of 750 that had traveled for months from California. All soldiers now had experience in killing Indians. From California to Owens Valley, across Nevada, and now into Utah, his forces targeted Indians. They had recently "put to death" an unspecified number along the Humboldt, nine of whom were killed as they "attempted to escape by jumping in the river."[167] As in Owens Valley, another group was executed when their family members did not "bring in Indians who were engaged" in recent attacks on overland travelers.[168]

Before the war, such killing had been commonplace in California but occurred in localized environments. Connor, equipped with horses, artillery, and firearms, controlled an increased capacity for violence, and in November he established Camp Douglas on a bluff overlooking the Mormon capital. Lest any Mormon civilians doubt the potential for violence, Connor trained his cannons on the town.

The events of the next two months came as no surprise to Connor and his forces. Throughout the fall, they lobbied for opportunities to fight more campaigns. Being based out of Utah gave them new possibilities. Between November and January, they pursued Northwestern Shoshonis in campaigns similar to those along the Humboldt. Subsequent Shoshoni raids upon Mormon ranches and immigrants fueled calls for retribution. On January 22, 1863, Connor mobilized seventy men, two howitzers, and fifteen wagonloads of supplies for a four-day trek to Bear River, Idaho. Their moment of national service had arrived.

Despite having their "hands . . . benumbed with cold" and "without regard to hunger, cold, or thirst," Connor's forces attacked, pushed on by their leader. He applauded their resolve afterward. They released "not a murmur," he reported; "Their uncomplaining endurance . . . from Camp Douglas to the battle field is worthy of the highest praise."[169]

The broad plain along the river held hot springs and served as a site for Shoshoni dances and winter camps. Connor's morning assault had almost failed to encircle two large Shoshoni encampments under the leadership of Bear Hunter and Sagwitch. After destroying both encampments, Connor's forces returned to Salt Lake, where they were received by Mormon settlers, although several later reported acts of disfigurement, rape, and torture.[170] Writing in March from Washington, Major General Henry Halleck congratulated Connor "on their heroic conduct." He also shared: "You are this day appointed a brigadier-general."[171]

The Long Walk and Confinement at Bosque Redondo

News of Connor's "brilliant victory" spread south to New Mexico, where other California volunteers were stationed.[172] They conducted similar campaigns in the service of the Union. Unlike those in California, Nevada, and Utah, however, the Southwest's campaigns were more protracted. They included seasons-long efforts to subjugate Native nations, many of which, such as the Diné, maintained thousands of soldiers. Many were also expert in the use of guns and horses. Others, such as the Apache, resisted in smaller bands and perfected guerrilla warfare tactics. Thousands of soldiers after the war would be required to subdue them.[173]

After Sibley's defeat at Glorieta Pass, Union leaders shifted their focus to campaigns against Native nations. They aimed in particular to destroy Diné subsistence economies, to subjugate their leaders, and to confine them indefinitely. As New Mexican governor James Carleton explained, "The purpose now is never to relax the application of force."[174] Upon confinement, he predicted, "they will acquire new habits, new ideas, new modes of life: the old Indians will die off and carry with them all latent longings."[175] The application of force and the anticipation of removal became Union policy, and the results brought misery and devastation.

Diné bands had dominated the western borderlands of New Mexico for centuries. Since the seventeenth century, their incorporation of horses and domestic livestock had initiated equestrian and pastoral change that made them mobile and self-sufficient. Spread across Dinétah (Navajo Country), they maintained spheres of autonomy that Spanish, Mexican, and U.S. leaders recognized. Raids and counter-raids had characterized their relations along the Rio Grande, as did extended periods of coexistence, trade, and diplomacy.[176]

As James Calhoun had reported before the war, U.S. dominion required more than the end of Diné raids. It necessitated a commensurate diminishment of their autonomy and mobility. As Union policies now shifted toward

Indigenous subordination, Carleton organized a campaign to invade, subdue, and relocate thousands of Diné families. He enlisted Pueblo and Ute auxiliaries and California volunteers. He appointed the region's most famous settler, Indian agent Christopher Carson, to head this invasion. No military force had successfully occupied Diné territories since the early 1700s.[177]

Throughout the eighteenth century, Diné strongholds had formed across the central canyons of Dinétah. Along the Chuska Mountain chain, bands combined herding and farming in a region home to numerous mountain passes and defensive locations, including Canyon de Chelly, where irrigation and horticulture had long sustained families.[178] Families partnered seasonal farming and pastoralism with craft production, expanding a regional textile trade that further linked Dinétah with settlements along the Rio Grande through the transmission of wools, dyes, and designs between Nuevomexicano, Pueblo, and Diné weavers.[179]

As with other Native nations, Diné connections to their homelands extend beyond politics, economics, and even culture. The depth of these ties resonates across communities and within tribes, whose collective memories, stories, and identities locate themselves—"the people"—at the center of their ancestors' landscapes. Their ties to these homelands became particularly tested during the 1860s. Using scorched-earth techniques, including killing livestock, seizing watering holes, and burning fields and orchards, Carson's forces exacted deadly tolls upon Diné families. As he reported in January 1864, "They must have been without any description of food. This is owing to the destruction of their grain [corn] amounting to about two Million of Pounds by my command . . . which they depended on for their Winter's Sustenance. . . . The generality of the Navajos are completely destitute."[180] As they had done against the Confederacy, Union forces targeted the institutions of society that sustained sovereign authority and autonomy. Like Union generals, Carson sought unconditional surrender. As Carleton had ordered him in September 1863: "*All* must go to the Bosque Redondo [Fort Sumner]. . . . There is to be no other alternative. . . . Say to them . . . 'Go . . . or we will pursue and destroy you.'"[181]

Many Diné leaders fought with an uncommon resolve against the Carson campaigns, and they resisted their indefinite confinement afterward. Soldiers under the leadership of Chief Manuelito heard his adjurations to resist removal and, if needed, die in defense of their homelands. "Just because they capture you," Manuelito instructed, "and even take your life, it's just you and not all your people who will suffer. . . . When you get captured, you just tell them, 'Go ahead and kill me, and I will shed my blood on my own land.'"[182]

Numerous Native nations were defeated during the war—but not destroyed. Despite the particular hardships inflicted upon their nation, Diné leaders maintained an unbroken commitment to their homelands and their "latent" beliefs and practices. Starting in 1863, Diné families endured years of invasion, their forced removal in 1864, known as "the Long Walk," and a four-year confinement thereafter at Fort Sumner, New Mexico, along the Pecos River far to the east. Incarceration took two thousand additional lives, nearly a quarter of those who had survived the removal.[183]

As Diné historian Jennifer Nez Denetdale suggests, Diné memories of this era "are filled with such anguish, pain, and humiliation."[184] Manuelito's son-in-law, Dághá Chíí Bik'is, recalled that many "wept from day-to-day. . . . Many of them died from starvation . . . [and] from homesickness."[185] Conditions at Fort Sumner were so sparse, he continued, that "people had no shelter so they would dig out a hollow space or bank and . . . lived there."[186] Not until after the war would civilian control return to the region's Indian affairs. In July 1868 the U.S. Senate ratified a new treaty negotiated at Fort Sumner that established a reservation in Dinétah for the Navajo Nation, ending their confinement under military authorities and returning surviving families to their beloved homelands.[187]

Like the West's many Indian wars, the Long Walk formed critical phases of the larger project of U.S. state formation. During the Civil War, the U.S. government not only devastated Indigenous communities but also subordinated them to institutions of federal authority. U.S. sovereignty was extended through violence and maintained thereafter by new political and legal regimes. As we shall see in chapter 10, warfare and what was essentially surveillance became interwoven, and new laws and policies now restricted Indigenous authority on reservations that were established by treaty. Negotiations, however, were often conducted under the threat of continued military action. The Navajo Treaty of 1868, for example, was negotiated with General William Tecumseh Sherman, whose practice of total war during the March to the Sea informed his leadership of subsequent Indian campaigns. Similarly, Connor sat alongside Utah governor and superintendent of Indian Affairs James Doty at two of the four treaties negotiated with Shoshone leaders throughout 1863, as did multiple officers of the Third Infantry of California Volunteers.[188]

The Road to Sand Creek

These campaigns and treaty negotiations were part of larger federal efforts to vanquish Indigenous autonomy. As Union victories flowed after Gettysburg, U.S. powers also grew in the West. Carleton and Carson not only confined approximately ten thousand Diné (as well as hundreds of Apache) captives at Fort Sumner but also participated in subsequent campaigns across the southern Plains in 1864 and 1865. These targeted Kiowa, Comanche, and Plains Apache communities.[189] Meanwhile, Connor extended his efforts at Camp Douglas across the Rockies into Colorado, where he helped to extend U.S. sovereignty over Ute, Cheyenne, and Arapaho communities. Indeed, Connor brought his practices of indiscriminate violence from California, Nevada, and Bear River, deepening Colorado's existing military commitments and imperatives. In March 1865, he became the first commander of the Department of the Plains, which expanded the Military District of Utah through Colorado and into Nebraska.[190]

Governor John Evans welcomed Connor's support, as did Colonel John Chivington, commander of the Military District of Colorado. Each had spent much of 1863 plotting against the Cheyenne and Arapaho. A Methodist doctor from Chicago who was appointed by Lincoln as the territory's second governor, Evans had arrived in May 1862 shortly after the battle at Glorieta, but he was more focused on economic development than campaigns against the Confederacy.

As a board member of the newly formed Union Pacific, Evans believed that no other part of the Union offered "such opportunities for the vast accumulation of wealth" as Colorado.[191] He envisioned Denver as the logical hub along the continental railroad. His primary obstacle in fueling this growth, however, was not the distance between the territory's thirty thousand settlers and their suppliers in Kansas to the east. Nor was it the specter of Sibley's army back in Texas. Evans's primary challenges were the southern Cheyenne and Arapaho Nations, whose elimination he now sought.[192]

Chivington had related concerns. An aspiring officer, he had long felt—like Connor—that his forces were being insufficiently used. As leader of Colorado's forces at Glorieta, he had gained recognition for assaults against Sibley and for pursuing retreating Confederate forces south to Albuquerque on their eventual retreat to Texas. Chivington felt that Union commanders had insufficiently engaged Sibley. He believed western forces deserved a greater role in the Union's battles and desired to launch more campaigns from Colorado. Unlike Connor, he resisted efforts to have his forces sent to other military theaters. As the Confederacy weakened, Colorado's Indian affairs became the sole theater of opportunity for combat.[193]

Before the war, Colorado's Indian policies had generally followed goals established in Washington. Treaties, such as the 1851 treaty at Fort Laramie, had established recognized, if unenforceable, boundaries between the region's equestrian powers. It aimed to provide annuities, build institutions of redress, and establish adjudication for crimes initiated by immigrants as well as tribesmen.

Unlike across the northern Plains, these agreements were held with Cheyenne and Arapaho communities long familiar with travelers and traders.[194] Many Cheyenne communities had intermarried with traders across the region's riverways. Like the Ute and Navajo, they had engaged in generations of trading with New Mexicans.

After the deluge of the Colorado gold rush, however, new treaties were forced upon Cheyenne and Arapaho leaders. Raids upon immigrant parties escalated. Tensions deepened as tens of thousands passed into the region.

In another attempt at diplomacy, in February 1861 Union cavalry officer Jeb Stuart presided over a new treaty at Fort Wise before he resigned to join the Confederacy. The treaty at Fort Wise reduced both nations' recognized territory. As the first sentence of article 1 suggests: "The said . . . Arapahoe and Cheyenne tribes of Indians do hereby cede and relinquish to the United States all lands now owned, possessed, or claimed by them, wherever situated, except a tract to be reserved for the use of said tribes."[195] The treaty established a reservation to which Evans eventually commanded all members of each nation to relocate. A radical redefinition of tribal jurisdiction was now underway in Colorado's Indian affairs.

Evans's arrival in May 1862 coincided with a series of challenges. While Sibley's forces had not reached Colorado, worries persisted across the Plains, especially as Union losses accumulated in the South. When news of the Dakota War reached the Front Slope, anxieties only deepened further, especially as communication lines stretched hundreds of miles and prices for supplies fluctuated in a region home to miners and merchants, not self-sufficient farmers.[196] Struggles between regional commanders erupted in 1863 when Union leaders opposed Evans's and Chivington's requests to keep their forces in the region. In December Evans headed to Washington to lobby for more soldiers to assist in overland travel. In March 1864 he heard that commanders in Kansas were requesting forces to stem potential Confederate movements south of the Arkansas River. Colorado, Evans feared, would be left out in the cold.[197]

In April simmering tensions exploded. After reports of stolen livestock along the South Platte River filtered into Denver, Evans and Chivington mobilized Colorado's cavalry units. Chivington now issued orders to "kill Cheyennes wherever and whenever found."[198]

From one perspective, the March withdrawal of forces shocked Colorado's leaders, sending them into a panic. Anti-Indian sentiments were fanned throughout the spring and summer as soldiers harassed Cheyenne, Arapaho, and their Lakota allies in the region. Cheyenne leader Lean Bear, for example, had visited Washington the previous year and received written notices recognizing his continued commitments to peace. He carried them proudly and displayed them frequently. As he rode out, however, in May to meet onrushing cavalry units, he and another leader were shot dead.[199] Like leaves of betrayal, his documents blew across the Plains.

Retaliations followed. They included a June killing of a ranch manager and his family. As he had in April, Evans took these responses as an indication of larger warfare. "Indians hostilities on our settlements [have] commenced," he wrote to Secretary of War Edward Stanton. "We are at war with a powerful combination of Indian tribes. . . . One settlement devastated. . . . Our troops near all gone."[200] As neighbors of the family carried their corpses into Denver, Evans ordered a citywide curfew in preparation for anticipated attacks, which never came. Nonetheless, panic reigned throughout the settlement even after Arapaho and Cheyenne leaders such as Black Kettle heeded Evans's mandate to file into local forts and reservations or risk "being killed through mistake."[201] By August, as Evans wrote to Stanton, "The alliance of Indians . . . is now undoubted. A large force, say 10,000 troops, will be necessary to defend the lines and put down hostilities. Unless they can be sent at once we will be cut off and destroyed."[202]

Unlike Connor and Carson, Evans and Chivington had not spent years in the West. They were newcomers in a region full of transplanted settlers, and they selectively listened to those with actual experiences fighting in the region. In New Mexico, for example, not only had Confederate forces been driven away from the region altogether but Carleton and Carson's campaigning had carried violence into Dinétah, targeting raiders who had never attacked white towns and doing so with coordinated movements of hundreds, not thousands, of forces, including the use of Indian auxiliaries. Evans's request for ten thousand uniformed men far exceeded those ever used by Carson, Connor, or his predecessor William Gilpin, Colorado's first governor. Such a request was fantasy and reflected paranoia.

The primary lesson that Evans and Chivington learned was that which Connor and other Californians had perfected: the use of indiscriminate violence against unsuspecting villagers. Killing Indians "wherever and whenever" and even "through mistake" had become a long-standing practice among Californian militiamen and volunteers. Throughout the summer and fall, both now developed ideological justifications that fanned the flames of racial hatred among the region's settlers.

Chivington's days-long march to Fort Lyon in November 1864 followed military and political strategies similar to Connor's march to Bear River in January 1863. Chivington, however, commanded far more men than Connor, approximately seven hundred. He had multiple officers under his command when he rode to Black Kettle's peaceful encampments at Sand Creek. The Indians were encamped under the protection of nearby U.S. commanders at Fort Lyon, whose objections Chivington now overrode. He targeted the community on November 29, massacring as many as possible.

✦

The killing of Indian noncombatants by U.S. soldiers and officers characterized California, Nevada, Utah, Colorado, and New Mexico during the Civil War. Various military strategies were used to extend U.S. sovereignty in these recently acquired territories. The exponential growth of the Union army made such violence both possible and transformative, as the settler revolution of the 1850s tightened its grip across North America with force and fury.

What had started as a conflict to preserve the Republic turned into a reorientation in the Union's capacity to harness power. Outmatched in population and dependent upon a political economy of slave labor, the Confederacy was vanquished by the Union's centralized military, economy, and government and by the resistance of former slaves who not only fled their plantations but volunteered to fight against the Confederacy.

Everything seemingly became inverted in the 1860s. Regiments of black soldiers armed to fight white men would have seemed inconceivable and terrifying to Jefferson and the Republic's founders. Similarly, the power of the federal government to impose laws, policies, and imperatives upon an increasingly integrated society became another legacy of the era.

Some historians draw particular attention to the days following Lincoln's assassination to underscore these inversions. The Twenty-Second U.S. Colored Troops preceded his coffin down Pennsylvania Avenue. Secretary of War Stanton, Vice President Andrew Johnson, and General Ulysses S. Grant awaited its arrival into the White House, a clear sign that the ceremony had become the responsibility of the federal government rather than Lincoln's family.[203]

Fittingly, a train carried the president from Washington to Illinois. It now ran along universal gauges and at an intentional pace of only five miles an hour. Onlookers throughout northern towns—Albany, Buffalo, Cleveland, Columbus, Indianapolis, and Chicago—witnessed the solemn spectacle. At many stations, thirty-six black sashes were outfitted for youth to wear. Each sash represented the now thirty-six states of the preserved Union.[204]

Few would have known much about the Civil War in the West or of the transformations that had occurred since candidate Lincoln's first train ride. They were residents now of what was becoming the most politically powerful region of the Union: its Midwest. All but two of the remaining presidents of the century would hail from Ohio; the Old Northwest was now known as both the Midwest and the "heartland."

The power of the Union exploded throughout the decades that followed. Economics and politics informed each other and bred a particularly extractive political economy in western North America. As the Civil War consolidated the power of settlers over Native peoples, the postwar era witnessed a commensurate rise in the power of the federal government to assert its authority over western citizens, lands, and Native peoples. Congressmen in particular would soon establish a "plenary power" over Indian affairs, and policy makers developed a campaign of assimilation that soon targeted the most intimate and everyday forms of Indian life.[205] They sought especially to seize Indian lands and, most painfully, children.

10 • Taking Children and Treaty Lands

Laws and Federal Power during the Reservation Era

The Indians boast of their freedom, and say they would
sooner die than be treated as beasts of burden.
—*Kahkewaquonaby (Peter Jones) (1861)*

Like hot summer winds, the years after the Civil War brought swift and blinding changes to Native American communities. The settler revolutions that had begun before the war developed with even greater fury as more and more Native peoples become confined to bounded lands. Every day, they watched their previous territories become white farms, homesteads, and properties.

Throughout the West, new towns, territories, and states emerged. In southern Arizona, Yuma grew rapidly. One of eight posts between San Antonio and San Diego in 1857, it welcomed in 1870 its first railway—the Southern Pacific—which now bridged the Colorado River.[1] Tracks connected Arizona not only with California but with northern Mexico, and in the years that followed, hundreds of thousands of migrants traveled by rail across the region, the majority of them Mexican families heading to Los Angeles.[2] Railway travel in fact became so common that only 7 percent of those migrating to Los Angeles arrived via the traditional land ports of Calexico and San Ysidro or the ocean ports of San Diego and San Francisco.[3] Trains now ruled the region, and stations such as Yuma's Southern Pacific Depot formed the center of countless towns.[4]

The connections that linked Mexico, Yuma, and Los Angeles mirrored other transformations. From 1865 until 1924, immigrants from nearly every continent arrived. They came from Mexico and other nations of Latin America; Asia and the Pacific Islands; the American Midwest, East, and South; and Europe and the Middle East. Not since the Revolution had such a diversity of peoples lived together upon the American continent, and many struggled with the racial constraints placed upon them.[5]

As thousands made their way to California, many settled in Yuma itself, including two women from very different geographies and backgrounds whose lives became inextricably intertwined: Mary H. Taylor and Lucía Martínez.

A white woman from Georgia, Taylor still carried much of the Confederacy's ideology with her. Recognized as an "unreconstructed rebel" by many settlers, she found social connections among the region's growing numbers of transplanted southerners, including King S. Woolsey.[6]

Born in Alabama in the 1830s, Woolsey had migrated west as a teenager. He soon became a leader among the "Indian fighters" of the borderlands and organized campaigns against Apache communities.[7] He had led unsuccessful mining efforts in California before establishing a burgeoning freight and ranching business in Arizona's Gila River Valley, where he became among the territory's most visible leaders. He controlled multiple ranches, businesses, and properties. He was elected to the first territorial legislature and was reelected five times.

Woolsey and Taylor married in 1871, and Taylor assisted in his businesses thereafter. She ran their merchandising store at Stanwix Station, where she was fondly remembered by its settlers, many of whom shared loyalty to the Democratic Party and antipathy to Republican-led Reconstruction efforts. Most remembered Taylor from shared meals and social encounters: "Many a time she has gotten up at midnight and cooked us something to eat when we have come in after chasing Indians," one settler recalled. "Woolsey was pretty sharp, but she was sharper."[8]

Taylor proved adept at assisting her husband's businesses and then consolidating his estate after his unexpected death in 1879. Childless, the widow now worked to exclude her husband's biological children from his inheritance. In the process, she came into conflict with Martínez, their Yaqui (Yoeme) mother who had been Woolsey's servant since he captured her during one of his Apache campaigns.[9]

Martínez was only ten when she was seized by Woolsey in 1864. Among the thousands of Indigenous children—overwhelmingly young girls—caught in the centuries-old borderlands network of captive raiding that arrived on the heels of Spanish colonialism, she had endured prior servitude at the hands of her Apache captors.[10]

Like many Yaqui, Martínez had lost family members in their Mexican homelands where military officials led campaigns against Yaqui villages. As in the United States, communally controlled Indigenous lands frustrated state leaders during nineteenth-century processes of economic liberalization. Mexican leaders killed, detained, and deported Yaqui leaders. Such violence was justified in part, according to Mexican intellectuals like Fortunato Hernández, because the Yaqui practiced "an absurd mixture" of antiquated, Indigenous-themed Catholicism. They worshipped, he maintained, "idols and wooden saints . . . like the phantoms of a nightmare in the brain of an idiot."[11] Their displacement was needed to build the Mexican Republic.

During her captivity to Woolsey, they had three children together. After his marriage to Taylor, however, she was driven away from his ranch. These white newlyweds had been raised in the largest slave society in modern history, and they understood how to mask the shame of enslaving others.[12] Exiled from her home, she was now technically free and fled into Yuma where other Indigenous families had sought refuge from the Apache and Yaqui wars raging across the region. She looked to find a way to retrieve her children, who remained under Woolsey's control.

Martínez worked as a domestic among the city's white community. Like many Indian captives, she was multilingual, speaking at least two Native languages—Yaqui and Apache—and two European languages—English and Spanish. Doubly burdened as both a woman and a Native, she sought available measures to subvert her own subordination and to a gain a modicum of support for her children. These included using the territory's new legal system, which provided all residents—even those who were not white or citizens—a space for adjudication. After years of determination, Martínez was ultimately successful in getting recognition of her rights as a parent as well as securing some financial support after Woolsey's death.

Martínez's experiences reveal an essential feature of western history—the clash between territorial versus federal laws. After she fled the ranch Woolsey had kept their children, arranging with neighboring ranchers to indenture their two daughters to be, like their mother, household servants in a form of unsalaried peonage authorized by the territory's new Howell Code of 1864, a five-hundred-page codex that governed the new territory.[13] Martínez, in turn, enlisted the assistance of local lawyers and sued for the release of their daughters. She filed a writ of habeas corpus, a legal protection required in all U.S. territories admitted to the Union under the Northwest Ordinance and reaffirmed by the Habeas Corpus Act of 1867, one of a series of new laws of the Reconstruction era.[14] Territorial and national laws thus came into conflict, and Martínez used initial rulings to make larger claims to Woolsey's estate after his death. Like hundreds of Indian plaintiffs in the years that followed, she drew upon federal laws to contravene state laws designed to subjugate Native peoples.

The West's New Legal Regimes

Woolsey held Martínez captive during the dawn of Reconstruction. Despite sharing a home and having three children together, they never married. Those who governed the West were building a settler society, and they placed racial restrictions on intermarriages, accepting as well established forms of gendered servitude such as Martínez's. Anti-miscegenation laws became common forms of lawmaking initiated to secure the rights of white men.[15] These laws were designed to prohibit the recognition of common-law marriages between settlers and Indian women and to ensure the protection of settlers' property. Marriage laws in the early West essentially favored the region's white male population which, as we have seen, mushroomed during the war.

Such laws enforced the West's new racial order. Vast and uncharted, Arizona in 1864 had only a few white settlements.[16] Even more than in New Mexico, the white population was only a fraction of the region's total population. Approximately six hundred white settlers ruled a territory that held thousands of ethnic Mexicans and untold numbers of tribal members.[17] Other than the region's topography, place-names, and diversity of Indigenous communities, little from this era resembled Arizona of the twentieth century. Social, economic, and legal power became concentrated into the hands of settlers such as Woolsey and Arizona governor John Goodwin, both of whom advocated for the "extermination" of Indians.[18] As federal judge Joseph Pratt Allyn noted upon his 1863 appointment in the region, a war of extermination against the Apache was already underway.[19] Hatred pervaded the region; "Indians are shot wherever seen," he wrote.[20] Allyn struggled to find words to describe the atmosphere. "It is difficult to convey the intensity of this [anti-Indian] feeling."[21]

During the Civil War, territorial leaders, newspaper writers, and business leaders worked to maintain and harness the aggression. They drew upon discourses of manhood that carried expectations of martial defense, patriarchy, and racial solidarity.[22] The Howell Code is full of provisions that upheld the authority of white men, the only members of the territory who could practice law.[23] Settler fathers held exclusive legal authority to determine the marital choices for daughters under eighteen, and the code established criminal charges for women who did not carry pregnancies to term.[24] None of the territory's five courts, including Allyn's, could issue a divorce—only the territorial legislature could annul a marriage.[25] Non-whites could not testify in criminal cases, and restrictive prohibitions limited interactions between Natives and settlers.

After the war, new law making became among the most enduring transformations that attended U.S. conquest. In the generations that followed, the legal redefinition of Native lands, families, and jurisdictions altered the balance of power across the region and established the foundations of settler society. After decades of racial coexistence, the West witnessed the rise of a new racial order. Like the region's burgeoning settlements and ranches, whiteness flowered across this new West.

This emergent racial order, however, was under constant threat. As Governor Goodwin relayed to the legislature, "The large number of Indians in our midst . . . must compel us to avail ourselves of all means of self-defense and protection."[26]

As Martínez's experiences attest, the law became an essential arena in the contest of western race relations. Without the support of family or tribal members and after nearly a decade under Woolsey's control, she nonetheless found avenues of redress, as even the West's most disenfranchised constituents had, at times, limited access to power. The passage of Reconstruction laws and new constitutional amendments created momentary possibilities for increased forms of racial justice, and Martínez became one of the few Indian mothers who successfully used the legal system to retrieve her children.

Her example, however, stands in marked contrast to the experiences of others within Native communities. Indeed, in the half century that followed, new national policies and doctrines of jurisprudence emerged that restricted the possibilities of equal protections for Native peoples. A new campaign of assimilation soon targeted the foundations of Native nations as a myriad of new laws extended the federal government's "absolute jurisdiction and control" over Native lands, eventually establishing Congress's oversight of Indian affairs as a defining feature of the new West.[27]

New Land and Educational Policies

These laws particularly targeted reservation lands and Indian children. Ratified by the Senate's treaty power and provisioned by Congress through its appropriations authority, reservations established unique, if limited, forms of

Indigenous sovereignty. While the federal government holds title to reservation lands, it does so in concert with tribal nations, whose jurisdiction extends over the land and its members.

Newly appointed superintendents and agents, however, redefined these practices. They assumed unbridled power. They oversaw the distribution of resources and worked to establish schools, hospitals, and churches. They built farms and instructional facilities, and they allocated as well as withheld the distribution of annuities, which became lifelines for communities removed from traditional homelands. Patronage appointments, these officials were subject to limited oversight from local settlers—let alone tribal members—as a new political system emerged upon reservation lands. With jurisdiction over a hundred million acres, competing views of land use soon defined this new era as Indigenous economic and cultural practices conflicted with U.S. notions of private property.[28]

Prior to reservation confinement, complex protocols and practices governed Indigenous use of natural resources. Access to hunting and fishing grounds and the authority to harvest and distribute resources were acquired socially. On the Northwest coast, hereditary and familial standing ensured that specified families held access to specified marine and territorial places, while across California and the Great Basin patrilineal leaders oversaw annual pine-nut harvests and rabbit drives.[29] Tribal ownership rights differed from western notions of individual property. Land and natural resources could not be alienated because the natural world was not to be commodified.

Throughout the Reservation Era (1879–1934), new laws redefined the use of reservation lands. They radically changed the structure of federal-Indian relations and reduced Indian land holdings. Under the 1887 General Allotment Act—known also as the Dawes Act after its author, Massachusetts senator Henry Dawes—new policies worked to subvert existing Native structures of power. Allotment divided reservation lands into individual parcels of 160 acres for heads of household and opened the remainder to sale and development. Individual tribal members, not communal bodies or governments, received title as the federal government aimed to alienate individuals from collective structures of tribal governance. From roughly 138 million acres of lands in 1887, Native-governed landholdings fell to 48 million acres in 1934, the year Congress disestablished the allotment system.[30] Two generations of continued dispossession followed the destruction and warfare of the nineteenth century. Such laws differed from those operating in earlier periods of Indian policy. Before the Civil War, the Senate and executive handled most Indian policies, with the Indian Office (and its commissioner) answering to the president's cabinet. Treaties and federal land policies—including Supreme Court rulings like those of the Marshall Court—also recognized tribal authority across communally governed reservation lands, which stood outside the jurisdiction of states and territories. Established by treaties, reservations fell under the exclusive jurisdiction of the Senate and the executive.

During Reconstruction, however, the U.S. House of Representatives began making laws that contravened earlier periods of Indian policy. With allotment, Congress began a process of land alienation that subdivided reservations. New laws violated treaties, although these remain "the supreme law" of the United States under the U.S. Constitution.[31] A major constitutional concern after the war was whether Congress could pass laws that undermined national treaty obligations.

Throughout Reconstruction, as Congress expanded the administrative capacity of the federal government, it assumed a new power to abrogate the Republic's treaty commitments. Treaties were no longer binding. Their provisions could now be broken with legislative impunity—a "plenary power" eventually authorized by the Supreme Court. What had been a percolating doctrine across much of the nineteenth century now boiled over, as Congress developed powers over Indian affairs that earlier justices, such as Marshall, had considered inappropriate.[32] As relayed in chapter 7, federalist leaders had long feared that interior settlement pressures would disrupt national Indian policies, and they had worked to limit the authority of territorial and congressional representatives over Indian affairs. The early history of the United States would look radically different if states and their representatives had been able to dispossess Indian nations.

Coupled with the decline of game, Congress's new land policies made the second half of the nineteenth century a time of continued deprivation across Native America. No one seemed able to address a growing crisis, as congressmen, intellectuals, and social reformers grew convinced of the need to solve a national "Indian problem."

Starting in the 1870s, government officials developed new ideas that aimed to eradicate Native American cultures. They then built the necessary institutions to do so. In charge of overseeing Indian prisoners of war, Captain Richard Henry Pratt witnessed how military-style discipline, dress, and regimentation aided in the pacification of Native captives and students. His vision quickly informed national policies.

By 1879 Pratt had developed pedagogies that used military-style education

Several hundred students stand in front of dormitories and classroom buildings in this 1892 photograph of the Carlisle Indian School student body. Photographs such as these helped to assimilate American Indians by obscuring their individual tribal identities and conveying a shared social, racial, and political identity as subjects of American dominion in need of transformation. In their uniforms, students seem to blend into one another, forming a sea of indistinct faces and identities. Over ten thousand students from 142 different Indigenous nations attended Carlisle between 1879 and 1918. (Courtesy of Cumberland County Historical Society.)

to discipline Native children. He also secured congressional funding to transform the former army barracks at Carlisle, Pennsylvania, into the Carlisle Indian Industrial School.[33] At Carlisle, he professed, the Indian child "could learn to march in line with America as a very part of it, head up, eyes front, where he could see his glorious future of manly competition in citizenship."[34] Such efforts aimed to ensure that there was no "Indian in [children] when they are grown."[35]

Pratt and other reformers hoped that assimilation would impart "civilization" to children. They viewed their work as beneficent, believing that Indian families were deficient and needed to be restructured. Native peoples, as the Supreme Court ruled in *Lone Wolf v. Hitchcock* (1903), were an "ignorant and dependent race."[36] Tribal governments, kinship networks, and cultural practices exerted negative influences over Indian youth, limiting their potential development as individuals and integration into American society. It was in fact, as Pratt remarked, "our duty . . . to advise them to do those things that would enable them to quit being tribesmen."[37]

While "being tribesmen" was not technically a crime, it nonetheless subjugated Native families to Pratt's new policies. As with Mexico's assaults against Yaqui lands, the United States used its administrative capacities to disestablish tribally controlled lands, to sever cultural connections between family members, and to prosecute the religious and political practices that governed Native nations.[38] After Reconstruction, the full force of the U.S. military and the federal government turned to Indian communities.

Indians, the Fourteenth Amendment, and the Growth of the Federal Government

Assimilation programs were part of a larger transformation of the federal government. From 1865 to 1900, Congress increased its jurisdiction over the West and its Native peoples through new ideologies and institutions. Guaranteed Indian treaty protections were disregarded, as were the complaints of Native parents protesting their children's seizure. A new American state was emerging, one in which, as Senator Orville Platt of Connecticut blithely noted, "the red man has no rights which the white man is bound to respect, and . . . no treaty or contract made with him is binding."[39]

This growth in federal power accompanied the "Greater Reconstruction" of the Union.[40] By destroying slavery and occupying the Confederacy, the Union army reasserted federal sovereignty and established new forms of national authority. In doing so, Congress rewrote the Constitution in a process that Republican leader Carl Schurz termed a "constitutional revolution."[41]

This revolution was as consequential as the American Revolution itself. To destroy slavery, Congress needed to restructure the Constitution. It began to do so through the Thirteenth Amendment, which established legal emancipation, extending the principles of the Emancipation Proclamation.[42] This revolution continued with the Fourteenth and Fifteenth Amendments, each of which strengthened the authority of the national government. After having not revised the Constitution in sixty years, Congress, starting in 1865, amended it three times in five years. It was the most intensive period of national law making since the ratification of the Constitution itself.

These amendments heralded a new era. Unlike the Constitution and Bill of Rights—which divide powers between branches of government and ensure that individual rights remain protected from federal interference—these amendments increased governmental powers over individuals and states. In addition to outlawing slavery and "involuntary servitude," they extended rights of citizenship, due process, and voting to all men regardless of "race, color, or previous condition of servitude." Each amendment increased the power of Congress and ends with the mandate: "Congress shall have the power to enforce" each "by appropriate legislation."

Before the war, Congress had been the most divided legislative branch of government; after it, it became the most powerful arm of government. Landmark legislation also accompanied the passage of each amendment and strengthened Congress's growing powers. In 1866, by example, it passed a new Freedman's Bureau bill, the nation's first Civil Rights Act, and then the Fourteenth Amendment. Each brought historic expansions of federal authority and carried broad new governmental protections for former slaves.[43] The Fourteenth Amendment's due process clause also made equal protection under the law an essential component of modern jurisprudence.

As was true of the original Constitution, such protections did not extend to Native peoples. Indians remain excluded from these landmark amendments, outside the nation's "second founding." Section 2 of the Fourteenth Amendment specifies representation among the states "according to their respective numbers, counting the whole number of persons, excluding Indians not taxed."

By excluding Native peoples, the Fourteenth Amendment thereby maintains the ambiguous legal provisions established during the Constitutional Convention. As we have seen, such legal ambiguities continued throughout the Removal Era when southern states ran roughshod over federal treaties and even Supreme Court rulings, such as *Worcester v. Georgia*. Similarly, Indians are also excluded from the Civil Rights Act of 1866, which declared all persons born in the United States, other than "Indians not taxed," citizens.[44]

The landmark congressional achievements of 1866 continued patterns of exclusion within the nation's body politic. The Civil Rights Act and Fourteenth Amendment did not therefore apply, as has been argued, to "virtually everyone born in the country."[45] Removed from the Republic's first civil rights laws and the Constitution, Native peoples remained excluded from the rights and liberties of U.S. citizens. As in Arizona, where their disfigured bodies were draped from trees as signs of the expanding sovereignty of white settlers, Indians could be hunted, killed, seized, and indentured with impunity.[46] Indian children could also be taken from their families. Native peoples had, as Senator Platt stated, "no rights which the white man is bound to respect."

As Native nations continued to inhabit a legal ambiguity within the Republic, they remained political outsiders. They were not entitled to the rights of citizens; however, they were still protected by the constitution. Their rights were not individual but collective, enshrined through treaties. The federal government recognized Native sovereignty and provided resources to individual nations. Such aid was embedded in treaties that also included provisions for communal health, education, and agricultural and economic assistance. These collective rights contrasted with the individual rights of U.S. citizens as designed by the Constitution and the Reconstruction amendments.

As Congress assumed greater authority during Reconstruction, however, treaty provisions were routinely broken. Starting in the last months of the Civil War and gaining momentum throughout the remainder of the century, Congress eroded existing Indian policies. New national policies—such as allotment—aimed at reforming the everyday livelihoods of Native peoples, and they conflicted with treaty provisions. That conflict defined the half century of federal Indian affairs after Reconstruction.

Treaty Making during Reconstruction

Neither Native nor federal leaders foresaw the rapid dispossession of Indian lands that defined the postwar era. As in Arizona, much of western North America lacked white settlements, and roads and railways were yet to be constructed. Governor Goodwin's first message to the Arizona territorial legislature, for example, largely concerned the construction of toll roads.[47]

Moreover, after years of warfare, many believed that peace had finally arrived. The West was as vast as it was bountiful. Much of it had already been recognized through treaties as Indian homelands, and many believed that coexistence was possible, if not preferred.

During the war, the Senate ratified 37 treaties with American Indian communities—10 percent of the 369 total ratified treaties between Native Americans and the U.S. government.[48] These treaties were the "supreme law of the land," and they recognized Native sovereignty over large portions of the Plains, Northwest and Plateau, Southwest, and Inter-Mountain West. As Arapaho leader Black Coal informed federal commissioners about Arapaho and their Lakota allies' ties to the Black Hills, "This is the country in which we were brought up, and it has also been given to us by treaty. . . . This is my country, and the Great Father has allowed the Arapahoe people to live here."[49] Arduous diplomacy accompanied each negotiation, as government and tribal leaders understood the stakes of such solemn commitments.

Few histories fully capture the extent of the federal government's recognition of Indian treaty lands during this era. As Black Coal stated, treaties recognized extensive tracts as Indian territories, as he witnessed in 1868. That year, Lakota, northern Cheyenne, and northern Arapaho leaders all signed treaties at Fort Laramie that brought an end to Red Cloud's War, which had erupted across the Bozeman Trail in Montana in 1866.

Among the most extensive in U.S. history, the Lakota Treaty established the Great Sioux Reservation west of the Missouri River for the "absolute and undisturbed use and occupation" by Lakota people.[50] Across two hundred miles and over nearly fifty thousand square miles, the federal government recognized Lakota sovereignty. One could now travel days on end without ever leaving the reservation. Moreover, in articles of the treaty, the federal government committed to annuities, agricultural and educational assistance, and other negotiated guarantees.[51]

Similar treaties with the Ute of Colorado, Crow of Montana, Shoshoni of Utah and Idaho, Nimiipuu (Nez Percé) of Washington and Idaho, and Diné (Navajo) of Arizona and New Mexico were also negotiated in 1868.[52] In each treaty, the U.S. committed to similarly sizable homelands, though the Crow and Nimiipuu treaties went unfulfilled. All were negotiated by high-ranking U.S. Army officers. General William Tecumseh Sherman, who now served as the nation's Indian peace commissioner, negotiated nearly all of these agreements.[53]

Treaties professed to establish peace between respective signatories, but peace meant different things to each signatory. "From this day forward all war between the parties to this agreement shall forever cease," reads the first line of article 1 of the Lakota Treaty.[54] For the Lakota, peace required limiting raids and mobilizations against immigrants while recognizing Lakota hunting territories west of the reservation on Montana's plains. For the Navajo, peace required an end to their imprisonment at Fort Sumner and a return to their homelands in Dinétah.[55]

The details of such treaty making are dizzying. In the years after Appomattox, the federal government negotiated dozens of treaties covering millions of

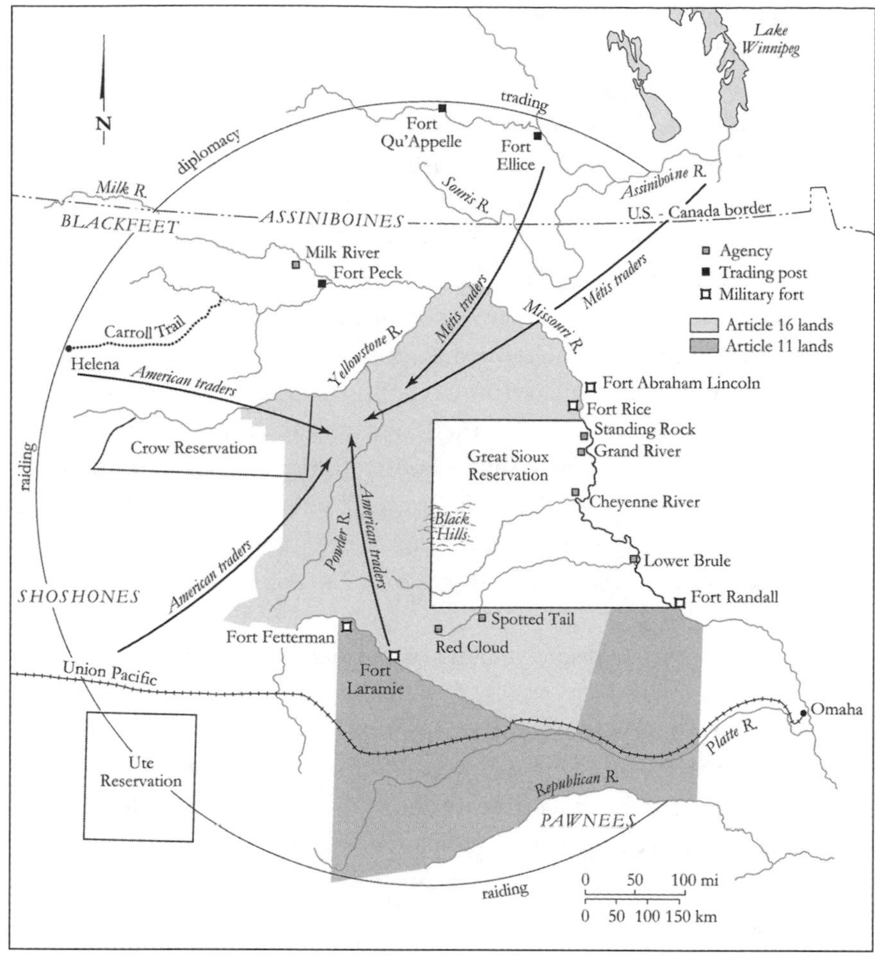

acres with the West's largest Indian tribes. Comparable to the treaty-making initiatives of the 1790s—discussed in chapter 7—that fueled the practices of U.S. diplomacy, the 1860s became among the most consequential periods of federal-Indian statecraft.

In Oklahoma, the government additionally redesigned the future of Indian Territory. In separate treaties with the Seminole, Choctaw, Chickasaw, Creek, and Cherokee Nations, the federal government recognized each of these nations' inherent tribal sovereignty while also extinguishing each nation's previous "treaty with the so-called Confederate States."[56] This reestablished federal authority over Indian Territory, helping to deepen the national government's reassertion of its national sovereignty more broadly. According to article 9 of the 1866 Seminole treaty, for example, "The United States *re-affirms* and *re-assumes* all obligations of treaty stipulations entered into before the treaty of said Seminole Nation with the so-called Confederate States."[57]

Unlike in earlier treaties, however, the authority of the federal government resonates throughout these agreements. A new vision for Oklahoma's future was forming. In particular, these treaties include provisions about the redistribution of existing reservation lands. Such articles concern railway development, the transformation of Indian lands into individual properties and allotments and, ominously, the seizure of existing reservation land for other tribes. "The United States may settle," according to article 15 of the 1866 Cherokee treaty, "Indians, friendly with the Cherokee and adjacent tribes, within the Cherokee country, on unoccupied lands."[58] Originally designed as a refuge for eastern tribes, Indian Territory was now being opened by the federal government for removals of a different kind. Federal officials now believed they had "acquired the rights to locate other Indian tribes within the limits of . . . Indian Country."[59]

Starting with the Delaware Indians of Kansas in 1866, dozens of western Indian nations were removed to Indian Territory. Such removals resembled those of the antebellum era in that federal forces coerced Indian leaders to leave their homelands, confined them and their families at military forts, and then relocated them to agencies in Indian Territory. They differed, however, in the rapidity of their implementation. Western removals now relied upon railway lines that transported Indian families from across the continent. Armed Union soldiers stood guard.

Such removals befell the Modoc of northern California, Cheyenne-Arapahos from the northern Plains and, most famously, Apaches from Arizona, including Geronimo's Chiricahua band, imprisoned in 1886 after years of resistance. Federal agents oversaw Chiricahua imprisonment for twenty-seven years thereafter at forts in Texas, Florida, Alabama, and finally at Fort Sill in Indian Territory. Hundreds, including Geronimo, died in exile, while Apache children were sent to Carlisle. Similarly, when Nimiipuu (Nez Percé) leaders, including Chief Joseph, surrendered to the U.S. Army in October 1877 at Bear's Paw Mountains near the Canadian border in Montana, they were marched east past Fort Berthold and then railroaded to St. Paul, where they awaited transport before being sent to Indian Territory. Like the Chiricahua, they were confined at federal prisons and transported by railway cars. Nearly five hundred spent a decade away from their homelands in Indian Territory struggling annually to find a way to return to Idaho.[60]

Not all removals were driven by the military, but the threat of violence lurked behind federal policies. For example, the Delawares' 1866 treaty states that the secretary of the Interior now required notification when each tribal member "is ready to remove to the Indian country, to provide for his removal to, and to enable him to make improvements on his new home therein."[61] Throughout the postwar era, a growing number of Indian treaties now diminished tribal lands and facilitated Natives' removal to Indian Territory.

Nevertheless, most postwar treaties still included U.S. policies designed to make local coexistence with settlers not only possible but preferable. In the 1867 Treaty of Medicine Lodge, for example, Apache, Comanche, Kiowa, Cheyenne, and Arapaho leaders exchanged their claims to nearly 90 million acres for 3 million acres in Indian Territory. Recognizing Indian land in exchange for peace had been a long-standing federal practice, and although local settlers such as Woolsey took pride in their violence, many national leaders understood that genocide was as destabilizing as it was immoral. As President Ulysses Grant told Congress in 1869, "The extinction of a race is too horrible for a nation to adopt." Like his predecessors, he knew that frontier killings bred lawlessness. "Engendering in the citizen a disregard for human life," he continued, becomes "dangerous to society" as a whole. Citizens, he concluded, should not "disregard . . . the rights of others."[62] Such rights were developed and defined by treaties.

Infrastructure and Environmental Change

As in the early Republic, such treaty negotiations reconfigured the administrative and governing structures of the United States. It had taken centuries for imperial powers to secure the continent up to the Missouri River, and now the United States used the railroads and treaty cessions to incorporate the rest. As the transcontinental railway spanned the continent, it left little doubt about the capacity of the government to move soldiers, supplies, settlers, and other resources. Indeed, a fundamental reconfiguration of continental travel was underway. Lines of power, communications, and trade now moved mainly east to west, rather than north to south or along major riverways.[63]

Gaining title to Indian lands in order to secure railway development had guided Indian policy before the Civil War, and the goal was quickly achieved during it. In a complex process of mediation, starting in 1861, the federal government acted as a broker selling Indian treaty lands to the Leavenworth, Pawnee, and Western Railroad Company. In a financial agreement transferring nearly 250,000 acres from the "Delaware tribe of Indians" to the federal government, the Senate ratified the Delaware Treaty of 1861. The government subsequently sold these lands for nearly $1 per acre, purportedly taking this action "for the benefit of said Delaware Indians."[64] On June 10 President Lincoln even wrote a four-paragraph addendum to the treaty authorizing its implementation, and on October 4 he signed the treaty upon ratification. "I have caused the seal of the United States to be hereto affixed," he wrote, while "having signed the same with my hand."[65] Five years prior to their removal to Indian Territory, the Delaware lost title to over 100,000 acres of lands. Like many tribes, their homelands remained coveted by settlers and railway developers, both of whom appealed to the federal government to dispossess the Indians.[66]

As railways linked East and West, they accelerated economic integration. Home to 107,000 settlers at the time of statehood in 1861, Kansas saw its total population boom thereafter, and settlers spread north into Nebraska. Like other settler booms across the West, Kansas's populace was young; in 1861 only 1 percent was over forty-four years. As a sign of the integration to come, within twenty years, a majority lived on farms mortgaged by eastern banks in an intertwined process of dual economic and settler colonization that required the migration of not only people but also credit. Nebraska's population similarly exploded, quadrupling in a decade after statehood in 1867.[67]

With the Delawares' removal to Indian Territory, Kansas became a hub for railway development, new town construction, and cattle ranching. It also became a major site of buffalo slaughter. Harvested across the southern Plains, buffalo hides now provided an export boom.[68] For the first time in history, bison were killed only for their hides. Their corpses littered the southern Plains in an "industrial hunt" that prioritized the swiftness of killing and skinning. By 1871 the Atchison Railway shipped 459,500 hides out of the region in a global tanning economy that fueled both U.S. and English industrialization. Such killings brought the near extermination of bison on the Plains and crippled Native economies.[69]

Invasive species—cattle, sheep, and wheat—quickly replaced bison as the region's primary export. As the railway moved east-west, a latticework of roads, depots, and herding trails remapped adjacent regions. The majority of Texan longhorn, for example, were not killed or processed in Texas. They were driven through Indian Territory in order to get to depots in Kansas. Not all cattle, however, were sent to slaughter. An inter-regional breeding economy also grew, ferrying younger steer to graze in the colder climates of Colorado, Wyoming, and Nebraska. As early as 1868, a herd of Texas longhorns reached Cheyenne.[70]

Throughout the postwar era, the railway unleashed permanent transformations. It conquered distances and solved the former challenges of seasonal travel. It spawned ranching and farming economies that transformed what one traveler called "a dry, treeless, unpeopled desert" into "an agricultural paradise."[71] The era of ox carts, stagecoach travel, and walking had ended. Roadhouses were forgotten, and the ruts of wagon wheels across the continent became initial signs of western nostalgia. The central Plains, in short, had become revolutionized by new technologies, peoples, and species.[72]

Amid such changes, little seemed certain about the future of Indian affairs. By 1868 the federal government had secured title to vast stretches of the Plains. Treaties drove Native nations north and south from the central Plains. New territories and states followed. The long-term future, however, of the nation's "Indian problem" remained far from clear.

The treaties of 1868 had formed giant reservations across the interior of the continent. Several, such as Ute, Navajo, and Lakota reservations, were so large that they resembled "independent states."[73] They remained governed by mobile communities. Only the force of the U.S. military and the power of congressional laws could exert federal authority upon them. In the generation to come, the fate of Indian Territory and the northern Plains established many of the legal foundations that carried Indian affairs into the twentieth century.

The Origins of the Great Sioux Reservation

North of Nebraska, the Great Sioux Reservation and its environs teemed with energy. In the two years before the 1868 treaty establishing it was signed, a confederation of Lakota bands had fought the U.S. military to a standstill along the Bozeman Trail in Montana. Known as Red's Cloud War, this conflict garnered wide press coverage and included notable losses, including the defeat of the entire U.S. command under Lieutenant William Fetterman on December 21, 1866, outside Fort Kearny. Many Lakota remembered this season as the "winter of the Hundred Slain."[74]

In the treaty of 1868, U.S. and Lakota leaders promised each other peace, and the treaty is full of signs of this commitment. Among its many provisions, it stipulates that the federal government would establish new reservation agencies; begin distributions of cattle, manufactured goods, and other annuities; and offer agricultural lessons to those who desire them. The Lakota, in return, relinquished claims to lands south of the Nebraska border, accepted the reservation's new borders, and agreed to "permit the peaceful construction of any railroad not passing over their reservation," among other negotiated agreements.[75]

Despite extended provisions for allotments and subsidies for farming, most Lakota did not choose to become farmers. As the treaty permits, they returned to the Plains to hunt remaining bison herds, renew alliances and friendships, and participate in seasonal and ceremonial cycles of life.[76] Many bands chose to live there year-round rather than at the agencies emerging along the Missouri River on the reservation's eastern edges. These agencies became sites of fraud and disruption, particularly as white agents monopolized government annuities and allowed illicit alcohol traders to operate.

As during the Dakota War of 1862, government traders were not to be trusted. They worked to line their pockets and stood in contrast to the generations of Métis, French, and earlier fur traders who married into Indian communities, learned Native languages, and understood the social dimensions of life across the Plains. As Mathó Wathákpe (Charging Bear) expressed in 1876, a government trader did not "trade with us at the same prices that he trades with the whites. . . . I want a trader . . . that will not charge an Indian more than he does a white man. . . . Send a man in his place who is acquainted with Indians and with Indians ways, a man who can live with the Indians."[77]

The Lakota Treaty was distinct in establishing federal recognition of adjacent territories. Article 16 provides federal sanction for continued seasonal migrations. It designates lands "east of the summit of the Bighorn Mountains" and "north of the Platte River" as under Lakota jurisdiction.[78] Including the Powder River Country in Montana and the western Black Hills, these were prime horse-grazing, bison-hunting, and ceremonial locations in the Lakota's migratory cycle.

The Plains north of the reservation stretching into Canada remained similarly recognized as Lakota hunting grounds. Article 16 further "stipulates and agrees that no white person or persons shall be permitted to settle upon or occupy any portion of the same; or without the consent of the Indians first," and that "the military posts now established in the territory . . . shall be abandoned, and that the road leading to them . . . shall be closed."[79]

Although technically outside the reservation, these lands remained under

Lakota oversight. They were now protected by treaty by the federal government. The most desired homelands for many Lakota bands were within unceded territories. These were to be held by the government for the exclusive use of Lakota communities.

Across these "article 16 lands," Lakota encampments proliferated. They included Cheyenne and Arapaho allies and numbered in the thousands. Families grazed horse herds that reached into the tens of thousands. Summer encampments attracted traders from all directions who brought goods to exchange for horses, hides, dried meats, and other wares processed throughout the winter. These summer gatherings continued generations-old economic and social practices and outnumbered white settlements between the Missouri River and Montana's gold fields. As they had for generations, Métis fur traders from Canada and Hudson's Bay continued to travel south to ferry English-made metals, guns, and wares to Lakota hunters.[80] The arrival of new arms, however, made strong impressions on federal officials, one of whom noted in 1866 that modern guns had now transformed the Lakota (and their allies) "from an insignificant, scarcely dangerous adversary into as magnificent a solider as the world can show."[81]

By establishing an autonomous Lakota homeland that included adjacent territories, the treaty heralded a new era in Plains Indian diplomacy. Like other treaties from the 1860s, it brought federal government recognition of Indigenous lands to be ruled by specified Indian leaders, hundreds of whom signed treaties in 1868. The first decade after the treaty, however, brought assaults against its provisions, soon returning the region to war. Much like the Delaware loss of lands in the 1860s, the Great Sioux Reservation shrank due to the pressures of white settlers who streamed into the region to gain lands and resources.

Lakota leaders fumed at the duplicity that followed implementation of the treaty. Visiting the White House in June 1870, three delegations of Lakota leaders, including those led by Red Cloud and Spotted Tail, were stunned to find themselves presented with new versions of the treaty.[82] They had come to voice their complaints about violations of the recent treaty, not to renegotiate. Now the unceded lands were not to remain theirs in perpetuity. As they heard for the first time, Lakota jurisdiction over the article 16 territories was to last only "so long as the buffalo may range thereon in such numbers as to justify the chase."[83] The leaders' invitation to dine with President Grant was no recompense for this betrayal.

The conditions now articulated had not been included at Fort Laramie nor upon the treaty's ratification in the Senate. Like other treaties, the Lakota Treaty had been conducted with the solemnity and protocols commensurate with ambitions to end war. Red Cloud and other leaders had struggled to accept its initial provisions; now confronted with these new terms, they found them unacceptable.

The government had already restricted Lakota lands. Within a region of diminishing bison herds, strains within their communities had formed, particularly among soldiers who believed they could defeat federal forces once more. Sensing such troubles, Red Cloud insisted that they return immediately, while other leaders, according to the *New York Times*, claimed that they "might as well die here . . . as they had been swindled."[84] Lakota leaders understood the new threats of federal negotiations. When Mathó Wathákpe negotiated with government leaders again in 1876, he insisted: "I want a copy of this agreement left with me."[85]

While the Grant administration offered gifts and promises, Lakotas understood that their off-reservation viability as a sovereign power was now in question. Their western homelands held essential resources—both spiritual and economic. Every month they watched waves of new threats forming around them: railway lines, roads, and bison hunters.

Lakota leaders understood that their rights were under assault. They did not, however, realize the extent of the threat. Diplomacy had continued since 1868, and while the power of the United States had vastly increased, Lakota leaders remembered defeating U.S. forces during Red Cloud's War and dictating many of the terms at Fort Laramie.

The power of the federal government was changing, however. Ominously, at one of the many events scheduled to impress the Lakota delegations, Red Cloud watched from the Senate gallery as congressional leaders debated the Indian Appropriations Act. It came to include a rider to curb further Indian treaty making altogether.[86] Passed in 1871, this act extinguished the United States' treaty-making authorizations with Native nations—another sign of the expansion of congressional authority. Unbeknown to the visiting delegates, such extinguishment was linked with the growing efforts of reformers to turn Indians into wards of the government.[87]

The Great Sioux War and Centennial America

While limiting the practice of treaty making, the Appropriations Act of 1871 still recognized the supremacy of existing treaties. It specifies that "nothing herein contained shall be construed to invalidate or impair the obligation of any treaty heretofore lawfully made and ratified."[88] Treaties governed Indian affairs; however, Congress was changing the federal government's longest-standing diplomatic practice.

Congress's new vision marked a shift in U.S. history. It moved from recognizing the distinctiveness of tribal nations outside the jurisdiction of federal authority to enforcing national laws upon tribal members under its jurisdiction.[89] As we have seen, the Constitution "excluded" Indians from taxation, state and federal laws, and citizenship. Indians remained outside the boundaries of the nation—not "subject to the jurisdiction thereof," as the Fourteenth Amendment suggests. During Reconstruction, however, these practices shifted. They now took new form: forcible inclusion and assimilation. While the 1871 act upholds the supremacy of treaties, Congress soon passed multiple statutes that worked "to invalidate or impair" the obligations of treaties.

All Native nations struggled to understand the increasing power of Congress over them.[90] For the Lakota, this growing increase in federal authority over them soon prompted another war. Political and legal challenges brewed over the fate of the nation's Indian peoples, particularly their lands and jurisdiction.

Few years in American history have been as iconic, contested, and determinative as 1876. In March U.S. Army generals launched campaigns against Lakota villages that escalated into the Great Sioux War. On the Fourth of July the United States celebrated its centennial, and in November the contested election of Rutherford B. Hayes brought an end to Reconstruction and extended nearly a half century of Republican Party rule.

The election had become a referendum on reunion, and its outcome signaled a betrayal of Reconstruction.[91] In the election's aftermath, known as the Compromise of 1877, Republican leaders—in securing Hayes's presidency—offered the withdrawal of remaining Union soldiers from the South, signaling a return to unbridled white supremacy. Southern whites had so resented Reconstruction that even after the wave of elected Democrats into statehouses and governorships, the "anger of the majority," according to one reporter, continued to "threaten a new civil war."[92]

White anger against the government also resonated across the Plains. With the discovery of gold in the Black Hills in 1875, prospectors flooded into federally protected lands of the Great Sioux Reservation. Eight hundred miners a week arrived to the Deadwood mines, where, according to one early promotional account, "the average to the miners on each claim was $300 to $700 per day."[93]

This invasion violated the treaty of 1868. While Lakota leaders had not received written copies of the original treaty, they remembered that its first article specifies that if "men among the whites, or among other people subject to the authority of the United States, shall commit any wrong upon the person or property of the Indians, the United States will . . . proceed at once to cause the offender to be arrested and punished."[94] The article also promises federal remedies for redress. In the event of "any wrong upon the person or property of the Indians," the government pledged to "re-imburse the injured person for the loss sustained."[95]

Wrongs now accumulated by the hour, and the federal government made no effort to limit the invaders. Their numbers altered this ecological "oasis," as General George Crook called it: "The Black Hills was then a most . . . beautiful country . . . here was a broken piece of country covered with a beautiful growth of time, filled with game of all kinds."[96] According to the *Pacific Tourist*, it was a "land of which the eye never tires."[97]

Prospectors leveled trees for fuel. They killed or drove off the game, and they consumed the region's water for themselves and their herds. Their technologies leached mercury and related chemicals. They hated the Lakota, who they felt were not using the lands appropriately and like the farmers they harbored antipathies toward the government and the railroads, which they believed profited the most. "The minute you crossed the Missouri River your fate," one settler remembered, "was in their hands and they robbed us of all we produced. . . . Many of the early settlers filled early graves on account of being ill nourished and ill clad while the wealth they produced was being coldly calculated."[98] Following the economic Panic of 1873, western farmers, settlers, and miners formed a powerful constituency.[99]

Violence and then war followed. Outraged by the invasion, many Lakota leaders refused to return to the reservation and its dreaded agencies. Others fled north into Canada. White lawlessness and Indian raids followed, which soon brought punitive military campaigns. Army officials such as Crook "received instructions to compel the Sioux and Cheyenne Indians, who were off their reservation, to go on it. They were consequently notified that they must either go on the reservation . . . or else the troops would attack them wherever found."[100]

In a nation celebrating a century of independence, Crook's campaign of 1876 generated little notice. Lakota resistance was as unsurprising as it was familiar. They "declined to be restrained in their freedom," as Crook matter-of-factly reported.[101] As in previous U.S.-Lakota wars, however, the accumulated losses on both sides soon shocked the Republic. These included the defeat of the Seventh Cavalry under George Armstrong Custer on June 26, 1876.

News of Custer's defeat reached eastern newspapers just as centennial celebrations were beginning. Hundreds of thousands had gathered at the Philadelphia Centennial Exposition—the largest gathering in U.S. history. Across eighty miles of asphalt walkways, the city celebrated new museums, gardens, and technologies, including Alexander Graham Bell's "new apparatus operated by the human voice," the telephone.[102] A new era of communications, electricity, and transportation had arrived, although the majority of reservations would not benefit from this "overwhelmingly American" process until the late twentieth century.[103]

As the exhibition opened, the city received news of the defeat of nearly three hundred soldiers along the Little Big Horn River. It was the largest loss of Union soldiers since the Civil War. For a nation that still lacked a national anthem, the defeat confirmed certain truths. Despite a century of expansion and a cataclysmic war of unification, the United States remained as divided as it was uneven. With eight western territories, including the Dakota Territory, still home to autonomous Native nations, and eleven southern states struggling to reestablish white supremacy, the Republic was defined by asymmetries. The United States had begun as an agrarian nation, but cities and concentrated wealth now shaped its future.[104]

Empowered by a decade of law making, Congress broadened its authority after the Compromise of 1877. It turned in particular to the West and to taking Indian lands. As army forces encircled Lakota bands and "compelled" them onto the reservation, Congress responded to Custer's defeat on August 15. It exercised its most commonly used constitutional authority: cutting funding for Lakota annuities. Known as the "starve or sell" rider, it made land cessions a precondition for renewed federal support.[105] Then, on February 28, 1877, Congress passed a new law altogether, the 1877 Lakota Act, "to ratify an agreement with certain bands of the Sioux Nation of Indians."[106] Laws from Congress—not treaties ratified by the Senate—now fueled federal-Indian affairs. Despite Congress having abandoned treaty making in 1871, this congressional act resembles the 1868 treaty with a preamble, a set of articles, and hundreds of Lakota signatories. It was also drafted by a commission that conducted negotiations among the Lakota the previous summer, and it targeted Lakota lands and jurisdiction. The act's first article revokes the off-reservation territories of the Lakota. Its third article diminishes the original treaty even further: "The said Indians also agree that they will hereafter received all annuities . . . at such points and places on the said reservation."[107]

By diminishing the size of the reservation and anchoring annuities to its agencies, Congress established a new geography of power that fostered fur-

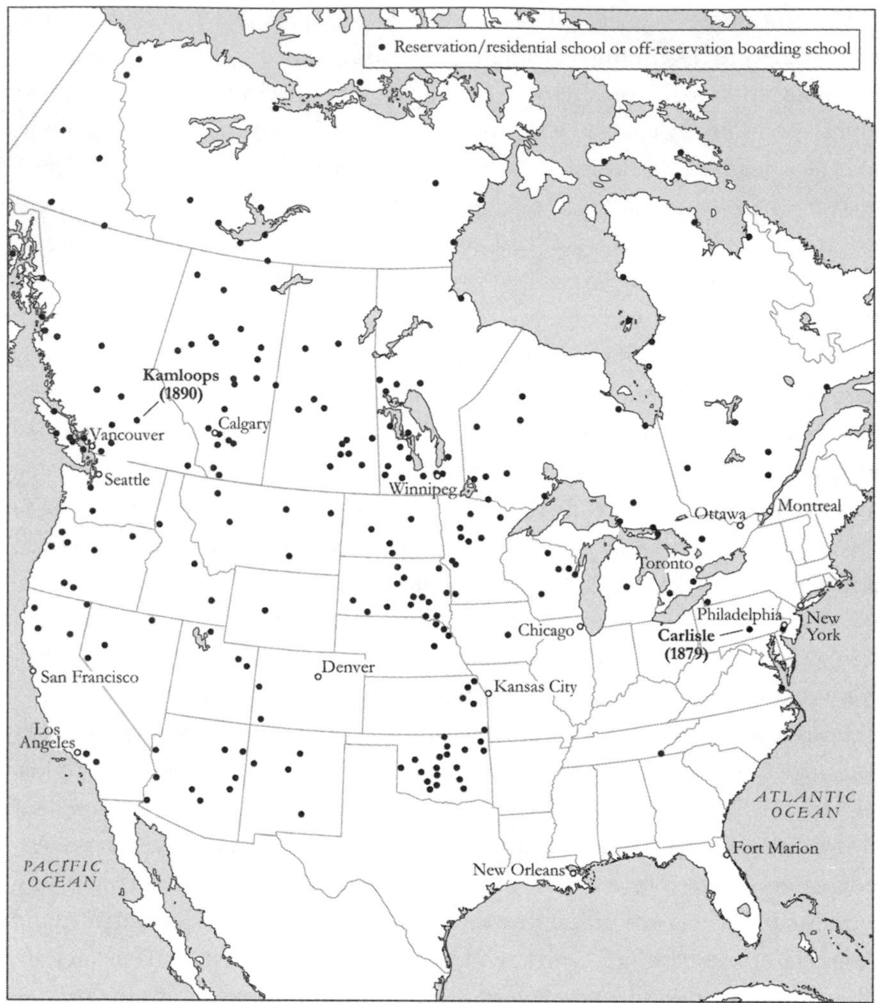

ther dependency and dispossession. An uncommon hybrid in a century-long process of treaty making, the legislation resembled the structure of a treaty and mimicked the earlier diplomatic practices that Congress had outlawed in 1871. Congress was now adopting new authorities for itself. It was assuming the exercise of power to acquire and revoke lands—a power that had previously been held solely by the Senate and executive. It also worked in concert with the army for enforcement.

This unbridled authority—Congress's "plenary power"—overrode existing treaty commitments. However, as Congress exercised these new powers, it did so in the shadows of constitutional ambiguity, because nowhere in the U.S. Constitution is Congress given the power to abrogate national treaty commitments—the "supreme law of the land." Such unbridled congressional power did not go unchallenged by Native peoples, who believed their treaty-protected lands to be irrevocable. An enduring legal conflict has followed, shaping federal Indian policies across the nineteenth, twentieth, and now twenty-first centuries.

The Challenges of Assimilation

With new reservation land policies and a continental-wide system of boarding schools, the United States entered the twentieth century committed to eradicating Native Americans. Officials targeted Indian lands and children in a campaign designed not to exterminate Native peoples but to eliminate their cultures. The goal, as Pratt famously quipped, was to "kill the Indian, and save the man."[108] As he also suggested, "All the Indian there is in the race should be dead."[109] His perspective was echoed by Dawes, reservation agents, and social reformers, many of whom advocated for humane forms of cultural erasure. They stood in opposition to other leaders, such as Theodore Roosevelt, who believed in the inferiority of Native peoples. As Roosevelt remarked in New York in 1886: "I don't go so far as to think that the only good Indians are the dead Indians, but I believe nine out of every ten are." And, he concluded, "I shouldn't like to inquire too closely into the case of the tenth."[110]

Native peoples resisted the assimilation programs that targeted their lands, economies, religions, and politics. They did so by continuing forms of political and cultural authority in the face of new governing structures. After their settlement in 1877 onto the Wind River Reservation in Wyoming, Arapaho leaders adapted their age-based political systems, establishing sets of intermediary council chiefs and more elderly "ritual leaders" on the reservation. Such adaptations maintained pre-reservation leadership systems in which elderly men held ceremonial and cultural authority and younger men were expected to serve their community's needs under the elders' guidance.[111] Similarly, among the Crow of Montana, venerable leaders such as Plenty Coups and Medicine Crow maintained communal authority despite the placement of younger men into positions of power, such as reservation police officers, by superintendents.[112]

Such adaptations curbed only certain aspects of the assimilation program. Each year it became more difficult to shield the children, especially as reservation officials developed new strategies of removal. On the Navajo Nation, officials targeted children when parents and extended family members were herding, as parents were forced to choose between maintaining their pastoral economies and keeping their children. As Tall Woman (also known as Rose Mitchell) recalled, "Children were snatched up and hauled [away] because the policemen came . . . while they [parents] were out herding. . . . So we started to hide ourselves in different places whenever we saw strangers coming to where we were living."[113]

Child removal became institutionalized in other ways. As Superintendent of Indian Schools Estelle Reel reported, "Some reservations withhold the rations until the parents place their children in the schools, and so strong is the opposition to this that in many cases they have held out against it until their families were on the verge of starvation."[114] A new politics of hunger emerged across the West, as economically vulnerable Native communities confronted the choice of protecting their children from removal or feeding them.

Boarding schools targeted children as young as four. Many were taken from their families, communities, and cultures for years on end. Bitterness followed these removals. "I was happy living with my grandparents in a world of our own," remembered Lame Deer from the Rosebud Reservation.

> But it was a happiness that could not last. . . . One day the monster came—a white man from the Bureau of Indian Affairs. I guess he had my name on a list. He told my family, "This kid has to go to school. If your kids don't come by themselves the Indian police will pick them up." . . . I hid behind Grandma. My father was like a big god to me and Grandpa had been a warrior at the Custer fight, but they could not protect me now.[115]

Protection was also absent within the schools themselves. Children were plunged into what Pratt termed "the swim of American citizenship," and many drowned in this state-sponsored struggle.[116] Students faced immediate and enduring impositions: forced to learn English, wear woolen clothing, and maintain regimented work schedules. Boys' heads were shorn upon arrival, and all had their handmade clothing and moccasins burned. Students were beaten for speaking their languages or had their mouths washed with soap. Untold numbers suffered physical and sexual abuse, and thousands died due to disease, overly strict discipline, and deprivation.[117]

Such losses were necessary from Pratt's perspective. Civilization and assimilation necessitated cultural isolation and regimen. "Day after day," he

Memorial outside St. Paul's Cathedral in Saskatoon, Saskatchewan. In May 2021 the Tk'emlúps te Secwépemc Nation announced the discovery of 215 unmarked gravesites at a former residential school near Kamloops, British Columbia. In the wake of this discovery, hundreds of unmarked graves have been found at other schools across North America. Boarding school survivors in the United States and residential school survivors in Canada have protested the traumatic legacies of forced assimilation on Indigenous communities as well as the failure of states and churches to take responsibility for these violent institutions. Many place children's shoes on the steps of former boarding schools, churches, and legislative buildings to express mourning for the young lives lost and a desire for accountability. (Tenille K Campbell, sweetmoon photography.)

proclaimed, Indian children were becoming "saturated with the spirit . . . [and] the touch" of American freedom.[118] "Dear boys and girls," the Carlisle student newspaper attempted to reassure its students: "Be content that you are where you can get the education that will save you."[119]

Expansion of the Assimilation Campaign: 1880s–1920s

Until the New Deal, Congress imposed laws that diminished reservation lands, removed children, and imposed additional assimilative measures, such as the persecution of Indian religions. These burdens compounded existing challenges for Native families, particularly those associated with malnutrition and disease. Dependent on government assistance and corrupt officials, countless communities struggled to feed themselves and sustain their economies.

During the Assimilation Era, U.S. policy makers targeted reservations because they believed that Indian lands and families needed to be changed. Only through the adoption of Christianity, the English language, and Anglo-American practices could Native people become incorporated into the Republic. While railway companies, settlers, and corporate leaders viewed reservations as sources of unrealized property, reformers targeted Indians in order to transform them, believing that they were bringing new opportunities to individuals rather than destroying them. Thomas Morgan of the Commission of Indian Affairs reported in 1890: "The reservation system is an anachronism which has no place in our modern civilization. . . . That which is fundamental . . . is the recognition of the complete manhood of the Indians. . . . They should be free to make for themselves homes wherever they will."[120]

Assimilation was also referred to as "Americanization," and it motivated other movements during the Progressive Era. As the United States received millions of non-Protestant and non-Anglophone immigrants, reformers sought to Americanize both immigrant and Indigenous communities. In the case of the latter, this meant that reservations were not conceived of as the autonomous sovereign homelands that Native nations knew them to be but as communities requiring new familial social structures; in the case of immigrants, housing and educational reforms were proposed.

Anglo-American gender norms drove these reform efforts, which spread north and influenced Canadian First Nations policies.[121] Domesticity dominated the discourse of reformers, who dismissed existing social practices in favor of patriarchal understandings of authority.[122] Echoing the individualism articulated by Pratt, Dawes, and other federal officials, Morgan summarized: "They must stand or fall as men and women, not as Indians."[123]

As gender relations became a principal battleground for assimilation, government impositions conflicted with the beliefs of Indian communities. Native familial structures placed value on extended familial structures, not nuclear households. Reservation homes included the elderly, who rarely lived alone or away from their relatives. Within matrilineal kinship networks, women's authority structured households and family units.

Among the Crow of Montana, women's authority also extended intergenerationally. Through social and cultural processes, women determined clan and kin relationships as well as forms of child care.[124] Crow women controlled much of their family's wealth and possessions; 75 percent of wills left by Crow women in the early twentieth century include no provisions for their husbands.[125]

As in other tribes, Crow women often had more than one husband in their lifetimes. They lived in intergenerational homes and preferred birthing their children with midwives and family, away from agency hospitals. A nursing graduate of Franklin County Memorial Hospital in Massachusetts, Susie Yellowtail returned to Montana to practice medicine in her community. She remarked the cultural insensitivities and negligence of white nurses and doctors, who often expressed indifference to their patients. Reservation doctors at the Crow Agency Hospital were always "in a hurry," she remembered. In one particularly traumatic birth, one doctor "just cut the umbilical cord [too short] and left," causing extensive bleeding and leaving Yellowtail to fight to save the child's life and comfort the mother.[126]

Reformers believed that Indian familial structures were insufficient for raising children. Additionally, because they occupied lands communally, Native nations were thought to practice "primitive" forms of land management and needed to adopt an ethos of private property. Dismantling reservations, removing children to faraway schools, and establishing property ownership as a path to citizenship defined this era. As among the Lakota, however, disaster, rather than "uplift," ensued.

The Lakota Act of 1877 was one of a series of laws that abrogated treaty commitments. A dizzying number of laws and "riders" followed that further subdivided reservations. For decades, Congress passed statute after statute that disaggregated reservations. Minnesota's White Earth Anishinaabe's 1867 treaty stipulated that they were to retain all lands within their reservation, but a series of laws and riders—such as the Clapp Riders of 1904 and 1906—diminished their land base.[127]

Such dispossession devastated White Earth's subsistence economies, which had provided maple sugar, wild rice, and hunting resources in an annual migratory cycle. These laws also opened the reservation's most commodified resources—lumber, farming lands, and tourist sites such as lakefronts for summer cabins—to external development. Many laws drafted by congressional representatives targeted specific Native nations and their resources, as with the Lakota and White Earth; others, including the 1887 General Allotment Act, targeted all Native nations.

Not all Native nations were so dramatically impacted. Some navigated allotment challenges through a combination of ingenuity, diplomacy, and unified leadership. Neighboring Anishinaabe leaders at Red Lake, Minnesota, successfully resisted the allotment pressures. They retained comparatively autonomous control over their reservation, waters, and resources. Unlike at White Earth, they prevented allotment as well as the relocation of other Native peoples upon their homelands. As Medwe-ganoonind (He Who Is Spoken To) repeated to officials, "We wish to live alone on our premises; we do not wish any other Indians to come here."[128]

With the military supporting the implementation of these laws, most Native nations had few choices but to comply. During the Great Sioux War (1876–77), army leaders seized all horses and guns within the reservation agencies. They confined hungry families while depriving them of their capacity to hunt. Meanwhile, Generals Crook and Nelson A. Miles conducted a war of attrition to subdue remaining resistance fighters.[129] The Lakota Act of 1877 was enforced by the military.

Violence, land seizures, and further treaty violations characterized this conflict, and over a century of legal challenges followed. In 1980 the U.S. Supreme Court in *United States v. Sioux Nation of Indians* affirmed a court of claims ruling that "the 1877 Act . . . effected a taking of tribal property which had been set aside by the Fort Laramie Treaty." Such a "taking," the Court found, "implied an obligation on the Government's part to make just compensation to the Sioux. That obligation, including an award of interest, must now be paid."[130]

The Court identified additional problems with congressional actions. Given that treaties remain the "supreme law of the law," the House of Representatives lacks the authority to revoke treaty commitments made by the Senate and executive branch. While the 1877 act resembled previous treaties, it did not achieve the required consent of "at least three-fourths of the adult male Sioux population . . . for the cession of any part of the reservation," as stipulated in article 12 of the Lakota Treaty.[131] The commission had obtained only 230 required signatures, or roughly 10 percent of the eligible Lakota population. Congress's law was in effect unconstitutional and led to an illegal seizure of Lakota lands.

Facing military attacks, withheld provisions, and growing settlement pressures, many prominent leaders, such as Red Cloud, agreed to the new impositions. The majority of Lakota leaders, however, refused to accept what amounted to the uncompensated loss of over 7 million acres of land. Nonetheless, despite failure to obtain Lakota consent, Congress attached a preamble to this "alleged 'agreement' and declared it law."[132]

The next decades of federal Indian policy proved to be among the darkest years for the Lakota and other Native nations. South Dakota became a state in 1889, the same year that the federal government further divided the Great Sioux Reservation. Through another statute, Congress subdivided the reservation into six smaller reservations, in the process gaining additional title to 13 million acres of treaty lands. Statehood fostered more dispossession. Upon lands where Lakota herds once grazed, white settlements and state jurisdictions now arrived. As Phizí (Gall), a Lakota leader noted sadly, "The whites have now got our lands, and I hope they will be satisfied and let us live in peace."[133]

With the military stationed across the region, the Bureau of Indian Affairs oversaw the reservation's new policies. From annuity distributions to the issuing of passes to leave the reservation, officials such as Valentine McGillycuddy now dominated the everyday lives of the Lakota.[134] Assuming command over Pine Ridge in 1879, he doled out resources, favors, and passes to select Lakota headmen—and meted out punishments as well—in an attempt to divide the community.

A supporter of Pratt's boarding school movement, McGillycuddy began targeting Lakota children, 120 of whom were removed to Carlisle in 1879. Such large numbers initially troubled Pratt, who protested the arrival of such a large number from one community, complaining that he "had never met these discontented . . . Indians; [and] that they were then in a hostile attitude toward the government."[135] Pratt had envisioned some degree of tribal consent to his new efforts. As a military officer, he nonetheless followed, as well as understood, commissioner of Indian Affairs Ezra Hayt's recent directive "because the children would be hostages for the good behavior of their people."[136]

The Supreme Court Affirms the Plenary Power Doctrine

While the Assimilation Era transformed Indian reservations geographically and politically, few understood the specific nature of this policy reversal. Confusion reigned. Reservation officials, Indian signatories to treaties, and federal judges all understood the era's policies differently. When territories such as Arizona imposed state authority upon reservation lands and tribal members, questions arose. How could the Apache communities Woolsey hunted possess a political authority beyond that of the state? How could treaties bring legal protections for tribal members? For many settlers, sovereignty resided only with them. It was theirs exclusively and did not extend to tribal lands that many considered "a barren waste, yielding nothing that the white man cared for."[137]

Innumerable questions flowed from the incorporation of Indian lands. Were Native people citizens of the United States? Could they vote, hold property, or testify in courts? Were Indians subject to the criminal laws of states or those of the federal government, or were they governed by their own laws and customs? Could Indians contest state prohibitions, like miscegenation laws and the Howell Code? Who ultimately governed Indian lands and how? Such questions took decades to address and were answered within an emergent legal system that struggled to uphold existing agreements, redress crimes, and maintain forms of justice and equity. While many of these questions would remain unanswered until after World War I, a series of rulings offered partial explanations.

In 1865 the Comanche and the Lakota dominated much of the southern and northern Plains. Each fought military campaigns with the U.S. Army and contested the diminution of their jurisdictions thereafter. They attempted to compel federal officials to uphold their treaty agreements, resulting in two of the most consequential rulings of the era.

In 1883 the Supreme Court ruled in *Ex Parte Crow Dog* that Crow Dog, a convicted Lakota leader, was being held illegally by the Dakota Territory even though he had allegedly committed murder. This ruling led to his release. However, the Court also ruled that Congress held the power to override tribal authority should it pass statutes specifically aimed at resolving ambiguities in criminal law, which it did in the Major Crimes Act of 1885.[138] Congress's authority thereafter overrode the power of treaties in matters of criminal law, as a number of "major crimes" came under federal jurisdiction.

Similarly, in 1903 the Court ruled in *Lone Wolf v. Hitchcock* that Kiowa treaty provisions were not binding if Congress determined otherwise. The Comanche Treaty of 1867 negotiated at Medicine Lodge holds that any changes to the Comanche's land policies require a three-fourths approval of all eligible Comanche men. When a series of Oklahoma land acts took possession of tribal lands without such approval, tribal members sued; however, the Supreme Court ruled that Congress holds an inherent power that supersedes the authority of treaties. Despite assurances in the U.S. Constitution that treaties were the "supreme law of the land," Congress now held "full administrative power . . . over Indian tribal property," Justice White wrote in the majority opinion.[139]

Such rulings redirected the course of federal Indian policy and continue to wield influence upon contemporary Native nations. Before the Civil War, Congress passed few laws affecting Indian communities. Now it developed new powers that targeted the most intimate forms of Indian life. Individual law makers such as Dawes also began driving federal Indian policy.[140] Starting in the 1870s, he and other members of Congress passed an assembly of laws designed to remake Indian lands, families, and communities. Such active and intrusive law making made the last decades of the century among the most challenging years of federal Indian policy.[141]

A century after the United States achieved independence, a new structure of Indian affairs had emerged in the country: unbridled congressional authority held sway. Rooted in a body of precedents stretching back to the Taney Court, an "inherent doctrines power" had emerged that justified congressional actions.[142] This doctrine of plenary power contradicted the visions of retained tribal sovereignty outlined by many leaders of the early Republic and the Marshall Court. It upholds the exercise of congressional legislative authority upon all territories within the geographical limits of the United States and diminishes the jurisdiction of tribal communities therein. It became distilled in a series of additional Supreme Court cases during the Reservation Era, including *United States v. Kagama* (1886), which upheld the constitutionality of the Major Crimes Act of 1885.

The taking of Indian children and treaty lands defined many reservation experiences, and a diminishment of tribal jurisdiction accompanied these intrusions, as tribal communities increasingly lost full control over their lands and resources. Laws from this era shaped federal policies for generations. The Major Crimes Act gives the federal government criminal jurisdiction over a series of seven "major crimes" committed on reservations.[143] It was a legislative response to an exertion of tribal autonomy through the court system. In *Ex Parte Crow Dog* (1883), the Supreme Court called for the release of Crow Dog, a Lakota police officer who had been convicted of murder by a South Dakota court. Recognizing that states and territories hold no jurisdiction upon reservation lands and that tribes were best able to adjudicate their own inter-tribal disputes, the High Court ordered his release in a ruling that affirmed the jurisdiction of tribes over crimes committed by their members.[144] There were generations of treaties, customary practices, and even cultural imperatives within tribal communities that either sanctioned his behavior or established the exclusive authority of tribal communities to adjudicate crimes within their respective communities. Crow Dog's "imprisonment is illegal," concluded Justice Matthews in the unanimous decision.[145] While displaying language that disparaged Indian social practices, the ruling nonetheless provided affirmation of Marshall's view of Indian sovereignty: tribes retain jurisdiction over the governance of their lands and members. It was, however, the last nineteenth-century ruling to uphold that right.[146]

In response to *Crow Dog*, Congress intervened. In the Major Crimes Act, it claimed such jurisdiction for itself. The wave of plenary power was now cresting, and it soon crashed into the most remote areas of jurisdiction and legal practice. Central questions, however, still remained about whose authority governed crimes on reservations, especially those between tribal members. As Matthews had suggested in *Crow Dog*, to give territorial courts the authority to impose jurisdiction on tribes "would be to reverse . . . the general policy of the government towards the Indians, *as declared in many statutes and treaties*, and recognized in many decisions of this court, from the beginning to the present time. To justify such a departure . . . requires a clear expression of the intention of congress, and that we have not been able to find."[147]

The constitutionality of the act—and of congressional power over Indian affairs—was considered the next year in *United States v. Kagama* (1886). After Native defendants on the Hoopa Valley Reservation in California were convicted under the act, they, like Crow Dog, used the court system to challenge their imprisonment. In a key opinion, however, the Court upheld the new laws. It also ruled more broadly on congressional authority to legislate Indian affairs, articulating a new vision of "exclusive" U.S. sovereignty.

This vision mirrored that of conquest. According to *Kagama*, only two forms of sovereign authority reside in the United States: the sovereignty of the federal governments and of state governments. "There exist with in the broad domain of sovereignty but these two," Justice Samuel Miller wrote. "The power of the General Government over these remnants of a race once power[ful] . . . is necessary to their protection."[148] The jurisdiction of tribes over their lands and members, in short, could be now overridden by congressional power.

Joining the Appropriations Bill of 1871, the Lakota Act of 1877, and the Allotment Act of 1887, the Major Crimes Act became another piece of legislative intrusion into Indian affairs. It was designed to expand national powers upon Indian communities in response to an affirmation of Indian sovereignty issued in *Crow Dog*. These laws deprived tribes of lands and jurisdiction. They established through statute new forms of constitutional practice, and they were developed after the Civil War when the federal government expanded its authorities through the congressional usurpation of treaty powers.

As it had with the Reconstruction amendments, Congress now changed the nation's constitutional meanings. It also acquired far-ranging jurisdictional powers once held by other branches of government, as Congress orchestrated a remaking of the Republic's oldest diplomatic practices, those stipulated "in many statutes and treaties." A doctrine of congressional plenary power had now formed.[149]

The Wounded Knee Massacre of 1890

In 1890, the U.S. Census declared the national "frontier" to be officially closed, ending for the first time in U.S. history recognition of the availability of unincorporated western lands. Settlers, traders, government officials, and missionaries now encircled Indian homelands, confirming to many a sense of an impending apocalypse. Amid a growing dependency on the government and evoking the lives of ancestors lost over the generations, a millennialist cultural revitalization known as the Ghost Dance empowered many across the West to abandon the debilitating influence of whites.

Gathered to share teaching and ceremonies, worshippers danced throughout the year. "At Pine Ridge," Lakota historian Josephine Waggoner later recounted, "the dancing was continually kept up, [and] great chiefs . . . were all swept into the new belief."[150] As with other revitalization movements, such as those led by Neolin, they pledged to abandon their reliance on trader products, particularly alcohol, and to abandon the practices of Christianity. They also prized handmade, ceremonial clothes over those provided at agencies and believed them to hold sacred power.[151] Men continued to wear their hair long in defiance of prescriptions flowing from boarding schools, and many shared sacred songs that crossed tribal boundaries and carried within them the potential for communing with one's lost ancestors.

In the fateful winter of 1890, the Ghost Dance again seared South Dakota and the Lakota into the Republic's history. Three days after Christmas renewed violence befell the region. Believing a band of worshippers under Big Foot to be hostile, members of the Seventh Cavalry—Custer's former unit—

confined them along the Wounded Knee Creek on the Pine Ridge Reservation. They forced them to surrender their arms, and upon the discharge of a concealed rifle, the cavalry attacked, charges unleashing mortar fire from Hotchkiss cannons stationed above them. Revenge for Custer's defeat was now obtained against women, children, and the elderly. Historians debate the extent of the number of those killed, as hundreds either died or fled across the frozen winter landscape, hiding in whatever shelters they could find.[152]

"When I saw the soldiers going out," recalled Nicholas Black Elk in a 1931 interview, "I knew there would be trouble."[153] Encamped nearby, Black Elk was moving on horseback to the scene of the conflict as the cannons sounded. "I felt it right in my body," he remembered.[154] He was fortunate to evade the subsequent conflicts, but his experience of being numbed by the sight of those wounded and massacred stayed with him forever.

✦

Many currents of U.S. history converged in 1890 across the former Great Sioux Reservation, now divided into five separate reservation communities. Red Cloud's war had influenced the reservation's initial creation in 1868, and a subsequent decade of warfare and failed governmental protections contributed to its eventual dismantling. The Lakota Treaty of 1868 had specified the reservation's massive form, slowly eroding by subsequent congressional statutes that brought once unimaginable territorial diminishment. For Black Elk, Waggoner, and other community members, life had irrevocably changed, as a depth of betrayal, loss, and suffering settled across their beloved homelands.

11 • Indigenous Twilight at the Dawn of the Century

Native Activists and the Myth of Indian Disappearance

> There are old Indians who have never seen the inside of a classroom whom I consider far more educated than the young Indian with his knowledge of Latin and algebra. There is something behind the superb dignity and composure of the old . . . there is something in the discipline of the Red Man . . . there to remain separate and distinct . . . against all time, against all change.
>
> —*Laura Cornelius Kellogg (1911)*

The summer of 1879 was a busy time for the Reverend David Craft. For twenty-five years, he had served as pastor of the Presbyterian church of Wyalusing, Pennsylvania, on the Susquehanna River south of the New York border. He had preached during the Civil War, counseling widows, Union veterans, and others who lost family members, and afterwards distilled from the pulpit the new wonders and temptations of modern life. He likely attended the Centennial Exhibition in nearby Philadelphia and enjoyed the majesty of its visions of the future. Patriotic undertones accompanied the exhibition's most arresting addition: a recent delivery from France of the torch for a massive "statue of liberty."

The 1870s were a time of centennial celebrations, and Craft led a series of these in New York in August and September. They commemorated not independence but the revolutionary struggle behind it. They centered not on Philadelphia or other colonial centers but on western New York. Throughout the summer of 1879, Craft commemorated the centennial conquest of the Iroquois Confederacy begun by revolutionary general John Sullivan in 1779.[1]

"Seized with an enthusiastic desire to learn all about the campaign," Craft delivered lengthy addresses at Elmira, Waterloo, Geneso, and Aurora.[2] He also authored an 80-page historical study that accompanied a 579-page publication commissioned by the New York legislature, "of which ten copies shall be furnished and distributed to . . . each Senator and Member of the Assembly."[3]

Rescued from the "obscurity of a century," the Sullivan expedition now became the founding event in these towns' collective history. According to the marble tablet laid beneath Elmira's newest monument, the expedition formed the central moment that "assured to the United States their existence as an INDEPENDENT NATION."[4] To Craft, Sullivan's campaign "determined in a single blow, whether white men or red men should hold domination over these fertile vales and along these streams. . . . At a single stroke it solved the question, whether the American Indian . . . was longer to stand in the way of human progress . . . or whether he must go down before the antagonism of another race."[5] Soon thereafter settlers established what many believed to be an ideal society.[6] As the region's most famous author, James Fenimore Cooper, had suggested in *The Pioneers*, New York's "neat and comfortable farms" created an idyllic world of "beautiful and thriving villages" inhabited by "a moral and reflecting people."[7] Craft extended Cooper's visions back to what he believed were their origins: Sullivan and the revolutionary era.

Before the 1890 Census declared the frontier to be "closed" and before Chicago held the nation's largest commemoration—the Columbian Exhibition of 1893—sweeping new visions of American history proliferated. With each monument, celebratory parade, and commemorative publication, visions of a confident and certain past deepened across the nation's historical consciousness.[8] As Craft suggested, "the question" of American history had been answered. "Progress" defined American history, not an "undisguised hatred" or "unconquerable aversion to civilization." Progress had arrived triumphantly and in a "single stroke" with Sullivan.[9]

The destruction of Iroquois villages and farms needed to be studied in order to be celebrated and celebrated in order to be studied. His extensive research aside, Craft already understood the lessons from this past. Sullivan had removed barriers to "civilization" and also liberated the lands themselves. His campaign brought to New York those "New England troops, who had been accustomed to the rocky soil and the steep hillsides of their native states."[10] Upon Iroquois homelands, New Englanders "built their homes and reared their children, planted the institutions of liberty and religion."[11] In New York, New Englanders built "an empire."[12] As confident in his version of the past as he was in his belief in scripture, Craft interwove them, lionizing the region's settlers, for whom "these broad and fertile valleys seemed like another Eden."[13]

Across the United States, mythological visions of history gained currency. Everywhere, citizens celebrated the origins of the Republic and equated its history with progress, if not Providence.[14] Even the nation's first trained historians shared Craft's truisms. They, too, located the defining characteristics of U.S. history in the colonial era and believed that the conquest of Indian lands formed the basis of America's historical fulfillment. Ironically, in the world's first constitutional democracy, settlements far away from the state defined the American experience.

Most notably, Francis Parkman and Frederick Jackson Turner offered visions of "frontier" societies and the Indigenous obstacles that had stood in their way. Parkman's seven-volume history of "France in the New World," as he initially termed it, was the most thorough attempt to fashion a history of Anglo-American distinctiveness.[15] It did so through a vilification of Indigenous actors and their French allies, whose loyalties to "Feudalism, Monarchy, and Rome" hindered North America's destiny.[16] Similarly, Turner offered a explanatory thesis on "the Significance of the Frontier in American History." Delivered in Chicago during the Columbian Exhibition, it argues that the colonization of interior lands transformed settlers into self-governing citizens, thereby forming the headwaters of American democracy.[17] His less famous dissertation had examined the first "institution" of the Euro-American economy, "the trading post," which "made the Indian dependent on the white man's supplies."[18] For Turner, despite centuries of Indigenous adaptation across the Great Lakes, small, interior trading posts prepared Native nations for an inevitable disappearance—"the stage of civilization that could make a gun and gunpowder was too far above the bow and arrow to be reached by the Indian."[19]

Parkman's, Turner's, and Craft's new orthodoxies hardened at the dawn of the twentieth century, as scholars and religious, civic, and state leaders celebrated visions of U.S. history. In a morality play with foregone conclusions, the United States emerged from the conquest of Indian lands and achieved its destiny through continental expansion. A consciousness of the American interior fueled not only the nation's historical production but also its scholarly infrastructure. The Mississippi Valley Historical Association formed in 1907 and began its journal in 1914, creating the antecedents for the Organization of American Historians and the *Journal of American History*.[20]

Within such studies, Indians were not simply outside of American "civilization" but antithetical to it. They remained naturalized in "another time" and represented the obverse to the nation's fulfillment.[21] "It is only from the study of barbarous and partially cultivated nations that we are able to comprehend man as a progressive being," summarized Hubert Howe Bancroft in his five-volume series, *The Native Races*.[22] From Iroquoia to Alaska, scholars sought to identify how Indigenous peoples differed from "civilized" man. Despite differences between them, all Native peoples shared commonalities below those of "progressive" man. As Bancroft detailed among the Alutiiq of Kodiak Island, their "domestic manners are of the lowest order. . . . They have no idea of morality" and live simply "in filth."[23]

On the scale of white supremacy, Native peoples inhabited the lowest rungs of humanity. They remained members of a "vanishing race" in need of reform. Like the nation, they too shared in a destiny: if they could not reform, they were destined to disappear. The new century was dawning, but Native people still inhabited the twilight of the past.

This vision of history reached into all corners of America. It became so ubiquitous that it inspired endless commemorations and also national holidays, first celebrating Thanksgiving and then Columbus himself.[24] From school books to monuments, within advertisements to the earliest motion pictures, an endless stream of historical production flowed across the nation.[25]

In a remarkable fusion, Native Americans became viewed as both noble and savage. Despite impeding the march of progress, they nonetheless possessed aesthetic, ethnographic, or experiential arts that needed to be "captured," "salvaged," or "marketed." Artists, writers, and photographers joined in commemorating the closing of the frontier, while scholars and anthropologists rushed to grasp evidence of this historical experience in order to preserve its "authenticity." At new national parks, weekend visitors witnessed performances by Native peoples at Yellowstone, Glacier, and Yosemite, each of which had formed in part through the dispossession of resident Indian nations.[26] In the Southwest, travelers entered trading posts and railway markets for Navajo and Pueblo weavings, jewelry, and pottery, while across the Pacific Northwest's agricultural fields, Native families posed for photographs with the region's settlers, who were interested in observing them while they worked.[27] At work and at play, Native people had to confront the expectations of outsiders.[28]

The phenomenon of being Indian—of being both familiar and forgotten—became an overarching feature of the ideological terrain upon which Native peoples had to navigate life in modern America. Starting in the late nineteenth century, a new generation of Native leaders emerged that confronted this ideology, challenging the foundational mythology of America. Often educated in boarding schools as well as U.S. colleges, they hailed from across the continent and had different ideas of nations and of the United States itself. Raised with distinctive cultural practices, kinship networks, and differ-

This 1912 portrait of Laura Cornelius Kellogg of the Oneida Nation of Wisconsin was published in the *Report of the Executive Council on the Proceedings of the First Annual Conference of the Society of American Indians* along with the paper she presented at the conference, "Industrial Organization for the Indian." She argued that Indigenous self-determination was best promoted by developing robust industries on Native lands rather than by Indians becoming wage earners in settler-controlled economies.

ent understandings of history, they responded to this intellectual formation in sustained and powerful ways. As Oneida reformer Laura Cornelius Kellogg asked in her 1920 work, *Our Democracy and the American Indian*, "What shall I say to you now, America of my Americans? Shall I fawn upon you with nauseating flattery, because you are rich and powerful?"[29] "We are 'dubbed' a race of beggars before the world," she explained, encouraging Native peoples to "refuse to allow" such representations to go unchallenged.[30]

Kellogg was one of the founding members of the Society of American Indians (SAI), an inter-tribal political association that took aim at Richard Henry Pratt's educational philosophies and the government's related programs of assimilation. SAI founders, including Henry Roe Cloud (Ho-Chunk) and Elizabeth Bender Cloud (Ojibwe), worked within their own and other tribal communities.[31] They challenged federal policies and national myopia. They wrote books, delivered sermons, held meetings, traveled widely, went to court and to Washington. The Clouds even opened their own school—the American Indian Institute—to foster advanced academics for Native students.[32]

While focused on particular policies or community concerns, this generation worked collectively to create an American future that included Native peoples. They challenged the grammar of white supremacy in words and action. Many lobbied for Indian citizenship. Others, such as Kellogg, pressed for land reforms and treaty rights. Few in number and understudied, they laid the institutional, political, and ultimately ideological foundations for national reforms that became legislated in the 1930s under the "Indian New Deal."

World's Fairs and the Politics of Representation

While Indian history formed the foundations for the nation's modern historical consciousness, contemporary Indian peoples remained living embodiments of its fading agrarian heritage. Within most reservation communities, opportunities for travel, employment, and autonomy were so circumscribed that thousands sought work within staged human exhibitions at world's fairs, Wild West–themed traveling shows, and related tourist sites. Within five years, for example, Chicago (1893), Atlanta (1895), and Omaha (1898) organized fairs that attracted tens of millions of visitors—St. Louis (1904), Portland (1905), Seattle (1909), and San Francisco (1915) followed thereafter.[33]

Each held permanent displays of Indians living within the fair grounds or within "midway" spectacles led by the famed showman William "Buffalo Bill" Cody. Omaha's "Indian Congress" attracted over five hundred Native people from approximately three dozen tribes who spent three months living in a four-acre section within the exposition grounds. The undertaking was subsidized by $40,000 from the federal government, down from the original request of $100,000 following the outbreak of the Spanish-American War in April 1898.[34]

While these performers were viewed as primitives, complex adaptations characterized their lives. Some came willingly. Others were compelled by government officials or by economic need. As the Apache leader Geronimo recalled about his time selling handmade arrows at the 1904 Louisiana Purchase Fair in St. Louis, "I had plenty money—more than I had ever owned."[35]

By sequestering Native peoples together and limiting their use of modern conveniences, such spectacles attempted to provide visual proof of the historical suggestions made by Craft, Turner, and Bancroft. Fair organizers hoped that the exhibitions would offer a "university for the masses," and they believed that real Indians offered the best object lessons for the racial and historical superiority of Euro-Americans.[36] In Atlanta in 1895, as Cherokee historian Theda Purdue suggests, "The lifeless models and inert objects on display at the Cotton States Exposition conveyed the primitivism and savagery of indigenous peoples but not nearly as dramatically as the real Indians who appeared on the midway."[37] Eighteen years had passed since Cody had last visited Georgia, and his performances in Chicago in 1893 and at Queen Victoria's Silver Jubilee in 1887 had now made him a global celebrity. Cody's performances offered a celebration of frontier history with a modern emphasis on the showman's cult of personality.[38]

While performers like Cody and Geronimo attracted attention, many Native participants used their time in these urban spaces to publicize their community's concerns, to critique governmental policies, and to counteract public misconceptions. Lakota leader Henry Standing Bear, for example, wrote to the commissioner of Indian Affairs that members of his community wanted to attend the fair but "they want to come as men and not like cattles driving to a show. . . . They do not wish [that anyone] . . . will misrepresent our race."[39] Similarly, Medicine Horse, who performed with Cody in Chicago, remained committed to ensuring that fairgoers developed a positive impression of Native people. According to one account, he displayed "an apparent eagerness to talk. He is very interesting to listen to, and the information he gives . . . is of much interest and value."[40] These Lakota performers understood that Cody and the fair's organizers discounted even the possibility that Indian people might occupy the same time and space as their audiences.[41]

Politics accompanied Native participation at these expositions, and Indian leaders developed strategies designed to counteract stereotypes and advance community needs. They confronted, however, deep-seated mythologies of disappearance and inevitability. As a prominent history of Chicago published in 1881 boldly declared:

> Never before in the history of the world has the ambition of man been stimulated to such an extent as here. . . . Only the Indians . . . [were] left to contend against the Americans. A prolonged struggle ensured on their part for existence, and on ours for advancement. . . . Few of their offspring are left among the living of to-day. . . . [Nothing] could save them.[42]

To challenge such myopia, Native participants drew increased attention to contemporary affairs. They developed practices that subsequent activists followed. In Chicago, Potawatomi author Simon Pokagon circulated protests concerning his community's long-standing land claims, and he achieved broad public notice.

As discussed in chapter 7, Potawatomi leaders had suffered dispossession and removal following the Chicago Treaty of 1833, which Pokagon's father Leopold had attended. The city's 1893 homage to Columbus amounted, according to Pokagon, to nothing less than a celebration of "our own funeral, the discovery of America."[43] In his manifesto *The Red Man's Rebuke*, which he issued in handmade birch-bark binding, a testament to the region's literary methods that predated the Euro-American alphabet, Pokagon wrote pointedly, "We have no spirit to celebrate with you."[44]

As his denunciations garnered growing audiences, Pokagon was soon introduced to Chicago mayor Carter Harrison, who invited him to additional celebrations during the city's new holiday of Chicago Day. Interested in enlisting powerful allies for his cause, Pokagon joined Harrison in an unsuccessful effort to garner his support. He left the city having failed to leverage the federal government to return tribal lands lost sixty years earlier at the Chicago Treaty.

Other participants used different strategies to highlight their community's concerns. From the northern tip of Vancouver Island, Canada, George Hunt traveled to Chicago with a delegation of Kwakwaka'wakw dancers in part to protest "potlatch" laws that criminalized Northwest communal practices and giveaways.[45]

As in the United States, Canadian officials had targeted Native children in a broader "war on Aboriginal families" that prohibited religious and ceremonial practices.[46] As Prime Minister John Macdonald informed the House of Commons in 1883, when children are "surrounded by savages," they cannot effectively "acquire the habits and modes and thoughts of white men." He recommended they "be withdrawn . . . [to] central training industrial schools."[47] Macdonald drew his views from other officials, including Nicholas Flood Davin, who had traveled to Washington in 1879 to learn how American officials were developing Indian policies. "If anything is to be done with the Indian," Davin reported, "we must catch him very young."[48]

In 1884 Parliament outlawed the potlatch. For decades thereafter, state officials imposed fines, imprisoned individuals, and limited communal gatherings. Championed by missionaries, these laws targeted redistributive practices that conferred honor, standing, and genealogical meanings. Across the Pacific Northwest, lamented one official, Native villages resisted these bans, expressing "a decided dislike for anything approaching reform."[49] Reform, of course, meant adopting the "habits and modes and thoughts of white men" and did not sanction cultural celebrations in which families demonstrated their social power and genealogical standing by giving away their possessions. Such gift exchanges were the opposite of private property and individualism, values that were reinforced through assimilation.

Unlike Pokagon, Medicine Horse, and Standing Bear, Hunt used outlandish performances to critique his community's suppression and did so by embellishing his audience members' expectations. He proudly claimed to be performing "cannibalistic" dances. As the *Chicago Tribune* complained, "right in the midst" of a fair intended to mark "the progress of mankind were these ceremonies of this strange and semi-barbarous race."[50] The dances, in fact, soon "caused an international outcry."[51]

Cognizant of the institutional divisions among the fair's organizers, Hunt intended to upset Canadian officials who had sponsored national exhibits that celebrated industry and ingenuity. Lurid tales of savage dances did not conform with their official image, designed to attract settlers and investors.[52] Shunned by governmental officials but assisted by ethnographers, Hunt brought the everyday realities of religious persecution to fairgoers' attention, performing dances, such as the *Hamatsa*, that he knew were outlawed in Canada. He understood that performances generated government sanctions and drew attention to his community's concerns against them. Newspapers from Victoria, London, and New York all reported on the controversy.[53]

Like Pokagon, Hunt also established ties with institutional leaders, particularly the anthropologists who led various cultural exhibitions. He navigated these relationships in order to find spaces to articulate broader critiques of colonialism, even presenting an academic paper with the influential German anthropologist Franz Boas at the International Congress of Anthropology that opened in August.[54] Chicago in many ways was just the beginning of Hunt's activism, as over the next thirty years, he continued to co-author ethnographies with Boas; worked with other ethnographers and artists, including the photographer and filmmaker Edward Curtis; and helped Chicago's Field Museum and New York's Museum of Natural History assemble vast collections of Northwest coast artifacts.[55] He essentially saw in other places, peoples, and institutions possibilities for preserving the Native artwork and cultural forms that were prohibited in Canada and enlisted others in disseminating his ideas.

Hunt's efforts helped to make the Kwakwaka'wakw and other Northwest Native nations among the most heavily studied Native peoples. His ability to immerse outsiders within his community's cultural traditions subverted prevailing ideologies of Indigenous inferiority. Like many of anthropology's "informants," Hunt contributed to the development of new forms of cultural analyses, including those long attributed to Boas, that came to view cultural difference horizontally rather than vertically.[56] In a theory of cultural relativism, Boas articulated how cultures developed with their own internal logic and were best understood on their own terms rather than in disaggregated hierarchies. Differences between "peoples" were thus not innate but relative. Race was not a natural condition of inferiority but a status assigned by colonizers to assist global imperialism. Like the masks, songs, and dances of transformation that Hunt had introduced to him, Boas learned from Hunt that ethnic and cultural values were fluid rather than fixed. They could also bridge rather than divide communities.[57]

Rooted within their respective communities and working in their defense, Hunt and Pokagon articulated Indigenous visions that were broad, humanistic, and uncompromising. They offered defiant and impassioned critiques that challenged the mythology of Indian disappearance. A subsequent generation broadened these efforts to reformulate the national laws that continued to target Indian lands, families, and children for assimilation.

American Imperialism and Growing Movements of Indigenous Resistance

Indigenous critiques of American colonialism accelerated throughout the 1890s, particularly after the United States supported the 1893 overthrow of Queen Lili'uokalani and the Hawaiian monarchy while adding imperial possessions during the Spanish-American War. For the first time since 1842, when President John Tyler "recognized the kingdom's independence," the United States disaffirmed the sovereignty of the Hawaiian kingdom.[58]

From Puerto Rico to the Philippines, the United States now spanned the globe. It added distant harbors, territories, and millions of non-white subjects. This expanding empire changed the nation, particularly its ways of governing non-citizens.[59] Across its empire, the United States expanded its administrative capacities, which included a dramatic expansion in the role of the federal government in the governance of non-white subjects.[60]

New racial classifications informed American imperialism, and new institutions of territorial control, resource extraction, and political subordination followed. Such colonial infrastructure not only resembled the institutions of federal Indian affairs, it was also staffed by many of the same individuals. Religious leaders, military officials, and state officials who had staffed Indian administrative agencies now used similar forms of education, policing, and military surveillance across the American empire.

New England missionaries, in particular, had planted the earliest seeds of America's global empire. Members of the American Board of Commissioners for Foreign Missions (ABCFM) plied the Pacific shortly after the organization's founding in 1810, reaching Hawaii in 1819. A member of the ABCFM, Richard Armstrong worked with Hawaiian royal family members, including King Kamehameha III, to establish missionary and industrial schools across the kingdom. A graduate of Princeton Theological Seminary, he carried forth the board's missionary zeal from Maui to the Marquesas Islands.[61]

Missionary children such as Samuel Chapman Armstrong learned the practices of industrial education from their parents.[62] Samuel grew up within early Christian communities in Hawaii, educated in their new churches and schools. He sought to replicate them after serving in the Civil War, establishing the Hampton Institute in Virginia, where he worked with former slaves and mentored Booker T. Washington.[63] Between 1878 and 1893, Hampton also recruited Indian students. Such education attracted interested social reformers, including Richard Henry Pratt, whom Armstrong advised on the values of industrial education. Pratt's 1878 visit to Hampton, in fact, strengthened his faith in his work and facilitated his request to Congress to fund Carlisle.[64]

By the time Hampton welcomed Theodore Roosevelt as its commencement speaker in 1906, American imperialism had broadened. It also encountered new challenges, especially in the Philippines, where revolutionary forces continued their struggle for independence.[65] As Roosevelt championed, the ideologies that had guided U.S. continental expansion also sanctioned imperialism: "The reasoning which justifies our having made war against Sitting Bull also justifies our having checked the outbreak of Aguinaldo and his followers."[66] If the United States "were morally bound to abandon the Philippines," he continued, "we were also morally bound to abandon Arizona to the Apaches."[67]

U.S. military practices drew upon experiences with Indian warfare. In the Philippines, the U.S. Army prioritized the use of local scouts, the establishment of reservations to control native civilians, and attacks on villages to undermine Indigenous economies.[68] All of these practices had expanded across Indian Country since the end of the Civil War.

Policing became another extension of federal oversight into the Pacific. In a particularly violent thirteen-month period from May 1900 to June 1901, over five thousand Filipinos were killed as a result of combat operations, while another thirty thousand were captured or surrendered.[69] After subjugating the Filipino revolutionary movement under the leadership of Emilio Aguinaldo, the U.S. civil administration, known as the Philippine Commission, established the Philippines Constabulary. Using a locally recruited force, it infiltrated civil society, limited public discourse, and placed leaders under surveillance.[70]

Such policing paralleled systems developed during the Indian wars. As in the Philippines, Indian police forces grew from the scouts who had fought in military campaigns. At reservation agencies, officers such as Captain Theodore Schwan at Cheyenne River, South Dakota, recruited local Lakota officers. In 1878 Schwan chose twenty Lakota soldiers who had fought in the Great Sioux War. Through inspections, drills, parading, and salaries, the unit became institutionalized. Such practices, he reported, "are absolutely essential to the efficiency and discipline of the force."[71]

Indian police units were often despised within their own communities. They enforced governmental laws and were commanded by outside military officers or civilian officials. They arrested individuals for leaving reservations "without permission" or for traveling between reservations to visit relatives.[72] Such crimes left prisoners in jail, hobbled with irons and denied food. To many, these new institutions embodied the worst aspects of the "Indian Service." They became a focal point for cascading criticisms of federal Indian policy.

The "Indian Service" included all forms of federal services offered by the Office of Indian Affairs, which was founded in 1824 and renamed the Bureau of Indian Affairs in 1947.[73] It administered federal policies on reservations. It also took children away to boarding schools, which it also administered and funded. It paid police and oversaw annuity distributions mandated by treaties. It governed essential areas of everyday life: housing, food, education, and healthcare. Governed by reservation superintendents and under the jurisdiction of the commissioner of Indian Affairs, such collective practices formed an authoritarian administrative infrastructure. It brought, according to Kellogg, "a reign of terror" to reservations, a despotism comparable to imperial projects abroad.[74]

Kellogg's critiques echoed those of previous generations. A member of the Iroquois Confederacy, her community, the Oneida Nation of Wisconsin, was formed in the 1820s by migrating Oneida families seeking refuge from the onslaught of New York settlement, and her family had years of experience confronting the challenges of retaining their lands. Due to allotment, for example, over 90 percent of the Oneida reservation had been alienated by 1920.[75] Her critiques, however, also articulated new concerns. White officials such as Schwan now accumulated unjust powers, and in some cases they were joined by allied Indians. Such Native employees came from what she termed "the Indian Bureau School of Sycophants."[76] These graduates of the boarding schools, she argued, reinforced the Indian Service's programs of assimilation. Radical change was needed to reform national policies as well as the institutions of reservation governance that they had spawned. Others soon shared her vision, and worked to refine it.

The Society of American Indians

Kellogg led a great debate in the early twentieth century about how best to resolve the nation's Indian affairs. Begun in the late 1870s, the federal campaign to assimilate Native peoples showed no signs of slowing. As Kellogg understood, the campaign was in fact gaining momentum. It became more expensive and expansive each year. Congress appropriated $3 million for Indian schools in 1901, more than double the amount funded in 1890. More than 23,000 students attended these institutions, nearly double the number in 1890. Over the next two decades, Congress appropriated more money to these institutions, over $4 million a year on average.[77] From the time Pratt visited Hampton and advocated for $20,000 to open Carlisle, Congress by 1920 had allocated $113,755,357 to government-run boarding schools.[78] By 1926, 77,577 Native students attended these schools, and the annual costs had grown further to $7,264,145—the nation's largest school, Haskell Indian Institute in

Kansas, welcomed 8,000 for its homecoming and alumni weekend. By 1926, its annual entering class averaged more than 400.[79] Assimilation was destructive and costly. It was also nowhere near complete.

Kellogg knew "the Indian Bureau" well. She had grown up on the Oneida Reservation during the Allotment Era and had worked for two years at Sherman Institute in Riverside, California, teaching within the system that Pratt designed. She lectured and wrote widely and attended college in Wisconsin, California, and New York City. Through her work and travels, she became convinced that national policies were misguided. "I know the ideas that prevail in regards to Indian life," she relayed in 1903.[80] The same year her poem "A Tribute to the Future of My Race" was reprinted in boarding school newspapers, including Carlisle's *The Red Man.*[81] An impassioned 147-line work, it critiques American mythology using "the famous trochaic tetrameter meter" found in Henry Wadsworth Longfellow's epic *The Song of Hiawatha.*[82] Unlike Longfellow, Kellogg does not eulogize the disappearance of Native peoples; she envisions a different symmetry between Native and non-Native peoples, one in which Native peoples again "will extend the wampum strand made of friendships, purest pearl, made of gratitude, deep-rooted, made to last eternal summers."[83]

Known for her lyricism and leadership, Kellogg toured England in 1908, where she received extensive news coverage. One reporter wrote that she "spoke with enthusiasm of the flattering reception she had received from the most exclusive set in London society . . . [and that] it is her intention to begin a movement in America to recognize Indian affairs."[84]

As in other anti-colonial struggles, the problems of Indian communities were more apparent than their solutions. Nearly all Indian leaders understood that child removal programs, land allotment, underemployment, and stereotypes damaged families, communities, and individuals. The origins of these problems lay with the government's treatment of Indian peoples and in the history of land loss, resource alienation, and settler violence. Not everyone, however, shared the same answers to solving these systemic problems.

Kellogg wrote poetry and plays, lectured and performed, taught and studied, and traveled in order to "begin a movement." She was soon joined by other authors, educators, and intellectuals. In 1911, two years after the founding of the National Association for the Advancement of Colored People, she was one of six founders of the Society of American Indians, which held its inaugural meetings on Columbus Day in Columbus, Ohio. The founders first met in June in Kellogg's Wisconsin home to begin preparations for organizing what would become the first inter-tribal, or "pan-Indian," political association led by Native people. Kellogg served on the founding executive committee and became its secretary, the primary leadership position in the organization.[85]

Among the countless considerations confronting SAI organizers, whether to make the association open to non-Native peoples and to employees of the "Indian Service" generated much debate.[86] The society aspired to be unlike other "Indian rights" associations. Led by white ministers and social reformers, these largely Protestant-led groups had become assimilation's biggest champions.[87] Kellogg and the other founders rejected such philosophies. As they wrote:

> To-day the white man does not believe in Indian capacity—does not believe that he has either the intelligence or the dignity to hold such a Conference. . . . The Association seeks to bring about a condition whereby the white race and all races may have a better and broader knowledge of the red race [and] . . . its ability to contribute materially and spiritually to modern civilization.
>
> One of its high aims is to see the development of conditions whereby the Indian as an individual and as a race may take his place as a man among men, as an active member of the great commonwealth.[88]

It is unclear how Kellogg, the only woman among the SAI's founders, understood the patriarchal assumptions guiding the society's first pronouncements. The language and metaphors of a global "family of man" had guided imperialism for generations while also providing a tool for organizing colonized populations.[89] Assimilationist ideologies linked manhood and citizenship, and individualism with civilization. Allotment had become the culmination of nearly a century of efforts to impose Jeffersonian ideals of agrarian society and patriarchy onto Natives.

Euro-American gender norms were so pervasive that prominent SAI members, including Dr. Carlos Montezuma (Yavapai), debated whether the society should be exclusively male, despite the contributions of Kellogg and a generation of women activists including Emma Johnson (Potawatomi), Elizabeth Bender Cloud (Ojibwe), and Marie Louise Bottineau Baldwin (Ojibwe), among others. All were early SAI members, as was author Zitkála-Šá, or Gertrude Simmons Bonnin (Yankton Dakota), who retorted to Montezuma's suggestion: "Am I not as an Indian woman as capable to think on serious matters and as thoroughly interested in the race—as any one or two of your men put together? Why do you dare to leave us out?"[90]

Indigenous female advocacy became, in fact, a defining feature of the society. While membership concerns and public responses to developments in Indian Country characterized much of the SAI's first years, Kellogg, Zitkála-Šá, and others pressed for broader political reforms. Kellogg did so by calling for the restoration of traditional political forms that drew upon her community's centuries-long membership within the Iroquois Confederacy.

Kellogg's invocation of a durable "wampum strand . . . made to last eternal summers" was more than poetic. It referenced covenants made between nations, particularly treaties made by the United States and the Six Nations Council of the Confederacy. As discussed in chapter 3, the council was composed of members selected by Iroquois clan mothers whose matriarchal systems of political governance predated European contact.[91] For Kellogg, Native nations understood how to run their communities and maintained more equitable social and gender relations than those of Victorian Americans. Moreover, tribes possessed long-standing recognition of such capabilities. Their sovereignty was enshrined into American law through treaties as well as recognized internationally through long-standing diplomacy with England.

Progressive Era ideologies of individual uplift, personal restraint, and related moral emphases intruded upon Indigenous principles. They also counteracted the recognition of tribal sovereignty. When Kellogg spoke at the first meeting of the Society of American Indians in 1911, she rejected the tropes of modernization and civilization. Unlike many participants, she did not see herself as a "Red Progressive," as Indian reformers were often viewed.[92] As she proclaimed, "I am not the new Indian; I am the old Indian adjusted to new conditions."[93] She considered cultural continuity, not assimilation, to be essential to reforming Indian affairs. Political adaptation, rather than abandonment, informed her strategies for rebuilding reservation communities.

Drawing initially fifty members to Columbus, the SAI had over two hundred members at its 1913 meeting in Denver. Many, including Bottineau Baldwin, had received one of the society's initial four thousand invitations mailed in 1911. Raised in North Dakota and a longtime employee of the Education Division within the Indian Service, Bottineau Baldwin had met many of the society leaders in Washington before joining its executive committee. Though she was unable to travel to Kellogg's home for the first meeting, she sent letters that were read aloud. She was part of an emerging "urban Indian" community that drew members from across Indian Country and often confronted misconceptions on a daily basis. When census takers arrived at her home, for example, she failed to convince them that she was in fact an American Indian who resided in Washington. There was no space for Indians on the census form or in the imagination of those who oversaw it.[94]

Like other Native people navigating the challenges of modern America, Bottineau Baldwin was eager to join in the society. It was led by Native peoples, many of whom had found professional success and worked to use their education on behalf of Native America. She carried closely the invitation that followed. "Dear Fellow Indian," it began. "What is to be the future of the American Indian?"[95]

Among its many achievements, the society published a quarterly journal. Renamed in 1916 the *American Indian Magazine*, it initially published only articles written by Native authors. The society also proposed the creation of a national American Indian Day, which several states adopted, and it began "a community center movement to be instituted on the various reservations . . . [in order to bring] reservation Indians into a better understanding and more harmonious relationship with the civilization of the country."[96] Zitkála-Šá oversaw the first of its centers at Fort Duchesne, Utah, on the Uintah-Ouray Ute Reservation. In under a decade, the society held yearly conferences, drew increased attention to Native affairs and, for the first time in American history, offered a national Indian political organization.

The Vexed Place of Citizenship: Communal Sovereignty versus Individualism

Many of the Society's greatest legacies came after its demise in 1923. Formed to curb assimilation's most damaging practices and to rehabilitate tribal communities "materially and spiritually," the SAI deployed a host of strategies during its thirteen-year operation. In order to raise support for American Indian Day, Red Fox James of Montana rode on horseback to multiple state capitols to garner gubernatorial endorsements, which he presented to President Woodrow Wilson.[97] Others lectured about the harmful effects of U.S. commemorations that perpetuated racist ideologies, like Columbus Day. As its first "Report of the Executive Council" remarked, the society targeted that "part of the white race [that believed] that it has inherently superior rights and was morally justified in oppressing" Native peoples.[98]

So wide ranging were its concerns and so varied its strategies that the society ultimately succumbed to challenges of funding, leadership, and factionalism.[99] Regional and class divisions also divided the society, particularly regarding the expansion of the Native American Church. An inter-tribal religious movement that utilized peyote in its religious practices, the church attracted a wide and varied following. Many of its members in Oklahoma, Arizona, and Nebraska differed from the "educated, middle-class" SAI leaders who had more fully embraced Protestant denominations—several of them even became ministers.[100]

American ideologies of Indigenous disappearance remained so pervasive that arguing against them was often futile. Even seemingly positive commemorations offered variants of this pernicious dogma. As New York's *Evening Sun* reported in 1913 during the city's effort to build a "National American Indian Memorial" in its harbor larger than the Statue of Liberty, the Indian "race, whose practical disappearance from the continent can be but a matter of a few more years, should be perpetuated at least in memory."[101] As suffragist Anna Howard Shaw remarked upon the unveiling of a statute of Sacagawea at the Lewis and Clark Centennial and American Pacific Exposition and Oriental Fair in Portland, "Your tribe is fast disappearing from the land of your fathers. May we, the daughters of an alien race who slew your people and usurped your country, learn the lessons of calm endurance . . . in our efforts to lead men through the Pass of Justice."[102]

Confronting such representations strained society members. In its final years, many shifted their attention to Washington and spent increased time there hosting Indian delegations and lobbying Congress to achieve citizenship. Zitkála-Šá, for example, moved from Fort Duchesne to Washington in 1917 to lead lobbying efforts. At the society's annual meeting in 1919, the conference's theme was "American Citizenship for the Indians."[103]

As discussed in chapter 10, Indians were "excluded" from the Fourteenth Amendment and remained outside the nation's constitutional definitions of citizenship. They remained recognized political communities upon lands held in trust by the federal government, a relationship akin to a ward and its guardian. Many wondered how citizenship might complicate that relationship. Could tribal members be protected by the U.S. Constitution and remain dependent wards of the federal government, particularly if they lived within communities deemed by court officials to be outside "the customs and habits of civilization," as the Minnesota Supreme Court ruled in 1917, limiting Indian voting eligibility?[104]

Congress had the power to grant citizenship. In 1884, in yet another sign of the growth of congressional plenary power, the Supreme Court had ruled in *Elk v. Wilkins* that only an act of Congress could confer citizenship on Native peoples.[105] What such conferral would actually entail remained, however, to be determined.

In 1924 SAI lobbying helped advance the American Indian Citizenship Act, which ended the 137-year history of excluding Native Americans. This legislation followed the passage of the Nineteenth Amendment in 1920, another historic struggle, this one establishing women's suffrage. Many society members had worked to advance the passage of both, and after 1920 Zitkála-Šá and others urged suffragists to also push for Indian citizenship. Bottineau Baldwin spoke and marched at suffragist rallies, choosing to represent herself in either Ojibwe women's regalia or in her recently earned law school commencement robes.[106]

Indian service in World War I aided the cause to obtain citizenship. After Zitkála-Šá had been elected secretary of the SAI and became editor of its journal, she often justified the call for Indian citizenship by evoking the heroism of Native soldiers. Some of the most decorated veterans from the war were Indians. Three Choctaw soldiers in the Thirty-Sixth Division of the American Expeditionary Force, for example, won the French Croix de Guerre for their bravery, including Joseph Oklahombi from Oklahoma, who "under a violent barrage . . . rushed on Machine Gun nests, capturing 171 prisoners."[107] Choctaw runners and "code-talkers" were among Indians in several tribes who used their respective languages to transmit secure messages. Society members argued that such dedicated servicemen deserved the right to become U.S. citizens. "The Sioux are not picketing," one society article read, in a "campaign for rights and notes. . . . Their battle is broader. Their finest men are picketing on the war front in France and asking the world court if the defender of liberty is not entitled to its privileges."[108]

Citizenship, however, meant different things to various Native people. Not everyone agreed about its importance or meaning. Zitkála-Šá, who testified before the Senate during her lobbying efforts, considered her work getting the "Act through Congress granting citizenship to all Indians" among her greatest life achievements.[109] She spent several years after the society's demise working within reservation communities "to organize Indian voters." As she stated, "Only when the Indian wields his vote effectively will the system be reformed."[110]

Voting rights mattered more in the West than they had in earlier generations, and policy making had changed following statehood for Oklahoma (1907), Arizona (1912), and New Mexico (1912). Each holds large Indian populations. Once the domain of eastern reformers, Indian policy formation was becoming the province of western representatives.[111] Eighteen new senators had arrived from the West since 1889, and many society members participated in these elections.

In 1928 the Republican Party nominated Senator Charles Curtis from Kansas as Herbert Hoover's vice presidential candidate. A descendent of the Kaw Nation, which had been removed to Oklahoma in 1873, Curtis visited his tribe after winning the nomination. Chief Lucy Tayiah Eads presided over the festivities. She joined other council members in reminding Curtis of the tribe's outstanding land claims against the government, which totaled $15 million.[112]

Many believed that Curtis's election would lead to greater oversight and reform of Indian affairs. Zitkála-Šá joined other SAI members in helping to advise the Republican Party platform. Their recommendations included the creation of a national committee to advise the administration on the "repeal of any law and the termination of any administrative practice which may be inconsistent with Indian citizenship," while reminding that "the treaty and property rights of the Indians of the United States must be guaranteed."[113]

Despite her enthusiasm for Curtis and Indian voting, Zitkála-Šá held a complex view of citizenship. Her call for "layered citizenships" for Native peoples invoked a central paradox.[114] Citizenship was often seen as a form of political assimilation comparable to the individualization sought by allotment. Citizenship for her, however, was better than being a ward. As she wrote in *American Indian Stories* (1921), "Wardship is no substitute for American citizenship."[115] Being a ward of the United States government not only discriminated against Indian communities but also fostered graft:

> Do you know what *your* Bureau of Indian Affairs, in Washington, D.C., really is? . . . Behind the sham protection, which operated largely as a blind to publicity, have been at all times great wealth in the form of Indian fund[s] to be subverted; valuable lands, mines, oil fields, and other natural resources to be despoiled or appropriated. . . . This has been the situation in which the Indian Service has been for more than a century—the Indian during all this time having his rights and properties to greater or less extent neglected. . . . There is . . . an inducement to fraud, corruption, and institutional incompetence almost beyond the possibility of comprehension.[116]

Like Kellogg, Zitkála-Šá spent decades working at Indian schools, lecturing, publishing, and advocating for improved Indian affairs. U.S. citizenship appeared to her a necessary remedy for a broader illness. Citizenship alone could not resolve the structural problems that she so readily identified. Wardship was not working, but something more than citizenship would also be needed. As she suggested: "The Many treaties made in good faith with the Indian . . . we would like to see equitably settled."[117]

Treaties between Native nations and the federal government mandate alternative forms of political resolution for Native peoples. Native "rights" are collective, not individual. They have been negotiated with the federal government since its founding. Treaties ceded lands, established jurisdiction over them, and outlined structures of power between sovereigns. Native peoples have long prioritized communal power and autonomy over the rights of individuals.

While imposing draconian policies during Reconstruction, U.S. leaders had long recognized treaty commitments, which predated the Assimilation Era and remained legally binding. Treaties established the political boundaries of reservation communities, and for many Native leaders, "equity" necessitated ensuring that their respective jurisdictions remained in force. Moreover, reforming the "institutional incompetence" of the Indian Service did not mean abolishing it entirely, because the Office of Indian Affairs remained the only administrative agency capable of overseeing such reforms. Many SAI leaders had come to recognize this administrative burden and believed that legislative reforms and legal protections were essential steps toward building improved bilateral symmetry with Native nations. But although they were important steps, they were only partial ones.

Building reservation capacities remained equally important. Poverty and underemployment remained chronic problems across Indian Country. In 1929 Montana senator Burton Wheeler took to the radio after touring Indian reservations and juxtaposed the challenges confronting reservation families with those of "the wealthiest of all governments."[118]

Even Indian heroes, such as Jim Thorpe and Joseph Oklahombi, struggled to find employment. The Depression took particular toll on Oklahoma's Indian nations where each was raised. Thorpe was the most decorated U.S. Olympian of his generation and a prominent professional football organizer. Like many Oklahomans, he was forced to migrate during the Depression. He took a job as a security guard for Ford Motor Company in Dearborn, Michigan, and traveled often for various appearance fees. "All of my earnings," as he complained to former teammate Gus Welch (Ojibwe), "seem to be burning up on the road." Trouble with agents and divorce left him nearly propertyless:

"There can't be anything left for them to . . . take," he wrote.[119] War hero Oklahombi eventually found work loading lumber and coal for $2 a day, but he was laid off and forced to seek a veteran's pension to provide for his family.[120]

Such chronic hardships made policy reforms challenging, and challenges became even more difficult after "more than a century" of government mismanagement. Did Native activists believe that they could reform the Indian Service from within? After *Kagama, Lone Wolf,* and other Supreme Court rulings affirming the power of Congress to abrogate treaties, did activists think that they could use the legal system to address treaty violations? Were there other remedies for leveraging support for the ongoing injustices confronting Native peoples?

More questions than answers remained after the war. SAI leaders had organized an effective inter-tribal political association composed of members educated in Western schooling. Most were fluent in both their Native languages and English. They took pride in their bilingualism and cultural heritage and posed a stark collective rejoinder to the expectations of disappearance articulated by Pratt.

Their formal dress and contemporary styles also countered stereotypes of savagery and backwardness. The annual meetings, publications, and constant communications had also created an infrastructure for assessing national concerns. Citizenship had been conferred. The prospects, however, of regaining lost lands, curbing assimilation, and reforming the Indian Service remained distant. Land claims in particular required legal fees and took endless hours of time, lasting for years and even decades, especially within the U.S. legal system where the study of Indian law had little space.

Enduring reforms, however, did follow. They were led by former society members, particularly Kellogg and Roe Cloud, who continued their activism to advance their communities' individual and collective concerns. Meanwhile, across the country, other Native people drew inspiration from the SAI's years of organization and advocacy. They, too, mounted campaigns for land return that brought unexpected reforms.

Laura Cornelius Kellogg's Internationalism and Iroquois Advocacy

The end of World War I brought a flood of international attention to debates around "self-determination." President Wilson's vision of a postwar order run by the League of Nations seemed to offer opportunities for political representation, and for a few seasons after 1918, imperialism everywhere appeared to be teetering. The tsarist Russian empire was overthrown in March 1918, and waves of strikes swept Egypt, West Africa, and South Asia thereafter as anticolonial struggles emerged in the openings posed by inter-imperialist rivalries.[121]

Native leaders attempted to lodge their concerns within such arenas. Zitkála-Šá lobbied Wilson to appoint a Native representative for the postwar negotiations in Paris. "Who shall represent," she asked, our "cause at the World's Peace Conference?"[122] For centuries, Iroquois leaders had traveled the Atlantic, and on August 17, 1919, Kellogg was headed to Europe to, as a newspaper headline put it, "plead [the] cause of the Indians before the League of Nations."[123] Cayuga leader Levi General, or Deskaheh, also organized a visit to the League of Nations in 1920 as a delegate of the Confederacy Council at Six Nations Reserve in Canada.[124]

Kellogg wanted reform to be centered upon the Oneida community and others of the Iroquois Confederacy, which, as she wrote, "originated . . . about 600 years ago" and "planted the first seed of civilization" on the continent.[125] Iroquois leaders understood New York's history differently than had the audiences gathered for the Sullivan centennial. The Confederacy had not been vanquished. It maintained continued governing practices. Moreover, their treatment at the hands of Sullivan, Washington, and other revolutionary leaders was not only unjust but illegal. The seizure of their lands in upstate New York violated treaties made between the Confederacy and the early Republic; these were unconstitutional usurpations by the State of New York. Kellogg and other Iroquois leaders wanted their lands returned, particularly those taken from the Oneida. This dispossession had fueled the forced migration of Oneida families who eventually resettled in Wisconsin, including Kellogg's.[126]

Calls for the return of stolen lands have long animated Native American politics. Simon Pokagon attended the Chicago World's Fair in part to seek allies in his efforts to get Potawatomi lands returned under the provisions of the Treaty of Chicago of 1833. Obtaining the return of lands requires not just allies but also lawyers, courts, and above all judges who might see history differently. "Just look over the land," Kellogg pleaded, "and count the billions that have gone" into national "temples of worship," such as Mount Rushmore, whose construction started in 1927.[127]

Land claims challenges are not only costly but time consuming. As outlined in chapter 10, Lakota claims against the federal government for violations of the 1868 Fort Laramie Treaty only received judgment in the Supreme

Court in 1980. Oneida claims are even older. They predate the Constitution to 1785, when New York officials began twenty-seven land cessions against the tribe, only two of which had consent or approval from the federal government.[128] Only the federal government has the constitutional authority to take Indian lands into trust, making New York's seizure of Oneida lands illegal. For Kellogg, "Securing ties to the land, or at minimum collecting damages for illegal treaties, would provide a way for Oneidas and other Haudenosaunee people to become self-supporting."[129]

The economy, as Kellogg reminded, provides "the structure upon which all things depend." Any proposal to create a "social order which intends to rebuild a broken people . . . must have business."[130] Reestablishing economic self-sufficiency remained at the heart of her efforts at land reform.

The emphasis on the economy was rooted in notions not of individual progress but of collective empowerment. White leaders often believed that Indians remained unable to adopt ethics of thrift and savings. "The savage is concerned only with the immediate necessities of life, while the civilized man looks . . . only to the future," wrote railway man Walter Camp in his 1920 report "The Condition of Reservation Indians."[131] Camp criticized Native people for "lacking . . . industry. . . . The dearth of capital is an effect not the cause of his poverty," concluding matter-of-factly that "the Indian is not a capitalist."[132]

Kellogg's economic philosophies took aim at such presumptions. Binary assumptions about "savage" versus "civilized" have doomed Indians to disappearance, thereby erasing contemporary land and economic concerns. Unlike the myths of American history, Indian land transfers and economic challenges occurred at actual times and places. These histories were recorded, translated into legal documents that concerned real lands and property. An archive of both knowledge and documentary power flows from each land cession, a process established by Native and non-Native participants alike.

Federal Indian law reflects a different vision of history than that animating popular and scholarly discourses. Indian law's genealogy is rooted in the land, in treaties and negotiations, and in documents. New York's many land seizures did not matter to Craft during the Sullivan Centennial, but they have mattered to Iroquois leaders since the eighteenth century. In 1795, for example, Oneida leaders settled their first suit against New York's Madison and Oneida Counties over county-owned lands. They have filed subsequent suits ever since.[133] By 1920, Kellogg had worked on land concerns across the country. In Wisconsin, much of her efforts centered not on reacquiring title to the many reservation allotments recently lost but on the one-hundred-acre Oneida Boarding School. Built in 1893, it was home to 160 students and twenty-four employees in 1914. It closed in 1919 and was sold to the Catholic Diocese of Green Bay. Kellogg tried to convince the superintendent to turn the facility into a day school in order to keep its operations running. Unlike Carlisle and off-reservation boarding schools, reservation boarding schools educated students within rather than outside their communities. They also generally educated students from the same community rather than from across the continent.

Kellogg had an ambitious vision to turn the school into a revenue-generating facility with a canning factory and farm. Unlike their nearby Menominee neighbors in central Wisconsin, the Oneida had been hit hard by allotment, and economic self-sufficiency seemed a necessary step for survival. As detailed in chapter 12, the Menominee had, in contrast, a vibrant lumber economy and an incorporated mill that generated both revenue and jobs.[134]

Kellogg was a part of a network fighting for land reforms and economic improvement. Whether acquiring title to a former school—which her tribe eventually purchased in 1984—or pursuing recognition at the League of Nations, Iroquois activists devised various strategies aimed at regaining lost territories. Many of these battles were costly, and Kellogg organized the Six Nations Club to raise awareness and funds. "We had not the means at our disposal to fight [fully] for our heritage," the *Milwaukee Journal* reported her saying in 1923 under the headline "Council Fires Blaze Again; Oneidas Astir."[135]

The Six Nations Club had approached the Iroquois Confederacy Council at Onondaga to garner support. The organization aimed to build a network across Iroquois communities—in New York, Wisconsin, Oklahoma, and Canada—to raise funds from individual tribal members. Similar to the forms of African American community empowerment articulated by Marcus Garvey and his Universal Negro Improvement Association, it was to be, in Kellogg's view, an Iroquois-wide "business model of identifying investors to fund the litigation of the claim; these 'investors' would then share in any reward, as members of the Six Nations Confederacy."[136] They issued enrollment cards as receipts to contributing members.

The "claim" at the time was a recent decision by the U.S. Circuit Court of Appeals for the Second Circuit, *United States v. Boylan* (1920). In 1919 Iroquois leaders had encouraged federal lawyers to file suit on their behalf over a contested thirty-two-acre parcel of land that Oneida leaders claimed had never been dispossessed. The state of New York had tried to sell it off and evict Oneida members. The court ruled that the lands in question could not be sold as the state of New York lacked jurisdiction over Oneida lands; the federal government possessed "sole authority to dispose Indian lands."[137] The decision was upheld on appeal, and in 1942 the court further decreed that New York had no jurisdiction over Seneca lands, reaffirming the *Boylan* decision.

Legal advocacy characterized much of Kellogg's efforts after *Boylan*. She continued her fund-raising activities and joined efforts led by New York assemblyman Edward A. Everett to clarify the state's outstanding Iroquois land claims. The resulting commission and its 1922 report affirmed Oneida claims at issue in *Boylan* and outlined other potential Iroquois claims, such as Mohawk claims at Akwesasne (St. Regis) along the Canadian border.[138] Kellogg and others had now established an effective land rights strategy, and she continued to build ties across Iroquoia. She also sought to revive Oneida leadership titles associated with matrilineal lineages and hosted delegations of leaders in Wisconsin.[139]

Kellogg's tireless advocacy prompted government scrutiny and tribal dissent. Many rejected her defiance and sought more stable ways of navigating reservation life, especially after the Great Depression deepened the tribe's challenges.[140] Kellogg had called, for example, for tribal members not to pay allotment taxes, and she advocated for the abolishment of the Indian Service. Kellogg's fund-raising also brought charges of fraud, leading to her arrest in Canada.

Notwithstanding such allegations, Kellogg offered an emancipatory vision of the future that differed from those of policy makers. Unlike other SAI leaders, who focused on legislative reforms, she advocated for land returns. For her, reservation priorities took precedence, and she worked to provide immediate relief to reservation families. When in 1929 the Senate solicited testimony for its "Survey of Conditions of Indians in the United States," Kellogg outlined her concerns in a statement that embodied much of her activist philosophy: "The effect upon the social life, upon the everyday life, of these Indians in these reservations is something that we cannot endure and we will not endure."[141]

Allotment, Race, and the Meriam Report's "Problem of Indian Administration"

By the end of the 1920s, reservation concerns had attracted national scrutiny. Partly due to SAI activism, "America's Indian Problem," as Zitkála-Šá titled her last essay in *American Indian Stories* (1921), now garnered media coverage and the focus of policy makers.[142] Magazines, such as *Forum* in 1924, ran opposing articles debating "the question of whether the Indian should be encouraged to preserve his individuality, tradition, arts, and customs, or be received into the melting pot."[143]

After half a century, the campaign for assimilation had failed to incorporate Native peoples. Tribal communities maintained cultural ties and communal traditions that defied assimilationist efforts. Although they lost extensive tracts of their reservations due to allotment, they continued to welcome their children home, helping them reintegrate into tribal life after their many seasons away.[144] Many maintained their children's Indian names, rejecting those imposed by white teachers. Blackfeet names, for example, "were rich with meaning and significance. Names expressed the intertwined and interwoven histories and stories of relationships between humans and the supernatural world. Told collectively, Blackfeet names constituted a continuous narrative of the people, places, events, and history."[145]

Boarding school graduates had endured years of discipline, loneliness, and deprivation. Untold thousands died in institutional settings that became prone to disease. Some graduated and never returned. Others tried to find strength in their experiences. Zitkála-Šá never forgot her hardships as a young girl taken away from her Dakota family to a missionary school, where on her first day she was "dragged out [of her room] . . . carried downstairs and tied fast in a chair. . . . I cried aloud, shaking my head all the while until I felt the cold blades of scissors against my neck, and hear[d] them gnaw off one of my thick braids."[146] It was then, she wrote, that "I lost my spirit. Since the day I was taken from my mother I had suffered extreme indignities. . . . No one came to comfort me. . . . Not a soul reasoned quietly with me . . . I was only one of many little animals driven by a herder."[147] As for her conversion to Christianity, when presented with a Bible after returning home, she "took it from her [mother's] hand . . . but . . . did not read it. . . . My enraged spirit felt more like burning the book."[148] *American Indian Stories* indicts the assimilation campaign and underscores many of the paradoxes of federal policy, as those who endured assimilation's educational practices became its most vocal critics.

Similar indictments informed a series of policy reviews. The chronic economic disparities across reservations, researchers concluded, were the result of federal policy, not intrinsic "to the nature of the Indian."[149] Allotments had devastated Indian economies, as had the federal mismanagement of reservation oil, timber, and grazing leases. Begun in the 1870s with paternalistic discourses about uplift, the assimilation campaign by 1920 had devolved into a campaign to integrate native resources into the American economy.[150] While the Indian Service acted as trustees in these leases, it failed to guarantee that the Indians received the maximum return from their lands.[151]

The "institutional incompetence" that Zitkála-Šá critiqued was often intentional. Reservation superintendents, railway developers, and western ranchers conspired to use Indian lands for their gain, doing so with little thought for the development of tribes. Such collusion was common. For example, superintendent Henry Armstrong at the Crow Agency rented a massive tract of reservation lands to ranchers in 1884.[152] Unfortunately for Armstrong, he had leased to ranchers from Colorado—not Montana—provoking the ire of cattlemen from the Billings Board of Trade who expected local ranchers to be the beneficiaries of reservation lands.

Assimilation, in short, benefited whites and failed Indians. It had also become a national disgrace. Throughout the 1920s, Indian activists, policy makers, and concerned citizens identified faults in the government's policy. Such attention, however, disappeared during the Great Depression as economic hardship became a national experience that pushed Indian affairs outside the media. From 1929 to 1934, no national magazines or the *New York Times* carried any coverage of Indian economic issues.[153] Before then, however, the focus was different. Reservation communities stood in such stark contrast to the nation's affluence, a juxtaposition that opened potential windows of reform. Kellogg's invitation to testify to the Senate, for example, followed a furious twenty-four months of policy review, including the delivery to Congress of the 1928 Meriam Report, named after its survey director Lewis Meriam. The Senate Committee on Indian Affairs had also conducted a survey between 1928 and 1933 that brought senators to large reservations to investigate complaints against the Indian Service.[154]

Begun in 1926 by the secretary of the Interior and conducted by the Brookings Institution, the Meriam Report leveled a devastating critique of federal policy. It provided the most thorough assessment of federal Indian policy ever produced. As the opening sentence of the nearly nine-hundred-page report, *The Problem of Indian Administration*, states, "An overwhelming majority of Indians are poor, even extremely poor, and they are not adjusted to the economic and social system of the dominant white civilization."[155]

The research team chronicled the innumerable challenges of reservation economies, concluding, "There is little evidence of anything which could be termed an economic program."[156] Allotments had failed to bring about socioeconomic development. Individual properties had become taxed, alienated, and divided among heirs. Inheritance, moreover, was difficult "to be determined. . . . In some case the heirs were numerous and records of their relationship poor."[157] Any money gained from leases confronted similar problems—the costs of wills were prohibitive. In short, rather than generating development, individual capital and property fueled divisions among families and created costly administrative problems. Allotment's goal of individual self-sufficiency had become harmful and unjust.

While family relations, kinship structures, and gendered age-grade societies varied across Native America, by and large Indians did not live within nuclear family structures. Many lived in interrelated households where male and female authority operated within overlapping but discrete realms. Grandparents and elders usually lived with children and relatives, often in adjoining cabins or lodges.

Allotment targeted such family structures and their domestic economies. It attempted to turn men into landowners and heads of patriarchal households. Tribes such as the Blackfeet resisted such efforts. They fought to get their "surplus" lands allotted to other tribal members rather than exclusively male heirs. Bands within the tribe also defied efforts to compete with one another in annual contests between the reservation's twenty-nine agricultural districts. The prize in these competitions was an imported steer, and districts could lose points if they failed to maintain the "appearance of home" or owned less valued household animals, particularly dogs, which continued to run freely across the reservation.[158]

Moreover, families continued their communal economies, such as seasonal fishing in the Northwest, wild rice and maple sugar gatherings in the Great Lakes, and herding in the Southwest. "I am real anxious to have her here while we make maple sugar," a father from Cass Lake, Minnesota, wrote to his daughter's boarding school in spring 1924.[159] Another parent encouraged administrators to "do the right thing" and send their child home for gatherings.[160]

Wage earning and allotments challenged communal practices. They imposed external economic and gender values upon tribal communities. As always, racial assumptions guided these impositions. Indians who farmed, wore Western clothes, lived in single-family households, and spoke English more resembled white citizens. Government understandings of race rewarded "white" behavior. Even the simple preference of where to sit became a sign of the era's new dialectics of race and resistance. Just as delegates to Washington, such as Red Cloud in 1870, insisted on sitting on the floor, Blackfeet families tended to keep much of their living room empty of furniture, as elders did not like to sit on chairs.[161]

Race had facilitated allotment's formation, but determining who was eligible for allotments brought new challenges. Reservation census taking facilitated such processes. Starting in the late 1800s and continuing throughout the twentieth century, the Indian Service oversaw censuses that used fractional determinations of "Indian blood," or "blood status," to determine tribal membership rolls.[162]

Like allotment, such racial determinations devastated Indian Country. Race divided individuals and families based on external understandings of ethnicity. As discussed in chapter 10, some tribes lost over 80 or even 90 percent of their reservations during the Assimilation Era. "Blood rolls" facilitated and furthered such alienation by limiting the number of descendants eligible for inheritance and by establishing fixed racial assessments for such eligibility. Not coincidentally, the fewer people eligible for allotment, the more "surplus" reservation lands could be opened to external development.

Census rolls fueled what eventually became known as degrees of Indian "blood quantum."[163] Tribal censuses established external forms of "Indian blood" that posed additional "problems of administration." Designed by policy makers with the goal of incorporating Indian bodies and lands into the nation, such laws continue to challenge Native nations.

Henry Roe Cloud and Elizabeth Bender Cloud's Shared Visions of Empowerment

Unlike other members of the Meriam Commission, Henry Roe Cloud lived through many of these experiences. Born and raised on the Winnebago (Ho-Chunk) Reservation in Nebraska within a community removed from its Wisconsin homelands, he was the commission's only Native author.[164] By 1928 he and Elizabeth Bender Cloud had each devoted twenty years to reforming federal Indian policy. Like other SAI members, they hoped to reverse assimilation and institute policies that would strengthen tribal autonomy. "There is a close relationship between the loss of land and the health and prosperity of the Indian people," Roe Cloud stated in a speech at Pine Ridge, South Dakota.[165] Improving the "health and prosperity of the Indian people" became the Clouds' lifelong commitment.

Even before Roe Cloud joined the commission, the Clouds developed prac-

An aerial view of the American Indian Institute. In contrast to boarding schools run by the Bureau of Indian Affairs or those administered by missionaries, at the institute Native students learned from Native teachers who prioritized tribal knowledge and encouraged students to take pride in their Indigenous identities. (*American Indian Institute [Roe Institute] from Above, Wichita, Kan.*, G.E.E. Lindquist Papers, The Burke Library Archives [Columbia University Libraries] at Union Theological Seminary, New York.)

tices that challenged the mythology of Indigenous disappearance. They did so by educating students at the American Indian Institute, which opened in 1915 in Wichita, Kansas, and transformed a generation of students. They ran the school until fund-raising became too challenging during the Depression.[166]

The Clouds hoped to strengthen tribal capacities by educating young Indian men differently, and they had planned to expand the school to include women. They emphasized academic pedagogy and also prioritized, rather than punished, tribal knowledge. As articulated in the Meriam Report, the Clouds countered prevailing notions that "some Indian children [are] 'not worthy of an education beyond the grades.'"[167]

The institute hired Native teachers who incorporated oral traditions, folk tales, and Indian languages into the curriculum. Roe Cloud urged students to analyze their own creation stories and to compare them with European folklore. Some, he noted, are "romantic, some heroic, some satire, humor and adventure, and a great many of them teach moral allegiance."[168]

The Clouds understood that the failures of Indian education were not intrinsic to Native people but to the vocational, punitive structures of boarding schools. As Roe Could wrote in 1914, "The difficulty lies in the system rather than in the race."[169] The Clouds knew this faulty system well. A graduate of Mount Hermon School in Massachusetts and Yale University, Roe Cloud began his schooling at Nebraska's Winnebago Industrial School.[170] At age five, he had seen his older brother "seized" by police and taken away to school.[171] The same soon happened to him. Washing clothes in the school laundry, however, did not provide much learning, and he "nursed a growing hatred" of the monotony of vocational education. "Such work is not educative," he later argued. "It begets a hatred of work, especially where there is no pay. . . . The Indian will work under such conditions [only] because he is under authority."[172] Such "industrial" education exploited youth and did nothing to prepare them "to grapple with" their communities' problems.[173]

Elizabeth Bender was from northern Minnesota near the White Earth Reservation. One of ten children, she attended Catholic school at age ten before being sent to the Pipestone Industrial School. As she recalled, "I had two sisters and two brothers there. . . . We had to spend a term of three years before we were allowed to return home."[174] In 1903 she joined four siblings at Hampton Institute. They all likely heard Theodore Roosevelt's commencement address in 1906.

While each had spent time in faraway institutions, the Clouds maintained ties to their families and tribal communities. They returned in summers and whenever they could. They also became devoted to other Native peoples in their new environments. They helped to form "hubs" for intellectual and social development, using new social relationships in their advocacy.[175]

Roe Cloud drew upon his ties to missionaries and Yale alumni to fund the institute, while Bender Cloud followed her sister Anna into the Indian Service. She taught on the Blackfeet Reservation and worked as a nurse at Fort Belknap, where she advocated for treatment of the reservation's trachoma. "Nearly thirty percent of Indian children are in danger of becoming blind," she wrote in 1915 in the *Southern Workman*.[176] An educator and healthcare provider, she oversaw much of the institute's affairs, particularly during Roe Cloud's travels. "All the responsibility of school affairs seems to fall on my shoulders," she wrote.[177]

Housed in a college basement in its first year, the institute's campus grew to include multiple dormitories, a teacher's cottage, a barn and agricultural facilities, an entryway driveway, and the Cloud family home. It accepted over a dozen students a year. Roe Cloud traveled more frequently throughout the 1920s, particularly during his work on the commission.

Fund-raising required constant travel, as did working with Ho-Chunk leaders, whom he accompanied to Washington in 1912 after graduating from Yale in 1910.[178] Roe Cloud prided himself on his friendship with President Howard Taft's son, future senator Robert Taft, against whom he debated and won prizes. Such competition drew upon long-standing traditions of Ho-Chunk soldier cultural responsibilities: "I began to realize that I can do things just as this man can and somehow my spirit became ready for . . . any sort of battle."[179]

His educational attainment distinguished Roe Cloud from other Native guests in Washington, often dramatically. In March 1911 Hopi leaders visited to protest their community's incarceration for refusing to accept boarding school programs. Some had been sent to government prisons, such as Alcatraz, for refusing instruction, and internal divisions had divided their community at Orayvi.[180] As Chief Yukeoma implored Taft, "We don't want schools and school teachers. We want to be let alone to live as we wish . . . without the white man always there to tell us what we must do."[181]

Hopi leaders struggled to find solutions to these impositions, developing unique solutions. One leader, Tawaquaptewa, successfully pleaded to accompany seventy Hopi children to Sherman Indian Institute in 1906, while in 1907 eleven prisoners agreed to attend Carlisle together, including Louis Tewanima, a future U.S. Olympian.[182]

The American Indian Institute offered alternatives to these problems. Native students applied, were not restrained, and could return to their communities to visit family or attend ceremonies. There was no corporal punishment. The Clouds' fluency in navigating government institutions offered opportunities for students, but challenges remained. Meriam understood that the commission was well served by Henry's involvement: "Mr. Cloud has a wide acquaintanceship among the Indians . . . and had been active for years in constructive work on their behalf. The result was the one hoped for, namely, that Indians would come to him . . . [as] part of the work of the survey."[183] In fact, many believed that his leadership, experience, and visibility positioned Roe Cloud to become commissioner of Indian Affairs, a position he desired. In 1933 Navajo leaders requested that he be appointed.[184]

Roe Cloud had even written to Meriam "asking for the endorsement from the survey" members.[185] Meriam, however, expressed doubts. "I do not think the position would bring anything but bitterness and disappointment. . . . The job would be a deadly one, and particularly for Henry . . . because he would feel that tremendous responsibility to his own race."[186]

Despite his respect for Roe Cloud, Meriam was ambivalent about the request. So, too, was commission member Edward Dale, a professor at the University of Oklahoma who had studied under Frederick Jackson Turner and worked for decades to expand Turner's theory of frontier history.[187] While professing his admiration for Henry, whom he considered "like a Brother," Dale wrote to Meriam, "I do not think that Henry is the man for the job. . . . [He] would undoubtedly be subject to pressures and demands that would be very puzzling to him."[188]

Notwithstanding their years of working together under Meriam and Roe Cloud's unwavering dedication to the cause—in summer 1927 he moved his family to Maryland in order to complete the report—his white colleagues were not convinced that he possessed the capability to oversee the Indian Service. Despite his commitment, his recognition across the Capitol, and his years of leadership at the institute, Roe Cloud was passed over for commissioner. Even outperforming President Taft's son Robert was apparently insufficient training for such an appointment.

The Great Depression and the Indian New Deal

The year 1929 brought tragedy to countless American families, including the Clouds, who suffered a very personal loss as well. Their only son, Henry Jr., died of pneumonia at age three. They commemorated his life and engraved above the fireplace at their institute home: "To the memory of 'Little Henry' and the glory of all childhood."[189]

Love for family and other Native people guided the Clouds during the institute's operations. "Never be ashamed that you are an American Indian or Native of Alaska," Roe Cloud told the graduating class of 1949 in Mount Edgecumbe, Alaska.[190] Such love and pride stood in perpetual contrast to boarding schools and their indiscriminate and arbitrary authority. As he reported from the Rosebud Boarding School in South Dakota, conditions were awful and punishments severe. Runaways were common. Several boys, he wrote, "froze to death by running away. This year three girls ran away. . . . One girl was made to carry a ball and chain around her ankle, and push a wheelbarrow for hours in front of the whole school."[191]

Breaking the punitive structure of education was imperative, and upon his appointment in 1933 as superintendent of Haskell Indian Institute, Roe Cloud instituted new philosophies and practices. In his first act, he closed the Haskell jail, a common feature of the military-styled facilities established by Pratt.[192] He dismissed school employees known for their harsh discipline and broke Haskell's long-standing ties with the local National Guard unit, which had supplied military uniforms, officers, and drilling equipment, a practice that other schools followed.[193] A new era at the institution had begun, and in 1935, after only two years as superintendent, he helped twenty-eight students gain admission to the University of Kansas.[194]

Destructive educational, land, and cultural practices had guided the assimilation campaign since its inception. Stories of Hopi fathers imprisoned at Alcatraz, Lakota girls in shackles, and the frozen bodies of children running to their families were shared by generations of Indian families. All Native nations experienced related forms of shame, punishment, and deprivation. Such injustices had fueled a generation of activism.

These negative outcomes, however, were the goal of the federal government. Unless national policies changed, assimilation would continue. New laws were needed. By comparison, Canada shared many similar educational policies; however, its government did not fund schools as extensively as in the United States, delegating oversight to Christian denominations. As the Depression crippled the economy, funding became restricted, and the cost of food rose. Accordingly, many schools, such as the Presbyterian school at Kenora, Ontario, adopted austere policies, such as selling bread to its students.[195] Inspectors toured these facilities and made damning reports that students were being "insufficiently fed," and that "the only meal I have actually seen was one at mid-day which consisted of a piece of bread and a raw carrot."[196] With limited national oversight, children suffered. The complaints of their parents were even censured by school administrators. As the Canadian Truth and Reconciliation Commission, begun in 2008, concluded, austerity and neglect underscored "the government's failure to provide schools with the resources needed to feed students adequately. . . . It was the students who paid the price—in more ways than one."[197]

In the United States, by contrast, the assimilation campaign began to unravel during the Depression. Like the disasters wrought by the nation's unregulated economy, the failures of assimilation exposed the need for more than incremental reform.[198] The Senate's 1929 survey of Indian affairs had toppled the administration of Commissioner Charles Burke, who had served since 1921 and was now replaced by Charles Rhoads, not Henry Roe Cloud. A former president of the Indian Rights Association, Rhoads left a limited legacy in office—that is, until he returned to Indian policy after World War II and reaffirmed his belief that "assimilation must be the dominant goal of public policy."[199] By 1930 the Depression so destroyed the popularity of Hoover that there was little his commissioner could accomplish. As in Canada, Congress withdrew funding for Indian affairs, and malaise and malnutrition stalked Native nations.

Republicans like Taft and Hoover had dominated a half century of U.S. politics. In addition to the racist evaluations from Meriam, Roe Cloud's close ties with the Taft family and their Republican allies likely contributed to Roe Cloud not being considered for federal appointments, and like many, the Clouds spent the first years of the Depression trying to keep their careers at the institute stable while continuing to work for the Indian Service. In the years ahead, Henry accepted more government assignments: in 1932 he was sent to Neah Bay, Washington, to review complaints made by the Makah against their reservation's superintendent, whom the tribal council had petitioned for removal. Often absent and beholden to local traders who profited from the tribe's timber and fishing beds, the superintendent, Roe Cloud described, "thunders out authority and commands without obedience from any sources."[200] Meticulous and expansive, his report recommended not only the superintendent's removal but also a reorganization of the region's superintendencies, recommendations that Commissioner Burke accepted.

After his appointment at Haskell, Roe Cloud continued to advocate for Indian reforms under the new commissioner of Indian Affairs, John Collier. While the Meriam Report failed to propel its authors into positions of national leadership, its critiques resonated with reformers such as Collier. Active in social welfare circles in New York and California, Collier moved to New Mexico in 1920 and became involved with Indian policy reforms. He joined Pueblo land rights and religious freedom campaigns and worked in the newly formed American Indian Defense Association, which targeted Burke's administration, whose mismanagement of Pueblo lands, water rights, and religious freedoms generated national attention.

For example, upon Burke's arrival to Taos Pueblo in 1924 with Interior secretary Hubert Work, the superintendent informed Burke of the tribe's refusal to send all of their children to school. As they had for centuries, they kept a number of young men home in order to offer rites of religious initiation. Congress, however, had passed a 1920 law requiring all Indian children to attend schools and instructing the commissioner of Indian Affairs "to make and enforce such rules and regulations as may be necessary to secure the enrollment . . . of eligible Indian children who are wards of the government."[201] Congress additionally authorized the commissioner of Indian Affairs to "forcibly" enroll them at "whatever government boarding schools" he should designate. The superintendent now advised Burke to do just that and to "arrest the governor and a few of the leading men and incarcerate them in jail."[202] Conflict, rather than partnership, characterized the situation; as the All-Pueblo Council later wrote, Burke and Secretary Work had allegedly also "called us 'half-animal.'"[203]

As the Clouds and other reformers maintained, violence accompanied assimilation, and Collier's critiques extended such advocacy. Before becoming commissioner, his proposals did three important things: they echoed SAI suggestions, amplified those from the Meriam Report, and added further pressure for national reform. When Collier moved to Washington to lobby Congress, he gained entry into policy circles that eventually positioned him for his selection as commissioner in 1933.[204] His administration quickly became the most consequential in U.S. history.

Like other New Deal leaders, Collier pushed a series of legislative reforms through Congress. In short succession, he and others in the Department of the Interior, including its assistant solicitor Felix Cohen, wrote and achieved passage of the Pueblo Relief Bill (1933) and the Indian Reorganization Act (1934). Each brought statutory reforms in land, funding, and political practices.

Collectively, these initial reforms sparked an ideological reorientation of federal Indian policy. Cohen gained more and more understanding of the challenges confronting both tribes and the federal government, prompting an interpretive revolution in the study of federal Indian law. Having initially "never given the 'Indian problem' a shred of thought," by the time he resigned from the Interior in 1946, he had institutionalized the practice and study of federal Indian law through his litigation on behalf of tribes, drafting of legislation, and the "monumental task" of authoring the *Handbook of Federal Indian Law* (1941).[205] Few employees of the federal government have ever so heavily impacted Indian affairs.

Among its key provisions, the Indian Reorganization Act (IRA) ended the allotment system, encouraged self-government and the drafting of tribal constitutions, and closed numerous schools while increasing resources of local education. Additionally, by providing relief to Pueblo and other tribes for lost lands, the Collier administration validated long-standing land claims concerns. Significantly, the IRA also attempted to reorganize the existing political structures governing tribal communities and to enshrine into federal law recognized self-governance for tribal communities operating with their own constitutions.

Each piece of legislation was an achievement for Indian reformers. Their collective passage represented a sea change in federal Indian policy. For the first time in U.S. history, the federal government used its administrative powers, legislative authority, and budgetary resources to support Native American self-governance. It recognized tribal rights to land, cultural autonomy, and oversight over their own communities. In words, actions, and beliefs, federal officials worked with Native nations, which were no longer seen as disappearing from the American body politic. While popular culture and scholarly discourses still contributed to the mythology of Indian disappearance, within the federal government, partnerships with tribal communities emerged and in some cases even flourished. The Supreme Court soon followed suit: in 1941 it tackled the pressing question of whether the taking of federally protected reservation lands was constitutional.

Activism at the Local and National Levels: The Origins of the Hualapai Decision

Activism took many forms during the half century of efforts to reverse assimilation. Countless reservation families developed strategies to mitigate the effects of land loss, child removal, and repression. Navajo leaders including Chief Manuelito implored their community to "learn new things from the Americans" but to do so selectively, maintaining communal values and practices while accessing U.S. education as a ladder upon which the Navajo "would again rise to independence."[206] Subsequent Navajo leaders such as Chee Dodge continued Manuelito's teachings, reminding, "Education is the ladder. Tell our people to take it."[207]

Remembering the harshness of the boarding school experiences, however, many families avoided schooling for their children. In 1919 only 2,089 out of an estimated 9,613 children from the Navajo Nation attended schools.[208] In countless acts of everyday resistance, families hid their children from government officials to limit the damaging effects of assimilation.

Many SAI members had worked as teachers, nurses, and administrators within the Indian Service. Thousands of other Indian peoples also labored as staff and vocational instructors. Ironically, despite their rhetoric, which claimed to train students to live in mainstream society, boarding schools actually prepared Indian students for employment within the Indian Service.[209] Over time a generation had worked within it. In 1888 only 25 Native people were employed by boarding schools; by 1905 453 worked within them.[210] In

1906 16 graduates of the Chilocco Indian School alone were working in government schools as printers, matrons, and harness makers, though rarely as teachers.[211] Native people, in short, staffed the schools designed to assimilate them.

When reservation members sought remedies to their problems, they encountered superintendents who rarely provided relief. In fact, as the Hopi disputes at Orayvi indicated, superintendents often used force to suppress dissent and enforce policies. The endless stream of Indian delegations to Washington signaled an inability of reservation officials to address their concerns. Moreover, the government directed its resources—budgets, staffing, and infrastructure—to advancing assimilation, not reforming Indian affairs, and few federal employees were attentive to structural concerns or possessed the requisite authority to mitigate them. Their authority enforced existing assimilation laws and disciplined reservation members into compliance.

Reservation leaders understood such imbalances. They sought strategies to reverse them. Many anticipated that boarding school graduates would return to their community to improve the punitive systems around them. Crow leaders encouraged Robert and Susie Yellowtail to attend distant schools in California and Massachusetts before returning to Montana. As mentioned in chapter 10, Susie returned home to practice nursing at the Crow Agency Hospital, while Robert became superintendent of Crow Agency during the New Deal, the first Native person to hold such a position within their own community.[212] "This is something I never dreamed of," remarked interim superintendent Warren L. O'Hara as he watched Yellowtail's inauguration along with three thousand tribal members.[213]

Yellowtail attended Sherman Indian School in Riverside, California. He possibly took classes with Kellogg, who started teaching there in 1902. The employment of Indian teachers inspired Native students, and the Yellowtails' advocacy soon resembled that of SAI leaders and earlier generations of Crow leaders, including the venerable leader Plenty Coups, whose multiple trips to Washington had positioned him alongside world leaders.[214] In 1932, when Yellowtail greeted his reservation's new superintendent, he echoed many SAI pronouncements. Just as Kellogg had testified to the Senate, he declared that tribes maintained "rights which we insist shall be respected by the Washington officials and their subordinates in the field."[215]

In what would become a key feature of twentieth-century Native American politics, local and national advocacy efforts developed ongoing connections during the Assimilation Era. Reservation leaders and national reformers increasingly reinforced one another's advocacy, often outside of public notice. While the SAI often focused on policy reforms, reservation members concentrated on largely local issues. Such leaders included Fred Mahone, a former Chilocco student, World War I veteran, and concerned Hualapai tribal member.[216]

As he awaited deployment overseas in 1918, Mahone wrote to the commissioner of Indian Affairs Cato Sells announcing his intentions to persuade Native people to "make up our mind to be . . . modern in the History of today."[217] His letter included a proposal for a new tribal organization for his community, and upon his return from service he became his tribe's most vocal spokesperson.

Like other veterans and SAI members, Mahone connected modernity with pride in his community and a commitment to fight against injustices. Raised in the Hualapai Nation of Arizona along the Colorado River, Mahone dedicated decades to redressing the seizure of one-third of his tribe's reservation by the Atchison, Topeka and Santa Fe Railroad. The company had received land grants that cut across millions of acres of tribal lands, including Navajo, Pueblo, Havasupai, Yavapai, Chemehuevi, Mojave, and Hualapai lands south of the Grand Canyon.[218] The railway laid its first tracks in 1883, shortly after the reservation was established by executive order on January 4—twelve years after Congress ended the treaty-making process.

Trains consume much water, and the spring well at Peach Springs, which the tribe had historically used, became a key station for the company. However, when tribal members came to water their herds or gather for their gardens, the company charged them for it. Railway leaders pointed to early land sales from local non-Indians as the basis for their use of Peach Springs. Tribal members disagreed with the railway, pointing out that the springs were clearly within the reservation's boundaries. Absent a formal treaty, however, federal officials paid little initial notice. Hualapai leaders remembered earlier run-ins with the superintendent. Like nearby Hopi families, one of their leaders, Quiwhatanava, had also been sent to Alcatraz for resisting federal policies.[219]

Unsurprisingly, like many Native nations, the Hualapai confronted reservation agents allied against them. At best, superintendents expressed sympathy for the conditions confronting the tribe but did little about them. At worst, they imprisoned their leaders, rented their lands to corporations and outsiders, and then left for other appointments or jobs. Additionally, as happened with so many grievances sent to Washington, Sells did not respond to Mahone's letter. His administration, like Burke's, espoused assimilation, and in 1919 the railway was also among the most powerful corporations in the West.

Mahone's activism, however, was unrelenting, as was his faith in his cause. As he and other tribal members knew, the railway was using lands that did not belong to it. Regaining the use of their lands and developing them for themselves became their focus. President "Chester A. Arthur set aside and reserved [these lands] for the use and occupancy of the Hualapai Indians," Mahone wrote. "It is our desire to make this [reservation] our everlasting home for ourselves and our future generations."[220] Much like Kellogg and other SAI leaders, Mahone understood, as Roe Cloud stated, the "close relationship between the loss of land and the health and prosperity" of his tribe.

The Hualapai believed that their reservation, to which they held exclusive title for use and occupancy, had been illegally seized by the railway. They drew upon history—the tribe's 1883 executive order, their historic use of the springs, their recognition as a distinct and free community—to establish their claims. They countered government and corporate assertions that they were nomads who possessed no practices of land use, self-governance, or even civilization.[221] Holding views so often espoused by whites, Arizona's political leaders believed that the tribe was destined to disappear, that they were, as Senator Carl Hayden remarked, "a dying race."[222]

The tribe's case attracted local, regional, and national advocates, among them the Mission Indian Federation of California, a pan-Indian political association for California and Colorado River tribes. Soon, New Deal officials joined them, including Collier and Cohen.

The tribe, however, also confronted powerful adversaries, such as Hayden, who worked closely with the railway. Scholars such as historian Herbert Eugene Bolton employed by the railway testified that the tribal members were not landowners and did not use their reservation lands as property.[223] A series of lower court rulings offered varied judgments but failed to determine not only whether the Hualapai—and by extension other Native nations—held possession over their lands but also, if so, where such authority originated.

The resulting Supreme Court decision, *United States v. Santa Fe Pacific Railroad Co.* (1941), became the twentieth century's first major articulation of Native American land rights. It quickly propelled postwar Indigenous land claims processes across the United States and eventually served as precedent in numerous international cases—in 1973 the Supreme Court of Canada overturned a seventy-five-year precedent in *Calder v. Attorney General*, ruling that the Nisga'a of northern British Columbia held the rights to their land. Justice Hall specifically referenced the Hualapai case, which "must be considered the leading modern judgement on the question of aboriginal rights."[224]

Like so many moments in Native American history, the Hualapai decision occurred in the shadows of other events. No Washington or national newspapers covered the ruling, which was handed down on December 8, 1941, only hours after the United States declared war on Japan. A unanimous decision, the ruling upheld Hualapai rights to their lands and declared that even without clear recognition of land title by treaty, Native nations hold "aboriginal title" to their lands based on occupancy since time immemorial. Echoing the Marshall Trilogy and extending its doctrines into the twentieth century, the decision offered a landmark affirmation of Indian land rights.

The ruling also projected a different understanding of history itself. Cohen presented the case before the Court. He represented the federal government, which holds reservation lands in trust and often litigates tribal concerns. As examined in chapter 10, since the 1870s, the federal government had abrogated its trust relationship with tribes, passing laws that violated treaties and fostering assimilation policies. By 1941, however, Collier's New Deal administration had reversed many programs. It had reinterpreted the "trust relationship" and, ultimately, the place of Native nations within the United States.[225] Cohen's *Handbook*, for example, provided the first compilation and interpretation of Indian rights, precedent-setting cases, and Native systems of government. Before this few resources had existed—other than the treaties themselves—to draw upon.

They were informed by Native leaders. Collier and Cohen had taken an early interest in Mahone's work, and dozens of Indian reformers such as Roe Cloud traveled the nation's highways explaining Collier's proposals to reservation leaders. Roe Cloud also helped to draft the IRA statute itself, while Robert Yellowtail oversaw New Deal policies upon his reservation. This practice of mutuality—long ascribed to Collier—sprang from Native roots and the broader history of Indian activism. It flowered throughout the New Deal into a powerful force that slowed the damages of assimilation.

✦

Autonomous, self-governing tribal communities working in partnership with the federal government rejected asymmetry as the basis of federal policy and attempted to unmake the violence wrought by assimilation. The idea was not universally accepted across Indian Country—far from it—as many tribes remained so distrustful of federal initiatives that they rejected the IRA. Even in rejecting the IRA, however, tribal communities were exercising their powers of self-governance. The Supreme Court became a part of this effort just as Native nations began to fight alongside non-Native citizens in World War II. For a brief period, a new era of federal Indian affairs had emerged, one that was radically challenged after 1945 when assimilationist forces again aimed to eliminate the distinct sovereignty of Native nations.

12 • From Termination to Self-Determination

Native American Sovereignty in the Cold War Era

I am fervently hopeful that you will guide this nation into more responsible discharge of its trusteeship obligations towards Indians rather than give support to the idea of mass, premature withdrawal of essential federal services.
—*Elizabeth Bender Cloud to the secretary of the Interior (1952)*

The reforms of the Indian New Deal became more apparent, and more politically threatening, over time. The advocacy of Society of American Indian members, the reversal of the government's land and educational philosophies, and the beginning of favorable Supreme Court rulings made the Roosevelt administration a focal point of Indian policy formation. In one of its last acts, the Interior Department lobbied for the passage of the Indian Claims Commission Act (1946), which followed the Supreme Court's 1941 ruling in *United States v. Santa Fe Pacific Railroad Co.* that tribes possessed occupancy rights over definable territories and the Hualapai Indian Nation of Arizona held title to its reservation lands, not the railway. With this law, Congress established a mechanism for adjudicating outstanding land claims and offering financial restitution of alienated reservation lands. The Hualapai quickly filed suit, as did over one hundred tribes.[1]

Much, however, had changed over the course of the New Deal. The United States had gone to war. It now oversaw occupations of Germany and Japan. Foreign affairs dominated the nation's attention, and a new world order consisting of "First," "Second," and soon-to-be-called "Third World" nations recast international diplomacy.[2] The United Nations had formed in 1945, its charter defining its purpose as "to develop friendly relations among nations based on the respect for the principle of equal rights and self-determination of peoples."[3]

Anxieties and tensions grew across postwar America. Millions of veterans returned home in need of reintegration into the economy. Northern cities such as Detroit witnessed violent racial and labor conflicts, while images of atomic mushroom clouds made the threat of nuclear war a household preoccupation. Then, as waves of prosperity arrived, they put further distance between the Depression and postwar America, bringing many individuals and families into a new national economy and culture.[4]

For many American families, a new culture of leisure and affluence followed. Policy makers worked to subsidize the expansion of American prosperity, offering educational, housing, and financial benefits, in particular to veterans, that extended government protections established during the New Deal.

U.S. history after 1945 illuminates the nation's changing place in the world. In 1940 the United States possessed an inconsequential standing army. By war's end, over 7 million had served, and hundreds of thousands of soldiers remained stationed in Germany and Japan. The U.S. Navy now held supremacy across the seas and included the largest, fastest, and most advanced ships ever built. The U.S. Air Force policed the skies and now possessed nuclear weaponry within its arsenal.

Taking a different approach than after World War I, U.S. leaders worked to reshape the postwar order, as *Time* editor Henry Luce argued, in order "to create the first great American century."[5] San Francisco—not Paris—witnessed the formation of the United Nations, which opened its General Assembly in New York. The United States received a permanent seat on its Security Council. Meanwhile, the U.S.-led Marshall Plan led to the rebuilding of Europe while U.S. administrators oversaw the reconstruction of Japan. In under four years, the United States and its allies had defeated two fascist empires, and they now governed their occupied territories.

Native Americans are usually missing from this global history, just as Indians rarely appear in narratives of modern America. They inhabit "another time" that is incongruous with modernity and at odds with the idea of the Atomic Age. This absence is important not just because it shapes how we understand the past but because it informed policies toward Native nations aimed to assimilate them into American society. These policies seized Native lands and resources, as well as Native children in new forms of removal effected through welfare and adoption agencies.

In countless ways, Native Americans shaped "the American Century." Undiscovered at the war's beginning, the majority of the nation's uranium reserve lay under portions of the Navajo Nation.[6] Pueblo lands near Los Alamos and unceded Western Shoshone lands in Nevada provided the basis for atmospheric nuclear testing, while Southern Paiutes and other "downwinders" suffered disproportionate fallout from over one hundred detonations.[7] In order to develop the "fissionable material necessary to make a bomb," as physicist Niels Bohr informed his U.S. colleagues, they would need to turn the "whole country into a factory" for plutonium enrichment and hydro development.[8] Massive dams were built, flooding the Columbia, Colorado, and Missouri watersheds and inundating reservation communities therein. Leaders of industry and social reformers lobbied for these "democratic pyramids," promising that they would bring electricity to the nation and replace older forms of energy such as oil and coal.[9] Far from being outside the currents of the era, Native peoples were at the center of them.

Congress led the way in this remaking of Native America. Across the West, federal agencies cooperated with one another, while private and public utilities coordinated new infrastructure. The Pick-Sloan Plan and Flood Control Act (1944) authorized the construction of dams across the Upper Missouri that aimed to bring water to more farmlands and to limit droughts and floods. The U.S. Army Corps of Engineers worked with other federal agencies to build damns that flooded over 600,000 acres in North and South Dakota alone, including 150,000 acres of the Three Affiliated Tribes (Mandan, Hidatsa, and Arikara) of North Dakota.[10]

For countless Plains Indian families, the Missouri River and its banks provided the sustenance of everyday life, offering water for families and herds, shelter for settlements, and trees for fuel. After subsidizing the near extinction of the bison, the federal government had forced reservation communities into agricultural and ranching economies. Now, state-controlled reservoirs submerged entire villages, creating "new towns" on the shores of human-made lakes. This single piece of legislation, according to Dakota scholar Vine Deloria Jr., became "without a doubt, the single most destructive act ever perpetrated on any tribe by the United States."[11] It linked with larger national efforts to implement "high-modernist agriculture," especially its reliance on mono-cropping, hybrids, commercial fertilizers, and pesticides.[12]

While dams, reservoirs, nuclear testing, and uranium mining impacted Native nations adversely, other Cold War developments seized Native lands and resources. Hydroelectric plants and coal from the Colorado plateau brought electricity to growing western cities like Los Angeles and Phoenix. Like uranium, the coal deposits—estimated at 5 billion tons—lay underneath Navajo and Hopi homelands. Federal agencies oversaw the construction of massive furnaces that by 1975 generated annually nearly eight thousand megawatts of electricity and nearly two-thirds of the electricity consumed in Arizona, New Mexico, and Southern California. Furnaces released untold tons of nitrogen oxide and sulfur dioxide. Every year the Four Corners Generating Station, located on Navajo land, deposited over eighty thousand tons of pollutants. Every day, forty-two hundred tons of coal were unearthed through dynamite blasts. A vast toxic lake accompanied its construction as pumps removed water from the river to return it to the plant for coolant.[13]

Native nations were once again confronted with threats brought about by technological development and globalization. How could they reverse the effects of such environmental, economic, and social disruptions? In the American century, what future awaited them? Government leaders had the answer, and it was final.

Starting after the war, congressional leaders became convinced that reservation communities were their own worst enemy and that they stood in the way of the nation's broader goals of democracy and capitalist development. As Utah senator Arthur Watkins described to visiting Native leaders, "We do not recognize within the confines of the United States any foreign nations. You have now become citizens of the one nation. . . . *You cannot be both*; you cannot be an American citizen and a foreigner at the same time."[14] In a period characterized by a war against communism, Native nations that governed themselves and managed their own lands communally posed threats to U.S. interests.

With the first Republican administration in twenty years, Congress in 1953 began to unravel the Collier-era commitments to self-governance and cultural autonomy. It instituted a policy called "termination" that worked to "terminate" federal obligations to Native peoples. Termination intended to extinguish the federal government's centuries-long relationship with Native nations and to curb its treaty commitments and trust doctrine. This form of political assimilation shaped two decades of federal Indian policy.

Few Native leaders anticipated termination's arrival but they understood its implications. They knew that the government sought, again, to assimilate Indians into American society by terminating its treaty obligations. Rather than removing children to boarding schools, the government worked to urbanize families, developing a federally funded "relocation" program that sent over one hundred thousand individuals to cities for vocational training and employment assistance. Individuals received one-way bus tickets from their reservations in exchange for promises of better lives, and urban Indian communities expanded in every corner of the country.

Native leaders now confronted the new commissioner of Indian Affairs, Dillon Myer, who had led the Wartime Relocation Authority that incarcerated 120,000 Japanese Americans. Myer understood the changes he hoped to institute: "I made it quite clear . . . that I felt very strongly that the Bureau of Indian Affairs should get out of business as quickly as possible."[15] Defunding reservations became his mandate, and liquidating reservation lands became national policy. As termination and relocation incentivized individuals to leave their communities, they forecast an end to a federal Indian Affairs organization altogether. As Deloria Jr. explained about the conflict at hand, "If we lose this one, there won't be another."[16]

When Congress passed House Concurrent Resolution 108 (1953), it codified the new policy. Terminated tribes were stripped of their political autonomy, and state governments assumed jurisdiction over tribal lands, healthcare, and education. Members of terminated tribes became individual property owners or shareholders in newly incorporated entities. Companies and trusts—not elected tribal governments—now governed reservation lands. As the pendulum of federal Indian policy again swung to assimilation, over a hundred tribes were terminated, while throughout the postwar era half a million tribal members migrated to cities, where urban poverty often replaced reservation poverty.

As with earlier assimilation policies, termination sowed the seeds of its own failure. Not all "urban Indians" assimilated into modern America. Like SAI members before them, many formed inter-tribal political communities. Students, veterans, and "relocatees" joined activist movements, including the American Indian Movement (AIM). A generation of Native intellectuals such as Deloria Jr. developed ideologies of Indigenous liberation and "Red Power" that connected with other social and environmental movements.

The ideas and texts of Red Power spread widely. Deloria Jr.'s *Custer Died for Your Sins: An Indian Manifesto* (1969) circulated widely and laid bare what it described as "the disastrous policy of termination."[17] Reservation leaders soon linked their struggle for self-determination with the plight of other colonized populations.[18] At the same time they differentiated their goals from those of the civil rights movement by insisting that the federal government honor its treaty commitments. They used the courts, national media, and Congress to insist on the government's trust responsibilities. Like other Indigenous peoples, Indian leaders rejected attempts to provide national citizenship rights "of whatever grade and quality" and fought against uniform policies at odds with how Indigenous people understood sovereignty.[19]

Together, by the mid-1970s, reformers and activists reversed the tide of termination. In the process, they did something broader: they had inaugurated the modern American Indian sovereignty movement. By strengthening treaty law, raising public awareness, and passing new legislation, they demonstrated that Native peoples could in fact be citizens of both their respective tribal nations *and* of the United States. Redefining American law and policy, the sovereignty movement envisioned new forms of power in modern America, and it worked to establish them within the confines of reservation homelands and under the jurisdiction of tribal governments.

Native Americans and World War II

In direct and indirect ways, Native Americans shaped the course of the Second World War. In both Germany and Japan, both of which had expanded their territories and attempted to govern subject populations, leaders drew inspiration from the history of the United States and its conquest of Indian lands.

In the late nineteenth century, a generation of Japanese immigrants migrated to North America where they encountered racial hierarchies and exclusionary forms of citizenship. Satō Torajirō was among them. Arriving at nineteen in 1885, he lived in San Francisco and Seattle, where he experienced the racist comments and rebukes that confronted Asian immigrants. When he moved to attend the University of Michigan, discrimination followed. Although he was successful on campus and even edited a student newspaper, *Dai Nippon* (Great Japan), white supremacy surrounded him. Upon returning to Japan in 1891, he used his family ties and English-language fluency to build a pearling business on the Torres Strait in Queensland, Australia. One thousand Japanese divers immigrated and worked under him.[20]

Continued racism extinguished Satō's business—but not his ambition. As in the United States, cries to expel Asian laborers fueled racist policies for a "White Australia." Anti-Asian sentiment was everywhere, and he became convinced that Japanese colonization—not immigration—was the key for the future. It was, he believed, the destiny of his race: "While the United States has dared to enforce its invasive Monroe Doctrine, we, the Japanese, shall rise up and carry out our Monroe Doctrine. . . . We shall rise up. . . . This is our manifest destiny."[21]

Satō's ethno-nationalism had been forged over sixteen years on the streets of America, in its university lecture halls, and in the British Commonwealth. Racial pride fueled his newfound passion. As a newspaper owner he articulated justifications for Japanese supremacy over the neighboring nations of China and Korea. These nations were less civilized than Japan, he wrote. They needed colonization: "The best policy to govern Korea would be to populate [its land] with as many [Japanese] people as possible to establish our solid [numerical] hegemony."[22]

Among the first generation of Japanese settlers who arrived in Seoul after the Russo-Japanese War, Satō spent fifteen years brokering Japanese and Korean interests before his death in 1928. In 1924 he helped to form the influential settler political association Dōminkai, which worked to entrench Japanese commercial and political interests.[23] His career encapsulated how a generation of settlers drove the construction of Japan's expanding commercial orbit. They laid the foundations of the Japanese empire drawing inspiration from the policies and practices of the U.S. policy of Manifest Destiny.[24]

Like the Japanese, Germans had a long-standing history of immigration to the Americas, but Adolf Hitler hoped to reverse it. He wanted to see German peasants become settlers closer to home.[25] Germany lacked colonies, and Hitler envied the United States. "One thing the Americans have and which we lack," he wrote, "is the sense of vast open spaces."[26] Germany's best prospects for colonization, he argued, lay in Europe.

Even before he assumed power, Hitler drew inspiration from American Indian policy. He praised the U.S. government for having "gunned down the millions" of Native Americans "to [only] a few hundred thousand" and for "keep[ing] the modest remnant under observation in a cage."[27] Such ideas resonated because they drew upon German cultural practices and prior forms of colonization. German children read Karl May, whose popular *Winnetou* tales chronicled the friendship between a German cowboy in America and his Apache friend. May, who became the best-selling author in the German language, projected simplistic versions of American history and conquest in which Indians befriended Europeans. May, wrote Hitler, opened "my eyes to the world."[28]

German colonization in Africa also drew justification from Native American history. A comparative latecomer to global colonialism, Germany concentrated its imperialism in Africa. When fourteen thousand troops arrived in 1904 to suppress Herero and Nama insurgents in Namibia, they used counter-insurgency campaigns that many consider to be "the first genocide of the modern period."[29] After tens of thousands died, German leaders invoked U.S. history to justify their violence. "Look at America," General Lothar von Trotha reminded. "The Native must give way."[30] Civilian leaders made similar arguments: "The history of the colonization of the United States, clearly the biggest colonial endeavor the world has ever known, had as its first act the complete annihilation of its native people."[31]

For Hitler, Germany's future lay not in African imperialism but in settler colonialism within Europe. "Our Mississippi must be the Volga," he instructed. He anticipated that Slavic peoples would fight "like Indians," and that eastern Europe needed to be remade just as North America had been.[32]

Nazi officials were inspired not just by American colonialism but also by American law. Forty-five Nazi lawyers traveled to New York in September 1935 for a "study trip" inspired by the Nazi lawyer Heinrich Krieger, who had returned from a year at the University of Arkansas. His article "Principles of the Indian Law and the Act of June 18, 1934," which appeared in the *George Washington Law Review* in 1935, examines the Indian Reorganization Act and traces variances in federal Indian policy in order to explain the seemingly incoherent fluctuations in Indian affairs.[33]

Such incoherence and variations were important for Krieger because they exposed what many Nazis believed to be America's "unacknowledged conviction" that Indians were in fact a different race and therefore must be required to submit to separate laws.[34] Krieger's subsequent study *Race Law in the United States* (1936) codified his thinking. The book examines how the United States established its racial orders based in law. His work influenced Germany's Ministry of Justice and other Nazi leaders who sought to establish "a fully realized race state."[35]

As the United States mobilized for war, the federal government centralized the nation's economy and population. More than forty thousand left the reservations during each of the war years to take jobs in ordnance depots, in aircraft factories, on the railroads, and in other war industries. These included Indian women, who left their homes to work in factories, and on ranches and farms.[36]

With the majority of Native American tribes in the West, the war became for most Native communities a Pacific-orientated conflict, although Native soldiers fought in every U.S. theater. By 1945 nearly forty-four thousand Native men and women had served in the armed forces, including 21,767 Indians in the Army, 1,910 in the Navy, 121 in the Coast Guard, and 723 in the Marines.[37] As the government publication *Indians in the War* (1945) noted, "The casualty lists are long. They come from theaters of war all over the world. There were many Indians in the prison camps in the Philippines. . . . There were Indians in the 45th Division in Sicily. . . . They were at Anzio, and they took part in the invasion on D-Day in Normandy. A Ute Indian, LeRoy Hamlin, was with a small troop which made the first contact with the Russians across the Elbe."[38]

Native soldiers also contributed to the dramatic final campaigns of the war. In early 1945 the United States organized for an anticipated invasion of Japan and the conquest of nearby islands in order to open supply and air routes. Among the targets was Iwo Jima, where daily trench warfare killed thousands throughout February. Moreover, suicide aircrafts had been incorporated into Japan's defense plans and sunk up to twenty-four U.S. ships a day.[39] The plan was to be carried out without "even the pretence" of Allied assistance, as English, French, and Russian forces remained committed to Europe.[40] Five million soldiers would be needed.

The intensity of combat was immortalized by photographer Joe Rosenthal, whose photo of six U.S. Marines raising the American flag on Mount Suribachi remains among the war's most iconic images. Only three of the men survived, including Ira Hayes (Pima) from Bapchule, Arizona.

Hayes's contribution is famous, but few accounts note that Louis Charlo (Flathead) from Montana had died in the effort to secure the mountain or that Clifford Chebahtah (Comanche) from Oklahoma, lay injured in a foxhole nearby. Like his peers, Chebehtah recalled, "When I saw our boys raise the flag, cold shivers ran down my spine."[41]

Thousands of Indians fought during the war, and many were killed or injured. At least 235 Lakota servicemen from South Dakota were casualties, including Howard Brandon, who also died on Iwo Jima.[42] In communities across the country, Native service was commemorated throughout the postwar era. Most notably, in November 1954, Hayes joined military and political leaders at the Marine Corps Memorial dedication in Washington to have his image cast in bronze alongside the other flag-raisers.[43] Countless other ceremonies were held for returning soldiers, as were more formal memorials. In September 1945, at Oregon's Klamath Agency, a local airstrip was dedicated in honor of Ray Enouf, a medic in the Marines who also died at Iwo Jima.[44]

The Early Cold War in Indian Country

When Hayes sat alongside President Dwight Eisenhower at the memorial dedication, they gazed upon a nation different than that which had welcomed each home from service. Family incomes had nearly doubled since 1941, and by 1956 there were more white-collar workers than manual laborers.[45] But reservation communities still struggled to participate in the prosperity generated by the nation's consumer economy.[46] The United States had become an affluent society, but within this "consumer's republic," Indians had faded largely into mythology.

During the Cold War, Indian history offered morality tales that reassured the nation in uncertain times. Eisenhower had barely won the Republican nomination over Henry Roe Cloud's classmate Robert Taft, and fears of inflation dominated his party's platform, which decried the "wanton extravagance and inflationary policies" of the New Deal.[47] Many in fact compared New Deal programs to an illness that required treatment. "Depression-born thinking," to many, now constituted a "psychosis."[48] The remedy: "balanced budgets, restrictive monetary policy, and government pressures to restrain wage increases."[49]

Race relations also deepened the challenges of demilitarization. President Harry Truman had integrated the military, but southern resistance made the postwar era a period of prolonged struggle. Eisenhower's first appointment to the Supreme Court, Earl Warren, had stunned the nation by presiding over a unanimous ruling in *Brown v. Board of Education* to desegregate American schools. Unlike Andrew Jackson and the *Worcester* ruling, the president would soon use national troops to enforce this ruling, as the African American freedom struggle remade America.

The morality tales of the Cold War were mainly visual. The western dominated movies and television. In 1954 twenty-four Hollywood films featured Indian characters; however, these were not movies about contemporary Indians. As was common in the industry, producers cast white actors as Indian subjects and set their films in the reassuring familiarity of the past. Apaches were particularly popular that year as Burt Lancaster starred in *Apache* (United Artists) and Rock Hudson in *Taza, Son of Cochise* (Universal).[50]

Westerns went well beyond simply casting white actors. They showed Indians using invented languages, grunts, and gibberish.[51] When Indians played supporting characters, they uttered monosyllabic lines that were "ungrammatical, or full of anger."[52] Moreover, in contrast to boarding schools, where musical programs brought varied sounds and traditions together, westerns employed repetitive, threatening scores that became widely recognized.[53] Sounds of cavalry charges, "tom-tom" drumming, and racist war whoops filtered across school yards, sporting arenas, and new amusement centers. Disneyland's "Frontierland" opened in 1955 only two years after the debut of *Peter Pan,* which Americanized the English tale *Peter and Wendy* and incorporated Indian characters and music in its depictions of Never Never Land. Similar to Karl May's influence with children in Germany, Walt Disney linked American childhood with Native peoples.

The sounds of the western shaped young and old. Westerns became so widespread that they spawned a stable of popular and masculine metaphors. Throughout society the genre introduced new expressions: showdown, last stand, hired gun, round up.[54] By 1958 Hollywood was churning out a western a week. When families gathered after sundown around their electronic campfires for evening chow, they fancied watching a western, eight of which were among the top ten shows of 1959.[55]

In actuality, throughout the Cold War, Native peoples confronted political structures even more damaging than the representations around them. The postwar ideology of limiting federal spending hit the Office of Indian Affairs hard. Starting in 1946, Congress began pressuring its leaders to identify specific tribes ready for the removal of federal oversight. When Commissioner William Zimmerman refused, the Senate subpoenaed him and directed him to identify tribes to be "removed at once" from federal supervision.[56] The Eightieth Congress had entered Washington with ambitions of reducing federal spending. It intended to extinguish Indian Affairs. Termination was now beginning.

Ideology versus Practice: The Twisted Implementation of Termination

Many congressional leaders believed that the Indian Claims Commission (ICC) would settle long-standing land concerns. Many also hoped it would do more and lead to the removal of all remaining federal supervision. Watkins chaired the Senate's Subcommittee on Indian Affairs and wrote the original termination legislation. He believed that the ICC would assure "final settlement of all obligations—real or purported—of the federal government to the Indian tribes."[57]

Once claims were settled, there would be no need for federal recognition of individual communities. Senator George Malone of Montana went even further. He believed that the efforts of the New Deal had fostered un-American, "socialistic" governments that were working with the Indian Bureau to "entwist and entangle . . . the tree of liberty." He argued, "We are spending billions of dollars fighting communism . . . [and] perpetuating the systems of Indian reservations and tribal government, which are natural Socialist environments."[58]

Most tribes would have agreed that federal oversight had been a disaster. Even with the adoption of constitutional governments and the New Deal's support for arts and cultural programs, few things had improved. Tribes remained the poorest communities in North America. Infant mortality was two to three times the national average.[59] Federal officials exercised "a nearly unfathomable degree of authority," as the BIA served as reservations' "banker, educator, doctor, and land manager."[60] Such federal control fostered demoralization and divisions. There were often as many proposed solutions as there were opinions on how to improve conditions.

Divisions had characterized many reservations for generations. Across the Columbia Plateau in eastern Washington, numerous bands of related tribes had been congregated onto reservations, sometimes living together for the first time. On the vast Colville Reservation, twelve bands agreed in 1872 to live together, eventually creating a "confederated" tribe out of bands that had not previously formed a confederacy.

As was common during the Allotment Era, their reservation became quickly dispossessed. Its northern half became alienated through a combination of shoddy deals and transfers. Many blamed the federal government and one another. Land loss and dissention became so severe that it in many ways "defined" the Colville Reservation thereafter.[61]

Colville history illuminates how federal policies devastated tribes in ways that made subsequent policies even worse. In a descending spiral, policies perpetuated generations of harm. The Allotment Era created such distrust that the tribe rejected the Indian Reorganization Act in 1934. Like many, Colville members voted down Collier's proposals because of anti-government feeling that followed the loss of their lands.

In 1938 the tribe did draft a constitutional government. For the first time, tribal members ceded autonomy to an institutionalized "confederated" council; however, only a third of tribal members voted. More than a thousand voiced their opposition by not participating. Some even wrote to President Roosevelt about their distrust of their newly elected leaders and of the election process that centralized authority in the tribe. "We have leaders or Chiefs in our own districts," one member wrote. "We want our old laws" restored.[62]

The passage of the ICC exacerbated these divisions and deepened the distrust. After 1953 such divisions paved the way for termination as many Colville members believed that remedies to their land claims were forthcoming. As the federal government grew powerful and spent billions rebuilding Europe and Asia, many Native people believed that the ICC would offer compensation for their lands. Land claims settlements might finally bring economic recovery.

Federal leaders also believed that mismanagement blocked tribal self-sufficiency. They argued that economic autonomy would never emerge as long as federal officials governed the reservation. Tribes needed to be "freed" from the constraints of their political dominion. As House Concurrent Resolution 108 outlined, "It is the policy of Congress, as rapidly as possible, to make Indians . . . subject to the same laws and entitled to the same responsibilities as are applicable to other citizens."[63]

Throughout the first decade of termination, settlement claims assisted the policy's implementation. Watkins and other senators reminded tribes that in order to recover damages for lost property, they would have to vote to accept termination. Individuals would receive compensation for outstanding claims. Communally governed lands would be sold. Once Indian claims were resolved and their lands alienated, there would be no need for federal recognition. Tribal members could finally enjoy the "same laws" as "other citizens." They would remain "Indians," of course, but not members of federally recognized tribal communities with jurisdiction over reservation lands; eligibility for treaty guarantees in health, education, and housing; or with recognized hunting or fishing rights, among other entitlements.

As federal leaders tied land claims settlements to termination, they fostered individual hopes for monetary gain, pitting individuals against the political survival of their communities. Pro-termination council members among the Colville voted to receive compensation from the sale of their reservation. A survey mailed to each tribal member posed a single question: "Do you favor termination and liquidation of the tribal owned reservation assets at fair value, with the proceeds distributed equally to the members of the tribes?"[64] Sixty-two percent of members on the reservation approved, as did 82 percent of those living away. Making funds available to individual members facilitated the implementation of termination.

In countless other ways, federal officials also fostered individual ambitions against tribal solidarity. Alluring promises and new programs flowed from Washington. In 1956 Congress passed the Indian Vocational Training Act, which formalized housing, jobs, and educational benefits in exchange for relocation.[65] BIA promotional flyers touted the benefits of urbanization over reservation life. Glossy photos displayed young Indian families gathered around kitchen tables with new appliances, enticements meant to attract reservation youth away from their tribes. With funding for travel and temporary housing, relocation funded the urbanization of one hundred thousand tribal members. Unsurprisingly, Colville members living away from the reservation favored liquidation. Like termination, relocation intended to diminish loyalties to tribes.

Problems, however, accompanied tribal members into cities or developed upon arrival. In Los Angeles, as many as four young women sometimes shared a single hotel room. The BIA's Relocation Office worked to find temporary housing for recent arrivals; however, so did the state of California's Department of Corrections—which used the same hotels for its recently released inmates.[66] "Menial jobs" were the only positions offered to most Indian women, as gender doubly bound Indian women into employment as domestic workers, beauticians, or office secretaries. As LaNada Means from the Shoshone-Bannock Nation of Fort Hall, Idaho, recalled, "I wanted to try college," but she was told by her local vocational coordinator that she was being "irrational and unrealistic."[67]

Like many, Means found herself without family, friends, or focus. As during the Assimilation Era, individuals often left reservation communities with limited preparation. Some had never seen freeways, taken public transportation, or navigated shopping centers. Their alienation and isolation often became consuming. "The Indian who has come to the city is like a man without a country," Means concluded. "You hang around with other Indians, but they are as bad off as you are . . . living in the slums."[68]

While extinguishing Indian sovereignty and alienating lands eventually generated community responses, the 1950s were a time of shock across Native America. Meanwhile, automation and automobiles drove the rest of the nation down highways of productivity and leisure. In many ways, it was like the movies where Native peoples faded into the horizon or died quickly at the hands of more powerful actors.

In the years ahead, denunciations against termination began to spread, particularly from larger tribes, who first encountered the Watkins-led policies. They began fighting to get their recognition by the federal government "restored." In the process, they joined a larger movement for Indigenous liberation.

Reservation Resources and Menominee Termination

Termination promised tribes a move from the economic margins into the mainstream. A triad of federal policies supported this promise: (1) the potential for claims settlements, (2) the prospects of urbanization, and (3) the ultimate extinguishment of federal supervision of tribal communities. Combined, the three would end the federal recognition of tribal communities and "free" tribal members from the "limitations" of being Indians. Over one hundred tribes, including the Colville, accepted the false promises of the federal government. They became terminated.

Losing recognition meant losing resources. Tribes such as the Menominee Nation of Wisconsin understood this but they saw few alternatives. Like the Colville, the Menominee had struggled for decades to get compensation for the mismanagement of their lands. Termination provided a possibility for such claims.

Menominee grievances extended to the nineteenth century when superintendents first began using reservation forest resources for their self-interests. Most reservations across the upper Midwest had been clear-cut by nineteenth-century timber industries; however, several tribes, including the Menominee and the Red Lake Ojibwe of Minnesota, resisted such pressures. Through advocacy and often ingenuity, they fought off these phases of capitalist development. In the 1890s Menominee lumbermen entered into government-backed contracts that culled timber from the reservation's timber reserve. They did so despite the growing "collusion" between reservation and state leaders who, as the Indian Rights Association alleged, intended to initiate a "robbery" of the reservation's vast forest treasure.[69]

When severe storms damaged reservation forests in 1905, Wisconsin senator Robert La Follette drafted legislation that mandated the construction of a reservation-based lumber mill for Menominee workers.[70] Previously, white-owned lumber companies, nearby farmers, and others often seized reservation timber without paying for it. Menominee leaders protested that they did so also without justification, as the reservation's resources remained under their jurisdiction.

In the early 1920s Menominee leaders organized the tribe to take ownership of the lumber economy. Leaders such as William Kershaw, an SAI member and Milwaukee attorney, pressured the Office of Indian Affairs to provide greater autonomy for the tribe.[71] In 1924 the tribe drafted its own constitution. It lobbied for an Advisory Council to have a veto over the lumber mill's budget, a self-governing power that Collier authorized in 1934.

In a rare example of autonomy, self-sufficiency, and conservation, the Advisory Council governed the 233,000-acre reservation, preserved its forests, and employed tribal members. Any "man who wanted a job could find one at the mill," remembers Ada Deer, former Menominee chairwoman and anti-termination leader.[72] Unlike the owners of nearby mills, the Menominee sustainably "reduced the percentage of the forest harvested annually in order to ensure trees—and the jobs they brought—were always available."[73] Milling provided seasonal labor and allowed tribal workers to fish, hunt, and pursue other opportunities in the off season. While the BIA did not support such a communitarian business model, the tribe insisted upon it.[74]

Menominee self-sufficiency contrasted with conditions in the state's other tribes. Clear-cutting and allotment had devastated the nearby Oneida Nation. Wisconsin's Ho-Chunk and Ojibwe communities, which engaged in commercial fishing, seasonal agricultural, and even tourist economies combined seasonal wage labor with subsistence hunting.[75] Despite their comparative advantages, the Menominee still lagged behind white farms and industries. The Department of the Interior estimated that most reservation families made $2,300 annually; some estimates were only half as much.[76]

Born in 1935, Deer grew up in a log cabin built by her family at a time when timber-harvesting and home construction were incentivized on the reservation, and most houses on the reservation were self-fashioned. Hers included a nearby barn with several cows and horses that her father bred with neighboring farmers. He worked at the mill. Winters were cold and poverty apparent.

In 1951 the tribe succeeded in getting restitution for decades of timber theft; among other frauds, superintendents had limited the production of Menominee millwork in order to drive up the value of neighboring white-owned production. The U.S. court of claims awarded $8.5 million to the tribe. The Menominee now sought authorization to award onetime distributions of $1,500 to its 3,270 members. Optimistic leaders traveled to Washington to negotiate the settlement.[77]

When Senator Watkins learned of Menominee settlement prospects, he traveled to Wisconsin and informed tribal members that in order for them to get their settlement they would need to accept termination. The tribe's economy, he assured them, would prosper without federal bureaucracies overseeing them. The government was doing a "bad job," he continued, "and we don't want to get sued again for $8,500,000."[78]

Only a small percentage of the tribe voted to support Watkins's measure. Some believed they were voting to receive settlements. Many felt pressured to extinguish their treaty relations, and few understood the consequences of the reservation becoming a county in the state. Congress passed legislation in 1954 to terminate the tribe even though Wisconsin state officials had no idea how that process would proceed. At hearings in Washington, Watkins attempted to reassure the tribe that termination was not taking away reservation lands but "trying to give it to" individual tribal members.[79] As one member recalled: "We became convinced that there was *no* alternative to accept termination. . . . All we pleaded for was adequate time to plan this sudden and revolutionary change in our lives."[80]

In Indian Country, jurisdiction is everything. Which government—state, federal, tribal, county, or municipality—possesses authority over crimes, contracts, and funding defines the contours of sovereignty. Sovereignty, moreover, is experienced as well as legislated. For terminated tribes, this "sudden and revolutionary" change arrived like a thunderclap. In under twenty-four months, tribes in Utah, California, and Oregon were no longer recognized Indian communities. They had been terminated.

With smaller tribes, the BIA quickly had their lands appraised and then sold. Many never again became federally recognized. Larger tribes, including the Menominee and Klamath, had detailed administrative plans developed that attempted to ease this transition, but termination still wrought irrevocable harm. As Klamath tribal member Lynn Schonchin recalled:

> What it did to the tribe . . . was . . . horrible. To see our tribe, we broke apart, we moved away, family units broke down, some folks went through

> the loss of identity, they didn't feel comfortable with who they were. . . . Even the [other] tribes looked at us as, "You're not Indian any more." And that's basically what the Termination Act said, "They will no longer be Indians." How do you deal with that?[81]

For the Menominee, whose termination did not finally arrive until 1961, federal contracts disappeared. Wisconsin state taxes were levied on reservation lands. Hospital repairs grew costly, and signs of a strange new corporate entity, Menominee Enterprise, Inc. (MEI), appeared. Its new managers instituted more extractive logging practices, which required more expensive trucks and equipment, and the mill increasingly lost money.[82]

Unlike other terminated tribes, the Menominee managed to avoid the immediate alienation of their land. Most tribes' termination required an individual act of Congress, but Menominee termination took several years to unfold, delayed by requests by the tribe for more time. During this crucial interlude, tribal members still maintained their homes, and the federal government continued to hold the land in trust until the final legislation went into effect. Tribal members continued their daily lives. They no longer, however, possessed a common government. Their national sovereignty was being diminished. A voting trust controlled the MEI, in which tribal members now held depreciating stock.

In one of the most chilling developments, thousands of acres of the tribe's most beloved lands surrounding reservation lakes were sold to pay accumulated taxes. Developers purchased these properties to make summer cottages for the wealthy. They also planned to dam smaller lakes in order to build properties on larger lakeshores. As Deer recalls, "In a community where there had been few strangers, outsiders now transformed the landscape and ecosystem in ways that inflicted a severe wound on the tribal psyche. . . . Our leaders had little experience developing policies or programs."[83] They pleaded for more time and began to organize for more aggressive action.

The Cold War and the Racial Logic of Termination

For most Americans, Indian affairs seemed inconsequential. Few noticed that HRC 108 passed the House and Senate with unanimous support. If the Klamath, Menominee, or other tribes could turn a profit from the sale of their reservations, shouldn't they do so? Moreover, shouldn't they be allowed to do so? The nation's Indian policies and the federal trust doctrine remained outside the focus of most Americans. Like most laws, they were too complicated for popular engagement.

Pressing foreign affairs also dominated the headlines, particularly in the months after HRC 108's passage in 1953. Only days before the Marine Corps Memorial dedication in 1954, for example, national liberation fighters attacked French colonial outposts across Algeria. The decline of French colonialism in Southeast Asia had already forced the United States to assume the majority of expenses in Vietnam, where in May 1954 French forces had suffered their largest defeat at Dien Bien Phu. The Geneva Conference subsequently partitioned Vietnam into two nations, and soon the United States and its South Vietnamese allies confronted northern Vietnamese fighters. Civil War in China and the Korean War also dominated news coverage, as conflicts across the Asian rim escalated into the defining conflicts of the Cold War era.[84]

Additionally, everywhere America's closest allies confronted anti-colonial insurgencies even as it appeared that the nation's adversaries were growing stronger. Fears of attack "bordering on hysteria" pervaded policy circles, and U.S. leaders propped up anti-democratic regimes in Guatemala, Iran, and Indonesia.[85] In 1955 it also confronted the establishment of the Warsaw Pact and a "non-aligned movement" of twenty-nine independent nations that met in Bandung, Indonesia.[86] The early years of termination were, in short, dominated by international affairs and civil rights activism in the domestic sphere.[87]

Moreover, in its global battle against communism, the United States championed liberal economic and political practices that celebrated individualism. A "deification of the market" and capitalist ideologies dominated federal policy making.[88] Termination enjoyed such widespread support because it used the Cold War ideology of individual self-realization and contrasted it with visions of communal governance. "Socialist Democrats," railed South Dakota congressman E. Y. Berry, "are making much ado about fighting Communists and Communism throughout the world, and yet, the same Administration passed the Wheeler-Howard Act (IRA, 1934). . . . Talk about fighting Communism? No, they are bringing it right to America and Communizing the Indian just as thoroughly as if they were citizens of Russia."[89] Anti-communism so powerfully shaped national policies that few questioned termination, relocation, or the nation's extractive resource economies.

Racism and racial politics also fueled termination and relocation. States with large reservation populations, such as South Dakota, encouraged the extinguishment of federal supervision and the distant urbanization of tribal members. Berry expressed many of his constituents' concerns that Native nations limited white Americans' freedom in principle and in practice.

As sovereign nations with their reservation jurisdiction over non-Indians, Indians intruded upon the freedom of white people. Moreover, state residents did not want tribal members integrated into their towns: "We do not intend to let an Indian light around here at all," declared Mayor Herschel Melcher of Chamberlain, South Dakota. "If they come in here it will be necessary to declare an open season on Indians. . . . We do not want to live with them and we see no reason why we should, we don't want them in our schools. . . . That is the job of the Federal Government."[90]

Relocating Indians to cities and selling their lands benefited white citizens materially, emotionally, and ideologically. Termination promised to maintain existing racial orders and to extinguish reservation jurisdiction altogether. In fact, many western leaders believed that any federal support for Indian communities constituted a form of discrimination against whites. As Melcher continued, "We do not feel that we are entitled to this kind of abuse from the government."[91]

As the specter of integration exacerbated white fears, anti-government feeling grew in Cold War America. In a spiraling logic, Indians threatened the "American way of life." As Commissioner Myer suggested, "We can either lead the Indians toward more and more assimilation . . . or allow them to retrogress to the narrow and inbred way of life which has been customary of reservation living."[92] Either way, Indians posed problems to white authorities.

Native peoples and their allies viewed reservations differently—as homelands, not pathologies. Founded in 1944, the National Congress of American Indians (NCAI) began critiquing termination policy. Similar to the Society of American Indians in its orientation to national affairs, NCAI differed by drawing its leadership from elected tribal leaders. It now worked to provide legislative solutions to reverse termination. Garnering support from advocacy groups and legislators, including George McGovern from South Dakota, in 1957 NCAI helped to propose Senate Concurrent Resolution 3, which attempted to repeal HRC 108.[93] It failed to generate sufficient support but signaled to the Eisenhower administration tribes' growing concerns about termination.

By 1960 activism percolated across Indian Country. NCAI's 1960 conference theme, "Self-Determination—Not Termination," underscored its position.[94] Efforts to reach American Indian students and youth organizations followed, including the 1961 American Indian Chicago Conference at the University of Chicago, which drew over five hundred participants and received media coverage and a welcome from Mayor Richard Daley. An ambitious effort that built upon a series of regional meetings, the conference was the first national effort to bring together tribal leaders, urban Indians, academics, and nonrecognized Indian tribes. Among its central goals: to issue a "Declaration of Indian Purpose" to President John Kennedy.

It was a contentious effort. NCAI's initial support for the conference dissipated as some tribal leaders wondered whether university organizers might have communist sympathies. The declaration seemed to satisfy no one. A compromised pronouncement, it simultaneously critiqued federal Indian policy and included an "American Indian Pledge" of loyalty to the United States. This "Pledge within the Purpose" was designed to repudiate "the efforts of the promoters of any alien form of government" within Indian Country and was done to secure participation from Oklahoma's conservative Indian leaders.[95] Fears of communism—and national charges of "un-American" activities—remained so prevalent that they mitigated tribal attempts to reverse legislation that diminished their sovereignty.

Unlike many elected leaders, youth participants grew aggrieved by such apparent fidelity to the federal government. "It was sickening to see American Indians get up and just tell obvious lies about how well the federal government was treating them," recalled Clyde Warrior, a Ponca youth leader from Oklahoma. "What was happening was these tribal officials . . . were just going into that gear of appealing to the Great White Father again."[96] The declaration—which included statutory proposals, overviews of the effects of termination, and critiques of new dams and infrastructural developments—never made it to Kennedy. It was filed away in the Department of the Interior. Many left Chicago thinking that coalition politics and general efforts at national Indian unity were unlikely avenues for national reform.

Termination and Indian Child Welfare

In four years, NCAI had brought attention to damaging policies. From Washington to Chicago, NCAI members attempted to reverse termination's many threats. Despite limited results, NCAI's coordination with other groups highlighted a growing capacity for organizing and alliance-making that would eventually bring national reforms. Its inclusion of urban Indians and nonfederally recognized tribes, such as the Lumbee of North Carolina and the Mohegan of Connecticut, signaled a broader, more inclusive approach to Indian affairs.[97]

Notwithstanding these efforts, termination and relocation continued unabated. For most of the 1950s and 1960s, NCAI's advocacy, research, and proposals failed to alter national policy. Moreover, other challenges deepened the federal government's assault on tribes. In particular, state officials increasingly seized Native children. They targeted them, however, not for distant boarding schools but for adoption.

During termination, as states gained increased jurisdiction over tribes, they also gained new financial burdens. As among the Menominee, states assumed educational, housing, and healthcare responsibilities for terminated tribes. Tribes remained the most impoverished communities. Infant mortality and unemployment exceeded national averages, and life expectancy rates were lower. Indian newborns, for example, were six times more likely to die during their first year than non-Natives, while over 10 percent of Indian babies died at birth, compared to 2 percent for non-Natives.[98] Many tribal members relied upon government funding for housing, healthcare, and food. While cloaked in the language of individualism and benevolence, termination sought to extinguish tribal sovereignty in order to eliminate governmental costs and responsibilities established in treaties.

In 1958 BIA officials instituted a program designed to help offset state responsibilities. The Indian Adoption Project encouraged state welfare workers to expand their foster care and child placement programs. In an early model of the privatization of governmental services, adoptive and foster families—and not the federal or state governments—assumed the costs for caring for Indian children.[99] The results were immediate. In North Dakota, tribal members comprised less than 2 percent of the state's total population, but their children made up 50 percent of the state's foster population.[100] In Minnesota, Indian children made up nearly 10 percent of caseload for state child service cases even though tribal members constituted only 0.5 percent of the state's population.[101] The Indian Adoption Project instituted another national policy of Indian removal.

When tribal councils passed resolutions prohibiting the intrusion of county officials onto the reservation, state and county authorities cut off welfare payments to tribal members. State legislatures even passed laws that made "chronic dependency" on state assistance evidence of fostering an "unsuitable" home for children, thereby accelerating the justifications for child removal. Children living with "unwed" mothers or with extended family members were seen as living in "illegitimate" families. "Illegitimacy," as former BIA official Arnold Lyslo reported, "among Indian peoples is frequently acceptable."[102] As Aleta Brownlee of the BIA's new Welfare Branch continued, a new and more "desirable" family structure was needed, one in which "the father works and supports his family" and "the mother cares for her home and children."[103]

Placing children in non-Native families accomplished multiple policy objectives. It diminished state welfare to tribes, inculcated Indian adoptees into new forms of domesticity, and concomitantly punished tribal communities that practiced differential gendered or kinship systems. Adoption also encouraged broader efforts at urbanization by steering adoptees away from tribal communities.[104]

Starting in 1958, adoption programs worked in concert with the BIA. The Child Welfare League of America (CWLA) and the Adoption Resource Exchange of North America (ARENA) operated under federal contracts to arrange for private agencies to assist in placing Indian children into their programs. Lyslo left the BIA to work with CWLA. He oversaw its placement programs and toured reservation communities to assess available children; he concluded, "Only a small percentage should remain on reservations . . . for the majority, resources outside the reservations must be found."[105]

One of several adoption programs working in Indian Country, the CWLA oversaw the adoption of 650 children into non-Indian homes.[106] Lyslo even envisioned adoption programs for relocated mothers who, he proudly relayed, "are now being referred to social agencies by the workers of the Bureau of Indian Affairs. . . . The Indian Adoption Project has encouraged the development of these services."[107] He encouraged such "development" in Los Angeles, where over thirty thousand American Indians had relocated.[108]

Since adoption programs rarely reported to tribal authorities, family reunions became difficult. Gaining access to placement records proved difficult due to confidentiality laws. When mothers did visit their children in foster homes, they encountered challenges. Poverty and lack of transportation limited their travel, as did finding care for their other children. In 1973, for example, when one Standing Rock Sioux mother hitchhiked across the country to try to retrieve her two eldest children, she returned to find her remaining child had been placed into an adoptive family.[109]

Leaving children with extended family or older siblings potentially positioned them for removal. As Denise Altvater (Passamaquoddy) recalled, she was seven when she and her five sisters were taken to a foster home while their mother was out of the house. State officials "took all of our belongings and they put them in garbage bags. They herded us into station wagons and . . . left us" in a home where they were housed for several years and suffered abuses from their providers.[110] A quarter to a third of all American Indian children were removed from their families during the Termination Era and placed into adoptive families, foster homes, or orphanages. As a congressional report concluded in 1978: "The Indian child welfare crisis is of massive proportions and Indian families face vastly greater risks of involuntary separation than are typical in our society."[111]

Early in the twentieth century, when Indian children such as Elizabeth Bender Cloud or Zitkála-Šá attended off-reservation boarding schools, they sometimes had siblings or other tribal members around them. Despite the isolation and violence around them, boarding school students had one another, and throughout the twentieth century many boarding schools, such as Haskell Indian Institute, developed enriching curriculums with successful arts and athletic programs. In the 1930s Haskell placed dozens of its graduates into universities.[112]

In contrast, the vast majority of "lost birds," as Indian adoptees were known, had limited emotional and familial support. Many remained unaware of their tribal nationalities until they were old enough to review their adoption records. Their adoptive families often discouraged inquiry into their heritage. Difference followed them everywhere. "I was considered an oddity," Joan Kauppi (Red Lake Anishinaabe) recalls. "I always had a feeling I did not quite fit in. . . . I was forced to explain the concept of adoption to my friends . . . [who asked] why my real parents didn't want me. Of all my experiences, this was the most painful as I had to keep retelling and explaining my adoption."[113]

Feelings of loss, anger, and betrayal accompanied their placements. Abuse was common. In one study, nearly half of the participants indicated that their adoptive family abused them, and of these, 70 percent reported sexual abuse.[114] "What those Caucasians did to me I will never recover from," explains Evelyn Red Lodge (Lakota). "I was dispossessed of my language, culture, and traditions and had imposed on me the history and religion that was not mine." Despite the Christian rhetoric that pervaded the environment, abuse from her adoptive family confirmed to her flatly "that God would do nothing for me."[115]

Moreover, the legal system worked against family reunifications. When mothers sued to have their children returned, judges often awarded custody to adoptive families, upholding the rights of "psychological parents" over natural ones. When mothers won in court, adoptive families gained custody on appeal even in cases where "evidence of sexual abuse of the child by the foster father was offered."[116]

The connections between child removal and termination were clear to Indian leaders and their allies. The Devil's Lake Sioux in North Dakota became the front line in this new struggle. "The Devil's Lake Sioux people and American Indian tribes have been unjustly deprived of their lands and livelihood," proclaimed the Association on American Indian Affairs (AAIA) in 1968. An advocacy group based in New York that worked with NCAI, it generated awareness through its newsletter, *Indian Family Defense.* "Now they are being dispossessed of their children . . . [by] County welfare workers . . . without sufficient cause and without due process of law."[117]

Native peoples attempted to stall these assimilationist practices that intruded upon the most intimate relationships within tribes—those between parents and their children. They went to court, worked with advocacy groups, and called for national protections. Child welfare activists envisioned new laws to ensure that in the event of adoption or foster care, children's relatives, fellow tribal members, or even other Indian families would receive priority placements over non-Indians. New laws were needed to protect Indian families.

The Rising Tide of Red Power

Adoption, like termination and relocation, haunted reservations. It devastated Indian communities by taking away their most precious resource, their children. As the chief of the Mississippi Band of Choctaw Indians Calvin Isaac summarized, "The chances of Indian survival are significantly reduced if our children . . . are to be raised in non-Indian homes and denied exposure to the ways of their People."[118] Numerous Cold War policies threatened "Indian survival."

For different laws and policies to be fashioned, new ideas would be needed. Following the Chicago conference and during the Kennedy administration, a tide of change started to flow, and a new language of "survival" emerged. It grew in various locations: among youth movements, within communities of artists, and in activist takeovers. By 1969, when *Custer Died for Your Sins* was published, a new language and aesthetics of sovereignty had emerged. Three key developments heralded the rise of what became known as Red Power.

First, following the Chicago conference, students continued organizing. Understanding that their futures were threatened by the rapaciousness of termination, student leaders such as Clyde Warrior and Mel Thom (Walker River Paiute) met in Gallup in August 1961 and founded the National Indian Youth Council (NIYC), which dedicated "its activities and projects to attaining a greater future . . . derived from the values and beliefs of our ancestors."[119] As Thom stated, "We know the odds are against us, but we also realize that we are fighting for the lives of future Indian generations."[120]

Drawing inspiration from the African American freedom struggle, NIYC organized a series of protests and direct actions. It distanced itself ideologically from NCAI and emphasized the urgency of the situation. As Deloria Jr. noted, "NIYC inclines to the spectacular . . . rather than the extended program."[121] He knew such distinctions well, having become NCAI's executive director in 1964.[122]

As they had in Chicago, NIYC members rejected the politics of accommodation. They argued for fundamental, not incremental, change. Indians, as Warrior proclaimed,

> are not free. We do not make choices. . . . Choices and decisions are made by federal administrations, bureaucrats, and their "yes men," euphemistically called tribal governments. . . . We must be free in the most literal sense of the word, not sold or coerced into accepting programs for our own good, not of our own making or choice.[123]

As Warrior suggested, an ideological change was underway. Advocating for autonomy outside the constraints of federal oversight, Indian students, artists, and intellectuals argued for a "greater future" in the United States. Their vision differed from assimilation. It celebrated not only Indigenous "values and beliefs" but also sovereignty. As NIYC leader Hank Adams (Assiniboine-Sioux) suggested before heading into the army, "I owe and swear first allegiance to the sovereignty of my tribes and my people."[124] Staging protests, teach-ins, and related forms of public awareness, NIYC brought Indian affairs into the nation's consciousness. It created a grammar of Indian politics rooted in cultural pride and sovereignty.

No place embodied this changing intellectual climate more than the Institute of American Indian Arts (IAIA), a federally funded school for arts education established in Santa Fe in 1962. The outgrowth of various initiatives sponsored by the BIA—including the establishment of the Indian Arts and Crafts Board during the New Deal—IAIA in its inaugural semester drew 130 students from sixty-nine tribes.[125] Lloyd Kiva New (Cherokee) served as its arts director, and instructors such as Allan Houser (Chiricahua Apache) and Fritz Scholder (Luiseño) joined as studio teachers.

Initially housed on the campus of the Santa Fe Indian School, the institute attracted students from across North America. By 2012 over four thousand had attended, including hundreds of Navajo, Pueblo, and Iroquois students.[126] The institute now maintains a separate campus outside of town, while the Museum of Contemporary Native Arts operates downtown.

In the institute's early days, many hoped to advance new directions in Indian arts that combined modernist forms with traditional cultural aesthetics.[127] As museum director Richard Hill (Tuscarora) recalled, students "studied tribal art styles from across the Americas as well as historical and contemporary Euro-American art history. This resulted in cross-cultural experiments and exchanges that created new avenues for express[ion]."[128]

For many, the experience was transformative. "The two years I studied at IAIA gave me more than an education in the arts," recalled Larry Desjarlais (Turtle Mountain Chippewa). "It helped me find myself."[129] As former IAIA president Della Warrior (Otoe-Missouria) learned from her alumni conversations, "In almost every instance, the people we interviewed said that the institute was a life-changing force."[130] Self-discovery, cultural pride, and above all creative expression defined the institute. With new facilities for printmaking, textile arts, and theater performances, IAIA fostered an explosion of artistic production. Across a variety of media and employing a range of styles, students initiated a new style of art, often referred to as the "New Indian Art movement."[131]

T. C. Cannon (Caddo/Kiowa) became one of the school's earliest successes. Born in 1946 near Rainy Mountain, Oklahoma, he enrolled in 1964, the same year that Scholder began teaching. The two became accomplished painters, each deploying abstract figurations in bold and often jarring coloration. Cannon's *Indian Man* (1967) presaged many of Scholder's subsequent portraits of ghostly and deracinated subjects, and within five years the two were exhibiting together in Washington while holding residencies in the Ivy League.[132]

Themes of uncertainty, defiance, and discomfort resonate in their work. "I have tried to paint the torture that it seems to me the Indians have had to go through," Scholder explained. "I have painted the Indian real, not red."[133] His *Indian with Beer Can* (1969) exploded familiar representations and offered a visual accompaniment to the militancy of the era, "only darker and scarier."[134]

Advancing an aesthetics of vibrancy and futurity, artists at IAIA developed visions that both defined an era and reimagined the future.

Last, Indian activists began protests in 1964 that shaped a decade of subsequent reforms. At a series of "fish-ins" around Puget Sound, Adams, Billy Franks Jr. (Nisqually), and other activists staged protests against state officials who criminalized Indian fishing. They proclaimed that such criminalization was illegal since the Nisqually Treaty of 1854 "secured" the rights of Natives to fish at "usual and accustomed grounds and stations."[135] The state, moreover, lacked jurisdiction over Indian affairs. Natives fishing without a license was not a crime, as the state contended. Nonetheless, officials imprisoned Indian fishers, arguing that Indian fishing threatened the salmon industry. Franks was arrested over fifty times, while Adams had been shot in the stomach while standing watch. Countless families fished at night to avoid arrest.[136]

Protests in Olympia, Washington, started to generate awareness, and the arrival of NIYC leaders brought national awareness. Two thousand marched to the state capitol in March 1964 to demand a cessation of state repression. Celebrities such as Marlon Brando soon joined, visiting Franks' Landing—the family's "station"—to publicize their cause. As Franks recalled, "This was a war," and it raged at the landings, in Olympia, and eventually in the courts.[137]

Calls for upholding treaty law echoed across the nation. While many viewed the Indian activist movements as offshoots of the civil rights movement, the laws that inspired activists were particular to Native communities. Treaties guaranteed those rights, and when the federal government closed its prison on Alcatraz Island in 1963, a provision in the Lakota Treaty of 1868 became justification for the occupation of the island. As in the Northwest, treaty law drove Indian activism.

Like many from her community, Belva Cottier (Lakota) had migrated to San Francisco from South Dakota. Even in the city, she understood that her nation's relationship with the government included guarantees that had not been upheld.[138] Included in article 6 of the Lakota Treaty is a provision that Lakotas living on federal lands outside the reservation "shall be entitled to receive from the United States a patent," or title, provided that they make "improvements thereon."[139]

When Cottier and other Lakota members staged a short-lived occupation of Alcatraz in 1964, they drew upon their treaty rights. Their takeover inspired other students and activists, including Richard Oakes (Mohawk), who had moved to the region in the late 1960s. As Cottier told Oakes, treaty law justified Indians taking unused federal lands. Throughout the fall, Oakes worked with students at Bay Area campuses to organize another takeover. On November 20, they again seized Alcatraz, inaugurating a period of hope and militancy.

The Road to Self-Determination: 1969–78

The occupation of Alcatraz formed a fitting conclusion to the turbulence of the 1960s. In an era when Indians rarely appeared in public media, young and defiant Native peoples were in the news. An international chorus of media responses followed. "You have no idea how much publicity this has had in Europe," reported San Francisco mayor Joseph Alioto upon his return from abroad. "Everywhere I went I was asked about Alcatraz and the Indians."[140] For the first time in the twentieth century, Native Americans dominated the headlines.

Surprise, shock, and also sympathy followed. Alioto continued, "They're using Alcatraz as a means of negotiating their serious and in my opinion justifiable claims. The Indians and the federal government will have to work out their differences . . . between themselves."[141] Here were eighty American Indians defying U.S. Coast Guard and federal officials and claiming vacant land in order to build an "Indian city."[142] For eighteen months, they worked to transform the old prison into a new community with a school, museum, religious center, radio station, and facilities run by Indians. Indians from across North America arrived to support one another. They also launched new actions of their own and joined organizations, such as AIM, that led subsequent takeovers at Fort Lawton, Seattle (1970), the BIA headquarters in Washington, D.C. (1972), and Wounded Knee, South Dakota (1973).

Alcatraz heightened national consciousness and led to the re-shaping of national policy toward self-determination. The result of a generation of collective activism, it became articulated as national intent on July 8, 1970, when President Nixon addressed Congress, declaring that "forced termination is wrong" and that a new "goal of . . . national policy toward the Indian people [was needed] to strengthen the Indian's sense of autonomy." Never before had a U.S. president offered such a public rebuke of existing Indian policy as well as an endorsement of tribes becoming free of "federal control."[143]

While articulate and media-savvy leaders led activist takeovers, the policies of self-determination centered more on reservation communities than urban environments. Few specific national laws formed in response to activist takeovers. Expanding federal commitments to Indian communities and fighting for increased protections for treaty rights characterized two streams of transformation.

In a stark reversal of termination's politics of austerity, President Lyndon Johnson's "War on Poverty" poured resources into Indian affairs. Communities such as the Navajo Nation received grants from the Office of Economic Opportunity and began running their own institutions. Navajo leaders such as Ned Hatathli worked to build tribally administered schools, including the Rough Rock Demonstration School and Navajo Community College. Each incorporated a culturally enriched curriculum. Each prioritized the hiring of Indian educators. Rough Rock became the first "successful contract school" that allowed tribes to administer their own federal contracts, inspiring other communities to do the same.[144] As Philip S. Deloria (Standing Rock) of the American Indian Law Center emphasized, "It was through the Great Society program that Indian tribes became widely recognized by federal agencies as legitimate governments."[145]

Funding flowed into Indian communities from multiple sources, not exclusively the Bureau of Indian Affairs. Multiple government agencies, such as Housing and Urban Development and the Department of Education, expanded opportunities to Indian communities. This administrative expansion constituted a revolution in Indian affairs. It opened new avenues for education, housing, health, and land management. It also loosened the BIA's stranglehold over tribes. Even national parks began collaborations with tribes that created new employment opportunities for tribal members.[146]

While a new era was forming, its future still remained unclear. Buoyed by heightened awareness and greater funding, tribal leaders pressed for precise new legislation. They also sought legal remedies in the courts. In short order, they got both. A sweep of landmark legislation—including a series of "restoration" bills—and favorable court rulings followed, solidifying the legal foundations of self-determination. Two moments in particular stood out.

Throughout the Termination Era, court rulings had generally disadvantaged tribes, upholding the doctrine of plenary power. The Supreme Court had undercut Native sovereignty in cases such as *Tee-Hit-Ton v. United States* (1955), which denied Tlingit efforts in Alaska to receive compensation for the destruction of their habitat by the U.S. Forest Service. As Justice Stanley Reed noted, Indians were only "permitted to occupy portions of territory over which they had previously exercised sovereignty. . . . This is not a property right but amounts to a right of occupancy which . . . may be terminated."[147] The establishment of the Tongass National Forest by executive order in 1909, Reed reasoned, had terminated Tlingit title and did not entail any obligation by the United States to offer compensation or restitution.

But what of treaty rights that were never formally relinquished or extinguished? The Northwest fishing rights case in *U.S. v. Washington* (1974) provided some answers. District Court judge George Boldt presided, and his ruling differed in spirit and form from Reed's. In an affirmation of treaty law, Boldt held that tribes possess rights to fish at "usual and accustomed" grounds and to do so "in common" with non-Native residents.

These rights had never been fully clarified, but a decade of protests had raised their visibility. As was the case with the takeover of Alcatraz, a media storm accompanied the trial. Franks stood in the back of the courtroom, while Adams appeared on behalf of the Nisqually. Each understood that questions of jurisdiction and equity were under review. No one, however, anticipated the breadth of Boldt's judgment.

Drawing on a trial transcript of 4,600 pages, Boldt offered a 203-page decision that sided with the tribes on nearly all points. According to Boldt, tribes had rights that the state could not abridge. The state's prosecutions of Native fishing were thus unconstitutional. Moreover, Boldt held that tribes were entitled to an equal allocation of the region's salmon harvest, a "50-50" split that tribal governments would now regulate "in common" with the state's non-Indians.[148]

A clarion call spread across the nation. Tribes possessed not only recognized treaty rights but also off-reservation authority. The Boldt decision also reaffirmed the limited jurisdiction of state governments over "treaty areas" and highlighted renewed capacities of tribal governments to exercise treaty rights in modern America.

The decision was upheld by the federal court of appeals and denied certiorari by the Supreme Court in 1979. Adams and Franks Jr. soon took leadership roles within the inter-tribal Northwest Indian Fisheries Commission (NIFC), which began to regulate an allocation regime between twenty tribes involved in the management of tribal fisheries.[149] The commission's complex work, however, encountered resistance, as enraged local leaders, state officials, and white fishers whose boats lost profitability vilified Indians and Boldt. As the Supreme Court noted in its denial of the state's appeal, state leaders had developed "extraordinary machinations in resisting the decree." "Except for some desegregation cases," the Court continued, these actions comprised "the most concerted . . . efforts to frustrate a decree of federal court witnessed this century."[150]

Contemporary Indian self-governance is determined by tribal members working together and, ideally, in partnership with the federal government. Throughout the 1970s, tribes gained increased control over their natural resources, membership criteria, and hiring preferences within federal agencies. Court rulings supported these increases, but getting federal agencies to fund them remained a problem. While the Johnson administration provided the money, growing inflation during Nixon's second term increasingly imperiled it. The passage of the Indian Self-Determination and Education Assistance Act (ISDEAA) of 1975 remedied this issue and embodied the transformations of the new era. It ultimately transferred a "miraculous" amount of power from the federal government to tribal communities.[151]

Passing laws and appropriating funding are two essential responsibilities of Congress. With the ISDEAA, Congress established more secured forms of funding from federal agencies to tribes, broadening the "contracts" systems initiated with the Office of Economic Opportunity. Tribes now had legislative power behind their requests to federal agencies. Tribal representatives lobbied Congress for funding, which they administered themselves.

The Quinault Reservation on the Olympic Peninsula was one of dozens of communities that now witnessed the dramatic reversals brought by self-determination. Termination had decimated much of the tribe's old-growth forests. Clear-cutting and road construction created erosion into the Quinault River and damaged fish spawns. Throughout the 1960s, tribal leaders attempted to limit further destruction. In 1971 they blocked timber company access by blockading the reservation's main bridge.[152]

While less famous than other activist takeovers, the Quinault barricade sent a jolt through the community. Relying less on the BIA and timber companies, tribal leaders developed their own studies on deforestation and ecological degradation. They pressured federal officials for increased authority over land management, and after the passage of the ISDEAA they secured contracts that gave the tribe authority over their lands, resources, and decision-making processes. "I think all we're saying," President Joe DeLaCruz stated, "is that what we have left is ours. . . . Let us alone . . . [to] rebuild it."[153]

President of the Quinault for a quarter century, DeLaCruz also served as

NCAI leader, and he heard many of the proclamations of the activist years. He saw outsiders destroy forests and salmon runs, and he knew that increased tribal power could limit such intrusion. Like many tribal leaders, he followed the national developments of activists while attempting to improve local conditions. His imperative to be left "alone" resonated with one of the suggestions from *Custer Died for Your Sins*. Deloria concludes chapter 1 with an answer to the common question of the era, "What do you Indians want?"

> The primary goal and need of Indians today is not for someone to feel sorry for us. . . . Nor do we need to be classified as semi-white and have programs and policies made to bleach us further. Nor do we need further studies to see if we are feasible. We need a new policy by Congress acknowledging our right to live in peace, free from arbitrary harassment. . . . What we need is a cultural leave-us-alone agreement, in spirit and in fact.[154]

Expansion and Backlash: Self-Determination in the Late Twentieth Century

From Washington to Maine, tribes secured new resources and governed on their own. Such practices did not constitute complete independence, but they indicated sovereignty nonetheless. Indeed, the language of sovereignty deployed by Adams, Warrior, and Deer resonated across society, reaching even into the Supreme Court, where Justice Thurgood Marshall reasoned in 1973: "It must always be remembered that the various Indian tribes were once independent and sovereign nations, and that their claim to sovereignty long predates that of our Government."[155]

Making decisions communally, fighting to secure funding, and stewarding lands through tribally run governments characterized the new politics of self-determination. Moreover, ideas of Indigenous self-governance flowed across national boundaries, particularly between the United States and Canada, where Native communities confronted similar challenges. Indians, according to George Manuel's *The Fourth World* (1974), now shared common cause to "carry on [their] own administration, and to develop [their] own policies and programs." As he explained, "I am struck by the similarity" of positions taken by "Indian groups across Canada and the United States," as First Nations and U.S. Native leaders increasingly communicated and followed their respective challenges.[156]

As tribes secured more power, however, they also faced new forms of resistance. In the United States, state governments did not give up jurisdiction easily. Attorneys general in the 1970s, such as Washington's Slade Gorton, fought to limit tribal authority. As a U.S. senator, Gorton continued efforts to curtail tribal sovereignty into the 1990s.[157]

While Gorton's office lost its appeal of the Boldt decision, it succeeded in limiting tribal jurisdiction in other areas. In 1973 state officials challenged the right of tribes to arrest non-Indians. As during the Removal Era, criminal law became a determinative arena for clarifying the parameters of tribal jurisdiction.

Did the tribe possess the authority to prosecute non-Indians who committed crimes against Indians? As with the Boldt decision, courts decided the outcome. In 1978 in *Oliphant v. Suquamish Indian Tribe*, the Supreme Court said tribes do not possess such authority. In an opinion written by then associate justice William Rehnquist, the Court held that once they submitted to "the overriding sovereignty of the United States, Indian tribes therefore necessarily give up their power to try non-Indian citizens of the United States except in a manner acceptable to Congress."[158] *Oliphant* began a series of court rulings that called into question the retained nature of tribal sovereignty. As Rehnquist further noted in 1981, "This court has retreated from the position that Indians are sovereigns."[159]

As the contrasting opinions of Rehnquist and Marshall reveal, opposing legal doctrines accompanied the federal government's shift from termination to self-determination. Indeed, conflicting ideas about the place of modern Indian nations have created clouds of uncertainty, and tribal communities stand constant guard against threatening new rulings and legislation. The removal of criminal jurisdiction established by *Oliphant*, for example, has required tribal leaders to pressure Congress for increased statutory powers to prosecute non-Indians, especially those who endanger women and children. Tribal advocacy led to new provisions in the Violence against Women Act (2013) that authorized tribal courts to seek prosecutions against non-Indian assailants and abusers.[160] Thousands of non-Indians reside on reservation lands, and clarifying the legal contours of tribal jurisdiction over "non-Indians" remains a constant challenge.

Backlashes against tribal authority have long characterized American Indian political formations and the exertion of tribal sovereignty. The broad and shifting arc of twentieth-century Indian policy underscores how the fluctuations between tribal communities and the federal government have bred uncertainty, confusion, and contestation.

Of all areas of tribal governance, economic development remains a constant challenge. Tribes have worked hard to remedy their underemployment. Many moved quickly throughout the 1970s to take advantage of new federal initiatives. Grants for education, housing, and infrastructure offered tribal leaders new opportunities. Well into the 1980s, tribes secured funding to build new schools and roads, hire tribal employees, and establish language and cultural programs aimed at reversing generations of neglect. Sovereignty both followed and flowed from such efforts.

The 1980s, however, began a new phase of self-determination. After nearly a generation of federal funding, the streams ran dry. Reagan-era cutbacks slashed funding and deepened the precarity of tribes, as the Bureau of Indian Affairs' annual budget was slashed by nearly 50 percent in under three years.[161] Per capita income had risen for Native peoples in the 1970s but fell throughout the 1980s.[162] Loans for development came due while uncompleted infrastructure projects sat idle. Tribal employment rolls shrank, and a general economic malaise again threatened the viability of numerous communities. Many leaders were thrown out of office or fought to hold on to their positions through creative and at times illegal means.

The gains of self-determination, however, did not simply disappear. Prescient leaders devised new strategies that maximized the jurisdictions of tribes to attract capital. Exempt from state taxation, for example, tribal members sold fireworks in the summer and cigarettes and gasoline year-round. They often did so at makeshift or small-scale venues so as not to invite surveillance. Given the jurisdictional questions, many worried about potential state prosecution.

Along with "black market" businesses on reservations came suggestions of lawlessness that played into existing stereotypes of Indians. But sometimes these activities attracted loosely regulated industries and organized crime.[163] In southern Florida and California, tribal initiatives attracted both. The Seminole Nation and Cabazon Band of Mission Indians used their sovereignty to run, respectively, bingo and poker cardroom facilities.

Tribal economies are unregulated by state laws. One can hunt or fish on a reservation using tribal as opposed to state licenses. When the Seminole and Cabazon Band began their respective recreational initiatives designed to attract seasonal "snow birds," state and county officials closed their facilities and confiscated their proceeds.[164] The Seminole had seen how churches and other nonprofits in Broward County ran similar efforts to generate revenue. In both regions, multiple sovereigns—the tribes, the states of California and Florida, and Broward and Riverside Counties—were in conflict.

Ironically, these small-scale gaming efforts bred the largest economic development in contemporary American Indian history. While tribal gaming was criminalized by each state, tribal leaders defended their sovereignty and sought injunctions. The Cabazon argued that California incentivized gaming through state lottery practices and cardrooms and that their jurisdiction did not extend to reservation lands. Each tribe also began collaborating with other tribes to seek enhanced gaming authority. Eventually, the Supreme Court concurred in *Cabazon v. California* (1987), and in 1988 Congress passed another milestone legislation—the American Indian Gaming and Regulatory Act (AIGRA).[165] It established a national framework for states and tribes to enter into agreed-upon compacts in order to regulate gaming initiatives and to share revenues. What had once been a million-dollar industry among scattered communities grew into a billion-dollar business involving over one hundred tribes.

In 1992, upon the five-hundredth anniversary of the Columbian encounter, few envisioned tribal communities developing such expansive and profitable economies. The Oneida Nation of Wisconsin, for example, employs more workers in Green Bay County than the Green Bay Packers, while the Seminole Nation of Florida has acquired international companies, including the Hard Rock Hotel and Casino franchise. In the Northeast, the Mashantucket Pequot Tribe and Mohegan Nation have generated hundreds of millions of dollars for their tribal communities and for the state of Connecticut.

As tribes expanded their institutional capacities, they became more effective at governing. However, the majority of the nearly six hundred federally recognized tribes do not offer gaming, and of those that do, the majority do not run profitable facilities. Inter-tribal competition, online gaming, and new state and municipal casinos have weakened markets and diminished the initial comparative advantages of gaming tribes.

Collectively, however, gaming revenues and inter-tribal advocacy have yielded powerful results. At the tribal level, new schools, language programs, and health centers are among many recent tribal initiatives, while nationally, lobbying and inter-tribal coalitions have helped pass new laws and legislative reforms. Indeed, as with the Violence against Women Act reauthorization in 2013, legislative advocacy has become an effective political strategy, one that is less costly and less threatening than litigation.

Ironies abound. They became particularly apparent to those who navigated the turbulent years of earlier activism. When Ada Deer succeeded in getting the Menominee Restoration Act passed in 1973, Indian Country remained rife with tensions. Educational, health, and social disparities affected

Standing at the right, Ada Deer watches as U.S. secretary of the Interior Rogers Morton signs documents that returned land to the Menominee Nation of Wisconsin, a major step in the implementation of the Menominee Restoration Act of 1973. Deer described the transfer as "the epitome of Indian self-determination." (Wisconsin Historical Society, WHI-45437.)

all tribes. Additionally, among the Menominee, "a generation had grown up without a tribe." Due to termination, she recalled, "their parents and grandparents had lost their government, their schools, their hospital, their power plant, their phone company, and their control over their forest and mill."[166]

Congress had restored the tribe's federal recognition and placed it again under the sovereign protection of the United States. That protection, which had been so damaging in the 1950s, became by 1975 the basis for new partnerships and initiatives. Indeed, it paved the way for a new future, one in which Deer became not only the first woman elected tribal chairperson of her tribe but also eventually assistant secretary of the Interior for Indian affairs. Taking the oath in Washington in August 1993 on her fifty-eighth birthday, she assumed charge of an office that served over 1 million Native people across more than 40 million acres of tribal lands. It included twelve area offices, eighty-three agency offices, and thousands of employees.[167]

In under a year, Secretary Deer had toured many of the agencies and helped to organize a tribal leaders' summit at the White House. President Clinton received over three hundred elected tribal leaders. "Welcome to the White House. Welcome home," he began. "This great historic meeting today must be the beginning of our new partnership."[168] With Cherokee principal chief Wilma Mankiller and Lac Courte Oreilles chairman Gaiashkibos presiding, Cheyenne River Sioux chairman Greg Bourland addressed his colleagues: "Sovereignty burns in my heart," he declared, "I look around me and I see sovereignty."[169] He received a standing ovation, and Clinton signed two new executive orders.

✦

By the end of the century, the dark days of termination had faded. A series of "new partnerships" had begun. As Deer knew well, however, nearly a third of all tribal members lived below the poverty line, as the challenges of health, educational obtainment, and economic development continued to impair tribal nations. Language loss, continued ecological destruction, and innumerable legacies of colonialism endure, making the challenges of Native America among the most enduring.

Tribes had reversed the most threatening policies of the Cold War era. Few outside Indian Country understood this historic reversal of fortune, while even fewer grasped the hard-fought gains of the modern sovereignty movement. As the twenty-first century began, continued challenges to those sovereign gains reappeared as congressional law makers, court justices, and other concentrations of power again took aim at Indian lands, jurisdiction, and resources.

OKLAHOMA
1 Miami
2 Ottawa
3 Peoria
4 Seneca-Cayuga
5 Shawnee
6 Modoc
7 Quapaw
8 Eastern Shawnee
9 Cherokee
10 Keetoowah (Cherokee)
11 Osage
12 Kaw
13 Ponca
14 Tonkawa
15 Otoe Missouria
16 Pawnee
17 Iowa
18 Sac & Fox Nation
19 Muscogee (Creek)
20 Alabama-Quassarte
21 Thlopthlocco
22 Kialegee
23 Seminole
24 Chickasaw
25 Choctaw
26 Absentee-Shawnee
27 Kickapoo
28 Cheyenne and Arapaho
29 Caddo
30 Wichita and Affiliated Tribes
31 Delaware Nation
32 Fort Sill Apache
33 Comanche
34 Apache
35 Kiowa
36 Wyandotte
37 Delaware Tribe of Indians
38 Citizen Potawatomi Nation
Tribal Jurisdictional Areas
Port Gamble S'Klallam
Jamestown S'Klallam
Lower Elwha
Makah
Quileute
Hoh
Quinault
Skokomish
Squaxin Island
Shoalwater
Chehalis
Lummi
Samish
Nooksack
Upper Skagit
Swinomish
Stillaguamish
Sauk-Suiattle
Tulalip
Snoqualmie
Muckleshoot
Puyallup
Nisqually
Cowlitz
Yakama
Suquamish (Port Madison)
Grande Ronde
Siletz
Warm Springs
Umatilla
Colville
Kootenai
Kalispel
Spokane
Coeur D'Alene
Nez Perce
Blackfeet
Salish-Kootenai (Flathead)
Rocky Boy's
Fort Belknap
Little Shell
Fort Peck
Turtle Mountain
Fort Berthhold
Spirit Lake
Red Lake
Bois Forte
Leech Lake
White Earth
Fond du Lac
Mille Lacs
Standing Rock
Northern Cheyenne
Crow
Sisseton-Wahpeton Oyate
Upper Sioux
Lower Sioux
Flandreau
Shakopee Mdewakanton Sioux
Cheyenne River
Lower Brule
Crow Creek
Rosebud Sioux
Yankton
Oglala Sioux
Ponca
Santee
Winnebago
Omaha
Coos, Lower Umpqua, & Siuslaw
Umpqua (Cow Creek)
Coquille
Burns Paiute
Klamath
Fort McDermitt
Fort Hall
Shoshone (Wind River)
Arapaho (Wind River)
Duck Valley
Summit Lake
Pyramid Lake
Reno-Sparks
Winnemucca
Battle Mountain
Wells
Northwestern Shoshoni
Lovelock
Carson
Stewart
Elko
South Fork
Goshute (Skull Valley)
Fallon
Yomba
Walker River
Yerington
Washoe Ranches
Dresslerville
Goshute
Uintah and Ouray
Ely
Duckwater
Kanosh
Koosharem
Indian Peaks
Shivwitz
Cedar
Moapa River
Kaibab
Ute Mountain Ute
Southern Ute
Jicarilla Apache
See key at top right for Nations in California
Las Vegas
Havasupai
Hualapai
Navajo
Hopi
San Juan Southern Paiute
Yavapai-Apache
Yavapai-Prescott
Tonto Apache
Colorado River
Santa Clara
San Ildefonso
Taos
Picuris
Ohkay Owingeh
Pojoaque
Nambe
Tesuque
Cochiti
Kewa
San Felipe
Santa Ana
Jemez
Zia
Zuni
Acoma
Laguna
Sandia
Isleta
White Mountain Apache
San Carlos
Gila Bend
Ak Chin
Salt River
Gila River
Cocopah
Tohono O'odham
Pascua Yaqui
Mescalero Apache
Ysleta Del Sur
Sac & Fox
Iowa
Kickapoo
Prairie Band Potawatomi
See key at top left for Nations in Oklahoma
Alabama-Coushatta
Kickapoo Traditional
PACIFIC OCEAN
Contemporary State and Federally Recognized Native Nations and Lands in the Contiguous United States
Federally recognized tribes
Federal reservations
State recognized tribes
Map does not include tribal communities seeking federal and/or state recognition

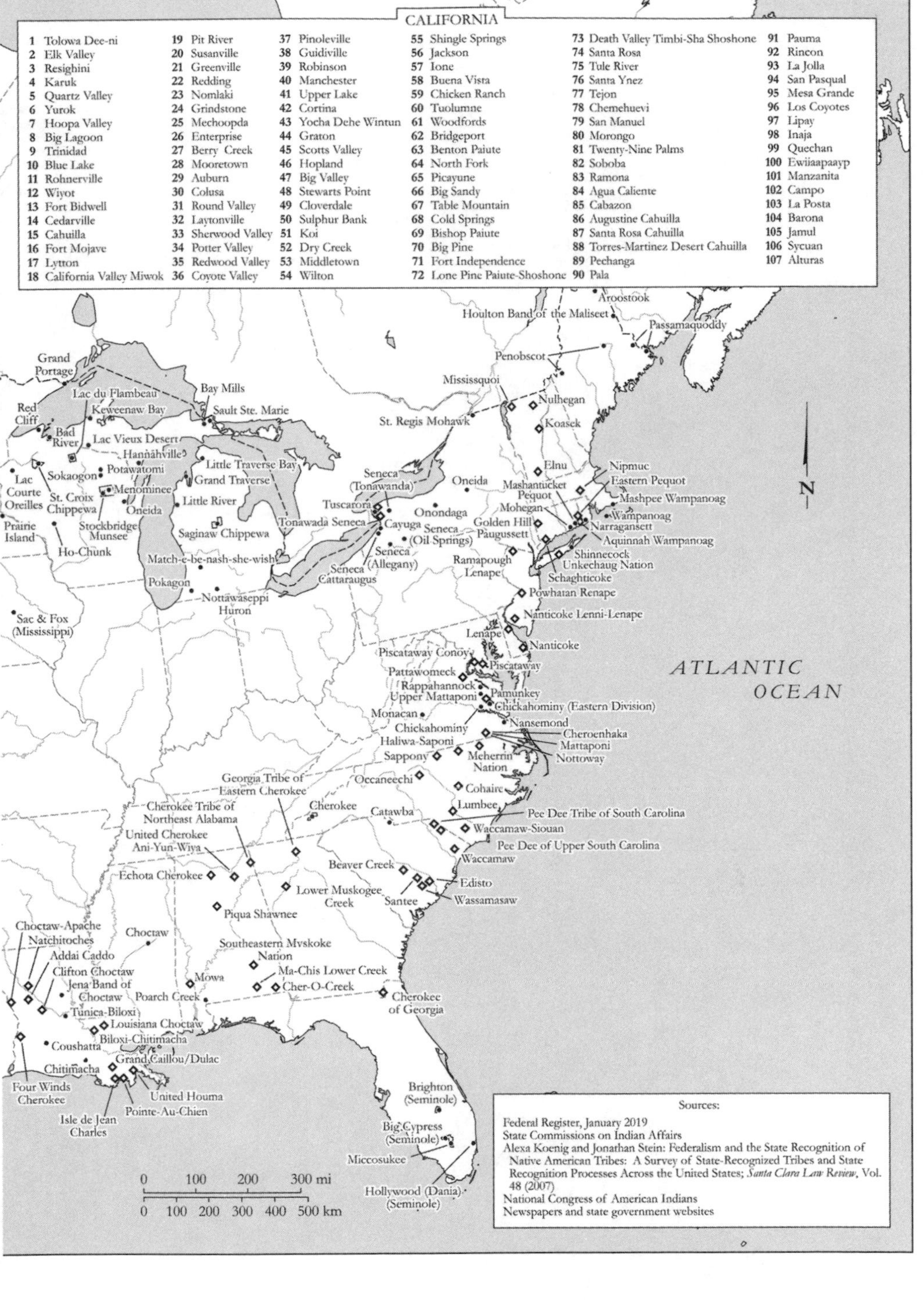

CALIFORNIA
1 Tolowa Dee-ni
2 Elk Valley
3 Resighini
4 Karuk
5 Quartz Valley
6 Yurok
7 Hoopa Valley
8 Big Lagoon
9 Trinidad
10 Blue Lake
11 Rohnerville
12 Wiyot
13 Fort Bidwell
14 Cedarville
15 Cahuilla
16 Fort Mojave
17 Lytton
18 California Valley Miwok
19 Pit River
20 Susanville
21 Greenville
22 Redding
23 Nomlaki
24 Grindstone
25 Mechoopda
26 Enterprise
27 Berry Creek
28 Mooretown
29 Auburn
30 Colusa
31 Round Valley
32 Laytonville
33 Sherwood Valley
34 Potter Valley
35 Redwood Valley
36 Coyote Valley
37 Pinoleville
38 Guidiville
39 Robinson
40 Manchester
41 Upper Lake
42 Cortina
43 Yocha Dehe Wintun
44 Graton
45 Scotts Valley
46 Hopland
47 Big Valley
48 Stewarts Point
49 Cloverdale
50 Sulphur Bank
51 Koi
52 Dry Creek
53 Middletown
54 Wilton
55 Shingle Springs
56 Jackson
57 Ione
58 Buena Vista
59 Chicken Ranch
60 Tuolumne
61 Woodfords
62 Bridgeport
63 Benton Paiute
64 North Fork
65 Picayune
66 Big Sandy
67 Table Mountain
68 Cold Springs
69 Bishop Paiute
70 Big Pine
71 Fort Independence
72 Lone Pine Paiute-Shoshone
73 Death Valley Timbi-Sha Shoshone
74 Santa Rosa
75 Tule River
76 Santa Ynez
77 Tejon
78 Chemehuevi
79 San Manuel
80 Morongo
81 Twenty-Nine Palms
82 Soboba
83 Ramona
84 Agua Caliente
85 Cabazon
86 Augustine Cahuilla
87 Santa Rosa Cahuilla
88 Torres-Martinez Desert Cahuilla
89 Pechanga
90 Pala
91 Pauma
92 Rincon
93 La Jolla
94 San Pasqual
95 Mesa Grande
96 Los Coyotes
97 Lipay
98 Inaja
99 Quechan
100 Ewiiaapaayp
101 Manzanita
102 Campo
103 La Posta
104 Barona
105 Jamul
106 Sycuan
107 Alturas
Aroostook
Houlton Band of the Maliseet
Passamaquoddy
Penobscot
Mississquoi
Nulhegan
Koasek
St. Regis Mohawk
Elnu
Nipmuc
Eastern Pequot
Mashantucket Pequot
Mohegan
Mashpee Wampanoag
Wampanoag
Narragansett
Aquinnah Wampanoag
Golden Hill Paugussett
Shinnecock
Unkechaug Nation
Schaghticoke
Ramapough Lenape
Powhatan Renape
Nanticoke Lenni-Lenape
Lenape
Nanticoke
Grand Portage
Bay Mills
Sault Ste. Marie
Lac du Flambeau
Keweenaw Bay
Red Cliff
Bad River
Lac Vieux Desert
Hannahville
Sokaogon
Potawatomi
Little Traverse Bay
Grand Traverse
Lac Courte Oreilles
St. Croix Chippewa
Menominee
Oneida
Little River
Prairie Island
Stockbridge Munsee
Saginaw Chippewa
Ho-Chunk
Match-e-be-nash-she-wish
Pokagon
Nottawaseppi Huron
Sac & Fox (Mississippi)
Seneca (Tonawanda)
Oneida
Tuscarora
Onondaga
Tonawada Seneca
Cayuga
Seneca (Oil Springs)
Seneca (Allegany)
Seneca Cattaraugus
ATLANTIC OCEAN
N
Piscataway Conoy
Piscataway
Pattawomeck
Rappahannock
Pamunkey
Upper Mattaponi
Chickahominy (Eastern Division)
Monacan
Nansemond
Chickahominy
Cheroenhaka
Haliwa-Saponi
Mattaponi
Nottoway
Sappony
Meherrin Nation
Occaneechi
Georgia Tribe of Eastern Cherokee
Cohaire
Cherokee Tribe of Northeast Alabama
Cherokee
Lumbee
Catawba
Pee Dee Tribe of South Carolina
United Cherokee Ani-Yun-Wiya
Waccamaw-Siouan
Pee Dee of Upper South Carolina
Waccamaw
Beaver Creek
Echota Cherokee
Edisto
Lower Muskogee Creek
Santee
Wassamasaw
Piqua Shawnee
Choctaw-Apache
Natchitoches
Choctaw
Addai Caddo
Southeastern Mvskoke Nation
Clifton Choctaw
Ma-Chis Lower Creek
Jena Band of Choctaw
Mowa
Cher-O-Creek
Poarch Creek
Cherokee of Georgia
Tunica-Biloxi
Louisiana Choctaw
Biloxi-Chitimacha
Coushatta
Grand Caillou/Dulac
Chitimacha
Four Winds Cherokee
United Houma
Pointe-Au-Chien
Isle de Jean Charles
Brighton (Seminole)
Big Cypress (Seminole)
Miccosukee
Hollywood (Dania) (Seminole)
0 100 200 300 mi
0 100 200 300 400 500 km
Sources:
Federal Register, January 2019
State Commissions on Indian Affairs
Alexa Koenig and Jonathan Stein: Federalism and the State Recognition of Native American Tribes: A Survey of State-Recognized Tribes and State Recognition Processes Across the United States; Santa Clara Law Review, Vol. 48 (2007)
National Congress of American Indians
Newspapers and state government websites

Notes

Introduction

1. Linda Tuhiwai Smith, *Decolonization Methodologies: Research and Indigenous Peoples*, 2nd ed. (London: Zed Books, 2012); Patrick Wolf, "Settler Colonialism and the Elimination of the Native," *Journal of Genocide Research* (December 2006): 387–409. For an application of "settler colonialism" to U.S. history, see Roxanne Dunbar-Ortiz, *An Indigenous Peoples' History of the United States* (Boston: Beacon, 2014). The terms *Indigenous, Native American*, and *American Indian* all generally refer to the first peoples of the Americas and are used interchangeably herein. While problematic in their homogenization of distinctions, these terms offer insights into the histories of power and difference that comprise foundational chapters in the history of global colonialism.

2. For an overview of U.S. history without attention to settler colonialism or ongoing processes of Indigenous dispossession, see Jill Lepore, *These Truths: A History of the United States* (New York: Norton, 2018).

3. As quoted in Carroll Smith-Rosenberg, "Dis-Covering the Subject of the 'Great Constitutional Discussion,' 1786–1789," *Journal of American History* (December 1992): 841 (emphasis added).

4. Only in 2012 did the American Historical Association include a state of the field essay on Native American history in its essays on U.S. historiography. See Eric Foner and Lisa McGirr, eds., *American History Now* (Philadelphia: Temple University Pres, 2012). For previous editions, see Eric Foner, ed., *The New American History: Revised and Expanded Edition* (Philadelphia: Temple University Press, 1997); and Foner, ed., *The New American History* (Philadelphia: Temple University Press, 1990).

5. See, e.g., Bernard Bailyn et al., *The Great Republic: A History of the American People*, 2nd ed. (Lexington, Mass.: D. C. Heath, 1981), 5.

6. Ann Laura Stoler, *Duress: Imperial Durabilities in Our Times* (Durham: Duke University Press, 2016), 10–17.

7. As quoted in Toby Lester, "1507—The Name 'America' Appears on a Map," in Greil Marcus and Werner Sollors, eds., *A New Literary History of America* (Cambridge, Mass.: Harvard University Press, 2009), 5.

8. As quoted in Lester, "1507," 3.

9. For discussion of history textbook production and the absence of American Indians, see Frederick E. Hoxie, "The Indian versus the Textbooks: Is There Any Way Out?" Occasional Papers in Curriculum Series (Chicago: Newberry Library, 1984).

10. See Susan Sleeper-Smith et al., eds., *Why You Can't Teach United States History without American Indians* (Chapel Hill: University of North Carolina Press, 2015).

11. Charles J. Kappler, ed., *Indian Affairs: Law and Treaties*, 5 vols. (Washington, D.C.: Government Printing Office, 1904), 2:55–807.

12. See chapters 8–10 for Civil War–era conflicts. For 40 percent, see Charles Wilkinson, *Blood Struggle: The Rise of Modern Indian Nations* (New York: Norton, 2005), 285.

13. Akhil Reed Amar, *America's Constitution: A Biography* (New York: Random House, 2005), 20; Sven Beckert and Seth Rockman, eds., *Slavery's Capitalism: A New History of American Economic Development* (Philadelphia: University of Pennsylvania Press, 2016), 1.

14. Lepore, *These Truths*, 38.

15. Russell Thornton, "The Demography of Colonialism and 'Old' and 'New' Native Americans," in Russell Thornton, ed., *Studying Native America: Problems and Prospects* (Madison: University of Wisconsin Press, 1998), 17–24. See also Alan Taylor, *American Colonies: The Settling of North America* (New York: Viking Penguin, 2001), 39–44.

16. Wolf, "Settler Colonialism and the Elimination of the Native," 401–3. As Boyd Cothran suggests, "Settler colonialism is the logic that gives meaning to the history of North America." See Cothran, *Remembering the Modoc War: Redemptive Violence and the Making of American Innocence* (Chapel Hill: University of North Carolina Press, 2014), 16.

17. See Jean M. O'Brien, *Firsting and Lasting: Writing Indians out of Existence in New England* (Minneapolis: University of Minnesota Press, 2010); Jodi A. Byrd, *The Transit of Empire: Indigenous Critiques of Colonialism* (Minneapolis: University of Minnesota Press, 2011); and Manu Karuka, *Empire's Tracks: Indigenous Nations, Chinese Workers, and the Transcontinental Railroad* (Oakland: University of California Press, 2019).

18. See Jeff Benvenuto et al., "Colonial Genocide in Indigenous North America," in Andrew Woolford et al., eds., *Colonial Genocide in Indigenous North America* (Durham: Duke University Press, 2014), 1–25.

19. See Benjamin Madley, *An American Genocide: The United States and the California Indian Catastrophe* (New Haven: Yale University Press, 2016), 1–15, 336–59.

20. Tiffany Lethabo King, *The Black Shoals: Offshore Formations of Black and Native Studies* (Durham: Duke University Press, 2019), 11.

21. See Lisa Lowe, *The Intimacies of Four Continents* (Durham: Duke University Press, 2015); and Frederick E. Hoxie, "Retrieving the Red Continent: Settler Colo-

nialism and the History of American Indians in the US," *Ethnic and Racial Studies* (2008): 1160.

22. Allan Greer, "Settler Colonialism and Empire in Early America," *William and Mary Quarterly* (2019): 383–90.

23. James Belich, *Replenishing the Earth: The Settler Revolution and the Rise of the Anglo-World, 1783–1939* (New York: Oxford University Press, 2009).

24. See Robert Warrior, "Organizing Native American and Indigenous Studies," *PMLA* (2008): 1683–91; and Shari Huhndorf, "Literature and the Politics of Native American Studies," *PMLA* (2005): 1618–27. "Native America constitutes an essential dimension of colonial studies, but it necessitates an analysis of the changing nature of and responses to colonialism proper . . . as well as forms of domestic imperialism" (1624).

25. "Editors' Introduction," *NAIS* (Spring 2014): 1. See also Robert Warrior, "2010 NAISA Presidential Address: Practicing Native American and Indigenous Studies," in the same issue, 3–24. The formation of NAISA continued long-standing efforts by Native American intellectuals and activists to establish enduring academic infrastructure. See, e.g., *Indian Voices: The First Convocation of American Indian Scholars* (San Francisco: Indian Historian Press, 1970); and *The Native American Today: The Second Convocation of Indian Scholars* (San Francisco: Indian Historian Press, 1971).

26. Gerald Vizenor, *Manifest Manners: Postindian Warriors of Survivance* (Middletown, Conn.: Wesleyan University Press, 1993).

27. Ned Blackhawk, *Violence over the Land: Indians and Empires in the Early American West* (Cambridge, Mass.: Harvard University Press, 2006).

28. Lepore, *These Truths*, xi.

29. https://www.archives.gov/founding-docs/declaration-transcript.

30. Amy Lonetree, *Decolonizing Museums: Representing Native America in National and Tribal Museums* (Chapel Hill: University of North Carolina Press, 2012), 16–21.

31. See Alyssa Mt. Pleasant et al., "Materials and Methods in Native American and Indigenous Studies: Completing the Turn," *William and Mary Quarterly* (April 2018): 207–36.

32. Randall K. Q. Akee et al., "The Indian Gaming Regulatory Act and Its Effects on American Indian Economic Development," *Journal of Economic Perspectives* (Summer 2015): 185–208.

33. Vine Deloria Jr. and Clifford Lytle, *The Nations Within: The Past and Future of American Indian Sovereignty* (New York: Pantheon Books, 1984), 244–64.

34. Walter R. Echo-Hawk, *In the Courts of the Conqueror: The 10 Worst Indian Law Cases Ever Decided* (Golden, Colo.: Fulcrum, 2010), 13.

35. See Mary Sarah Bilder, "Without Doors: Native Nations and the Convention," *Fordham Law Review* 89, no. 5 (2021): 1707–59.

36. House Resolution 18166, Public Law No. 219, House of Representatives, 1912, 14.

Chapter 1. American Genesis

1. Ted J. Warner, ed., *The Domínguez-Escalante Journal: Their Expedition through Colorado, Utah, Arizona, and New Mexico in 1776*, trans. Fray Angelico Chavez (Salt Lake City: University of Utah Press, 1995), 83.

2. Warner, *The Domínguez-Escalante Journal*, 83–84.

3. See Joseph P. Sanchez, *Explorers, Traders, and Slavers: Forging the Old Spanish Train, 1678–1850* (Salt Lake City: University of Utah Press, 1997), 55–79.

4. Warner, *The Domínguez-Escalante Journal*, 119–20. For legacies of their exploration to western cartography, see Gloria Griffen Cline, *Exploring the Great Basin* (Reno: University of Nevada Press, 1988), 43–56.

5. Warner, *The Domínguez-Escalante Journal*, 128–29.

6. Warner, *The Domínguez-Escalante Journal*, 129.

7. Warner, *The Domínguez-Escalante Journal*, 130, 129.

8. Warner, *The Domínguez-Escalante Journal*, 117.

9. For an overview of Hopi-Spanish relations following the Pueblo Revolt, see James F. Brooks, *Mesa of Sorrows: A History of the Awat'ovi Massacre* (New York: Norton, 2016), 68–86.

10. Alfonso Ortiz, introduction to Alfonso Ortiz, ed., *New Perspectives on the Pueblos* (Santa Fe: School of American Research, 1972), xv. See also Albert H. Schroeder, "Rio Grande Ethnohistory," in the same volume, 47–49.

11. Tamar Herzog, *Frontiers of Possession: Spain and Portugal in Europe and the Americas* (Cambridge, Mass.: Harvard University Press, 2015), 1.

12. J. H. Elliott, *Empires of the Atlantic World: Britain and Spain in America, 1492–1830* (New Haven: Yale University Press, 2006), 198.

13. For debates about the Native American demography in the pre-contact era, see Russell Thornton, "The Demography of Colonialism and 'Old' and 'New' Native Americans," in Russell Thornton, ed., *Studying Native America: Problems and Prospects* (Madison: University of Wisconsin Press, 1998), 17–24. See also Alan Taylor, *American Colonies: The Settling of North America* (New York: Viking Penguin, 2001), 39–41.

14. David G. Sweet and Gary B. Nash, *Struggle and Survival in Colonial America* (Berkeley: University of California Press, 1981). "We must not be misled by the impressive examples of hegemonic mechanisms that did exist in the colonies . . . into accepting the notion that the establishment of such mechanisms guaranteed hegemony" (7).

15. Brian P. Owensby and Richard J. Ross, eds., *Justice in a New World: Negotiating Legal Intelligibility in British, Iberian, and Indigenous America* (New York: New York University Press, 2018), 2.

16. Brian P. Owensby, *Empire of Law and Indian Justice in Colonial Mexico* (Palo Alto: Stanford University Press, 2008).

17. See Pekka Hämäläinen, *The Comanche Empire* (New Haven: Yale University Press, 2008); Ned Blackhawk, *Violence over the Land: Indians and Empires in the Early American West* (Cambridge, Mass.: Harvard University Press, 2006).

18. As quoted in Taylor, *American Colonies*, 413.

19. See Maurice Crandall, *These People Have Always Been a Republic: Indigenous Electorates in the U.S.-Mexico Borderlands, 1598–1912* (Chapel Hill: University of North Carolina Press, 2019); Juliana Barr, *Peace Came in the Form of a Woman: Indians and Spaniards in the Texas Borderlands* (Chapel Hill: University of North Carolina Press, 2007).

20. Lauren Benton, *A Search for Sovereignty: Law and Geography in European Empires, 1400–1900* (New York: Cambridge University Press, 2010), 2.

21. Estimates vary widely regarding the demography of sixteenth-century Pueblo nations. See, e.g., Elinore M. Barrett, *Conquest and Catastrophe: Changing Rio Grande Pueblo Settlement Patterns in the Sixteenth and Seventeenth Centuries* (Albuquerque: University of New Mexico Press, 2002), 12.

22. Joe S. Sando, *Eight Centuries of Pueblo History* (Santa Fe: Clear Light, 1992), 22–35.

23. Matthew Liebmann, *Revolt: An Archaeological History of Pueblo Resistance and Revitalization in 17th Century New Mexico* (Tucson: University of Arizona Press, 2012), 30.

24. Sando, *Eight Centuries of Pueblo History*, 43.

25. See Eleanor B. Adams and Fray Angelico Chavez, eds. and trans., *The Missions of New Mexico, 1776: A Description by Fray Francisco Atanasio Dominguez with Contemporary Documents* (Albuquerque: University of New Mexico Press, 1956), xiv–xv.

26. Benton, *A Search for Sovereignty*, 286–87.

27. Lauren Benton, "In Defense of Ignorance: Frameworks for Legal Politics in the Atlantic World," in Owensby and Ross, *Justice in a New World*, 275.

28. Warner, *The Domínguez-Escalante Journal*, 40.

29. For the evolution of Spanish legal and political claims to jurisdiction over Spain's expanding American territories, see Elliott, *Empires of the Atlantic World*, 119–30.

30. Nancy E. van Deusen, *Global Indios: The Indigenous Struggle for Justice in Sixteenth-Century Spain* (Durham: Duke University Press, 2015), xi.

31. As quoted in van Deusen, *Global Indios*, xii.

32. See, e.g., Herbert E. Bolton, *The Spanish Borderlands: A Chronicle of Old Florida and the Southwest* (New Haven: Yale University Press, 1921), 4; Charles Gibson, *Spain in America* (New York: Harper & Row, 1966), 25.

33. As J. H. Elliott writes, "Spain's American territories, unlike those of the English, were not called 'colonies.' They were kingdoms in possession of the Crown of Castile, and they were inhabited, not by *colonos*, but by conquerors (*conquistadores*) and their descendants, and by *pobladores*, or settlers, the name given to all later arrivals." *Empires of the Atlantic World*, 9.

34. As quoted in Tzvetan Todorov, *The Conquest of America: A Question of the Other* (New York: Harper & Row, 1982), 47–48.

35. Andrés Reséndez, *The Other Slavery: The Uncovered Story of Indian Enslavement in America* (New York: Houghton Mifflin Harcourt, 2016), 17. See also 13–45 for overviews of this "Caribbean Debacle."

36. Kathleen Deagan, "Native American Resistance to Spanish Presence in Hispaniola and La Florida, ca. 1492–1650," in Matthew Liebmann and Melissa S. Murphy, eds., *Enduring Conquests: Rethinking the Archaeology of Resistance to Spanish Colonialism in the Americas* (Santa Fe: School of Advanced Research Press, 2010), 41.

37. For the carnage relayed by Las Casas, see Todorov, *The Conquest of America*, 138–42. Quoting Las Casas: "To see the wounds which covered the bodies of the dead and dying was a spectacle of horror and dread: indeed . . . the Spaniards . . . everywhere . . . wielded their weapons upon these stark naked bodies. . . . Six hundred, including the cacique, were thus slain like brute beasts. . . . Vasco ordered forty of them to be torn to pieces by dogs" (141). The violence and cruelty, for Todorov, signal more than military or strategic gains: "If the word genocide has ever been applied to a situation with some accuracy, this is here the case" (133). See also Gibson, *Spain in America*, 40–43.

38. Elliott, *Empires of the Atlantic World*, 7.

39. As quoted in Reséndez, *The Other Slavery*, 39.

40. Deagan, "Native American Resistance to Spanish Presence," 46. See also Woodbury Lowery, *The Spanish Settlements within the Present Limits of the United States, 1513–1561* (New York: G. P. Putnam's Sons, 1911), 132.

41. As quoted in Lowery, *The Spanish Settlements within the Present Limits of the United States*, 133.

42. Lowery, *The Spanish Settlements within the Present Limits of the United States*, 133–34.

43. "Having asserted their authority with such difficulty at home, they were not inclined to let their subjects get the better of them overseas." Elliott, *Empires of the Atlantic World*, 22. See also Taylor, *American Colonies*, 25–32. "The stunning expansion of European power, wealth, and knowledge would have seemed improbable in 1400, when Europeans were a parochial set of peoples preoccupied with internal and interminable wars" (25).

44. Lyle N. McAlister, *Spain and Portugal in the New World, 1492–1700* (Minneapolis: University of Minnesota Press, 1984), 79.

45. Matthew Restall, *Seven Myths of the Spanish Conquest* (New York: Oxford University Press, 2003), 27–43.

46. Gibson, *Spain in America*, 48–67.

47. Jill Lepore, *These Truths: A History of the United States* (New York: Norton, 2018), 7. For an overview of the demographic estimates and decline of Hispaniola's

Indigenous population—"seemingly one of the greatest of all genocides"—see William M. Denevan, ed., *The Native Population of the Americas in 1492*, rev. ed. (Madison: University of Wisconsin Press, 1992), 35.

48. For overviews of the varying ethnonyms, Aztec, Mexica, and Nahuas, see Matthew Restall, *When Montezuma Met Cortés: The True Story of the Meeting That Changed History* (New York: HarperCollins, 2018), xii. See also James Lockhart, *The Nahuas After the Conquest: A Social and Cultural History of the Indians of Central Mexico, Sixteenth through Eighteenth Centuries* (Palo Alto: Stanford University Press, 1992); and Camilla Townsend, *Fifth Sun: A New History of the Aztecs* (New York: Oxford University Press, 2019), 30–32. As Pete Sigal suggests, the use of Nahua, as opposed to Aztec, "prioritizes linguistic unity . . . [and] has become a term used by many . . . to describe the bulk of the Indigenous peoples of central Mexico." Pete Sigal, *The Flower and the Scorpion: Sexuality and Ritual in Early Nahua Culture* (Durham: Duke University Press, 2011), xv.

49. Townsend, *Fifth Sun*, 71–84.

50. Lockhart, *The Nahuas After the Conquest*, 1.

51. Restall, *When Montezuma Met Cortés*, 4–5. For Seville's prominence in Spanish exploration, see Andrés Reséndez, *A Land So Remote: The Epic Journey of Cabeza de Vaca* (New York: Basic Books, 2007), 39–42. "As Spain's only port licensed to do business with the American colonies, Seville became a protagonist in the history of discovery, the starting and end point of all transatlantic voyages" (39).

52. Lockhart, *The Nahuas After the Conquest*, 14. See also 14–58.

53. Townsend, *Fifth Sun*, 27–30.

54. Lockhart, *The Nahuas After the Conquest*, 15–16.

55. Restall, *When Montezuma Met Cortés*, xxviii. Restall refers to their encounter as "the Meeting," proper noun, a convention that is followed hereafter.

56. Townsend, *Fifth Sun*, 113–28.

57. Gibson, *Spain in America*, 38.

58. Matthew Restall argues for a broader temporality for "the Conquest of Mexico," and distinguishes between the Spanish-Aztec War and Spanish-Mesoamerican War. See *When Montezuma Met Cortés*, xxix.

59. For the construction of "indio" as a racial and legal category, see van Deusen, *Global Indios*, esp. 224–28. See also Ethelia Ruiz Medrano, *Mexico's Indigenous Communities: Their Lands and Histories, 1500–2010*, trans. Russ Davidson (Boulder: University of Colorado Press, 2010); and Brian P. Owensby, *Empire of Law and Indian Justice in Colonial Mexico* (Palo Alto: Stanford University Press, 2008): "During the early decades after conquest the word *indio* rarely appeared as a loanword in Nahuatl texts. 'Indians' preferred to speak of themselves as residents of this or that altepetl, town, or pueblo, insisting on their 'microethnicities' *over and above all other labels*. In calling them *indios*, Spaniards were not merely recognizing and naming an existing dif-

ference between themselves and these New World others, so much as they were creating new categories: they were 'inventing' the Indians and thus themselves" (24) (emphasis added).

60. Restall, *Seven Myths of the Spanish Conquest*, 41–42.

61. Restall, *Seven Myths of the Spanish Conquest*, 42.

62. As quoted in Reséndez, *The Other Slavery*, 62.

63. Clay Mathers et al., eds., *Native and Spanish New Worlds: Sixteenth-Century Entradas in the American Southwest and Southeast* (Tucson: University of Arizona Press, 2013). See also Dennis Reinhartz and Oakah L. Jones, "*Hacia el Norte!* The Spanish *Entrada* into North America, 1513–1549," in John Logan Allen, ed., *North American Exploration: A New World Disclosed*, 3 vols. (Lincoln: University of Nebraska Press, 1997), 1:241–91.

64. David J. Weber, *The Spanish Frontier in North America* (New Haven: Yale University Press, 1992), 49. See also Richard Flint, *Great Cruelties Have Been Reported: The 1544 Investigation of the Coronado Expedition* (Dallas: Southern Methodist University Press, 2002), 27–36.

65. For the first English interior explorations, see Clarence Walworth Alvord and Lee Bidgood, *The First Explorations of the Trans-Allegheny Region by the Virginians, 1650–1674* (Cleveland: Arthur H. Clark, 1912); and J. Ralph Randolph, *British Travelers among the Southern Indians, 1660–1763* (Norman: University of Oklahoma Press, 1973).

66. Lowery, *The Spanish Settlements within the Present Limits of the United States*, 146–50.

67. Bolton, *The Spanish Borderlands*, 71. See also Lowery, *The Spanish Settlements within the Present Limits of the United States*, 243–44; Charles Hudson, *Knights of Spain, Warriors of the Sun: Hernando de Soto and the South's Ancient Chiefdoms* (Athens: University of Georgia Press, 1997); and Paul E. Hoffman, "Introduction: The De Soto Expedition, a Cultural Crossroads," in Lawrence A. Clayton et al., eds., *The De Soto Chronicles: The Expedition of Hernando De Soto to North America, 1539–1543*, 2 vols. (Tuscaloosa: University of Alabama Press, 1993) 1:5–13.

68. Clayton et al., *The De Soto Chronicles*, 1:135–36.

69. Restall, *Seven Myths of the Spanish Conquest*, 71. See also Lowery, *The Spanish Settlements within the Present Limits of the United States*, 146–71, 213–52; Weber, *The Spanish Frontier in North America*, 49–55; and Robin A. Beck Jr. et al., "Limiting Resistance: Juan Pardo and the Shrinking of Spanish La Florida, 1566–68," in Liebmann and Murphy, *Enduring Conquests*, 19–39.

70. By contrast, southern anthropologists have offered sustained inquiries into the fate of many Native communities impacted by de Soto's violent journey. See, e.g., Thomas J. Pluckhahn and Robbie Ethridge, eds., *Light on the Path: The Anthropology and History of the Southeastern Indians* (Tuscaloosa: University of Alabama Press, 2006).

71. As Matthew Liebmann suggests, borderlands encounters defy simple binaries of accommodation and resistance. See Liebmann, "The Best of Times, the Worst of Times: Pueblo Resistance and Accommodation during the Spanish *Reconquista* of New Mexico," in Liebmann and Murphy, *Enduring Conquests*, 200–201.

72. Weber, *The Spanish Frontier in North America*, 51.

73. Paul Kelton, "The Great Southeastern Smallpox Epidemic, 1696–1700: The Region's First Major Epidemic?" in Robbie Ethridge and Charles Hudson, eds., *The Transformation of the Southeastern Indians, 1540–1760* (Jackson: University Press of Mississippi, 2002), 22–23. See also Ann F. Ramenofsky and Patricia Galloway, "Disease and the Soto Entrada," in Patricia Galloway, ed., *The Hernando de Soto Expedition: History, Historiography, and "Discovery" in the Southeast* (Lincoln: University of Nebraska Press, 1997), 259–79; and Dale L. Hutchinson, "Entradas and Epidemics in the Sixteenth-Century Southeast," in Mathers et al., *Native and Spanish New Worlds*, 140–51.

74. Robin A. Beck Jr. et al., "Limiting Resistance: Juan Pardo and the Shrinking of Spanish La Florida, 1566–68," in Liebmann and Murphy, *Enduring Conquests*, 22–23.

75. Robbie Ethridge, "Creating the Shatter Zone: Indian Slave Traders and the Collapse of Southeastern Chiefdoms," in Pluckhahn and Ethridge, *Light on the Path*, 207–18.

76. Stephen A. Kowalweski, "Coalescent Societies," in Pluckhahn and Ethridge, *Light on the Path*, 94–96.

77. For the centrality of the monopolization of violence and the use of violence in the formation of state power, see Meyer Kestbaum and George Ritzer, eds., *The Wiley-Blackwell Companion to Sociology* (Malden, Mass.: Wiley-Blackwell, 2012), 588–608.

78. Ruiz Medrano, *Mexico's Indigenous Communities*, 18.

79. Ruiz Medrano, *Mexico's Indigenous Communities*, 18.

80. Kelly McDonough, "Indigenous Remembering and Forgettings: Sixteenth-Century Nahua Letters and Petitions to the Spanish Crown, *NAIS* (Spring 2018): 72–73.

81. Restall, *Seven Myths of the Spanish Conquest*, 72.

82. Michael C. Meyer and William L. Sherman, *The Course of Mexican History*, 4th ed. (New York: Oxford University Press, 1991), 147.

83. Ida Altman, *The War for Mexico's West: Indians and Spaniards in New Galicia, 1524–1550* (Albuquerque: University of New Mexico Press, 2010). See also Philip Wayne Powell, *Soldiers, Indians, and Silver: The Northward Advance of New Spain, 1550–1600*, rev. ed. (Berkeley: University of California Press, 1969). For the ethnography of north-central Mexico north of Mesoamerica, see also William B. Griffen, "Southern Periphery: East," in Alfonso Oritz, ed., *Southwest*, vol. 10 of *Handbook of North American Indians* (Washington, D.C.: Smithsonian Institute, 1983), 329–42.

84. J. Lloyd Mecham, *Francisco de Ibarra and Nueva Vizcaya* (New York: Greenwood, 1968), 32–33.

85. Ida Altman, "Conquest, Coercion, and Collaboration: Indian Allies and the Campaigns in Nueva Galicia," in Laura E. Matthew and Michel R. Oudijk, eds., *Indian Conquistadors: Indigenous Allies in the Conquest of Mesoamerica* (Norman: University of Oklahoma Press, 2007), 145–74. See also Oakah L. Jones, *Nueva Vizcaya: Heartland of the Spanish Frontier* (Albuquerque: University of New Mexico Press, 1988), 17–21.

86. P. J. Bakewell, *Silver Mining and Society in Colonial Mexico: Zacatecas, 1546–1700* (New York: Cambridge University Press, 1971), 4–6. See also Powell, *Soldiers, Indians, and Silver,* 4–9. For lower estimates of auxiliaries, see Altman, "Conquest, Coercion, and Collaboration," 160–61.

87. Colin M. MacLachlan and Jaime E. Rodriquez O., *The Forging of the Cosmic Race: A Reinterpretation of Colonial Mexico,* rev. ed. (Berkeley: University of California Press, 1990), 99.

88. Powell, *Soldiers, Indians, and Silver,* 3–4.

89. For an outstanding overview of de Guzmán's campaign, see Altman, "Conquest, Coercion, and Collaboration," 147–59. See also Altman, *The War for Mexico's West,* 34–53.

90. Bakewell, *Silver Mining and Society in Colonial Mexico,* 8–9. See also Powell, *Soldiers, Indians, and Silver.* Powell suggests that Cristóbal de Oñate was acting governor during the Mixtón War (11).

91. Reséndez, *The Other Slavery,* 103.

92. Taylor, *American Colonies,* 63. Taylor suggests the total tonnage of silver from the colonial era at 16,000 tons, or 32 million pounds.

93. Taylor, *American Colonies,* 63.

94. Gibson, *Spain in America,* 122.

95. Gibson, *Spain in America,* 121.

96. Elliott, *Empires of the Atlantic World,* 94.

97. Elliott, *Empires of the Atlantic World,* 95.

98. Paradoxically, Spanish overreliance on mineral wealth fueled its underdevelopment, as nascent mercantilist and commercial institutions formed outside of Iberia rather than within it. "Real prosperity was to be measured by national productivity, and not by a fortuitous inflow of bullion." Elliott, *Empires of the Atlantic World,* 26.

99. For an overview of such Indigenous settlement patterns, see MacLachlan and Rodriquez O., *The Forging of the Cosmic Race,* 168–71. For an introduction to "settler colonialism" as applied to U.S. history, see Roxanne Dunbar-Ortiz, *An Indigenous Peoples' History of the United States* (Boston: Beacon, 2014), esp. 1–10.

100. As quoted in George P. Hammond and Agapito Rey, *Don Juan de Oñate: Colonizer of New Mexico, 1595–1628* (Albuquerque: University of New Mexico Press, 1953), 6.

101. For New Mexico and northern Mexico's interconnected economies, see Reséndez, *The Other Slavery,* 116–24.

102. Gibson, *Spain in America,* 60. See also 57–67.

103. Gibson, *Spain in America*, 72–77.

104. Edward H. Spicer, *Cycles of Conquest: The Impact of Spain, Mexico, and the United States on the Indians of the Southwest, 1533–1960* (Tucson: University of Arizona Press, 1962), 22–24.

105. France V. Scholes, "Church and State in Colonial New Mexico, 1610–1650," *New Mexico Historical Review* (1936): 297–349.

106. Hammond and Rey, *Don Juan de Oñate*, 318.

107. Spicer, *Cycles of Conquest*, 156. For overviews of the Oñate expedition, see also 152–58 in Spicer's work; Weber, *The Spanish Frontier in North America*, 77–87; and Hammond and Rey, *Don Juan de Oñate*, 5–16.

108. Hammond and Rey, *Don Juan de Oñate*, 340.

109. Hammond and Rey, *Don Juan de Oñate*, 340.

110. Barrett, *Conquest and Catastrophe*, 12.

111. Hammond and Rey, *Don Juan de Oñate*, 17–18.

112. Hammond and Rey, *Don Juan de Oñate*, 340.

113. For an overview of the joint religious and political structures within Pueblo society, see Alfonso Ortiz, *The Tewa World: Space, Time, Being, and Becoming in a Pueblo Society* (Chicago: University of Chicago Press, 1969), 79–119.

114. John L. Kessell, *Pueblos, Spaniards, and the Kingdom of New Mexico* (Norman: University of Oklahoma Press, 2008), esp. 51–72.

115. Hammond and Rey, *Don Juan de Oñate*, 339.

116. Hammond and Rey, *Don Juan de Oñate*, 450.

117. Hammond and Rey, *Don Juan de Oñate*, 446.

118. Hammond and Rey, *Don Juan de Oñate*, 21.

119. Hammond and Rey, *Don Juan de Oñate*, 447.

120. Hammond and Rey, *Don Juan de Oñate*, 466.

121. Hammond and Rey, *Don Juan de Oñate*, 477–78.

122. Hammond and Rey, *Don Juan de Oñate*, 478.

123. Hammond and Rey, *Don Juan de Oñate*, 478–79.

124. Reséndez, *The Other Slavery*, 118. Throughout the sixteenth century, the Spanish monarchy had "allowed the capture of Indians taken in 'just wars'" as slaves (42).

125. Heather B. Trigg, *From Household to Empire: Society and Economy in Early Colonial New Mexico* (Tucson: University of Arizona Press, 2005), 88–133.

126. Barrett, *Conquest and Catastrophe*, 68–69.

127. Ortiz, *The Tewa World*, 98.

128. Barrett, *Conquest and Catastrophe*, 54.

129. Barrett, *Conquest and Catastrophe*, 62.

130. As quoted in Barrett, *Conquest and Catastrophe*, 78. The term *cocolitzli* can be interpreted as either a virulent form of smallpox—the fulminating type—or as a major disease outbreak with generally more than one disease involved.

131. Barrett, *Conquest and Catastrophe*, 78.

132. Charles Wilson Hackett, *Revolt of the Pueblo Indians of New Mexico and Otermín's Attempted Reconquest, 1680–1682,* 2 vols. (Albuquerque: University of New Mexico Press, 1942), 1:11–12.

133. Joe S. Sando, "The Pueblo Revolt," in Joe S. Sando and Herman Agoyo, eds., *Po'Pay: Leader of the First American Revolution* (Santa Fe: Clear Light, 2005), 13–15.

134. Sando, "The Pueblo Revolt," 13.

135. As quoted in Kurt E. Dongoske and Cindy K. Dongoske, "History in Stone: Evaluating Spanish Conversion Efforts through Hopi Rock Art," in Robert W. Preucel, ed., *Archaeologies of the Pueblo Revolt: Identity, Meaning, and Renewal in the Pueblo World* (Albuquerque: University of New Mexico Press, 2002), 118.

136. John L. Kessell, *Kiva, Cross, and Crown: The Pecos Indians and New Mexico, 1540–1840* (Washington, D.C.: National Park Service, 1979), 122–29, 307.

137. Sando, "The Pueblo Revolt," 40.

138. Michael V. Wilcox, "Social Memory and the Pueblo Revolt: A Postcolonial Perspective," in Preucel, *Archaeologies of the Pueblo Revolt,* 175.

139. Sando, "The Pueblo Revolt," 40–41.

140. Barrett, *Conquest and Catastrophe,* 91–92.

141. Elizabeth John, *Storms Brewed in Other Men's Worlds: The Confrontation of Indians, Spanish, and French in the Southwest, 1540–1795* (College Station: Texas A&M University Press, 1975), 98–154.

142. Blackhawk, *Violence over the Land,* 88–112.

143. Peter Whiteley, "Re-imaging Awat'ovi," in Preucel, *Archaeologies of the Pueblo Revolt,* 154.

144. Weber, *The Spanish Frontier in North America,* 168.

145. For an introduction to the racial diversity and distinct ethnic formations across eighteenth-century New Spain, see Magali M. Carrera, *Imagining Identity in New Spain: Race, Lineage, and the Colonial Body in Portraiture and Casta Paintings* (Austin: University of Texas Press, 2003). "Numerous edicts, laws, and ordinances of the 1750s through 1790s also refer to the general population of New Spain less often as castas and more often as people marked by calidad and class" (48).

146. Schroeder, "Rio Grande Ethnohistory," 62.

147. For an overview of the gendered systems of domesticity and power in colonial New Mexico, see Ramon A. Gutíerrez, *When Jesus Came, the Corn Mothers Went Away: Marriage, Sexuality, and Power in Colonial New Mexico, 1500–1846* (Palo Alto: Stanford University Press, 1991).

148. Ethridge, "Creating the Shatter Zone," 207–18. See also Robbie Ethridge, *From Chicaza to Chickasaw: The European Invasion and the Transformation of the Mississippian World, 1540–1715* (Chapel Hill: University of North Carolina Press, 2010).

149. See Warren L. Cook, *Flood Time of Empire: Spain and the Pacific Northwest, 1542–1819* (New Haven: Yale University Press, 1973), esp. 44–84. See also Freeman M.

Tovell, *At the Far Reaches of Empire: The Life of Juan Francisco de la Bogeda y Quadra* (Vancouver: University of British Columbia Press, 2008).

Chapter 2. The Native Northeast and the Rise of British North America

1. Lawrence C. Wroth, *The Voyages of Giovanni da Verrazzano, 1524–1528* (New Haven: Yale University Press, 1970), 137.

2. As Lisa Brooks suggests, "a decolonial process might reverse" narrative perspectives on the region's settlement history "by resisting containment and opening possibilities for Native presence." See *Our Beloved Kin: A New History of King Philip's War* (New Haven: Yale University Press, 2018), 6.

3. "Four [mutually intelligible] distinct languages, each with several dialects" were spoken by northeastern Algonquian communities, including the Narragansett. See Neal Salisbury, *Manitou and Providence: Indians, Europeans, and the Making of New England, 1500–1643* (New York: Oxford University Press, 1982), 21; and Jean M. O'Brien, *Dispossession by Degrees: Indian Land and Identity in Natick, Massachusetts, 1650–1790* (New York: Cambridge University Press, 1997), 21. As Christine DeLucia writes, "There is not a single, universally shared Algonquian word for this region, though occasionally commentators use 'Dawnland.'" See *Memory Lands: King Philip's War and the Place of Violence in the Northeast* (New Haven: Yale University Press, 2018), 24. See also Coll Thrush, *Indigenous London: Native Travelers at the Heart of Empire* (New Haven: Yale University Press, 2016), 52–61; Salisbury, *Manitou and Providence*, 26–27; Wendy Warren, *New England Bound: Slavery and Colonization in Early America* (New York: Norton, 2016), 27, 84; and Neal Salisbury, "The Atlantic Northeast," in Frederick E. Hoxie, ed., *The Oxford Handbook of American Indian History* (New York: Oxford University Press, 2016), 335.

4. Wroth, *Voyages of Giovanni da Verrazzano*, 140. For "Southern New England, as a cultural region," see Bert Salwen, "Indians of Southern New England and Long Island: Early Period," in Bruce G. Trigger, ed., *The Northeast*, vol. 15 of *Handbook of North American Indians* (Washington, D.C.: Smithsonian Institute, 1978), 160–76. For an overview of the northeastern homelands of the Mi'kmaq, Wulstukwiuk, Passamaquoddy, and Wabanaki Confederacy members, see Jeffers Lennox, *Homelands and Empires: Indigenous Spaces, Imperial Fictions, and Competition for Territory in Northeastern North America, 1690–1763* (Toronto: University of Toronto Press, 2017), 15–25.

5. Wroth, *Voyages of Giovanni da Verrazzano*, 138.

6. Wroth, *Voyages of Giovanni da Verrazzano*, 139.

7. See Andrew Lipman, *The Saltwater Frontier: Indians and the Contest for the American Coast* (New Haven: Yale University Press, 2015), 19–53.

8. Wroth, *Voyages of Giovanni da Verrazzano*, 137. As Neal Salisbury suggests, "His-

torians and others have described the English conquest of Indian New England many times over, but with nearly always the same underlying assumption. Implicitly or explicitly, they have presupposed that the outcome was inevitable." *Manitou and Providence,* 3. As Christine DeLucia writes, "Archiving has been a cornerstone of New Englanders' claims to territorial and political authority. . . . The very sources upon which scholars rely to reconstruct Northeastern pasts have been inflected by historical contingencies and settler colonialism." *Memory Lands,* 13.

9. For an effort to expand early American history beyond "English-speaking men confined to the Atlantic seaboard," see Alan Taylor, *American Colonies: The Settling of North America* (New York: Viking Penguin, 2001), x. While "Virginia was the largest of the new United States, in territory, in population, and in influence," its slave economy proliferated during the eighteenth century. See Edmund S. Morgan, *American Slavery, American Freedom: The Ordeal of Colonial Virginia* (New York: Norton, 1975), 5.

10. Mark Peterson, *The City-State of Boston: The Rise and Fall of an Atlantic Power, 1630–1865* (Princeton: Princeton University Press, 2019), 14.

11. Taylor, *American Colonies,* 159. See also Richard S. Dunn, *Sugar and Slaves: The Rise of the Planter Class in the English West Indies, 1624–1713* (Chapel Hill: University of North Carolina Press, 1972), 10.

12. As quoted in Warren, *New England Bound,* 85.

13. Benjamin Madley, "Reexamining the American Genocide Debate: Meaning, Historiography, and New Methods," *American Historical Review* (February 2015): 98–139.

14. Francis Jennings, *The Invasion of America: Indians, Colonialism, and the Cant of Conquest* (Chapel Hill: University of North Carolina Press, 1975), 178.

15. Karen Ordahl Kupperman, *Indians & English: Facing off in Early America* (Ithaca: Cornell University Press, 2000), 214.

16. DeLucia, *Memory Lands,* 11.

17. "Throughout New England before 1700," as Margaret Ellen Newell writes, "Native Americans represented the dominant form of nonwhite labor." *Brethren by Nature: New England Indians, Colonists, and the Origins of American Slavery* (Ithaca: Cornell University Press, 2015), 5.

18. Robert C. Winthrop, ed., *Life and Letters of John Winthrop,* 2 vols. (Boston: Ticknor & Fields, 1867), 2:54. For Virginia correspondences, see Warren, *New England Bound,* 20. For Virginia's underdevelopment vis-à-vis other colonies, especially Bermuda, see Michael J. Jarvis, *In the Eye of All Trade: Bermuda, Bermudians, and the Maritime Atlantic World, 1680–1873* (Chapel Hill: University of North Carolina Press, 2010), 26–29.

19. Richard B. Sheridan, "The Domestic Economy," in Jack P. Greene and J. R. Pole, eds., *Colonial British America: Essays on the New History of the Early Modern Era* (Baltimore: Johns Hopkins University Press, 1984), 43.

20. Morgan, *American Slavery, American Freedom.* See also Sheridan, "The Domestic Economy," 45–46.

21. Jennings, *Invasion of America,* 27.

22. "To a large degree, it may be said the Americans bought their independence with slave labor." Morgan, *American Slavery, American Freedom,* 5.

23. "In the sixteenth century at least 650,000 indigenous peoples were enslaved and forced to relocate to foreign lands throughout the inter-American and transatlantic Iberian world." Nancy E. van Deusen, *Global Indios: The Indigenous Struggle for Justice in Sixteenth-Century Spain* (Durham: Duke University Press, 2015), 2. Focus upon the "approximately 175 Indians and Inuit who are known to have journeyed to the British Isles" has limited comparative analysis of the transatlantic Indigenous slave trade. See, for example, Alden T. Vaughan, *Transatlantic Encounters: American Indians in Britain, 1500–1776* (New York: Cambridge University Press, 2006), xi.

24. See chapter 3 for displacement of Algonquian-speaking communities.

25. Alan Gallay, *The Indian Slave Trade: The Rise of the English Empire in the American South, 1670–1717* (New Haven: Yale University Press, 2002), 7–8. See also Robbie Ethridge, "Global Capital, Violence, and the Making of a Colonial Shatter Zone," in Andrew Woolford et al., eds., *Colonial Genocide in Indigenous North America* (Durham: Duke University Press, 2014), 49–69.

26. Stephen Greenblatt, *Marvelous Possessions: The Wonder of the New* (Chicago: University of Chicago Press, 1991), esp. 52–118.

27. "As Indians and English came to know each other along America's east coast, nothing mattered more than religion." Kupperman, *Indians & English,* 110. See also Karen Ordahl Kupperman, *The Jamestown Project* (Cambridge, Mass.: Harvard University Press, 2007), 12–42.

28. Michael P. Winship, *Godly Republicanism: Puritans, Pilgrims, and a City on a Hill* (Cambridge, Mass.: Harvard University Press, 2012), 5.

29. Acts 16:12, King James Bible.

30. Steve Pincus, *1688: The First Modern Revolution* (New Haven: Yale University Press, 2009), 92.

31. As quoted in Peterson, *City-State of Boston,* 12.

32. John Cotton, *God's Promise to His Plantation* (London: William Jones, 1630), 6.

33. Peterson, *City-State of Boston,* 15–16.

34. Winship, *Godly Republicanism,* 227.

35. Cotton, *God's Promise to His Plantation,* 8.

36. Peterson, *City-State of Boston,* 17. See also Warren, *New England Bound,* 85–87. For discussion of the environmental suggestions found in the Great Seal, see John Demos, *The Unredeemed Captive: A Family Story from Early America* (New York: Vintage Books, 1995), 4.

37. Cotton, *God's Promise to His Plantation,* 13.

38. Virginia DeJohn Anderson, "New England in the Seventeenth Century," in

Nicholas Canny, ed., *The Origins of Empire: British Overseas Enterprise to the Close of the Seventeenth Century*, vol. 1 of Wm. Roger Louis, ed., *The Oxford History of the British Empire* (New York: Oxford University Press, 1998), 193.

39. Kupperman, *Jamestown Project*, 14. See also Reginald Horsman, *Race and Manifest Destiny: The Origins of American Racial Anglo-Saxonism* (Cambridge, Mass.: Harvard University Press, 1981), esp. 80–85.

40. See Barry O'Connell, ed., *A Son of the Forest and Other Writings* (Amherst: University of Massachusetts Press, 1992).

41. "Many colonists . . . were highly motivated to find ways to expand their claim to neighboring lands. They were not averse to cattle, pigs, and horses, as members of their households, doing that work for them, on the front lines of colonization." Brooks, *Our Beloved Kin*, 56.

42. Daniel R. Madnell, ed., *Early American Indian Documents: Treaties and Laws, 1607–1789*, 19 vols. (Bethesda: Congressional Information Services), 19:7.

43. Neal Salisbury, "Squanto: Last of the Patuxets," in David G. Sweet and Gary B. Nash, eds., *Struggle and Survival in Colonial America* (Berkeley: University of California Press, 1981), 233. See also Salisbury, *Manitou and Providence*, 51–84.

44. Membertou's quote in Salisbury, *Manitou and Providence*, 57. See also William Cronon, *Changes in the Land: Indians, Colonists, and the Ecology of New England*, rev. ed. (New York: Hill & Wang, 2003), 90.

45. As quoted in O'Brien, *Dispossession by Degrees*, 18; see also 14–17.

46. Cronon, *Changes in the Land*, 94–95.

47. Lipman, *Saltwater Frontier*, 27. See also 25–33 for an overview of the social dynamics of "corn and fish" within northeastern Native communities.

48. Salisbury, "Squanto," 237.

49. As quoted in Daniel K. Richter, *Facing East from Indian Country: A Native History of Early America* (Cambridge, Mass.: Harvard University Press, 2001), 60. See also Cronon, *Changes in the Land*, 67–90.

50. As quoted in Cronon, *Changes in the Land*, 162.

51. Jennings, *Invasion of America*, 15.

52. As quoted in Thrush, *Indigenous London*, 42. See also, Lipman, *Saltwater Frontier*, 79–80; and Margaret Ellen Newell, *Brethren by Nature: New England Indians, Colonists, and the Origins of American Slavery* (Ithaca: Cornell University Press, 2015), 18.

53. Lipman, *Saltwater Frontier*, 86.

54. Salisbury, *Manitou and Providence*, 90–95.

55. Edward Arber, ed., *Travels and Works of Captain John Smith*, 2 vols. (Edinburgh: John Grant, 1910), 1:219. For the traffic of English captives to Spanish slave markets, see van Deusen, *Global Indios*, 44–45. Margaret Newell suggests that Hunt enslaved "twenty-seven Pawtuxet and Nauset Indians." *Brethren by Nature*, 19.

56. DeLucia, *Memory Lands*, 294.

57. Jace Weaver, *The Red Atlantic: Indigenes and the Making of the Modern World* (Chapel Hill: University of North Carolina Press, 2014).

58. DeLucia, *Memory Lands,* 291.

59. Thrush, *Indigenous London,* 44.

60. "In total, perhaps a little more than forty made up Algonquian London in the Tudor-Stuart era." Thrush, *Indigenous London,* 44. Alden Vaughan suggests a total of five Eastern Abenakis were "abducted" by George Waymouth. See *Transatlantic Encounters,* 57.

61. As quoted in Thrush, *Indigenous London,* 42; see also 57.

62. Newell, *Brethren by Nature,* 19.

63. Vaughan, *Transatlantic Encounters,* 57–65.

64. As Margaret Newell suggests, "Somehow Indian slavery virtually disappeared from post–World War I scholarship on New England. . . . The history of slavery in general and of Indian slavery in particular remains stubbornly absent." *Brethren by Nature,* 4.

65. Salisbury, *Manitou and Providence,* 92n15, 265–66. See also "Gorges, Ferdinando, 1568–1647," in The Yale Indian Papers Project (YIPP), https://yipp.yale.edu/bio/bibliography/gorges-ferdinando-1568-1647.

66. Van Deusen, *Global Indios,* 210–26.

67. Kathleen Brown, "Native Americans and Early Modern Concepts of Race," in Martin Daunton and Rick Halpern, eds., *Empire and Others: British Encounters with Indigenous Peoples, 1600–1850* (Philadelphia: Literary University of Pennsylvania Press, 1999), 79–100; and Ed White, "Invisible Tagkanysough," *PMLA* (2005): 751–67.

68. As quoted in Alexander Young, *Chronicles of the Pilgrim Fathers of the Colony of Plymouth, from 1602 to 1625,* 2nd ed. (Boston: Charles C. Little & James Brown, 1864), 190–91.

69. As quoted in Betty Booth Donohue, *Bradford's Indian Book: Being the True Roote & Rise of American Letters as Revaeled by the Native Text Embedded in "Of Plimoth Plantation"* (Gainsville: University Press of Florida, 2011), xiv. For "spetiall" quote, see 96. Based on readings of nineteenth-century sources, Donohue provides an alternative biography for Tisquantum, one that suggests an earlier date of enslavement (96n12, 156.

70. As quoted in Young, *Chronicles of the Pilgrim Fathers,* 301.

71. As quoted in Young, *Chronicles of the Pilgrim Fathers,* 301.

72. Lipman, *Saltwater Frontier,* 100

73. As quoted in Young, *Chronicles of the Pilgrim Fathers,* 190. There is debate as to whether Dermer returned with Tisquantum to England or came directly to the Northeast. See, for example, Lipman, *Saltwater Frontier,* 100. See also Vaughan, *Transatlantic Encounters,* 66–67; and Salisbury, "Sqaunto," 237.

74. As Alden Vaughan writes, by "1620 . . . [Tisquantum] had completed at least two round trips to Europe, perhaps three, conceivably four." *Transatlantic Encounters,* 71. For focus on one-way European migration, see Warren, *New England Bound,* 21.

75. Van Deusen, *Global Indios,* 139.

76. Lipman, *Saltwater Frontier,* 100–101.

77. As quoted in Vaughan, *Transatlantic Encounters,* 65.

78. Salisbury, "Squanto," 236–37.

79. Salisbury, "Squanto," 237.

80. Lipman, *Saltwater Frontier,* 100–101.

81. Lipman, *Saltwater Frontier,* 103. See also Salisbury, *Manitou and Providence,* 122–23.

82. Anderson, "New England in the Seventeenth Century," 197.

83. "The feasting was meant to celebrate the shared harvest and alliance; it was not a proper Christian Thanksgiving at all. We think of it that way thanks to late nineteenth-century writers who rediscovered the long-obscure feast and reinterpreted it as a providential moment of cross-cultural cooperation." Lipman, *Saltwater Frontier,* 101.

84. Anderson, "New England in the Seventeenth Century," 196.

85. Hilary McD. Beckles, "The 'Hub of Empire': The Caribbean and Britain in the Seventeenth Century," in Canny, *Origins of Empire,* 221, 219. See also Dunn, *Sugar and Slaves,* 17–19.

86. Brooks, *Our Beloved Kin,* 36–39.

87. Salisbury, *Manitou and Providence,* 114–19.

88. J. Franklin Jameson, ed., *Narratives of New Netherland, 1609–1664* (New York: Charles Scribner's Sons, 1909), 43. See also Salisbury, *Manitou and Providence,* 147.

89. Salisbury, "The Atlantic Northeast," 341. See also Robert E. Dewar and Kevin A. McBride, "Remnant Settlement Patterns," in J. Rossignol, et al., eds., *Space, Time, and Archaeological Landscapes* (New York: Springer, 1992), 227–55; Lucianne Levin, "Coastal Adaptations in Southern New England and Southern New York," *Archaeology of Eastern North America* (1998): 101–20; and Kevin A. McBride, "The Historical Archaeology of the Mashantucket Pequot, 1637–1900: A Preliminary Analysis," in Laurence M. Hauptman and James D. Wherry, eds., *The Pequots in Southern New England* (Norman: University of Oklahoma Press, 1990), 96–116.

90. Lipman, *Saltwater Frontier,* 104.

91. Brooks, *Our Beloved Kin,* 27.

92. Salwen, "Indians of Southern New England and Long Island," 167. See also Brooks, *Our Beloved Kin,* 27–71, 124–31, 322–26.

93. David J. Silverman, *Thundersticks: Firearms and the Violent Transformation of Native America* (Cambridge, Mass.: Harvard University Press, 2016), 92–120.

94. Michael P. Winship, *Seers of God: Puritan Providentialism in the Restoration and Early Enlightenment* (Baltimore: Johns Hopkins University Press, 1996), 10.

95. As quoted in Lipman, *Saltwater Frontier,* 115.

96. Winthrop, *Life and Letters of John Winthrop,* 2:54.

97. Taylor, *American Colonies,* 206; see also 134–37; and Beckles, "The 'Hub of Empire,'" 221–25.

98. Peter C. Mancall, "Native Americans and Europeans in English America, 1500–1700," in Canny, *Origins of Empire,* 333.

99. Winship, *Godly Republicanism,* 206–14.

100. Allan Greer, *Property and Dispossession: Natives, Empires, and Land in Early Modern North America* (New York: Cambridge University Press, 2018), 200, 4; see also 1–23, 191–237. See also Warren, *New England Bound*, 89–90; and Cronon, *Changes in the Land*, 56–72.

101. A "debate over whether colonial farmers engaged in subsistence or commercial agriculture goes back at least to [Frederick Jackson] Turner." Cronon, *Changes in the Land*, 250–51. See also Taylor, *American Colonies*, 188–97.

102. S. T. Livermore, *A History of Block Island: From Its Discovery, in 1514, to the Present Time, 1876* (Hartford: Case, Lockwood, & Brainard, 1877), 10; Lipman, *Saltwater Frontier*, 96–97.

103. Neal Salisbury, William Cronon, Andrew Lipman, and Kathleen Bragdon all use the term *revolution* to describe this economic change. See Bragdon, *Native People of Southern New England, 1500–1650* (Norman: University of Oklahoma Press, 1996), 100; Salisbury, *Manitou and Providence*, 147; Lipman, *Saltwater Frontier*, 109; and Cronon, *Changes in the Land*, 95.

104. See Elizabeth Tooker, "The League of the Iroquois: Its History, Politics, and Ritual," in Trigger, *Northeast*, 422–24; and William N. Fenton, *The Great Law and the Longhouse: A Political History of the Iroquois Confederacy* (Norman: University of Oklahoma Press, 1998), 224–39. Drawing upon a 1646 transaction, Andrew Lipman suggests that "purple wampum was not common in early trade." *Saltwater Frontier*, 290n38.

105. Margaret M. Bruchac, "Broken Chains of Custody: Possessing, Dispossessing, and Repossessing Lost Wampum Belts," *Proceedings of the American Philosophical Society* (March 2018): 56–105.

106. Cronon, *Changes in the Land*, 95.

107. Jon Parmenter, *The Edge of the Woods: Iroquoia, 1534–1701* (East Lansing: Michigan State University Press, 2010), 17.

108. As quoted in Lynn Ceci, "Native Wampum as a Peripheral Resource in the Seventeenth-Century World System," in Hauptman and Wherry, *Pequots in Southern New England*, 58.

109. Fenton, *Great Law and the Longhouse*, 224.

110. Cronon, *Changes in the Land*, 95–96.

111. Joost Joner and Keetie Slutyerman, *At Home on the World Markets: Dutch International Trading Companies from the Sixteenth Century until the Present* (The Hague: Sdu Uitgevers, 2000), 50–51.

112. As Pierre Bourdieu suggests, economic determinism often reduces social relations "to a sort of epiphenomenal manifestation of economic" forces that ignores "the specifically symbolic effectiveness of representation." This "inability to *historicize*" remains a consistent challenge within such analyses. See *Language and Symbolic Power* (Cambridge, Mass.: Harvard University Press, 1991), 182, 288n11 (emphasis in original).

113. Livermore, *History of Block Island*, 13–14.

114. Lipman, *Saltwater Frontier*, 110.

115. In 1641 the Dutch offered "20 fathoms of wampum for every head of the [rival] Indians . . . on Staten Island." As quoted in Madley, "Reexamining the American Genocide Debate," 114–15. The wampum trade is often not recognized in Dutch economic histories. See, for example, Joner and Slutyerman, *At Home on the World Markets*.

116. As quoted in Lipman, *Saltwater Frontier*, 110.

117. Cronon, *Changes in the Land*, 94–95. See also Salisbury, *Manitou and Providence*, 141–47.

118. Salisbury, *Manitou and Providence*, 151–65.

119. "The transition from trade to settlement as the dominant mode of European activity was facilitated by an epidemic." Salisbury, *Manitou and Providence*, 209.

120. Salisbury, *Manitou and Providence*, 204–10.

121. Within the early years of Plymouth colony, conflicts over stolen "trifles" did often prompt threats of violence from Puritan leaders. See Ben Kiernan, *Blood and Soil: A World History of Genocide and Extermination from Sparta to Darfur* (New Haven: Yale University Press, 2007), 226.

122. As quoted in Lipman, *Saltwater Frontier*, 132.

123. Lipman, *Saltwater Frontier*, 134.

124. Lipman, *Saltwater Frontier*, 134.

125. Richard Dunn et al., eds., *The Journal of John Winthrop, 1630–1649* (Cambridge, Mass.: Harvard University Press, 1996), 183.

126. Dunn et al., *Journal of John Winthrop*, 183.

127. Dunn et al., *Journal of John Winthrop*, 184.

128. Dunn et al., *Journal of John Winthrop*, 184.

129. Dunn et al., *Journal of John Winthrop*, 184.

130. As quoted in Madley, "Reexamining the American Genocide Debate," 121.

131. Dunn et al., *Journal of John Winthrop*, 191.

132. Dunn et al., *Journal of John Winthrop*, 191.

133. Dunn et al., *Journal of John Winthrop*, 191.

134. Lipman, *Saltwater Frontier*, 129.

135. Dunn et al., *Journal of John Winthrop*, 213.

136. As quoted in Madley, "Reexamining the American Genocide Debate," 121.

137. Lipman, *Saltwater Frontier*, 138.

138. Perry Miller, *Errand into the Wilderness* (Cambridge, Mass.: Harvard University Press, 1956), 217–39. "The Puritans . . . were medieval men . . . and cherished still the vision of a glorious consummation" (218).

139. As quoted in Madley, "Reexamining the American Genocide Debate," 121.

140. Lipman, *Saltwater Frontier*, 134.

141. As quoted in Madley, "Reexamining the American Genocide Debate," 121.

142. Such battles, massacres, and the continued bounties for Pequot heads constituted, as Ben Kiernan suggests, "genocidal measures." *Blood and Soil*, 232.

143. Dunn et al., *Journal of John Winthrop,* 221. See also Lipman, *Saltwater Frontier,* 136–37.

144. As quoted in Kiernan, *Blood and Soil,* 232. See also Madly, "Reexamining the American Genocide Debate," 121–23.

145. Dunn et al., *Journal of John Winthrop,* 221–22.

146. As quoted in Kiernan, *Blood and Soil,* 232.

147. Lipman, *Saltwater Frontier,* 141.

148. As quoted in Lipman, *Saltwater Frontier,* 140.

149. Dunn et al., *Journal of John Winthrop,* 226. A complex "Indigenous cartography" across the Northeast provided numerous sites of refuge for Native peoples that held foods, medicines, fuels, and other resources for survival. According to Christine DeLucia, the designation of "swamp" used to describe such refuges has remained a centuries-long practice of erasing such tribal "memoryscapes." See *Memory Lands,* 121–200. As in the battle of Long Island Sound, such "swamps" became sites of military conflicts throughout the seventeenth century, particularly during King Philip's War. See Brooks, *Our Beloved Kin,* 238–52.

150. Dunn et al., *Journal of John Winthrop,* 226–27.

151. Dunn et al., *Journal of John Winthrop,* 227–28.

152. Dunn et al., *Journal of John Winthrop,* 238.

153. Taylor, *American Colonies,* 168.

154. As quoted in Taylor, *American Colonies,* 175.

155. Taylor, *American Colonies,* 177.

Chapter 3. The Unpredictability of Violence

1. Daniel K. Richter, *Before the Revolution: America's Ancient Pasts* (Cambridge, Mass.: Harvard University Press, 2011), 5. See also Russell Thornton, *American Indian Holocaust and Survival: A Population History since 1492* (Norman: University of Oklahoma Press, 1987); William M. Denevan, ed., *The Native Population of the Americas in 1492,* rev. ed. (Madison: University of Wisconsin Press, 1992); and David S. Jones, "Population, Health, and Public Welfare," in Frederick E. Hoxie, ed., *The Oxford Handbook of American Indian History* (New York: Oxford University Press, 2016), 413.

2. Bernard Bailyn, *The Barbarous Years: The Conflict of Civilizations, 1600–1675* (New York: Knopf, 2012), 528.

3. Richard White, *The Middle Ground: Indians, Empires, and Republics in the Great Lakes Region, 1650–1815,* rev. ed. (New York: Cambridge University Press, 2011), 11.

4. Brian DeLay, "Independent Indians and the U.S.-Mexican War," *American Historical Review* 112, no. 1 (February 2007): 35–68. See also Michael Witgen, *An Infinity of Nations: How the Native New World Shaped Early America* (Philadelphia: University of Pennsylvania Press, 2012).

5. Elisabeth Tooker, "The League of the Iroquois: Its History, Politics, and Ritual," in Bruce G. Trigger, ed., *The Northeast,* vol. 15 of *Handbook of North American*

Indians (Washington, D.C.: Smithsonian Institute, 1978), 418–29; Daniel K. Richter, *Ordeal of the Longhouse: The Peoples of the Iroquois League in the Era of European Colonization* (Chapel Hill: University of North Carolina Press, 1992), 14–49; Matthew Dennis, *Cultivating a Landscape of Peace: Iroquois-European Encounters in Seventeenth-Century America* (Ithaca: Cornell University Press, 1993), 76–115; Timothy J. Shannon, "Iroquoia," in Hoxie, *The Oxford Handbook of American Indian History*, 200–203. See also Francis Jennings, *The Ambiguous Iroquois Empire: The Covenant Chain Confederation of Indians Tribes with English Colonies from its Beginnings to the Lancaster Treaty of 1744* (New York: Norton, 1984), 25–41; Taiakeke Alfred, *Peace, Power, and Righteousness: An Indigenous Manifesto* (Don Mills, Ont.: Oxford University Press, 1999), 89–103; and William N. Fenton, *The Great Law and the Longhouse: A Political History of the Iroquois Confederacy* (Norman: University of Oklahoma Press, 1998), 51–84.

6. Jon Parmenter, *The Edge of the Woods: Iroquoia, 1534–1701* (East Lansing: Michigan State University Press, 2010), 289.

7. W. J. Eccles, *The Canadian Frontier, 1534–1760*, rev. ed. (Albuquerque: University of New Mexico Press, 1983), 83.

8. Gilles Havard, *The Great Peace of Montreal of 1701: French-Native Diplomacy in the Seventeenth Century* (Montreal: McGill-Queens University Press, 2001), 4. See also Parmenter, *The Edge of the Woods*, 3–31; and David Hackett Fischer, *Champlain's Dream* (New York: Simon & Schuster, 2008), 227–342.

9. Eccles, *The Canadian Frontier, 1534–1760*, 13–14.

10. Colin G. Calloway, *One Vast Winter Count: The Native American West Before Lewis and Clark* (Lincoln: University of Nebraska Press, 2003), 215. See also Parmenter, *The Edge of the Woods*, 11–18.

11. Gary W. Crawford, "Northeast Plants"; and Bonnie W. Styles, "Northeast Animals," in Douglas H. Ubelaker, ed., *Environment, Origins, and Population*, vol. 3 of *Handbook of North American Indians* (Washington, D.C.: Smithsonian Institution, 2006), 405–11; 412–27.

12. Helen Hornbeck Tanner, ed., *Atlas of Great Lakes Indian History* (Norman: University of Oklahoma Press, 1987), 37. See also Allan Greer, ed., *The Jesuit Relations: Natives and Missionaries in Seventeenth-Century North America* (New York: Bedford/St. Martin's, 2000), 1–19.

13. Frank Norall, *Bourgmont: Explorer of the Missouri, 1698–1725* (Lincoln: University of Nebraska Press, 1988), 3.

14. For an overview of seventeenth-century French cartography of western North America, see Carl I. Wheat, *Mapping the Transmississippi West*, 6 vols. (San Francisco: Institute of Historical Cartography, 1957) 1:48–60.

15. Historians have long debated the limits of French "possession" across the Great Lakes. See Witgen, *Infinity of Nations*, 68.

16. H. P. Biggar, ed., *The Works of Samuel de Champlain*, 6 vols. (Toronto: Champlain Society, 1925), 2:326. See also Wheat, *Mapping the Transmississippi West*, 1:49.

17. Biggar, *Works of Champlain*, 2:345.

18. Colin G. Calloway, *New Worlds for All: Indians, Europeans, and the Remaking of Early America* (Baltimore: Johns Hopkins University Press, 1997), 92.

19. Biggar, *Works of Champlain*, 2:96–97.

20. Hackett Fischer, *Champlain's Dream*, 3.

21. Biggar, *Works of Champlain*, 2:98–100.

22. Coll Thrush, *Indigenous London: Native Travelers at the Heart of Empire* (New Haven: Yale University Press, 2016).

23. For an "effort to analyze innovative change over time in Iroquois spatial practices," see Parmenter, *The Edge of the Woods*, xii–xv, 41–75.

24. Tooker, "The League of the Iroquois," 424–28.

25. Charles T. Gehring and William A. Starna, eds. and trans., *A Journey into Mohawk and Oneida Country, 1634–1635: The Journal of Harmen Meyndertsz Van Den Bogaert*, rev. ed. (Syracuse: Syracuse University Press, 2013), 4.

26. Bruce G. Trigger, "Early Iroquoian Contacts with Europeans," in Trigger, *The Northeast*, 347–49.

27. Biggar, *Works of Champlain*, 2:13. See chapter 1 for additional analysis of the 1513 Spanish "Requirement" laws.

28. Biggar, *Works of Champlain*, 2:70. For sociological assessment of "proximity senses" and the sensory dimensions of Algonquian-French relations, see Denys Delage, *Bitter Feast: Amerindians and Europeans in Northeastern North America, 1600–64* (Vancouver: University of British Columbia Press, 1993), 76–77.

29. Hackett Fischer, *Champlain's Dream*, 518.

30. "No one engaged in thought about history and politics can remain unaware of the enormous role violence has always played in human affairs." Hannah Arendt, *On Violence* (New York: Harcourt, Brace & World, 1970), 8. "Moreover . . . violence harbors within itself an additional element of arbitrariness . . . [an] all-pervading unpredictability, which we encounter the moment we approach the realm of violence" (4–5).

31. Thomas Hobbes provides an analysis of violence and political sovereignty—"because the command of the *militia*, without other institution, maketh him that hath it sovereign." See Michael Oakeshott, ed., Thomas Hobbes, *Leviathan: Or the Matter, Forme and Power of a Commonwealth Ecclesiastical and Civil* (New York: Simon & Schuster, 2008), 139. See also Martin Shaw, "Violence," in Bryan S. Turner, ed., *The Cambridge Dictionary of Sociology* (New York: Cambridge University Press, 2006), 652–53.

32. David J. Silverman, *Thundersticks: Firearms and the Violent Transformation of Native America* (Cambridge, Mass.: Harvard University Press, 2016), 90.

33. Trigger, "Early Iroquoian Contacts with Europeans," 347–48. See also Alain Beaulieu, "La naissance de l'alliance franco-amérindienne," in Raymonde Litalien and Denis Vaugeois, eds., *Champlain: La naissance de l'Amérique française* (Sillery: Les Éditions du Septentrion, 2004), 153–61.

34. Harold Blau, Jack Campisi, and Elisabeth Tooker, "Onondaga," in Trigger, *The Northeast*, 491. See also Trigger, "Early Iroquoian Contacts with Europeans," 349–50; Parmenter, *The Edge of the Woods*, 25–27; and James W. Bradley, *Evolution of the Onondaga Iroquois: Accommodating Change, 1500–1655* (Syracuse: Syracuse University Press, 1987).

35. Biggar, *Works of Champlain*, 3:66. Estimates of this village size are based on the illustration of the battle along with van den Bogaert's descriptions of Mohawk and Oneida "castles" in 1634–35. See Gehring and Starna, *A Journey into Mohawk and Oneida Country*, 4.

36. According to Christian Le Clercq's 1691 history of New France, "Victory would have been infallible, if our Hurons . . . [had not broken] their promise to wait for the signals and orders from Monsieur de Champlain." See Christian Le Clercq, *First Establishment of the Faith of New France*, 2 vols., ed. and trans. John G. Shea (New York: John G. Shea, 1881), 1:104.

37. Biggar, *Works of Champlain*, 3:67.

38. Biggar, *Works of Champlain*, 3:67. See also Parmenter, *The Edge of the Woods*, 26–27.

39. Le Clercq, *First Establishment*, 1:104.

40. Le Clercq, *First Establishment*, 1:104.

41. Dean R. Snow, *The Iroquois* (New York: Blackwell, 1994), 108.

42. Bruce G. Trigger describes 1615–29 as "the Quiet Years," a period that followed a "smooth course." See Bruce G. Trigger, *The Children of Aataentsic: A History of the Huron People to 1660* (Montreal: McGill-Queens University Press, 1976), 1:331; see also 331–433.

43. Richter, *Ordeal of the Longhouse*, 51. For English colonization, see chapter 2. For Dutch colonization, see Alan Taylor, *American Colonies: The Settling of North America* (New York: Viking Penguin, 2001), 248–57; and Susanah Shaw Romney, *New Netherland Connections: Intimate Networks and Atlantic Ties in Seventeenth-Century America* (Chapel Hill: University of North Carolina Press, 2014), 128–45.

44. Bruce G. Trigger, "The Mohawk-Mahican War (1624–1628): The Establishment of a Pattern," *Canadian Historical Review* 51 (September 1971): 277. See also Delage, *Bitter Feast*, 122.

45. For overviews of Mahican and Delaware histories, see T. J. Brasser, "Mahican"; and Ives Goddard, "Delaware," in Trigger, *The Northeast*, 198–212; 213–39.

46. Taylor, *American Colonies*, 105.

47. Taylor, *American Colonies*, 253–54. See also Romney, *New Netherland Connections*, 66–121.

48. Romney, *New Netherland Connections*, 124.

49. For the expansion of Indigenous empires as a unifying theme of early American history, see Pekka Hämäläinen, "The Shape of Power: Indians, Europeans, and North American Worlds from the Seventeenth through the Nineteenth Centuries," in Juliana Barr and Edward Country, eds., *Contested Spaces of Early America* (Philadel-

phia: University of Pennsylvania Press, 2014), 31–68. See also Kathryn Magee Labelle, *Dispersed but Not Destroyed: A History of the Seventeenth-Century Wendat People* (Vancouver: University of British Columbia Press, 2013), 5–6.

50. D. W. Meinig, *Atlantic America, 1492–1800*, vol. 1 of *The Shaping of America: A Geographical Perspective on 500 Years of History* (New Haven: Yale University Press, 1986), 291.

51. Francis Jennings, ed., *The History and Culture of Iroquois Diplomacy: An Interdisciplinary Guide to the Treaties of the Six Nations and Their League* (Syracuse: Syracuse University Press, 1985), 158.

52. Jaap Jacobs, *New Netherland: A Dutch Colony in Seventeenth-Century America* (Leiden: Brill, 2005), 37–40.

53. Brasser, "Mahican," 202–3.

54. As quoted in J. Franklin Jameson, ed., *Narratives of New Netherland: 1609–1664* (New York: Charles Scribner's Sons, 1909), 84–85.

55. As quoted in Jameson, *Narratives of New Netherland*, 84–85. See also Charles T. Gehring and William A. Starna, introduction to Gehring and Starna, *A Journey into Mohawk and Oneida Country*, xxiv–xxv. For the West Indian Company's economic policies, see Donna Merwick, *The Shame and the Sorrow: Dutch-Amerindian Encounters in New Netherland* (Philadelphia: University of Pennsylvania Press, 2006), esp. 48–55.

56. As quoted in Gehring and Starna, *A Journey into Mohawk and Oneida Country*, 4.

57. For effects of disease in the Mohawk-Mahican War, see Dennis, *Cultivating a Landscape*, 132.

58. Silverman, *Thundersticks*, 25.

59. Silverman, *Thundersticks*, 27.

60. As quoted in Gehring and Starna, *A Journey into Mohawk and Oneida Country*, 11.

61. As quoted in Gehring and Starna, *A Journey into Mohawk and Oneida Country*, 6.

62. As quoted in Gehring and Starna, *A Journey into Mohawk and Oneida Country*, 16, 43n82.

63. Parmenter, *The Edge of the Woods*, 56–61.

64. Silverman, *Thundersticks*, 21.

65. Labelle, *Dispersed but Not Destroyed*, 14–15.

66. Jones, "Population, Health, and Public Welfare," 421. See also 420–23 for a critique of popular suggestions about the inevitability of Indian demographic decline.

67. Jones, "Population, Health, and Public Welfare," 422. See also Paul W. Sciulli and James Oberly, "Native Americans in Eastern North America: The Southern Great Lakes and Upper Ohio Valley," in Richard H. Steckel and Jerome C. Rose, eds., *The Backbone of History: Health and Nutrition in the Western Hemisphere* (New York: Cambridge University Press, 2002), 440–80.

68. Parmenter, *The Edge of the Woods*, 289–91.

69. Robert Michael Morrissey, "The Terms of Encounter: Language and Contested Visions of French Colonization in the Illinois Country, 1673–1702," in Robert Englebert and Guillaume Teasdale, eds., *French and Indians in the Heart of North America, 1630–1815* (East Lansing: Michigan State University Press, 2013), 43–75.

70. Recent studies use the term "Wendake." See Thomas Peace and Kathryn Magee Labelle, introduction to Peace and Labelle, eds., *From Huronia to Wendakes: Adversity, Migration, and Resilience, 1650–1900* (Norman: University of Oklahoma Press, 2016), 3–15.

71. Labelle, *Dispersed but Not Destroyed,* 2. See also Conrad E. Heidenreich, "Huron," in Trigger, *The Northeast,* 368–69; Bruce C. Trigger, "The French Presence in Huronia: The Structure of Franco-Huron Relations in the First Half of the Seventeenth Century," *Canadian Historical Review* 49, no. 2 (June 1968): 107–41; Trigger, *The Children of Aataentsic,* 1:31–32, 90–91; and Gary Warrick, *A Population History of the Huron-Petun, A.D. 500–1650* (New York: Cambridge University Press, 2008), 152–53.

72. Reuben Gold Thwaites, ed., *The Jesuit Relations and Allied Documents: Travels and Explorations of the Jesuit Missionaries in New France, 1610–1791,* 73 vols. (Cleveland: Burrows Brothers, 1898), 13:117–19. See also Labelle, *Dispersed but Not Destroyed,* 15–16.

73. Thwaites, *Jesuit Relations,* 13:217–23. See also Labelle, *Dispersed but Not Destroyed,* 18–25. Labelle uses English versions of the French spellings of these leaders—Tarentandé and Aenons.

74. Thwaites, *Jesuit Relations,* 12:197–99.

75. Thwaites, *Jesuit Relations,* 15:43.

76. Alfred Goldsworthy Bailey, *The Conflict of European and Eastern Algonkian Cultures, 1504–1700: A Study in Canadian Civilization,* 2nd ed. (Toronto: University of Toronto Press, 1969), 79.

77. Thwaites, *Jesuit Relations,* 12:243.

78. Trigger, "Early Iroquoian Contacts with Europeans," 351.

79. Labelle, *Dispersed but Not Destroyed,* 25–27.

80. Thwaites, *Jesuit Relations,* 12:197.

81. Thwaites, *Jesuit Relations,* 12:197.

82. Thwaites, *Jesuit Relations,* 12:201–3. See also José António Brandão, *Your Fire Shall Burn No More: Iroquois Policy toward New France and Its Native Allies to 1701* (Lincoln: University of Nebraska Press, 1997), 146.

83. Thwaites, *Jesuit Relations,* 12:207–9. See also Parmenter, *The Edge of the Woods,* 48–49.

84. Parmenter, *The Edge of the Woods,* 49.

85. Thwaites, *Jesuit Relations,* 12:215.

86. Parmenter, *The Edge of the Woods,* 80.

87. For Iroquoian raids as far north as James Bay, see Arthur J. Ray, "The Northern Interior: 1600 to Modern Times," in Bruce G. Trigger and Wilcomb E. Washburn,

eds., *The Cambridge History of the Native Peoples of the Americas*, vol. 1, *North America*, part 2 (New York: Cambridge University Press, 1996), 274. See also Bruce G. Trigger, *Natives and Newcomers: Canada's "Heroic Age" Reconsidered* (Montreal: McGill-Queens University Press, 1986), 259–73.

88. Colin G. Calloway, *The Western Abenakis of Vermont, 1600–1800: War, Migration, and the Survival of an Indian People* (Norman: University of Oklahoma Press, 1990), 67. See also Alice N. Nash, "The Abiding Frontier: Family, Gender and Religion in Wabanaki History, 1600–1763" (Ph.D. diss., Columbia University, 1997), 211–12; and J. A. Mauault, *Historie des Abenakis: Depuis 1605 jusqu'á nos jours* (Sorel, Quebec: Gazette de Sorel, 1866), 125–27.

89. Labelle, *Dispersed but Not Destroyed*, 49–140. See also Trigger, *The Children of Aataentsic*, 2:634–788.

90. Conrad E. Heidenreich, "Re-establishment of Trade, 1654–1666," in R. Cole Harris, ed., *Historical Atlas of Canada: From the Beginning to 1900*, vol. 1 (Toronto: University of Toronto Press, 1987), plate 37.

91. As quoted in Parmenter, *The Edge of the Woods*, 47.

92. Bacqueville de la Potherie, *Histoire de l'Amérique septentrionale*, 4 vols. (Paris: Jean-Luc Nion and Francois Didot, 1722), 3:1; "nothing in the world as cruel": as quoted in Parmenter, *The Edge of the Woods*, 41. See also Havard, *Great Peace of Montreal*, 202.

93. See also Emma Helen Blair, ed. and trans., *The Indian Tribes of the Upper Mississippi Valley and Region of the Great Lakes: As Described by Nicolas Perrot, French Commandant in the Northwest; Bacqueville de la Potherie, French Royal Commissioner to Canada; Morrell Marston, American Army Officer; and Thomas Forysth, United States Agent at Fort Armstrong*, 2 vols. (Cleveland: Arthur Clark, 1911), 2:135.

94. Trigger, "Early Iroquoian Contacts with Europeans," 354; and Trigger, *Children of Aataentsic*, 2:604.

95. Snow, *Iroquois*, 96–100. See also Parmenter, *The Edge of the Woods*, 289–91.

96. Parmenter, *The Edge of the Woods*, 81.

97. Thwaites, *Jesuit Relations*, 12:215.

98. Martin Fournier, *Pierre-Esprit Radisson: Merchant Adventurer, 1636–1710* (Sillery: Les Éditions du Septentiron, 2002), 20–24.

99. Brett Rushforth, *Bonds of Alliance: Indigenous and Atlantic Slaveries in New France* (Chapel Hill: University of North Carolina Press, 2012), 15–71.

100. See Roland Viau, "Enfants du néant et mangeurs d'âmes: Guerre, culture et société, en Iroquoisie l'époque de la colonization européenne" (Ph.D. diss., Université de Montréal, 1994), 269; and Fournier, *Pierre-Esprit Radisson*, 41.

101. Arthur T. Adams., ed., *The Explorations of Pierre Esprit Radisson* (Minneapolis: Ross & Haines, 1961), 18. See also Parmenter, *The Edge of the Woods*, 83–84, 331–32n15.

102. Brandão, *Your Fire Shall Burn No More*, 73–74.

103. Blair, *The Indian Tribes of the Upper Mississippi Valley,* 1:146.

104. White, *The Middle Ground,* 1.

105. Trigger, *The Children of Aataentsic,* 2:752.

106. Trigger, *The Children of Aataentsic,* 2:752–53.

107. Trigger, *The Children of Aataentsic,* 2:729. See also George T. Hunt, *The Wars of the Iroquois: A Study in Intertribal Relations* (Madison: University of Wisconsin Press, 1940); and Trigger, *Natives and Newcomers,* 271–77.

108. Brandão, *Your Fire Shall Burn No More,* 77.

109. Trigger, *The Children of Aataentsic,* 2:767–70.

110. Thwaites, *Jesuit Relations,* 36:177.

111. Trigger, *The Children of Aataentsic,* 2:770–79.

112. See also White, *The Middle Ground,* 46.

113. Marian E. White, "Neutral and Wenro"; and "Erie," in Trigger, *The Northeast,* 407–17.

114. White, *The Middle Ground,* 11. See also Pekka Hämäläinen, *Lakota America: A New History of Indigenous Power* (New Haven: Yale University Press, 2019), 21–28.

115. For perspectives that highlight continuities rather than disruptions, see Rushforth, *Bonds of Alliance,* 24; Heidi Bohaker, *Doodem and Council Fire: Anishinaabe Governance through Alliance* (Toronto: University of Toronto Press, 2020); Heidi Bohaker, "'Nindoodemag': The Significance of Algonquian Kinship Networks in the Eastern Great Lakes Region, 1600–1701," *William and Mary Quarterly* (January 2006): 23–52; Witgen, *Infinity of Nations;* Michael A. McDonnell, *Masters of Empire: Great Lakes Indians and the Making of America* (New York: Hill & Wang, 2015); and Michael A. McDonnell, "Rethinking the Middle Ground: French Colonialism and Indigenous Identities in the *Pays d'en Haut,*" in Gregory D. Smithers and Brooke N. Newman, eds., *Native Diasporas: Indigenous Identities and Settler Colonialism in the Americas* (Lincoln: University of Nebraska Press, 2014), 79–108.

116. White, *The Middle Ground,* 14.

117. Patty Loew, *Indian Nations of Wisconsin: Histories of Survival and Renewal,* 2nd ed. (Madison: State of Wisconsin Historical Society Press, 2011).

118. Richter, *Ordeal of the Longhouse,* 74.

119. For an overview of the "agricultural revolution" that swept eastern North America, see Richter, *Before the Revolution,* 20–24.

120. Trigger, *Natives and Newcomers,* 271.

121. Trigger, *Natives and Newcomers,* 273–78. See also Gunlog Fur, *A Nation of Women: Gender and Colonial Encounters among the Delaware Indians* (Philadelphia: University of Pennsylvania Press, 2009), 47–50.

122. For estimates on the corn cultivation capacities of the Wendat, see Conrad Heidenreich, *Huronia: A History and Geography of the Huron Indians, 1600–1650* (Toronto: McClelland & Stewart, 1971), 168–200. See also Trigger, *The Children of Aataentsic,* 1:165–68.

123. The Iroquois had "shattered the trading network on which New France depended for its economic prosperity, creating despair throughout the colony." Trigger, *Natives and Newcomers*, 273.

124. Robert A. Goldstein, *French-Iroquois Diplomatic and Military Relations, 1608–1701* (The Hague: Mouton, 1969), 79–84.

125. Joyce Marshall, ed., *Word from New France: The Selected Letters of Marie De L'Incarnation* (Toronto: Oxford University Press, 1967), 225, 227. See also Trigger, *Natives and Newcomers*, 277–80.

126. Richter, *Ordeal of the Longhouse*, 105–25.

127. Trigger, *Natives and Newcomers*, 279.

128. W. J. Eccles, *Essays on New France* (Toronto: Oxford University Press, 1987), 111. See also Marcel Trudel, *La population du Canada en 1663* (Montreal: Éditions Fides, 1973), 11–28.

129. As quoted in Jack Verney, *The Good Regiment: The Carignan-Salières Regiment in Canada, 1665–1668* (Montreal: McGill-Queen's University Press, 1991), 3.

130. Verney, *The Good Regiment*, 4.

131. Verney, *The Good Regiment*, 4. See also Goldstein, *French-Iroquois Diplomatic and Military Relations*, 86–89.

132. McDonnell, *Masters of Empire*, 33.

133. "Appendix B: Nominal Roll" in Verney, *The Good Regiment*, 145–85. In the 1660s, 623 French women also migrated to New France, more than in all previous decades combined. See Harris, *Historical Atlas of Canada*, 118.

134. Goldstein, *French-Iroquois Diplomatic and Military Relations*, 166–97.

135. Steve Pincus, *1688: The First Modern Revolution* (New Haven: Yale University Press, 2009), 307.

136. "Mémoire de Mr De Salieres," in Régis Roy and Gérard Malchelosse, *Le Régiment de Carignan: Son organisation et son expédition au Canada, 1665–1668* (Montreal: G. Ducharme, 1925), 48.

137. Mémoire de Mr De Salieres," 63. See also Parmenter, *The Edge of the Woods*, 119–20.

138. "Civil and ecclesiastical authorities in New France," Parmenter writes, "could barely contain their joy" upon the arrival of the regiment. See Parmenter, *The Edge of the Woods*, 118–19.

139. Marshall, ed., *Word from New France*, 317.

140. McDonnell, *Masters of Empire*, 39.

141. Parmenter, *The Edge of the Woods*, 167.

142. Parmenter, *The Edge of the Woods*, 172–73, 182. For campaigns of 1687 and 1693, see 189–226.

143. Parmenter, *The Edge of the Woods*, 246–48.

144. McDonnell, *Masters of Empire*, 34.

145. Silverman, *Thundersticks*, 50–55.

146. Havard, *Great Peace*, 190–209. See chapter 4 for the centrality of Anishinaabe-French relations to New France.

147. Bohaker, *Doodem and Council Fire*, 24–69.

148. Havard, *Great Peace*, 211. See also Goldstein, *French-Iroquois Diplomatic and Military Relations*, 196–97.

149. Bohaker, *Doodem and Council Fire*, 67–69.

150. Bohaker, *Doodem and Council Fire*, 61.

151. White, *The Middle Ground*, 50–185.

152. Richard Weyhing, "'Gascon Exaggerations': The Rise of Antonie Laumet de Lamothe, Sieur de Cadillac, the Foundation of Colonial Detroit, and the Origins of the Fox Wars," in Englebert and Teasdale, *French and Indians in the Heart of North America*, 77–112.

Chapter 4. The Native Inland Sea

1. Elizabeth Fenn, "The Mandans: Ecology, Population, and Adaptation on the Northern Plains," in Edward Countryman and Julianna Barr, eds., *Contested Spaces of Early America* (Philadelphia: University of Pennsylvania Press, 2014), 96–99.

2. Fenn, "The Mandans," 98.

3. Lawrence J. Burpee, ed., *Journals and Letters of Pierre Gaultier de Varennes de La Vérendrye and His Sons* (Toronto: Champlain Society, 1927), 367.

4. Burpee, *Journals and Letters of Pierre Gaultier de Varennes de La Vérendrye*, 366.

5. Burpee, *Journals and Letters of Pierre Gaultier de Varennes de La Vérendrye*, 369.

6. As Elizabeth Fenn writes: "Surely there were ten thousand Mandans in the sixteenth century. . . . But numbers as high as fifteen or twenty thousand also seem possible." See Elizabeth A. Fenn, *Encounters at the Heart of the World: A History of the Mandan Peoples* (New York: Hill & Wang, 2014), 24–26.

7. Gary B. Nash, *The Urban Crucible: The Northern Seaports and the Origins of the American Revolution*, rev. ed. (Cambridge, Mass.: Harvard University Press, 1986), 1.

8. For overviews of Cahokia and Mississippian-era "chiefdoms," see Robbie Ethridge, *From Chicaza to Chickasaw: The European Invasion and the Transformation of the Mississippian World, 1540–1715* (Chapel Hill: University of North Carolina Press, 2010), 3–25; and Timothy R. Pauketat, *Cahokia: Ancient America's Great City on the Mississippi* (New York: Penguin Group, 2009), 1–10. See also Francis Jennings, *The Founders of America: From the Earliest Migrations to the Present* (New York: Norton, 1993), 56–67.

9. Gary E. Moulton, ed., *The Journals of the Lewis and Clark Expedition*, 12 vols. (Lincoln: University of Nebraska Press, 1987), 3:238.

10. See, e.g., Pekka Hämäläinen, *Lakota America: A New History of Indigenous Power* (New Haven: Yale University Press, 2019), 50–84.

11. Fenn, *Encounters at the Heart of the World*, 41–47. See also Brett Rushforth, *Bonds of Alliance: Indigenous and Atlantic Slaveries in New France* (Chapel Hill: Univer-

sity of North Carolina Press, 2012), 34n25; Scott Berthelette, "The Making of a Manitoban Hero: Commemorating La Vérendrye in St. Boniface and Winnipeg, 1886–1938," *Manitoba History* 74 (Winter 2014): 15–25; and Berthelette, "La Vérendrye's 'Middle Ground': Village and Imperial Politics in the Northwest, 1731–1743," *Strata* 5 (2013): 1–31.

12. Burpee, *Journals and Letters of Pierre Gaultier de Varennes de La Vérendrye*, 1.

13. See chapter 3 for French-Iroquois relations and the Grand Settlement of 1701.

14. Burpee, *Journals and Letters of Pierre Gaultier de Varennes de La Vérendrye*, 481. See also William H. Goetzman and Glyndwr Williams, *The Atlas of North American Exploration: From the Norse Voyages to the Race to the Pole* (Norman: University of Oklahoma Press, 1998), 96–97.

15. See chapter 5 for the frontier conflicts that sparked the American Revolution.

16. See frontispiece map and accompanying tables in Heidi Bohaker, *Doodem and Council Fire: Anishinaabe Governance through Alliance* (Toronto: University of Toronto Press, 2020). For state and federally recognized Anishinaabe tribes, see also "Appendix A: State and Federally Recognized Tribes," in Charles Wilkinson, *Blood Struggle: The Rise of Modern Indian Nations* (New York: Norton, 2005), 493–97.

17. Brenda J. Child, *Holding Our World Together: Ojibwe Women and the Survival of Community* (New York: Penguin, 2012), xiv. See also Michael Witgen, *An Infinity of Nations: How the Native New World Shaped Early America* (Philadelphia: University of Pennsylvania Press, 2012), esp. 15–21.

18. Child, *Holding Our World Together*, 23–27. For subsequent nineteenth- and twentieth-century changes to such gendered labor systems, see Brenda Child, *My Grandfather's Knocking Sticks: Ojbiwe Family Life and Labor on the Reservation* (St. Paul: Minnesota Historical Society Press, 2014), esp. 161–91; and Lucy Eldersveld Murphy, *Great Lakes Creoles: A French-Indian Community on the Northern Borderlands, Prairie du Chien, 1750–1860* (New York: Cambridge University Press, 2014), 27–64.

19. Fred Anderson, *Crucible of War: The Seven Years' War and the Fate of Empire in British North America, 1754–1766* (New York: Knopf, 2000), 7.

20. A. P. Nasatir, *Before Lewis and Clark: Documents Illustrating the History of the Missouri, 1782–1804*, 2 vols. (St. Louis: St. Louis Historical Documents Foundations, 1952), 1:31.

21. Gilles Havard, *The Great Peace of Montreal of 1701: French-Native Diplomacy in the Seventeenth Century* (Montreal: McGill-Queens University Press, 2001), 193–206.

22. R. David Edmunds and Joseph L. Peyser, *The Fox Wars: The Mesquakie Challenge to New France* (Norman: University of Oklahoma Press, 1993), 5.

23. Leslie Choquette, "Center and Periphery in French North America," in Christine Daniels and Michael V. Kennedy, eds., *Negotiated Empires: Centers and Peripheries in the Americas, 1500–1820* (New York: Routledge, 2002), 197.

24. William N. Fenton, *The Great Law and the Longhouse: A Political History of the Iroquois Confederacy* (Norman: University of Oklahoma Press, 1998), 289.

25. Burpee, *Journals and Letters of Pierre Gaultier de Varennes de La Vérendrye*, 481.

26. Francis Jennings, *The Ambiguous Iroquois Empire: The Covenant Chain Confederation of Indian Tribes with English Colonies from Its Beginnings to the Lancaster Treaty of 1744* (New York: Norton, 1984), 142.

27. As quoted in Daniel K. Richter, *Ordeal of the Longhouse: The Peoples of the Iroquois League in the Era of European Colonization* (Chapel Hill: University of North Carolina Press, 1992), 206.

28. Fenton, *The Great Law and the Longhouse,* 382–83. See also Jennings, *Ambiguous Iroquois Empire,* 258–60.

29. Tiya Miles, *The Dawn of Detroit: A Chronicle of Slavery and Freedom in the City of the Straits* (New York: New Press, 2017), 7–12.

30. As Francis Jennings has suggested, "Repeated imperial wars created disastrous Indian casualties." See *The Creation of America: Through Revolution to Empire* (New York: Cambridge University Press, 2000), 119.

31. Timothy J. Shannon, *Iroquois Diplomacy on the Early American Frontier* (New York: Penguin, 2008), 55–68.

32. As quoted in Havard, *Great Peace,* 33.

33. Richard White, *The Middle Ground: Indians, Empires, and Republics in the Great Lakes Region, 1650–1815,* rev. ed. (New York: Cambridge University Press, 2011), 51.

34. White, *The Middle Ground,* 53.

35. George Irving Quimby, *Indian Life in the Upper Great Lakes: 11,000 B.C. to A.D. 1800* (Chicago: University of Chicago Press, 1960). "There was a population of at least 100,000 Indians occupying the Upper Great Lakes region" (108).

36. White, *The Middle Ground,* 135–36. See also George Irving Quimby, *Indian Culture and European Trade Goods* (Madison: University of Wisconsin Press, 1966), 117–39; and Michael S. Nassaney, William M. Cremin, and LisaMarie Malischke, "Native American-French Interactions in Eighteenth-Century Southwest Michigan: The View from Fort St. Joseph," in Charles Beatty-Medina and Melissa Rinehart, eds., *Contested Territories: Native Americans and Non-Natives in the Lower Great Lakes, 1700–1850* (East Lansing: Michigan State University Press, 2012), esp. 62–72.

37. Carol Devens, *Countering Colonization: Native American Women and Great Lakes Missions, 1630–1900* (Berkeley: University of California Press, 1992), 32.

38. Michael Witgen, "The Rituals of Possession: Native Identity and the Invention of Empire in Seventeenth-Century Western North America," *Ethnohistory* 54, no. 4 (Fall 2007): 641–47. See also Witgen, *An Infinity of Nations.*

39. As quoted in Christian Le Clercq, *First Establishment of the Faith of New France,* 2 vols., ed. and trans. John G. Shea (New York: John G. Shea, 1881), 2:131.

40. White, *The Middle Ground,* 128–31. For conceptualization of "entangled histories," see Eliga H. Gould, "Entangled Histories, Entangled Worlds: The English-Speaking Atlantic as a Spanish Periphery," *American Historical Review* 112, no. 3 (June 2007): 764–86.

41. David J. Silverman, *Thundersticks: Firearms and the Violent Transformation of Native America* (Cambridge, Mass.: Harvard University Press, 2016).

42. As quoted in Havard, *Great Peace*, 206 (emphasis added). See also Reuben Gold Thwaites, ed., *The French Regime in Wisconsin, 1634–1727* (Madison: Wisconsin State Historical Society, 1902), 245.

43. For the disruptive impacts of gun technologies, see R. D. Crosby, *The Musket Wars: A History of Inter-Iwi Conflict, 1806–1845*, rev. ed. (Auckland: Libro International, 2012); and Silverman, *Thundersticks*.

44. Bacqueville de la Potherie, *Histoire de l'Amérique septentrionale*, 4 vols. (Paris: Jean-Luc Nion & Francois Didot, 1722) 2:87. See also Havard, *Great Peace*, 33.

45. Kathleen DuVal, "Cross-Cultural Crime and Osage Justice in the Western Mississippi Valley, 1700–1826," *Ethnohistory* 54, no. 4 (Fall 2007): 701–2.

46. As quoted in J. H. Schlarman, *From Quebec to New Orleans: The Story of the French in America* (Belleville, Ill.: Buechler, 1930), 226.

47. As quoted in Schlarman, *From Quebec to New Orleans*, 229.

48. As quoted in Schlarman, *From Quebec to New Orleans*, 227, 230.

49. As quoted in Schlarman, *From Quebec to New Orleans*, 227.

50. As quoted in Schlarman, *From Quebec to New Orleans*, 231, 225. See also White, *The Middle Ground*, 92.

51. Reuben Gold Thwaites, ed., *The Jesuit Relations and Allied Documents: Travels and Explorations of the Jesuit Missionaries in New France, 1610–1791*, 73 vols. (Cleveland: Burrows Brothers, 1898), 12:117.

52. Robert Michael Morrissey, "The Terms of Encounter: Language and Contested Visions of French Colonization in the Illinois Country, 1673–1702," in Robert Englebert and Guillaume Teasdale, eds., *French and Indians in the Heart of North America, 1630–1815* (East Lansing: Michigan State University Press, 2013), 44–49; Helen Hornbeck Tanner, ed., *Atlas of Great Lakes Indian History* (Norman: University of Oklahoma Press, 1987), 37.

53. Francis Parkman, *The Jesuits in North America in the Seventeenth Century*, rev. ed. (Lincoln: University of Nebraska Press, 1997), ix.

54. See Parkman, *Jesuits in North America in the Seventeenth Century*, v–xvii.

55. Parkman, *Jesuits in North America*, 3–4.

56. Michael A. McDonnell, *Masters of Empire: Great Lakes Indians and the Making of America* (New York: Hill & Wang, 2015), 53–54. See also James Axtell, *Natives and Newcomers: The Cultural Origins of North America* (New York: Oxford University Press, 2001), 163.

57. Annette S. Lee et al., eds., *Ojibwe Sky Star Map Constellation Guide: An Introduction to Ojibwe Star Knowledge* (Cloquet, Minn.: Avenue F., 2014), 32.

58. Reuben Gold Thwaites, ed., *The French Regime in Wisconsin, 1727–1748* (Madison: Wisconsin State Historical Society, 1906), 9. For "Lakota Star Knowledge," see Ronald Goodman, *Lakota Star Knowledge: Studies in Lakota Stellar Theology*, 2nd ed. (Mission, S.D.: Sinte Gleska University, 1992).

59. Lee et al., *Ojibwe Sky Star Map Constellation Guide.*

60. As quoted in Schlarman, *From Quebec to New Orleans*, 230.

61. Frank Norall, *Bourgmont: Explorer of the Missouri, 1698–1725* (Lincoln: University of Nebraska Press, 1988), 84.

62. See Bohaker, *Doodem and Council Fire*, 26–27.

63. Sylvia Van Kirk, *Many Tender Ties: Women in Fur-Trade Society, 1670–1870* (Norman: University of Oklahoma Press, 1983), 29.

64. Murphy, *Great Lakes Creoles*, 25.

65. Jill Doerfler, *Those Who Belong: Identity, Family, Blood, and Citizenship among the White Earth Anishinaabeg* (East Lansing: Michigan State University Press, 2015), 12–15.

66. White, *The Middle Ground*, 60.

67. White, *The Middle Ground*, 60.

68. Le Clercq, *First Establishment*, 132–35. See also Pierre Margry, ed., *Découvertes et établissements des Français dans l'ouest et dans le sud de l'Amérique septentrionale*, 6 vols. (Paris: Imprimerie D. Jouaust, 1875), 1:488. "On les accuse d'estre adoonez au péché contra nature et d'avoir dés homes destinez, des leur enfance, à cet usage."

69. Jenny L. Davis, "More Than Just 'Gay Indians': Intersecting Articulations of Two-Spirit Gender, Sexuality, and Indigenousness," in Lal Zimman et al., eds., *Queer Excursions: Retheorizing Binaries in Language, Gender, and Sexuality* (New York: Oxford University Press, 2014), 64. See also references therein for "the most cited texts on berdache identity" (esp. 79n4).

70. Le Clercq, *First Establishment*, 134.

71. Edmunds and Peyser, *The Fox Wars*, 176; see also 119–201; Rushforth, *Bonds of Alliance*, 197–221; and White, *The Middle Ground*, 149–75. Despite the centrality of such conflicts to these studies, few scholars have taken up Edmunds and Peyser's suggestions that the French policy toward the Fox constituted "genocide." See Edmunds and Peyser, *The Fox Wars*, 158–201.

72. See Gottfried Hotz, *The Segesser Hide Paintings: Masterpieces Depicting Spanish Colonial New Mexico* (Santa Fe: Museum of New Mexio Press, 1991); and Thomas E. Chavez, "The Villasur Expedition and the Segesser Hide Paintings," in Ralph H. Vigil et al., eds., *Spain and the Plains: Myths and Realities of Spanish Exploration and Settlement on the Great Plains* (Niwot: University of Colorado Press, 1994).

73. Richard White, *The Roots of Dependency: Subsistence, Environment, and Social Change among the Choctaws, Pawnees, and Navajos* (Lincoln: University of Nebraska Press, 1983), 34–68. See also James Axtell, *The Indians' New South: Cultural Change in the Colonial Southeast* (Baton Rouge: Louisiana State University Press, 1997), 61.

74. Rushforth, *Bonds of Alliance*, 193–252.

75. Rushforth, *Bonds of Alliance*, 245–46.

76. As quoted in Rushforth, *Bonds of Alliance*, 194. These visiting leaders were identified as "Sioux" within French sources, and as Rushforth notes, "I use the term 'Sioux' rather than . . . 'Dakota' because the latter term excludes those Sioux who are Lakota or Nakota and because 'Sioux' is a much more widely recognized term among

Anglophone readers" (15–16n1). I choose to use Dakota since they remained the most eastern of the Siouan-speaking "Sioux" communities and were as equestrian in the 1740s as their Lakota and Nakota kin.

77. Rushforth, *Bonds of Alliance.*

78. As quoted in Edmunds and Peyser, *The Fox Wars*, 180. See also White, *The Middle Ground*, 171–73.

79. Edmunds and Peyser, *The Fox Wars*, 181.

80. White, *The Middle Ground*, 174–202.

81. For the limits of European geographic knowledge of the eighteenth-century West, see Paul W. Mapp, *The Elusive West and the Contest for Empire, 1713–1763* (Chapel Hill: University of North Carolina Press, 2011).

82. Norall, *Bourgmont*, 87.

83. As quoted in Eric Hinderaker, *Elusive Empires: Constructing Colonialism in the Ohio Valley, 1673–1800* (New York: Cambridge University Press, 1997), 38.

84. George F. G. Stanley, *New France: The Last Phase, 1744–1760* (Toronto: McClelland & Stewart, 1968), 4–14.

85. Michael N. McConnell, *A Country Between: The Upper Ohio Valley and Its Peoples, 1724–1774* (Lincoln: University of Nebraska Press, 1992), 61–82.

86. McConnell, *A Country Between*, 67–121.

87. Anderson, *Crucible of War*, 28.

88. Hinderaker, *Elusive Empires*, 40.

89. McConnell, *A Country Between*, 78–81; Shannon, *Iroquois Diplomacy on the Early American Frontier*, 87–102.

90. Alan Taylor, *American Colonies: The Settling of North America* (New York: Viking Penguin, 2001), 154.

91. As quoted in Hinderaker, *Elusive Empires*, 41.

92. Anderson, *Crucible of War*, 25.

93. As quoted in McConnell, *A Country Between*, 82–83.

94. As quoted in Stanley, *New France*, 278n4; see also 37–38; and Donald H. Kent, *The French Invasion of Western Pennsylvania, 1753* (Harrisburg: Pennsylvania Historical and Museum Commission, 1981), 7–10.

95. As quoted in Stanley, *New France*, 38.

96. Anderson, *Crucible of War*, 26.

97. As quoted in McConnell, *A Country Between*, 86.

98. Mapp, *The Elusive West and the Contest for Empire*, 1–5.

99. William P. Cumming, *The Southeast in Early Maps*, 3rd ed. (Chapel Hill: University of North Carolina Press, 1998), 27. Few English military and boundary surveys detailed "the general topographical knowledge of the interior," which "increased . . . but little" before the Revolution (28).

100. Anderson, *Crucible of War*, 50.

101. McConnell, *A Country Between*, 121.

102. As Allan Greer suggests, "Land speculation was, of course, nothing new . . . but it had entered a new phase as of the mid-eighteenth century. Men with access to capital and political influence had begun organizing themselves into associations, such as the Ohio Company, which through grants and purchases accumulated claims to vast tracts with the sole purpose of later extracting a profit from settlers. Several future revolutionary heroes such as Patrick Henry and George Washington were among the most active speculators. *Property and Dispossession: Natives, Empires, and Land in Early Modern North America* (New York: Cambridge University Press, 2018), 384.

103. Anderson, *Crucible of War*, 52–53.

104. As quoted in McConnell, *A Country Between*, 89.

105. Anderson, *Crucible of War*, 56–58.

106. Anderson, *Crucible of War*, 7.

107. As quoted in Anderson, *Crucible of War*, 53.

108. McConnell, *A Country Between*, 119–20.

109. Anderson, *Crucible of War*, 62.

110. Anderson, *Crucible of War*, 61.

111. As quoted in Anderson, *Crucible of War*, 60.

112. White, *The Middle Ground*, 223.

113. McConnell, *A Country Between*, 109.

114. Shannon, *Iroquois Diplomacy on the Early American Frontier*, 150.

115. McConnell, *A Country Between*, 110.

116. Anderson, *Crucible of War*, 62.

117. As quoted in Anderson, *Crucible of War*, 63.

118. As quoted in Anderson, *Crucible of War*, 65.

119. James H. Merrell, "Shamokin, 'the Very Seat of the Prince of Darkness': Unsettling the Early American Frontier," in Andrew R. L. Clayton and Fredrika J. Teute, eds., *Contact Points: American Frontiers from the Mohawk Valley to the Mississippi, 1750–1830* (Chapel Hill: University of North Carolina Press, 1998), 50.

120. Anderson, *Crucible of War*, 410.

121. Colin G. Calloway, *The Scratch of a Pen: 1763 and the Transformation of North America* (New York: Oxford University Press, 2006), 15.

122. Anderson, *Crucible of War*, 212–13.

123. As quoted in Merrell, "Shamokin," 53. For overviews of English fort construction at Fort Augusta along the Susquehanna River, see 50–56.

124. As quoted in Merrell, "Shamokin," 55.

125. As quoted in Merrell, "Shamokin," 55.

126. As quoted in Merrell, "Shamokin," 50.

127. As quoted in Merrell, "Shamokin," 51.

128. As quoted in Merrell, "Shamokin," 51.

129. As quoted in Merrell, "Shamokin," 55.

130. Anderson, *Crucible of War*, 80. See also Jill Lepore, *These Truths: A History of the United States* (New York: Norton, 2018), 65–71.

131. Anderson, *Crucible of War*, 85.

132. Robert Dale Parker, ed., *Changing Is Not Vanishing: A Collection of American Indian Poetry to 1930* (Philadelphia: University of Pennsylvania Press, 2011), 50–51.

133. Jane Johnston Schoolcraft, "Lines Written at Castle Island, Lake Superior," in Parker, *Changing is Not Vanishing*, 63.

134. Schoolcraft, "Lines Written at Castle Island, Lake Superior," 63.

135. Richard Wilworth Rust, ed., *The Pathfinder: or, The Inland Sea* (Albany: State University of New York Press, 1981), 7–9.

Chapter 5. Settler Uprising

1. As quoted in Alan Taylor, *Liberty Men and Great Proprietors: The Revolutionary Settlement on the Maine Frontier, 1760–1820* (Chapel Hill: University of North Carolina Press, 1990), 61.

2. Peter Cunningham, ed., *The Letters of Horace Walpole: Fourth Earl of Orford* (Edinburgh: John Grant, 1906), 5:49, 35.

3. As quoted in Taylor, *Liberty Men and Great Proprietors*, 61. For an overview of the centrality of landowners to colonial notions of "personal independence," see also T. H. Breen, *American Insurgents, American Patriots: The Revolution of the People* (New York: Hill & Wang, 2010), 30, 25–41. For overviews of expanding settlements of the early 1760s, see Eric Hinderaker and Peter C. Mancall, *At the Edge of Empire: The Backcountry in British North America* (Baltimore: Johns Hopkins University Press, 2003), 150–54.

4. As quoted in Alan Taylor, *American Revolutions: A Continental History, 1750–1804* (New York: Norton, 2016), 11.

5. As quoted Taylor, *American Revolutions*, 50–51.

6. Eliga H. Gould, *The Persistence of Empire: British Political Culture in the Age of the American Revolution* (Chapel Hill: University of North Carolina Press, 2000), 1–71.

7. Fred Anderson, *Crucible of War: The Seven Years' War and the Fate of Empire in British North America, 1754–1766* (New York: Knopf, 2000), esp. 587–685.

8. Gregory Evans Dowd, *War under Heaven: Pontiac, the Indian Nations, and the British Empire* (Baltimore: Johns Hopkins University Press, 2002).

9. As quoted in Taylor, *American Revolutions*, 40.

10. As quoted in Taylor, *American Revolutions*, 57.

11. As quoted in Colin G. Calloway, *The Indian World of George Washington: The First President, the First Americans, and the Birth of the Nation* (New York: Oxford University Press, 2018), 135. See also Colin G. Calloway, *The Scratch of a Pen: 1763 and the Transformation of North America* (New York: Oxford University Press, 2006), 6, 168.

12. Gary B. Nash, *The Urban Crucible: The Northern Seaports and the Origins of the American Revolution*, rev. ed. (Cambridge, Mass.: Harvard University Press, 1986), 152–55.

13. Nash, *The Urban Crucible*, 152. See also Taylor, *American Revolutions*, 44–45;

and W. J. Eccles, *France in America*, rev. ed. (Markham, Ont.: Fitzhenry & Whiteside, 1990), 221–23.

14. Catherine Cangany, *Frontier Seaport: Detroit's Transformation into an Atlantic Entrepôt* (Chicago: University of Chicago Press, 2014), 26. See also Dowd, *War under Heaven*; and J. Clarence Webster, ed., *The Journal of Jeffery Amherst: Recording the Military Career of General Amherst in America from 1758 to 1763* (Toronto: Ryerson, 1931), 264–65.

15. As quoted in Taylor, *American Revolutions*, 59.

16. Richard White, *The Middle Ground: Indians, Empires, and Republics in the Great Lakes Region, 1650–1815*, rev. ed. (New York: Cambridge University Press, 2011), 269–314.

17. Patrick Spero, *Frontier Rebels: The Fight for Independence in the American West, 1765–1776* (New York: Norton, 2018), 183.

18. Robert G. Parkinson, *The Common Cause: Creating Race and Nation in the American Revolution* (Chapel Hill: University of North Carolina Press, 2016), 22.

19. As quoted in Patrick Spero, *Frontier Country: The Politics of War in Early Pennsylvania* (Philadelphia: University of Pennsylvania Press, 2016), 4.

20. Joseph Doddridge, *Notes on the Settlement and Indian Wars of the Western Parts of Virginia and Pennsylvania from 1763 to 1783, Inclusive, Together with a Review of the State of Society and Manners of the First Settlers of the Western Country* (Parson, W.V.: McClain, 1976), 171.

21. Parkinson, *The Common Cause*, 24. See also Colin G. Calloway, *The American Revolution in Indian Country: Crisis and Diversity in Native American Communities* (New York: Cambridge University Press, 1995).

22. Parkinson, *The Common Cause*, 186–87.

23. See, for example, Benjamin Franklin, *A Narrative of the Late Massacres, in Lancaster County, of a Number of Indians, Friends of This Province, by Persons Unknown. With Some Observations on the Same.* (Philadelphia: Anthony Armbruster, 1764).

24. Doddridge, *Notes on the Settlement and Indian Wars*, 168.

25. Doddridge, *Notes on the Settlement and Indian Wars*, 168.

26. As quoted in Peter Silver, *Our Savage Neighbors: How Indian War Transformed Early America* (New York: Norton, 2008), 154.

27. As Gordon S. Wood argues, "The Revolution brought respectability and even dominance to ordinary people . . . and gave dignity to their menial labor in a manner unprecedented." *The Radicalism of the American Revolution: How a Revolution Transformed a Monarchial Society into a Democratic One Unlike Any That Had Ever Existed* (New York: Knopf, 1992), 8.

28. Colin G. Calloway, *The Indian World of George Washington: The First President, the First Americans, and the Birth of the Nation* (New York: Oxford University Press, 2018), 14.

29. See Eliga H. Gould, *Among the Powers of the Earth: The American Revolution*

and the Making of a New World Empire (Cambridge, Mass.: Harvard University Press, 2012), esp. 30–33. For early U.S. Indian policy, see also chapter 6.

30. By 1775 the British Army occupied seventy-nine forts and posts across North America. See Douglas Edward Leach, "The British Army in America, Before 1775," in Jack P. Greene and J. R. Pole, eds., *The Blackwell Encyclopedia of the American Revolution* (Cambridge: Basil Blackwell, 1991), 150.

31. Nash, *The Urban Crucible*, 153.

32. As quoted in Jack M. Sosin, *Whitehall and the Wilderness: The Middle West in British Colonial Policy, 1760–1775* (Lincoln: University of Nebraska Press, 1961), 36.

33. Webster, *Journal of Jeffery Amherst*, 261.

34. Daniel P. Barr, *A Colony Sprung from Hell: Pittsburgh and the Struggle for Authority on the Western Pennsylvania Frontier, 1744–1794* (Kent: Kent State University Press, 2014). See also P. J. Marshall, "The British in Asia: Trade to Dominion," in P. J. Marshall, ed., *The Eighteenth Century*, vol. 2 of Wm. Roger Louis, ed., *The Oxford History of the British Empire* (New York: Oxford University Press, 1998), 499.

35. Leach, "The British Army in America," 148.

36. Anderson, *Crucible of War*, 317–18. For an overview of Massachusetts's farming-based economy on the eve of the Seven Years' War, see Fred Anderson, *A People's Army: Massachusetts Soldiers and Society in the Seven Years' War* (Chapel Hill: University of North Carolina Press, 1984), esp. 28–39.

37. Benjamin Franklin, "To the Printer of the London Chronicle," December 28–30, 1758, in Leonard W. Labaree, ed., *The Papers of Benjamin Franklin*, vol. 8 (New Haven: Yale University Press, 1965), 214.

38. Taylor, *American Revolutions*, 44–51.

39. Taylor, *American Revolutions*, 50–51.

40. Taylor, *American Revolutions*, 62–65.

41. Vincent Brown, *Tacky's Revolt: The Story of an Atlantic Slave War* (Cambridge, Mass.: Harvard University Press, 2020).

42. Taylor, *American Revolutions*, 46.

43. Gould, *The Persistence of Empire*, 110.

44. Keith R. Widder, *Beyond Pontiac's Shadow: Michilimackinac and the Anglo-Indian War of 1763* (East Lansing: Michigan State University Press, 2013), 18.

45. Dowd, *War under Heaven*, 34.

46. Tiya Miles, *The Dawn of Detroit: A Chronicle of Slavery and Freedom in the City of the Straits* (New York: New Press, 2017), 21–27.

47. Cangany, *Frontier Seaport*, 71–105.

48. Dowd, *War under Heaven*, 282n4.

49. See chapter 4 for Franco-Algonquian relations in the Great Lakes region after 1701.

50. Brenda J. Child, *Holding Our World Together: Ojibwe Women and the Survival of Community* (New York: Penguin, 2012), 49–58. "The Ojibwe who lived along Gichiga-

miing (Lake Superior) conceived of themselves in autonomous bands at locations the French had named. . . . Hereafter, the federal government lumped them together under the name Lake Superior Ojibwe. . . . These classifications did not reflect Ojibwe ideas about political organization; they were merely categories created by the federal bureaucracy. . . . The Ojibwe language was [still] the 'universal language of the territory' even as late as the 1830s, when children . . . had books in Ojibwemowin" (49–50, 57).

51. Webster, *Journal of Jeffery Amherst*, 265.

52. Webster, *Journal of Jeffery Amherst*, 265.

53. Dowd, *War under Heaven*, 59–63.

54. For an overview of Detroit's economic development, see Cangany, *Frontier Seaport*, 8–26. See also Miles, *Dawn of Detroit*, 27–33.

55. Albert T. Volwiler, *George Croghan and the Western Movement, 1741–1782* (Cleveland: Arthur H. Clark, 1926), 146.

56. Cangany, *Frontier Seaport*, 1–4. See also Barr, *A Colony Sprung from Hell*, 1–10.

57. As quoted in Widder, *Beyond Pontiac's Shadow*, 19–20.

58. Dowd, *War under Heaven*, 62.

59. As quoted in Dowd, *War under Heaven*, 62. See also Volwiler, *George Croghan and the Western Movement.*

60. Barr, *A Colony Sprung from Hell*, 6. See also Ian K. Steele, *Setting All the Captives Free: Capture, Adjustment, and Recollection in Allegheny Country* (Montreal: McGill-Queen's University Press, 2013), 432.

61. Spero, *Frontier Country*, 116. See also Kevin Kenny, *Peaceable Kingdom Lost: The Paxton Boys and the Destruction of William Penn's Holy Experiment* (New York: Oxford University Press, 2009).

62. As quoted in Dowd, *War under Heaven*, 64.

63. Dowd, *War under Heaven*, 72.

64. "If generosity and reciprocity defined alliance, none existed with the continent's new overlords." Daniel K. Richter, *Facing East from Indian Country: A Native History of Early America* (Cambridge, Mass.: Harvard University Press, 2001), 192.

65. Webster, *Journal of Jeffery Amherst*, 306.

66. As quoted in Steele, *Setting All the Captives Free*, 144.

67. Child, *Holding Our World Together*, 56–62.

68. Dowd, *War under Heaven*, 20–21. For the persistence of Catholicism after 1760 among Michigan Indians, see 109–11. See also chapter 4 for further assessments of Franco-Algonquian social and religious ties.

69. Scholars studying Indian religions have not only paid attention to millennialist practices among communities suffering from cultural stresses but have also established lasting paradigms of religious study. The term *cultural revitalization* emerged in the 1950s and helps to explain Native religious expression occurring during periods of extreme economic and political transformation. See Anthony F. C. Wallace, *The*

Death and Rebirth of the Seneca (New York: Knopf, 1970). See also Anthony F. C. Wallace, "Revitalization Movements: Some Theoretical Considerations for Their Comparative Study," *American Anthropologist* (1956): 264–81.

70. Anderson, *Crucible of War*, 536.

71. C. A. Weslager, *The Delaware Indians: A History* (New Brunswick: Rutgers University Press, 1972), 184.

72. As quoted in James H. Merrell, *Into the American Woods: Negotiators on the Pennsylvania Frontier* (New York: Norton, 1999), 83.

73. As quoted in Dowd, *War under Heaven*, 100.

74. Jane Merritt, *At the Crossroads: Indians and Empires on a Mid-Atlantic Frontier* (Chapel Hill: University of North Carolina Press, 2003), 202.

75. Merrell, *Into the American Woods*, 83–92.

76. See chapter 4 for the Indigenous settlement of the Ohio River Valley in the eighteenth century.

77. Merritt, *At the Crossroads*, 172–74.

78. Steele, *Setting All the Captives Free*, 3.

79. Dowd, *War under Heaven*, 41–42, 90. See also chapter 4.

80. Merritt, *At the Crossroads*, 124.

81. Francis Jennings, "Iroquois Alliances in American History," in Francis Jennings et al., eds., *The History and Culture of Iroquois Diplomacy: An Interdisciplinary Guide to the Treaties of the Six Nations and Their League* (Syracuse: Syracuse University Press, 1985), 44–46.

82. As quoted in Dowd, *War under Heaven*, 91.

83. As quoted in Dowd, *War under Heaven*, 91.

84. Anderson, *Crucible of War*, 536.

85. Other French and English spellings of Pontiac include Pontiak, Pondiag, and Pondiac. See Widder, *Beyond Pontiac's Shadow*, 275n19.

86. Webster, *Journal of Jeffery Amherst*, 18n18.

87. As quoted in Richter, *Facing East from Indian Country*, 192.

88. As quoted in Calloway, *The Indian World of George Washington*, 173.

89. Calloway, *The Indian World of George Washington*, 173. For Tamaqua's captive returns, see Steele, *Setting All the Captives Free*, 255–56, 279–89.

90. Calloway, *The Indian World of George Washington*, 174.

91. Steele, *Setting All the Captives Free*, 282.

92. Calloway, *The Indian World of George Washington*, 172. "In many ways and for most of his life, George Washington's Indian world *was* the Ohio country" (45; emphasis in original).

93. Spero, *Frontier Country*, 150.

94. Anderson, *Crucible of War*, 537.

95. As quoted in Richter, *Facing East from Indian Country*, 195–96. See also Dowd, *War under Heaven*, 94–105.

96. Miles, *Dawn of Detroit*, 32–34.

97. Webster, *Journal of Jeffery Amherst*, 299.

98. As quoted in Anderson, *Crucible of War*, 538. For the capture of Fort Augustus, see 539.

99. Spero, *Frontier Country*, 113–15. See also Richter, *Facing East from Indian Country*, 191.

100. For an assessment of regional communication networks, see Alejandra Dubcovksy, *Informed Power: Communication in the Early American South* (Cambridge, Mass.: Harvard University Press, 2016). "Maintaining these complicated [inter-tribal] networks required constant adaptation and reevaluation" (181).

101. Dowd, *War under Heaven*, 115.

102. Dowd, *War under Heaven*, 97–112.

103. As quoted in Dowd, *War under Heaven*, 98.

104. Dowd, *War under Heaven*, 126. See also Widder, *Beyond Pontiac's Shadow*, 141–49. Lacrosse has had many names, including baggatiway (141, 287n5).

105. Dowd, *War under Heaven*, 132. See also Anderson, *Crucible of War*, 538–42.

106. Anderson, *Crucible of War*, 548.

107. Webster, *Journal of Jeffery Amherst*, 307.

108. Spero, *Frontier Country*, 151.

109. Spero, *Frontier Country*, 114.

110. Nicole Eustace, "The Sentimental Paradox: Humanity and Violence on the Pennsylvania Frontier," *William and Mary Quarterly* (January 2008): 29–64.

111. As quoted in Spero, *Frontier Country*, 117.

112. As quoted in Spero, *Frontier Country*, 151.

113. Spero, *Frontier Country*, 152.

114. Silver, *Our Savage Neighbors*, 193–202.

115. As quoted in Spero, *Frontier Country*, 152.

116. Thomas Agostini, "'The Provincials Will Work Like Giants': British Imperialism, American Colonial Troops, and Trans-Atlantic Labor Economics during the Seven Years' War," *Early American Studies* 15, no. 1 (2017): 64–98.

117. As quoted in Anderson, *Crucible of War*, 542.

118. As quoted in Anderson, *Crucible of War*, 542.

119. As quoted in Anderson, *Crucible of War*, 542. See also Dowd, *War under Heaven*, 211.

120. Webster, *Journal of Jeffery Amherst*, 325.

121. David J. Silverman, *Thundersticks: Firearms and the Violent Transformation of Native America* (Cambridge, Mass.: Harvard University Press, 2016), 121–54.

122. Kenny, *Peaceable Kingdom Lost*, 130–32.

123. As quoted in Merrell, *Into the American Woods*, 62.

124. Kenny, *Peaceable Kingdom Lost*, 41–49. See also chapter 4.

125. Anderson, *Crucible of War*, 278. See also Merritt, *At the Crossroads*, 249–51.

126. Spero, *Frontier Country*, 121–22.

127. See, e.g., Colin G. Calloway, *The Scratch of a Pen: 1763 and the Transformation of North America* (New York: Oxford University Press, 2006), 92–111.

128. As quoted in Anderson, *Crucible of War*, 568.

129. Anderson, *Crucible of War*, 566.

130. Nash, *The Urban Crucible*, 158.

131. "In 1763 the settlers' fears took form." Merritt, *At the Crossroads*, 272.

132. As quoted in John R. Dunbar, ed., *The Paxton Papers* (The Hague: Martinus Nijhoff, 1957), 17.

133. Leonard W. Labaree, Introduction to Labaree, *Papers of Benjamin Franklin*, vol. 11 (1976), 44.

134. Dunbar, *Paxton Papers*, 17n13. See also Anderson, *Crucible of War*, 552.

135. As quoted in Dunbar, *Paxton Papers*, 17.

136. For an introduction to the Conestoga settlement community, see Francis Jennings, "Susquehannock," in Bruce G. Trigger, ed., *The Northeast*, vol. 15 of *Handbook of North American Indians* (Washington, D.C.: Smithsonian Institute, 1978), 366–67. See also Weslager, *The Delaware Indians*, 196–97; and Kenny, *Peaceable Kingdom Lost*, esp. 43–46.

137. Several attackers from the December 1763 massacre filed a collective "Apology of the Paxton Volunteers" in 1764 along with sets of sworn testimonies from individual participants. See Dunbar, *Paxton Papers*, 185–95.

138. As quoted in Dunbar, *Paxton Papers*, 23.

139. As quoted in Dunbar, *Paxton Papers*, 23n2.

140. Anderson, *Crucible of War*, 612.

141. Nash, *The Urban Crucible*, 177–78.

142. Anderson, *Crucible of War*, 612. See also Merrell, *Into the American Woods*, 235–40.

143. Eustace, "Sentimental Paradox," 40.

144. As quoted in Silver, *Our Savage Neighbors*, 222.

145. Silver, *Our Savage Neighbors*, 225–26.

146. As quoted in Eustace, "Sentimental Paradox," 56.

147. Dunbar, *Paxton Papers*, 29.

148. McConnell, *A Country Between*, 190.

149. Dunbar, *Paxton Papers*, 35–37. See also Lorett Treese, *The Storm Gathering: The Penn Family and the American Revolution* (University Park: Pennsylvania State University Press, 1992), 37–38.

150. Dunbar, *Paxton Papers*, 37.

151. Treese, *Storm Gathering*, 38.

152. Nash, *The Urban Crucible*, 179–80.

153. Labaree, *Papers of Benjamin Franklin*, vol. 10 (1966), 406–7.

154. Labaree, *Papers of Benjamin Franklin*, vol. 11 (1967), 43n3.

155. Franklin, *A Narrative of the Late Massacres*. See also Labaree, *Papers of Benjamin Franklin*, vol. 11 (1967), 47–69.

156. Labaree, *Papers of Benjamin Franklin*, vol. 11 (1967), 67–69.

157. Labaree, *Papers of Benjamin Franklin*, vol. 11 (1967), 55, 64–65.

158. Silver, *Our Savage Neighbors*, 203. "In 1764, Philadelphia's printers put out twice as many pamphlets as in any year before" (191).

159. As quoted in Anderson, *Crucible of War*, 620.

160. As quoted in Spero, *Frontier Rebels*, 81. See also Spero, *Frontier Country*, 103–96; and Patrick Griffin, *American Leviathan: Empire, Nation, and Revolutionary Frontier* (New York: Hill & Wang, 2007), esp. 74–94.

161. As quoted in Spero, *Frontier Rebels*, 181.

162. Calloway, *Indian World of George Washington*, 182–190.

163. Dowd, *War under Heaven*, 229–30.

164. James Smith, *An Account of the Remarkable Occurrences in the Life and Travels of Col. James Smith, during His Captivity with the Indians in the Years 1755, '56, '57, '58, and '59*, rev. ed. (Cincinnati: Robert Clark, 1870), 107.

165. Griffin, *American Leviathan*, 65–77. See also Richter, *Facing East from Indian Country*, 201–10; and Kenny, *Peaceable Kingdom Lost*, 205–9.

166. Smith, *An Account of the Remarkable Occurrences in the Life and Travels of Col. James Smith*, 106. See also Spero, *Frontier Rebels*, 31. "Greater representation, resentment of and hostility toward Native American groups, a desire to physically remove all Indians from the colony, a sense of being taken for granted by easterners, and a desire for a highly regulated Indian trade—those were the driving beliefs of the frontier people" fueling the western rebellion of 1765 (45).

167. As quoted in Spero, *Frontier Rebels*, 32.

168. As quoted in Spero, *Frontier Rebels*, 53.

169. Hinderaker and Mancall, *At the Edge of Empire*, 155. For overviews of Scots-Irish migration after 1750, see Patrick Griffin, *The People with No Name: Ireland's Ulster Scots, America's Scots Irish, and the Creation of a British Atlantic World* (Princeton: Princeton University Press, 2001); and T. M. Devine, *To the Ends of the Earth: Scotland's Global Diaspora, 1750–2010* (Washington, D.C.: Smithsonian Books, 2011).

170. As quoted in Volwiler, *George Croghan and the Western Movement*, 170. See also 168–171 for the 1764 trip to England.

171. Spero, *Frontier Rebels*, xix.

172. Smith, *An Account of the Remarkable Occurrences in the Life and Travels of Col. James Smith*, 110.

173. Smith, *An Account of the Remarkable Occurrences in the Life and Travels of Col. James Smith*, 109.

174. As quoted in Richter, *Facing East from Indian Country*, 202.

175. Steele, *Setting All the Captives Free*, 210, 378–79.

176. As quoted in Spero, *Frontier Rebels*, 235n35; see also 67.

177. Smith, *An Account of the Remarkable Occurrences in the Life and Travels of Col. James Smith*, 110–11.

178. As quoted in Spero, *Frontier Country*, 182.

179. Spero, *Frontier Country*, 182. See also Silver, *Our Savage Neighbors*, 158–59.

180. Lisa Ford, *Settler Sovereignty: Jurisdiction and Indigenous People in America and Australia, 1788–1836* (Cambridge, Mass.: Harvard University Press, 2010).

181. As quoted in Spero, *Frontier Rebels*, 111.

182. Silver, *Our Savage Neighbors*, 159.

183. "The beginning of the end for British empire in America occurred not in Boston or Philadelphia but on the Pennsylvania frontier . . . on March 6, 1765." Griffin, *American Leviathan*, 74.

184. Smith, *An Account of the Remarkable Occurrences in the Life and Travels of Col. James Smith*, 111–13.

185. Edmund S. Morgan and Helen M. Morgan, *The Stamp Act Crisis: Prologue to Revolution* (Chapel Hill: University of North Carolina Press, 1953), 144–45.

186. Eric Hinderaker, *Boston's Massacre* (Cambridge, Mass.: Harvard University Press, 2007), 4.

187. Bernard Bailyn, *Faces of Revolution: Personalities and Themes in the Struggle for American Independence* (New York: Knopf, 1990), 207.

188. William C. Armor, *Lives of the Governors of Pennsylvania* (Philadelphia: James K. Simon, 1872), 187–88. "Experience, rather than political theory, drove the delegates crafting the new constitution." Spero, *Frontier Rebels*, 187.

189. As quoted in Jonathan Israel, *The Expanding Blaze: How the American Revolution Ignited the World, 1775–1848* (Princeton: Princeton University Press, 2017), 8.

190. As quoted in Spero, *Frontier Rebels*, 187–88.

191. Spero, *Frontier Rebels*, 188.

192. As quoted in Silver, *Our Savage Neighbors*, 226.

193. Armor, *Lives of the Governors of Pennsylvania*, 188.

194. Silver, *Our Savage Neighbors*, 226.

195. Spero, *Frontier Country*, 172.

Chapter 6. Colonialism's Constitution

1. Erica Armstrong Dunbar, *Never Caught: The Washington's Relentless Pursuit of Their Runaway Slave, Ona Judge* (New York: Simon & Schuster, 2017), 15.

2. Pauline Maier, *Ratification: The People Debate the Constitution, 1787–1788* (New York: Simon & Schuster, 2010), 6.

3. John Ferling, *A Leap in the Dark: The Struggle to Create the American Republic* (New York: Oxford University Press, 2003), 238–49.

4. Lance Banning, *The Sacred Fire of Liberty: James Madison and the Founding of the Federal Republic* (Ithaca: Cornell University Press, 1995), 15, 29–49.

5. As quoted in Ferling, *A Leap in the Dark*, 254.

6. Gregory Ablavksy, "The Savage Constitution," *Duke Law Journal* (February 2014): 1039.

7. Ferling, *A Leap in the Dark*, 234.

8. Ferling, *A Leap in the Dark*, 254; Banning, *The Sacred Fire of Liberty*, 45.

9. William T. Hutchinson and William M. E. Rachal, eds., *The Papers of James Madison*, 15 vols. (Chicago: University of Chicago Press, 1971), 7:412.

10. Hutchinson and Rachal, *Papers of James Madison*, 7:412.

11. As quoted in Gordon S. Wood, *The Idea of America: Reflections on the Birth of the United States* (New York: Penguin, 2011), 232.

12. As quoted in Woody Holton, *Unruly Americans and the Origins of the Constitution* (New York: Hill & Wang, 2007), 6.

13. As quoted in Alan Taylor, *American Revolutions: A Continental History, 1750–1804* (New York: Norton, 2016), 319. See also Ferling, *A Leap in the Dark*, 254–55.

14. Thomas Paine, *Common Sense* (Alexandria, Va.: TheCapitol.Net, 2009), 68.

15. Gary B. Nash, *Race and Revolution* (Lanham, Md.: Rowman & Littlefield, 1990), 60.

16. Maya Jasanoff, *Liberty's Exiles: American Loyalists in the Revolutionary World* (New York: Random House, 2011), 89. For immigration to Sierra Leone, see 284–300. For additional runaways from the Washington family, see Dunbar, *Never Caught*.

17. As quoted in Taylor, *American Revolutions*, 322. See also Jasanoff, *Liberty's Exiles*, 295.

18. Stephen Aron, *How the West Was Lost: The Transformation of Kentucky from Daniel Boone to Henry Clay* (Baltimore: Johns Hopkins University Press, 1996), 58–81; Sami Lakomåki, *Gathering Together: The Shawnee People through Diaspora and Nationhood, 1600–1870* (New Haven: Yale University Press, 2014), 102–22.

19. Ablavksy, "The Savage Constitution," 1002.

20. Woody Holton, *Forced Founders: Indians, Debtors, Slaves, and the Making of the American Revolution* (Chapel Hill: University of North Carolina Press, 1999), xv–9.

21. Colin G. Calloway, *The American Revolution in Indian Country: Crisis and Diversity in Native American Communities* (New York: Cambridge University Press, 1995).

22. Calloway, *American Revolution in Indian Country*, 198–212, 134–57.

23. Anthony F. C. Wallace, *The Death and Rebirth of the Seneca* (New York: Vintage Books, 1969), 125–48.

24. As quoted in Colin G. Calloway, "The Continuing Revolution in Indian Country," in Frederick E. Hoxie et al., eds., *Native Americans and the Early Republic* (Charlottesville: University Press of Virginia, 1999), 15.

25. As quoted in Taylor, *American Revolutions*, 247.

26. "Treaty with the Cherokee, 1785," in Charles J. Kappler, ed., *Indian Affairs: Law and Treaties*, 2 vols. (Washington, D.C.: Government Printing Office, 1904), 2:9.

27. As quoted in Claudio Saunt, *A New Order of Things: Property, Power, and the*

Transformation of the Creek Indians, 1733–1816 (Cambridge: Cambridge University Press, 1999), 61.

28. "Report on the Committee of Indians Affairs," in Colin G. Calloway, ed., *Revolution and Confederation*, vol. 18 of Alden T. Vaughn, gen. ed., *Early American Indian Documents: Treaties and Laws, 1607–1789* (Bethesda, Md.: University Publications of America, 1994), 290.

29. Frederick E. Hoxie, introduction to Hoxie et al., *Native Americans and the Early Republic*, ix.

30. Brian DeLay, "Independent Indians and the U.S.-Mexican War," *American Historical Review* (2007).

31. Nelson Vance Russell, *The British Régime in Michigan and the Old Northwest, 1760–1796* (Northfield, Minn.: Carleton College, 1939), 230.

32. "Speech of the United Indian Nations to Congress," in Calloway, *Revolution and Confederation*, 356.

33. Robert G. Parkinson, *The Common Cause: Creating Race and Nation in the American Revolution* (Chapel Hill: University of North Carolina Press, 2016), 534.

34. Susan Sleeper-Smith, *Indigenous Prosperity and American Conquest: Indian Women of the Ohio River Valley, 1690–1792* (Chapel Hill: University of North Carolina Press, 2018), 286. See also Alan Taylor, *The Civil War of 1812: American Citizens, British Subjects, Irish Rebels, and Indian Allies* (New York: Vintage Books, 2010).

35. As Colin Calloway suggests, "Burning homes, razing fields, and killing noncombatants does not necessarily destroy people's will to fight or even their ability to win." *American Revolution in Indian Country*, 272.

36. Calloway, *Revolution and Confederation*, 279. See also Bethel Saler, *The Settlers' Empire: Colonialism and State Formation in America's Old Northwest* (Philadelphia: University of Pennsylvania Press, 2015), 29–30.

37. As quoted in Maier, *Ratification*, 11–18.

38. Ferling, *A Leap in the Dark*, 255.

39. P. J. Marshall, "Britain's American Problem: The International Perspective," in Edward G. Gray and Jane Kamensky, eds., *The Oxford Handbook of the American Revolution* (New York: Oxford University Press, 2013).

40. Eric Hobsbawm, *The Age of Revolution, 1789–1848*, rev. ed. (New York: Vintage Books, 1996), 9.

41. Hobsbawm, *The Age of Revolution*, 42–43, 53–76.

42. Maier, *Ratification*, 12–13.

43. James P. Ronda, *Astoria and Empire* (Lincoln: University of Nebraska Press, 1990). See also chapter 7.

44. Hutchinson and Rachal, *Papers of James Madison*, 7:425.

45. Jacob F. Lee, *Masters of the Middle Waters: Indian Nations and Colonial Ambitions along the Mississippi* (Cambridge, Mass.: Harvard University Press, 2019), 196.

46. Allan Greer, *Property and Dispossession: Natives, Empires, and Land in Early Modern North America* (New York: Cambridge University Press, 2018), 389–415.

47. Aron, *How the West Was Lost,* 77–78.

48. Lee, *Masters of the Middle Waters,* 199.

49. As quoted in Aron, *How the West Was Lost,* 80.

50. William G. McLoughlin, *Cherokee Renascence in the New Republic* (Princeton: Princeton University Press, 1986), 18.

51. William A. Hunter, "History of the Ohio Valley," in Bruce G. Trigger, ed., *The Northeast,* vol. 15 of *Handbook of North American Indians* (Washington, D.C.: Smithsonian Institute, 1978), 590–93.

52. As quoted in Aron, *How the West Was Lost,* 2.

53. See chapter 9.

54. As quoted in Claudio Saunt, "The Age of Imperial Expansion, 1763–1821," in Frederick E. Hoxie, ed., *The Oxford Handbook of American Indian History* (New York: Oxford University Press, 2016), 85.

55. Colin G. Calloway, *The Indian World of George Washington: The First President, the First Americans, and the Birth of the Nation* (New York: Oxford University Press, 2018), 300.

56. Ablavksy, "The Savage Constitution," 1008.

57. Holton, *Unruly Americans,* 8.

58. Holton, *Unruly Americans,* 8–23.

59. As quoted in Holton, *Unruly Americans,* 144.

60. As quoted in Sleeper-Smith, *Indigenous Prosperity and American Conquest,* 261.

61. Gregory Ablavsky, "'With the Indian Tribes': Race, Citizenship, and Original Constitutional Meanings," *Stanford Law Review* (2018): 1026–76.

62. As quoted in Calloway, *The Indian World of George Washington,* 295.

63. Taylor, *American Revolutions,* 344. See also Calloway, *Indian World of George Washington,* 262–63.

64. John C. Fitzpatrick, ed., *The Writings of George Washington: From the Original Manuscript Sources, 1745–1799* (Washington, D.C.: Government Printing Office, 1938), 27:486.

65. Calloway, *Indian World of George Washington,* 288.

66. Hutchinson and Rachal, *Papers of James Madison,* 7:427.

67. Sleeper-Smith, *Indigenous Prosperity and American Conquest,* 175–209.

68. Thomas L. McKenny and James Hall, *History of the Indian Tribes of North America, with Biographical Sketches and Anecdotes of the Principal Chiefs Embellished with One Hundred and Twenty Portraits from the Indian Gallery in the Department of War, at Washington,* rev. ed. (Kent, Ohio: Volair), 1978.

69. Sleeper-Smith, *Indigenous Prosperity and American Conquest,* 197.

70. Sleeper-Smith, *Indigenous Prosperity and American Conquest,* 197.

71. Sleeper-Smith, *Indigenous Prosperity and American Conquest,* 197.

72. Sleeper-Smith, *Indigenous Prosperity and American Conquest*, 198–202.

73. Sleeper-Smith, *Indigenous Prosperity and American Conquest*, 214.

74. Calloway, "The Continuing Revolution in Indian Country," 13. See also Sleeper-Smith, *Indigenous Prosperity and American Conquest*, 215.

75. Saler, *Setters' Empire*, 26–27.

76. As quoted in Russell, *The British Régime in Michigan and the Old Northwest*, 228. See also 217–29 for Spanish and French challenges to the boundaries drawn after the Treaty of Paris.

77. Taylor, *American Revolutions*, 339.

78. Jack N. Rakove, *The Beginnings of National Politics: An Interpretive History of the Continental Congress* (New York: Knopf, 1979), 179.

79. Frank Pommersheim, *Broken Landscape: Indians, Indian Tribes, and the Constitution* (New York: Oxford University Press, 2009), 17–21.

80. As quoted in Ablavksy, "The Savage Constitution," 1019.

81. Colin G. Calloway, *Pen & Ink Witchcraft: Treaties and Treaty Making in American Indian History* (New York: Oxford University Press, 2013), 68–102.

82. "Governor Clinton to the U.S. Indian Commissioners," in Calloway, *Revolution and Confederation*, 301 (emphasis added).

83. As quoted in Daniel K. Richter, "Onas, the Long Knife: Pennsylvanians and Indians," in Hoxie et al., *Native Americans and the Early Republic*, 190; and Taylor, *American Revolutions*, 342.

84. "Treaty with the Six Nations, 1784," in Kappler, *Indian Affairs*, 2:5.

85. "Treaty with the Six Nations, 1784," 2:6.

86. Maier, *Ratification*, 13. See also Ablavsky, "The Savage Constitution," 1023–24.

87. As quoted in Maier, *Ratification*, 13.

88. Richter, "Onas, the Long Knife," 139.

89. Ablavksy, "The Savage Constitution," 1024.

90. Adam Tate, "James Madison, 1780–1787: Nationalism and Political Reform," in Stuart Leibiger, ed., *A Companion to James Madison and James Monroe* (Madlen, Mass.: Wiley-Blackwell, 2013), 48–53.

91. Robert A. Rutland and William M. E. Rachal, eds., *The Papers of James Madison*, 15 vols. (Chicago: University of Chicago Press, 1971), 8:113.

92. Rutland and Rachal, *Papers of James Madison*, 8:116–17.

93. Joseph T. Glatthaar and James Kirby Martin, *Forgotten Allies: The Oneida Indians and the American Revolution* (New York: Hill & Wang, 2006).

94. Rutland and Rachal, *Papers of James Madison*, 8:99.

95. As quoted in Holton, *Unruly Americans*, 24.

96. Sleeper-Smith, *Indigenous Prosperity and American Conquest*, 246. See also Calloway, *Indian World of George Washington*, 172–73. Virginian planters "knew they had to diversify to protect themselves from the boom-and-bust cycles that plagued the tobacco economy" (172).

97. "From Thomas Jefferson," in Rutland and Rachal, *Papers of James Madison*, 8:128.

98. As quoted in Calloway, *Indian World of George Washington*, 294.

99. Maier, *Ratification*, 8.

100. Maier, *Ratification*, 8.

101. Calloway, *Indian World of George Washington*, 172.

102. Maier, *Ratification*, 8.

103. Calloway, *Indian World of George Washington*, 297.

104. Calloway, *Indian World of George Washington*, 294–97.

105. As quoted in Calloway, *Indian World of George Washington*, 294.

106. Donald Jackson and Dorothy Twohig, eds., *The Diaries of George Washington* (Charlottesville: University of Virginia Press, 1978) 4:18.

107. Jackson and Twohig, *Diaries of George Washington*, 4:18.

108. Jackson and Twohig, *Diaries of George Washington*, 4:21.

109. Fitzpatrick, *Writings of George Washington*, 27:486.

110. Fitzpatrick, *Writings of George Washington*, 27:486.

111. W. W. Abbot and Dorothy Twohig, eds., *The Papers of George Washington*, 8 vols. (Charlottesville: University of Virginia Press, 1992), 2:170.

112. As quoted in Saler, *Settlers' Empire*, 27–28.

113. Fitzpatrick, *Writings of George Washington*, 27:486–87 (emphasis added).

114. Historian Joseph Ellis, as quoted in Calloway, *Indian World of George Washington*, 297.

115. See Jackson and Twohig, *Diaries of George Washington*, 4:21–58.

116. Jackson and Twohig, *Diaries of George Washington*, 4:66.

117. As quoted in Sleeper-Smith, *Indigenous Prosperity and American Conquest*, 245.

118. Jackson and Twohig, *Diaries of George Washington*, 4:57.

119. Fitzpatrick, *Writings of George Washington*, 27:486.

120. Gordon S. Wood, *Empire of Liberty: A History of the Early Republic, 1789–1815* (New York: Oxford University Press, 2009), 123. See also chapter 7.

121. On "the double nature of the American Republic," see Saler, *Settlers' Empire*, 27.

122. "Resolutions on Western Law Enforcement and Mississippi Navigation," in Rutland and Rachal, *Papers of James Madison*, 8:124–25.

123. "Treaty with the Cherokee, 1785," in Kappler, *Indian Affairs*, 2:9 (emphasis added).

124. Lisa Ford, *Settler Sovereignty: Jurisdiction and Indigenous People in America and Australia, 1788–1836* (Cambridge, Mass.: Harvard University Press, 2010), 60.

125. Fitzpatrick, *Writings of George Washington*, 27:487.

126. Fitzpatrick, *Writings of George Washington*, 27:486.

127. Fitzpatrick, *Writings of George Washington*, 27:487.

128. Adam Dahl, *Empire of the People: Settler Colonialism and the Foundations of Modern Democratic Thought* (Lawrence: University of Kansas Press, 2018), 34–35.

129. As quoted in Dahl, *Empire of the People*, 35.

130. As quoted in Dahl, *Empire of the People*, 35–36.

131. Calloway, *Indian World of George Washington*, 7.

132. Abbott and Twohig, *Papers of George Washington*, 2:144.

133. Abbott and Twohig, *Papers of George Washington*, 2:171.

134. For Madison's port bills from 1784, see Tate, "James Madison, 1780–1787," 80.

135. Abbott and Twohig, *Papers of George Washington*, 2:166.

136. Abbott and Twohig, *Papers of George Washington*, 2:171.

137. As quoted in Daniel P. Barr, *A Colony Sprung from Hell: Pittsburgh and the Struggle for Authority on the Western Pennsylvania Frontier, 1744–1794* (Kent: Kent State University Press, 2014), 256.

138. William Findley, *History of the Insurrection in the Four Western Counties of Pennsylvania* (Spartanburg, S.C.: Reprint Company, 1984), ix. See also Steven R. Boyd, ed., *The Whiskey Rebellion: Past and Present Perspectives* (Westport, Conn.: Greenwood, 1985), 77–95.

139. Abbott and Twohig, *Papers of George Washington*, 2:171–72.

140. Ferling, *A Leap in the Dark*, 259.

141. Taylor, *American Revolutions*, 340.

142. Greer, *Property and Dispossession*, 408. See also chapter 7.

143. Ferling, *A Leap in the Dark*, 257–64.

144. As quoted in Taylor, *American Revolutions*, 340.

145. As quoted in Holton, *Unruly Americans*, 144.

146. Wood, *The Idea of America*, 184. See also Saler, *The Settlers' Empire*, 30–32.

147. See chapter 10 for an analysis of the Fourteenth Amendment as regards Indians.

148. Ablavsky, "The Savage Constitution," 1050.

149. Sayler, *The Settlers' Empire*, 30.

150. As quoted in Ablavsky, "The Savage Constitution," 1048.

151. As quoted in Ablavsky, "The Savage Constitution," 1049.

Chapter 7. The Deluge of Settler Colonialism

1. As quoted in Ronald Takaki, *A Different Mirror: A History of Multicultural America* (Boston: Little, Brown, 1993), 96.

2. Matthew L. M. Fletcher, "Avoiding Removal: The Pokagon Band of Potawatomi Indians," in Suzan Shown Harjo, ed., *Nation to Nation: Treaties between the United States & American Indian Nations* (Washington, D.C.: Smithsonian Institution, 2014), 86–87. See also Jeffrey Ostler, *Surviving Genocide: Native Nations and the United States from the American Revolution to Bleeding Kansas* (New Haven: Yale University Press, 2019), 311–17.

3. Fletcher, "Avoiding Removal," 86.

4. "Treaty with the Chippewa, etc., 1833," in Charles J. Kappler, ed., *Indian Affairs: Law and Treaties,* 2 vols. (Washington, D.C.: Government Printing Office, 1904), 2:402.

5. "Between 1829 and 1851, eighty-six ratified treaties were signed with twenty-six . . . tribes in New York, the Old Northwest, and the immediate trans-Mississippi area. . . . Potawatomi Indians alone were involved in nineteen." Francis Paul Prucha, *American Indian Treaties: The History of a Political Anomaly* (Berkeley: University of California Press, 1994), 184.

6. Office Commissary General Subsistence, "To Lieutenant L. F. Carter, Washington, November 30, 1830," in *Correspondence on the Subject of the Emigration of the Indians between the 30th November, 1831, and 27th December, 1833,* vol. 1 (Washington, D.C., 1834), reprinted as *The Indian Removals,* 5 vols. (New York: AMS, 1974), 1:5.

7. "Treaty with the Potawatomi, 1826"; "Treaty with the Potawatomi, 1827"; "Treaty with the Winnebago, etc. 1828"; "Treaty with the Potawatomi, 1828"; "Treaty with the Chippewa, etc., 1829"; "Treaty with the Potawatomi, [October 20,] 1832"; "Treaty with the Potawatomi, [October 26,] 1832"; and "Treaty with the Potawatomi, [October 27,] 1832"; in Kappler, *Indian Affairs,* 2:273–77, 283–84, 292–94, 294–97, 297–300, 353–56, 367–70, 372–75.

8. For an overview of early U.S. state efforts at Indigenous dispossession in southern Michigan, see Tiya Miles, *The Dawn of Detroit: A Chronicle of Slavery and Freedom in the City of the Straits* (New York: New Press, 2017), 203–12.

9. Susan Sleeper-Smith, *Indigenous Prosperity and American Conquest: Indian Women of the Ohio River Valley, 1690–1792* (Chapel Hill: University of North Carolina Press, 2018).

10. Sleeper-Smith, *Indigenous Prosperity and American Conquest.*

11. Francois Furstenberg, "The Significance of the Trans-Appalachian Frontier in Atlantic History," *American Historical Review* (June 2008): 650.

12. Adam Dahl, *Empire of the People: Settler Colonialism and the Foundations of Modern Democratic Thought* (Lawrence: University of Kansas Press, 2018); and Roxanne Dunbar-Ortiz, *An Indigenous Peoples' History of the United States* (Boston: Beacon, 2014), esp. 78–132.

13. "Indian Removal Act," May 28, 1830, in Francis Paul Prucha, ed., *Documents of United States Indian Policy,* 3rd ed. (Lincoln: University of Nebraska Press, 2000), 52.

14. "Andrew Jackson, State of the Union Address, December 6, 1830," in Theda Perdue and Michael D. Green, eds., *The Cherokee Removal: A Brief History with Documents,* 2nd ed. (Boston: Bedford St. Martin's, 2005), 127.

15. Prucha, *American Indian Treaties,* 168–207.

16. Eric Foner, *The Fiery Trial: Abraham Lincoln and American Slavery* (New York: Norton, 2010), 4.

17. Miles, *Dawn of Detroit,* 99–100.

18. Foner, *The Fiery Trial*, 6.

19. E. P. Thompson, *The Making of the English Working Class* (New York: Vintage Books, 1966), 191.

20. Daniel Walker Howe, *What Hath God Wrought: The Transformation of America, 1815–1848* (New York: Oxford University Press, 2007).

21. "In the North, the building of canals and the advent of steamboats and, later, railroads sets in motion economic changes that created an integrated economy of commercial farms and growing urban and industrial centers. In the South, the market revolution, coupled with the military defeat and subsequent removal of the Native American population, made possible the westward expansion of the slave system and the rise of the great Cotton Kingdom of the Gulf states." Foner, *Fiery Trial*, 9.

22. Claudio Saunt, *A New Order of Things: Property, Power, and the Transformation of the Creek Indians, 1733–1816* (New York: Cambridge University Press, 1999), 62.

23. As quoted in Saunt, *A New Order of Things*, 63.

24. Walter Johnson, *River of Dark Dreams: Slavery and Empire in the Cotton Kingdom* (Cambridge, Mass.: Harvard University Press, 2013), 34–40.

25. Dahl, *Empire of the People*, 2.

26. Joyce Appleby, *Liberalism and Republicanism in the Historical Imagination* (Cambridge, Mass.: Harvard University Press, 1992), 58.

27. As quoted in Eric Foner, *Free Soil, Free Labor, Free Men: The Ideology of the Republican Party Before the Civil War* (New York: Oxford University Press, 1970), 39.

28. Karl Polanyi, *The Great Transformation: The Political and Economic Origins of Our Time*, as quoted in Appleby, *Liberalism and Republicanism in the Historical Imagination*, 58.

29. Andrew J. Torget, *Seeds of Empire: Cotton, Slavery, and the Transformation of the Texas Borderlands, 1800–1850* (Chapel Hill: University of North Carolina Press, 2015), 137.

30. Howe, *What Hath God Wrought*, 118.

31. Takaki, *A Different Mirror*, 81.

32. Sven Beckert, *The Monied Metropolis: New York City and the Consolidation of the American Bourgeoisie, 1850–1896* (New York: Cambridge University Press, 2001), 16–19.

33. Howe, *What Hath God Wrought*, 120. See also Sean Wilentz, *Chants Democratic: New York City and the Rise of the American Working Class, 1788–1850* (New York: Oxford University Press, 1984), 25.

34. Sven Beckert, *Empire of Cotton: A Global History* (New York: Knopf, 2014), 131–36.

35. See David J. Wishart, *The Fur Trade of the American West, 1807–1840: A Geographical Synthesis* (Lincoln: University of Nebraska Press, 1979), 53–78.

36. James P. Ronda, *Astoria and Empire* (Lincoln: University of Nebraska Press, 1990), 2.

37. Ronda, *Astoria and Empire*, 218–19.

38. Daniel J. Hulsebosch, *Constituting Empire: New York and the Transformation of Constitutionalism in the Atlantic World, 1664–1830* (Chapel Hill: University of North Carolina Press, 2005), 263.

39. As quoted in Amalia D. Kessler, *Inventing American Exceptionalism: The Origins of American Adversarial Legal Culture, 1800–1877* (New Haven: Yale University Press, 2017), 47.

40. For growing social ties across class, see Gordon S. Wood, *The Radicalism of the American Revolution: How a Revolution Transformed a Monarchical Society into a Democratic One Unlike Any That Had Ever Existed* (New York: Knopf, 1992), esp. 124–45.

41. Philip D. Morgan, *Slave Counterpoint: Black Culture in the Eighteenth-Century Chesapeake and Lowcountry* (Chapel Hill: University of North Carolina Press, 1998), 271.

42. Alan Taylor, *American Revolutions: A Continental History, 1750–1804* (New York: Norton, 2016), 357–61.

43. Howe, *What Hath God Wrought*, 121.

44. Clare A. Lyons, *Sex among the Rabble: An Intimate History of Gender and Power in the Age of Revolution; Philadelphia, 1730–1830* (Chapel Hill: University of North Carolina Press, 2006), 290.

45. Lyons, *Sex among the Rabble*, 309.

46. Lyons, *Sex among the Rabble*, 290.

47. Howe, *What Hath God Wrought*, 34.

48. Lyons, *Sex among the Rabble*, 244.

49. As quoted in Dahl, *Empire of the People*, 37. See also Bethel Saler, *The Settlers' Empire: Colonialism and State Formation in America's Old Northwest* (Philadelphia: University of Pennsylvania Press, 2015), 19–26.

50. Saler, *The Settlers' Empire*, 307. "Antipathy to control" is from Frederick Jackson Turner, as quoted in Saler's book.

51. Dahl, *Empire of the People*, 37.

52. As quoted in Lawrence H. Fuchs, *The American Kaleidoscope: Race, Ethnicity, and the Civic Culture* (Hanover: University Press of New England, 1990), 13. See also Hulsebosch, *Constituting Empire*, 186–87.

53. Fuchs, *The American Kaleidoscope*, 15. See also Takaki, *A Different Mirror*, 80.

54. Foner, *The Fiery Trial*, 16.

55. Jaqueline Jones, *A Dreadful Deceit: The Myth of Race from the Colonial Era to Obama's America* (New York: Basic Books, 2013), 95.

56. Foner, *The Fiery Trail*, 7. See Ibram X. Kendi, *Stamped from the Beginning: The Definitive History of Racist Ideas in America* (New York: Nation Books, 2016), 117.

57. Kendi, *Stamped from the Beginning*, 120.

58. David Waldstreicher, *Slavery's Constitution: From Revolution to Ratification* (New York: Hill & Wang, 2009), 156. See also Jones, *A Dreadful Deceit*, 83–95.

59. Robert G. Parkinson, *The Common Cause: Creating Race and Nation in the American Revolution* (Chapel Hill: University of North Carolina Press, 2016), 661.

60. As quoted in Kendi, *Stamped from the Beginning*, 104–5.

61. For an overview of Enlightenment principles that highlights the "varieties" and multiplicities of "American enlightened" thought, see Caroline Winterer, *American Enlightenments: Pursuing Happiness in the Age of Reason* (New Haven: Yale University Press, 2016).

62. See, e.g., David R. Roediger, *The Wages of Whiteness: Race and the Making of the American Working Class* (New York: Verso, 1991), 26. See also Ronald Takaki, *Iron Cages: Race and Culture in 19th-Century America* (New York: Oxford University Press, 1990).

63. As quoted in Dahl, *Empire of the People*, 86.

64. As quoted in Dahl, *Empire of the People*, 87.

65. Ernest Renan, "Qu-est-ce qu'une nation?" in John Hutchinson and Anthony D. Smith, eds., *Nationalism* (New York: Oxford University Press, 1994). Renan offered the enduring suggestion that "nations are not something eternal. . . . They have begun," in part from a shared "past . . . a rich legacy of remembrances." Such remembrances provide "a grand solidarity constituted by the sentiment of sacrifices which one has made and those that one is disposed to make again" (17–18).

66. Colin G. Calloway, *The Indian History of an American Institution: Native Americans and Dartmouth* (Hanover: Dartmouth College Press, 2010), 26.

67. Parkinson, *The Common Cause*, 648.

68. As quoted in Calloway, *The Indian History of an American Institution*, 27.

69. Winterer, *American Enlightenments*, 11.

70. Winterer, *American Enlightenments*, 11.

71. Benedict Anderson, *Imagined Communities: Reflections on the Origin and Spread of Nationalism* (London: Verso, 1983), 187–206.

72. As quoted in Dahl, *Empire of the People*, 2–3.

73. Dahl, *Empire of the People*, 3–4.

74. Dahl, *Empire of the People*, 3.

75. As quoted in Dahl, *Empire of the People*, 2. See also Winterer, *American Enlightenments*, 209–10.

76. As quoted in Takaki, *Iron Cages*, 38.

77. Annette Gordon-Reed and Peter S. Onuf, *"Most Blessed of the Patriarchs": Thomas Jefferson and the Empire of the Imagination* (New York: Liveright, 2016).

78. Kendi, *Stamped from the Beginning*, 102. See also Richard Drinnon, *Facing West: The Metaphysics of Indian-Hating and Empire-Building* (Minneapolis: University of Minnesota Press, 1980), 90–116.

79. As quoted in Alan Taylor, *Thomas Jefferson's Education* (New York: Norton, 2019), 50.

80. As quoted in Drinnon, *Facing West*, 93.

81. As quoted in Takaki, *Iron Cages*, 36.

82. Foner, *Fiery Trial*, 15; Kendi, *Stamped from the Beginning*, 121.

83. Kendi, *Stamped from the Beginning*, 109. See also Taylor, *Thomas Jefferson's Education*, 133–60.

84. Taylor, *Thomas Jefferson's Education*, 141.

85. As quoted in Lisa Ford, *Settler Sovereignty: Jurisdiction and Indigenous Peoples in America and Australia, 1788–1836* (Cambridge, Mass.: Harvard University Press, 2010), 24.

86. As quoted in Winterer, *American Enlightenments*, 113; see also 112–14.

87. Reginald Horsman, "The Indian Policy of an 'Empire for Liberty,'" in Frederick E. Hoxie et al., eds., *Native Americans and the Early Republic* (Charlottesville: University Press of Virginia, 1999), 37–61.

88. See Horsman, "The Indian Policy of an 'Empire for Liberty.'"

89. As quoted in Horsman, "The Indian Policy of an 'Empire for Liberty,'" 45.

90. Claudio Saunt, *Unworthy Republic: The Dispossession of Native Americans and the Road to Indian Territory* (New York: Norton, 2020), 22–24. The "so-called civilization policy was distinct from the political and bureaucratic operation in the 1830s to deport tens of thousands of people" (23).

91. Herman J. Viola, *Thomas L. McKenney: Architect of America's Early Indian Policy, 1816–1830* (Chicago: Sage Books, 1974), 6–20.

92. "President Washington on Government Trading Houses, December 3, 1793," in Prucha, *Documents of United States Indian Policy*, 16 (emphasis added).

93. Calloway, *The Indian History of an American Institution*, 58–66. See also William G. McLoughlin, *Cherokees and Missionaries, 1789–1839* (New Haven: Yale University Press, 1984), 21–24.

94. David S. Heidler and Jeanne T. Heidler, *Indian Removal: A Norton Casebook* (New York: Norton, 2007), 3–9.

95. As quoted in Saunt, *Unworthy Republic*, 23.

96. Calloway, *The Indian History of an American Institution*, 7–23. For Cornwall, see John Demos, *The Heathen School: A Story of Hope and Betrayal in the Age of the Early Republic* (New York: Knopf, 2014), 36–43.

97. As quoted in Horsman, "The Indian Policy of an 'Empire for Liberty,'" 41, 43.

98. As quoted in Kendi, *Stamped from the Beginning*, 112.

99. Taylor, *Thomas Jefferson's Education*, 135–36.

100. Kendi, *Stamped from the Beginning*, 111–17. "Jefferson may have privately justified his relations with Sally Hemmings by reminding himself that everyone did it, or tried to do it. . . . Master/slave rape or intercourse seemed 'natural,' and enslaving one's children seemed normal in slaveholding America" (130).

101. See, e.g., Wilson Jeremiah Moses, *Thomas Jefferson: A Modern Prometheus* (New York: Cambridge University Press, 2019).

102. As quoted in Taylor, *Thomas Jefferson's Education*, 134.

103. Jeremy D. Popkin, *You Are All Free: The Haitian Revolution and the Abolition of Slavery* (New York: Cambridge University Press, 2010), 12.

104. As quoted in Kendi, *Stamped from the Beginning,* 123.

105. For an overview of the political reactions to the Haitian Revolution within the Washington presidency, see Popkin, *You Are All Free,* 289–326.

106. Lyons, *Sex among the Rabble,* 195. See also Bruce Dian, *A Hideous Monster of the Mind: American Race Theory in the Early Republic* (Cambridge, Mass.: Harvard University Press, 2002), 84. For an introduction to the history of U.S. fugitive slave laws, see R. J. M. Blackett, *The Captive's Quest for Freedom: Fugitive Slaves, the 1850 Fugitive Slave Law, and the Politics of Slavery* (New York: Cambridge University Press, 2018).

107. Julius S. Scott, *The Common Wind: Afro-American Currents in the Age of the Haitian Revolution* (New York: Verso, 2018), 188.

108. Popkin, *You Are All Free,* 310–18.

109. As quoted in Kendi, *Stamped from the Beginning,* 126.

110. As quoted in Kendi, *Stamped from the Beginning,* 144. See also Robert Pierce Forbes, *The Missouri Compromise and Its Aftermath: Slavery and the Meaning of America* (Chapel Hill: University of North Carolina Press, 2007), 27–28.

111. As quoted in Taylor, *Thomas Jefferson's Education,* 138.

112. Dian, *A Hideous Monster of the Mind,* 91. For an overview of the founding of Sierra Leone, see also Jones, *A Dreadful Deceit,* 88–93.

113. Forbes, *The Missouri Compromise,* 27. On colonization efforts during Jefferson's presidency, see 28.

114. Ostler, *Surviving Genocide,* 120–21.

115. There are debates about the number of soldiers killed by forces under the Miami chief Little Turtle. See Walter LaFeber, *The American Age: United States Foreign Policy at Home and Abroad since 1750* (New York: Norton, 1989), 47. For slightly lower estimates, see Ostler, *Surviving Genocide,* 108.

116. As quoted in Ostler, *Surviving Genocide,* 108.

117. As quoted in Ostler, *Surviving Genocide,* 108.

118. Jeffrey Ostler, "'Just and Lawful War' as Genocidal War in the (United States) Northwest Ordinance and Northwest Territory, 1787–1832," *Journal of Genocide Research* 18 (2016): 1, 5–7.

119. See, e.g., Carl Benn, ed., *John Norton—Teyoninhokarawen: A Mohawk Memoir from the War of 1812* (Toronto: University of Toronto Press, 2019), 19–23.

120. As quoted in D. W. Meinig, *Continental America, 1800–1867,* vol. 2 of *The Shaping of America: A Geographical Perspective on 500 Years of History* (New Haven: Yale University Press, 1993), 10.

121. "Treaty with the Osage, 1808," in Kappler, *Indian Affairs,* 2:95–99. For the Osage treaty, see also Robert Warrior, *The People and the Word: Reading Native Nonfiction* (Minneapolis: University of Minnesota Press, 2005), 62.

122. "Treaty with the Ottawa, etc., 1807," in Kappler *Indian Affairs,* 2:92–95.

123. Carole Goldberg et al., eds., *Indian Law Stories* (New York: Foundation, 2011), 2.

124. For extended discussion on the evolution of congressional authority vis-à-vis treaty making, see David M. Golove, "Treaty-Making and the Nation: The Constitutional Foundations of the Nationalist Conception of the Treaty Power," *Michigan Law Review* (Spring 2000): 1075–1319.

125. Prucha, *American Indian Treaties*, 106.

126. As quoted in Furstenberg, "The Significance of the Trans-Appalachian Frontier in Atlantic History," 655.

127. "Doubt rather than certainty was the constant companion of enlightened hope." Winterer, *American Enlightenments*, 16.

128. For the classic study of how treaties shaped the practices of the U.S. Senate, see Ralston Hayden, *The Senate and Treaties, 1789–1817: The Development of the Treaty-Making Functions of the United States Senate during Their Formative Period* (New York: Macmillan, 1920). See also Prucha, *American Indian Treaties*, 70–79.

129. Margot Canaday, *The Straight State: Sexuality and Citizenship in Twentieth-Century America* (Princeton: Princeton University Press, 2009), 3.

130. Hayden, *The Senate and Treaties*, 11–16.

131. Taylor, *American Revolutions*, 392.

132. As quoted in Taylor, *American Revolutions*, 393.

133. As quoted in Prucha, *American Indian Treaties*, 71. For the treaty, see "Treaty with the Wyandot, etc., 1789," in Kappler, *Indian Affairs*, 2:18–23.

134. As quoted in Hayden, *The Senate and Treaties*, 14.

135. As quoted in Prucha, *American Indian Treaties*, 71–72; and in Hayden, *The Senate and Treaties*, 15.

136. See Kappler, *Indian Affairs*, 2:18–45.

137. Thomas Bender, *A Nation among Nations: America's Place in World History* (New York: Hill & Wang, 2006), 106.

138. "Treaty with the Wyandot, etc., 1795," in Kappler, *Indian Affairs*, 2:39–45.

139. "Treaty with the Wyandot, etc., 1795," 2:39–45.

140. Michael Witgen, *An Infinity of Nations: How the Native New World Shaped Early America* (Philadelphia: University of Pennsylvania Press, 2012), 219. See also Michael Wigten, "A Nation of Settlers: The Early American Republic and the Colonization of the Northwest Territory," *William and Mary Quarterly* 76 (2019): 391–98.

141. "Treaty with the Wyandot, etc., 1795," 2:42. See also Witgen, "A Nation of Settlers," 397–98.

142. See chapter 8 for *Johnson v. M'Intosh* decision.

143. Taylor, *American Revolutions*, 406.

144. Bender, *A Nation among Nations*, 107.

145. LaFeber, *The American Age*, 47.

146. Moses, *Thomas Jefferson*, 441–43. See also Gordon-Reed and Onuf, "*Most Blessed of the Patriarchs*," 198–99.

147. As quoted in Everett Somerville Brown, *The Constitutional History of the Louisiana Purchase* (Berkeley: University of California Press, 1920), 7n17.

148. Taylor, *American Revolutions*, 385.

149. As quoted in Brown, *The Constitutional History of the Louisiana Purchase*, 7n17 (emphasis added). "Piarningo" is likely a reference to a specific Chickasaw ally of the United States, "Piomingo," who opposed military actions against the United States and supported interior diplomatic efforts, such as the Treaty of San Lorenzo. There were two leaders among the Chickasaw so named, though no scholar has traced the connections between Jefferson's use of this name (in March 1796) to those mentioned in treaty councils. See Jason Herbert, "'To Treaty with All Nations': Invoking Authority within the Chickasaw Nation, 1783–1795," *Ohio Valley History* (Spring 2018): 27–29.

150. For "the contrast between the attitudes of Presidents Adams and Jefferson towards Haiti," see Moses, *Thomas Jefferson*, 454–57. See also Bender, *A Nation among Nations*, 108–9; and Taylor, *American Revolutions*, 429.

151. Peter J. Kastor, *The Nation's Crucible: The Louisiana Purchase and the Creation of America* (New Haven: Yale University Press, 2004), 40.

152. Taylor, *American Revolutions*, 419–23.

153. As quoted in Ford, *Settler Sovereignty*, 24.

154. As quoted in Brown, *The Constitutional History of the Louisiana Purchase*, 23.

155. As quoted in Brown, *The Constitutional History of the Louisiana Purchase*, 23.

156. As quoted in Brown, *The Constitutional History of the Louisiana Purchase*, 26.

157. As quoted in Brown, *The Constitutional History of the Louisiana Purchase*, 26.

158. Foner, *Fiery Trial*, 71.

159. Walter Johnson, *Soul by Soul: Life inside the Antebellum Slave Market* (Cambridge, Mass.: Harvard University Press, 1999), 5.

160. As quoted in Saunt, *Unworthy Republic*, xiv.

161. Johnson, *Soul by Soul*, 6.

162. Maureen Konkle, *Writing Indian Nations: Native Intellectuals and the Politics of Historiography, 1827–1863* (Chapel Hill: University of North Carolina Press, 2004), esp. 42–96.

163. For deaths during removal within deportation centers, see Saunt, *Unworthy Republic*, 148–55. See also Ostler, *Surviving Genocide*.

164. See Francis Paul Prucha, ed., *Atlas of American Indian Affairs* (Lincoln: University of Nebraska Press, 1990), 94–97. These distinctions are based on non-Atlantic military posts.

165. Prucha, *Atlas of American Indian Affairs*, 98.

166. Julie L. Reed, *Serving the Nation: Cherokee Sovereignty and Social Welfare, 1800–1907* (Norman: University of Oklahoma Press, 2016), esp. 38–59. See also Saunt, *A New Order of Things*, 38–185.

167. Reed, *Serving the Nation*, 5.

168. Saunt, *Unworthy Republic*, 48.

169. As quoted in Ford, *Settler Sovereignty*, 134.

170. As quoted in Ford, *Settler Sovereignty*, 134.

171. As quoted in Ford, *Settler Sovereignty*, 135.

172. Saunt, *Unworthy Republic*, 48.

173. As quoted in Ford, *Settler Sovereignty*, 141.

174. As quoted in Ford, *Settler Sovereignty*, 135.

175. Reed, *Serving the Nation*, 30. For an overview of Boudinot's education at Cornwall, see Ralph Henry Gabriel, *Elias Boudinot: Cherokee and His America* (Norman: University of Oklahoma Press, 1941), 49–65. The scholarship on Sequoyah is vast. For an overview with extensive citations, see Konkle, *Writing Indian Nations*, 78–96.

176. As quoted in Saunt, *Unworthy Republic*, 49.

177. As quoted in Keith Richotte Jr., *Federal Indian Law and Policy: An Introduction* (St. Paul, Minn.: West Academic, 2020), 60.

178. As quoted in Saunt, *Unworthy Republic*, 163.

179. As quoted in Saunt, *Unworthy Republic*, 163.

180. As quoted in Saunt, *Unworthy Republic*, 164–65.

Chapter 8. Foreign Policy Formations

1. "Table A3.9: Building Construction at San Gabriel Mission," in Robert H. Jackson and Edward Castillo, *Indians, Franciscans, and Spanish Colonization: The Impact of the Mission System on California Indians* (Albuquerque: University of New Mexico Press, 1995), 149.

2. As quoted in Steven W. Hackel, "Sources of Rebellion: Indian Testimony and the Mission San Gabriel Uprising of 1785," *Ethnohistory* 50 (2003): 648, 662n21.

3. As quoted in Richard F. Pourande, *Anza Conquers the Desert: The Anza Expeditions from Mexico to California and the Founding of San Francisco, 1774 to 1776* (San Diego: Copley Books, 1971), 179.

4. Also know as Kumivit, the Tongva have resided across Tovaangar (the Los Angeles Basin) since time immemorial. They lived in 1770 in an estimated fifty independent village communities comprising five thousand. See Hackel, "Sources of Rebellion," 648. See also Edward D. Castillo, "Gender Status Decline, Resistance, and Accommodation among Female Neophytes in the Missions of California: A San Gabriel Case Study," *American Indian Culture and Research Journal* 18 (1994): 67–93.

5. Steven W. Hackel, *Children of Coyote, Missionaries of Saint Francis: Indian-Spanish Relations in Colonial California, 1769–1850* (Chapel Hill: University of North Carolina Press, 2005), 266.

6. "Table A1.10: Livestock Reported at San Gabriel Mission, 1780–1832," in Jackson and Castillo, *Indians, Franciscans, and Spanish Colonization*, 126; Hackel, *Children of Coyote*, 266n74.

7. Hackel, *Children of Coyote*, 65–80.

8. Edward Dallam Melillo, *Strangers on Familiar Soil: Rediscovering the Chile-California Connection* (New Haven: Yale University Press, 2015), 17.

9. As quoted in in Jackson and Castillo, *Indians, Franciscans, and Spanish Colonization*, 74–75.

10. As quoted in Claudio Saunt, *West of the Revolution: An Uncommon History of 1776* (New York: Norton, 2014), 70. See also Saunt, "'My Medicine Is Punishment': A Case of Torture in Early California," *Ethnohistory* 57 (2010): 679–708.

11. As quoted in Pourande, *Anza Conquers the Desert*, 179.

12. Saunt, *West of the Revolution*, 59.

13. M. Kat Anderson et al., "A World of Balance and Plenty: Land, Plants, Animals, and Humans in a Pre-European California," in Ramón A. Gutiérrez and Richard J. Orsi, eds., *Contested Eden: California Before the Gold Rush* (Berkeley: University of California Press, 1998), 12–47.

14. Hackel, *Children of Coyote*, 266. See also George Harwood Phillips, *Vineyards and Vaqueros: Indian Labor and the Economic Exploitation of Southern California, 1771–1877* (Norman: University of Oklahoma Press, 2010), 115–17.

15. Hackel, *Children of Coyote*, 266.

16. John Ryan Fischer, *Cattle Colonialism: An Environmental History of the Conquest of California and Hawai'i* (Chapel Hill: University of North Carolina Press, 2015), 66–69.

17. Despite a paucity of records, Toypurina has emerged a celebrated as well as a fictionalized Indigenous leader. See Hackel, "Sources of Rebellion," 663–64; Antonia I. Castañeda, "Engendering the History of Alta California, 1769–1848: Gender, Sexuality, and the Family," in Gutiérrez and Orsi, *Contested Eden*, 230–59; Castañeda, "Malinche, Calafia, y Toypurina: Of Myths, Monsters and Embodied History," in Linda Heidenreich, ed., *Three Decades of Engendering History: Selected Works of Antonia I. Castañeda* (Denton: University of North Texas Press, 2014), 75–78; and Isabelle Allende, *Zorro* (New York: HarperCollins, 2005).

18. Fischer, *Cattle Colonialism*, 127.

19. Melillo, *Strangers on Familiar Soil*, 10.

20. As quoted in Melillo, *Strangers on Familiar Soil*, 26.

21. As quoted in D. W. Meinig, *Continental America, 1800–1867*, vol. 2 of *The Shaping of America: A Geographical Perspective on 500 Years of History* (New Haven: Yale University Press, 1993), 158–59.

22. Daniel Walker Howe, *What Hath God Wrought: The Transformation of America, 1815–1848* (New York: Oxford University Press, 2007), 809.

23. George Harwood Phillips, *Indians and Intruders in Central California, 1769–1849* (Norman: University of Oklahoma Press, 1993).

24. Benjamin Madley, "California and Oregon's Modoc Indians: How Indigenous Resistance Camouflages Genocide in Colonial Histories," in Andrew Woolford et al., eds., *Colonial Genocide in Indigenous North America* (Durham: Duke University Press,

2014), 98–130; and Madley, *An American Genocide: The United States and the California Indian Catastrophe* (New Haven: Yale University Press, 2016), 12; see also 362–528; and chapter 9 in this volume.

25. "Some 310,000 Indians lived within the boundaries of the present state just before Spanish colonization." Hackel, *Children of Coyote,* 21.

26. James C. Scott, *The Art of Not Being Governed: An Anarchist History of Upland Southeast Asia* (New Haven: Yale University Press, 2009), 22.

27. Hackel, *Children of Coyote,* 263. See also Rose Marie Beebe and Robert M. Senkewicz, *Junípero Serra: California, Indians, and the Transformation of a Missionary* (Norman: University of Oklahoma Press, 2015), 362–64.

28. Fischer, *Cattle Colonialism,* 73. See also William J. Bauer Jr., "California," in Frederick E. Hoxie, ed., *The Oxford Handbook of American Indian History* (New York: Oxford University Press, 2016), 282–83.

29. Hackel, *Children of Coyote,* 263–64.

30. Hackel, *Children of Coyote,* 263; Hackel, "Sources of Rebellion," 652.

31. Erika Pérez, *Colonial Intimacies: Interethnic Kinship, Sexuality, and Marriage in Southern California, 1769–1885* (Norman: University of Oklahoma Press, 2018), 6.

32. Bauer, "California," 284–85. See also Phillips, *Vineyards and Vaqueros,* 95–100.

33. Hackel, *Children of Coyote,* 310–11.

34. As quoted in Phillips, *Vineyards and Vaqueros,* 115.

35. Claudio Saunt, "The Age of Imperial Expansion, 1763–1821," in Hoxie, *The Oxford Handbook of American Indian History,* 80.

36. As quoted in Hackel, *Children of Coyote,* 266. See also Hackel, "Sources of Rebellion," 650–51.

37. Saunt, *West of the Revolution,* 60–64; Hackel, *Children of Coyote,* 260.

38. For prohibitions at San Gabriel, see Hackel, *Children of Coyote,* 264n71; at San Diego, see Hackel, "Sources of Rebellion," 651.

39. As quoted in Hackel, *Children of Coyote,* 263.

40. As quoted in Pérez, *Colonial Intimacies,* 43.

41. Lisbeth Haas, ed., *Pablo Tac, Indigenous Scholar: Writing on Luiseño Language and Colonial History, c. 1840* (Berkeley: University of California Press, 2011), 192.

42. As quoted in Lynn H. Gamble, *The Chumash World at European Contact: Power, Trade, and Feasting among Complex Hunter-Gatherers* (Berkeley: University of California Press, 2008), 115.

43. O.H.K. Spate, *The Spanish Lake: The Pacific since Magellan* (Canberra: Australian National University Press, 1979), 66.

44. As quoted in Gamble, *The Chumash World at European Contact,* 166. See also W. Michael Mathes, *Vizcaíno and Spanish Expansion in the Pacific Ocean, 1580–1630* (San Francisco: California Historical Society, 1968), 92.

45. Antonia I. Castañeda, "Sexual Violence in the Politics and Policies of Conquest: Amerindian Women and the Spanish Conquest of Alta California" in Heidenreich, *Three Decades of Engendering History,* 204; see also 201–28.

46. Castañeda, "Engendering the History of Alta California," 232–35.

47. Cutcha Risling Baldy, *We Are Dancing for You: Native Feminisms and the Revitalization of Women's Coming-of-Age Ceremonies* (Seattle: University of Washington Press, 2018).

48. Baldy, *We Are Dancing for You*, 57.

49. As quoted in Fischer, *Cattle Colonialism*, 68.

50. Hackel, "Sources of Rebellion," 657.

51. Hackel, "Sources of Rebellion," 654–57.

52. As quoted in Hackel, "Sources of Rebellion," 655.

53. Hackel, "Sources of Rebellion," 657–58.

54. Hackel, "Sources of Rebellion," 658–59, 669n90.

55. Gamble, *The Chumash World at European Contact*, 236–39.

56. Juan Crespí, "1769: The Santa Barbara Channel," in Rose Marie Beebe and Robert M. Senkewicz, eds., *Lands of Promise and Despair: Chronicles of Early California, 1535–1846* (Berkeley: Heyday Books, 2001), 121.

57. Gamble, *The Chumash World at European Contact*, 4–8, 223–34.

58. Hackel, *Children of Coyote*, 282.

59. Alan K. Brown, ed. and trans., *Gaspar de Portolá: Explorer and Founder of California* (Lerida: Instituto de Estudios Ilerdenses, 1983), 243.

60. Theodore H. Hittell, ed., El Triunfo de la Cruz*: A Description of the Building by Father Juan Ugarte of the First Ship Made in California* (San Francisco: Book Club of California, 1977), 11–12.

61. As quoted in Meinig, *Continental America*, 168.

62. As quoted in Malcolm J. Rohrbough, *Rush to Gold: The French and the California Gold Rush, 1848–1854* (New Haven: Yale University Press, 2013), 43.

63. As quoted in Melillo, *Strangers on Familiar Soil*, 20–21.

64. As quoted in Melillo, *Strangers on Familiar Soil*, 21.

65. Melillo, *Strangers on Familiar Soil*, 21. See also Susan Delano McKelvey, *Botanical Exploration of the Trans-Mississippi West, 1790–1850* (Jamaica Plain, Mass.: Arnold Arboretum of Harvard University, 1955), 3–10.

66. Julius S. Gassner, ed. and trans., *Voyages and Adventures of La Pérouse: From the Fourteenth Edition of the F. Valentine Abridgment* (Honolulu: University of Hawaii Press, 1969), 47.

67. Warren L. Cook, *Flood Tide of Empire: Spain and the Pacific Northwest, 1543–1819* (New Haven: Yale University Press, 1973), 111–12. See also Gassner, *Voyages and Adventures of La Pérouse*, 30–38.

68. Cook, *Flood Time of Empire*, 113.

69. McKelvey, *Botanical Exploration of the Trans-Mississippi West*, 6; see also 6n5, for plant identifications.

70. As quoted in Melillo, *Strangers on Familiar Soil*, 24.

71. As quoted in Melillo, *Strangers on Familiar Soil*, 24.

72. McKelvey, *Botanical Exploration of the Trans-Mississippi West*, 6.

73. McKelvey, *Botanical Exploration of the Trans-Mississippi West*, 9.

74. P. A. Tikhmenev, *A History of the Russian-American Company*, ed. and trans. Richard A. Pierce and Alton S. Donnelly (Seattle: University of Washington Press, 1978). *Promyshlennik* is translated as "a Russian trapper, hunter, or trader" (505). See also Ilya Vinkovetsky, *Russian America: An Overseas Colony of a Continental Empire, 1804–1867* (New York: Oxford University Press, 2011), 124–26.

75. James R. Gibson, *Otter Skins, Boston Ships, and China Goods: The Maritime Fur Trade of the Northwest Coast, 1785–1841* (Montreal: McGill-Queen's University Press, 1992), 12–16.

76. Gibson, *Otter Skins, Boston Ships, and China Goods*, 17–18.

77. As quoted in Cook, *Flood Tide of Empire*, 113.

78. Melillo, *Strangers on Familiar Soil*, 25.

79. Tikhmenev, *A History of the Russian-American Company*, 99. See also Cook, *Flood Tide of Empire*, 496–99.

80. Cook, *Flood Tide of Empire*, 499–506.

81. Vinkovetsky, *Russian America*, 91–92.

82. Colin G. Calloway, *The Indian History of an American Institution: Native Americans and Dartmouth* (Hanover: Dartmouth College Press, 2010), 55–56.

83. As quoted in Melillo, *Strangers on Familiar Soil*, 25.

84. Gibson, *Otter Skins, Boston Ships, and China Goods*, 18–21.

85. Melillo, *Strangers on Familiar Soil*, 25.

86. As quoted in Gibson, *Otter Skins, Boston Ships, and China Goods*, 19.

87. Iris H. W. Engstrand, "Seekers of the 'Northern Mystery': European Exploration of California and the Pacific," in Gutiérrez and Orsi, *Contested Eden*, 86–87; Spate, *The Spanish Lake*, 214–28.

88. Pourande, *Anza Conquers the Desert*. See also Natale A. Zappia, *Traders and Raiders: The Indigenous World of the Colorado Basin, 1540–1859* (Chapel Hill: University of North Carolina Press, 2014), 69–75.

89. Illona Katzew, *Casta Painting: Images of Race in Eighteenth-Century Mexico* (New Haven: Yale University Press, 2004), 42.

90. Hackel, *Children of Coyote*, 180–81.

91. William S. Simmons, "Indian Peoples of California," in Gutiérrez and Orsi, *Contested Eden*, 56.

92. See chapter 1 for use of Indigenous auxiliaries in the conquest of New Mexico.

93. "From Investigations of Occurrences at Mission San Gabriel on the Night of October 25, 1785," in Beebe and Senkewicz, *Lands of Promise and Despair*, 248.

94. Hackel, "Sources of Rebellion," 656.

95. Pérez, *Colonial Intimacies*, 44.

96. As quoted in Pourande, *Anza Conquers the Desert*, 178.

97. As quoted in Pérez, *Colonial Intimacies*, 42.

98. For estimates of 18,770 neophytes and "as many as 200,000" non-Christianized

Indians, see Robert Ryal Miller, *Juan Alvarado, Governor of California, 1836–1842* (Norman: University of Oklahoma Press, 1998), 3.

99. David J. Weber, *Bárbaros: Spaniards and Their Savages in the Age of Enlightenment* (New Haven: Yale University Press, 2005), 5–12.

100. Iris H. W. Engstrand, *Spanish Scientists in the New World: The Eighteenth-Century Expeditions* (Seattle: University of Washington Press, 1981), 44–75.

101. McKelvey, *Botanical Exploration of the Trans-Mississippi West*, 15–43.

102. Cook, *Flood Time of Empire*, 129–275.

103. "The 1775 Journal of Juan Francisco de la Bodega y Quadra," in Herbet K. Beals et al., eds., *Four Travel Journals: The Americas, Antarctica and Africa, 1775–1874* (London: Hakluyt Society, 2007), 81–83.

104. Cook, *Flood Tide of Empire*, 506.

105. "Appendix E: Nationality of Vessels Visiting the Northwest Coast, 1774–1820," in Cook, *Flood Tide of Empire*, 551. By 1848 British maintained a dozen warships exclusively housed in Pacific ports. See Paul M. Kennedy, *The Rise and Fall of British Naval Mastery* (New York: Charles Scribner's Sons, 1976), 171.

106. As quoted in James P. Ronda, *Astoria and Empire* (Lincoln: University of Nebraska Press, 1990), 6; see also 4–18.

107. James P. Ronda, *Lewis and Clark among the Indians* (Lincoln: University of Nebraska Press, 1984).

108. Bradford Perkins, *The Creation of a Republican Empire, 1777–1865* (New York: Cambridge University Press, 1993), 145.

109. Cook, *Flood Tide of Empire*, 506.

110. For an overview of Northwest Coast Indigenous-imperial diplomacy from 1770 through the 1840s, see Joshua L. Reid, *The Sea Is My Country: The Maritime World of the Makahs* (New Haven: Yale University Press, 2015), 26–105.

111. Reid, *The Sea Is My Country*, 4–12; Richard White, *The Organic Machine: The Remaking of the Columbia River* (New York: Hill & Wang, 1995), 3–12.

112. Reid, *The Sea Is My Country*, 7.

113. Cole Harris, *The Resettlement of British Columbia: Essays on Colonialism and Geographic Change* (Vancouver: University of British Columbian Press, 1997), 26–30.

114. Cook, *Flood Tide of Empire*, 271–326.

115. Reid, *The Sea Is My Country*, 30–31.

116. Alice W. Shurcliff and Sarah Shurcliff Ingelfinger, eds., *Captive of the Nootka Indians: The Northwest Coast Adventure of John R. Jewitt, 1802–1806* (Boston: Back Bay Books, 1993), 48.

117. David J. Silverman, *Thundersticks: Firearms and the Violent Transformation of Native America* (Cambridge, Mass.: Harvard University Press, 2016), 161.

118. Reid, *The Sea Is My Country*, 21.

119. As quoted in Harris, *The Resettlement of British Columbia*, 66.

120. Harris, *The Resettlement of British Columbia*, 33.

121. Harris, *The Resettlement of British Columbia*, 39, 66.

122. Gray H. Whaley, "American Folk Imperialism and Native Genocide in Southwest Oregon, 1851–1859," in Woolford et al., *Colonial Genocide in Indigenous North America*, 131–48.

123. White, *The Organic Machine*, 16–18.

124. Harris, *The Resettlement of British Columbia*, 20.

125. Shurcliff and Shurcliff Ingelfinger, *Captive of the Nootka Indians*, 46.

126. Charlotte Coté, *Spirits of Our Whaling Ancestors: Revitalizing Makah and Nuu-chah-nulth Traditions* (Seattle: University of Washington Press, 2010), 20.

127. Shurcliff and Shurcliff Ingelfinger, *Captive of the Nootka Indians*, 47.

128. Coté, *Spirits of Our Whaling Ancestors*, 6.

129. As quoted in Silverman, *Thundersticks*, 160.

130. Shurcliff and Shurcliff Ingelfinger, *Captive of the Nootka Indians*, 5.

131. Shurcliff and Shurcliff Ingelfinger, *Captive of the Nootka Indians*, 112–13.

132. Reid, *The Sea Is My Country*, 81.

133. Reid, *The Sea Is My Country*, 81.

134. Colin G. Calloway, *One Vast Winter Count: The Native American West Before Lewis and Clark* (Lincoln: University of Nebraska Press, 2003), 404.

135. Andrei Val'Terovich Grinëv, *Russian Colonization of Alaska: Baranov's Era, 1799–1818*, trans. Richard L. Bland (Lincoln: University of Nebraska Press, 2020), 192.

136. Nora Marks Dauenhauer et al., eds., *Anóoshi Lingít Aaní Ká: Russians in Tlingit America; The Battles of Sitka 1802 and 1804* (Seattle: University of Washington Press, 2008).

137. As quoted in Silverman, *Thundersticks*, 184–86.

138. Silverman, *Thundersticks*, 189.

139. Hackel, *Children of Coyote*, 97.

140. Hackel, *Children of Coyote*, 96–118.

141. As quoted in Fischer, *Cattle Colonialism*, 51.

142. Hackel, *Children of Coyote*, 104; Robert H. Jackson, *Indian Population Decline: The Missions of Northwestern New Spain, 1687–1840* (Albuquerque: University of New Mexico Press, 1994), 125.

143. As quoted in Hackel, *Children of Coyote*, 116.

144. Richard A. Pierce, ed., *Remarks and Observations on a Voyage around the World from 1803 to 1807*, 2 vols., ed. and trans. Victoria Joan Moessner (Fairbanks: Limestone Press, 1993), 2:124–25.

145. Robert Boyd, *The Coming of the Spirit of Pestilence: Introduced Infectious Diseases and Population Decline among Northwest Coast Indians, 1774–1874* (Seattle: University of Washington Press, 1999), 21–60.

146. Paul Hackett, *A Very Remarkable Sickness: Epidemics in the Petit Nord, 1670 to 1846* (Winnipeg: University of Manitoba Press, 2002), 93.

147. As quoted in Harris, *The Resettlement of British Columbia*, 17.

148. Elizabeth Fenn, "The Mandans: Ecology, Population, and Adaptation on the Northern Plains," in Edward Countryman and Julianna Barr, eds., *Contested Spaces of Early America* (Philadelphia: University of Pennsylvania Press, 2014), 112–13.

149. As quoted in Ryan Hall, *Beneath the Backbone of the World: Blackfoot People and the North American Borderlands, 1720–1877* (Chapel Hill: University of North Carolina Press, 2020), 44.

150. Harris, *The Resettlement of British Columbia*, 18–26.

151. As quoted in Gray H. Whaley, *Oregon and the Collapse of* Illahee*: U.S. Empire and the Transformation of an Indigenous World, 1792–1859* (Chapel Hill: University of North Carolina Press, 2010), 47–48.

152. Whaley, *Oregon and the Collapse of* Illahee, 77.

153. See, e.g., Brian DeLay, *War of a Thousand Deserts: Indian Raids and the U.S.-Mexican War* (New Haven: Yale University Press, 2008).

154. William H. Goetzmann and Glyndwr Williams, *The Atlas of North American Exploration: From the Norse Voyages to the Race to the Pole* (Norman: University of Oklahoma Press, 1992), 136–59.

155. David J. Weber, *The Mexican Frontier, 1821–1846* (Albuquerque: University of New Mexico Press, 1982), 9–14.

156. As quoted in Robert Pierce Forbes, *The Missouri Compromise and Its Aftermath: Slavery and the Meaning of America* (Chapel Hill: University of North Carolina Press, 2007), 33.

157. As quoted in Forbes, *The Missouri Compromise and Its Aftermath*, 43.

158. As quoted in Walter Johnson, *The Broken Heart of America: St. Louis and the Violent History of the United States* (New York: Basic Books, 2020), 84.

159. As quoted in Forbes, *The Missouri Compromise and Its Aftermath*, 65.

160. Jay Sexton, *The Monroe Doctrine: Empire and Nation in Nineteenth-Century America* (New York: Hill & Wang, 2015). "The creation of the Monroe Doctrine was not a single event in 1823, but rather a contested process that lasted throughout the nineteenth century" (4).

161. Deborah A. Rosen, *Border Law: The First Seminole War and American Nationhood* (Cambridge, Mass.: Harvard University Press, 2015), 11–39.

162. As quoted in Angela Pulley Hudson, *Creek Paths and Federal Roads: Indians, Settlers, and the Making of the American South* (Chapel Hill: University of North Carolina Press, 2010), 57.

163. Alan Taylor, *American Republics: A Continental History of the United States, 1783–1850* (New York: Norton, 2021), 138.

164. Rosen, *Border Law*, 17–19.

165. As quoted in Kathleen DuVal, *Independence Lost: Lives on the Edge of the American Revolution* (New York: Random House, 2015), 236.

166. DuVal, *Independence Lost*, 256.

167. As quoted in DuVal, *Independence Lost*, 321.

168. As quoted in DuVal, *Independence Lost*, 338.

169. As quoted in Taylor, *American Republics*, 127.

170. As quoted in Samuel Flagg Bemis, *John Quincy Adams and the Foundations of American Foreign Policy* (New York: Knopf, 1949), 120n26.

171. As quoted in Calloway, *One Vast Winter Count*, 430.

172. As quoted in Sexton, *The Monroe Doctrine*, 40.

173. DuVal, *Independence Lost*, 256–69.

174. Alejandra Dubcovksy, *Informed Power: Communication in the Early American South* (Cambridge, Mass.: Harvard University Press, 2016), 168–69, 196–97.

175. Rosen, *Border Law*, 34–35.

176. Bemis, *John Quincy Adams and the Foundations of American Foreign Policy*, 307. For Adams's earlier support of the Louisiana Purchase and the incorporation of Spanish subjects as U.S. citizens, see 118–22.

177. Taylor, *American Republics*, 135–39. The battle for New Orleans "fell in the middle of a longer war that erupted in 1810 and persisted until 1819, primarily on America's southwestern frontier" (135).

178. As quoted in Rosen, *Border Law*, 35.

179. Rosen, *Border Law*, 70.

180. Sexton, *The Monroe Doctrine*, 37.

181. As quoted in Rosen, *Border Law*, 135.

182. Sexton, *The Monroe Doctrine*, 74–82. "Designed to strengthen the Union, the American system . . . had the opposite effect, triggering sectional objections" (77).

183. As quoted in Forbes, *The Missouri Compromise and Its Aftermath*, 206. For the Panama Congress of 1824, see also 191–92, 203–9; Bemis, *John Quincy Adams and the Foundations of American Foreign Policy*, 544–61.

184. As quoted in Julius S. Scott, *The Common Wind: Afro-American Currents in the Age of the Haitian Revolution* (New York: Verso, 2018), 210.

185. For overviews of Monroe's various colonization efforts, see Forbes, *The Missouri Compromise and Its Aftermath*, 28–32, 199–206.

186. As quoted in Scott, *The Common Wind*, 210.

187. As quoted in Rosen, *Border Law*, 132.

188. As quoted in Rosen, *Border Law*, 132.

189. As quoted in Bemis, *John Quincy Adams and the Foundations of American Foreign Policy*, 557.

190. As quoted in Bemis, *John Quincy Adams and the Foundations of American Foreign Policy*, 313.

191. Bemis, *John Quincy Adams and the Foundations of American Foreign Policy*, 314–15.

192. As quoted in Maggie Blackhawk, "Federal Indian Law as Paradigm within Public Law," *Harvard Law Review* 132 (May 2019): 1827. "A war powers doctrine" in U.S. constitutional law and practice emerged from such nineteenth-century campaigns against Native nations, one "grounded in the Indian Wars" (1829).

193. Taylor, *American Republics*, 137–38.

194. As quoted in DeLay, *War of a Thousand Deserts*, 2–3.

195. As quoted in Bemis, *John Quincy Adams and the Foundations of American Foreign Policy*, 308.

196. As quoted in Bemis, *John Quincy Adams and the Foundations of American Foreign Policy*, 308.

197. Meinig, *Continental America*, 36–37, 72–74, 297–99. See also Bemis, *John Quincy Adams and the Foundations of American Foreign Policy*, 317–40.

198. As quoted in Walter LeFeber, *The American Age: United States Foreign Policy at Home and Abroad since 1750* (New York: Norton, 1989), 78. See also Weber, *The Mexican Frontier*, 11–13.

199. As quoted in Meinig, *Continental America*, 34.

200. Meinig, *Continental America*, 35.

201. As quoted in Perkins, *The Creation of a Republican Empire*, 152.

202. As quoted in LeFeber, *The American Age*, 82.

203. Perkins, *The Creation of a Republican Empire*, 159. See also LeFeber, *The American Age*, 81–85.

204. As quoted in Perkins, *The Creation of a Republican Empire*, 160.

205. As quoted in LeFeber, *The American Age*, 84.

206. Christian W. McMillen, *Making Indian Law: The Hualapai Land Case and the Birth of Ethnohistory* (New Haven: Yale University Press, 2007), 86–103; Walter R. Echo-Hawk, *In the Courts of the Conqueror: The 10 Worst Indian Law Cases Ever Decided* (Golden, Colo.: Fulcrum, 2010), 5–84.

207. As quoted in Forbes, *The Missouri Compromise and Its Aftermath*, 94–95.

208. McMillen, *Making Indian Law*, 88–89.

209. McMillen, *Making Indian Law*, 89.

Chapter 9. Collapse and Total War

1. As quoted in Elliott West, *The Contested Plains: Indians, Goldseekers, and the Rush to Colorado* (Lawrence: University of Kansas Press, 1998), 208, 211.

2. For "the conquest of distance," see Cole Harris, *The Resettlement of British Columbia: Essays on Colonialism and Geographic Change* (Vancouver: University of British Columbia Press, 1997).

3. As quoted in West, *Contested Plains*, 214.

4. As quoted in West, *Contested Plains*, 214–15.

5. As quoted in West, *Contested Plains*, 215.

6. As quoted in David Blight, *Frederick Douglass: Prophet of Freedom* (New York: Simon & Schuster, 2018), 332.

7. As quoted in Eric Foner, *The Fiery Trial: Abraham Lincoln and American Slavery* (New York: Norton, 2010), 146.

8. As quoted in Foner, *The Fiery Trial*, 88.

9. As quoted in Blight, *Frederick Douglass*, 356.

10. Eric Foner, *Reconstruction: America's Unfinished Revolution, 1863–1877* (New York: Harper & Row, 1988), 7.

11. Foner, *Reconstruction*, 7.

12. As quoted in Blight, *Frederick Douglass*, 381.

13. As quoted in Foner, *The Fiery Trial*, 237.

14. Foner, *The Fiery Trial*, 237.

15. Foner, *Reconstruction*, 462.

16. James Belich, *Replenishing the Earth: The Settler Revolution and the Rise of the Anglo-World, 1783–1939* (New York: Oxford University Press, 2009), 85–89.

17. Brenda J. Child, *Holding Our World Together: Ojibwe Women and the Survival of Community* (New York: Penguin, 2012), xiv. See also chapter 4.

18. As quoted in Belich, *Replenishing the Earth*, 335.

19. Belich, *Replenishing the Earth*, 341.

20. Foner, *Reconstruction*, 23.

21. Heather Cox Richardson, *West from Appomattox: The Reconstruction of America After the Civil War* (New Haven: Yale University Press, 2007), 5.

22. Foner, *Reconstruction*, 23.

23. Richardson, *West from Appomattox*, 2.

24. Foner, *Reconstruction*, 603.

25. Heather Cox Richardson, *Wounded Knee: Party Politics and the Road to an American Massacre* (New York: Basic Books, 2010), 30. For an overview of changing federal financial powers, see 28–32.

26. For a list of the "Names of the Condemned Dakota Men," see Waziyatawin Angela Wilson, ed., *In the Footsteps of Our Ancestors: The Dakota Commemorative Marches of the Twenty-First Century* (St. Paul: Living Justice, 2006), 25. See also Gary Clayton Anderson, *Kinsmen of Another Kind: Dakota-White Relations in the Upper Mississippi Valley, 1650–1862* (Lincoln: University of Nebraska Press, 1984), 261–79.

27. "Treaty with the Sioux—Sisseton and Wahpeton Bands, 1851," in Charles J. Kappler, ed., *Indian Affairs: Law and Treaties*, 2 vols. (Washington, D.C.: Government Printing Office, 1904), 2:588–89. See also David A. Nichols, *Lincoln and the Indians: Civil War Policy and Politics* (Columbia: University of Missouri Press, 1978), 76.

28. As quoted in Nichols, *Lincoln and the Indians*, 73, 75.

29. "Letter from John Pope to Col. H. H. Sibley, September, 28, 1862," in *The War of the Rebellion: A Compilation of the Official Records of the Union and Confederate Armies* (Washington, D.C.: Government Printing Office, 1885), series 1, vol. 13:685–86.

30. "Report of Lieut. James P. Martin, June 27, 1861," in *War of the Rebellion*, series 1, vol. 50, part 1:20.

31. "Report of Col. P. Edward Connor, February 6, 1863," in *War of the Rebellion*, series 1, vol. 50, part 1:186–87.

32. As quoted in West, *Contested Plains*, 301.

33. As quoted in West, *Contested Plains,* 300.

34. Adam Rotham, "Slavery, the Civil War, and Reconstruction," in Eric Foner and Lisa McGirr, eds., *American History Now* (Philadelphia: Temple University Press, 2011), 79.

35. As quoted in Benjamin Madley, *An American Genocide: The United States and the California Indian Catastrophe* (New Haven: Yale University Press, 2016), 293.

36. As quoted in Madley, *An American Genocide,* 292.

37. Alvin M. Josephy Jr., *The Civil War in the American West* (New York: Knopf, 1992), 241.

38. Madley, *An American Genocide,* 299.

39. Josephy, *The Civil War in the American West,* 239–40.

40. Josephy, *The Civil War in the American West,* 265.

41. Josephy, *The Civil War in the American West,* 240.

42. Madley, *An American Genocide,* 530–32.

43. Madley, *An American Genocide,* 286.

44. As quoted in Madley, *An American Genocide,* 289.

45. Madley, *An American Genocide,* 289.

46. "Indian Troubles in Mendocino," in Robert F. Heizer, ed., *The Destruction of California Indians: A Collection of Documents from the Period 1847 to 1865 in Which Are Described Some of the Things That Happened to Some of the Indians of California* (Santa Barbara: Peregrine Smith, 1974), 253.

47. Madley, *An American Genocide,* 290–93.

48. "Report of Lieut. James P. Martin, June 27, 1861," 20.

49. As quoted in Madley, *An American Genocide,* 294.

50. As quoted in Madley, *An American Genocide,* 297.

51. As quoted in Madley, *An American Genocide,* 296–97.

52. William J. Bauer Jr., *We Were All Like Migrant Workers Here: Work, Community, and Memory on California's Round Valley Reservation, 1850–1941* (Chapel Hill: University of North Carolina Press, 2009), 6–7, 30–57.

53. Bauer, *We Were All Like Migrant Workers Here,* 33.

54. As quoted in Madley, *An American Genocide,* 296.

55. As quoted in Madley, *An American Genocide,* 298.

56. As quoted in Madley, *An American Genocide,* 299.

57. As quoted in Madley, *An American Genocide,* 299.

58. Madley, *An American Genocide,* 299–300.

59. Nichols, *Lincoln and the Indians,* 5–24.

60. "Report of the Commissioner of Indian Affairs," in *Annual Report of the Commissioner of Indian Affairs* (Washington, D.C.: U.S. Government Printing Office, 1862), 33.

61. Francis Paul Prucha, *The Great Father: The United States Government and the American Indians,* 2 vols. (Lincoln: University of Nebraska Press, 1984), 1:411–78.

62. As quoted in Prucha, *The Great Father,* 1:413.

63. As quoted in Foner, *The Fiery Trail,* 262.

64. Foner, *The Fiery Trail,* 261–62. See also Josephy, *The Civil War in the American West,* 227–68.

65. As quoted in Blight, *Frederick Douglass,* 486.

66. Belich, *Replenishing the Earth,* 555.

67. West, *Contested Plains,* 147.

68. Harlan D. Fowler, *Camels to California: A Chapter in Western Transportation* (Palo Alto: Stanford University Press, 1950), 74–75.

69. Richard White, *Railroaded: The Transcontinentals and the Making of Modern America* (New York: Norton, 2011), 2.

70. See David J. Weber, *The Taos Trappers: The Fur Trade in the Far Southwest, 1540–1846* (Norman: University of Oklahoma Press, 1971).

71. As quoted in Elliott West, *The Way to the West: Essays on the Central Plains* (Albuquerque: University of New Mexico Press, 1995), 5.

72. As quoted in Pekka Hämäläinen, *The Comanche Empire* (New Haven: Yale University Press, 2008), 245. See also West, *The Way to the West,* 32–33.

73. Thomas G. Andrews, "Tata Antanasio's Unlikely Tale of Utes, Nuevo Mexicanos, and the Settling of Colorado's San Luis Valley," *New Mexico Historical Review* (2000): 4–41.

74. As quoted in West, *The Way to the West,* 31.

75. Ned Blackhawk, *Violence over the Land: Indians and Empires in the Early American West* (Cambridge, Mass.: Harvard University Press, 2006), 184–225.

76. West, *Contested Plains,* 256.

77. West, *Contested Plains,* 255–57.

78. Richard White, *The Roots of Dependency: Subsistence, Environment, and Social Change among the Choctaws, Pawnees, and Navajos* (Lincoln: University of Nebraska Press, 1983), 207.

79. West, *The Way to the West,* 33.

80. See Francis Paul Prucha, ed., *Atlas of American Indian Affairs* (Lincoln: University of Nebraska Press, 1990), 90–91.

81. West, *Contested Plains,* 88.

82. Jean Barman, *Iroquois in the West* (Montreal: McGill-Queen's University Press, 2019), 117; see also 115–68.

83. Weber, *The Taos Trappers,* 192–227. See also Janet Lecompte, *Pueblo, Hardscrabble, Greenhorn: The Upper Arkansas, 1832–1856* (Norman: University of Oklahoma Press, 1978), 87–126.

84. "James S. Calhoun to Commissioner of Indian Affairs Luke Lea," December 28, 1850, in Annie Heloise Abel, ed., *The Official Correspondence of James S. Calhoun* (Washington, D.C.: Government Printing Office, 1915), 280.

85. See Maurice Crandall, *These People Have Always Been a Republic: Indigenous*

Electorates in the U.S.-Mexico Borderlands, 1598–1912 (Chapel Hill: University of North Carolina Press, 2019), 177–207.

86. "Calhoun to Lea," December 28, 1850, 280–81.

87. Deena J. González, *Refusing the Favor: The Spanish-Mexican Women of Santa Fe, 1820–1880* (New York: Oxford University Press, 1999).

88. Phillip B. Gonzales, *Política: Nuevomexicanos and American Political Incorporation, 1821–1910* (Lincoln: University of Nebraska Press, 2016), 183.

89. See Foner, *The Fiery Trial*, 148.

90. As quoted in Gonzales, *Política*, 243 (emphasis in the original).

91. "Charles Beaubien to Calhoun," June 11, 1851," in Abel, *The Official Correspondence of James S. Calhoun*, 358, 357.

92. Gonzales, *Política*, 184.

93. Paul VanDevelder, *Savages and Scoundrels: The Untold Story of America's Road to Empire through Indian Territory* (New Haven: Yale University Press, 2009), 161.

94. See "Treaty of Fort Laramie with Sioux, etc., 1851," in Kappler, *Indian Affairs*, 2:594–96.

95. As quoted in VanDevelder, *Savages and Scoundrels*, 162.

96. VanDevelder, *Savages and Scoundrels*, 165–66.

97. "Treaty of Fort Laramie," 2:594.

98. Frederick E. Hoxie, *Parading through History: The Making of the Crow Nation in America, 1805–1935* (New York: Cambridge University Press, 1995), 85–87.

99. Hoxie, *Parading through History*, 88.

100. As quoted in Hoxie, *Parading through History*, 88.

101. "Matȟó Thučhúhu, Bear Ribs," in "Lives of the Chiefs and Other Biographies," in Josephine Waggoner, *Witness: A Húnkpapȟa Historian's Strong-Heart Song of the Lakotas*, ed. Emily Levine (Lincoln: University of Nebraska Press, 2013), 332–33.

102. Foner, *The Fiery Trial*, 142–48.

103. For Lincoln's fear of Cuba annexations, see, e.g., Foner, *The Fiery Trial*, 154; for Crittenden Plan, see 148.

104. Foner, *The Fiery Trial*, 147.

105. Blight, *Frederick Douglass*, 378–82.

106. As quoted in Howard Roberts Lamar, *The Far Southwest, 1846–1912: A Territorial History* (New Haven: Yale University Press, 1966), 110.

107. Lamar, *The Far Southwest*, 115. See also Josephy, *The Civil War in the American West*, 61–92.

108. As quoted in Foner, *The Fiery Trial*, 155.

109. Lamar, *The Far Southwest*, 110. See also William H. Goetzman, *Exploration and Empire: The Explorer and the Scientist in the Winning of the American West*, rev. ed. (New York: History Book Club, 2006), 281–93.

110. Josephy, *The Civil War in the American West*, 233.

111. Josephy, *The Civil War in the American West*, 236–38.

112. For an overview of the creation of Indian Territory, see Jeffrey Burton, *Indian Territory and the United States, 1866–1906* (Norman: University of Oklahoma Press, 1995), 3–25. See also Prucha, *The Great Father,* 1:271–79. For the incorporation of African American slavery into the Choctaw and Chickasaw Nations, see Barbara Krauthamer, *Black Slaves, Indians Masters: Slavery, Emancipation, and Citizenship in the Native American South* (Chapel Hill: University of North Carolina Press, 2013), 17–45. For slavery within the Creek Nation, see David A. Chang, *The Color of the Land: Race, Nation, and the Politics of Landownership in Oklahoma, 1832–1929* (Chapel Hill: University of North Carolina Press, 2010), 19–38.

113. See Prucha, "The Southern Indians and the Confederate States," in *The Great Father,* 1:415–36.

114. Krauthamer, *Black Slaves, Indians Masters,* 80.

115. As quoted in Prucha, *The Great Father,* 1:417.

116. As quoted in Prucha, *The Great Father,* 1:418.

117. Josephy, *The Civil War in the American West,* 324–27.

118. As quoted in Prucha, *The Great Father,* 1:423.

119. Robert J. Conley, *The Cherokee Nation: A History* (Albuquerque: University of New Mexico Press, 2005), 174–77.

120. As quoted in Prucha, *The Great Father,* 1:429.

121. Josephy, *The Civil War in the American West,* 330.

122. Julie L. Reed, *Serving the Nation: Cherokee Sovereignty and Social Welfare, 1800–1907* (Norman: University of Oklahoma Press, 2016), 89.

123. "The Constitution and Laws of the Cherokee Nations: Passed at Tahlequah, Cherokee Nation, 1839–1851," in *Laws of the Cherokee Nation Adopted by the Council at Various Periods: Printed for the Benefit of the Nation,* 2 parts (Wilmington, Del.: Scholarly Resources, 1973), 2:73–74.

124. "Constitution and Laws of the Cherokee Nation," 2:7.

125. As quoted in Prucha, *The Great Father,* 1:425.

126. As quoted in Prucha, *The Great Father,* 1:425.

127. Josephy, *The Civil War in the American West,* 319–23.

128. As quoted in Reed, *Serving the Nation,* 95.

129. Prucha, *The Great Father,* 1:425–27.

130. Conley, *The Cherokee Nation,* 176.

131. Burton, *Indian Territory and the United States,* 25.

132. Belich, *Replenishing the Earth,* 324.

133. West, *Contested Plains,* 226.

134. Belich, *Replenishing the Earth,* 310. See also Andrew C. Isenberg, *Mining California: An Ecological History* (New York: Hill & Wang, 2005), 23–51.

135. Belich, *Replenishing the Earth,* 323.

136. West, *Contested Plains,* 224–25.

137. Peggy Pascoe, *What Comes Naturally: Miscegenation Law and the Making of Race in America* (New York: Oxford University Press, 2009), 78.

138. Alexander Saxton, *The Indispensable Enemy: Labor and the Anti-Chinese Movement in California* (Berkeley: University of California Press, 1971).

139. Belich, *Replenishing the Earth*, 307. See also Isenberg, *Mining California*, 23.

140. "William P. Dole, Commissioner of Indian Affairs, to J. P. Usher, Secretary of the Interior," October 31, 1863, in Dale L. Morgan, *Shoshonean Peoples and the Overland Trails: Frontiers of the Utah Superintendency of Indian Affairs, 1849–1869*, ed. Richard L. Saunders (Logan: Utah State University Press, 2007), 314–15.

141. Belich, *Replenishing the Earth*, 307.

142. As quoted in Richardson, *West from Appomattox*, 32.

143. Belich, *Replenishing the Earth*, 307.

144. Charles Neider, ed., *The Complete Essays of Mark Twain* (New York: Da Capo, 2000), 477, 482.

145. Harriet Elinor Smith, ed., *Autobiography of Mark Twain*, vol. 1 (Berkeley: University of California Press, 2010), 447.

146. Blackhawk, *Violence over the Land*, 274–76.

147. Neider, *The Complete Essays of Mark Twain*, 482.

148. Smith, *Autobiography of Mark Twain*, 461. Orion received his appointment after the selection of his longtime acquaintance Edward Bates in the Lincoln administration.

149. Richardson, *West from Appomattox*, 24–25.

150. Richardson, *West from Appomattox*, 25.

151. Belich, *Replinishing the Earth*, 247.

152. Damon B. Akins and William J. Bauer Jr., *We Are the Land: A History of Native California* (Oakland: University of California Press, 2021), 148.

153. Madley, *An American Genocide*, 311. See also George Harwood Phillips, *"Bringing Them under Subjection": California's Tejón Indian Reservation and Beyond, 1852–1864* (Lincoln: University of Nebraska Press, 2004).

154. Madley, *An American Genocide*, 309–12.

155. As quoted in Madley, *An American Genocide*, 312.

156. Madley, *An American Genocide*, 312.

157. Phillips, *"Bringing Them under Subjection,"* 244–48.

158. Madley, *An American Genocide*, 314.

159. As quoted in Madley, *An American Genocide*, 315. See also Phillips, *"Bringing Them under Subjection,"* 245.

160. As quoted in Phillips, *"Bringing Them under Subjection,"* 245.

161. Phillips, *"Bringing Them under Subjection,"* 246–47.

162. Josephy, *The Civil War in the American West*, 251–53.

163. As quoted in Josephy, *The Civil War in the American West*, 253–54.

164. Josephy, *The Civil War in the American West*, 251.

165. As quoted in Josephy, *The Civil War in the American West*, 254.

166. As quoted in Josephy, *The Civil War in the American West*, 254.

167. "Report of Major Edward McGarry, October 31, 1862," in *War of the Rebellion*, series 1, vol. 50, part 1:179.

168. "Report of Major Edward McGarry, October 31, 1862," 179.

169. "Report of Col. P. Edward Connor, February 6, 1863," 186.

170. Darren Parry, *The Bear River Massacre: A Shoshone History* (Salt Lake City: Common Consent, 2019).

171. "Letter of Henry W. Halleck, March 29, 1863," in *War of the Rebellion*, series 1, vol. 50, part 1:87.

172. "Letter of Henry W. Halleck, March 29, 1863," 187.

173. For overviews of Apache-U.S. military relations, see Thomas A. Britten, *The Lipan Apaches: People of Wind and Lightning* (Albuquerque: University of New Mexico Press, 2009), 217–34; Josephy, *The Civil War in the American West*, 276–84, Dan L. Thrapp, *Victorio and the Mimbres Apaches* (Norman: University of Oklahoma Press, 1974); Matthew Babcock, *Apache Adaptation to Hispanic Rule* (New York: Cambridge University Press, 2016), 254–58; and Karl Jacoby, *Shadows at Dawn: An Apache Massacre and the Violence of History* (New York: Penguin Group, 2008), 220–72.

174. As quoted in Jennifer Nez Denetdale, *Reclaiming Diné History: The Legacies of Navajo Chief Manuelito and Juanita* (Tucson: University of Arizona Press, 2007), 70. See also Lawrence Kelly, *Navajo Roundup: Selected Correspondence of Kit Carson's Expedition against the Navajo, 1863–1865* (Boulder: Pruett, 1970), 57.

175. As quoted in Denetdale, *Reclaiming Diné History*, 70.

176. See Frank McNitt, *Navajo Wars: Military Campaigns, Slave Raids, and Reprisals* (Albuquerque: University of New Mexico Press, 1972); and Brian DeLay, "Blood Talk: Violence and Belonging in the Navajo-New Mexican Borderland," in Julianna Barr and Edward Countryman, eds., *Contested Spaces of Early America* (Philadelphia: University of Pennsylvania Press, 2014), 229–56.

177. Blackhawk, *Violence over the Land*, 213–23.

178. Denetdale, *Reclaiming Diné History*, 56.

179. Peter Iverson, *Diné: A History of the Navajos* (Albuquerque: University of New Mexico Press, 2002), 32.

180. As quoted in Kelly, *Navajo Roundup*, 93.

181. As quoted in Kelly, *Navajo Roundup*, 52.

182. As quoted in Denetdale, *Reclaiming Diné History*, 73.

183. For an overview of the Long Walk, see L. R. Bailey, *The Long Walk: A History of the Navajo Wars, 1846–68* (Pasadena: Westernlore, 1978).

184. Denetdale, *Reclaiming Diné History*, 74.

185. As quoted in Denetdale, *Reclaiming Diné History*, 74.

186. As quoted in Denetdale, *Reclaiming Diné History*, 74.

187. For the negotiation of the 1868 treaty, see Bailey, *The Long Walk*, 228–35.

188. For the Navajo Treaty of 1868, see "Treaty with the Navaho, 1868," in Kappler, *Indian Affairs,* 2:1015–20. For the 1863 treaties of James J. Doty, superintendent of Indian Affairs in Utah, see "Treaty with the Eastern Shoshoni, 1863"; "Treaty with the Shoshoni-Northwestern Band, 1863"; "Treaty with the Western Shoshoni, 1863"; and "Treaty with the Shoshoni-Goship, 1863," in Kappler, *Indian Affairs,* 2:848–50; 850–51; 851–53; 859–60.

189. Josephy, *The Civil War in the American West,* 288–91.

190. Brigham D. Madsen, *Glory Hunter: A Biography of Patrick Edward Connor* (Salt Lake: University of Utah Press, 1990), 121–35.

191. As quoted in Josephy, *The Civil War in the American West,* 294. See also Lamar, *The Far Southwest,* 240–41.

192. Josephy, *The Civil War in the American West,* 295.

193. Josephy, *The Civil War in the American West,* 84–89.

194. See, e.g., Lamar, *The Far Southwest,* 242–43.

195. "Treaty with the Arapaho and Cheyenne, 1861," in Kappler, *Indian Affairs,* 2: 807.

196. Lamar, *The Far Southwest,* 243.

197. Josephy, *The Civil War in the American West,* 298–99.

198. As quoted in Josephy, *The Civil War in the American West,* 300.

199. Stan Hoig, *The Peace Chiefs of the Cheyennes* (Norman: University of Oklahoma Press, 1980), 63.

200. As quoted in Josephy, *The Civil War in the American West,* 300–301.

201. As quoted in Josephy, *The Civil War in the American West,* 301.

202. As quoted in Josephy, *The Civil War in the American West,* 303.

203. Richard White, *The Republic for Which It Stands: The United States during Reconstruction and the Gilded Age, 1865–1896* (New York: Oxford University Press, 2017), 14.

204. White, *The Republic for Which It Stands,* 16.

205. Maggie Blackhawk, "Federal Indian Law as Paradigm within Public Law," *Harvard Law Review* 132 (May 2019): 1811–25.

Chapter 10. Taking Children and Treaty Lands

1. Clifford E. Trafzer, *Yuma: Frontier Crossing of the Far Southwest* (Wichita: Western Heritage Books, 1980), 98–99.

2. George J. Sánchez, *Becoming Mexican American: Ethnicity, Culture and Identity in Chicano Los Angeles, 1900–1945* (New York: Oxford University Press, 1993), 65.

3. Sánchez, *Becoming Mexican American,* 65.

4. Trafzer, *Yuma,* 121.

5. "Between 1878 and 1944, Chinese, Burmese, Armenian, Japanese, South Asian, Hawaiian, Mexican, and Filipino applicants [for U.S. naturalization] all had

their racial eligibility to naturalize challenged in the courts." Sarah M. Am. Gualtieri, *Between Arab and White: Race and Ethnicity in the Early Syrian American Diaspora* (Berkeley: University of California Press, 2009), 2.

6. As quoted in Katrina Jagodinsky, *Legal Codes and Talking Trees: Indigenous Women's Sovereignty in the Sonoran and Puget Sound Borderlands, 1854–1946* (New Haven: Yale University Press, 2016), 37. See also Karl Jacoby, *Shadows at Dawn: An Apache Massacre and the Violence of History* (New York: Penguin, 2009), 111–14.

7. Jacoby, *Shadows at Dawn*, 112.

8. As quoted in Jagodinsky, *Legal Codes and Talking Trees*, 46.

9. Jagodinsky, *Legal Codes and Talking Trees*, 26–27. Also known as Yoemem, Yaquis dominated the Yaqui River Valley and faced recurring assaults by Mexican nationalist interests in the late nineteenth and early twentieth centuries, including state-sanctioned deportation campaigns. See Evelyn Hu-DeHart, *Yaqui Resistance and Survival: The Struggle for Land and Autonomy, 1821–1910* (Madison: University of Wisconsin Press, 1984), 155–200; David Delgado Shorter, *We Will Dance Our Truth: Yaqui History in Yoeme Performances* (Lincoln: University of Nebraska Press, 2009), 5–10; Raphael Brewster Folsom, *The Yaquis and the Empire: Violence, Spanish Imperial Power, and Native Resilience in Colonial Mexico* (New Haven: Yale University Press, 2014), 209–16; Maurice Crandall, *These People Have Always Been a Republic: Indigenous Electorates in the U.S.-Mexico Borderlands, 1598–1912* (Chapel Hill: University of North Carolina Press, 2019), 243–57; and Andrew Offenburger, *Frontiers in the Gilded Age: Adventure, Capitalism, and Dispossession from Southern Africa to the U.S.-Mexican Borderlands, 1880–1917* (New Haven: Yale University Press, 2019), 147–96.

10. Andrés Reséndez, *The Other Slavery: The Uncovered Story of Indian Enslavement in America* (Boston: Houghton Mifflin Harcourt, 2016), esp. 149–265.

11. As quoted in Folsom, *The Yaquis and the Empire*, 214.

12. Eric Foner, *The Second Founding: How the Civil War and Reconstruction Remade the Constitution* (New York: Norton, 2019), 24.

13. Jagodinsky, *Legal Codes and Talking Trees*, 35–36.

14. Jagodinsky, *Legal Codes and Talking Trees*, 39–41.

15. Peggy Pascoe, *What Comes Naturally: Miscegenation Law and the Making of Race in America* (New York: Oxford University Press, 2009), 77.

16. See James M. Murphy, *Laws, Courts, and Lawyers through the Years in Arizona* (Tucson: University of Arizona Press, 1970), 71–75.

17. Jagodinsky, *Legal Codes and Talking Trees*, 276n38.

18. As quoted in Jacoby, *Shadows at Dawn*, 113.

19. Paul Conrad, *The Apache Diaspora: Four Centuries of Displacement and Survival* (Philadelphia: University of Pennsylvania Press, 2021), 188–90.

20. As quoted in Jacoby, *Shadows at Dawn*, 112.

21. As quoted in Jacoby, *Shadows at Dawn*, 112.

22. Amy Kaplan, *The Anarchy of Empire in the Making of U.S. Culture* (Cambridge, Mass.: Harvard University Press, 2006), 23–50.

23. Murphy, *Laws, Courts, and Lawyers through the Years in Arizona*, 41.

24. Jagodinsky, *Legal Codes and Talking Trees*, 30.

25. Murphy, *Laws, Courts, and Lawyers through the Years in Arizona*, 73.

26. As quoted in Jagodinsky, *Legal Codes and Talking Trees*, 28–29.

27. House Resolution 18166. Public Law No. 219. House of Representatives, 1912, 14.

28. For the growth of the federal government and agencies across the U.S. West, see Richard White, *"It's Your Misfortune and None of My Own": A New History of the American West* (Norman: University of Oklahoma Press, 1991), 85–297.

29. Joshua L. Reid, *The Sea Is My Country: The Maritime World of the Makahs* (New Haven: Yale University Press, 2015), 137–53; Steven J. Crum, *The Road on Which We Came: A History of the Western Shoshone* (Salt Lake: University of Utah Press, 1994), 6–7.

30. N. Bruce Duthu, *American Indians and the Law* (New York: Viking Penguin, 2008), 75.

31. Duthu, *American Indians and the Law*, 76–82.

32. Maggie Blackhawk, "Federal Indian Law as Paradigm within Public Law," *Harvard Law Review* (2019): 1815–25.

33. David Treuer, *The Heartbeat of Wounded Knee: Native America 1890 to the Present* (New York: Riverhead Books, 2019), 132–37.

34. Richard Henry Pratt, *Battlefield and Classroom: Four Decades with the American Indian, 1867–1904*, ed. Robert M. Utley (New Haven: Yale University Press, 1964), 303.

35. As quoted in Margaret Jacobs, *White Mother to a Dark Race: Settler Colonialism, Maternalism, and the Removal of Indigenous Children in the American West and Australia* (Lincoln: University of Nebraska Press, 2009), 73.

36. As quoted in Duthu, *American Indians and the Law*, 76.

37. Pratt, *Battlefield and Classroom*, 306.

38. Stephen Skowronek, *Building a New American State: The Expansion of National Administrative Capacities, 1877–1920* (New York: Cambridge University Press, 1982).

39. As quoted in David E. Wilkins, *American Indian Sovereignty and the U.S. Supreme Court: The Masking of Justice* (Austin: University of Texas Press, 1997), 116.

40. Elliott West, "Reconstructing Race," *Western Historical Quarterly* (2003): 6–26.

41. As quoted in Foner, *The Second Founding*, xx.

42. Foner, *The Second Founding*, 24.

43. Foner, *The Second Founding*, 63–68. See also David Blight, *Frederick Douglass: Prophet of Freedom* (New York: Simon & Schuster, 2018), 545–49.

44. Stephen Kantrowitz, "Jurisdiction, Civilization, and the Ends of Native American Citizenship: The View from 1866," *Western Historical Quarterly* (2021): 203–4.

45. As Eric Foner suggests, the Civil Rights Act "for the first time put into national law the principle of birthright citizenship. . . . [It], in other words, severed citizenship from race. . . . It applied . . . not only to blacks but to *virtually everyone born in the country.*" *The Second Founding*, 63–64 (emphasis added). Despite his recognition that the

exclusion of "Indians not taxed" formed a legal understanding that "considered [Indians to be] members of their own sovereignties, not the nation," Foner misunderstands the exclusion of Native peoples from the American polity. The inability of the federal government to enforce its own recognition doctrines of Native sovereignty and to establish corresponding protections for treaty provisions is a legal and constitutional failing comparable to the exclusion of other racialized Americans. The constitutionally directed seizure of Native American lands and corresponding state-sanctioned removal of thousands of Native peoples are failures of justice and equality.

46. Article 8 of the Treaty of Guadalupe Hidalgo of 1848 extended the rights of U.S. citizenship to any Mexican citizen living in the conquered territory of what became the United States. Very few Indigenous peoples of the Mexican borderlands had voted in Mexican elections or held property under Mexican laws. See Crandall, *These People Have Always Been a Republic*, 7–12, 177–282.

47. Howard Roberts Lamar, *The Far Southwest, 1846–1912: A Territorial History* (New Haven: Yale University Press, 1966), 440–41. For the cycle of settler "booms" in population after 1865, see James Belich, *Replenishing the Earth: The Settler Revolution and the Rise of the Anglo-World, 1783–1939* (New York: Oxford University Press, 2009), 88.

48. See Charles J. Kappler, ed., *Indian Affairs: Laws and Treaties*, 5 vols. (Washington, D.C.: U.S. Government Printing Office, 1904), 2:807–909. Vine Deloria Jr. and Raymond J. DeMallie identify a series of methodological concerns about Kappler's work and provide an alternative "Chronological List of Ratified or Valid and Operable Treaties," which includes California and other "valid" treaties. See Deloria and Demallie, eds., *Documents of American Indian Diplomacy: Treaties, Agreements, and Conventions, 1775–1979*, 2 vols. (Norman: University of Oklahoma Press, 1999), 1:181–232. As they note, "Both scholars and students have a difficult time locating an accurate or official list of Indian treaties" (1:181). See also Francis Paul Prucha, *American Indian Treaties: The History of a Political Anomaly* (Berkeley: University of California Press, 1994), 446–502.

49. Black Coal (Arapahoe), "The Black Hills Is Our Country: Testimony to a Federal Commission, September, 1876," in Wayne Moquin and Charles Van Doren, eds., *Great Documents in American Indian History* (New York: Praeger, 1973), 230. Long recognized as "the spiritual center and homeland" of allied Lakota, Nakota, and Dakota communities—collectively known as the Oceti Sakowin (Seven Council Fires people)—the Black Hills form a "breathtakingly beautiful ecosystem" that rises "out of the northern Plains like an ocean island." See Craig Howe et al., eds., *He Sapa Woihanble: Black Hills Dream* (St. Paul: Living Justice, 2011), 3.

50. "Treaty with the Sioux—Brulé, Oglala, Miniconjou, Yanktonai, Hunkpapa, Blackfeet, Cuthead, Two Kettle, Sans Arcs, and Santee—and Arapahoe, 1868," in Kappler *Indian Affairs*, 2:999.

51. "Treaty with the Sioux, 1868," 2:998–1003.

52. Kappler, *Indian Affairs*, 2:996, 998–1025.

53. On June 20, 1867, Congress established the United States Indian Peace Commission, which began a more centralized process of federal treaty making. For an overview of the commission, see Prucha, *American Indian Treaties*, 279–85.

54. "Treaty with the Sioux, 1868," 2:998.

55. "Our homeland, called Dinétah or Diné Bikéyah, means Navajo Land or Navajo Country and is bounded by the four sacred mountains: Dzil Hajin in the east; Tso´dziil in the south; Dookóósliid in the west; and Dibénitash in the north." Jennifer Nez Denetdale, *Reclaiming Diné History: The Legacies of Navajo Chief Manuelito and Juanita* (Tucson: University of Arizona Press, 2007), 10.

56. "Treaty with the Cherokee, 1866," in Kappler, *Indian Affairs*, 2:942.

57. "Treaty with the Seminole, 1866," in Kappler, *Indian Affairs*, 2:914 (emphasis added).

58. "Treaty with the Cherokee, 1866," 2:946.

59. "Treaty with the Delawares, 1866," in Kappler, *Indian Affairs*, 2:937.

60. J. Diane Pearson, *The Nez Perces in the Indian Territory: Nimiipuu Survival* (Norman: University of Oklahoma Press, 2008). "The first detailed census of the prisoners was finally ordered at St. Paul. . . . It records that the army held 431 Nimipuu and Palus prisoners: 79 men, 178 women, and 174 children" (75). For attempts to send these children to eastern boarding schools, see 222–50. For an overview of the Chiricahuas' removal, see Paul Andrew Hutton, *The Apache Wars: The Hunt for Geronimo, the Apache Kid, and the Captive Boy Who Started the Longest War in American History* (New York: Broadway Books, 2016), 386–424.

61. "Treaty with the Delawares, 1866," *Indian Affairs*, 2:938.

62. As quoted in Norman J. Bender, *"New Hope for the Indians": The Grant Peace Policy and the Navajos in the 1870s* (Albuquerque: University of New Mexico Press, 1989), 8.

63. Richard White, *Railroaded: The Transcontinentals and the Making of Modern America* (New York: Norton, 2011), 455–59.

64. "Treaty with the Delawares, 1861," in Kappler, *Indian Affairs*, 2:814–15.

65. "Treaty with the Delawares, 1861," 2:821, 824.

66. Manu Karuka, *Empire's Tracks: Indigenous Nations, Chinese Workers, and the Transcontinental Railroad* (Oakland: University of California Press, 2019), 149–84.

67. Belich, *Replenishing the Earth*, 205, 334.

68. Despite its inefficiencies—characterized by millions of discarded bison corpses—the bison trade, like the western fur trade earlier, formed an initial boom for economic growth across the Plains during the great "settler booms" of the nineteenth century. Belich, *Replenishing the Earth*, 206.

69. For an overview of the central Plains railway and the extermination of American bison, see White, *Railroaded*, 462–66.

70. White, *Railroaded*, 468.

71. As quoted in White, *Railroaded*, 460.

72. See chapter 9 for overviews of overland travel from Kansas to the West.

73. Belich, *Replenishing the Earth*, 332.

74. "Maȟpíyalúlta, Red Cloud," in Josephine Waggoner, *Witness: A Húŋkpapȟa Historian's Strong-Heart Song of the Lakotas*, ed. Emily Levine (Lincoln: University of Nebraska Press, 2013), 450–51. See also Pekka Hämäläinen, *Lakota America: A New History of Indigenous Power* (New Haven: Yale University Press, 2019), 279–81.

75. "Treaty with the Sioux, 1868," 2:1002.

76. Nick Estes, *Our History Is the Future: Standing Rock versus the Dakota Access Pipeline, and the Long Tradition of Indigenous Resistance* (New York: Verso, 2019), 106.

77. John Grass (Blackfoot Sioux), "Indian Conditions for Treaty Renewal, October 11, 1876," in Moquin and Van Doren, *Great Documents in American Indian History*, 234. See also, "Mathó Watȟákpe, John Grass," in Waggoner, *Witness*, 321–23.

78. "Treaty with the Sioux, 1868," 2:1002.

79. "Treaty with the Sioux, 1868," 2:1002–3.

80. Michel Hogue, *Metis and the Medicine Line: Creating a Border and Dividing a People* (Chapel Hill: University of North Carolina Press, 2015), 81–83.

81. As quoted in Hämäläinen, *Lakota America*, 299.

82. George E. Hyde, *Spotted Tail's Folk: A History of the Brulé Sioux* (Norman: University of Oklahoma Press, 1961), 162–63.

83. As quoted in Hämäläinen, *Lakota America*, 311.

84. As quoted in Hämäläinen, *Lakota America*, 311.

85. John Grass (Blackfoot Sioux), "Indian Conditions for Treaty Renewal, October 11, 1876," 233.

86. Katharine C. Turner, *Red Men Calling on the Great Father* (Norman: University of Oklahoma Press, 1951), 121.

87. Prucha, *The Great Father*, 528.

88. Kappler, *Indian Affairs*, 4:1153.

89. In 1866 and 1868, Congress and the Supreme Court had deliberated upon the relative power of Congress to tax Indians, prompting a redefinition of policy. As David Wilkins suggests, "Whether tribes . . . may be *included* or *excluded* under the scope of general laws enacted by Congress" became a central concern throughout the Reconstruction era. "The documentary evidence—including the preexisting political status of tribes (a status not created by or subject to the United States Constitution), prior Supreme Court precedent, the treaty relationship, and the constitutional clauses acknowledging the distinctive status of tribal polities—clearly supports exclusion." *American Indian Sovereignty and the U.S. Supreme Court*, 55 (emphasis in original).

90. The "end [of the treaty system] came as the result of a conflict of authority between the House of Representatives and the Senate. The fundamental problem was that making treaties was a function of the president and the Senate, and if dealings

with the Indians were confined to treaties the House of Representatives was left out completely except to appropriate funds." Prucha, *The Great Father,* 530.

91. David W. Blight, *Race and Reunion: The Civil War in American Memory* (Cambridge, Mass.: Harvard University Press, 2001), 135–39.

92. As quoted in Heather Cox Richardson, *West from Appomattox: The Reconstruction of America After the Civil War* (New Haven: Yale University Press, 2007), 178; see also 174–78.

93. As quoted in Richardson, *West from Appomattox,* 165–66.

94. "Treaty with the Sioux, 1868," 2:998.

95. "Treaty with the Sioux, 1868," 2:998.

96. Martin F. Schmitt, ed., *General George Crook: His Autobiography,* 2nd ed. (Norman: University of Oklahoma Press, 1960, 189.

97. As quoted in Richardson, *West from Appomattox,* 166.

98. As quoted in Richardson, *West from Appomattox,* 161.

99. Richardson, *West from Appomattox,* 165.

100. Schmitt, *General George Crook,* 189.

101. Schmitt, *General George Crook,* 189.

102. As quoted in Candice Millard, *Destiny of the Republic: A Tale of Madness, Medicine, and the Murder of a President* (New York: Anchor Books, 2011), 11.

103. For U.S. telephone development, see Jurgen Osterhammel, *The Transformation of the World: A Global History of the Nineteenth Century* (Princeton: Princeton University Press, 2015), 720.

104. For an overview of urbanization and its many inequalities, see Richard White, *The Republic for Which It Stands: The United States during Reconstruction and the Gilded Age, 1865–1896* (New York: Oxford University Press, 2017), 481–517. The United States across both its rural and urban communities remained "a land of pervasive poverty in the midst of progress" (481).

105. Wilkins, *American Indian Sovereignty and the U.S. Supreme Court,* 221.

106. Kappler, *Indian Affairs,* 1:168. See also Prucha, *The Great Father,* 2:632–33.

107. Kappler, *Indian Affairs,* 1:168.

108. As quoted in Treuer, *The Heartbeat of Wounded Knee,* 133.

109. As quoted in Treuer, *The Heartbeat of Wounded Knee,* 133.

110. As quoted in Wolfgan Mider, "'The Only Good Indian Is a Dead Indian': History and Meaning of a Proverbial Stereotype," *Journal of American Folklore* (Winter 1993): 45–46.

111. Loreta Fowler, *Arapahoe Politics, 1851–1978: Symbols in Crises of Authority* (Lincoln: University of Nebraska Press, 1982), 153–56.

112. Frederick E. Hoxie, *Parading through History: The Making of the Crow Nation in America, 1805–1935* (New York: Cambridge University Press, 1995), 233–38.

113. As quoted in Brianna Theobald, *Reproduction on the Reservation: Pregnancy,*

Childbirth, and Colonialism in the Long Twentieth Century (Chapel Hill: University of North Carolina Press, 2019), 22.

114. As quoted in Jacobs, *White Mother to a Dark Race*, 159.

115. As quoted in quoted in Jacobs, *White Mother to a Dark Race*, 160.

116. As quoted in Treuer, *The Heartbeat of Wounded Knee*, 133.

117. See Paul C. Rosier, "Surviving in the Twentieth Century, 1890–1960," in Frederick E. Hoxie, ed., *The Oxford Handbook of American Indian History* (New York: Oxford University Press, 2016), 112–17. The boarding "school program was characterized by authoritarian methods, racism, and neglect. Faced with substandard living conditions, sexual abuse, and rigid attendance policies that often precluded family visits for years, many homesick students simply ran away. School graveyards were filled with young boys and girls who died of suicide or diseases such as tuberculosis and influenza, their effects intensified by malnutrition and overwork." (116). See also, Preston McBride, "Lessons from Canada: The Question of Genocide in US Boarding Schools for Native Americans," in Ben Kiernan, general ed., Ned Blackhawk, Ben Kiernan, Benjamin Madley, and Rebe Taylor, volume eds., *The Cambridge World History of Genocide, Volume II: Genocide in the Indigenous, Early Modern and Imperial Worlds, c.1535 to World War One* (3 vols., Cambridge: Cambridge University Press, 2022), 434–60.

118. As quoted in Treuer, *The Heartbeat of Wounded Knee*, 133.

119. As quoted in John W. Troutman, *Indian Blues: American Indians and the Politics of Music, 1879–1934* (Norman: University of Oklahoma Press, 2009), 109.

120. As quoted in Mark Rifkin, *When Did Indians Become Straight? Kinship, the History of Sexuality, and Native Sovereignty* (New York: Oxford University Press, 2011), 151.

121. Beth H. Piatote, *Domestic Subjects: Gender, Citizenship, and Law in Native American Literature* (New Haven: Yale University Press, 2013), 29–38.

122. Rifkin, *When Did Indians Become Straight?* 146–47.

123. As quoted in Rifkin, *When Did Indians Become Straight?* 149.

124. Theobald, *Reproduction on the Reservation*, 19.

125. Hoxie, *Parading through History*, 192–94.

126. As quoted in Theobald, *Reproduction on the Reservation*, 79–80.

127. Melissa L. Meyer, *The White Earth Tragedy: Ethnicity and Dispossession at a Minnesota Anishinaabe Reservation* (Lincoln: University of Nebraska Press, 1994), 137–72.

128. As quoted in Anton Treuer, *Warrior Nation: A History of the Red Lake Ojibwe* (St. Paul: Minnesota Historical Society Press, 2015), 83. For Red Lake diplomacy against allotment and the Nelson Act of 1888, see 78–103.

129. Hämäläinen, *Lakota America*, 373.

130. As quoted in Howe et al., *He Sapa Woihanble*, 174. See also Wilkins, *American Indian Sovereignty and the U.S. Supreme Court*, 217–34. "While an affirmation of the Court of Claims case would constitute a financial victory of sorts for the Lakota . . . it in no way provided any of the much needed clarification as to the actual basis

of the Lakota/United States political relationship. The majority, by refusing to question whether the Congress could take the land . . . failed to inspire much hope for justice among the Lakota or other tribes with treaty-based claims before the Supreme Court" (228–29).

131. "Treaty with the Sioux, 1868," 2:1002.

132. Wilkins, *American Indian Sovereignty and the U.S. Supreme Court*, 221.

133. As quoted in Heather Cox Richardson, *Wounded Knee: Party Politics and the Road to an American Massacre* (New York: Basic Books, 2010), 105–6.

134. Jeffrey Ostler, *The Plains Sioux and U.S. Colonialism: From Lewis and Clark to Wounded Knee* (New York: Cambridge University Press, 2004), 203–12.

135. Pratt, *Battlefield and Classroom*, 220.

136. Pratt, *Battlefield and Classroom*, 220.

137. As quoted in Jacoby, *Shadows at Dawn*, 229.

138. Sidney L. Harring, *Crow Dog's Case: American Indian Sovereignty, Tribal Law, and the United States Law in the Nineteenth Century* (New York: Cambridge University Press, 1994).

139. As quoted in Wilkins, *American Indian Sovereignty and the U.S. Supreme Court*, 115.

140. "The intimate lives of indigenous peoples—the ways they cared for and raised their children, their dwellings, their sexuality, their marriage practices, their gender relations, even the ways they adorned their bodies and styled their hair—eventually came under the scrutiny and condemnation of their colonizers." Jacobs, *White Mother to a Dark Race*, 24.

141. Wilkins, *American Indian Sovereignty and the U.S. Supreme Court*, 64.

142. Blackhawk, "Federal Indian Law as Paradigm," 1829–31.

143. The crimes are murder, manslaughter, rape, assault with intent to kill, arson, burglary, and larceny. Wilkins, *American Indian Sovereignty and the U.S. Supreme Court*, 68–69.

144. Harring, *Crow Dog's Case*, 141.

145. "*Ex Parte Kan-Gi-Shun-Ca (Otherwise Known as Crow Dog)*," in Robert T. Anderson et al., eds., *American Indian Law: Cases and Commentary*, 4th ed. (St. Paul: West Academic, 2020), 95.

146. Harring, *Crow Dog's Case*, 118–41. "The unanimous opinion . . . strongly supports the traditional [legal] conception that treaties are made between nations of people, and it interprets the Sioux treaties . . . in ways that give greatest effect to tribal sovereignty. The *Crow Dog* opinion was a watershed, the legal divide where a traditional Indian policy that recognized the equality of tribal peoples and respected their national sovereignty last stood against the rise of the BIA policy of assimilation" (129–30).

147. "*Ex Parte Kan-Gi-Shun-Ca (Otherwise Known as Crow Dog)*," 95 (emphasis added).

148. "*U.S. v. Kagama*," in Keith Richotte Jr., *Federal Indian Law and Policy: An Introduction* (St. Paul: West Academic, 2020), 138.

149. David E. Wilkins and K. Tsianina Lomawaima, *Uneven Ground: American Indian Sovereignty and Federal Law* (Norman: University of Oklahoma Press, 2001), 98–116.

150. Waggoner, *Witness*, 222–23.

151. Raymond J. DeMallie, ed., *The Sixth Grandfather: Black Elk's Teachings Given to John G. Neihardt* (Lincoln: University of Nebraska Press, 1984), 272.

152. Ostler, *The Plains Sioux and U.S. Colonialism*, 326–337.

153. DeMallie, *The Sixth Grandfather*, 271.

154. DeMallie, *The Sixth Grandfather*, 271.

Chapter 11. Indigenous Twilight at the Dawn of the Century

1. For an overview of the Sullivan campaign, see chapter 6. See also Rhiannon Koehler, "Hostile Nations: Quantifying the Destruction of the Sullivan-Clinton Genocide of 1779," *American Indian Quarterly* (Fall 2018): 427–53.

2. Frederick Cook, ed., *Journals of the Military Expedition of Major General John Sullivan against the Six Nations of Indians in 1779 with Records of Centennial Celebrations* (Auburn, N.Y.: Knapp, Peck, & Thompson, 1887), 335–36.

3. Cook, *Journals of the Military Expedition of Major General John Sullivan*, xi.

4. Cook, *Journals of the Military Expedition of Major General John Sullivan*, 392–93 (emphasis in original).

5. Cook, *Journals of the Military Expedition of Major General John Sullivan*, 336.

6. Alan Taylor, *William Cooper's Town: Power and Persuasion on the Frontier of the Early American Republic* (New York: Knopf, 1995), 432.

7. As quoted in Taylor, *William Cooper's Town*, 432.

8. For the contested meanings of Indigenous commemoration, see, e.g., Lisa Blee and Jean M. O'Brien, *Monumental Mobility: The Memory Work of Massasoit* (Chapel Hill: University of North Carolina Press, 2019); and Ari Kelman, *A Misplaced Massacre: Struggling over the Memory of Sand Creek* (Cambridge, Mass.: Harvard University Press, 2013).

9. Cook, *Journals of the Military Expedition of Major General John Sullivan*, 336.

10. Cook, *Journals of the Military Expedition of Major General John Sullivan*, 379.

11. Cook, *Journals of the Military Expedition of Major General John Sullivan*, 380.

12. Cook, *Journals of the Military Expedition of Major General John Sullivan*, 380.

13. Cook, *Journals of the Military Expedition of Major General John Sullivan*, 379.

14. For the "vital vernacular" provided by regional productions, see Jean M. O'Brien, *Firsting and Lasting: Writing Indians out of Existence in New England* (Minneapolis: University of Minnesota Press, 2010), xi–xxvi.

15. Mark Peterson, *The City-State of Boston: The Rise and Fall of an Atlantic Power, 1630–1865* (Princeton: Princeton University Press, 2019), 628.

16. As quoted in Peterson, *The City-State of Boston,* 629.

17. David M. Wrobel, *The End of American Exceptionalism: Frontier Anxiety from the Old West to the New Deal* (Lawrence: University of Kansas Press, 1993), 1–3.

18. Frederick Jackson Turner, *The Character and Influence of the Indian Trade in Wisconsin: A Study of the Trading Post as an Institution,* ed. David Harry Miller and William W. Savage (Norman: University of Oklahoma Press, 1977), 78.

19. Turner, *The Character and Influence of the Indian Trade in Wisconsin,* 78.

20. Ellen Fitzpatrick, *History's Memory: Writing America's Past, 1880–1980* (Cambridge, Mass.: Harvard University Press, 2002), 49.

21. Johannes Fabian, *Time and the Other: How Anthropology Makes Its Object* (New York: Columbia University Press, 1983), 143.

22. Hubert Howe Bancroft, *The Native Races,* 5 vols. (San Francisco: A. L. Bancroft, 1883), 1:3.

23. Bancroft, *Native Races,* 1:81.

24. David Silverman, *This Land Is Their Land: The Wampanoag Indians, Plymouth Colony, and the Troubled History of Thanksgiving* (New York: Bloomsbury, 2019).

25. In the genre of "silent westerns," film producers "thought of Indians mostly as scenic elements, and . . . effectively pushed them into the background." See Andrew Brodie Smith, *Shooting Cowboys and Indians: Silent Western Films, American Culture, and the Birth of Hollywood* (Boulder: University of Colorado Press, 2003), 219.

26. Mark David Spence, *Dispossessing the Wilderness: Indian Removal and the Making of the National Parks* (New York: Oxford University Press, 1999).

27. Erika Marie Bsumek, *Indian-Made: Navajo Culture in the Marketplace, 1868–1940* (Lawrence: University of Kansas Press, 2008); Paige Raibmon, *Authentic Indians: Episodes of Encounter from the Late-Nineteenth-Century Northwest Coast* (Durham: Duke University Press, 2005), 74–115.

28. Philip J. Deloria, *Indians in Unexpected Places* (Lawrence: University of Kansas Press, 2004), 12.

29. Kristina Ackely and Cristina Stanciu, eds., *Laura Cornelius Kellogg: Our Democracy and the American Indians and Other Works* (Syracuse: Syracuse University Press, 2015), 73.

30. Ackely and Stanciu, *Laura Cornelius Kellogg,* 76–77.

31. Renya K. Ramirez, *Standing Up to Colonial Power: The Lives of Henry Roe and Elizabeth Bender Cloud* (Lincoln: University of Nebraska Press, 2018).

32. Ramirez, *Standing Up to Colonial Power,* 98–120.

33. See, e.g., David M. Beck, *Unfair Labor? American Indians and the 1893 World's Columbian Exposition in Chicago* (Lincoln: University of Nebraska Press, 2019); Theda Purdue, *Race and the Atlanta Cotton States Exposition of 1895* (Athens: University of

Georgia Press, 2010); and Akim Reinhardt, "Indigenous Identities in the Imperialist Imagination," in Wendy Jean Katz, ed., *The Trans-Mississippi and International Expositions of 1898–1899* (Lincoln: University of Nebraska Press, 2018), 262–97.

34. Reinhardt, "Indigenous Identities in the Imperialist Imagination," 263.

35. As quoted in Beck, *Unfair Labor?* 198.

36. As quoted in Frederick E. Hoxie, *A Final Promise: The Campaign to Assimilate the Indians, 1880–1920*, rev. ed. (New York: Cambridge University Press, 1989), 86. For the strategies informing Chicago's exhibitions of Native people, see 87–91.

37. Purdue, *Race and the Atlanta Cotton States Exposition of 1895*, 79.

38. Deloria, *Indians in Unexpected Places*, 72.

39. As quoted in Beck, *Unfair Labor?* 10.

40. As quoted in Beck, *Unfair Labor?* 16.

41. Deloria, *Indians in Unexpected Places*, 67.

42. Rufus Blanchard, *Discovery and Conquests of the North-west, with the History of Chicago* (Wheaton, Ill.: R. Blanchard, 1881), 4.

43. As quoted in Beck, *Unfair Labor?* 7.

44. As quoted in Beck, *Unfair Labor?* 7.

45. Raibmon, *Authentic Indians*, 23–33.

46. Truth and Reconciliation Commission of Canada, *Canada's Residential Schools: The History, Part 1, Origins to 1939*, 6 vols. (Montreal: McGill-Queen's University Press, 2015), 1:164.

47. As quoted in Truth and Reconciliation Commission, *Canada's Residential Schools*, 1:164.

48. As quoted in Truth and Reconciliation Commission, *Canada's Residential Schools*, 1:157.

49. As quoted in Christopher Bracken, *The Potlatch Papers: A Colonial Case History* (Chicago: University of Chicago Press, 1997), 46.

50. As quoted in Hoxie, *A Final Promise*, 89.

51. Beck, *Unfair Labor?* 109.

52. Raibmon, *Authentic Indians*, 61.

53. Beck, *Unfair Labor?* 110–12.

54. Beck, *Unfair Labor?* 112.

55. For Hunt's influence on Boas and the development of "museum anthropology," see Douglas Cole, *Captured Heritage: The Scramble for Northwest Coast Artifacts* (Norman: University of Oklahoma Press, 1985), 156–64. For Hunt's relationship with Curtis, see Mick Gidley, *Edward S. Curtis and the North American Indian, Incorporated* (New York: Cambridge University Press, 1998), 88–94.

56. Ned Blackhawk and Isaiah Lorado Wilner, introduction to Blackhawk and Wilner, eds., *Indigenous Visions: Rediscovering the World of Franz Boas* (New Haven: Yale University Press, 2018), ix–xxii.

57. Isaiah Lorado Wilner, "Transformation Masks: Recollecting the Indigenous Origins of Global Consciousness," in Blackhawk and Wilner, *Indigenous Visions*, 3–41.

58. J. Kéhaulani Kauanui, *Paradoxes of Hawaiian Sovereignty: Land, Sex, and the Colonial Politics of State Nationalism* (Durham: Duke University Press, 2018), 14.

59. Daniel Immerwahr, *How to Hide an Empire: A History of the Greater United States* (New York: Farrar, Straus & Giroux, 2019), 79–87.

60. Alfred W. McCoy, Francisco A. Scarano, and Courtney Johnson, "On the Tropic of Cancer: Transitions and Transformation in the U.S. Imperial State," in McCoy and Scarano, eds., *Colonial Crucible: Empire in the Making of the Modern American State* (Madison: University of Wisconsin Press, 2009), 3.

61. Lee D. Baker, *Anthropology and the Racial Politics of Culture* (Durham: Duke University Press, 2010), 35–38.

62. Baker, *Anthropology and the Racial Politics of Culture*, 35.

63. Baker, *Anthropology and the Racial Politics of Culture*, 39–42.

64. Hoxie, *A Final Promise*, 56.

65. For the challenges of U.S. state building in the Philippines, see Immerwahr, *How to Hide an Empire*, 88–107.

66. As quoted in Hoxie, *A Final Promise*, 274n45.

67. As quoted in Hoxie, *A Final Promise*, 106–7.

68. Nick Estes, *Our History Is the Future: Standing Rock versus the Dakota Access Pipeline, and the Long Tradition of Indigenous Resistance* (New York: Verso, 2019), 91–92.

69. Brian McAllister Linn, "The Impact of the Philippine Wars (1898–1913) on the U.S. Army," in McCoy and Scarano, *Colonial Crucible*, 463.

70. Alfred W. McCoy, *Policing America's Empire: The United States, the Philippines, and the Rise of the Surveillance State* (Madison: University of Wisconsin Press, 2009), 35.

71. As quoted in Willam T. Hagan, *Indian Police and Judges: Experiments in Acculturation and Control* (New Haven: Yale University Press, 1966), 84.

72. Hagan, *Indian Police and Judges*, 85.

73. Robert M. Kvasnicka and Herman J. Viola, eds., *The Commissioners of Indian Affairs, 1824–1977* (Lincoln: University of Nebraska Press, 1979).

74. Ackely and Stanciu, *Laura Cornelius Kellogg*, 77.

75. Arlinda Locklear, "The Allotment of the Oneida Reservation and Its Legal Ramifications," in Jack Campisi and Laurence M. Hauptman, eds., *The Oneida Indian Experience: Two Perspectives* (Syracuse: Syracuse University Press, 1988), 85.

76. Ackely and Stanciu, *Laura Cornelius Kellogg*, 76.

77. "Congressional Appropriations for Indian Schools, 1877–1920," in Hoxie, *A Final Promise*, 253–54.

78. "Congressional Appropriations for Indian Schools, 1877–1920," 253–54.

79. Kim Cary Warren, *The Quest for Citizenship: African American and Native American Education in Kansas, 1880–1935* (Chapel Hill: University of North Carolina Press, 2010), 21, 145–54.

80. As quoted in Ackely and Stanciu, *Laura Cornelius Kellogg*, 8.

81. Ackely and Stanciu, *Laura Cornelius Kellogg*, 114.

82. Robert Dale Parker, ed., *Changing Is Not Vanishing: A Collection of American Indian Poetry to 1930* (Philadelphia: University of Pennsylvania Press, 2011), 256–57.

83. Laura M. Cornelius, "A Tribute to the Future of My Race," in Parker, *Changing Is Not Vanishing*, 256.

84. As quoted in Ackely and Stanciu, *Laura Cornelius Kellogg*, 16.

85. Cathleen D. Cahill, *Recasting the Vote: How Women of Color Transformed the Suffrage Movement* (Chapel Hill: University of North Carolina Press, 2020), 266.

86. Hazel W. Hertzberg, *The Search for an American Indian Identity: Modern Pan-Indian Movements* (Syracuse: Syracuse University Press, 1971), 36–38.

87. See, e.g., Francis Paul Prucha, *American Indian Policy in Crisis: Christian Reformers and the Indian, 1865–1900* (Norman: University of Oklahoma Press, 1976); and William T. Hagan, *The Indian Rights Association: The Herbert Welsh Years, 1882–1904* (Tucson: University of Arizona Press, 1985).

88. As quoted in Cahill, *Recasting the Vote*, 92.

89. Beth H. Piatote, *Domestic Subjects: Gender, Citizenship, and Law in Native American Literature* (New Haven: Yale University Press, 2013), 144.

90. As quoted in Cahill, *Recasting the Vote*, 92.

91. Susan M. Hill, *The Clay We Are Made Of: Haudenosaunee Land Tenure on the Grand River* (Winnipeg: University of Manitoba Press, 2017), 15–76.

92. Hertzberg, *The Search for an American Indian Identity*, 31–36.

93. As quoted in Ackely and Stanciu, *Laura Cornelius Kellogg*, 9.

94. Cahill, *Recasting the Vote*, 89–90.

95. As quoted in Cahill, *Recasting the Vote*, 92.

96. As quoted in Hertzberg, *The Search for an American Indian Identity*, 138.

97. Hertzberg, *The Search for an American Indian Identity*, 128–29. (No tribal identification is provided.)

98. As quoted in Cahill, *Recasting the Vote*, 92n40, 297.

99. For factionalism within the SAI, see Hertzberg, *The Search for an American Indian Identity*, 55–58, 135–54.

100. Hertzberg, *The Search for an American Indian Identity*, 239.

101. *New York Evening Sun*, February 22, 1913, as quoted in *The National American Indian Memorial—Harbor of New York* (New York: n.p., 1913), 3.

102. As quoted in Cahill, *Recasting the Vote*, 22.

103. Hertzberg, *The Search for an American Indian Identity*, 184.

104. As quoted in Hoxie, *A Final Promise*, 233.

105. Keith Richotte Jr., *Federal Indian Law and Policy: An Introduction* (St. Paul: West Academic, 2020), 258–63.

106. Cahill, *Recasting the Vote*, 100–102.

107. As quoted in Thomas A. Britten, *American Indians in World War I: At Home and at War* (Albuquerque: University of New Mexico Press, 1997), 81.

108. As quoted in Cahill, *Recasting the Vote*, 189.

109. As quoted in Cahill, *Recasting the Vote*, 256.

110. As quoted in Cahill, *Recasting the Vote*, 257.

111. Hoxie, *A Final Promise*, 108.

112. Cahill, *Recasting the Vote*, 259, 251.

113. As quoted in Cahill, *Recasting the Vote*, 258–59.

114. As quoted in Cahill, *Recasting the Vote*, 247.

115. Zitkala-Sa, *American Indian Stories* (Washington, D.C.: Hayworth, 1921), 187.

116. Zitkala-Sa, *American Indian Stories*, 192–93.

117. Zitkala-Sa, *American Indian Stories*, 187.

118. As quoted in Alexandra Harmon, *Rich Indians: Native People and the Problem of Wealth in American History* (Chapel Hill: University of North Carolina Press, 2010), 211–12.

119. As quoted in Sally Jenkins, *The Real All Americans: The Team That Changed a Game, a People, a Nation* (New York: Doubleday, 2007), 312.

120. Britten, *American Indians in World War I*, 165–66.

121. Manu Karuka, *Empire's Traces: Indigenous Nations, Chinese Workers, and the Transcontinental Railroad* (Berkeley: University of California Press, 2019), 56.

122. As quoted in Cahill, *Recasting the Vote*, 191.

123. As quoted in Ackely and Stanciu, *Laura Cornelius Kellogg*, 264n1.

124. Laurence M. Hauptman, *The Iroquois and the New Deal* (Syracuse: Syracuse University Press, 1981), 16.

125. As quoted in Ackely and Stanciu, *Laura Cornelius Kellogg*, 71, 73.

126. Jack Campisi, "The Oneida Treaty Period, 1783–1838," in Campisi and Hauptman, *The Oneida Indian Experience*, 48–64.

127. As quoted in Ackely and Stanciu, *Laura Cornelius Kellogg*, 74.

128. Arlinda F. Locklear, "The Oneida Land Claims: A Legal Overview," in Christopher Vecsey and William A. Starna, eds., *Iroquois Land Claims* (Syracuse: Syracuse University Press, 1988), 147.

129. Ackely and Stanciu, *Laura Cornelius Kellogg*, 47.

130. As quoted in Ackely and Stanciu, *Laura Cornelius Kellogg*, 81.

131. As quoted in Hoxie, *A Final Promise*, 240.

132. As quoted in Hoxie, *A Final Promise*, 240.

133. Locklear, "The Oneida Land Claims," 141–53.

134. For Menominee land tenure and lumber industry, see chapter 12.

135. As quoted in Ackely and Stanciu, *Laura Cornelius Kellogg*, 48n110, 263.

136. Ackely and Stanciu, *Laura Cornelius Kellogg*, 48.

137. Locklear, "The Oneida Land Claims," 151.

138. Hauptman, *The Iroquois and the New Deal*, 16–17.

139. Ackely and Stanciu, *Laura Cornelius Kellogg*, xxvii. See also Hauptman, *The Iroquois and the New Deal*, 76–77.

140. For varied Oneida responses to Kellogg, see Doug Kiel, "Competing Visions of Empowerment: Oneida Progressive-Era Politics and Writing Tribal Histories," *Ethnohistory* (2014): 419–44.

141. As quoted in Ackely and Stanciu, *Laura Cornelius Kellogg*, 212.

142. Zitkala-Sa, *American Indian Stories*, 185–95.

143. As quoted in Hertzberg, *The Search for an American Indian Identity*, 205.

144. See Brenda J. Child, *Boarding School Seasons: American Indian Families, 1900–1940* (Lincoln: University of Nebraska Press, 1998).

145. Rosalyn R. LaPier, *Invisible Reality: Storytellers, Storytakers, and the Supernatural World of the Blackfeet* (Lincoln: University of Nebraska Press, 2017), 120.

146. Zitkala-Sa, *American Indian Stories*, 55–56.

147. Zitkala-Sa, *American Indian Stories*, 55–56.

148. Zitkala-Sa, *American Indian Stories*, 73.

149. As quoted in Hoxie, *A Final Promise*, 240.

150. Hoxie, *A Final Promise*, 187.

151. Graham D. Taylor, *The New Deal and American Indian Tribalism: The Administration of the Indian Reorganization Act, 1934–1945* (Lincoln: University of Nebraska Press, 1980), 6.

152. Frederick E. Hoxie, *Parading through History: The Making of the Crow Nation in America, 1805–1935* (New York: Cambridge University Press, 1995), 144.

153. Harmon, *Rich Indians*, 212.

154. Taylor, *The New Deal and American Indian Tribalism*, 14.

155. Institute for Government Research, *The Problem of Indian Administration: Report of a Survey Made at the Request of Honorable Hubert Work, Secretary of the Interior* (Baltimore: Johns Hopkins University Press, 1928), 3.

156. Institute for Government Research, *The Problem of Indian Administration*, 14.

157. As quoted in Taylor, *The New Deal and American Indian Tribalism*, 6.

158. As quoted in LaPier, *Invisible Reality*, 125.

159. As quoted in Child, *Boarding School Seasons*, 53.

160. As quoted in Child, *Boarding School Seasons*, 54.

161. As quoted in Katharine C. Turner, *Red Men Calling on the Great White Father* (Norman: University of Oklahoma Press, 1951), 121. See also LaPier, *Invisible Reality*, 120.

162. Melissa L. Meyer, *The White Earth Tragedy: Ethnicity and Dispossession at a Minnesota Anishinaabe Reservation* (Lincoln: University of Nebraska Press, 1994), 170.

Such blood rolls "rested on a methodological foundation devised by experts who pioneered the science of eugenics."

163. See Joanne Barker, *Native Acts: Law, Recognition, and Cultural Authenticity* (Durham: Duke University Press, 2011), esp. 3–24, 81–97. "The administration of allotment required that those individuals recognized by their tribal governments to be members were officially registered on census rolls that recorded their blood quantum" (88).

164. For ties between the Winnebago Indian Tribe of Nebraska and the Ho-Chunk Nation of Wisconsin, see Ramirez, *Standing Up to Colonial Power*, 23–25.

165. As quoted in Ramirez, *Standing Up to Colonial Power*, 140.

166. For the American Indian Institute, see Ramirez, *Standing Up to Colonial Power*, 98–120. The following paragraphs draw upon this section and continue its argumentation that the Clouds encouraged "students to transform a Christian, individualized, masculine identity into one that incorporated an educated warrior identity, encouraging them to fight for the well-being of tribes, to be of service to Native Americans, and to right the wrongs of the federal government" (102).

167. Institute for Government Research, *The Problem of Indian Administration*, 380n.

168. As quoted in Warren, *The Quest for Citizenship*, 169.

169. Henry Roe Cloud, "Education of the American Indian," in Frederick E. Hoxie, ed., *Talking Back to Civilization: Indian Voices from the Progressive Era* (New York: Bedford/St. Martin's, 2001), 60.

170. Ramirez, *Standing Up to Colonial Power*, 36–37.

171. As quoted in Ramirez, *Standing Up to Colonial Power*, 32.

172. Roe Cloud, "Education of the American Indian," 61.

173. Roe Cloud, "Education of the American Indian," 60.

174. As quoted in Ramirez, *Standing Up to Colonial Power*, 83.

175. For "the flexible and fluid notion of the hub" as a theoretical "diasporic concept" for assessing "Native-oriented strategies to challenge the U.S. and settler colonialism," see Ramirez, *Standing Up to Colonial Power*, 4–5.

176. Ramirez, *Standing Up to Colonial Power*, 91–92.

177. As quoted in Ramirez, *Standing Up to Colonial Power*, 109.

178. Warren, *The Quest for Citizenship*, 166.

179. As quoted in Ramirez, *Standing Up to Colonial Power*, 50.

180. Matthew Sakiestewa Gilbert, *Hopi Runners: Crossing the Terrain between Indian and American* (Lawrence: University of Kansas Press, 2018), 51–66.

181. As quoted in Turner, *Red Men Calling on the Great White Father*, 202.

182. Gilbert, *Hopi Runners*, 61–87.

183. As quoted in Ramirez, *Standing Up to Colonial Power*, 122.

184. Ramirez, *Standing Up to Colonial Power*, 131.

185. Ramirez, *Standing Up to Colonial Power*, 249n14.

186. As quoted in Ramirez, *Standing Up to Colonial Power,* 126–27.

187. Edward Everett Dale, "Memories with Frederick Jackson Turner," in Arrell M. Gibson, ed., *Frontier Historian: The Life and Work of Edward Everett Dale* (Norman: University of Oklahoma Press, 1975), 336–59.

188. As quoted in Ramirez, *Standing Up to Colonial Power,* 127.

189. Ramirez, *Standing Up to Colonial Power,* 132.

190. As quoted in Ramirez, *Standing Up to Colonial Power,* 104.

191. As quoted in Ramirez, *Standing Up to Colonial Power,* 124.

192. For Roe Cloud's work at Haskell, see Ramirez, *Standing Up to Colonial Power,* 134–39.

193. Kenneth William Townsend, *World War II and the American Indian* (Albuquerque: University of New Mexico Press, 2000), 21–22.

194. Warren, *The Quest for Citizenship,* 171.

195. Truth and Reconciliation Commission, *Canada's Residential Schools,* 1:502–9.

196. As quoted in Truth and Reconciliation Commission, *Canada's Residential Schools,* 1:502.

197. Truth and Reconciliation Commission, *Canada's Residential Schools,* 1:509.

198. For the Depression and efforts to reform the "crisis of corporate capitalism," see Alan Dawley, *Struggles for Justice: Social Responsibility and the Liberal State* (Cambridge, Mass.: Harvard University Press, 1991), esp. 297–417. "Social hierarchy remained surprisingly intact through the Depression. . . . The structures of corporate power, male dominance, and white supremacy were little disturbed" (295).

199. As quoted in Lawrence C. Kelly, "Charles James Rhoads," in Kvasnicka and Viola, *The Commissioners of Indian Affairs,* 270. See chapter 12 for the return to assimilation after World War II.

200. As quoted in Joshua L. Reid, *The Sea Is My Country: The Maritime World of the Makahs* (New Haven: Yale University Press, 2015), 254.

201. As quoted in Lawrence C. Kelly, *The Navajo Indians and Federal Indian Policy* (Tucson: University of Arizona Press, 1968), 172.

202. As quoted in Tisa Wenger, *We Have a Religion: The 1920s Pueblo Indian Dance Controversy and American Religious Freedom* (Chapel Hill: University of North Carolina Press, 2009), 189. "In 1920 Congress directed that education be made compulsory for all Indian children subject to federal jurisdiction. . . . The compulsory education program was launched in the fall of 1921 with the slogan 'Every eligible pupil in school.' . . . Children whose parents refused to send them to school were to be forcibly enrolled in whatever government boarding schools the commissioner of Indian affairs should designate." See Lawrence C. Kelly, "Charles Henry Burke, 1921–1929," in Kvasnicka and Viola, *The Commissioners of Indian Affairs,* 254.

203. As quoted in Wenger, *We Have a Religion,* 191.

204. Lawrence C. Kelly, *The Assault on Assimilation: John Collier and the Origins of Indian Policy Reform* (Albuquerque: University of New Mexico Press, 1983), 103–377.

205. Christian W. McMillen, *Making Indian Law: The Hualapai Land Case and the Birth of Ethnohistory* (New Haven: Yale University Press, 2007), 128, 152.

206. As quoted in Jennifer Nez Denetdale, *Reclaiming Diné History: The Legacies of Navajo Chief Manuelito and Juanita* (Tucson: University of Arizona Press, 2007), 78, 80.

207. As quoted in Denetdale, *Reclaiming Diné History*, 80.

208. Kelly, *The Navajo Indians and Federal Indian Policy*, 172.

209. K. Tsianina Lomawaima, *They Called It Prairie Light: The Story of Chilocco Indian School* (Lincoln: University of Nebraska Press, 1994), 18–19.

210. Cathleen D. Cahill, *Federal Fathers and Mothers: A Social History of the United States Indian Service* (Chapel Hill: University of North Carolina Press, 2011), 110.

211. Lomawaima, *They Called It Prairie Light*, 19.

212. See Brianna Theobald, *Reproduction on the Reservation: Pregnancy, Childbirth, and Colonialism in the Long Twentieth Century* (Chapel Hill: University of North Carolina Press, 2019), 79–80; Hoxie, *Parading through History*, 325–35.

213. As quoted in Hoxie, *Parading through History*, 326.

214. Plenty Coups spoke before one hundred thousand at the dedication of the Memorial of the Unknown Soldier in 1921 and attended the 1913 dedication of the National American Indian Memorial in New York Harbor. See Hoxie, *Parading through History*, 344–48; and *The National American Indian Memorial—Harbor of New York* (New York: n.p., 1913), 6.

215. As quoted in Hoxie, *Parading through History*, 327.

216. McMillen, *Making Indian Law*, 17–35.

217. As quoted in McMillen, *Making Indian Law*, 17.

218. McMillen, *Making Indian Law*, 12.

219. Gilbert, *Hopi Runners*, 59.

220. As quoted in McMillen, *Making Indian Law*, 33.

221. McMillen, *Making Indian Law*, 71.

222. As quoted McMillen, *Making Indian Law*, 161.

223. McMillen, *Making Indian Law*, 139.

224. As quoted in McMillen, *Making Indian Law*, 177–78. See also Glen Sean Coulthard, "A Fourth World Resurgent," in George Manuel and Michael Posluns, *The Fourth World: An Indian Reality*, rev. ed. (Minneapolis: University of Minnesota Press, 2019), xxvii.

225. For an overview of the trust relationship and trust responsibility, see David E. Wilkins and K. Tsianina Lomawaima, *Uneven Ground: American Indian Sovereignty and Federal Law* (Norman: University of Oklahoma Press, 2001), 64–97.

Chapter 12. From Termination to Self-Determination

1. Christian W. McMillen, *Making Indian Law: The Hualapai Land Case and the Birth of Ethnohistory* (New Haven: Yale University Press, 2007), 172–73. See also Da-

vid E. Wilkins, *Hollow Justice: A History of Indigenous Claims in the United States* (New Haven: Yale University Press, 2013), 49–70.

2. Vijay Prashad, *The Darker Nations: A People's History of the Third World* (New York: New Press, 2007), 3–15.

3. https://www.un.org/en/about-us/un-charter.

4. Joshua B. Freeman, *American Empire: The Rise of a Global Power, the Democratic Revolution at Home, 1945–2000* (New York: Viking Penguin, 2012), xi.

5. As quoted in Walter LaFeber, *The American Age: United States Foreign Policy at Home and Abroad since 1750* (New York: Norton, 1989), 380.

6. Andrew Needham, *Power Lines: Phoenix and the Making of the Modern Southwest* (Princeton: Princeton University Press, 2014), 13–14.

7. Kristen Simmons, "Settler Atmospherics," *Fieldsights* (2017), https://culanth.org/fieldsights/settler-atmospherics.

8. As quoted in Richard White, *The Organic Machine: The Remaking of the Columbia River* (New York: Hill & Wang, 1996), 81.

9. As quoted in Needham, *Power Lines*, 248.

10. Nick Estes, *Our History Is the Future: Standing Rock versus the Dakota Access Pipeline, and the Long Tradition of Indigenous Resistance* (New York: Verso, 2019), 134–67. For the role of federal agencies in expanding the post–World War II West, see also Richard White, *"It's Your Misfortune and None of My Own": A New History of the American West* (Norman: University of Oklahoma Press, 1991), 553–61.

11. As quoted in Estes, *Our History Is the Future*, 139.

12. James C. Scott, *Seeing Like a State: How Certain Schemes to Improve the Human Condition Have Failed* (New Haven: Yale University Press, 1998), 270–71.

13. Needham, *Power Lines*, 247–48, 155. See also Dana E. Powell, *Landscapes of Power: Politics of Energy in the Navajo Nation* (Durham: Duke University Press, 2018), 7–57.

14. As quoted in Joy L. Gritton, *The Institute of American Indian Arts: Modernism and U.S. Policy* (Albuquerque: University of New Mexico Press, 2000), 69–70 (emphasis added).

15. As quoted in Richard Drinnon, *Keeper of Concentration Camps: Dillon S. Meyer and American Racism* (Berkeley: University of California Press, 1987), 166.

16. As quoted in Charles Wilkinson, *Blood Struggle: The Rise of Modern Indian Nations* (New York: Norton, 2005), xiii.

17. Vine Deloria Jr., *Custer Died for Your Sins: An Indian Manifesto* (New York: Macmillan, 1969).

18. Glen Sean Coulthard, "A Fourth World Resurgent," in George Manuel and Michael Posluns, *The Fourth World: An Indian Reality*, rev. ed. (Minneapolis: University of Minnesota Press, 2019), ix–xxxiv. See also Daniel M. Cobb, *Native Activism in Cold War America: The Struggle for Sovereignty* (Chapel Hill: University of North Carolina Press, 2008). "The politics of tribal sovereignty and self-determination cannot

be understood apart from the larger global politics of modernization and decolonization" (4).

19. As quoted in Manuel and Posluns, *The Fourth World*, xxxix. As Aileen Moreton-Robinson suggests, "What Indigenous people have been given . . . is a white-constructed form of 'Indigenous' proprietary rights that are not epistemologically and ontologically grounded in Indigenous conceptions of sovereignty. Indigenous land ownership, under these legislative regimes, amounts to little more than a mode of land tenure that enables a circumscribed form of autonomy and governance within minimum control and ownership of resources, on or below the ground, thus entrenching economic dependence on the nation state." Aileen Moreton-Robinson, ed., *Sovereign Subjects: Indigenous Sovereignty Matters* (Crows Nest, Australia: Allen & Unwin, 2007), 4.

20. Eiichiro Azuma, *In Search of Our Frontier: Japanese America and Settler Colonialism in the Construction of Japan's Borderless Empire* (Berkeley: University of California Press, 2019), 70–72.

21. As quoted in Azuma, *In Search of Our Frontier*, 73.

22. As quoted in Azuma, *In Search of Our Frontier*, 74.

23. Jun Uchida, *Brokers of Empire: Japanese Settler Colonialism in Korea, 1876–1945* (Cambridge, Mass.: Harvard University Asia Center, 2011), 166–67, 408.

24. Uchida, *Brokers of Empire*, 401.

25. Timothy Snyder, *Black Earth: The Holocaust as History and Warning* (New York: Tim Duggan Books, 2015), 12.

26. As quoted in Snyder, *Black Earth*, 15.

27. As quoted in James Q. Whitman, *Hitler's American Model: The United States and the Making of Nazi Race Law* (Princeton: Princeton University Press, 2017), 9.

28. As quoted in Snyder, *Black Earth*, 15.

29. Norman M. Naimark, *Genocide: A World History* (New York: Oxford University Press, 2017), 66.

30. As quoted in Snyder, *Black Earth*, 15.

31. As quoted in Snyder, *Black Earth*, 16.

32. As quoted in Snyder, *Black Earth*, 20.

33. Whitman, *Hitler's American Model*, 115.

34. Whitman, *Hitler's American Model*, 115.

35. Whitman, *Hitler's American Model*, 135.

36. Office of Indian Affairs, *Indians in the War* (Chicago: U.S. Department of the Interior, 1945), 1, 49.

37. Office of Indian Affairs, *Indians in the War*, 1.

38. Office of Indian Affairs, *Indians in the War*, 1.

39. Peter Calvocoressi et al., *Total War: The Causes and Courses of the Second World War*, rev. ed., vol. 2 (New York: Pantheon Books, 1989), 1162–63.

40. Calvocoressi et al., *Total War*, 1161.

41. As quoted in Office of Indian Affairs, *Indians in the War*, 29.

42. Office of Indian Affairs, *Indians in the War*, 23–24, 37–40.

43. See David Treuer, *The Heartbeat of Wounded Knee: Native America from 1890 to the Present* (New York: Riverhead Books, 2019), 221–22.

44. Office of Indian Affairs, *Indians in the War*, 47.

45. Meg Jacobs, *Pocketbook Politics: Economic Citizenship in Twentieth-Century America* (Princeton: Princeton University Press, 2005), 249.

46. Lizabeth Cohen, *A Consumers' Republic: The Politics of Mass Consumption in Postwar America* (New York: Vintage, 2003), 119.

47. As quoted in Jacobs, *Pocketbook Politics*, 252.

48. As quoted in Jacobs, *Pocketbook Politics*, 254.

49. Jacobs, *Pocketbook Politics*, 254.

50. Liza Black, *Picturing Indians: Native Americans in Film, 1941–1960* (Lincoln: University of Nebraska Press, 2020), 310–11.

51. Black, *Picturing Indians*, 204–5.

52. Black, *Picturing Indians*, 204.

53. John W. Troutman, *Indian Blues: American Indians and the Politics of Music, 1879–1934* (Norman: University of Oklahoma Press, 2009), 117.

54. White, *"It's Your Misfortune and None of My Own,"* 613.

55. White, *"It's Your Misfortune and None of My Own,"* 613.

56. As quoted in Kenneth William Townsend, *World War II and the American Indian* (Albuquerque: University of New Mexico Press, 2000), 223. See also Edward Charles Valandra, *Not without Our Consent: Lakota Resistance to Termination, 1950–59* (Urbana: University of Illinois Press, 2006), 71–136.

57. As quoted in Laurie Arnold, *Bartering with the Bones of Their Dead: The Colville Confederated Tribes and Termination* (Seattle: University of Washington Press, 2012), 47.

58. As quoted in Gritton, *The Institute of American Indian Arts*, 70.

59. Institute for Government Research, *The Problem of Indian Administration: Report of a Survey Made at the Request of Honorable Hubert Work, Secretary of the Interior* (Baltimore: Johns Hopkins University Press, 1928), 198–99.

60. Wilkinson, *Blood Struggle*, 21.

61. Arnold, *Bartering with the Bones of Their Dead*, 3.

62. As quoted in Arnold, *Bartering with the Bones of Their Dead*, 12.

63. As quoted in Valandra, *Not without Our Consent*, 17.

64. As quoted in Arnold, *Bartering with the Bones of Their Dead*, 98.

65. Kent Blansett, *A Journey to Freedom: Richard Oakes, Alcatraz and the Red Power Movement* (New Haven: Yale University Press, 2018), 81–82.

66. Ned Blackhawk, "'I Can Carry on From Here': The Relocation of American Indians to Los Angeles," *Wicazo Sa Review* (1995): 16–17.

67. As quoted in Blansett, *A Journey to Freedom*, 82.

68. As quoted in Blansett, *A Journey to Freedom*, 82.

69. As quoted in Brian C. Hosmer, *American Indians in the Marketplace: Persistence and Innovation among the Menominees and Metlakatlans, 1870–1920* (Lawrence: University of Kansas Press, 1999), 74.

70. Hosmer, *American Indians in the Marketplace,* 86–88. See also Ada Deer, *Making a Difference: My Fight for Native Rights and Social Justice* (Norman: University of Oklahoma Press, 2019), 7, 44–45.

71. Hazel W. Hertzberg, *The Search for an American Indian Identity: Modern Pan-Indian Movements* (Syracuse: Syracuse University Press, 1971), 136.

72. Deer, *Making a Difference,* 47.

73. Deer, *Making a Difference,* 47.

74. David R. M. Beck, *The Struggle for Self-Determination: History of the Menominee Indians since 1854* (Lincoln: University of Nebraska Press, 2005), 59–62.

75. See, e.g, Grant Arndt, *Ho-Chunk Powwows and the Politics of Tradition* (Lincoln: University of Nebraska Press, 2016), 98–108; and Nancy Oestreich Lurie, *Wisconsin Indians,* rev. ed. (Madison: Wisconsin State Historical Society Press, 2002), 36–37.

76. Wilkinson, *Blood Struggle,* 71–72.

77. Deer, *Making a Difference,* 46.

78. As quoted in Deer, *Making a Difference,* 48.

79. As quoted in Wilkinson, *Blood Struggle,* 74.

80. As quoted in Wilkinson, *Blood Struggle,* 73 (emphasis in original).

81. As quoted in in Wilkinson, *Blood Struggle,* 81–82.

82. Beck, *The Struggle for Self-Determination,* 143–56.

83. Deer, *Making a Difference,* 64, 52.

84. Paul Thomas Chamberlin, *The Cold War's Killing Fields: Rethinking the Long Peace* (New York: HarperCollins, 2018), 1–19.

85. Odd Arne Westad, *The Global Cold War: Third World Interventions and the Making of Our Times* (New York: Cambridge University Press, 2005), 159.

86. Robert J. C. Young, *Postcolonialism: An Historical Introduction* (Malden, Mass.: Blackwell, 2001), 191–92.

87. Thomas Borstelmann, *The Cold War and the Color Line: American Race Relations in the Global Arena* (Cambridge, Mass.: Harvard University Press, 2001), 93.

88. Westad, *The Global Cold War,* 31.

89. As quoted in Valandra, *Not without Our Consent,* 24–25.

90. As quoted in Valandra, *Not without Our Consent,* 79.

91. As quoted in Valandra, *Not without Our Consent,* 79.

92. As quoted in Valandra, *Not without Our Consent,* 78.

93. Cobb, *Native Activism in Cold War America,* 16–22.

94. Cobb, *Native Activism in Cold War America,* 30.

95. As quoted in Cobb, *Native Activism in Cold War America,* 51.

96. As quoted in Cobb, *Native Activism in Cold War America,* 52–54.

97. For Lumbee struggles for federal recognitions, see Malinda Maynor Lowery,

The Lumbee Indians: An American Struggle (Chapel Hill: University of North Carolina Press, 2018), esp. 117–36.

98. Margaret D. Jacobs, *A Generation Removed: The Fostering and Adoption of Indigenous Children in the Postwar World* (Lincoln: University of Nebraska Press, 2014), 7.

99. Jacobs, *A Generation Removed*, 19.

100. Laura Briggs, *Taking Children: A History of American Terror* (Berkeley: University of California Press, 2020), 63.

101. Jacobs, *A Generation Removed*, 6.

102. As quoted in Jacobs, *A Generation Removed*, 24.

103. As quoted in Jacobs, *A Generation Removed*, 26.

104. Briggs, *Taking Children*, 63.

105. As quoted in Jacobs, *A Generation Removed*, 26.

106. Patricia Busbee and Trace A. Demeyer, eds., *Two Worlds: Lost Children of the Indian Adoption Projects* (Greenfield, Mass.: Blue Hand Books, 2012), 16.

107. As quoted in Jacobs, *A Generation Removed*, 27–28.

108. Blackhawk, "'I Can Carry on From Here,'" 16–22.

109. Briggs, *Taking Children*, 69.

110. As quoted in Jacobs, *A Generation Removed*, 269.

111. As quoted in Matthew L. M. Fletcher, "ICWA and the Commerce Clause," in Matthew L. M. Fletcher, ed., *Facing the Future: The Indian Child Welfare Act at 30* (East Lansing: Michigan State University Press, 2009), 34.

112. See chapter 11.

113. Joan Kauppi, "Red Lake Anishinaabe Split Feather," in Busbee and Demeyer, *Two Worlds*, 29–31.

114. Jacobs, *A Generation Removed*, 261.

115. Evelyn Red Lodge, "I Will Die with All the Damage Done to Me as My Legacy," in Busbee and Demeyer, *Two Worlds*, 20–21.

116. As quoted in Jacobs, *A Generation Removed*, 91.

117. As quoted in Briggs, *Taking Children*, 66.

118. As quoted in Fletcher, "ICWA and the Commerce Clause," 35.

119. As quoted in Paul Chaat Smith and Robert Allen Warrior, *Like a Hurricane: The Indian Movement from Alcatraz to Wounded Knee* (New York: New Press, 1996), 42.

120. As quoted in Troy Johnson et al., "American Indian Activism and Transformation: Lessons from Alcatraz," in Troy Johnson et al., eds., *American Indian Activism: Alcatraz to the Long Walk* (Urbana: University of Illinois Press, 1997), 14.

121. Deloria, *Custer Died for Your Sins*, 17–18.

122. As quoted in David Martínez, *Life of the Indigenous Mind: Vine Deloria Jr. and the Birth of the Red Power Movement* (Lincoln: University of Nebraska Press, 2019), 20.

123. As quoted in Smith and Warrior, *Like a Hurricane*, 55.

124. David E. Wilkins, ed., *The Hank Adams Reader: An Exemplary Native Activist and the Unleashing of Indigenous Sovereignty* (Golden, Colo.: Fulcrum, 2011), 7.

125. Gritton, *The Institute of American Indian Arts*, 103.

126. Colette Lemmon and Ryan Rice, *Under the Influence: Iroquois Artists at IAIA (1962–2012)* (Santa Fe: Museum of Contemporary Native Arts, 2012), 11.

127. Gritton, *The Institute of American Indian Arts*, 103–49.

128. Richard W. Hill, "The Institute of American Indian Arts and Contemporary Native Art," in Lowery Stokes Sims, ed., *Fritz Scholder: Indian/Not Indian* (New York: Prestel, 2008), 123.

129. As quoted in Hill, "The Institute of American Indian Arts and Contemporary Native Art," 121.

130. Della C. Warrior, "Education, Art, and Activism," in Daniel M. Cobb and Loretta Fowler, eds., *Beyond Red Power: American Indian Politics and Activism since 1900* (Santa Fe: School of Advanced Research, 2007), 298.

131. Karen Kramer, "A Declaration of Love and Guts: T. C. Cannon's Visual Language and the Art of Survivance," in Karen Kramer, ed., *T. C. Cannon: At the Edge of America* (Salem, Mass.: Peabody Essex Museum, 2018), 37.

132. *Native American Art at Dartmouth: Highlights from the Hood Museum of Art* (Lebanon: University Press of New England, 2011), 13–17.

133. As quoted in *Native American Art at Dartmouth*, 14.

134. Paul Chaat Smith, "Monster Love," in Sims, *Fritz Scholder*, 30.

135. "Treaty with the Nisqualli, Puyallup, etc., 1854," in Charles J. Kappler, ed., *Indian Affairs: Law and Treaties*, 2 vols. (Washington, D.C.: Government Printing Office, 1904), 2:662.

136. Wilkinson, *Blood Struggle*, 166–73. See also Wilkins, *The Hank Adams Reader*, 8–9.

137. As quoted in Wilkinson, *Blood Struggle*, 169.

138. Blansett, *A Journey to Freedom*, 106–7.

139. "Treaty with the Sioux . . . and Arapaho, 1868" in Kappler, *Indian Affairs* 2:1000.

140. As quoted in Blansett, *A Journey to Freedom*, 144.

141. As quoted in Blansett, *A Journey to Freedom*, 144.

142. Blansett, *A Journey to Freedom*, 136–65.

143. As quoted in Alvin M. Josephy Jr., ed., *Red Power: The American Indians' Fight for Freedom* (New York: McGraw-Hill, 1971), 214, 216.

144. Peter Iverson, *Diné: A History of the Navajos* (Albuquerque: University of New Mexico Press, 2002), 233.

145. Philip S. Deloria, "The Era of Indian Self-Determination: An Overview," in Kenneth R. Philp, ed., *Indian Self-Rule: First-hand Accounts of Indian-White Relations from Roosevelt to Reagan* (Salt Lake City: Howe Brothers, 1986), 199–200.

146. Vine Deloria Jr. and Clifford Lytle, *The Nations Within: The Past and Future of American Indian Sovereingty* (New York: Pantheon Books, 1984), 216–23.

147. As quoted in Walter R. Echo-Hawk, *In the Courts of the Conqueror: The 10 Worst Indian Law Cases Ever Decided* (Golden, Colo.: Fulcrum, 2010), 363.

148. Wilkinson, *Blood Struggle*, 199–202.

149. Wilkins, *The Hank Adams Reader*, 9.

150. As quoted in Wilkinson, *Blood Struggle*, 202.

151. Edmund J. Danziger Jr., "A New Beginning or the Last Hurrah: American Indian Response to Reform Legislation of the 1970s," *American Indian Culture and Research Journal* (1983): 73.

152. Wilkinson, *Blood Struggle*, 13–21, 318–320.

153. As quoted in Wilkinson, *Blood Struggle*, 320–21.

154. Deloria, *Custer Died for Your Sins*, 27.

155. As quoted in N. Bruce Duthu, *American Indians and the Law* (New York: Viking Penguin, 2008), 12.

156. Manuel and Posluns, *The Fourth World*, 124–25.

157. Duthu, *American Indians and the Law*, 124–25.

158. As quoted in Duthu, *American Indians and the Law*, 21.

159. As quoted in Duthu, *American Indians and the Law*, 24.

160. Keith Richotte Jr., *Federal Indian Law and Policy: An Introduction* (St. Paul: West Academic, 2020), 374–86.

161. Ronald L. Trosper, "American Indian Poverty on Reservations, 1969–1989," in Gary D. Sandefur et al., *Changing Numbers, Changing Needs: American Indian Demography and Pubilc Health* (Washington, D.C.: National Academy Press, 1996), 188.

162. Randall K. Q. Akee et al., "The Indian Gaming Regulatory Act and Its Effects on American Indian Economic Development," *Journal of Economic Perspectives* (2015): 189.

163. Akee et al., "The Indian Gaming Regulatory Act," 189.

164. Jessica R. Cattelino, *High Stakes: Florida Seminole Gaming and Sovereignty* (Durham: Duke University Press, 2008), 53–58.

165. Richotte, *Federal Indian Law and Policy*, 507–18.

166. Deer, *Making a Difference*, 109.

167. Deer, *Making A Difference*, 151–55.

168. As quoted in Deer, *Making a Difference*, 160.

169. As quoted in Deer, *Making a Difference*, 160.

Acknowledgments

Overviews of scholarly fields are inherently dependent on the findings of others, and I am immeasurably indebted to the countless scholars, archivists, librarians, and community members whose research has made visible critical aspects of American Indian history. Such work has often been done away from the centers of academic institutions, and it has been a great privilege to witness the recent realignments that have made Native American history a vibrant and engaging practice. I offer my deep thanks and appreciation to the many individuals, institutions, professional associations, and tribal centers that have initiated this rediscovery of American history and to those who have supported me and invited me to share my work. At its best, academic engagement is a collective endeavor, and it has been wonderful to be part of a generation that is refashioning commonplace approaches to the past.

This book has had many beginnings. Its formation and execution have occurred since I joined Yale University. I am fortunate to have many colleagues, students, and administrators who have supported the study of Native American history. Those who began the Yale Group for the Study of Native America created an institutional home for Native American and Indigenous studies, and in the years since many have continued these efforts with their impressive research and sustained engagement, including Christine DeLucia, Khalil Johnson, Holly Miowak Guise, Ryan Hall, Isaiah Wilner, Anya Montiel, Tiffany Hale, Summer Sutton Adparvar, Naomi Sussman, Tess Lanzarotta, Hannah Greenwald, Isabella Robbins, Taylor Rose, Max Clayton, Sandra Sánchez, and David Kerry. Staff and faculty associated with the Ethnicity, Race, and Migration Program have assisted with related programs, and members of the Native American Law Student Association have worked tirelessly with related campus efforts.

The McNeil Center for Early American Studies and the University of Pennsylvania Law School provided vital support in 2017–18, and Chris Rogers and

Adina Berk at Yale University Press have been wonderful supporters of this volume as well as those in the Henry Roe Cloud series. Chris offered initial support for both in our first conversations, and Adina has worked to oversee and enrich them. Her edits have been invaluable, especially in trimming an already extensive project.

Joshua Reid has been a valued partner in the series whose patience and insight routinely amaze me. He offered some of the first reactions to the earlier chapters, as did Allan Greer and Nancy Van Deusen. Their comments and feedback have been generative and generous, as has that of Benjamin Madley, who along with an anonymous press reviewer provided essential responses and corrections. Any inconsistencies or errors are solely my own.

Bill Nelson and David Lindroth provided vital cartographical help, and several former students, including Heidi Katter, Meghan Gupta, Madeleine Freeman, and Leah Shrestinian, have supported this research, often doing so on short notice. Heidi and Leah assisted with the maps and images, respectively, enabling the completion of the project.

I am immensely grateful to work with those associated with the Native American Cultural Center community. Yale president Peter Salovey, as provost, helped secure a permanent location for this community in 2013, and it has grown in exciting ways since. Nicota Stevenson may not remember class discussions of primary sources in the seminar room that helped in the development of chapter 1, one of numerous generative moments since the center's opening. I offer my abiding gratitude to those who have worked to make the NACC such a supportive and vibrant space.

My deepest appreciation is to my family. My wife Maggie has offered incomparable support and guidance. Her combination of integrity and intellect remains unparalleled, and I am continually inspired by her brilliance and dedication. Tobias and Eva Blackhawk continue to enrich our lives, while parenting an infant, Evan Aaron, during the pandemic has put life's most important priorities into perspective.

Index

Illustrations and maps are indicated by page numbers in italics.

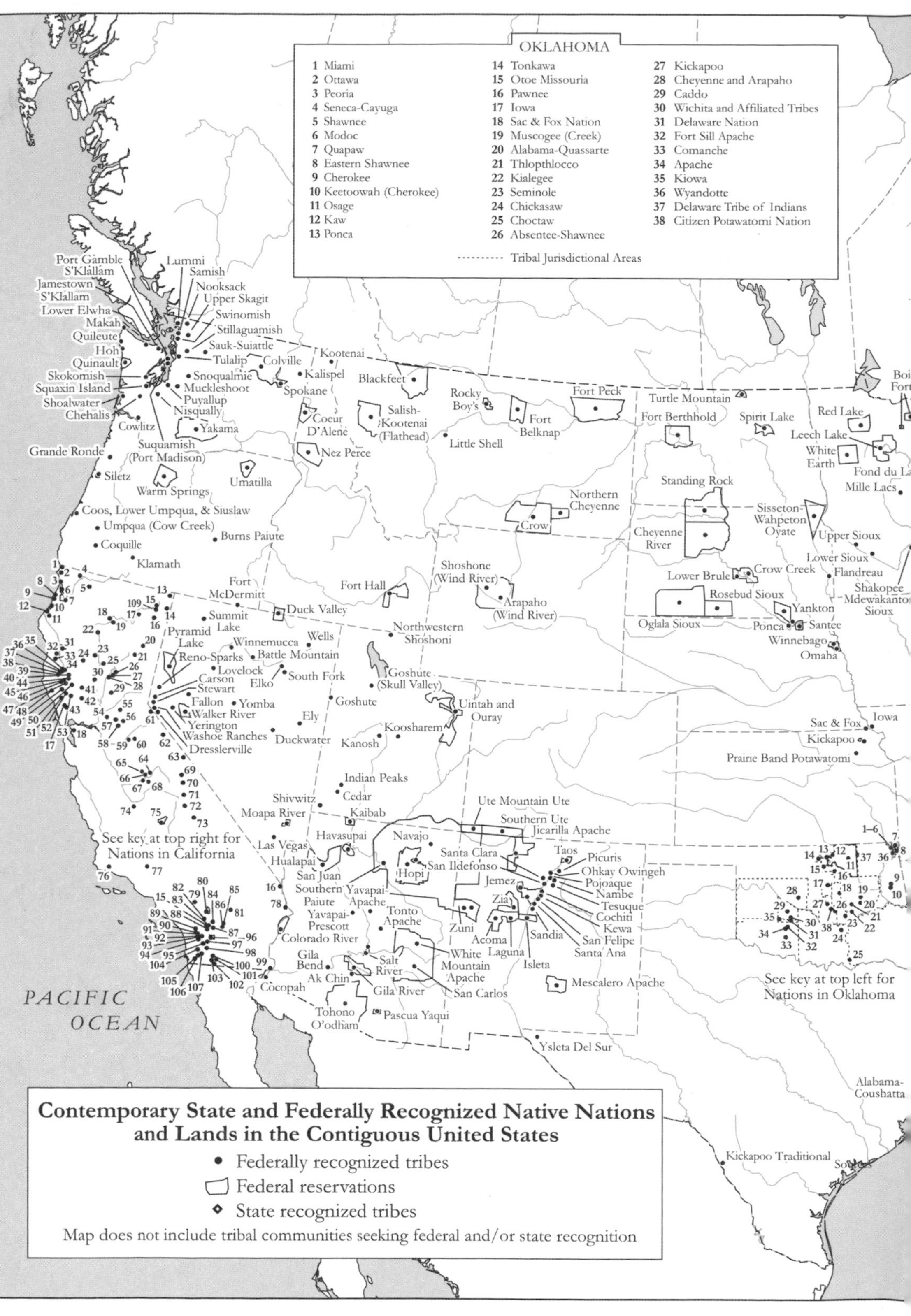

OKLAHOMA
1 Miami
2 Ottawa
3 Peoria
4 Seneca-Cayuga
5 Shawnee
6 Modoc
7 Quapaw
8 Eastern Shawnee
9 Cherokee
10 Keetoowah (Cherokee)
11 Osage
12 Kaw
13 Ponca
14 Tonkawa
15 Otoe Missouria
16 Pawnee
17 Iowa
18 Sac & Fox Nation
19 Muscogee (Creek)
20 Alabama-Quassarte
21 Thlopthlocco
22 Kialegee
23 Seminole
24 Chickasaw
25 Choctaw
26 Absentee-Shawnee
27 Kickapoo
28 Cheyenne and Arapaho
29 Caddo
30 Wichita and Affiliated Tribes
31 Delaware Nation
32 Fort Sill Apache
33 Comanche
34 Apache
35 Kiowa
36 Wyandotte
37 Delaware Tribe of Indians
38 Citizen Potawatomi Nation
Tribal Jurisdictional Areas
Port Gamble S'Klallam
Lummi
Samish
Jamestown S'Klallam
Nooksack
Upper Skagit
Lower Elwha
Swinomish
Makah
Stillaguamish
Quileute
Sauk-Suiattle
Hoh
Tulalip
Colville
Kootenai
Quinault
Kalispel
Skokomish
Snoqualmie
Squaxin Island
Muckleshoot
Spokane
Blackfeet
Shoalwater
Puyallup
Chehalis
Nisqually
Cowlitz
Yakama
Coeur D'Alene
Salish-Kootenai (Flathead)
Rocky Boy's
Fort Belknap
Fort Peck
Little Shell
Suquamish (Port Madison)
Grande Ronde
Nez Perce
Siletz
Warm Springs
Umatilla
Coos, Lower Umpqua, & Siuslaw
Umpqua (Cow Creek)
Coquille
Burns Paiute
Klamath
Northern Cheyenne
Crow
Turtle Mountain
Fort Berthhold
Spirit Lake
Red Lake
Leech Lake
White Earth
Fond du La
Mille Lacs
Bois Fort
Standing Rock
Cheyenne River
Sisseton-Wahpeton Oyate
Upper Sioux
Lower Sioux
Flandreau
Shakopee Mdewakanton Sioux
Crow Creek
Lower Brule
Rosebud Sioux
Yankton
Oglala Sioux
Ponca
Santee
Winnebago
Omaha
Fort McDermitt
Fort Hall
Shoshone (Wind River)
Arapaho (Wind River)
Duck Valley
Summit Lake
Pyramid Lake
Reno-Sparks
Winnemucca
Wells
Battle Mountain
Lovelock
Carson
Stewart
Elko
South Fork
Northwestern Shoshoni
Goshute (Skull Valley)
Fallon
Yomba
Walker River
Yerington
Washoe Ranches
Dresslerville
Goshute
Ely
Duckwater
Uintah and Ouray
Koosharem
Kanosh
Sac & Fox
Iowa
Kickapoo
Prairie Band Potawatomi
Indian Peaks
Cedar
Shivwitz
Moapa River
Kaibab
Ute Mountain Ute
Southern Ute
Jicarilla Apache
See key at top right for Nations in California
Las Vegas
Havasupai
Navajo
Hualapai
Hopi
Santa Clara
San Ildefonso
Taos
Picuris
Ohkay Owingeh
Pojoaque
Nambe
Tesuque
Cochiti
Kewa
San Felipe
Santa Ana
Jemez
Zia
Sandia
Acoma
Laguna
Isleta
Zuni
San Juan Southern Paiute
Yavapai-Apache
Yavapai-Prescott
Tonto Apache
Colorado River
White Mountain Apache
San Carlos
Gila Bend
Salt River
Ak Chin
Gila River
Cocopah
Tohono O'odham
Pascua Yaqui
Mescalero Apache
Ysleta Del Sur
See key at top left for Nations in Oklahoma
PACIFIC OCEAN
Alabama-Coushatta
Kickapoo Traditional
Contemporary State and Federally Recognized Native Nations and Lands in the Contiguous United States
Federally recognized tribes
Federal reservations
State recognized tribes
Map does not include tribal communities seeking federal and/or state recognition